DEEP INTO THE SIXTIES

TALES OF A NEW JERUSALEM

AUSTERITY BRITAIN

A World to Build, 1945–48

Smoke in the Valley, 1948–51

FAMILY BRITAIN

The Certainties of Place, 1951–54

A Thicker Cut, 1954–57

MODERNITY BRITAIN

Opening the Box, 1957–59

A Shake of the Dice, 1959–62

On the Cusp: Days of '62

A Northern Wind, 1962–65

DEEP INTO THE SIXTIES

BRITAIN, 1965–66

David Kynaston

BLOOMSBURY PUBLISHING
LONDON • OXFORD • NEW YORK • NEW DELHI • SYDNEY

BLOOMSBURY PUBLISHING
Bloomsbury Publishing Plc
50 Bedford Square, London, WC1B 3DP, UK
Bloomsbury Publishing Ireland Limited,
29 Earlsfort Terrace, Dublin 2, D02 AY28, Ireland

First published in Great Britain 2026

A catalogue record for this book is available from the British Library

ISBN: HB: 978-1-5266-5764-0; EBOOK: 978-1-5266-5759-6

2 4 6 8 10 9 7 5 3 1

Typeset by Six Red Marbles India
Printed and bound in Great Britain by Clays Ltd, Elcograf S.p.A

FSC
www.fsc.org
MIX
Paper | Supporting responsible forestry
FSC® C018072

This book is dedicated to the memory
of Michael Burns (1937–2025), a good friend

Contents

PART THREE

Preface

Deep into the Sixties continues *Tales of a New Jerusalem*, a series intended to stretch from 1945 to 1979. Here, the narrative runs from February 1965 (a week after Churchill's funeral) to July 1966 (a famous day at Wembley). Harold Wilson's Labour government is crucified on the cross of the pound sterling; the Beatles play their last British tour; Twiggy is discovered; Alf Ramsey's England, blessed by providence, win the World Cup. Familiar enough landmarks in our collective historical memory – but at the heart of this treatment is the sequence of thematic chapters comprising Part Two: on the economy and the start of deindustrialisation; on the scars, social and psychological as much as physical, of urban redevelopment; on immigration and race relations, poised to move politically centre stage; above all on the reality or otherwise of 'The Sixties'.

All books are in some sense products of their time, and much of the thinking behind this one occurred in the messy and protracted aftermath of the 2016 vote for Brexit. That vote had, inevitably, a variety of causes. My own view is that at some fundamental level it represented, especially for older voters, a cry of despair – or, at the least, of profound discomfort – against modernity and the forces of change. Some of the deepest roots of that socially conservative lament lay, I would argue, in the 1960s, that much-publicised decade of broadly liberal and progressive actual or incipient change.

But, of course, any decade is in real time always more complicated than the banal AI summary; and increasingly, I have come to see this particular decade as a complicated mixture of what one might call 'chances' and 'habits'. In terms of the former, I do not for a moment deny, least of all as a child myself of the Sixties, that there was a certain buzz in the air, a feeling of things opening up, even of a changing of the guard. The music alone – never to be equalled – bears ample, irrefutable testimony. Yet in the end, I suspect that Dostoyevsky's precocious boy calls it right in *The Brothers Karamazov*. 'Have you observed, Smurov, that in the middle of winter, if it is fifteen or even eighteen degrees below zero, it seems not as cold as, for example, now, at the beginning of winter, when the freezing weather strikes suddenly, as now, with twelve degrees below, and there is not yet much snow?' Kolya reflects at one point. 'It's because people have not yet got used to it,' he goes on. 'With human beings habit is all, in everything, even in matters of nationhood and politics. Habit is the principal driving force.'

The old certainties are never coming back; but it is indeed only human to regret the loss of the reassurance, of an almost taken-for-granted underlying stability, they once provided.

PART ONE

I

Back in His Cage

'News not so good,' privately noted Keith McBride, a youngish civil servant at the Ministry of Defence, on 7 February 1965, eight days after Churchill's funeral. 'The Americans & N. Vietnamese are having a go at one another, & just when Kosygin [Russian foreign minister] has arrived in Hanoi. It almost looks as if both sides want a large-scale clash.' Different concerns that Sunday for two middle-aged female diarists. 'Another horrible day,' lamented Betty Allen, a doctor's wife living at Poulton-le-Fylde near the Lancashire coast. 'David at work this morning, in bed all afternoon, at chapel & his mother's at night – it's just a year ago since he said he'd devote his life to me!' But for Grace Taylor in Ruislip, some quiet domestic satisfactions. 'We saw a blue-tit go in the "Fence" Box. Bill did some of the picture frame . . . I mended pockets in Bill's suit.' That evening, on ITV's *Sunday Night at the London Palladium*, it was Dusty's moment, as she stole the show from the headline group. 'The details of her performance were perfect – the blackened, half-awake eyes, the intense gestures, the sudden kangaroo leaps,' acclaimed the poet Adrian Mitchell, doubling as TV critic for the recently launched, pre-Murdoch *Sun*. 'If Miss Springfield is fire,' he added cruelly but unarguably, 'the Shadows are milk and water.'[1]

Over the following week, the government announced a ban on TV advertising of cigarettes; George Brown, in charge of the Department of Economic Affairs, was guest of honour at a London Chamber of Commerce lunch, where much of the conversation turned on the notoriously poor labour relations in the docks and he was adamant that the employers were the 'n——s in the wood pile'; *Coronation Street*'s

Stan Ogden started his short-lived career as a milkman; the fortunes of a rival soap, *Compact*, continued to falter ('I see by this episode they are still at it – office romances and crises galore,' observed one by now only occasional viewer); Keith McBride used a book token to buy Ludovic Kennedy's *The Trial of Stephen Ward*, reflecting 'it's strange how completely the business has been forgotten'; C. P. Snow, by now a Labour minister and in the House of Lords, defended to his fellow peers his decision to send his son to Eton ('it seems to me that if one is living in a fairly prosperous home, it is a mistake to educate one's child differently from those one knows socially'); Joe Orton's hastily rewritten *Loot*, playing in Brighton after a disastrous week in Cambridge, had Kenneth Williams (Inspector Truscott) gloomy even by his standards ('the cast is demoralised and the script practically in rags and some of it complete nonsense'); a White Paper set out the government's plan for a prices and incomes board, still an essentially voluntary system; with a budget looming and sterling under familiar pressure, a Cabinet meeting prompted Richard Crossman to observe of the chancellor, James Callaghan, and other working-class ministers that 'one could see how, whether they belong to the Right or to the Left of the Party, they can be terrorized, and how weak and pliable they are in the hands of the City and of the Bank of England when a crisis of this kind blows up and they feel they must put the country before their class'; 'Ringo got married!' recorded a teenage diarist, Roger Darlington, of the surprise event, adding that 'at least somebody is happy'; and on Friday the 12th – as the *Salford City Reporter* revealed that Salford was set to put up one of the first factory-made prefabricated blocks of flats in the country; as the *Liverpool Echo* quoted 85-year-old Mrs George Stopforth about her rundown terraced cottage due to be demolished under compulsory purchase order ('I feel broken-hearted about having to move . . . I want to stay here in Aigburgh Vale . . . I have spent all my life here, and I love it'); and as twelve-year-old Julia McLaughlin enjoyed the annual 'House Party' at her convent school in Preston ('more and nicer food than last year') – Malcolm X visited Smethwick.[2]

He was a charismatic Black American civil rights activist; the West Midlands town had the previous October infamously swung Conservative – wholly against the national trend – following an explicitly racist campaign by the successful candidate, Peter Griffiths; and the visitor had travelled in a BBC car, with an accompanying BBC crew fronted by *Tonight*'s Julian Pettifer, eager to report any potential confrontation, above all between Malcolm X and Griffiths. In the event, the MP remained in London, so instead the focus was on Malcolm X's inspection of Marshall Street, where the Conservative-run local council was planning to buy houses in order to prevent it from becoming a 'coloured ghetto'. At some point, either before or after going to the street (accounts differ), he was asked by the press why he had come to Smethwick. 'I have come because I am disturbed by reports that coloured people in Smethwick are being treated badly,' he replied. 'I have heard that they are being treated as the Jews were under Hitler.' What would he do if that was true? 'I would not wait for the Fascist element in Smethwick to erect gas ovens.' In Marshall Street itself, Malcolm X very deliberately stood outside the house, belonging to Mrs Joyce Parkes, that Smethwick Council was planning to purchase as the first step in implementing its scheme; while later he was taken by his local host, the trade unionist and anti-racism activist Avtar Singh Jouhl, to one of the town's many racially segregated pubs, the Blue Gates, where in the smokers' room both men were refused service. It is fairly clear that the white reaction to Malcolm X's few hours in Smethwick was on the whole hostile. 'It's disgusting that the BBC should bring that man here,' a shopkeeper in Marshall Street, coming out to watch the filming, told a reporter. 'They are trying to stir up the trouble in this street.' 'Simply deplorable' were the words of the Conservative mayor, Alderman Clarence Williams; but Mrs Parkes took a milder tone: 'I had never heard of him before he came here. I don't know whether it was a good idea to bring him here and I shall be very glad when the whole issue of colour troubles in this street is finished.' And Malcolm X himself? Had his visit, he was asked before he left in order to address a meeting of Islamic students at Birmingham University, confirmed the fears he had earlier spoken of? 'I can't say yet,' he answered.[3]

Next day Frederick Ward near Bristol did his first gardening of the year ('I dug a trench and filled it with compost – that is for the first planting of peas'); on Sunday the Kinks arrived at London Airport, after a tour down under, to find 'Tired of Waiting for You' topping the charts; and on Monday the Scottish bankers were treated to a well-publicised lecture by the Bank of England's patrician, right-wing governor, Lord Cromer, demanding that the new Labour government curtail its spendthrift instincts – a lecture that next day had one minister, Barbara Castle, asking Callaghan what he proposed to do about it, to which 'he merely grinned and didn't look too displeased', albeit 'he did add that he must seek the right moment to deal with Cromer and it hadn't arrived yet'. On the stage that Tuesday, the continuing nightmare of *Loot* (by now in Oxford, where Williams noted a 'dreadful' performance, as 'the hysteria started mounting' with 'the laughter that comes from desperation and ludicrousness') contrasted with a triumphant first night at the Old Vic for Franco Zeffirelli's carnivalesque *Much Ado About Nothing*, with next morning the *Daily Mail*'s Bernard Levin a rare dissenting voice ('one of the most excruciatingly tedious evenings obtainable this side of Hull'). In the context of Islington Council's plans to redevelop the Packington Estate, comprising some 220 attractive early Victorian terraced houses, and replace them with linked six-storey blocks of flats, 'Why Demolish Good Houses?' was the *Evening Standard*'s understandably pained Wednesday headline, while at Emsworth in Hampshire it was a typically industrious, family-oriented day for Daphne Meryon, a naval commander's wife with an iron grip on her domestic economy:

> Peter had to catch 7.34 to spend day in London, so was up early and I saw to his breakfast before dressing. I made a stew and a cake this morning, finished letter to Judy [her daughter, studying at Exeter University], then spent 2 hours on raspberry bed, mainly weeding along edges. Mrs Newell spring cleaned Clare's bedroom. I spent afternoon listening to radio play and working at dressing table cover, having had late lunch. Peter home about 7.15. We sat in little room after supper and I wrote letters to France about Nonie's proposed stay there.

'The American Dream Is at the Expense of the American Negro' was the motion next evening for the televised debate at the Cambridge Union, as James Baldwin and William F. Buckley Jr locked horns, Simon Schama of Christ's acted as one of the tellers, and – in a sign of the shifting student mood a year after the Union had given its approval to the Douglas-Home government – Baldwin won by 544 votes to 380; Christopher Booker in the latest *Spectator* pondered the limited impact of the *Sun* ('it is still no more than an improved *Daily Herald*, its tone is generally little higher than that of the *Mirror* – and it certainly never began to be the sort of "left-wing *Guardian*" that some of its staff hoped it was to become'); watching on Saturday evening the fourth outing of Peter Cook and Dudley Moore's *Not Only . . . But Also*, viewers found the Leaping Nuns sketch 'almost hysterically funny'; next day's *Observer* colour magazine profiled the visionary, larger-than-life, Jaguar-driving 'Mr Newcastle', aka T. Dan Smith ('our city has to be equal to the demands of the twenty-first century, a city people will come to see and live in because we have solved the problem of the car and city environment'); and in Harlem, nine days after upsetting a Smethwick shopkeeper, Malcolm X was shot dead.[4]

The box in the corner rolled on regardless. 'Clearly very popular with the sample at large, Val Doonican himself was often described as a man of immense charm – delightfully relaxed and easy in manner and with a singing voice as pleasing and attractive as his personality,' ran the BBC audience research summary of viewer reaction to *Date with Doonican* on Monday the 22nd, though an electrician did grumble that 'I suppose it will please the old folk but drab sentimental slosh is not for me'; next evening saw limited overall enthusiasm for the *Monitor* special on Samuel Beckett ('held little or no appeal for about half its audience, who, in many cases, dismissed it as "dull, meaningless piffle" '); that week's *The Wednesday Play* was a debut for Dennis Potter, whose *The Confidence Course* (about self-motivation courses) earned an underwhelming Reaction Index (RI) of 49, with a typical response being 'not really a play, but a lecture and counter-lecture with trimmings'; the same day, *Punch*'s TV critic, Patrick Skene Catling, noted that the current series of *Dr Who* (still less than two years old) had 'descended from the wonder of daleks to the ludicrous bathos of giant cardboard ants'; and next day, the day of Jennie Lee's pioneering White Paper on the arts (demanding from government 'a more coherent, generous and imaginative approach'), *New Society* included a lengthy piece by David Robinson on *Coronation Street* (not yet five years old). After running through all the main characters – including Jack and Elsie Tanner at the Rover's Return; Albert Tatlock at No. 1; Minnie Caldwell at No. 5; Ken Barlow at No. 9; Elsie Tanner at No. 11; the Ogdens at No. 13; Ena Sharples, live-in caretaker at the Mission; Len Fairclough in Maudsley Street at the back of the Mission – he went on:

> Behind all this immediate life and present history, though, there spreads a communal memory, an imaginary past in which the viewer is invited to share. Generations have learned their alphabet at Bessy Street School, and sometimes the old ones recall the years there before the First World War. People recall the Depression and unemployment and the Silver Jubilee. And only a week or so ago Elsie Tanner was saying to Len Fairclough: 'When them sirens went 25 years ago it started a lovely war for me. I had a smashing time one way and another . . .' When an unexploded bomb was found last summer they all went down the Mission stokehole and ex-warden Ena put on her tin hat and sang 'Rock of Ages', and they remembered the good times and the comradeship of the war.

In short, and unanswerably, 'this past is all so alive'.[5]

TV also played its inevitable part on Saturday the 27th – debut for *The Worker* (Charlie Drake reporting each week to the Labour Exchange, a conversation with the long-suffering counter clerk Mr Pugh, then off to create innocent chaos); *Not So Much a Programme, More a Way of Life* (successor to *TW3*) provoking the Catholic establishment with a satirical sketch about birth control – but not to the exclusion of everything else. For Davy Jones & The Manish Boys, whose van had broken down, the day began with a difficult hitch from Portsmouth, as the long-haired future David Bowie and his two equally long-haired male companions met such driver resistance that eventually his father had to be summoned from Bromley to fetch them; in Peterborough, one shopper, J. Parsons of Dogsthorpe, was appalled by the appearance of '"Mod" girls' ('drab and unflattering outfits . . . hair cropped deplorably short, dry and lifeless . . . their faces repellent, for what complexion they had originally has been lost after many applications of very pale, unflattering make-up'); the writer J. R. Ackerley told a friend that Stan Laurel's death had 'saddened me more than the deaths of Edith [Sitwell], Eliot, or Churchill'; Philip Larkin, after noting how in a supermarket that day 'canned piano music provided a brisk version of *Waiting at the Church*', outlined to Monica Jones his plans for going to Lord's that summer ('I must say I resent paying £2.10 or whatever it is a day to watch the S. Africans, whom I remember as one of the peaks of boredom in a life liberally supplied with that commodity'); the Kinks that evening played a double-header, the Adelphi Ballroom in West Bromwich followed by the Smethwick Baths; and Kenneth Williams, no longer in the ingrate provinces, thankfully noted how 'an absolutely packed house' in Golders Green had given *Loot* a 'colossal reception'. Yet all this was not quite a full lid – for that afternoon at London Zoo, a seven-year-old male eagle called Goldie had made his escape while his cage was being cleaned, settling seventy feet high in a Regent's Park tree and, when darkness fell and high-powered beams sought to dazzle him into immobility, resisting all attempts at recapture. So, too, on Sunday, with Williams – about to head unhappily to Bournemouth for *Loot*'s next round – among those taking a walk in the park and spotting the golden eagle. 'It was', he recorded without comment but perhaps implicit sympathy, 'being harried by gulls and crows.'[6]

Goldie stayed free through the first day of March, the major news event being a contretemps with a Cairn terrier, while that Monday evening, shortly after Hugh Mortimer (John Bentley) had turned up at the *Crossroads* motel and met Meg Richardson (Noele Gordon) for the first time, things on the south coast went much as expected ('they sat shocked and stunned, gasping their "ohs" and "ahs" and we got a lukewarm reception'); next day, as the increasingly famous eagle showed no interest in the meat offered as bait and condemned his keepers to 'cold, wearying trudges' as they 'trailed him with their nets and food attached to a rope', a combination of seven dissenting Conservative MPs (including Norman St John Stevas, Aubrey Jones, Humphry Berkeley and Terence Higgins) and more than fifty abstaining ones (including Iain Macleod, Sir Edward Boyle and Jim Prior) ensured defeat for a motion put forward by Sir Cyril Osborne – a prominent backbench right-winger – calling for 'periodic and precise limits on immigration'; next morning's *Daily Express* included a Cummings cartoon in effect saying that Britain's over-lenient immigration policy would lead to race riots; Goldie's main foe on Wednesday was a black mongrel called Rex, while next day his aerial tour of victory featured flying over a snowbound Lord's cricket ground; this Thursday also saw the launch of *Nova*, a new, upmarket monthly magazine (Molly Parkin as fashion editor) explicitly aimed at 'the woman who wants more than tea and sympathy', but instead 'SOMETHING TO THINK ABOUT – ARGUE ABOUT – EVEN DISAGREE WITH'; and on Friday the 5th, as Goldie in Regent's Park risked alienating his many fans by devouring most of a black-and-white Muscovy duck in the grounds of the American ambassador's residence, the *Bournemouth Times* gave *Loot* the dustiest of reviews ('sinks to the level of lavatorial wit . . . altogether a thoroughly unsatisfactory evening'), the *Daily Express*'s more congenial cartoonist Osbert Lancaster had one upper-class lady in grave conversation with another ('You know, dear, I've a nasty feeling that very soon we're going to *have* to know the difference between Vietnam and Vietcong'), the Conservative spokesman for Home Affairs (Peter Thorneycroft, recently replacing the much more liberal Edward Boyle) used a party meeting to support a motion stating that 'Britain must for the moment reject the multi-racial State', an education lecturer at Sheffield University (Dr Dorothea Mowat) told the Sheffield Soroptimists' Club that the comprehensivisation of secondary education was being done in too sweeping a fashion ('I think the people who are so very much against the doing away of grammar schools would not resist so strongly if the whole was not to be changed at once'), Tariq Ali narrowly defeated Quintin Hogg's son Douglas to become president of the Oxford Union, and Brian Jones of the Rolling Stones, backstage at the Regal in Edmonton, commended his namesake Tom (about to go top with 'It's Not Unusual') as 'a straight Ernie' who 'you can talk to easily over a pint'.[7]

Saturday was Goldie's day for playing to the gallery ('under a blue sky, with sunlight sparkling on the Regent's Park snow, he seemed to be making his majestic flights from tree to not-too-distant tree whenever the admiring crowds below showed signs of restiveness'), while for the *New Statesman*'s John Morgan and the *Daily Mail*'s Virginia Ironside it was a day of contrasts. Perhaps rather unwillingly, Morgan found himself in Alvechurch, a large Worcestershire village of some 5,000 people, whose team had unexpectedly made it to the quarter-final of the Amateur Cup and were now pitted against Enfield in front of a crowd of some 10,000:

> It [the village] has a house in the middle of the street from a window in which an old woman peered at the mob of men striding with that

> hard, purposeful look of football crowds, through narrow lanes. Gnarled oak trees surrounded the small, sloping pitch. Boys and men sat on the branches – in one I counted 27 – like crows against the pale sky. Oil drums, builders' small scaffolds, mounds of bricks: men who had these blocked the view of those who didn't.

From early on it was clear that the visitors were going to win, which they did comfortably enough 3–1. 'The Alvechurch players looked big, raw country boys with long shorts,' concluded Morgan. 'A dark cloud came over the snow on the hill, the crowd moved away, the afternoon became very cold and it took half an hour to push the car out of a muddy field.' For Ironside, in Liverpool to see the Stones at the Empire, it was a mixture of work and pleasure: the obligatory interview with the group's by now undisputed main man ('skimpily built, with a mouth that seems to stretch wider than his shoulders') and an overall experience which she would recall wistfully six years later when mulling whether to try to get tickets for the Stones at the Roundhouse:

> After initially thinking how much I wanted to go, I decided eventually not to as I don't want to see them spoiled. I don't want to see them being clapped after each number and not mobbed. I want to remember them in Liverpool with the mods in their funny little navy blue suits and short cropped hair (girls) and the boys with their longish hair and sharp clothes, running towards the stage screaming Mick Mick! and being beaten off by heavies, and picked up physically by Stones 'helpers' (thugs, bodyguards more likely) back into the screaming groping mob. I want to remember having a drink in the Liverpool pub before the show and going out into the greyness and seeing the police chasing the mods down the cobbled alley, and I want to remember the compere screaming 'M' and the yells of response 'I!' (screams) 'C!' 'K!' 'MICK JAGGER!', his words drowned in screams and the whole stalls getting up in a force as Jagger leapt onto the stage screaming into the mike.

'I'm quite an unenthusiastic person, really,' Jagger himself had told her. 'It's not that I'm rude. The only thing I really get enthusiastic about is audiences.'

'The Eagle is still at large,' noted McBride on Sunday the 7th, after a day in which thousands had thronged Regent's Park, causing traffic jams on the Outer Circle, in order to watch keepers, police, fire-fighters and even the BBC's John Timpson (playing an enticing tune on his recently acquired Ethiopian bird pipe) try in vain to outwit Goldie – somehow a suitable backdrop for the start of *Round the Horne*, successor to *Beyond Our Ken*, co-written by Barry Took and Marty Feldman, and starring Kenneth Williams, Hugh Paddick, Betty Marsden and Bill Pertwee as well as Kenneth Horne himself. 'At a time when television viewing was a national obsession and radio very much the poor relation,' recalled Took's obituarist, 'the mass audience would return to sound broadcasting to enjoy the double-entendres of rustic folk singer Rambling Sid Rumpo, the grandiose ambitions of J. Peasemould Gruntfuttock and, best of all, the camp repartee of Jule and Sand [Julian and Sandy], the out-of-work queens of the acting profession who were for ever turning up to do odd jobs for the urbane Horne'. This particular week, few laughs on the Monday – the trial starting at the Old Bailey of the Kray twins, Reginald and Ronald, for demanding money with menaces; Sir Kenneth Clark addressing National Trust members at the Royal Festival Hall and telling them that 'with the help of our democratic institutions, our local authorities and planning committees have done more in a few years than time, neglect or enemy action had done in centuries to obliterate history and destroy the visible beauty of England'; those knocking on doors in Stevenage to collect for the Churchill Memorial Fund being rebuffed, often rudely, by almost three-quarters of those asked – but at least Goldie was still a beacon of liberty, albeit on the Tuesday thwarted by the crowd, who chased him away after he had swooped down on a tasty-looking snow goose. Finally, soon after dawn on Wednesday the 10th, a week and a half after his great escape, the end came:

> He was caught [reported the *Daily Telegraph*'s Kathleen Welsh] by Mr Joe McCorry, deputy head keeper of birds of prey at the Zoo, without even the help of a snare. His capture was a triumph for the bird psychology of the experts. He was caught on one of their food lures, a dead rabbit, as they had predicted from the first that he would be, when he grew hungry enough to take it. He was captured

> when they had said he would be, in the early morning, before sightseers were around to distract him . . .

It was not exactly a case of national mourning; but as McBride regretfully recorded, probably echoing the sentiments of most, 'Goldie the eagle has been caught & is back in his cage, much to the general disgust'.[8]

Other diarists that day had other preoccupations, starting with Tony Benn (or Anthony Wedgwood Benn, as the Postmaster General was still better known) and his audience at Buckingham Palace with the Queen. The subject was the design of postage stamps – and, specifically, whether she would in principle be willing to have designs submitted for her consideration to include stamps which did not include her head. In the course of their conversation, the monarch 'indicated that she had never seen any of these stamps and would be interested to see them'. Whereupon:

> I said, 'Well, I've got some in my bag' (having brought David Gentleman's collection as provided this morning). The Queen wanted me to leave the new designs with her but I explained the difficulties and she agreed to see them on the spot.
>
> This was exactly what I had hoped would happen so I unlocked my bag and spread out on the floor twelve huge design models of the stamps provided by Gentleman and also brought out his album of foreign stamps. I then knelt on the floor and one after the other passed up to the Queen the Battle of Britain stamps bearing the words 'Great Britain' and no royal head on them. It was a most hilarious scene because I had my papers all over the place and she was peering at something that had obviously never been shown to her or even thought about at the Palace before . . .

'The fact is,' Benn reflected afterwards, 'the Palace is determined not to get into any controversy in which they might be seen to be responsible for holding back popular clamour for change.' Elsewhere, *Loot* was by now in the middle of another fairly dismal out-of-London week, this time at the Opera House in Manchester; and Williams, his heart no longer in it (if it ever had been), merely recorded, 'They made us take out "stopcock" and the rhumba gag 'cos the Watch Committee have objected to it here! Fantastic.' What about the political runes, some five months after Harold Wilson's narrow victory? Head of the Government Economic Service was Alec Cairncross, who in the evening gave a dinner party at which two of his guests (one of them Sir Geoffrey Crowther, a former editor of *The Economist*) 'said that they would vote Labour at an election tomorrow and had not done so last October'. 'This is in line', added Cairncross, 'with a lot of current thinking which is appalled at the poor showing of the Tories in opposition [still led by Sir Alec Douglas-Home] and correspondingly more willing to make allowances for the inexperience of the Labour Party in office.'

But for two final diarists, wholly non-public concerns. 'Saw the Blue Tits go in box again breakfast time,' gratefully noted Grace Taylor in Ruislip; while for the 55-year-old Frederick Ward, the highly conscientious manager of the Co-operative Wholesale Society's Bristol Grocery and Provisions Department as well as a palpably good citizen and family man, the usual factual record of his daily round was on this particular Wednesday in March 1965 replaced by an entry altogether more naked, a reminder perhaps of the abiding truth of Henry David Thoreau's dictum about most men leading lives of quiet desperation:

> In my private life I am always hoping something unusual will happen to break the monotony. When something happens in my business life which changes the daily pattern I become on edge and often start worrying. The sugar market is more jumpy than usual and I make my life miserable trying to do the impossible, that is trying to satisfy everyone. I want to avoid the criticism of the Directors and the lawyers, I want to make money for the CWS and the Societies. This creates a state of mind which makes me worry about the future and consider every personal expense as something which should be minimised or avoided. The next stage is concern about using leisure time to some advantage. What should I be learning and what skill should I be perfecting to equip myself for the protection of my income in the future?[9]

2

Why Didn't They Send Us *Hamlet* Instead?

'WOMAN GIVES CATHEDRAL ADDRESS' was the headline in the *Ripon Gazette* on Thursday the 11th; an opinion poll in that morning's *Daily Express* revealed that 88 per cent would be in favour of a state lottery whose profits went to good causes, with 79 per cent saying they would have a flutter either sometimes or every time; the report by Sir Milner Holland on London housing, which Sir Keith Joseph had commissioned after the Rachman revelations of 1963, contained an abundance of detailed evidence about landlords intimidating and generally abusing their tenants; a Cabinet discussion saw the government in tacit retreat from Labour's electoral stance of strong resistance to the railway closure programme of the 1963 Beeching Report; in the Commons, Richard Buchanan, a Glaswegian railway toolmaker who had become a Labour MP the previous year, urged ministers to impose a compulsory levy on the tobacco companies equivalent to the government grant towards cancer research; at Roundhay School's speech day, in Leeds, the headmaster 'criticised the G.C.E. "O" Level Examination for putting a straitjacket on curriculum, for placing a premium on facts, too closely directed and predigested work, dictated notes, and what has been called "scissors and paste" type of teaching'; at Cheltenham, the Irish-trained Arkle won the Gold Cup for the second time, trouncing his great rival, Mill House, by 20 lengths; at Layer de la Haye, near Colchester, the Revd James Allen decided to skip the local Amateur Dramatic Society at the village hall and reflected that the days of village drama were just about over ('when people see finished productions on the television – however poor the plays themselves may be – people are not content to put up with amateurishness'); the soon-to-be-legendary sculpture show *The New Generation: 1965* opened at the Whitechapel Gallery, with one reviewer noting that 'materials are synthetic, colours shrill, utility ignored'; and Sylvia Plath's posthumous *Ariel* was published. The critics were soon out in force – Al Alvarez hailing the poems as 'works of great artistic purity and, despite all the nihilism, great generosity'; Cyril Connolly less complimentary, calling her poems 'feminine and rather too ebullient and formless' – with perhaps the most resonant review being Macha Rosenthal's in the *Spectator*. After describing Plath as a poet with an 'absolute, almost demonically intense commitment by the end to the confessional mode', he ended: 'Thinking of this pitifully brief career, it is hard not to ask whether the cultivation of sensibility is after all worth the candle. The answer is yes, for reasons that I hope we all know – yet it seems important to raise the question anyway.'[1]

Over this next fortnight in March, *Ready, Steady, Go!* on the 12th featured Donovan singing his about-to-be-released debut single 'Catch the Wind', greeted by *Melody Maker*'s Ray Coleman as 'very Bob Dylanish, but once you've got over the shock of that, it's a really pleasant record'; next day, Eric Clapton walked out of the Yardbirds (accused by him of having gone 'too commercial'); George Best at Old Trafford 'induced an attack of vertigo' on his hapless marker (Chelsea's Eddie McCreadie); and in the 'very much enjoyed' viewers' stakes for *The Billy Cotton Band Show*, Russ Conway's 61 per cent compared very favourably with Tom Jones's 35 per cent, even though the Welshman had just gone No. 1 for the first time with 'It's Not Unusual'; 'only four in the congregation', noted James Allen without comment on the Sunday, adding that later he had watched *The Thirty-Nine Steps* on TV ('an actor called More took the part of Richard Hannay'); while a few days later, his diary focused on one of the more loyal members of his congregation, a sidesman and a reader who was chairman of the Churchyard Committee, as well as being an army colonel. Would he be willing, Allen had asked him, to attend the 'No Small Change' course during Lent? Sadly, 'he wrote to say that he dislikes discussion groups having been a soldier all his life!' No such hang-ups for the American expatriate Dee Wells (married to the philosopher A. J. Ayer), who that Wednesday evening, on Rediffusion's lively discussion programme *Three after Six*, caused a storm by effectively accusing the police of being thugs who wanted to beat people up; an hour or so later, on *Coronation Street*, Elsie Tanner began work at Gamma Garments, a day that began poorly (going out in the wrong shoes) and got worse; while around midnight the following evening, three of the Rolling Stones (after playing a show at Romford) pulled up in their Daimler at the Francis Service Station in Forest Gate and asked to avail themselves of the facilities, only to be told that the public lavatory was being 'reconditioned' and that the staff lavatory was out of bounds. At which point, as West Ham Magistrates Court would eventually hear before issuing fines, Messrs Jagger, Jones and Wyman urinated against the service station's boundary wall 'without taking steps to conceal this act'.[2]

'Nig-nog' and 'golliwog' were, at Elland Road on the afternoon of the 20th, among the terms directed at Leeds United's Albert Johanneson by his opponents. 'There was one point early in the game when one of the Everton players called me a "black bastard,"' he recalled. 'The referee was close at hand and heard the remark. I asked him if he was going to do something about it. "Nothing son, that's what they think you are though, a black bastard, so why worry?"' That Saturday evening, Kathy Kirby with 'I Belong' came second in Naples in the Eurovision Song Contest; Williams et al. ended at Wimbledon the final dismal week of *Loot*'s run, with no West End theatre in the offing; and Tamla Motown's UK tour – star-studded (the Supremes, Stevie Wonder, Smokey Robinson & the Miracles, Martha & the Vandellas) but under-publicised and poorly attended – began at the Finsbury Park Astoria, with Philip Larkin presumably never tempted, writing next day to his mother, 'I have a kind of phobia about London – I feel great West Indian & Pakistani germs hopping on me in the tubes . . .'; Crossman on Tuesday published his Rent Bill, a direct response to the Milner Holland report, seeking to give every tenant 'a reasonable security of tenure' but, perhaps inevitably, leading to a serious decline in the availability of private rented accommodation; John Fowles next day received from his ambitious publisher, Tom Maschler of Jonathan Cape, the telegram he was hoping for about what would become an era-defining novel – 'Was greatly entertained, intrigued and very very impressed by *The Magus*'; while that Wednesday night at Jedburgh Town Hall it was victory in the Roxburgh, Selkirk and Peebles by-election for the Liberals and David Steel, making him at twenty-six the youngest MP in the Commons. He had made Borders depopulation the big issue; his Conservative opponent, the wealthy and well-connected Robin McEwen, did his image few favours by wearing shooting gloves as he canvassed; and a family friend who came to the constituency to help McEwen would say afterwards, 'I had no idea that there were so many slums in Galashiels'.

Donovan was the subject this Thursday for Virginia Ironside's *Daily Mail* pop column ('with long curly hair, a funny little mouth and turned-up nose, he possesses a gentle ingenuousness that only just avoids being embarrassing'); Kevin Burke, a handsome nineteen-year-old Old Etonian, met seventeen-year-old Camilla Shand at her coming-out party in Knightsbridge, leading very soon afterwards to an affair which the following decade would disqualify her as a bride for the young Prince Charles; and the TV play of the day was Harold Pinter's *Tea Party*, starring Leo McKern (as a troubled businessman) and Pinter's wife, Vivien Merchant. 'A very good play indeed, written with extraordinary definition and clarity, and yet with all those strange undertones of the sinister and the absurd of which he is a master,' insisted the *Guardian*'s Mary Crozier; but from the BBC Viewing Panel, an RI of only 47. '"Absolute drivel and incomprehensible nonsense" was the description endorsed by many viewers who were apparently unable to detect any plot or any semblance of reality in the theme which, in addition, moved tediously and pointlessly to an ambiguous end.' Moreover, went on the audience research report, 'there was support for the contention that "the portrayal of a diseased mind" was neither interesting nor entertaining, and that the unpleasantness of the theme, with its emphasis on sex and its complex, abstract treatment, was both disagreeable and unintelligible'. Or as one viewer summed up their reaction to the hour and a quarter: 'After all the ballyhoo, I felt I must watch the play, but was bewildered by it. All it did for me was to make me feel an idiot. I had decided ages ago not to look at another Pinter play, and this one confirmed it. Never again.'[3]

Two contrasting new films were by this time either on the big screen or about to be. 'The most dreary and colourless performance I have seen in years' was the *Sunday Express*'s obtuse take on Michael Caine's Harry Palmer in *The Ipcress File* (based on Len Deighton's recent thriller), but most critics got the point of this emblematic anti-hero. 'He will never aspire to a sharkskin dinner-jacket and a tawny Brazilian mistress,' observed Kenneth Tynan, adding that Caine 'plays him with the right seedy coolness'; 'a cynical non-U character with a splendid knack of dead-pan insolence to authority', noted Richard Mallett; while according to *Sight & Sound*'s Geoffrey Nowell-Smith:

> For the first time in a British film heroism is no longer the prerogative of a tight-lipped aristocracy imbued with the public school ethos. Nor is it seen as a patriotic abnegation, the sacrifice of the individual to the nation. This cockney joker, a classic anti-hero if there ever was one, becomes a true hero through his will to survive. And his power of survival resides not in class conditioning . . . but in the assertion of his own individuality.

It was, through perfect casting, the film that made Caine into a major star – the cockney boy, with a rebellious streak, made good – but *The Sound of Music*'s Julie Andrews was already internationally famous. The critics generally found it tough going, typified by Tynan characterising its flavour as 'like that of a sugary, *spätlese* hock, left so long in the sun that it tastes like syrup'. None more so than the *Sunday Telegraph*'s Philip Oakes, for whom the 'fatuous' optimism and almost ceaseless singing ('barring the Nazis') comprised 'nearly three of the most punishing hours I've ever spent in the cinema'. There existed, he did not deny, 'an audience ready and waiting' for the film, the same audience 'which has kept the show running for four years on the London stage'. But, he went on, 'what they are keeping alive is a dodo' – a dodo which 'on the screen lays an almighty egg'. Almighty indeed, and in the event only *Sgt. Pepper's Lonely Hearts Club Band* would surpass the soundtrack to *The Sound of Music* as the decade's best-selling album.[4]

Optimism in the air at Elephant and Castle on Friday the 26th, as the Minister of Labour, Ray Gunter, opened the new, three-storey shopping centre, complete with bronze statue of an elephant carrying a castle on its back; late that evening, in a hotel lounge near Cardiff's New Theatre, the young drama critic Benedict Nightingale sat down to write a largely laudatory review of the world premiere of Harold Pinter's *The Homecoming* ('his gift is to imply a whole background, a near-lifetime, of emotional complications from a mere two hours of action on the stage'), while, he would recall, 'trying to ignore people yelping "Bloody disgusting", "What did it mean?" and "Why didn't they send us *Hamlet* instead?"'; and about the same time, on *Not So Much a Programme, More a Way of Life*, Bernard Levin described Sir Alec Douglas-Home as a 'cretin', an 'imbecile' and 'not equipped to conduct a bus let alone a great party', provoking next day a volley of attacks by Conservative MPs on the BBC ('Left-wing bias . . . exceeded the bounds of decency . . . disgusting and unseemly sensationalism'). Saturday was, more broadly, an international sort of day: a thrilling Grand National – billed as the last before the Aintree course was sold to property developers – won by the American horse Jay Trump, with American jockey and American owner; and, in London's Soho, the opening of the first Pizza Express, brainchild of the Italy-loving businessman Peter Boizot, shipping over an oven from Naples and undeterred by takings for the day of only £3. Sunday, the day in Wales of the long-expected, reservoir-creating flooding of the Tryweryn Valley that would provide water to Liverpool, saw a fateful conjunction: the sudden death of the Princess Royal, the Countess of Harewood (the Queen's aunt and Duke of Windsor's sister), followed by *Not So Much* . . . deciding to go ahead with a fairly feeble mock-operatic sketch about the Abdication crisis, causing an almost instantly jammed switchboard; and the upshot, announced on Monday evening after the hottest March day in half a century, was the BBC's decision to pull the plug on *TW3*'s successor once the current series ended on 11 April. 'The difficulty is to combine freedom of expression with a full sense of responsibility,' publicly reflected the director general, Sir Hugh Greene. 'I still think there is room for satire on the air but I do not think that we have the formula right yet.'[5]

'Pension increased 12/6 so everyone is pleased,' noted the elderly Gladys Hague on Tuesday. 'Have bought a green nylon raincoat.' She lived in Keighley, a long way in every sense from the Unity Theatre in NW3 where that evening David Halliwell's epic, high-energy, six-hour *Little Malcolm and His Struggle Against the Eunuchs* (Hitlerish, revenge-seeking anti-hero: Malcolm Scrawdyke, founder of the Party of Dynamic Erection) had, with Mike Leigh as director, its first outing. 'Although audiences were poor and the production doomed, the show was a watershed,' reckons Michael Coveney. 'It convinced Leigh that he should really only direct his own work. But the play has a rawness, rebelliousness and crude vitality that later became characteristics of Leigh's own stuff.' On Thursday, 1 April, the GLC (the Greater London Council, replacing the London County Council) marked its first full day by unveiling the route of the 'inner circle' of new urban motorways ('Ringways') it planned to ring central London, with such areas as Hampstead, Highgate, Islington, Greenwich, Blackheath and Battersea all earmarked to find themselves in the firing line: not at all what the gentrifiers had signed up for. The same day had the royal family at Harewood in Yorkshire for the burial of the Princess Royal. 'How Hanoverian Prince Charles looks,' thought James Allen after seeing him on television. 'It is strange that the "German" look continues to make itself apparent in the physiognomy of the Royal Family. There is, of course, so much German blood in them and it is to be hoped that the Prince of Wales will marry an English girl.'

One English girl now about to do her job alone was Cathy McGowan, for Friday the 2nd marked all change: the show renamed *Ready Steady Goes Live!*; no miming; no longer coming from Kingsway, but a much bigger studio at Wembley; and the less than cutting-edge Keith Fordyce quietly let go. 'The studio dance floor was jammed with boys and girls dressed to kill,' observed *Punch*'s Patrick Skene Catling. 'Cathy McGowan, pretty and bubbly with the thrill of it all, indicated that the moment had come to let the good times roll, and Manfred Mann, almost as realistically as on records, began a plaintive, groaning, passionate imitation of Ray Charles . . .' Other performers this evening included Zoot Money's Big Roll Band ('the vocalist, evidently a faithful student of the dialect of the underprivileged hog-callers of the Mississippi Delta, sang the pop creed: "Ya gotta live fuh yo-seff!"') and Donovan ('beautifully back-lighted so that an electric nimbus glowed around the edges of his luxuriant curls,' but his mouth-organ sounding 'as though he is blowing soup through a comb'). The star for Skene Catling? Undoubtedly Dionne Warwick, who 'sounded a discordant note of mature professionalism, but no new show is flawless'.[6]

Relatively few governments have a minister doubling as a diarist keeping an informal record of events; even fewer have a first-class diarist; but Harold Wilson's Labour government had, by happy if distorting chance, as many as three excellent diarists: Tony Benn, Barbara Castle (at Overseas Development) and the housing minister Richard Crossman. Distorting because all political diarists worth their salt give full value to personalities, rivalries and all the petty jealousies almost inherent in any collective endeavour. So if we tend to see that Labour government as especially fractious, it may well be that this is largely because we have an abundance of evidence usually much less available. No diarist more worth his salt in this particular respect than Crossman, arguably one of the great diarists – constantly engaged in an unresolvable quarrel with himself – of any genre. During the spring and early summer of 1965, he despaired of Wilson ('has not grown up since he went to Downing Street . . . is not developing into a strong Prime Minister . . . lacks both an inner Cabinet and a real strategy . . .'); complained that the chancellor, James (Jim) Callaghan, 'made no effort' to judge things 'from the point of view of Government strategy as a whole', but instead saw everything 'in strict Treasury terms'; identified in Benn 'an odd hardness which makes him sometimes unattractive as a colleague', even 'a kind of mechanical Nonconformist self-righteousness'; found Frank Cousins (Minister of Technology) 'a terrible old blatherer, talking on every subject and usually saying the obvious thing'; and dismissed almost out of hand Sir Frank Soskice (home secretary, 'ineffective'), Tom Fraser (Minister of Transport, 'pretty disastrous') and Douglas Houghton (Chancellor of the Duchy of Lancaster, 'I don't find him very impressive, and certainly he is a dreadful chairman').

What about George Brown, the man charged – at the Department of Economic Affairs – with the task of transforming the British economy into one of permanent high growth? Crossman during these months gave him fairly mild treatment, apart from wishing he was less dilatory about producing the much-anticipated National Plan; and it was instead left to another diarist, Alec Cairncross, to produce the definitive description of why Brown was ultimately, for all his gifts, such a high-maintenance operator. The occasion, in late March, was a dinner hosted by the Italian ambassador:

> G. Brown was there and about 40 others. He ragged Cromer [Lord Cromer, governor of the Bank of England] unmercifully at the table

> and passed messages to Lady C. comparing her with Mata Hari until Pieraccini, who sat between them and spoke no English, offered to change places with G.B., imagining he wanted to make eyes at Lady C. – although Mrs B. sat opposite, stern as a disapproving landlady.
>
> When the ladies left he divided his fire between C. and me saying he couldn't make up his mind which of us to nominate for the Consulate Generalship of the Yemen (a favourite threat of his I gather). Somebody suggested the Leeward Isles and George at once corrected the pronunciation (twice, in fact) to Looard . . .

During the dinner itself, Cairncross's wife, Mary, had sat next to Cromer, and she reported afterwards that, unsurprisingly, he had been 'very annoyed' by Brown's behaviour. Cromer was never going to be any Labour government's friend – but, given the parlous state of sterling, it was still not a great idea to provoke gubernatorial wrath.

As it happened, the budget to be presented by Callaghan was barely a week away; and only two days after the dinner, Cromer frankly warned the chancellor that, such was 'the acute lack of confidence in sterling', it was imperative not only that his fiscal thrust should be deflationary, but that he should think very hard about making any controversial tax changes. In the event, Cromer got half a loaf: significant public expenditure cuts, but the new capital gains and corporation taxes still going ahead. 'A most disgusting attack on anyone who wants to make his way in the world,' one City gentleman standing in Throgmorton Street told the television cameras soon after Callaghan had sat down. 'It's Marxism: they want a communist state. Personally, I shall fight like hell on the beaches, and on the streets and in the farms we will fight them.' Perhaps, though, what really stuck in his craw was the withdrawal of tax relief on business entertainment – a move condemned by the *Financial Times* as 'a clumsy way of getting at the minority who abuse it' and likely to 'create considerable (and justifiable) annoyance among the majority of businessmen who entertain for purely business purposes'. The City over the coming weeks continued to make negative noises, the trade gap continued to widen and Crossman by late May was lamenting, 'my God, the situation is against us', in particular that 'the pound has not been stabilised, despite the deflation we are carrying through'. June saw the gold reserves draining away and sterling still weakening under continuous pressure; but at the start of July, recorded Cairncross after a meeting at No. 10, the three key ministers – Wilson, Callaghan, Brown – were 'all united against devaluation as firmly as ever'.[7] Something, it was clear, was at some point going to have to give.

For a government with a tiny majority but big hopes invested in it, these were not easy times; and inevitably, as with almost any Labour government in almost any era, there was already a whiff of 'betrayal' in the air.

The slow burner, in the context of wage restraint being viewed as crucial just as much as public expenditure restraint if sterling was to be protected, was incomes policy. In theory the trade union movement was – just about – signed up to a policy of tempering its wage claims against the larger economic picture; but with George Brown in mid-March appointing Aubrey Jones to chair the embryonic National Board for Prices and Incomes (NBPI), things started to get serious. Jones himself was a Conservative MP (now giving up his seat) who in his way could hardly have been a more classic figure of his era: a one-nation Conservative, and the son of a South Wales miner, who as early as 1950 had defined the task of modern Conservatism as being 'to effect a reconciliation between industrialist and worker'; and that 'the last thing that Conservatism has ever stood for is "unrestricted private enterprise" – that is, economic liberalism'. His was an essentially corporatist vision – and not at all to the taste of a prominent unreconstructed Tory, Sir Gerald Nabarro, who on Jones's appointment attacked him as a 'jellyfish, without vertebrae, without muscle', who had been 'seduced by his opponents'. Predictably, Jones as a Conservative was also under fire from the unions, with John Boyd of the AEU (Amalgamated Engineering Union) calling him out as an enemy not only of the Labour Party, but of the working class generally. Jones for his part insisted that he was taking the job out of a sense of national duty. 'The party system which we have inherited in this country is, unfortunately, founded on class,' he told the press. 'I was being called upon, it seemed to me, as one who might overcome the rigidities of the present party system and if I were able to do this, I might be able to deflect British politics on to a new course.' Noble aspirations, somewhat undercut by the revelation that Jones had negotiated his salary up from £12,000 to £15,000 – or, put another way, £240 a week at a time when the average industrial weekly wage was barely £18.

A White Paper in early April made it clear that incomes policy would still be on a voluntary basis, with the NBPI making recommendations rather than anything more mandatory. Inevitably this meant in practice an invoking of the greater good. Even if a group of workers was able to make convincing claims of productivity improvements, warned the White Paper, 'exceptional increases should be kept to the minimum, bearing in mind that they will need to be balanced by lower than average increases to other groups if the increase in wages and salaries over the economy as a whole is to be kept within the norm' (that norm being rises of no more than 3–3½ per cent). The last day of April saw executives of 178 unions affiliated to the TUC meeting at Central Hall, Westminster, where – following a stirring address from Brown ('planning is the foundation of all we hope to achieve . . . we decisively reject the free-for-all, grab-all-you-can society'), in which he acknowledged that these were 'uncharted seas' for the trade union movement – the vote was more than three to one in favour of the government's prices and incomes policy. The main dissent came from the T&G (Transport and General Workers' Union), where Frank Cousins's left-wing heart still beat strongly even though he was no longer in post and was instead in government. He had already, inside and outside Cabinet, warned Brown that the incomes policy was untenable and would not work; that evening, an incensed Brown told Geoffrey Goodman, high-class labour correspondent and Cousins's future biographer, that 'if I am obstructed I will have to fight'; and as Goodman himself would observe, 'it was indeed an extraordinary situation that the largest union of all, whose general secretary was now sitting in the Cabinet, had ostentatiously opposed a central feature of the government's economic policy'. Moreover, quite apart from those charged dynamics, could a voluntary-style incomes policy realistically survive? By mid-June, reckoned Benn, certainly not in the public sector, as the only sector which the government directly controlled, with the only alternative being what he called 'some form of pay pause policy'. 'I can see this coming and it is going to pose terrible industrial problems and turn many people away from us,' he continued his pessimistic private reflection. 'But I frankly don't see the alternative unless we carry planning a great deal further and begin to control the economy in a true sense. Exhortation is too late.'[8]

Benn was not yet on the left of the Parliamentary Labour Party (PLP), but for those who were the issue of steel renationalisation had all antennae quivering. Back in the late 1940s, it had been the most controversial of the Attlee government's nationalisations; the post-1951 Conservative government had then denationalised most of the steel industry; and the Wilson government was now committed, through a manifesto pledge and in a detailed White Paper, to renationalising the fourteen biggest companies. The issue was, in short, a symbol of general radical intent, even of ideological purity. On 5 May, ahead of a Commons vote on the issue the following evening, Wilson assured the PLP that, if any 'minorities' tried to hold him to ransom, he would tell them 'to go to blazes' – a clear reference, in the context of the government's tiny parliamentary majority, to the two Labour right-wingers Woodrow Wyatt and Desmond Donnelly, both of whom had been arguing for weeks that state control (perhaps a 51 per cent holding in the relevant companies) rather than outright nationalisation was the way to go. In the event, both men did vote on the government's side – but only after Brown at the last minute had assured them that in the weeks ahead it would 'listen' to their concerns. Labour's left was appalled by this implicit retreat, with Michael Foot in their house magazine, *Tribune*, accusing Brown of 'remarkable political imbecility' and declaring that 'a dog which appeared to be wagged by Wyatt and Donnelly would be the most contemptible of curs'. Wilson's public stance remained unyielding; but given the exceedingly tight parliamentary arithmetic, given also that a recent Gallup poll had revealed a majority of electors in favour of the steel industry being in private hands, all his pragmatic instincts would increasingly be to push the troublesome issue into the long grass.

No one on the British left would have denied that wages policy and steel nationalisation were issues that mattered, but there was another issue now starting to carry a far greater emotional charge, certainly among the middle-class left. It concerned a distant country of which, before 1965, even most well-informed people knew relatively little: Vietnam. The decisive moment came in February when, to widespread criticism around the world, the US launched on North Vietnam a heavy bombing attack which went way beyond anything they had done previously – a policy of escalation given formal standing by late March, as the American ambassador in Saigon told an Italian paper that there were 'no limits set to the escalation' of the war. In the Commons, at the start of April, a pro-American speech by the foreign secretary, Michael Stewart, won cheers largely from the Tories, with Sir Tufton Beamish calling it 'courageous, eloquent, realistic, statesmanlike and constructive'; while Wilson for his part declared that 'so far as Her Majesty's Government are concerned, I'll repeat, as I have said many times before, that we have made absolutely plain our support for the American stand against Communist infiltration into South Vietnam'; and neither man was prepared to condemn the napalming of Vietnamese villages. Protests followed the next Sunday: in Manchester, a meeting of several hundred people, addressed by left-wing Labour MPs including Sydney Silverman, Stanley Orme and Frank Allaun, passing a motion condemning the government for 'encouraging the United States to continue warlike activities'; and in London, a demonstration outside the American Embassy, with the fifteen arrested including the Oxford Union's president-elect, 21-year-old Tariq Ali.

The anger continued to grow. 'VIETNAM: WILSON RIGHT BEHIND JOHNSON' was the headline on *Private Eye*'s cover at the end of April, occasion for a savage drawing by Gerald Scarfe showing the PM preparing to lick the presidential arse; a week later, Michael Foot declined a government position on the explicit grounds of being 'strongly critical' of the official British attitude to American policy in Vietnam; and mid-June saw a flurry of American-style 'teach-ins'. The first two were at Cambridge University and University College London, with the latter's event (organised in tandem with the LSE) more prominently covered. Speakers there, including such prominent public intellectuals as Isaac Deutscher, Eric Hobsbawm and Ralph Miliband, were overwhelmingly anti-American; so, too, was the audience of some 800 students ('teach-in with minds already made up', the *Guardian*'s sardonic headline), who hissed loudly when a letter from Wilson was read out justifying the British government's position; and rare dissenting viewpoints came from a young prospective Conservative candidate, John Selwyn Gummer, and the *Sunday Telegraph*'s Peregrine Worsthorne. 'Although they may look like barbarians and savages,' he reflected afterwards about the audience ('long-haired boys with pointed beards and leather jackets, girls dressed for Vespa tandems'), they had actually been 'much more interested and interesting than they seem'. Then inevitably, a few days later, it was Oxford's turn, as an eight-hour teach-in unfolded at the Union. Speakers included Stewart as well as Henry Cabot Lodge, former American ambassador to Saigon; the BBC covered the event on both TV and radio; and on the former, its chief political commentator, Ian Trethowan, unambiguously declared that the event had been a triumph for the foreign secretary and a drubbing for what he called the 'British Left'. 'Perhaps', caustically commented David Caute (young left-wing novelist and historian) after it was all over, 'we should be grateful to Mr Trethowan for his youthful distinction between Mr Stewart and the British Left.'[9]

Westminster eschewed a teach-in, but certainly there was plenty of unhappiness there, including among the diarists. 'Went to Cabinet determined to have a showdown about Vietnam,' noted Castle the day before the Oxford event. 'Opinion is mounting against the Americans as Johnson puts in thousands more ground troops and abandons all pretence that the Americans are there merely to "advise".' 'It has been getting worse and worse with the Americans becoming more and more deeply committed,' reflected Crossman the same day. 'It is having its effect inside the Parliamentary Party where the situation is growing very tense and not only left-wingers are beginning to organize letters and stage protests in their constituencies.' Meanwhile Benn a few days earlier had come to the conclusion that 'sooner or later we shall have to come out and say what we really think', given that 'the argument that we are keeping quiet in order to retain influence is of course fallacious' and that 'the real reason is quite different'. So indeed it was – to the extent that by July the president's special assistant, McGeorge Bundy, was emphasising to LBJ that 'we want to make very sure that the British get into their heads that it makes no sense for us to rescue the pound in a situation in which there is no British flag in Vietnam, and a threatened British thin-out both east of Suez and in Germany'. In short, as with the steel issue, pragmatism ruled; and Wilson would also not have been unaware of polling evidence in June to the effect that, despite minimal enthusiasm for British boots on the ground, only one in three actively believed that America should pull out of Vietnam.

Did he also, for all their increasingly large rhetoric, count on the ultimately cautious, domestic-focused instincts of his more left-wing MPs? That was certainly the view of one public intellectual, Raymond Williams, desperate to stop the Labour government supporting the American war in Indochina, albeit like many on the left underestimating Wilson's resolute refusal to send British troops there. 'This was during the period of the minority government [a slight exaggeration, but not much] and the left MPs could, if they had wanted to, have put tremendous pressure on the Cabinet on Vietnam because the Labour government completely depended on their votes,' he would ruefully recall in 1979 about the situation fourteen years earlier. 'To them it was unthinkable to risk bringing the government down over an issue like Vietnam. They were much more concerned about getting this or that bill through the Commons; they couldn't see that the alliance with the US over Vietnam was deciding the basic political character of the Labour government.' Or in the words of Wilson's largely admiring biographer Ben Pimlott, Vietnam was the issue on which 'the party of conscience seemed to lose touch with its soul'.[10]

'What most clearly distinguishes the comments about him is the frequent approving references to his sense of humour and witty asides,' noted an audience research report on reactions to Eddie Waring's rugby league commentary for *Grandstand* on the afternoon of Saturday, 3 April. 'His Northern accent, of course, received widespread notice but it never seems to have put viewers off. Significantly it was nearly always viewers in the *North* who objected to his "Northernness" . . .' The Stones were still topping the charts with 'The Last Time', and the sixteen-year-old Laurence Marks was knocked out by the 'amazing' Who when on Tuesday he went to see them at the 'dark, hot, sweaty' Marquee in Wardour Street ('for just a four-piece group they make more noise than any group I have ever heard before'), but a venerable voice from that prehistoric, pre-Beatles era was now poised for a run. 'We'll send on the Musical Express as I see it's all a great crisis as to whether Cliff is top or not,' the future novelist Penelope Fitzgerald wrote on the 7th, from her 'Squalid Council Estate' in Clapham, to a teenage daughter abroad, though in the event

'The Minute You're Gone' would have to defer for a week to Unit 4 Plus 2 ('Concrete and Clay') before taking top spot. Next day, the 8th, it was contrasting fortunes in the *Guardian* for Jacqueline du Pré and Glenda Jackson – the former's performance of Elgar's Cello Concerto at the Royal Festival Hall prompting Neville Cardus to acclaim her as 'a very precious advent into our music'; the latter, in *Love's Labour's Lost* at Stratford, described by Philip Hope-Wallace as 'an appealing face but a squawking voice' – while at Poulton-le-Fylde it was a crisp diary sentiment by doctor's wife Betty Allen: 'Have definitely decided to stop smoking & put the money in the Halifax!' Two days later, another diarist, Roger Darlington, 'watched "Thank Your Lucky Stars" which now has too much screaming on it, to make it worthwhile taping from'; a London conference on 'Changes in adolescent culture', organised by the Howard League for Penal Reform, heard from an expert in student health that drug-taking was now 'usurping the place of sex as a fundamental excitement or "kick" of youth'; and Paul Stephenson, who two years earlier had organised the Bristol bus boycott over racial discrimination, walked into the city's Bay Horse pub:

> I was initially served half a pint but then told to get out because they didn't serve black people. I said I hadn't done anything wrong. It was the manager who then said, 'We don't want you black people in here because you are a nuisance.' I refused to leave and he said he would call the police so I replied, 'Well call the police.'
>
> Eight police officers came with an inspector in a Land Rover. I was surprised by the number of police officers who arrived just to ask me to leave, which I duly did. I was then told that I would be arrested and charged for refusing to leave licenced premises. So I was taken to the Central Police Station, Bridewell at about 8 or 9 o'clock in the evening and I was released from the cell at midnight.

Sunday the 11th featured at Wembley's Empire Pool the *New Musical Express* 1964–65 Annual Poll-Winners' All-Star Concert, arguably the ultimate (all-white) pop jamboree of the entire decade – Moody Blues, Georgie Fame, Rolling Stones (Jagger 'whirling around at one moment like a berserk windmill'), Donovan, Them (Van and his men 'sounding like some ecstatic pop version of a Cossack dance'), Tom

Jones ('red shirt and black tight trousers'), Dusty Springfield ('a long, vivid orange skirt with a sequinned top that dazzled and winked as she moved'), Animals, Beatles ('the girl next to me fell to her knees weeping') and Kinks ('pounded through "Tired of Waiting" and "You Really Got Me" in terrific style'), with supporting roles (in posterity's eyes anyway) for Twinkle, Freddie and his Dreamers, Herman and his Hermits, Wayne Fontana and his Mindbenders, and Cilla Black ('ended her act with a soft but dramatic "I Think I'm Going Out of My Mind"') – before on TV that evening *Not So Much* . . . reluctantly bowed out, praised by viewers at the death because 'there were fewer "cheap jibes" than usual', albeit some 'protested that the discussion on sex went on far too long'. Next day, Stephenson was remanded on £10 bail until late April; the Tamla Motown tour, disappointing attendances to the last, ended at Portsmouth's Guildhall; and the Acton diarist Henry St John, a civil servant possessing a strictly limited engagement with humanity, painstakingly recorded that 'for the first time in my recollection the "Daily Telegraph" carried an advertisement by Ambrose Wilson, the mail order corsetry specialist, extolling the virtues of "the most comfy" corselet ever'.[11]

By this time BBC TV's *The Wednesday Play* was starting to make waves. The previous week it had attracted its largest audience so far – some eleven million viewers – for *Three Clear Sundays* by James O'Connor, a former convict who two decades earlier had narrowly avoided the gallows. Directed by Ken Loach, and marking a passionate plea against capital punishment at a time when abolition was not yet certain (despite the Commons vote the previous December), it ended with six one-second shots of a man being wrongly hanged. This particular Wednesday, though, no waves worth speaking of for Jack Russell's *The Interior Decorator*, a fantasy about a millionaire's wife being seduced in the course of a sumptuous refurbishment. 'I have seen some rotten plays over the years but this takes the prize for poppycock,' declared a disgruntled steel smelter; its RI was a pitiful 28; and the audience research report noted that 'its timing on the day of the announcement of the increase in the television licence fee seems to have further inflamed their anger'. What, then, was the way to a TV audience's heart? 'The most popular types of play are those featuring mystery or crime, comedy, family situations,' concluded a study of how, in the course of this April, ten plays across the channels had been received. 'To be acceptable to the majority a play must have plenty of action, and a happy, satisfactory ending.' While as to what to avoid: 'The principal dislikes, by the majority of play-viewers, are of plays featuring sex or violence, and plays that "leave you up in the air." These views reflect widespread moral conservatism among play-viewers and dislike of technical innovation (e.g. too many flashbacks) and of ambiguous endings.'[12]

The best of Easter came early in Chingford. 'We all tucked in to Chicken Dinner with roast pots and cauliflower au gratin,' recorded Judy Haines on Good Friday, the 16th. 'We wined, too, and opened our Easter Gifts, since John and I are off to Lancing [where John's parents lived] tomorrow':

> I received 1½ Terry's All Gold Eggs – the 1 from John and the half of same large egg from Pam. Ione, too, gave us a beauty between us. Actually it was a casket containing two eggs filled & surrounded by chocolates, huge and delicious. How generous they are.
>
> They liked their Terry's New World and John his Contrast from me.

Next afternoon at Elland Road saw English football's combative arrivistes – Don Revie's Leeds United, whose 'rugged determination' (in Tony Pawson's words) 'has offended the purists but enthused the city' – in an intense, top-of-the-table battle against Manchester United. The visitors won by the solitary goal, while the spectacle for the neutral was the dustiest of pitches, a gale-force wind, the most brutal, physically violent of contests, and altogether (as another high-end Sunday reporter, Brian Glanville, regretfully put it) 'a match thoroughly spoiling and negative'. The 1960s had their dark side, and one darkness was the turn that top club football took, with this perhaps as the decisive moment. A happier northern influence was almost simultaneously on show at the London Palladium, as Ken Dodd's *Doddy's Here* began its record-breaking, nine-month run. 'I'd seen what happened to Northern comedians when they went to the West End, and I was very loath to take what might have been this self-destructive step,' recalled the virtuoso himself in the 1970s. 'But in the end it was right. TV, being a great leveller, has broken down a lot of this North versus South thing.' TV, though, was also responsible for another comedian,

Ted Rogers, who after making his name guesting on *The Billy Cotton Band Show* now began on Easter Sunday his own series . . . *And So to Ted*, leaving one critic, Skene Catling, almost in awe of its 'frightful badness'. Next day, Judy Haines's daughters 'set off at 7.30 a.m. for Easter March of C.N.D., joining the main party at Acton' on its way to Aldermaston, but with no longer quite the emblematic quality it had once had. Instead, emblem-wise this Easter Monday, it was Joan Bakewell who stepped up, for the first time appearing on BBC2's *Late Night Line-Up*. 'Her job was to ask very earnest, pretentious questions, while tossing her glossy hair and deploying her endless legs to maximum seductive effect' would be the rather sour verdict of Lynn Barber four decades later; but in truth, she – and the unpredictable, free-form, boundaries-shifting programme – had far more to offer than that.[13]

Also moving increasingly into the limelight this month, and also destined to be iconic, were the East End twin gangsters Ronnie and Reggie Kray. On the 5th, a case at the Old Bailey, where they were accused of running a Soho protection racket that involved demanding money with menaces, ended against all the evidence in a not guilty verdict – an acquittal which, according to their biographer John Pearson, now gave them a feeling of invulnerability. 'The long, hard climb from Bethnal Green' was the headline for a *Sunday Times* profile on the 11th:

> The Krays were 'discovered' less than a year ago when they figured, as reluctant third parties, in Lord Boothby's £40,000 action against the *Sunday Mirror*. Ever since, stories of the Krays' prowess and business deals have become part of London folk-lore.
>
> In the East End, where Ronald and Reginald were born 31 years ago, the Kray myth has always been potent. The Boothby business gave it national coverage. But it is still essentially an East End story – early boxing success, some violent but small-scale crime in their youth, the graduation to club ownership and the cultivated 'in' with the show-business world. They still spend much of their time at their parents' tiny home in Vallance Road, Bethnal Green.
>
> They hold court in its cosy front parlour, flanked by boxing trophies and artificial flowers. A guitar-shaped mirror hangs on one wall reflecting a print of a Spanish flamenco dancer on another.

> A scrapbook of newspaper clippings is one of the family's prize possessions.

A résumé followed of the twins' business careers ('most of their enterprises, which range from an East End billiards hall to a Nigerian housing development, have had somewhat erratic histories'), but inevitably pulling its punches about the often unsavoury methods involved. Unmentioned in the profile was Reggie's imminent marriage, on the 20th at St James's, Bethnal Green, to a doomed 21-year-old, Frances Shea. Among the guests at 'the East End wedding of the year', as it was inevitably and invariably called, were the well-known boxers 'Kid' Lewis and Terry Spinks; David Bailey, arriving in a blue Rolls-Royce and wearing a blue velvet suit, took the photographs; and Ronnie was best man. 'Sing, fuck ya,' he hissed at one point at the congregation, leaving bride and groom at the altar as he stormed down the aisle.

Next day, Wednesday, was the Queen's thirty-ninth birthday. 'Nice photographs of Royal Family in paper,' noted Judy Haines, 'but wish Princess Anne would pretty herself up. She can.' 'I think she makes a good monarch but a little stiff and formal I think' was James Allen's take on the Queen herself. 'It would make things easier if she were more informal. The Royal Family I think needs to be more free and easy . . .' Well, full marks that evening as Elizabeth headed a royal party to the Comedy Theatre to see Spike Milligan in *Son of Oblomov*, with Peter Sellers seated between Charles (the Goons-obsessed probable originator of the expedition) and Margaret. Over the weekend, more than 500 bonfires and beacons were lit on Friday night to mark the start of the National Trust's Enterprise Neptune campaign to save hundreds of miles of coastline; Chelsea's 'Blackpool incident' involved eight players being summarily sent home by manager Tommy Docherty after spectacularly breaking an eve-of-match curfew; the Pennine Way, England's first national trail, opened; and, in South Shields, a sixteen-year-old future historian, Robert Colls, had a moment of epiphany:

> Imagine [he wrote several decades later] a street of Tyneside flats, two sides facing each other, one street in a grid of hundreds like it, all banking steeply down to the river. From an upstairs bedroom window on the higher side, imagine looking down across 20 yards

of cambered road to kerb and pavement, then a yellow doorstep and set of front doors up to an upstairs bedroom window the same as mine only slightly lower and facing me. My bed was wedged sideways against the window. I lay on it looking down. It was Saturday, late afternoon, around five o'clock. Over the way, some of the older residents were sitting on their doorsteps calling out to neighbours on my side doing the same. One man was reading the *Shields Gazette*. I recall he had a cup and saucer by his slippered feet. Up the road, the milkman's horse was pulling the cart and clopping and stopping, as she was trained to do, while Tommy got his money. I could hear some kids playing . . . To the right, about a hundred yards up and on the other side of the road, a knot of older women stood at the corner shop, talking calmly, all arms-folded except for one who, arm out straight, gently rocked a pram. Mothers like these held the streets from first morning message to last evening call.

What I saw that afternoon was a normal scene in a very small world. I knew it in every line and movement. I knew the cracks in the warm summer pavements, as I knew the stepped slate roofs with blue shipyard cranes beyond and the familiar river noises off – welding, blasting, drilling, with screeching seagulls wheeling in . . .

Then something happened. It took long enough just to think it. I saw that what I was looking at from the window was a 'community'. More, I saw that that community was, or had, or lived, or somehow encompassed, a culture. This flash of realization had everything to do with the book in front of me and nothing at all to do with what was happening down in the street – a street, I may say, that I had never thought about even though I had stepped into it a million times. The book was *The Uses of Literacy* by Richard Hoggart . . .

On Monday, a court in Bristol heard the prosecuting barrister claim that Paul Stephenson had, through his 'offensive' behaviour in the Bay Horse, 'made himself not a martyr but a fool'; Lindsay Anderson, watching next day Henry Miller's *The Crucible* at the Old Vic, found himself 'sickened and infuriated by that frightful, middle-class, bourgeois audience, philistine to a man'; 'The Sound of Motown' – a pre-recorded fifty-minute *Ready, Steady, Go!* special, fronted by Dusty Springfield and featuring the stars of the recent tour – went out on Wednesday evening; the *New Statesman*'s Paul Johnson, at

Lord's on Thursday or Friday, mingled with 'a scattering of bored spectators' and heard one say, 'Nice to think of that dreadful footer business being over for a bit, isn't it?'; definitely on Friday, magistrates at Bristol dismissed all charges against Stephenson of having behaved in a disorderly, quarrelsome manner; and that evening, Bob Dylan began his first English tour. 'They gathered', wrote one semi-sceptical journalist, Dan O'Neill, about the expectant audience, 'on the grime-encrusted steps of Sheffield's City Hall, blue-jeaned, bearded; many of them Jesus-haired, and they radiated a religious fervour suggesting they might have been happier feet-stomping at the River.' While afterwards, he wondered: 'So the bearded boys and the lank-haired girls, all eye-shadow and undertaker make-up, applaud the songs and miss perhaps the sermon. They are there: they are with it. But how remote they really are from protest marches, sit-in strikes, and scabs, and life.'[14]

The following day was May Day, when among the visitors in Padstow to see its traditional pagan celebrations was a young American, the future legendary record producer Joe Boyd. He had recently been in Glasgow ('the grime of the city was astounding – sooty black buildings loomed over me as I emerged from the station and the air was pungent with that peculiarly Scottish odour of coal smoke and granite'), but here in this Cornish fishing town it was a wholly pre-industrial world, as he watched 'two "hobby-horse" teams circulate for twenty-four hours, playing and singing a fertility-rite song', while 'the "horse" dances and twirls and tries to catch girls under the skirts of his costume'. Also gathered in Padstow were many of the leading singers (the Watersons, Martin Carthy, Cyril Tawney, Maddy Prior, Anne Briggs) of the growing English traditional folk revival. But the locals, recalled Boyd, 'had little use for tourists or publicity': 'Non-Cornish singers were grudgingly welcomed but a camera crew was dragged out of their hotel room and thrown – equipment and all – off the end of the dock. When the tide went out, a 16mm camera was revealed in the mud, waves lapping gently over it.'

Far from Cornwall, a bad day on Wednesday the 5th for Julia McLaughlin at her convent school in Preston. 'Was terrified of Mademoiselle,' she recorded. 'Left hat at school and met Mademoiselle when didn't have it. Had hiccups on the bus all the way home.' By Thursday, after playing in Liverpool, Leicester and Birmingham,

Dylan's tour had reached Newcastle's City Hall, where before the concert he was (in a scene captured in D. A. Pennebaker's documentary *Don't Look Back*) introduced to the furs-wearing High Sheriff's lady. 'I think the songs are very wonderful,' she gushed, 'and you write them yourself too, don't you, sometimes? . . . I think you're really a good example for the youth . . .' Dylan, who had just destroyed a student interviewer, listened to her with perhaps surprising patience and good humour – and rightly so, for in fact Theresa Russell was over the years a much-loved Newcastle figure, as a councillor for first Scotswood, later Byker, and was renowned for her commitment to social justice. Two days later came a Wembley triumph for Wigan's veteran, mixed-race winger Billy Boston ('tacklers bouncing like hailstones from his chest', in Geoffrey Nicholson's appreciative words), as his team narrowly overcame Hunslet in the Rugby League Challenge Cup Final, while Sunday was home-decorating day in Chingford:

> John and I were up with the lark and he worked hard on kitchen all day, taking only the minimum time off for meals. It is a wonderful transformation, paper covering cracks in plaster, too. Now we need sun blinds to keep kitchen as cool as it now looks with grey and pink design on white paper, and lino.
>
> What a day! 13 hours of it. I am so grateful for our lovely house and gardens. It is so nice to work at it and gradually emerge triumphant, as we seem to have done.
>
> Ione went to Albert Hall with Mick to see Bob Dylan. What a lot of travelling for 1 hour and 35 mins entertainment. They started at 5.30 and arrived home just before midnight.

But what an hour and thirty-five minutes . . . 'A small wisp of a figure in a black leather coat and jeans, his hair sticking up like feathers on a fledgling sparrow,' wrote a not wholly devout Virginia Ironside, 'Bob Dylan played to a silently appreciative audience who laughed in the right places and waited until the last whine had died away before bursting into applause. Squeals were soon stifled by the frowns of the folk fans.' The following evening he played the Albert Hall again, an extra concert added because of demand – and, in the event, probably his last solo concert ever. A few weeks earlier, on Good Friday, the release of Bert Jansch's first album had coincided with the opening of Les Cousins folk club in Soho: a double event which, according to Jansch's biographer Colin Harper, marked 'a line in the sand between the old order of "folksong" epitomised by Ewan MacColl and his left-wing agenda and the new dis-order of individual "folk singers" whose songs espoused largely personal politics'. Dylan himself had spent much of his English tour chafing publicly to cross that line – and, within weeks, he would. While as for the 300 or so folk clubs meeting regularly by this time all over Britain – their performers, according to Rory McEwen in *New Society*, 'a constantly shifting, travelling, galaxy of professional, semi-professional and amateur folk singers who range from elderly, genuine traditional singers to teenage coffee bar hipsters, with fantastic variations in between' – that, too, would, very broadly speaking, be their introspective, individualistic direction of travel.[15]

'Knife sharpener interrupted my pot of tea on lawn on this glorious day,' noted Haines on Wednesday the 12th, 'but I'm glad to have two pairs of scissors that will cut'; next day's *Country Life* had Geoffrey Grigson luxuriating in W. Keble Martin's *The Concise British Flora in Colour* ('here you have, for instance, asarabacca and birthwort, field cow-wheat, perhaps the most extravagant-looking of English flowers, and mountain specialities like creeping cudweed and mossy cyphel, and southern specialities such as the wild gladiolus of the New Forest, acrid lobelia, and the triangular-stemmed garlic of the Isles of Scilly'), the lifetime's work of a retired clergyman that was about to become the year's surprise best-seller; and at a party that evening at the American Embassy, Tony Benn encountered Groucho Marx. 'I like England and its people but this quaintness has gone too far and has got to be stopped,' he told the Postmaster General. 'I ordered a suit and it was four weeks before the first fitting. I asked about another firm of tailors who had made a suit years ago and they said, "It's still going but the head of the firm is dead at present".' 'This is how the world looks at us,' reflected Benn afterwards, 'but we are still resolutely blind to it.' On Saturday, Haines and her husband went to a day's county cricket at Brentwood ('had a "modern youth" beside me, tight with his money but tucking in to all the girl's family provided'), *Dr Who* got a lukewarm reception ('the Daleks were a good idea but they seem to have inexplicably developed enormously from being confined to one city to being able to roam through time and space'), and the last passenger train ran between Dowlais and Nelson (for some, observed John Humphreys for the *Merthyr Express*, 'no sentiment or emotion at the departure of the train – just a dread of complete isolation'); next day, a Sunday paper interviewed the up-and-coming self-made financier James (not yet 'Jim') Slater, who stressed the importance of 'gearing' to investment success, in other words obtaining as much credit as possible from banks and brokers; and on Monday, at Tonypandy's Cambrian Colliery in the Rhondda Valley, a blast killed thirty-one miners who were some 800 feet underground. 'They are stunned and saddened,' a local church minister said of the suddenly bereaved wives. 'But they know the risk is with them always. All they can do is carry on. There is nothing else they can do, because mining is their life.'[16]

'Jolly good,' reckoned one diarist, young Julia McLaughlin, about Ken Russell's *The Debussy Film*, co-scripted with Melvyn Bragg and, starring Oliver Reed, shown on BBC TV's *Monitor* strand on Tuesday the 18th; 'really quite horrid and sensual', thought another diarist, James Allen; 'superb boldness and technique', according to the *Daily Mail*'s Peter Black; and from the viewing panel, a respectable if not ecstatic RI of 56. Next evening, the performance by the Kinks at Cardiff's Capitol Theatre was aborted after only minutes, once a row between Mick Avory and Dave Davies had ended with the former using his hi-hat stand to knock down the latter – leading to hospitalisation, sixteen stitches to the head, and Avory, fearful of the others, holing out for several days at journalist Keith Altham's house in the suburban anonymity of New Malden, Surrey; *Not Only . . . But Also* had on Thursday its first outing on BBC1, and this time the audience (much larger than on BBC2) 'included a sizeable group who had no taste for this style of comedy', typified by one viewer calling the efforts of Peter Cook and Dudley Moore 'just a lot of unfunny rubbish and vulgar into the bargain'; next day Richard Crossman took satisfaction from opening a supermarket in Cowley's new shopping centre, 'a successful affair, done not by private developers but by the city [i.e. Oxford City Council] itself'; and on Monday the 24th the valuably preservationist Landmark Trust was founded by the banker John Smith (moved to action by the recent wanton demolition of Thomas Telford's Junction House on the Shopshire Union Canal), the press quoted the chairman of Richmond upon Thames's housing committee objecting to new blocks of flats for families from inner-city slum-clearance areas being built on his patch ('Richmond is a very nice residential area . . . People pay high rates to live here . . . If you build tower blocks in large number it would spoil the area . . .'), and Phyllis Willmott went to University College Hospital for her cervical smear test. 'I suppose inevitably one is apprehensive about such a thing,' she recorded. 'And the discomforts of the NHS service do not make it easier. It is nothing, we know, but all the same one does not enjoy waiting in a dreary corridor for such an intimate event. Being *interviewed* there – or partly so. Sitting in a dressing gown, and so on.'[17]

That afternoon the House of Lords considered a bill put forward by Lord Arran to legalise homosexual practices between adults in private – in effect, to implement the essence of what had been unsuccessfully recommended by the Wolfenden Committee eight years earlier. Prominent supporters on the day included the reliably outspoken Bishop of Southwark, Mervyn Stockwood ('the law as it stands is one of the most misguided, the most vicious and the most evil in its consequences'); only semi-enthusiastic Lord Attlee ('homosexuality is mainly a matter of physical condition; of misfortune rather than crime'); and, in a maiden speech that might have prompted from the shade of Oscar Wilde an ironic smile, the Marquess of Queensberry ('the best solution is that the homosexual should have the opportunity to lead a quiet, ordered life, finding, if he must, sexual satisfaction with another adult man'). For the other side, a former Lord Chief Justice, Lord Goddard, warned gravely that 'family life will run a serious chance of deterioration if it is known there are buggers in the family and they cannot be dealt with', but undeniably their main man was Field Marshal Viscount Montgomery, whose contribution prompted Noël Coward to reflect on how 'he so brilliantly commanded so many men and obviously knows nothing about them'. 'One might just as well condone the Devil and all his works,' declared 'Monty'. 'We are not French and we are not other nationals. We are British, thank God.' In the event, and perhaps surprisingly, the Lords voted 94–49 in Arran's favour. Two days later, following a motion put by the flamboyant Labour backbencher Leo Abse, the Commons was asked to decide whether to follow the example of the Lords. Abse's was only a ten-minute bill, so did not produce a full debate; and most of the noise was made by Cyril Osborne, the reactionary's reactionary, adamant that the vast majority of public opinion considered such practices 'wrong, unnatural, degrading and disgusting'. Moreover:

> To legalise this horrible, revolting practice would be against public security. This is an age of lawlessness, violence and crime. What we need is stronger discipline and not more licence. The greatest harm the Bill would do the country would be to send out from this House the message to our friends and allies that the character of the English people was going wrong.

As in the Lords, it was a free vote; and Osborne carried the day, 178–159, significantly helped by the veteran Labour MP and former minister Manny Shinwell managing to mobilise a phalanx of trade unionist MPs into voting against the reformism of the parliamentary party's increasingly high share of middle-class liberals. Even so, in terms of the bigger picture, this was not simply a case of the entrenched social conservatism of the working-class 'red wall' seats determining the outcome: for of those who voted against Abse's motion, well over two-thirds were Conservative MPs, mainly representing decidedly non-working-class constituencies.[18]

More explicitly party political was the increasingly high-profile matter – especially post-Smethwick – of race relations. 'There is no reason why they should abandon their own national culture and tradition – indeed they will enrich our society – but they must recognise that we have established in this country certain standards of behaviour, of sanitation and hygiene': such were the warning words, in an address on 4 April to the English Speaking Union, of Labour's Maurice Foley, recently tasked with coordinating policy on race relations and anxious, like many of his colleagues, to minimise the gap between well-intentioned government action on the one hand, and unreconstructed public opinion on the other.

The Race Relations Bill was published three days later, setting out measures for criminalising and fining those found guilty of discriminating on racial grounds in public places, but carefully avoiding the two key areas of housing and employment. 'LIBELLING BRITAIN' was the *Daily Telegraph*'s instant response, lamenting that 'native Britons will be prone to feel that they must watch their tongues and their doings when dealing with minority groups, and will find it hard not to be on their guard'; while over the next few weeks, the Conservatives successfully pressured the home secretary, Frank Soskice, into abandoning his intention to make discrimination in public places a criminal offence, with complaints instead to be handled by conciliation machinery operating at both a national and a local level. Even so, one Conservative backbencher remained predictably dissatisfied. 'The latest version of the bill', declared Smethwick's Peter Griffiths in late June, 'does not say there will be committees in every part of the country, but only when and where necessary. One great danger in this is that certain areas are going to be designated race-hate areas. Certain areas are sick and tired of being called race-hate areas already.' And, he added, 'I would not like to think that my own constituency, where there has never been a racial incident of any significance at all, would be designated an area of race-hate'.

Smethwick's shadow since the previous October had been long indeed. In January, when Patrick Gordon Walker was unexpectedly defeated again, this time in Leyton, the evidence was mixed about how much the cause had been dislike of a perceived Labour softness on non-white immigration; but Wilson by this time had little appetite for being outflanked by the Tories, resulting in the Commons spectacle in early February of Soskice, to Tory cheers, largely endorsing the Opposition's latest recommendations on tightening immigration controls. 'Ever since the Smethwick election,' reflected Crossman in a mood of grim realism as a West Midland MP all too aware of local feeling, 'it has been quite clear that immigration can be the greatest potential vote-loser for the Labour Party if we are seen to be permitting a flood of immigrants to come in and blight the central areas in all our cities'. In March another, much younger West Midlands MP, Roy Hattersley, was unusual among his colleagues in attempting to explain in the Commons why he found himself taking a tougher line so relatively soon after bitterly opposing the 1962 Commonwealth Immigrants Act put through by the Conservative government. The economic arguments, he emphasised, were still all in favour of increased immigration. But, he went on, 'I now believe that there are social as well as economic arguments'; and, after referring rather vaguely to 'social problems', he declared that 'we must impose a test which tries to analyse which immigrants . . . are most likely to be assimilated in our national life', adding that such a test would fall most heavily on Pakistanis. All Hattersley's natural instincts were pro-immigration, and so, too, were those of the recently elected Shirley Williams; but in late May, days after Enoch Powell had told a Conservative Women's coffee morning in Wolverhampton that it was an 'absurd anachronism' whereby 'the myriad inhabitants of African, Asian and American territories which were once under British rule could not be distinguished for any purpose from the citizens of Birmingham or Wolverhampton and possessed an identical right to enter this country at will', Benn was noting how 'Shirley thinks that race is going to be the dominant issue at the next Election and is rather pessimistic.'

Some six weeks later, in early July ahead of a White Paper due later in the summer, another bid – in the ongoing Dutch auction about which party could out-tough the other – came from the Tories, as Selwyn Lloyd, the former chancellor now chairing the party's policy group on immigration, publicly pushed the idea of 'one in, one out' for 'at least a period of years', accompanied generally by more stringent monitoring of immigrants. 'A sane approach', acclaimed the *Daily Mail*; while when the Cabinet met a few days later, there were apparently no remnants left of what Crossman called 'the 100 per cent pro-immigration line and arguments with which Hugh Gaitskell and George Brown opposed the Tory immigration Act lock, stock and barrel only three years ago'. 'The atmosphere', he hardly needed to add, 'has changed since then!'[19]

'They make mountains out of very small mole-hills' were the ungracious words on Wednesday, 26 May of Bangor's town clerk, W. Elwyn E. Jones, about the press, adding during a formal lunch of dignitaries at the Castle Hotel that it made local authorities such as his own into 'Aunt Sallys'; next day at London Zoo, Lord Snowdon formally opened the aluminium birdcage he had helped to design and which was named after him, conceding semi-cheerfully to a reporter that 'not everybody likes it'; that evening, viewers watching coverage, plagued by technical problems, of the Queen's visit to Berlin heard Richard

Dimbleby expostulate 'Jesus wept!', prompting an almost immediate apology from the BBC; around this time, while spending a week in Liverpool, Allen Ginsberg famously declared the city to be 'at the present time the center of the consciousness of the human universe'; on Saturday, interviewed by the *Evening Standard*'s Maureen Cleave, Pete Townshend explained how in essence what underpinned the Who's close bond with their fans was working-class anger ('we want to show the audience that we are frustrated characters, that we do want to get something out of our system and we wanna do it in front of them'); Veronica Lee, still a student in Leeds, went next day to the students' union cinema to watch *A Kind of Loving* ('as usual the Sunday night audience at the Uni tried to ruin it by laughing heartily all the way through'); 8,715 members of the National Federation of Women's Institutes gathered on Monday afternoon for a garden party at Buckingham Palace, with the high spot at four o'clock when the Queen and others came on to the lawns ('as the W.I. members surged towards the Royal party,' noted a watching member, 'one looked upon a sea of hats, fluffy, feathered and frilly, together with floating chiffon coats and silk suits'); June began in Birmingham with details, almost exultantly revealed by the local *Evening Mail*, of 'a spectacular 80 ft. high, eight-level traffic junction to be built at Gravelly Hill, to provide the main access between central and north Birmingham and the M6', soon to be known as Spaghetti Junction; the same issue of the paper reported how, in Theodore Close, Rowley Regis, the estate's all-white residents' association was trying to buy out and thereby get to move a recently arrived family 'because they are coloured and they fear the value of their property will fall'; and next day the latest *Wednesday Play*, David Mercer's *And Did Those Feet?*, broke almost all records with a stunningly low RI of 25. 'They might perhaps have forgiven the fantasy element if there had been "a story to follow," but it just, it was said, "meandered on and on" . . . "another weird play," one groaned, typically – "no more, please." '[20]

Thursday, 3 June was in its own ephemeral way a bumper day. Anthony Burgess, after two years as the *Listener*'s TV critic with a positively Leavisite disdain for commercialised popular culture, took his temporary leave with various potshots, including at David Jacobs ('the most dangerous man of them all, since he presents hogwash with a veneer of reason and culture') and the unnamed but clearly identifiable Jimmy Savile ('that explodable fool with the wig'); the film version of Ann Jellicoe's stage play *The Knack* was released, with the full 'swinging London' treatment by its director Richard Lester and nicely characterised by one critic, Philip Oakes, as 'a bold and jaunty comic moustache drawn blithely across the British Way of Sex'; at the British Motor Corporation's Morris Motors plant in Cowley, Oxford, seven trade unions issued a joint notice solemnly warning the workforce that 'we cannot support members who violate the Domestic Agreement which clearly states that before any stoppage of work takes place there must be full consultation with the Senior Shop Stewards'; and Pinter's *The Homecoming* had its London first night at the Aldwych:

> At first and even into the second, sadder half, the relentless ribaldry and poker-faced outrageousness was relished by the audience – or most of them [noted the *Guardian*'s Philip Hope-Wallace]. Gleeful squeals of joy greeted the unvarnished home-truths exchanged by cockney brothers in a widower's home, welcoming back a brother from America and his ex-model suburban British wife with a view to inducing her to go on the streets and keep them in comfort. But by the end I sensed some disappointment and shared it. The thing is perfectly turned, but to what end?

'Disappointment' did not quite capture it for one dedicated amateur critic in the audience. 'Repugnantly filthy almost to the point of obscenity,' Anthony Heap wrote straight afterwards in his diary, adding that 'otherwise it is very much the Pinter mixture for Pinter addicts as before', including 'the same banal, repetitive, drivelsome dialogue' and 'the same negligible and ludicrous apology for a plot'. Still, neither Hope-Wallace nor Heap recorded an audience walk-out, unlike earlier in Cardiff and then Brighton, at the point where Ruth (played by Vivien Merchant) declares that only by going 'on the game' will she be able to stay with the family. Even so, the day had a final and perhaps unexpected moralistic judgement yet to come. Ginsberg by now was back in London; and this evening at his birthday party – briefly attended by John Lennon and his wife Cynthia, as well as George Harrison and his girlfriend Patti Boyd – he got so drunk that he removed all his clothes except his Jockey shorts. Why did the two Beatles not stay any longer? Apparently, the answer lay in a handful of hissed words by Lennon: 'You don't do that in front of the birds!'[21]

Next day the *North Wales Chronicle* printed the unimpressed response of a Bangor citizen to the town clerk's grumbles on behalf of local authorities. ('let the Press press on regardless,' declared Idris Williams, 'and show up their bungling Aunt Sallys'); that evening, after the name of Cathy McGowan's show had reverted to its canonical *Ready, Steady, Go!*, viewing figures between seven and eight o'clock revealed *Take Your Pick* being watched by 22 per cent of the population (excluding, as usual, children under five), as against *Tonight*'s 8 per cent, and also *Emergency – Ward 10*'s 18 per cent share fairly comfortably ahead of *Compact*'s 13 per cent; away from the box, at the Aldwych during the interval, an indignant lady stalked into the foyer just behind the critic Ronald Bryden, fuming as she did so, 'They're exactly like animals!'; on Saturday evening, Val Doonican was back on BBC TV and, noted audience research, proved 'immensely popular with the vast majority of the sample', albeit 'viewers in the not insignificant group who did not enjoy Marianne Faithfull's contribution [singing 'This Little Bird'] variously reported that she was lacking in talent, sang in a monotonous style and did not present an attractive appearance', with one viewer especially critical of her 'stupid droopy look'; nothing relaxed next morning on the Isle of Skye, where on the quayside at Kyleakin a Free Church minister, Angus Smith, and what he called the 'cream of island morality' (including many crofters from the north of the island) protested forcibly against the arrival there of the first-ever Sunday ferry – in the words of Smith, who dramatically threw himself in front of the first car edging ashore, 'a sad, sad day for this God-fearing island of ours'; the irresistible forces of secularisation in evidence, too, next day in Manchester, where though some 13,000 Anglicans took part in the traditional Whit Walks, 'crowds were thinner along Market Street than in previous years, and veterans recalled the days when they walked six abreast'; but not yet all-consuming, twenty-first-century-style secularisation. 'I went down this morning to do the shopping, and found every shop shut,' recorded

Veronica Lee the day after Whit Monday Bank Holiday. 'The centre of Leeds was quite deserted. Very depressing, as it means we have to rely on snacks bought from odd post-offices & corner shops.' That was on the 8th; and at some point during June, though impossible to establish exactly when, the renowned, controversial psychoanalyst R. D. (Ronald) Laing and colleagues set up a community at Kingsley Hall, a large building in the East End (near Bromley-by-Bow station), to try to establish whether patients suffering from severe emotional damage could be helped through a drama of breakdown and rebirth. An early resident was 42-year-old Mary Barnes. 'Life soon became quite fantastic,' she would recall. 'Every night I tore off my clothes, feeling I had to be naked. Lay on the floor with my shits and water, smeared the walls with faeces. Was wild and noisy about the house or sitting on a heap on the kitchen floor. Half aware that I was going mad . . .' Ultimately, the process worked, to be commemorated in David Edgar's moving 1978 play, *Mary Barnes*.[22]

Back in June 1965 – on Friday the 11th, reviewing in the *Guardian* the 1965 edition of *The Socialist Register* – Alasdair MacIntyre highlighted 'a splendid essay by Edward [E. P.] Thompson', not only detailing his break three years earlier with the new regime at the *New Left Review*, but also pinpointing 'much that is wrong in the theoretical writings of [Perry] Anderson and [Tom] Nairn, showing how intractable the facts of social history remain when confronted with their *a priori* schematism'. The essay was called 'The Peculiarities of the English', most suggestive of titles; and in essence it amounted, in David Eastwood's apt later words, to 'a synoptic celebration of the English radical tradition' revealing 'the fundamental unity of Thompson's intellectual and political vision'. Radical visions, too, that Friday evening at the Royal Albert Hall, as a predominantly youthful audience of some 7,000 (handed on arrival daffodils, tulips, roses and greenery) witnessed the International Poetry Incarnation, organised by Michael Horowitz and filmed by Peter Whitehead for his subsequent documentary *Wholly Communion*. Of the many poets of widely varying quality who performed over the four hours, the stand-out Americans were Lawrence Ferlinghetti invoking the internationalism of love and a stoned Ginsberg intoning Tibetan chants; but according to one observer, it was the English poets who took the honours, sounding 'less self-absorbed, more precise and political', with the biggest cheer going to Adrian Mitchell for his 'savage ironies on Vietnam'. Altogether, added Kenneth Tynan, it was 'a partly embarrassing, partly inspiriting occasion'; but perhaps ultimately more the latter, catalyst as it would prove for the whole countercultural, underground scene of the next few years.

While the all-male poets performed, the news came out that each of the Beatles was to be awarded the MBE. Cue controversy. 'What have they done for this country?' was the indignant immediate reaction of Laurence Marks's mother in Finsbury Park; Noël Coward privately reckoning that 'some other decoration should have been selected to reward them for their talentless but considerable contributions to the Exchequer'; and over the next week or so, a handful of existing medal holders (not only MBEs) very publicly returning their gongs in protest. Several of them had a wartime background, including ex-Squadron Leader Paul Pearson, honoured for his part in sea-rescue operations. 'I know the war is old hat and I've got nothing against the Beatles, but they have been amply rewarded already,' he explained. 'All they do is exploit a basic jungle rhythm for money.' From the left, two critical voices – one private, the other public – belonged to Anthony Wedgwood Benn and the *New Statesman*'s editor Paul Johnson. 'The royal family love the idea that the honours list is popular because it all helps to buttress them and indirectly their influence is used to strengthen all the forces of conservatism in society,' complained Benn. 'I think Harold Wilson makes the most appalling mistake if he thinks that in this way he can buy popularity, for he is ultimately bolstering a force that is an enemy of his political stand.' Johnson's take on a 'fatuous decision' (appearing in the same column where he noted that he had been to see Pinter's *The Homecoming* and 'left the theatre feeling demeaned and sick') concentrated more on what he saw as its intrinsic lack of merit:

> It makes a mockery of everything the Labour Party fought for at the last election. Labour's main theme was that it was on the side of those who really earned money, as opposed who those who simply made it – and Wilson himself spoke repeatedly of 'raising the quality of life' in this country. Can he really claim that the Beatles have *earned* the millions of pounds their publicists boast about? And does he seriously suggest they have contributed to the quality of our lives?

As for the right, there was seemingly no more authentic, malcontent spokesman than the *Daily Telegraph*'s 'Peter Simple', aka Michael Wharton:

> A year ago, I think it was, I took a vow never to write about the Beatles in this column. The vulgar idiocy (or low cunning or whatever it is) of the present Government in paying them an official honour surely absolves me from the vow.
>
> Several people, I am glad to say, have already returned their insignia of the Order of the British Empire in protest. I hope their example will be followed by a multitude.
>
> Having said this, I can now renew my vow of silence for a further five years. By that time, I hope, the honour paid to these cosmic bores will be remembered only with shame and embarrassment, as an historical curiosity.

During these mid-June days, the *Telegraph*'s own letters page revealed a reasonably even spread of views. Yet, strikingly, when the correspondence closed just over a week after the original announcement, the paper noted that 'some 80 per cent of the very large number of correspondents on this subject have expressed approval of the award of the MBE to the Beatles'. Could there have been a clearer indication that they had by now become a thoroughly accepted – and in no way threatening – part of the national furniture? Or as Judy Haines put it, it was only the 'snobs' who had returned their medals.[23]

The announcement of birthday honours was followed on Saturday the 12th by Trooping the Colour, with the Wilsons inviting the Mandelsons, including eleven-year-old Peter, to watch it from No. 10 ('Marcia Williams, Harold's private secretary, fed me large quantities of triangular smoked-salmon sandwiches and asparagus rolls . . . she even took my hand and led me into the Cabinet Room, and briefly planted me in the Prime Minister's chair'); *Joan Baez in Concert* on BBC1 that evening earned an RI of 80 ('such a perfect singing voice', said a bank clerk, and every song 'made sense and really meant something'); over the following week, RSPCA officials expressed alarm about the high number of pets (especially cats) in the London area being abandoned by families moving into new council flats where animals were not permitted, the second series of *The Likely*

Lads started with an RI of 77 ('natural comedy of what happens in everyday life . . . typical of the amusing remarks made by ordinary working-class people . . .'), the first-night audience at the Duke of York's gave a 'wildly enthusiastic' reception to the pioneering lesbian drama *The Killing of Sister George* ('while I was never actually bored by the somewhat distasteful proceedings,' noted curmudgeonly Heap, 'I fail to find them in any way amusing or beguiling or touching'), the visiting Richard Crossman cast a baleful look at 'defunct' Derby ('that soulless industrial Victorian town with its pathetically ingrained Labour administration terrified of any change'), and the final outing of Cliff Michelmore's *Tonight*, way past its prime, starred John Lennon promoting the imminent publication of *A Spaniard in the Works* by reading aloud an extract from 'We Must Not Forget The General Erection'.[24]

'Funny sort of day – got suddenly sickened by all the humdrum cooking & housework – I hate it! – & went all depressed . . .' recorded Betty Allen in Poulton-le-Fylde on Saturday the 19th; late that evening, on the TV folk front, it was Dylan's turn (relatively modest RI of 55, and 'many viewers considered him a vastly overrated performer and failed to see what all the fuss was about'); many viewers also unhappy on Monday about the BBC's choice of tennis promoter-cum-commentator Jack Kramer to introduce Wimbledon highlights ('murdering the English language', according to a solicitor, who wondered why it had to be 'an American at all'); Birmingham's historic Bromford Bridge racecourse held that evening its final races (two winners for Lester Piggott), with the site to be converted into a largely high-rise council estate; two days later a nervous public broadcaster pulled at almost the last minute its *Wednesday Play*, due to be Dennis Potter's unflattering depiction of the political class, *Vote, Vote, Vote for Nigel Barton*; altogether less contentious, albeit dismissed by one viewer as 'poor man's Bond', was the debut next evening of *The Man from U.N.C.L.E.*; and the latest issue of *Private Eye* had Christopher Booker laying into an increasingly consumerist country that had lost all sense of 'serious purpose' and instead was giving itself over to caring about 'nothing more than the right colour of their shirts, the latest record in the Hit Parade, the most amusing way to cook paella or the most up-to-date model of sports car', enabling the rise of what he called 'a new aristocracy, that of the smart parasites, the photographers and model girls and dress designers and beat musicians'. No disagreement from Mary Whitehouse, who on the 29th described as 'extremely puzzling and distressing' the refusal of the BBC's chairman, Lord Normanbrook, to see a deputation from the 400,000-strong Clean-up TV Campaign; and, that Tuesday, two unusually acerbic comments from a Chingford housewife. 'In Woolworth's you not only help yourself to what you want but tell them the price,' noted Haines after shopping with her younger daughter. 'They have just enough spirit to take the money. Oooh!' While later, watching events on Centre Court: 'Christine Truman beat the peculiarly attired Nancy Richey of United States. Long shorts and large eye-shade, I ask you. She didn't deserve to win.'[25]

Another diarist ended June by attending a mass lobbying of Parliament, by some 4,000 people, in protest at the Vietnam War. 'We saw Bertrand Russell arrive in his palatial car,' recorded Veronica Lee. 'He is so old & looked as if he were about to break. He peered around him and we all clapped & sang. He tottered in to sign the petition & came out & was driven off. Yet he really moved me. To still care at 93 is wonderful, I think.' In early July, Melvyn Bragg's first novel – *For Want of a Nail*, about a scholarship boy from Cumberland – was reviewed by A. S. Byatt for the *TLS* ('begins well and holds the reader's attention until more than half-way through', before 'the last few chapters meander into reiterated descriptions of adolescent perturbation and are alternately over-intense and over-cynical'); privately educated Ed Stewart (aka Stewpot), formerly Edward Stewart Mainwaring, had his first show on the pirate station Radio London, virtually as Simon Dee became the first pirate DJ to work for the BBC, hosting *Midday Spin*; *Tomorrow's World* started life with not only the startling revelation by Raymond Baxter that a school had recently bought a computer, but an RI of 80 ('I thought it absolutely enthralling'); Ronnie Biggs, one of the Great Train Robbers, began his ascent to cult status by scaling a 30-foot wall to escape from Wandsworth prison ('Cor,' reflected Laurence Marks, 'that must have been brave'); and at Scarborough's Theatre-in-the-Round Library Theatre – and competing against Harry Worth at the Floral Hall, Max Jaffa at the Spa Grand Hall, William Douglas-Home's comedy *The Reluctant Debutante* at the Opera House, and all-star wrestling at the Olympia – Alan Ayckbourn's *Meet My Father* (an early version of *Relatively Speaking*) had its first night, the local paper's critic acclaiming 'this talented young playwright' for creating 'a feather-light farce' with dialogue full of 'brittle wit'. That was on the 8th. Five days later, on Tuesday the 13th, while Barbara Castle at Buckingham Palace was having an enjoyable, post-state-banquet chat with the Queen, interrupted only when 'a flunkey came and whispered in her ear and she excused herself, saying laughingly that "poor Charles" was doing his O-levels the next day and just wanted a bit of reassurance', the BBC showed a documentary about ten days in the life of Jimmy Savile, the typical responses to which ('a complete nut . . . he makes me feel sick . . . effeminate . . . completely grotesque . . . self-advertising mountebank . . . the world's highest-paid ignoramus') showed that he still had a very long way to go on the road to becoming a national treasure. And next day, the 14th, the Secretary of State for Education and Science, Anthony Crosland, issued to local education authorities a long-awaited circular – Circular 10/65 – 'requesting' them to produce, within a year, their plans for changing over (if they had not already done so) to the non-selective, comprehensive model of secondary schooling.[26]

3

One Huge Handicap Event

'Nowhere has the British passion for letting institutions just grow, and the British distaste for centralised control, been more evident than in the educational system,' declared Anthony Sampson in *Anatomy of Britain Today*, published in April 1965 less than three years after his original *Anatomy*. 'Yet,' he went on, 'education is the main instrument of change: it is the schools that mould the future attitudes of society, and must lay the foundation of new skills and adaptability.' Never more so, Sampson emphasised, than in this decade of persistent talk and fears about economic decline, as Britain's 'confident assumption of her superiority gave way, in the current malaise, to new doubts as to what kind of country she should be, and what kind of schooling was needed to change her.' One reviewer, the historian Asa Briggs, was sympathetic but sceptical. After noting how Sampson 'rests his optimism on educational transformation', he added: 'It will take a long time, however, for educational changes to produce large-scale social results, and in the meantime every educational change has produced and continues to produce not only embittered open debate but a great deal of concealed hostility. The self-perpetuating power of existing institutions is a force which must always be reckoned with.'

Certainly there was by this time no apparent shortage of debate, bitter or otherwise, over the issue of reorganising state secondary education along comprehensive lines – Labour's firm commitment on coming to power in October 1964, and very much in accordance with the direction of travel being currently established by many local education authorities (LEAs), especially but not only in the north of England. Controversy over the abolition of grammar schools was particularly fierce that autumn in Bristol and Liverpool, while in the closing days of 1964 the right-wing press began a sustained campaign against the whole process, with its fire initially directed at London's two 'showpiece' comprehensives. 'COMPREHENSIVE SCHOOL "A FAILURE": TEACHER ON LACK OF CONTACT' was *The Times*'s headline, quoting a teacher at Kidbrooke School in south-east London saying that such was 'the size of the school' that in practice 'the pulling-up thing just does not happen' – a quote, it soon emerged, less than fully representing her views; and then, in early January 1965, the *Sunday Telegraph* weighed in with 'TRAPPED IN THE D STREAM', a take-down of Holland Park School, to which the two oldest children of Tony Benn had, amid considerable publicity, been recently transferred from the fee-paying Westminster School. Bullying, swearing, smoking, general lack of discipline: one way and another, it was seemingly an environment in which 'the D-stream child has virtually no chance', while 'to many teachers these lower-stream children, particularly those in their last year, are a nightmare from which they pray for an early release'. The sequence ended on the 18th with a lengthy *Times* editorial ('Ignoring Too Much') on what it portrayed as the intrinsic absurdity of attempting, through the non-selective, comprehensive principle, to 'equalize' children from wholly different home backgrounds:

> The picture is grotesque from every point of view, but its most obvious distortion in the context of education is that it fails to take account of the fact that the family nexus promotes continuity from one generation to the next – dockers see that jobs at the docks go to dockers' sons; naval officers, with rather more interference from politicians, keep alive a naval tradition in their families; even politicians generate political families, and even in left-wing parties. Families can be grouped into distinguishable sub-cultures in any plural society like ours; and schools are an important instrument for transmitting the manners, codes, attitudes, ideals, and learning of broad sub-cultures within society.

'Of these,' concluded the paper with an eye firmly on its readership (smallish but ultra-influential), 'the middle classes are not the least important, and unless they have lost all self-confidence they will insist that they have the schools for that purpose.'[1]

Next day, Tuesday, 19 January, the Cabinet met to discuss the paper which the Education Secretary, Michael Stewart, had sent to them about his intention to issue a circular to LEAs concerning their plans to go comprehensive. Ahead of the meeting, over the weekend, a horrified reader of one specific aspect had been Richard Crossman – namely, the recommendation that (in his own words) 'we should firmly commit ourselves to legislation making the comprehensive compulsory in the next Session'. He had managed to get a rebuttal paper rapidly off to Wilson, and his reward came on Tuesday morning:

> At the Cabinet Harold Wilson started by describing Michael Stewart's paper as the model of what a Cabinet paper should be – something he approved in every way. Then he added that he wondered about the end. Should we really commit ourselves to this legislative compulsion in the coming Session? This seemed to him possibly to be a mistake. He used almost the words I had written to him . . . When Harold Wilson finished Douglas Houghton came in on roughly the same lines, and it was clear that the only support Michael Stewart got was from the old school teachers like Fred Peart and Willie Ross. Even the other members of the Social Services Committee immediately withdrew when the Prime Minister made his point of view clear. Instead of trying to dragoon the schools into action by legislation, the Government would take the line that while we weren't afraid of legislation in the last resort, we didn't think it necessary now, since our plans for encouraging the local authorities to go comprehensive of their own free will were going so well.

An undeniably cardinal moment, born no doubt of many elements, including a small parliamentary majority and an awareness that a hostile press was spoiling for a fight. Two days later, in the Commons, Stewart dutifully emphasised that he was content to rely on 'willing co-operation from the local authorities' and promised that he 'would not ask the House for legislative powers unless that were absolutely necessary for the continuation of policy'. It turned out to be almost his last act in post. Patrick Gordon Walker's defeat that same day in the Leyton by-election led on the Friday to a hasty reshuffle; Stewart became foreign secretary; and, after an unenthusiastic Roy Jenkins had turned down Wilson's offer, the new education secretary was Anthony Crosland.

The author of *The Future of Socialism* (1956) would not for one second have disagreed with Stewart's stirring list to the Commons of why 'separatism' was wrong – 'the damage to primary education, the fallibility and arbitrariness of the eleven-plus, the holding back of many children from furthering and developing their abilities in the way they really could, the depriving of the nation of a proper number of people of well-trained talent, and the general poisoning of the educational atmosphere by encouraging children at an early age to concentrate more on their differences than on their common humanity' – but there was a significant difference between the two men. Whereas Stewart's strong preference would have been for compulsion, Crosland's attachment to egalitarianism was always counterbalanced by an attachment to libertarianism, whether in his personal or his political life. Accordingly, over the next six or so months as he finalised what became Circular 10/65, he won a decisive battle against one of his junior ministers: Reg Prentice wanted his boss to 'require' local authorities to reorganise their secondary provision, but Crosland himself successfully insisted on the milder verb 'request'. Which absolutely did not mean any dilution of his commitment – ultimately on social rather than educational grounds – to the comprehensive principle, as his wife Susan would recall in arguably the most-quoted passage in any biography of any British politician:

> He was driven mad by the obtuseness of those who claimed grammar schools did not affect comprehensives despite the undeniable fact that the former creamed off the more gifted children. Following a dinner [probably quite soon after becoming education secretary] with four of the teachers' associations – 'Joint 4' – his tread was ominous as he mounted the stairs. He stopped at our bedroom door.
>
> 'Good evening. You'd better come in the study.'
>
> I put my novel aside and got smartly out of our bed, wondering what had caused this latest vexation.
>
> 'If it's the last thing I do, I'm going to destroy every fucking grammar school in England,' he said. 'And Wales. And Northern Ireland.'

'Why not Scotland?' I asked out of pure curiosity.

'Because their schools come under the Secretary of State for Scotland.' He began to laugh at his inability to destroy their grammar schools.

Deep down he was convinced that, whatever the multitude of practical problems involved, the tide of history was flowing his way – an understandable enough assumption, given that almost two-thirds of secondary school pupils in England and Wales *already* lived in areas where the LEA was implementing or planning a policy along essentially comprehensive lines. 'The fact is', he told an audience that spring with characteristic assurance, 'that there has been a growing movement against the 11+ examination and all that it implies. This movement has not been politically inspired or imposed from the centre. It has been a spontaneous growth at the grass roots of education, leading to a widespread conviction that separatism is an offence against the child as well as a brake on social and economic progress . . .' In short, and brooking no ambiguity, 'the whole notion of a selection test at this age belongs to the era when secondary education was a privilege of the few'.[2]

During these months, the story was indeed not just about Crosland. In February alone, the Lord Chancellor, Lord (Gerald) Gardiner, spoke eloquently to his peers about attending a packed-out meeting at Leicester's De Montfort Hall where 'the vast majority were parents and they were hopping mad because in the city they had secondary and grammar schools whereas the county had comprehensive schools', with Gardiner adding, 'I had always known that the 11-plus was not very popular but I had never known before the extent it was both hated and feared'; the *Liverpool Daily Post* welcomed a one-year delay in the city going comprehensive, but 'hoped that erstwhile critics will now prove the truth of their repeated assertions that it was not comprehensive education they opposed, but precipitancy'; and the first meeting was held of what would become the campaigning-cum-informational Comprehensive Schools Committee, with Benn's American wife Caroline at its very heart. Early in March, Margaret Thatcher confessed to her Finchley Association that she was 'very concerned indeed about the Government's intention to reorganise secondary education on comprehensive lines', a position in marked contrast to her party's more relaxed education spokesman, Sir Edward Boyle; late that month, Ernest Taylor, headmaster of Wolverhampton Grammar School and president of the Headmasters' Association, told the Liverpool Parents' Protest Committee that he remained convinced that 'most children' were 'rightly placed' in their respective schools at eleven ('we have allowed sympathy with the unfortunate misfits to blind us to the tremendous success of the experiment we started in 1944 with a resolve to provide secondary education for all according to age, ability, and aptitude'); while in the space of four days in April, Labour-controlled Luton decided to reject the ministry's advice that it should postpone until 1966 its scheme for going comprehensive ('a half-baked plan', according to a prominent local Conservative), the *Observer Magazine* ran a largely admiring profile of a pioneer comprehensive school in a Sussex new town ('Thomas Bennett takes the whole of one Crawley neighbourhood, and therefore gets its fair share of able children, stupid children, geniuses and psychopaths'), and Stoke-on-Trent's *Evening Sentinel* glumly concluded that 'the game is lost' after what it called 'a radically ideological authority' had in its determination to go comprehensive been 'backed up by the government in power'.

'Drawing into its maw every child over eleven' was how the even more hostile *Daily Express* described in May the comprehensive system; the June issue of the *British Journal of Sociology* had D. N. Holly examining the fortunes of late-1950s entrants to a London comprehensive (streamed throughout by ability) and finding that middle-class children benefited more than working-class children, with Holly reflecting that 'ironically meritocracy in this school is held at bay not – as many enthusiasts for the comprehensive school would have hoped – by a breakdown in the class-determined barriers to educational involvement but, on the contrary, by the very persistence of such barriers'; the same month, an assessment by Sussex University's Boris Ford of Bristol's newly approved plan for neighbourhood comprehensives claimed not only that the local authority had 'gone forward with astonishingly little detailed study, research experiment, testing and redesigning which would have seemed essential in so large a project', but also that the result, far from enhancing diversity in intake, was likely to prove the opposite; and July began with *New Society* publishing an analysis by George Taylor, chief education officer for Leeds, of how the vexed issue of catchment area policy was so far working out in practice. 'It would appear', he concluded, 'that parents selecting houses in the right areas have little to lose from comprehensive education; other parents of able children may be apprehensive.'[3]

Less than a fortnight later, on the 14th, Crosland's much-drafted, much-anticipated circular was at last published. 'The Government are aware', it declared,

> that the complete elimination of selection and separatism in secondary education will take time to achieve. They do not seek to impose destructive or precipitate change on existing schools. They recognize that the evolution of separate schools into a comprehensive system must be a constructive process requiring careful planning by local education authorities in consultation with all concerned. But the spontaneous and exciting progress which has been made in this direction by so many authorities in recent years demonstrates that the objective is not only practicable – it is also widely accepted.

Almost throughout, the circular's tone was studiously moderate and reassuring: an intention to preserve 'all that is valuable in grammar school education for those children who now receive it and to make it available to more children'; no one-size-fits-all method of implementation, but instead freedom for the LEA to choose (or perhaps even pick 'n' mix) from the half-dozen main types of comprehensive organisation currently emerging; and an emphasis on how 'the smooth inception and continuing success of any scheme of reorganisation will depend on the co-operation of teachers and the support and confidence of parents'. All in all, reckoned the *Guardian*'s education correspondent (and future editor), Peter Preston, it amounted to an 'amiably toothless tiger of a comprehensive circular', putting 'children and common sense first' and bowing to 'local ties, personal beliefs, individual concerns'. By contrast, the *Daily Telegraph* took the line that, for all the sweet talking, 'in essence the Government's policy remains the same, to foster the egalitarian trend', with 'the dogma kept inviolate'. That dogma remained fundamentally unacceptable. 'The common characteristic of children at grammar and public schools is that they can be presumed to be fit for higher education either on strict academic grounds or by general reason of their background,' insisted the paper. 'No such assumption can be made in relation to the pupils of comprehensive schools.' Accordingly, 'if there are merits in both comprehensive and segregated education they should be judged more by parents, less by Mr. CROSLAND'. Stern stuff, with instinctively little or no sympathy for the nearest that the circular had come to a truly New Jerusalem moment. 'A comprehensive school', it had declared, 'aims to establish a school community in which pupils over the whole ability range and with differing interests and backgrounds can be encouraged to mix with each other, gaining stimulus from the contacts and learning tolerance and understanding in the process.'[4]

Where did public opinion – especially parental opinion – really stand? How much, indeed, did the public really engage with the whole issue? After all, for every city like Bristol or Liverpool where feelings on both sides ran strong, there was at least another city like Sheffield, where public debate during the first half of 1965 had fairly rapidly fizzled out, with the organisers of a petition and counter-petition finding it appreciably easier to announce targets than to collect actual signatures. About this time, on the basis of surveys that his Research Services Ltd had conducted in recent years, Mark Abrams sought to unpick what he called a 'widespread complacency about our educational system'. 'Working-class people', he argued, 'approve of the present educational facilities because they fail to see the connection between educational privilege and social inequality; and middle-class people approve of the present educational structure because they *do* appreciate from direct personal experience the connection between educational privilege and social inequality.' Not long afterwards, in June, the *Guardian*'s Preston reported the findings of an Essex University research project, interviewing 135 mothers in Basildon and Brentwood who this year had children taking the 11-plus. Opinion divided two to one in favour of comprehensives; the dissenters were mainly middle-class mothers (criticising 'size, levelling down and grammar school abolition in roughly equal proportions') whose children were at primary schools 'with an enviable 11-plus record'; while more generally, added Preston, 'profound parental muddle and ignorance marked all stages of the inquiry', to the extent that 'only 57 per cent knew comprehensive schools were non-selective'. Another journalist with his nose close to the educational ground was

Paul Barker, soon to become long-serving editor of *New Society*. 'The supposed groundswell of public support for comprehensives was misleading,' he would reflect some thirty years later. 'One segment consisted of modestly placed parents who were well enough off to pay the pre-Butler grammar school fees, but couldn't afford public schools; their children were now shut out from grace if they failed the 11-plus. Another, larger segment were voting *against* the secondary modern schools, to which most who failed went, rather than *for* comprehensives.'

That seems plausible enough. Yet ultimately, given the prevailing quite high levels (speaking generally) of apathy, and perhaps even greater levels of ignorance, so much in practice depended upon the individual local authorities. And it is worth quoting – not as the last word on the subject, but suggestive nevertheless – the retrospective assessment of Martin Wilson, who in June 1965 retired as Salop County Council's successfully pro-comprehensive secretary for education: 'The new policy makers at least had their feet on the ground. They knew where the shoe pinched. They were fairly close to the customer. They were susceptible to the pressures as existed from the people – and from the teachers. They developed zest and ambition. Local pride worked powerfully in them.'

If there was an emblematic figure in the broader movement now under way, it was surely Harry Rée. Before the war he had taught at Penge Grammar School; after the war, he taught at Bradford Grammar School, before spending most of the 1950s as headmaster of Watford Grammar School, during which time he wrote a well-regarded book, *The Essential Grammar School* (1956), whose message was exactly as the title stated. By 1965 he was professor of education at the recently established University of York – and, to the surprise and consternation of many former colleagues, an impassioned advocate of the comprehensive revolution. 'What factors', the magazine *Where?* asked him that spring, 'made you reject the idea of separate grammar and secondary modern schools?'

> As the headmaster of a grammar school I began to get genuinely interested in secondary modern schools. When I visited them and showed I was interested this caused surprise. This surprise horrified me.

> I recognised that the job of a secondary modern school was a damn sight harder than that of a grammar school. When I realized the incredible handicaps that, in a racehorse sense, weigh down the secondary modern school I was appalled by the inequality. They have to deal with more difficult families; apart from saintly exceptions they attract less good teachers. They often suffer from having poor buildings and inadequate playing fields. Most important they are adversely affected by a general lack of public esteem.

Rée continued over the rest of the interview to pour out his opinions. 'Not only does selection divide families, it divides communities,' adding that 'most of us who were personally involved in selection in Hertfordshire came to loathe it because we knew we were making mistakes'. And: 'It seems to me that in the 'sixties the grammar school is failing in its social duty. In its social effects it is as guilty as the public school.' And: 'We must stop locking kids up in segregated schools before they have a chance to prove themselves. We mustn't be impressed by the transfer to grammar school at 13. The children who achieve this have had to contend against huge odds. There is only one answer. We must keep doors open all the way along and we must make them as easy to open for one child as for the next.' And finally, this most painfully targeted of Parthian shots: 'The grammar schools produce a large number of well-meaning solid citizens, who set limits on people who they think are beneath them.'[5]

On 14 July itself, as Circular 10/65 went definitive and public, Crosland spent the afternoon at Manchester's Free Trade Hall, where Manchester Grammar School (MGS) was holding a special speech day to mark its 450th anniversary. The *Guardian* next day printed a photo of Crosland holding a cup of tea as, after the formalities were over, he answered questions – but, sadly, with no further details. MGS was one of 179 direct grant schools (as compared with some 1,200 maintained grammar schools); most of their funding came from a mixture of fee-paying and a grant direct from central government; they were obliged to give at least a quarter of their places to children from state primary schools, without cost to their parents; and as Alec Clegg, president of the Association of Chief Education Officers, had pointed out in February, there was a big difference between on the one hand most of the direct grant schools, their intake comparable to that of the average maintained grammar school, and on the other what he labelled 'the big civic direct grant schools', such as in Manchester or Bradford or Leeds or Birmingham, where substantially over half the (all-male) pupils came from professional or clerical homes and whose non-fee-paying pupils were 'of extraordinarily high intelligence', unsurprisingly topping 'the "Oxbridge" scholarship league table' – a table which also saw high places for pupils from the twenty-two direct grant schools which were part of the Girls' Public Day School Trust (GPDST).

What to do about these 179 schools? In May, on the basis of a draft circular that Crosland had sent to local authorities, the *Observer* had revealed that they 'are not being forced into the comprehensive school system until the future of the public schools is settled'; and an explanation for this exemption had perhaps come three days later, when (according to Cabinet papers) Crosland had told colleagues that 'there was the likelihood that many of the better direct grant schools would become independent rather than merge into local comprehensive reorganisation'. Still, the continuing existence of these hybrid schools (half-private, half-state) was undeniably a problem if one believed in the comprehensive principle. And when in due course Circular 10/65 explicitly stated that Crosland had no present intention of withdrawing the direct government grant paid to them, yet at the same time requested LEAs to ask them to (in an undefined way) 'associate' themselves with LEA plans, it was, to quote the subsequent words of educational researcher Alun Griffiths, 'like asking the Athenaeum to consider ways in which it could become a Youth Centre'.[6]

As for the actual full-blown public (i.e. private) schools, Labour's promise ahead of the October 1964 election had been to 'integrate' them into the state system; and that autumn, starting at my own public school (Wellington College), I was aware even as a thirteen-year-old of some apprehension among the teachers about what lay ahead. 'Waiting to be Integrated' was the title in December of a *Spectator* piece by Richard Rhodes James. 'I teach in a public school,' he began. 'And so my world is less certain than it was. There is, in fact, precious little hush in the close these days. With the twang of guitars are mingled the arguments of those who would destroy us . . .' He did not deny the existing social and educational divisiveness that schools like his own caused, but wondered whether, when it came to it, he and his fellow teachers would *really* be 'willing to throw open the doors to all and sundry'. 'Nostalgia tends to return,' he admitted with commendable honesty. 'We think of happy days, and splendid boys, and we contemplate cockneys with a cold unease. We think of how we should operate a boarding school with boys who have never been taught the social disciplines that such a life entails. We wonder about the parents. We wonder about the sanitation. We try to conjure up Speech Day . . .' The following month, Crosland was the new education secretary; and, in the same magazine, a profile by Alan Watkins rightly noted how, in his seminal *The Future of Socialism* nine years earlier, 'the heart of the whole work was the conviction that a large private educational sector was the greatest single obstacle to social equality'. Even so, pondered Watkins, would he now have the 'political toughness' to be able to dismantle that obstacle? On that, Watkins was less categorical.

In the immediate event, precious little happened in the next six months. Susan Crosland would recall a conscious decision on her husband's part to prioritise the comprehensive issue, even telling her, 'I'm not frightfully interested in the public schools at this moment'; while one historian, Dennis Dean, argues that 'he was aware that this task [i.e. of tackling the public schools] was more difficult, but by settling the debate about selection in the maintained sector and promoting widely an ethos of opportunity he hoped to weaken the position of the public schools by isolation'. Accordingly, when in May Harold Wilson made cautious noises in favour of continuing to delay the appointment of a public schools commission to work out precisely how to resolve the issue ('there is a growing feeling in the country that we are stirring up too many things, not all of equal priority'), Crosland went quietly, accepting that 'the political grounds for postponement are over-riding'. The most revealing testimony arguably comes from the memoirs of one of his advisers, the sociologist A. H. ('Chelly') Halsey:

> Tony's love of freedom was fetishist, driven, immoderate. Alcohol, cigars, women, even opera, were avidly consumed . . . He wanted to see himself as the proponent of libertarian socialism and me as a stern egalitarian. I didn't see it like that: I saw us both as both. But the English sin in education, I thought, was inequality while

> his great fear was that we might impose unfreedom on those who wanted to send their children to schools in the private sector.

'Underneath,' adds Halsey, 'he was reluctant and convinced that nobody really cared about such things.' Perhaps so, with indeed that indifference, or anyway relative indifference, probably shared by most of Crosland's Cabinet colleagues. 'I don't see much point in setting up a commission or trying to improve the link between the public schools and the state system,' noted Richard Crossman in July when – the day after Circular 10/65 – Crosland did tell those colleagues about the intended eventual establishment of a public schools commission. While as for Crossman's own future as a fee-paying parent, 'I very much doubt whether this will make the faintest difference to Patrick's or Virginia's education.'

He, to be fair, was hardly alone. Back in January, when Wilson had invited Jenkins to replace Stewart as education secretary, the reason Jenkins gave for declining the offer was that all three of his children were at fee-paying schools and that this was surely a problem for any education minister in a Labour government. Whereupon, as Jenkins recalled, 'Wilson brushed this aside as being of no importance. "So were mine," he said.' Or take the aftermath of that awkward moment a few weeks later in the House of Lords, when C. P. Snow made such a ham-fisted mess of explaining why his own son was destined for Eton and failing to make the well-known, get-out-of-jail gag about Eton being one of the first comprehensives. Lord (David) Eccles for the Tory opposition immediately branded Snow a 'humbug'; a Labour MP, Fred Bellenger, called for his ministerial resignation; and crisis was averted only when Crosland depersonalised the issue by producing for the Commons the statistics which showed, across the parties, the low or relatively low percentages of MPs whose sons went to state schools. Nor, or course, was it just politicians. 'Lord Snow's dilemma as a father and a liberal intellectual is a very real one, shared at different levels of education by many other parents,' reflected the sociologist Dennis Marsden soon afterwards:

> In a society with the present system of priorities and school structure, how is one to make a humane choice, good for one's own child but also good for others? Lord Snow has reached 'the top'

> via grammar school and university. Yet having done so, he feels he doesn't want his child to have to climb up the whole difficult way that he has come. He sees now an easy consolidation of his gains, which as a good parent he will grasp.

In short, simply by sending his son to public school, he 'can make sure the boy *begins* at the top'.[7]

'The demand for degrees has hugely increased since the war, and with the growth of big corporations, the break-up of family firms, and the need for professional managers, "graduatisation" has spread through industry and even into parts of the City,' noted Sampson in his 1965 *Anatomy*. 'An Arts degree is no longer regarded as an agreeable cultivation before starting serious work, but more as a vital qualification for the higher rungs of government and industry.' Or as Frankie Howerd had put it much more succinctly a couple of years earlier on *TW3*, lamenting the seemingly irresistible incursion of graduates into hitherto no-go areas, 'in these days, anyway, you can't be filthy unless you've got a degree'. British universities, for so long educating a smaller proportion of their population than those in almost any other comparable country, were certainly now having a moment, as the new Labour government conscientiously and even enthusiastically fulfilled the expansionist promises of the 1963 Robbins Report, which itself had built on the decision back in the late 1950s to found a new generation – coming to fruition by this time as the famous seven of Sussex, York, East Anglia, Essex, Lancaster, Kent and Warwick. Back in 1960 there had been a total of 108,000 university students (up admittedly from the 82,000 in 1951, but not spectacularly so); by 1965 the total was 169,000; and by 1970 it would be up to 228,000.

'A brief and disastrous period, the years when a benign and sense-stealing sense of euphoria descended on dons everywhere and elephantiasis of the imagination was the most commonly encountered disease in university common rooms' was how in 1968 one dissenting academic, Donald Watt of the London School of Economics, rather sourly looked back on the mid-1960s. 'Confronted with statistics as to the numbers of students processed by American, European and Soviet universities, the university world of Britain plunged into schemes of expansion on a Stakhanovite scale.' He did have at least one ally. In April 1965, the same month that Sampson's new *Anatomy* quoted with evident approbation the dictum of Lord Bowden (former head of the Manchester College of Science and Technology, now the minister of state responsible for universities) that 'for the first time in recorded history the survival of the country depends upon the universities', the *Observer* ran a major report by Brian Jackson on the reasons behind what he viewed as the disturbingly and unnecessarily high one-in-seven drop-out rate from those universities. 'Obviously the problem includes everything from bone-idleness to mental illness,' he accepted, before declaring that '*most* university failures arise because of subjective feelings in university teachers about *how many* students *ought* to fail'. Few tears shed that Sunday in Maida Vale. 'Perhaps only you could have published a whole article on university failures that laid no weight on the almost invariable cause of failure: *insufficient ability*, or, alternatively, *excessive stupidity*' ran a letter to the editor the following week from Kingsley Amis. 'I was glad to learn from you, however, that as many as 14 per cent of people do fail. Evidently not all standards have been fully lowered everywhere yet. But your fashionable brand of sentimental mercy will hasten the process.'[8]

Happily for Amis's blood pressure, he did not yet know that the age of the 'poly' was about to dawn. Nine days later, on the 27th, Crosland made a speech at Woolwich which, though barely reported in the national press, was in its way as significant as the Robbins Report. In essence, to quote the educational historian Simon Dixon, he plotted the outlines of a path 'amalgamating colleges of art, technology, and commerce into polytechnics geared primarily to vocational provision' – a path which at the same time, and against apparent pre-election Labour policy, 'drove a wedge through higher education' through upholding the binary principle, that in other words these polytechnics would comprise a different sector from the universities and, unlike them, not be autonomous but instead under local authority control. In the event, thirty polytechnics were created over the next eight years; and it would not be until the 1990s that they became universities in their own right. Why the decision to go binary? No doubt it reflected in part Crosland's desire to undermine what he called in his speech 'our snobbish, caste-ridden, hierarchical obsession with university status'; while it is likely that he was influenced by one of his senior civil servants, Toby Weaver, seeing them as more cost-effective alternatives to universities at a time of rapidly increasing demand for higher education places. The backlash started early, including from the educationalist Robin Pedley, author two years earlier of a hugely influential Penguin Original, *The Comprehensive School*. A segregated system, he wrote stiffly to Crosland in early May, 'seriously conflicts with the philosophy of comprehensive education' and was therefore 'disastrous'. To which Crosland might have responded that his aim was for polytechnics to evolve as different beings from universities, but not lesser beings – the old dream, in fact, of 'parity of esteem' that the creators of the post-1944 state secondary system had had of the relationship between grammars and secondary moderns.

Even so, for all the ultimate futility of both dreams, there was still something undeniably noble about the original 1960s 'poly' vision (which itself found inspiration from such London institutions as the Regent Street Polytechnic, going back to the nineteenth century). 'Sooner or later this country must face a comprehensive form of education beyond school – a reform which will bring higher education out of the ivory towers and make it available to all.' Such was the clarion call of Eric Robinson – Labour Party activist, former adviser to Crosland, soon to become deputy director of North East London Polytechnic – introducing his 1968 book, *The New Polytechnics*. 'The shape and speed of this change to come', he added, 'depends on the success with which the polytechnics are established.' New institutions operating in the heart of urban, industrial, regional England; 'study with a purpose'; no expensive halls of residence; perhaps above all, a focused, unglamorous, productive style and atmosphere of higher education mercifully free of (in the indignant, heartfelt words of one of Robinson's 2011 obituarists) 'the whole grotesque panoply of research exercises, vice-chancellors and all the attendant mummery'.[9]

One embryonic educational institution was always going to be a university, not a poly. Back in 1962, Brian Jackson and Dennis Marsden in the closing pages of *Education and the Working Class* had written of the need to develop what they called 'the "open" university', a concept which would necessarily 'entail a large new working-class intake'; in September 1963, in a speech in Glasgow,

Harold Wilson had talked enthusiastically about a university of the air; a year later, Michael Young had written a paper for *Where?* magazine, 'Towards an Open University'; and on 2 April 1965, a few weeks before Crosland's Woolwich speech, the arts minister, Jennie Lee (widow of Nye Bevan), was telling the Commons about her intention to commission feasibility studies into the possibility of setting up a full-blown university of the air with degree courses provided through television. 'Above all,' she insisted, 'there would have to be a vice-chancellor of impeccable academic standing. I am not interested in a sort of Paddy-the-next-best thing, a kind of poor man's university of the air.' The immediate response was widespread scepticism. For the opposition, Geoffrey Johnson Smith, despite being a former star of *Tonight*, 'said the concept of a university of the air was an inflated one, and he proposed to take some of the gas out of it'; *The Times* next day declared it nothing other than 'misleading nonsense' to imagine that a television viewer would be 'offered the range and depth of courses open to the university student'; and even the *Guardian* was doubtful, pointing out that, in terms of a proper university education, broadcasts might be able to take the place of lectures, but not private reading, let alone tutorials or seminars.

In the end, of course, the doubters were proved wrong; Lee over the next few years was staunchly supported by Wilson; and the OU would admit its first students in 1971. Yet for all the justifiable pride that Wilson and Lee took in their creation, is it possible to be too Whiggish, too confident that the very best outcome prevailed? Perhaps. 'I supported the idea of the Open University very strongly, but I also thought it could be combined with a reshaping of adult education,' reflected Raymond Williams in conversation in 1979:

> There could be a connection between education by television, radio and correspondence courses, and the kind of tutorial class education which had been so well developed by the WEA [Workers' Educational Association]. It would not have been easy, and I am sure there were political reasons for wanting to push a prepared idea of the Open University through, against its many enemies on the right. But Jennie Lee later told me, at a *Guardian* dinner, the only time I ever met her, that as the Minister responsible she had decided to steer clear of the old types of adult education and set up what

> looked as much as possible like a conventional university, including the 'trimmings'. So that was it, that kind of assimilated even where radical initiative, and the Open University still has no properly based tutorial organization, and little of our old educational democracy.[10]

To a surprising extent, for all that its substance was much on the minds of 'activators' and others, the specific term 'social mobility' was used quite sparingly in the 1960s, certainly as compared to later decades. An exception was the American literary critic Lionel Trilling. 'I asked him about the people in the pub, all of whom seemed of the same class,' he reported back home in spring 1962 following a London conversation, in a pub near Sloane Street, with the English philosopher Stuart Hampshire:

> He said he thought they were mainly advertising people. I spoke about English social mobility and he said yes, but a little dubiously and went on to speak of the class lines that are still stringent. He said: 'I suppose not one of these people went to a really good school,' and then he looked around carefully and confirmed himself: 'No, not one.' (There must have been a hundred people jammed into that pub.) I said: 'How can you tell, by their faces?' And he replied with perfect simplicity, 'Oh yes.' And of course you *can*. Faces and voices and set of the shoulders really do show, and how long it will take before these things don't finally matter is hard to say. But I would guess not long: the new pressure is very great.

An optimistic guess? Or where British society was irresistibly heading? Certainly, when almost exactly three years later, in March 1965, Harold Wilson was asked in an interview to envisage the kind of Britain he would like to see in ten years' time, he had no hesitation in spelling out as one of his three top priorities – along with a country standing on its own feet economically and where poverty had been abolished – 'a Britain in which anyone who has anything to contribute can get to the top on merit and ability, not on social or family connections'. A classless society? Wilson did not actually use the utopian adjective, but undoubtedly that was the implicit thrust of his meritocratic and socially mobile vision.

However classless or otherwise things might turn out to be by 1975, there was little denying in the mid-1960s themselves that social class still to a large degree permeated the British education system – *even* ignoring the utterly class-dominated private school aspect. The fullest state-of-play overview, 'The Trend of Class Differentials in Educational Opportunity in England and Wales' by Alan Little and John Westergaard, appeared in the *British Journal of Sociology* in December 1964. 'The results are easily summarized,' they declared of their detailed comparison of pre-war and post-war educational opportunities:

> Social inequalities in access to selective secondary education have been somewhat reduced over the past 50–60 years. But the reduction has, in the first place, been small – so small as to disappear should one choose to look at the differentials in failure to obtain a grammar school type education, rather than the differentials in successful admission to such an education. In the second place, the reduction of social inequalities is not a new, post-1944 phenomenon, but the continuation of a long-term, gradual trend. And in the third place, it has been confined to entry into selective secondary education, while access to the universities has remained more or less unaffected.

It was a conclusion which played down the social-mobility implications of Rab Butler's 1944 Education Act; while in terms of the bigger sociological picture, Little and Westergaard reflected that 'the persistence of marked social inequalities in educational opportunity is in line with a good deal of other evidence on the relative constancy of class divisions in our society'. That persistence definitely included the universities, where quite apart from the continuing marked class – and gender-cum-ethnic – bias when it came to access, as well as a steep and unyielding hierarchy across the sector as a whole, there also remained distinct socially determined differences in the student experience itself. In 1965, on the basis of a study of university life at Edinburgh, Durham and Newcastle, the social anthropologist Joan Abbott found that class consciousness prevented, in each of those three student bodies, anything like a 'melting-pot', most notably on occasions like dances and parties. Indeed, as she was reported the following year as observing more generally, 'it is no longer monetary obstacles but cultural differences which distinguish the social classes in universities'.

None of this is to deny that educational opportunities for the working class had increased since the war – they palpably had. Nor is it to deny the emergence by the mid-1960s of a grammar school elite positioned to challenge the traditional privately educated elite. After all, whereas in 1959 the private schools had been responsible for 55 per cent of the Oxbridge intake, only eight years later that proportion was down to 38 per cent, with the majority of places going instead to the grammar schools, including the direct grants. Yet in any case, even if one accepts the 1980s long-run conclusion of Halsey, based on the 1972 evidence of the Oxford Mobility Study, that across the previous decades 'it appears that expansion has brought a slow and steady diminution of class inequality', there is the crucial larger point, understandably under-appreciated in the 1960s, that education itself was *not* the silver bullet, *not* the key driver of social mobility. The crux instead, it is now generally recognised, was the changing labour market – above all, an occupational structure in which blue-collar jobs were, in increasing rapidity, starting to be replaced by white-collar jobs, especially as management and professional employment grew, not least in the burgeoning public sector. In short, to quote the veteran sociologist John Goldthorpe looking back from a 2016 perspective on the so-called 'golden age' of social mobility, it had simply if prosaically been a case of more 'room at the top'.[11]

One can be a bit more specific. What Goldthorpe had in mind was what he called the 'service class' – comprising the professions, local and national government administration, the higher technical jobs, middle to senior management – which in the course of the 1960s and 1970s moved from roughly one in eight of the employed men in Britain to roughly one in four. Not that it was only men who were affected by the changing occupational structure, for the welfare state was by now becoming an increasingly large-scale employer of women, whether in healthcare or education or local government, a process that has been nicely described as 'the feminization of the state'. Even so, for all the changing labour market, major blockages remained, perhaps above all in the world of business. Through the 1960s, and beyond, a clear majority of the chairmen of Britain's leading industrial companies had been privately educated; similarly, a 1965 survey by the Institute of Directors of some 6,000 company directors found well over half to have been privately educated; a year earlier, when the London Chamber of Commerce surveyed its younger members (all under the age of forty, all holding executive positions), it emerged that a little under half had been privately educated, so perhaps, under the radar, things were just starting to change; in the City of London, 'who you know' rather than 'what you know' was still, with relatively few exceptions, the primrose path to success; and in advertising, a 1966 survey of the larger agencies revealed 20 per cent of staff to be privately educated, while at one well-known firm, Robert Sharpe & Partners, the three principals were all Old Etonians. Or take the civil service: there, analysis in 1967 showed that only 19 per cent of senior civil servants came from lower socio-economic backgrounds. Even in obscure and dusty archives, the right sort of personal background could be an invaluable asset, conferring competitive advantage. 'I went to the County Hall where I am currently trying to charm the pleasant custodian of the archives to let me see certain volumes of Church courts which are, because of their delicate state, technically "unfit for production"', the 23-year-old Alan Macfarlane (Sedbergh and Oxford) told his parents in June 1965 about his postgraduate progress. 'Working among these and other records I have become increasingly aware of the delicate pressures which come to bear even in strictly "academic research". If one has the right accent, comes from the right university, has contacts etc, one can see things that others can't . . . With strings all sorts of strong-room doors will slide open, where no amount of direct banging and pleading will open them.'[12]

What, then, faced by these competing social and economic forces, is the bigger picture about social mobility in the 1960s? Much depends on whether one means *absolute* social mobility – best defined as the percentage of the population who make it from one class into another – or the ultimately more telling *relative* social mobility, best defined as the likelihood that anyone from a given social class will make it to somewhere near the top. In terms of the former type of social mobility, it is unambiguously clear that it was significantly increasing; but in terms of the latter type, the evidence is more mixed, with two much-respected sociologists reaching somewhat different historical conclusions. Goldthorpe's central finding can be summarised quite bluntly: that through the whole of the twentieth century (including the 1960s), the chances of a working-class child making it into the middle class barely varied through time – and that during that century a child born middle class was some fifteen times likelier to end his life middle class than was a child born working class. The other sociologist, also examining the British experience of social mobility during the twentieth century, is Anthony Heath, employing the data from British Election Surveys going back to 1964. At the heart of his analysis is the question of what were the relative odds, as between men from middle-class ('salariat') origins and men from working-class origins, of reaching the salariat and avoiding working-class destinations – an odds ratio which in a society of 'perfect' social mobility should be 1:1, i.e. even odds. Inevitably, they were never that, or indeed anything remotely like it; but there *was*, according to Heath, some significant movement – so that whereas for men born in the 1920s and entering the labour market around the 1940s the odds ratio in favour of those born middle-class was 14:1, for the next cohort, born in the 1930s and entering the labour market around the 1950s, the odds had been reduced to 10:1; while for those born in the 1940s and entering the labour market around the 1960s, the odds were down to 6:1.[13] Even so, six to one . . . And for those who believed in the desirability of an ever more socially mobile society with increasingly equal life chances irrespective of birth, which for different reasons far from everyone in either the left or the right did believe in, there was still a way to go.

Against the backdrop of rising standards of living, of more or less full employment, of significantly if not dramatically greater equality of outcome, it is easy to understand why the 1960s *felt* like a golden age of social mobility. Perhaps especially if one lived in Wales, where (in the words of Martin Johnes) 'despite the fact that education and university degrees were unlikely to solve the problems of an industrial town, out of a mix of idealism, pragmatism and snobbery, they were widely esteemed in all Wales'. Take the holy trinity of Gerald Davies, Gareth Edwards and Barry John: all were sons of miners; all were playing rugby for Wales by 1966/7; and all were enabled by the growth of further and higher education to train as teachers rather than following their fathers down the pit. Generally, there was no shortage by the middle years of the decade of the upwardly mobile famous: David Bailey, Jean Shrimpton, Twiggy, Albert Finney, Tom Courtenay, Michael Caine, Terence Stamp, Sean Connery, Cilla Black, Lulu – to name but ten obvious examples, quite apart from the Beatles and the Stones (even if the social origins of neither group was quite as working-class as often assumed). John Fowles was a fascinated observer of the phenomenon. 'Terry [Stamp] has created a sort of dream life-style for himself,' he noted in March 1964 during the filming of *The Collector*. 'He says whatever comes into his head, does what he likes, lives like a sort of Hamlet without neurosis, eternally white-shirted, open-throated, thrusting, on the crest of the wave.' While at Cannes fourteen months later: 'Mike Caine. A Cockney boy made good – Terry's friend. He can't act, but takes himself very seriously: hot for birds, for the *dolce vita*, for prestige. Very ugly, these new ultra-hard young princes of limelight.' And of Stamp again in early 1967: 'He has that Prince Hamlet aura still and his absurd vanity, certainly no less than his chum Caine's, but so much more lightly carried. His charm is really in the air of happy freedom he carries with him; a sort of eighteenth-century swagger.'[14] A fascinated observer, indeed, but even in a supposedly more classless world, Fowles, a product of public school (Bedford) and Oxford, simply could not help the condescension.

In general, so many individual circumstances, so many individual destinies, so many individual emotions. **Jacqueline Angell**, a 1947 baby boomer, found herself, because of that year's demographic 'bulge', in a secondary modern and unable to access a grammar school, even though she and around half her class had actually passed the 11-plus; **Richard Banks** and most of his friends had failed the 11-plus in 1957 ('from that moment we were made to feel like second-class citizens fit only for second-class jobs'), but some dedicated teaching and a few O level passes led to the local authority compelling a grammar school to take four of them for A levels ('our presence was clearly resented by the headteacher who publicly announced that we were likely to spoil his proud exam record'), and Banks would eventually retire half a century later as a senior hospital consultant physician; **George Charlton**, born 1950 and brought up in Gateshead, would become a poet and reflect in later life how he was one of many working-class children born since the war who, at their grammar school, 'Suppressed the local accent in our voice, / Not to give ourselves away'; the future novelist **Mavis Cheek**, born 1948, failed her 11-plus and in 1964 left her school in Raynes Park with just one O level, but after answering an *Evening Standard* ad landed a job as a receptionist with the very upmarket Kensington print dealer, Editions Alecto ('they'd always employed Hooray Henriettas before, but suddenly thought they'd get a prole'); **Brian Cox** (born 1946), son of a small grocer in a poor part of Dundee and brought up in a tenement, got a place aged seventeen at the London Academy of Music and Dramatic Art ('people made it obvious they were happy that I was there . . . I loved the sense that I was allowed to be who I was and celebrated for coming from my class'); **Harold Evans**, born 1928, had by sheer ability and determination risen from being the son of a Manchester engine driver and failing to get to grammar school to become by the mid-1960s the editor of the *Northern Echo* – and, before long, almost a poster boy for post-war social mobility; the future playwright **John Godber** was brought up in a mining community near Pontefract, failed his 11-plus ('my father found it a great humiliation'), went in 1966 to the local secondary modern, and developed a hatred of the grammar school boys ('"Have you done your table tennis homework?" they used to shout at us'); **Philip Gould**, born 1950, grew up near Woking as the son of a primary school headmaster, prepared hard for the 11-plus before disaster struck ('I took one look at the paper and I just froze . . . I went home to lunch, to be greeted by my parents – my mother in tears, my father ashen – telling me I had failed already'), went to Knaphill Secondary Modern ('the school from hell . . . everybody knew they were a failure . . . always it was grindingly, gruesomely boring'), left school at sixteen with one O level, eventually after a chequered few years got to Sussex University – and became a quarter of a century later the architect of New Labour; a smoother upward trajectory for future historian **Tony Judt** (born 1948), a self-confessed classic post-war meritocrat who went to a direct grant (Emanuel School in Battersea) and then in 1966 to King's College, Cambridge, where among other grammar school boys he encountered was a future governor of the Bank of England, **Mervyn King**, whose father had been a railway porter before retraining after the war as a geography teacher; 'we qualified for free school meals, but I was made to collect the dining numbers from each class as I was told to earn my keep,' recalled **Jackie King-Owen** half a century (and five degrees between them) later about the experience of her brother and herself in the 1960s, attending grammar schools in Urmston, Trafford, as the children of a divorced mother who worked as a legal secretary; **Neil Kinnock** (born 1942) was by 1965, after a working-class childhood in Tredegar and then becoming in 1961 the first Kinnock to go to university, now president of the students' union at Cardiff University, having won his election on the irresistible slogan 'Kinnock for Efficiency, Initiative, Approachability, Experience'; the future Labour leader had passed his 11-plus, but not so the young **W. R. McCrindle**, future chairman of McCrindle Group Ltd, who had narrowly failed before he then, after studying at night school for his engineering qualifications, came third in a class of eighty-eight boys, many of whom had passed the 11-plus, and 'in a blinding flash realised I was not stupid', giving him the confidence to start his engineering company with £10 capital in April 1966; born in 1945 in a mining village near Bridgend in South Wales, son of a merchant seaman, speaking only Welsh for the first five years of his life, **Howard Marks** became in 1964 the first boy from Gawr Grammar School to win a place at Oxford University, where he read physics at Balliol College – ideal preparation for a career of drug smuggling fuelled by charm and social connection; four years younger, **Marjorie (Mo) Mowlam** had an intelligent but alcoholic father who became Coventry's increasingly unreliable assistant postmaster, a shrewd and determined mother who worked as a telephonist to maintain the family income, and was the only one among her siblings to pass the 11-plus and go to grammar school, where (detailed her future biographer) 'she trailed glory as a member of the county hockey team, a school athlete, a member of the debating team, the lead in the school play and, eventually, head girl'; the future historian **Roy Porter**, born 1946 and of the same stellar quality as Judt, was a jeweller's son who grew up in New Cross Gate ('a stable if shabby working-class community completely undiscovered by sociologists') before passing the 11-plus and treading the route from local grammar school to Cambridge via an inspirational English teacher; **Heather Rabbats**, born 1955 and future barrister, local authority chief and football bigwig, spent her 1960s first being bullied at primary school for being mixed-race, then failing her 11-plus and ('pretty much cast into the darkness') O levels; the future poet and critic **Craig Raine** (born 1944) was the son of a pub landlord, grew up in a prefab in Shildon, near Bishop Auckland, won a scholarship to the private Barnard Castle School, managed to expunge his broad Durham accent, and got to Oxford in 1963 ('I had to change my voice again because all my girlfriends laughed at what *I* had thought was an Oxford accent'); a future professor of Hispanic languages, **Malcolm Read** (born 1946), was a Derby boy who failed his 11-plus and ended up with little in the way of formal education ('at every step of the way to higher education, I was made to feel cheap and common, denigrated for my squat working-class body, my accent, spelling, table manners, in short, for my whole culture') before finally making it in 1964 to the alienating atmosphere of Bristol University ('most of the students moved through the world as if they owned it, which, to all intents and purposes, some of them, or at least their fathers, did . . . the university was an extension of their social round, with all the privileges that this entailed'); a few years later, the privately educated, son-of-a-bishop, exams-flunking **Jon Snow**, born 1947, acquired his university place rather differently ('my father was in his dog collar on a train, sitting next to a man who was a professor of law at Liverpool University – by the time the train pulled into Lime Street, he'd persuaded him to take me'); and for **Polly Toynbee**, born 1946 into the privilege of enlightened protest, a place in 1966 – after taking herself out of her detested private boarding school (Badminton) and doing her A levels at Holland Park Comprehensive under the mentorship of a wise teacher – at the worldlier of the two elite universities. 'The truth is, the Oxford scholarship exam of those days was designed to reward people of exactly my background and journalistic state of mind,' she reflected in 2023. 'It gave an underserved chance to shine to someone who had regularly done badly in exams through idle failure to learn theorems or foreign grammar by heart, ignoring what I found boring, studying only what I enjoyed. This heavily class-biased exam would disadvantage very clever applicants who had worked exceedingly hard at every subject at school but lacked the family or an Alan Bennett *History Boys* teacher or my Mr Stedman Jones to open their wings at this early stage in their life.'[15]

Failure – not least failure compared to a sibling – could cut deep indeed. 'In the early 1960s in Eastbourne I failed my 11-plus and went to a secondary modern school,' Gyr King wrote in 2023 to the *New European*:

> Despite their best efforts, the teachers could barely mask their acceptance of having to deal with 'failures', and of course as pupils we were acutely aware that we were very much second-class pupils. We were branded it on the badges on our school blazers and caps for all to see.
>
> At home I particularly felt I had let my (middle-class) parents down because my elder brother had passed his 11-plus and was able to actively participate in the school orchestra, classical plays, Latin classes, school trips and rugby. With the teachers wearing gowns, the place was really modelled on a minor public school.
>
> Despite passing my O-levels and going on to university via A-levels from a local technical college, the path towards achievement was much more difficult and the feeling of failure never really leaves you throughout your life.

'Now, a lifetime lived, having started and run a successful business employing more than 100 staff for many years,' ended King, 'I find it ironic that the opposite attitude engendered by passing the 11-plus – one of entitled success – so infected my brother, it seems, it has led to a point where in his 70s I bale him out from his impoverished state.'

Fortunately, we can be a bit more systematic about all this, on the basis of three evocative as well as informative studies. Mary Ingham's *Now We Are Thirty* is about herself and her peers who, having passed the 11-plus, started in September 1958 at the Girls' High School in 'a middle-sized midland town', leaving school in either 1963 or 1965; Roy Greenslade's *Goodbye to the Working Class* is also about the 11-plus successes of 1958, in his case focusing on what became of his fellow pupils who had gone that year to Dagenham County High School; and Peter Willmott's *Adolescent Boys of East London* is based on interviews in 1964 with almost 250 adolescent boys living in Bethnal Green, only about one in seven of whom were present or former pupils of grammar schools.

'The High School's reputation ironed on the moment you donned that distinctive dark uniform which made you the butt of taunts from former friends who'd been banished to the secondary modern,' recalls Ingham with only semi-affection. 'We were here because we were clever. But we were never allowed to lean back on our laurels. They constantly spurred us on to do better, dug out any pockets of complacency with their pickaxe criticisms.' Who were 'they'? 'The charioteers in this grim race', she goes on, 'were the clique of single women teachers, long hair firmly controlled under a hairnet and twisted into plaits or a bun, long box-pleated tweedy skirts and sturdy lace-up shoes. These were the women whose own education had been hardwon, in the teeth of opposition.' Accordingly, 'no wonder they were obsessed with qualifying and matriculating examinations'. Yet ultimately, the education provided at Ingham's grammar school seems to have had the effect of narrowing as much as broadening the horizons of its pupils. 'When we were little, however much time we spent tucking dolls up in bed, playing mothers and fathers, quite a few of us knew exactly what we wanted to be when we grew up, and the answer was never a housewife and a mother', with alternative ambitions including opera singer, doctor, explorer, pilot, astronomer and actress; some ambitions started palpably to wither by the third year, as streaming within the school took effect; career guidance, whether from parents or the school itself, was fairly nugatory; and although the sixth form was expanding, a significant proportion of girls still chose to leave after taking their O levels – mainly going into routine office work, and with an underlying assumption of marriage and motherhood sooner rather than later. What about those who stayed on? The picture Ingham draws is broadly one of her and her peers, admittedly with some exceptions, finding it difficult – whether still at school ('content to carry on in a dream state of indecision about our futures') or even, for those who got there, at university – to think realistically about life's larger possibilities. In the end, it is a portrait of a culturally determined, as opposed to self-determining, generation. 'Oh God, why am I not married and happy with two kids? Why am I aimlessly wasting away?' Ingham herself wrote in her diary in 1968, her final year at Liverpool University reading Social Science. Or again, this time (also in 1968) in a diary confession to her boyfriend: 'I see life stretching before me – endless hurdles too high for me to jump. Unless you could be there, lifting me over ...' Thirteen years later, writing her book, Ingham was almost devastatingly honest: 'Buried deep in my psyche was the hatchet of all those expectations, assumptions, rationalizations that had accompanied the privilege of my education. You got to the end of the conveyer belt and the man and the family were waiting. They knew the way.'

So, too, at Greenslade's Dagenham grammar, overwhelmingly working class in its intake and academically uninspiring. There, as soon as O levels were over, most of the early leavers were girls, even though their exam performance had been superior to that of the boys. 'Girls in working-class families were not encouraged to seek education beyond sixteen,' he reflected in his 1976 book, based like Ingham's on an impressively large range of interviews. 'Some went off to college to take one-year commercial courses; others took the best job their GCEs could win them. One or two said they seriously considered staying on but could not face the discipline when so many other girls of their age were enjoying independence, the independence that allowed them to put on make-up every morning, to dress in the latest fashion, to carry handbags in place of satchels.' In fact, out of Greenslade's overall sample of ninety-six who sat O levels, only twenty-two stayed on, of whom a mere seven were girls. As for the motivation of those twenty-two staying on, Greenslade reckons that 'nearly all had parents who were ambitious for their child's advancement, or who gave them complete freedom of choice'. His most striking finding is that for the boys especially – almost irrespective of what stream they had been in or whether they had stayed on – the simple fact of going to the locally prestigious and unwaveringly strict Dagenham County High School, as opposed to one of the area's secondary moderns ('infamous as training centres for hooliganism and anarchy'), almost always resulted in an adult journey away from that person's roots. 'In the case of most people,' he wrote after his 1973–4 interviews with his peers in their mid-twenties, 'this is a story of flight from their class and from their past.' And, helpfully, he gave a comprehensive list comparing son's job with father's job – for example, public health inspector (postman), Ford cost analyst (painter), shop manager (security guard), insurance broker (assembly liner), stockbroker's assistant (crane driver) and shipping broker (carpenter). 'Upward mobility of sorts has carried the working class away from their childhood status,' concluded Greenslade about the sociological lessons of his survey. 'They have said goodbye to the working class. Their values have altered and they are inclined to be embarrassed by the continuing link through their parents. However, they have not joined the varied middle classes. My contemporaries do not call themselves middle-class. They are wedged into the structure so that they form part of a new class . . .'

What about the products of the secondary modern? They were largely the subject of Willmott's Bethnal Green investigation, with most of his working-class interviewees having left school within the last few years; and they spoke with feeling:

> Most boys at my school, their attitude was this isn't going to help me when I leave school so I won't bother. The school didn't give you enough scope on trades – it was nothing to do with your job later on. Maths, history – all that crap: anyway half the time I didn't know what they were talking about, to tell you the truth.
>
> My favourite subject was arithmetic, which is fucking useless to me now.
>
> Fucking Napoleon and all that crap. You couldn't make a noise and then he'd start talking and then he'd be writing and he'd be nagging away about it and you'd have to write it all down. And it's very hard in a subject like that, because you know nothing of what people say and quotations and all that sort of junk. And we didn't know nothing about it – fucking Napoleon and some battle. We'd say, 'We ain't got no interest in this,' and he'd say, 'Then you've got to find interest; it may come in useful to you.' So I said, 'I ain't leaving the country,' and he said, 'Don't you ever read the papers? Perhaps it will help you to read what's in there.' Yes, he said all that junk would help you read the papers.
>
> I wish I'd got somewhere while I was at school. I can see my mistake now, but I didn't know what school meant at the time. I didn't realize about G.C.E.s and all that – I can see now that you're much better off if you can stay at school a bit longer and get G.C.E.s. But at my school there was only about one person in fifty who did G.C.E.
>
> They didn't tell us anything at school about G.C.E. being a big help in getting a job. Nobody bothered to explain about it. It's no

> use crying over spilt milk, but I wish now that I had had a better education – I realise now that I would have liked to have gone to a grammar school if I could.

An unskilled, or at best semi-skilled, future almost certainly lay ahead for the great majority of Willmott's interviewees. How much did they mind? Was there a nagging sense of life chances very unlikely to go beyond the strictly limited? Inevitably, the only quantitative assessment we have comes from Willmott himself, noting that 'in talking about the future – we asked them about the prospects ten years ahead – half said not only that they expected to be doing the same kind of work but also that they would "choose" to'. And he quoted a perhaps representative – or at least adequately representative – twenty-year-old: 'I'm a fish porter and that's what I expect to go on being. It's not really a promotion job at all. I suppose I could go on to be a salesman, but I'd rather have no worries. As it is, when I get home from work I'm finished. I prefer it like that.'

Approaching the last third of the twentieth century, not everyone was so relaxed about the state of play in opportunity (or otherwise) Britain. 'What do you think would most help your son in his career? Brains, hard work, or the right school tie?' Those were the questions posed on *Woman's Hour* in February 1964 by Marjorie Anderson to Mrs Hilary Haywood (living in London, two grown-up children) and Mrs Joyce Wood (also living in London, young family of four). Both plumped for hard work, though with Mrs Wood adding, 'you do find that the old school tie does help a lot, because it's inclined to break down the initial barrier'. Yet was it possible, wondered Anderson, that 'the new school tie, sort of red-brick versus Oxbridge, could be the bond?' 'I like to hope so,' responded Wood, 'but to be quite honest, I don't think so':

> I think old school tie will always be the same thing. Oxford and Cambridge, Eton and Harrow. Everyone hopes so, that it will – that the Universities will come into their own. They might turn out excellent students and hard-working people, because they're the people who've gone there to work, and not for the fun and games. But I have a sneaking feeling that they never quite hold the same position.

'What about you, Mrs Haywood?' asked Anderson. 'No,' she answered, 'I feel there's a chance that it might indeed, but I don't think perhaps in Mrs Wood's and my lifetime . . . our sons' lifetimes maybe.'[16]

In the end, and seemingly inescapably, so much came down to deeply entrenched assumptions, whether conscious or unconscious. Take this cumulative evidence – ultimately depressing – from a final trio.

'As a recipient of secondary modern education,' John Bird (born 1946, future founder of the *Big Issue*, ennobled 2015) recalled in 2025, 'I was among the ones that failed':

> The supposed clever workers were separated off to become the managing class through a grammar school education. For the rest of us, the problem was not so much the curriculum, but more the fact that none of us understood the significance of this learning and the potential that flowed from it. My class was largely semi-literate; after school leaving at 15 they went into labouring jobs that led nowhere in later life. I was fortunate, as I often say, to always be in trouble with the police, and in being locked up I was always taught new things, finally finishing off my reading education in a boys' prison aged 16. But the vast majority of people in the British working classes were not given the advantages of education in a young offenders institution; my five brothers were left behind to remain manual labourers.

'What the welfare state did not break', argues Bird, 'was the horrendous evils of the British class system': 'The middle and upper class, even in their fine thoughtfulness and kindness, saw us as a different species. And they catered for our low education and low social status, never taking a lead in breaking the powerlessness that undereducation condemns you to: to an unskilled and unfulfilled life.'

Almost nine years younger, Hanif Kureishi's account of going at secondary stage in 1966 to a technical school (in Bromley) comes without any explicit broader message, but in its way is just as dispiriting, just as revealing. After noting how the school 'put the emphasis on practical subjects such as woodwork, metalwork and technical drawing,' he goes on:

> Our class and position in society was made pretty clear from the first day. When not doing 'practical' learning, we were either copying from the blackboard or attempting to follow 'dictation'. We were not even oppressed by the imposition of moral or religious axioms, or even ideas of 'good' behaviour. We were aware that we were existing in a very banal dictatorship; this, in its way, might be described as educational. Otherwise, we were only filling paper, and filling time. There was nothing to be done with the information we received; it was inert, dead. How could it become part of a living system? Nobody knew, including the teachers, how to ask why we were there or what we should be doing.

'There were strange, sadistic and almost ritualistically weird beatings,' he adds about another aspect of the conditioning, 'where three or four boys would be bent forward at the front of the class while the maths teacher would stand over them, stick raised, asking the rest of us which bottom should be beaten. The teacher had two "beaters," of different lengths and thicknesses, called "big Willy" and "little Willy".'

The testimony of Laurence Marks (born 1948, attending a comprehensive in north London) comes from his teenage diary. 'This morning, we are told about our mock O level results and I am pleased to be able to take home the news that I passed all eight exams I sat for and so will be taking eight O levels in the summer,' he recorded in May 1965:

> When I do get home and tell my mum, she doesn't believe me. She shows no happiness with my achievement, not a sausage. Not even a pat on the back and a 'well done, son' as I was expecting. In fact, when I go off to my bedroom, I think that my success has upset her, and I don't know why. When dad gets home from work, I ask him what he thinks, and he doesn't know what I am talking about. My mum hasn't bothered to tell him I'm going to take eight O levels in the summer. He seems slightly more pleased than my mum. Nobody even asks me what subjects I passed, it's as if none of them care. Well, if they don't care, why should I?

Then a few weeks later, before the actual exams, came a 'careers' interview with the Latin teacher:

> I am sent to Mr Clarke's study, high up in the Old Building, and I sit outside waiting to be called. I see other boys I know coming out with bundles of pamphlets and when I hear Mr Clarke's distinctive voice shout for me, I get up and go in. Mr Clarke, a teacher that was also a pupil at Holloway County School, which means he has been here for most of his life, calls me to his desk then asks me to sit down. He looks at me and says,
>
> 'Assuming you get six O levels this summer, Marks, what do you then intend to do with them?'
>
> 'I haven't really thought about it, sir'.
>
> 'Well, when you step into the big old world outside, what job would you like to do?'
>
> I give it some thought and then say 'I think I would like to be a writer, sir.'
>
> 'You want to be an underwriter,' says Mr Clarke.
>
> 'I don't know what that is, sir. An underwriter. No, sir, I was thinking more of books or writing for a newspaper. I like reading newspapers. Could I do that, sir?'
>
> Mr Clarke gives me a strange look, not angry, more confused. He then says, 'Marks, writers are born, not made, now go away and think about something more sensible. Have you ever thought about shipping or insurance?'
>
> 'No, sir', I tell him.
>
> 'Well think about it and not this insane idea of being a writer, or journalist or anything like that.'
>
> This then is my careers talk. I don't leave Mr Clarke's room with an armful of pamphlets, all I leave his study with is a vague idea that he has crushed.

A cruel sequence followed in August:

> We sit down for supper and my mum tells me that she has written to my school's headmaster telling him that she is pulling me out of school. I am so surprised that I say nothing. It just doesn't sink in.

I leave my supper and hurry to my room. She doesn't give me any explanation. *(2 August)*

I haven't eaten properly since Monday [the 2nd], well not at home. I have just kept myself in my bedroom and wondered why my mum has pulled me out of school. What am I supposed to do when we have to go back in September? I have eaten at work [a holiday job he had managed to get in the *Private Eye* office]. Sandwiches and a cup of tea, but that's all. When I get home, I don't even talk to my mum. I know this is what she did to my brother and sister, particularly Shirley. She got into the best girls' school in north London: Camden School for Girls, and apparently my mum had to sign a form saying that Shirley would stay on until after her A levels. But Shirley was pulled out of school by my mum, and made to go off and work as a lift attendant at Fortnum and Mason, the posh grocery shop.

Malcolm was pulled out of Highbury County School at about 14 too. Whether he wanted to stay on, he has never told me, but I *do* want to stay on. I might have lots of O levels to my name soon and for what? Nothing. My mum keeps telling me I've got to eat something, but I just don't want to sit down at the kitchen table with her. She has destroyed my dreams. *(4 August)*

Tonight I really don't want to sit down at the table with my mum, what she has done is just unforgiveable. Without even asking me, she has told the school I am not coming back ever again.

So when she asks me, 'What is the matter with you?' I tell her what is the matter with me. She knew I wanted to stay on at school and see how far I could get. That is not what she wants. What she wants is another pay packet coming in. 'It is time you paid your way,' she tells me. 'Why?' My dad, who just wants a peaceful life when my mum is in full flow, says, 'You can't expect to live here forever for nothing.' 'Why?' I ask. 'You have stopped my education, and you didn't even ask me.' *(6 August)*

I just want to get out of the flat. I am starting to feel like I don't belong here anymore. And I'm only 16. I shall never forgive my mum for what she has done. There isn't even any football to go to. *(7 August)*

It's as we sit down in our lounge for Friday night supper, candles and all, no prayers though, we haven't done that in ages, and with

> me still not talking properly to my mum, she says 'We have got to talk about what we are going to do about you.' I don't understand what she's talking about. She tells me that I am going to have to get a proper job if I am not going to go back to school. 'But I want to go back to school,' I plead . . . Supper is had in near silence. The television is on and my dad is half-watching The Valiant Years, based on Winston Churchill's memoirs . . . My dad hasn't said anything at all about me finding a job and I wonder how he feels about me being pulled out of school just so I can give my mum thirty bob a week for my keep? He never says anything. He just sits and does his crossword. *(27 August, after getting his eight O levels)*

Marks asked *Private Eye* if he could stay on, to be told there was no permanent vacancy. No return to school either, so instead the resentful hunt for a job, until at last in early October:

> I have written so many job application letters that surely one of them will receive a reply. And it does. It arrives in the post this morning. The Chappell job [at the music publisher Chappell's] that I went for an interview for, want to see me again next Tuesday and they also make me the offer of the lowly job in their photocopying and photographic room. I showed the letter to my mum, and she is more pleased than I am. I should be back at school, preparing for my A levels in two years' time, but instead I have had my education stolen from me by my mum for no good reason. *(7 October)*

The sequence ends in early December, on Marks's seventeenth birthday, as he treats himself to a new book (Saul Bellow's *Herzog*) and starts reading it during his lunch break. 'It has got to be more interesting than this job my mum forced me into. And now she gets her thirty bob every Friday she doesn't even enquire about my job, what I do, whether I enjoy it. Well, it is boring and I don't enjoy it . . .' In the event, it all turned out fine, as through a mixture of talent and good fortune he became first a *Sunday Times* journalist and then one of the leading screenwriters of his generation. Yet, of course, for every eloquent and glorious Milton, there remained – in a host of different fields – many, many mute and inglorious ones, whose names we will never know.[17]

4
Broadstairs Boy Makes Good

'Temple Meads goods staff went on strike and there are 256 bales Danish Bacon of ours up there which no one will collect for us,' lamented the Bristol diarist Frederick Ward (a manager for the Co-operative Wholesale Society) on Wednesday, 14 July 1965. 'This has caused me a hectic day of worry and telephoning – thank heavens we are not in the middle of a heat wave,' he went on. 'What is so annoying is that every other bacon firm in Bristol can persuade their staff to co-operate in collecting its. Our perishers must support their trade union colleagues, but not their own firm which stands to lose thousands of pounds. It always seems to be bacon which gives me the biggest headaches.' Next day – as, despite continuing pressure on sterling, Callaghan promised in the Commons that he was 'resisting the temptation' to take any 'further measures which would have the effect of restricting the economy even more'; as Marigold Johnson in the *TLS* gave only qualified praise to Anne Tyler's first novel (*If Morning Ever Comes*), but anticipated that in time she would 'outgrow her hesitant efforts to produce big answers to emotional muddles'; as an article in the *Daily Telegraph* on children and TV ('the fact that they are being exposed to a dangerous and insidious influence is not immediately apparent') made a considerable impact on Mary Whitehouse; and as the Postmaster General went up the just-about-completed Post Office Tower, recording that 'the view is superb, but the organisation of the staircases and lifts is appalling' – Ward found 'some hope' that 'our bacon will be saved': 'It is being gradually taken into Cold Store. Thank goodness again for a N.E. wind that even at mid-day kept things very cool.'

Friday, too – while the press reported on a new study showing that issues of colour and immigration had become major matters of concern in at least two dozen parliamentary seats, especially in the Midlands, and while folk music purists gathered for a festival at Keele University ('we keep away from commercial songs . . . Bob Dylan will never be remembered for his protest songs 40 years from now') – was a day of some further relief for Ward ('I am assured that all the bacon is now moved from Temple Meads and we can only wait and see what condition it is in when we begin to draw it from Cold Store'), before a mercifully bacon-free weekend. By contrast, the economic adviser Alec Cairncross described Lord Cromer, governor of the Bank of England, as 'increasingly upset (almost hysterical)' in his opposition to Callaghan's apparent reluctance to go further down the deflationary road; Pat Scott in Barking had a Saturday of doing odd jobs about the house with her husband Ted ('we had an almighty row about him throwing the children's books etc away but it all blew over'); the teenage Roger Darlington in Manchester taped from ITV's *Lucky Stars* the soon-to-be-released new Beatles single ('It was called "Help!", dead different and absolutely great! Played it about a dozen times. If it reaches No. 1, I win 5/- off Dad – and it's certain to . . .'); and William Rees-Mogg in the *Sunday Times* laid into the increasingly beleaguered Leader of the Opposition, Sir Alec Douglas-Home, arguing that the opinion polling evidence was incontrovertible that the public 'look on Mr Wilson as a professional in the good sense and on Sir Alec as an amateur in the bad sense'.[1]

On Monday, the end of the bacon saga ('the first delivery of the bacon was made today and it is a relief to hear the condition is reasonable'), last-ever day at school for Worthing diarist Diana Griffith ('Read books in nearly all lessons! Saw a film – good. Tennis OK. Said "goodbyes" etc – lots of handshaking!!'), and the government announcing its broad approval of Sir Leslie Martin's Whitehall redevelopment plan, involving the demolition of the magnificent Foreign Office. On Tuesday, Owen Maclaren applying for a UK patent on his newly invented buggy (future nemesis of the Silver Cross pram), the writer B. S. Johnson not allowed to attend the birth of his son at Bart's, and Tony Benn's encounter with Robert Maxwell prompting an essentially unbitchy diarist to describe 'really rather a thrusting man who regards the House of Commons as a place where he can push himself'; and on

Wednesday the 21st, Benn again, this time explaining in detail to the Commons his intended introduction of a postal Giro service enabling free banking and transfer services ('rather sprang the word "Giro" on us,' complained *Punch*), while that evening, about the time that *The Likely Lads* ended its second season on BBC2 with a highest-yet RI score of 82, the diarist Anthony Heap was recording that the recently established GLC (Greater London Council) had decided to take no further action in relation to the move to ban smoking in cinemas that its predecessor body, the LCC (London County Council), had initiated but not implemented the previous year.

Next day, ahead of the start of the England v South Africa Test at Lord's, banners outside the ground proclaimed 'It's not cricket!' and 'Going to see the South African "whites only" cricket team?', as members of the anti-apartheid movement picketed the main gate and handed in a protest petition to Billy Griffiths, secretary of MCC – with one observer noting that 'though supervised by two amiable police sergeants, it was a very peaceful picket'. Later this Thursday, there were ten times more police in evidence at West Ham magistrates court, along with some 200 teenagers inside and outside, as three of the Stones – Mick, Brian and Bill – were fined £5 each for their late-night 'breach of the peace' pee back in March. In the City, sterling continued to take a hammering, involving losses of some £48 million. And at Westminster in the early evening, Douglas-Home told the 1922 Committee of backbenchers that he was stepping down as Tory leader. 'The rotters' eleven has won,' one palpably shocked 'Knight of the Shires' MP told a waiting journalist immediately afterwards, while the Keighley diarist Kenneth Preston commented that Sir Alec was 'probably too much of a gentleman for the dirty game of politics'. Another diarist, the clergyman James Allen near Colchester, took a different view. 'I think it is time that leaders with an aristocratic and "grouse moor" mentality should go in this our day and age,' he reflected after hearing the news on the radio. 'Politics is much too serious a business for the enthusiastic amateur.' Who, then, should step up? 'The names suggested for the leadership are those of Edward Heath and Reginald Maudling,' he continued. 'My own choice would be Heath as being a more honest and open type. Maudling seems to be too smooth a character – a typical politician.' This time round, two years on from the much-criticised secretive process from on high that had led to Douglas-Home's anointing, the result would be determined by secret ballot of Conservative MPs. Not everyone in the party was thrilled. 'Democracy doesn't suit the Conservatives,' John Profumo had recently informed the young historian Sheila Rowbotham, apparently with a twinkle in his eye. 'They prefer that all the old animals in the herd get together and make a decision.'[2]

Douglas-Home's announcement was still being digested when at 8.50, after the Thursday staples of *Top of the Pops* and *The Man from U.N.C.L.E.*, BBC1 showed the eighth in its summer series of *Comedy Playhouse*, essentially one-off pilots to test audience reaction. The previous seven had averaged a respectable but unremarkable RI of 54, but this one – *Till Death Us Do Part* – secured a promising 67, as viewers largely enjoyed Johnny Speight's depiction of a working-class family in London's docklands, with Warren Mitchell playing the opinionated-cum-bigoted middle-aged father, Una Stubbs his daughter, Anthony Booth his 'Scouse git' of a son-in-law, and Gretchen Franklin his long-suffering wife. 'Oh, how delightfully vulgar,' commented an electrical engineer. 'I laughed and laughed, yet in many ways it was all quite true to life.' Another viewer warmly commended Dad as a 'real character'. Even so, 'there were some who considered the show distasteful – the setting was hardly edifying, they remarked, the language was unnecessarily coarse at times and they rarely, in any case, found these working-class "slanging matches" particularly funny'. Still, no complaints on that front from one young viewer. 'It shows the working classes, just like we are in our council flats,' reflected an appreciative Laurence Marks. 'Most comedies are about people who we never meet here on our council estate. They all live in big houses, well furnished, they're well dressed and talk all posh. No one seems to worry about money. You can tell that Alf Ramsey [the name at this stage for the Warren Mitchell character] and his family count every penny and I like that.'

Next day, amid the torrent of print about the forthcoming Tory leadership election (first round due on Tuesday the 27th), the *Telegraph* reported from the lobbies the previous night 'a strong ground swell' for Enoch Powell, with MPs arguing that 'no-one in sight is better equipped to imbue the country with faith in sound Conservative principles, which might have more relevance than "personality" when the [general] election comes'; the *Mirror*'s powerful proprietor, Cecil King, received an entirely improper phone call from Cromer at the Bank of England, warning him that (in King's words) 'the foreign bankers regard Maudling as the architect of our present financial misfortunes and that, therefore, if he is chosen as leader the effect on the pound will be bad'; outside Lord's, very few paid heed to the demonstrators' increasingly forlorn demand that would-be spectators boycott the match; Crossman had a mixed sort of day visiting Wolverhampton, taking pleasure in the new housing estates ('not brilliant architecture but decently done and constantly improving, and inspired by a real socialist sense of municipal enterprise'), but far less so in the elderly Labour local eminences ('the whole atmosphere of the council is one of socialist decrepitude . . . they all feel on the down-grade'); and the *Evening Standard* sounded out popular opinion on the looming contest, with at this stage only Heath and Maudling officially standing, and the latter generally viewed as the favourite:

> Mr Powell is obviously a brilliant man, and the only one among the Tory candidates that offers the nation an alternative to Socialism. *(Raymond Harris, thirty-five, Canonbury, accountant)*
>
> Mr Heath looks a completely honest and dedicated man. *(Myfanwy Roach, Camden, Harris's secretary)*
>
> Mr Heath is shrewd and dedicated, and being a bachelor will enable him to give the absolutely undivided attention it needs to run the Party. *(Sheila Austin, twenty, Harold Park, secretary)*
>
> Mr Maudling has a sounder economic knowledge, and a better image I think than Mr Heath. *(Leslie Newton, forty-five, Reading, insurance official)*
>
> Maudling has got a good image, and although he seems a sociable chap I don't think he will be pushed around. *(Donald Pope, forty-one, Highams Park, bus inspector)*

'It's the image', added Pope, 'that counts nowadays.'[3]

The Scotts spent their weekend on Canvey Island, where they now had a holiday caravan. 'It was Carnival day & we saw procession,' noted Pat. 'Barking Carnival Queen was there & they all came to Club in the evening.' Generally, indeed, she was travelling more or less hopefully with their Canvey venture. 'A new cafe has opened at Lakeside. About time. It's clean & cheap & let's hope it stays open.' Also this weekend, the Campaign Against Racial Discrimination (CARD) held in London's Conway Hall its founding convention, which heard evidence from a committee of inquiry about how, the previous month, a Plaistow shopkeeper, Faizal Dad, had had his premises attacked three times in barely a week, as well as 'Wogs' being scrawled twice on the walls of his home. Passing by an overwhelming majority a resolution condemning the deterioration of the racial situation in Britain, the convention (chaired by David Pitt) also condemned a recent Department of Education circular on immigrant children for differentiating between white and coloured children, highlighted the increase of 'incidents involving harassment of coloured citizens by individual policemen', deplored the government's impending race relations legislation as not only ineffectual but too narrow in scope, and called overall for a campaign to stamp out the 'growing cancer' of racialism in British life. Matters of race played no part this weekend in Tory leadership manoeuvres, where the main development was recorded by the west London diarist Keith McBride. 'According to the news now in,' he wrote on Sunday evening, 'Powell has thrown his hat in the ring for the Tory leadership: he is a desperate private-enterprise man, but I don't think he has much following.' Philip Larkin was also keeping his eye on the political state of play. 'I'd vote for Oswald Mosley, or anyone who would stabilise prices & wages, keep out immigrants, bring back the birch, & abolish family allowances,' he told Monica Jones, probably after the news about Powell. 'But who will?' he asked. 'Not any of these lads.'

On Monday morning the press, including, of course, the *Mirror*, largely came out for Heath, typified by the *Mail* hailing him as 'a leader who is a man of action'. Benn's afternoon press conference on all-figure dialling – 'I tried to take the offensive and to explain that this was inevitable, that it would bring advantages in terms of increased capacity, technical improvements by sectorisation, and open the way for direct international subscriber dialling' – provided a flicker of interest, given the distinct public attachment to area-identifying letter codes, but for the most part it was a day of waiting. 'I have put a hundred guineas to win at evens, very good odds, I consider, a hundred guineas to win on Mr Edward Heath,' the Tory right-winger Sir Gerald Nabarro, temporarily out of the Commons because of illness, informed *Panorama*'s Robin Day, while declining to say whom he wanted to win. No such reserve from one veteran, *Express*-reading diarist. 'I looked at Enoch Powell's photo today, & wished he could have been the choice for P.M.,' rather wistfully recorded Barrow's Nella Last, well aware he was the rank outsider. 'Something about Churchill's resolution in his square jaw. I often think things must be worse than we know – & still wage demands are made for the same work done & prices of materials go up . . . We certainly need a "man" now as much as when Churchill took over [i.e. in 1940]. Someone ruthless & a real hell for leather leader.'[4]

Tuesday the 27th, last day of the South Africa Test (drawn), proved twice over a day of decision. On the economic front, the Cabinet met in the morning to discuss – nominally at least – the measures proposed by the near-omnipotent triumvirate of Wilson, Brown and Callaghan. 'What happened was as near to central dictatorship as one is likely to get in a British Cabinet,' complained Crossman. 'We were not given the time either to discuss the underlying strategy or even to consider the document as a whole. We were told to "take it or leave it as it stands". The chancellor revealed that there had been a run on sterling in the previous week and that a huge part of our reserves had disappeared. Unless a Statement was made that afternoon devaluation would be upon us.' The 'it' that the Cabinet had to take or leave essentially comprised a package of deflationary measures which included significant cuts in government spending (not least, in Crossman's words, 'abandoning the incomes guarantee for the lower paid'), as well as making mortgages more difficult to obtain and restricting hire purchase. Barbara Castle recorded a significant but far from overwhelming degree of opposition – Frank Cousins 'bitterly critical'; Crosland not only insisting that the package was heading the government 'straight into stagnation and Tory policies', but sceptical anyway whether 'these steps would do the trick'; Crossman saying that 'the constant nibbling at the problem was all wrong'; no one quite daring to come out explicitly in favour of devaluation – and attention turned eventually to the question of whether Wilson himself should make the Commons statement later in the day, resulting in, as Crossman noted with some pleasure, 'a two to one majority for making Callaghan do it'. This he duly did. 'The place was packed and Labour Members heard the news with dismay,' noted Benn. 'But Jim did as well as he could.' Dismay indeed, and later in the week many Labour backbenchers would probably agree with the *New Statesman*'s assertion (in an editorial headed 'A Black Week for Labour') that the nub of the dismal episode was having a prime minister who 'appears to see no alternative to submitting to the prejudices of the international financial community'. As for the future, the critical question, declared the *Statesman*, was whether the government had 'the moral resilience to re-think its economic strategy and so regain the offensive'. Much, it hardly needed to add, would depend upon Brown's National Plan, now expected for September.

The hours between the Cabinet meeting and the formal statement saw the Tory leadership contest being resolved. That morning the national press had anticipated a tight finish between Heath and Maudling, though with the *Telegraph* ('Slight Maudling Lead Likely'), the *Guardian* ('Mr Maudling's Prospects Grow Brighter') and the *Sun* ('The Tide Runs for Maudling') all identifying the latter as the likelier to come out on top in the first ballot. Moreover, according to National Opinion Poll (NOP) figures prominently quoted by the *Mail*, the sobering fact for Heath's closest supporters – who had by general consent run a far more energetic and better-organised leadership campaign than Maudling's – was not only that 48 per cent of Conservative voters backed Maudling compared to 31 per cent wanting Heath, but that among voters as a whole the margin was almost equally great in favour of Maudling, by 44 per cent to 28 per cent. Still, it was Conservative MPs, no one else, who had the say that mattered; and when the result was announced soon after lunch, Heath was ahead with 150 votes, Maudling behind with 133 votes, and Powell tailed off with just 15. It would have been within the rules for Maudling to have fought on, but sensibly enough he almost instantly conceded. For a man who had enjoyed a seemingly near-effortless rise to almost the very top, it was the bitterest of pills, completely unexpected to him and largely ruining the rest of his life. 'He sat morosely, alone in the Smoking Room' is how his biographer, Lewis Baston, memorably describes the later stages of that long Tuesday afternoon. 'His paralysed misery left a vivid, lifelong impression on several MPs, such as Edward Boyle; his colleagues were shocked to see the bluff, agreeable Reggie reduced to such a state. His public emotional bleeding was surely about showing them how deeply their personal rejection had hurt him. It was, to Reggie, as if he had been jilted at the altar.'[5]

Among the non-political diarists, Anthony Heap regretted the Tory MPs' choice – 'Maudling has a more genial and likeable personality which appeals to me regardless of party allegiance' – while McBride conceded that Heath had 'lots of good ideas', but struck him as 'somehow weak'. Two Labour diarists were broadly sanguine. 'Maudling would be much more frightening from our point of view,' reckoned Benn, 'and I think we shall be able to project Heath as a ruthless, ambitious machine politician without even the aristocratic backing of Home who could always count upon the deferential vote.' And according to Crossman, 'Maudling would have been a far better, wiser political leader', whereas 'all the disadvantages of Harold Wilson seem to me to be incorporated in Heath', though admittedly 'most of the advantages as well – his drive, energy, skill in debate, his dedication to politics'. The final diarist was the aged Supermac. 'I feel sure that Ted is the best choice,' noted Harold Macmillan. 'He is a stronger character than Maudling.' 'The vote', declared the *Telegraph* next day, 'has been for toughness and pugnacity, for absolute commitment and political professionalism'; the *Financial Times* argued that the outcome 'should convince even the most sceptical that in the current Conservative Party ability counts for more than wealth or an inherited position'; and the *Guardian* offered the unanswerable headline, 'Broadstairs Boy Makes Good'.

After three successive Old Etonian leaders of his party, themselves preceded by the most famous Old Harrovian of all, why had this grammar school-educated son of a carpenter and a lady's maid prevailed? Heath had, of course, been helped by his main opponent. 'I am sorry', Charles (Lord) Hill wrote with genuine regret about Maudling the previous year, 'that I have never seen him angry, for his equanimity suggests to some that he lacks fire in his belly, leading them to wonder whether the stuff of leadership is in him' – whereas, emphasised Hill, the man from Broadstairs was 'probably the toughest politician on either side of the House'. And when, after it was all over, Maudling asked Powell, an old friend, why he had lost, Powell simply replied that the former chancellor's decision to take on various remunerative directorships, in the immediate wake of the 1964 election, had naturally led his colleagues, presumably including Powell himself, to conclude that 'you weren't really interested any longer'. The key defection from the Maudling camp, all pundits were agreed, was that of Iain Macleod, former minister, now editor of the *Spectator*, probably taking as many as forty votes with him after letting it be known that he now viewed Heath as the more dynamic alternative. Not influenced by Macleod, but also changing horses, was Margaret Thatcher, in her case persuaded by Sir Keith Joseph to plump for Heath, essentially on the grounds that he had 'a passion to get Britain right'.

Yet ultimately, it was down to a combination of spirit of the age and immediate circumstances. 'The main difference between Reggie and Ted was in temperament,' reflects Baston. 'Reggie was almost impossible to dislike, a claim nobody has ever made for Ted. But the virtue of likeability was out of fashion in 1965, when many Conservatives yearned for an abrasive, tough leader who would take the fight to Harold Wilson.' And: 'The worry about electing Reggie was that he would drift along amiably and allow Wilson to get away with too much, and that his image as a slow, comfortable sort of man would suffer by comparison with Wilson's apparent dynamism. Heath was a moderniser ...' Or put another way, it was in significant part a marriage of convenience, including with the party's natural supporters. Edward du Cann, one of Heath's main political allies (though subsequently falling out), would recall a particularly telling episode, probably not all that long after he became leader. The occasion was Heath being guest of honour at a dinner of leading industrialists and deciding to wear a white dinner jacket. 'Our host, a peer and a chairman of one of the UK's most successful companies, turned to me and asked, "Who's that bloody waiter you've brought with you?" .'[6]

What of the third man? 'Mr Powell, the Piltdown Man of the Conservative Party, did his best to inject a conflict of issues into the contest,' noted the *Guardian*'s Ian Aitken the morning after the ballot. 'He was told, in effect, to take his principles elsewhere.' Those principles had been given full expression, above all in the economic field, in *A Nation Not Afraid*, a newly published and widely noticed collection of his speeches and articles. Among the reviewers, Rees-Mogg was dissatisfied with the lack of nuance ('much too simple, insufficiently pragmatic') in what he called Powell's 'stark black-and-white apology for capitalism, an apology which is almost as absolutist as the Marxism of a good Marxist'; Macleod declared himself a 'fellow traveller', albeit 'sometimes I leave Powell's train a few stations down the line, before it reaches, and sometimes crashes into, the terminal buffers'; the *Sunday Telegraph* editor, Donald McLachlan, hailed Powell for 'trying to cure the Tories' of their 'embarrassed reluctance to use with any conviction the vocabulary and arguments of capitalism'; Rudolf Klein in *New Society*, while acknowledging that the Conservative Party now in opposition was 'listening to Enoch Powell with more attention and respect than ever before', reckoned nevertheless that ultimately 'his uncompromising style of thinking is too alien to the traditional Conservative approach to politics to make it likely that this new Book of Enoch will be considered as part of the canonical text'; and *Punch*'s editor was outright hostile about 'this brand of *laissez-faire* mysticism'. 'Classical economics is a dead language, useful only as a key for ancient history and as an intellectual discipline,' declared the usually good-humoured Bernard Hollowood. 'It has no relevance in a society that believes in man's ability to climb above the chaotic tooth-and-claw animalism of its forebears.' In short, 'the thinking of Enoch Powell is nonsense'.

Still, whatever the value judgements, 'Powellism' had indisputably arrived – and, with its strong sense of Britain's national identity, was relevant not just to economic matters. Its spiritual home, as well as Powell's specific political home as a Wolverhampton MP, was the West Midlands; and when back in March his elevation to the chair of the government's new Prices and Incomes Board had compelled Aubrey Jones to resign his Hall Green seat in Birmingham, there were many in that constituency happy to see the back of someone far more tolerant of non-white immigration than were by this time the great majority of the region's Tory MPs. 'The old liberal image has gone and I'm glad of it: what we want is a return to real Conservatism,' a city councillor and local estate agent, Edward Hanson, who had already led a narrowly failed revolt against Jones and was proud of having got 10,000 signatures to his petition to retain the death penalty, told a national journalist. 'Get out among your people; on the buses, at work, out shopping, in their homes, then go back to Westminster and tell the whole country what they're thinking' was his trenchant advice to Jones's Hall Green successor.[7] The British right and a nationalist, inward-looking, socially conservative populism: a long, long journey lay ahead, taking well over half a century before completion, but here was an early intimation.

As it happened, the specific issue of immigration – from the Commonwealth – had a touchstone moment less than a week after the Tory leadership election. Entry vouchers for the unskilled to be discontinued, stricter tests of eligibility about dependants seeking to follow an immigrant, health checks at both ends of the process, greater government powers of repatriation – these were among the new proposals for controls announced on 2 August in the White Paper on Immigration, with the aim of bringing annual numbers down to 8,500. Crossman in his diary that day readily acknowledged that the measures were 'illiberal' and 'unpleasant', as well as economically illogical 'at a time when we have an acute shortage of labour'. Even so: 'I am convinced that if we hadn't done all this we would have been faced with certain electoral defeat in the West Midlands and the South-East. Politically, fear of immigration is the most powerful undertow today.' And: 'We felt we had to out-trump the Tories by doing what they would have done and so transforming their policy into a bipartisan policy. I fear we were right; and partly I think so because I am an old-fashioned Zionist who believes that anti-Semitism and racialism are endemic, but one has to deal with them by controlling immigration when it gets beyond a certain level.' The regret, nevertheless, was palpable, with Crossman adding that 'the White Paper will probably have a deeper undermining effect on the moral strength of Harold Wilson's leadership than any other thing that we have done'.

Yet, pragmatically speaking, he did indeed call it right. At the very moment that Heath's recent arrival as leader had given the Conservatives a significant fillip – putting them, according to Gallup, some 7.5 per cent ahead of Labour – this high-profile show of Labour 'toughness' halted that revival in its tracks: almost nine in ten voters, according to opinion polling evidence, approved of the proposed new measures; when further questioned, one in two felt that Britain had been harmed by Commonwealth immigrants; and within weeks Labour had regained its comfortable lead. A last word on the White Paper goes to Keith McBride's immediate take: 'The pretence that colour has nothing to do with it is still kept up.'[8]

On Monday the 2nd itself – five days after eighteen-year-old Janet Bull (later Street-Porter) left school, walked up to Putney Bridge and threw her 'loathed Lady Margaret panama hat' in the Thames; three days after the semi-lamented final episode of *Compact* (an informal party in the penthouse to celebrate the magazine's first French edition); two days after the last cigarette ad on British TV and the start of the first Cambridge Folk Festival; one day after Kenneth Tynan had assessed *Help!*, the fab four's new film, as 'brilliant, unboring but ferociously ephemeral' – the White Paper was not the only political story, as Heath took on Wilson for the first time: in a censure debate, following the previous week's economic measures, and by general consent coming out second best. Elsewhere, on a thoroughly wet day immediately justifying the decision to move August Bank Holiday from the first to the last Monday (on an experimental basis, to try to extend the summer period and thereby boost trade), the TV critic Peter Black had lunch with a thinner-than-usual Richard Dimbleby ('I am not pompous, really I'm not, and though I may not be clever, I am not an ass'); while in Barking, Pat Scott's son Stephen 'queued all afternoon to see Beatles in Help & then was told there would be no seats till after 5 so he came home soaked to the skin'. Next day, better luck for her daughter Susan, though she still had to queue for two hours before getting in; the Cabinet met to discuss Brown's National Plan, with Crosland candidly asking (in Crossman's words) 'how we could talk about a plan based on a 4-per-cent average increase of production each year when we now knew perfectly well that for the next eighteen months at least production wasn't going to rise by anything like that – in fact when the Government was actually cutting back production by its deflationary measures'; and Crossman himself that evening took his family out to the movie of the moment, presumably with no Barking-style queuing. 'I thought it was going to be awful but it turned out the best thing I have seen since the Marx Brothers. I adored it.'[9]

Two days later, Thursday the 5th, was the last day of term, before an increasingly querulous political class at last broke up for its holidays. Inevitably some attention was focused on Lord Devlin's official report into the docks – urging 'decasualisation', accepting with reference to the Transport and General Workers' Union (T&G) that 'a trade union leader is not a policeman who can be called in by employers to enforce the law', and urging the Minister of Labour 'to impose a scheme for regular employment in the industry' – but as so often it was matters of sterling that preoccupied, after the disobliging foreign exchange markets had been unconvinced by the recent measures. 'A gloomy session at the Bank,' noted Cecil King, one of the Bank of England's non-executive directors. 'There has been a run on gold and a run on sterling, and the reserves are in sight of exhaustion . . . The Governor thinks the only card left to play is a wage and price freeze. This might impress foreign opinion; nothing else would.' Gloom, too, in the Cabinet, as discussions continued about further possible public expenditure cuts. 'I talked to Tony Crosland afterwards and we agreed that the vital thing is to make Cabinet take the risk of deserting the pound for the sake of the social services,' recorded Crossman, his feet firmly back on the ground. 'But that is a very difficult thing to do because both James Callaghan and Harold Wilson are personally committed to the defence of the pound to a quite extraordinary degree.' So indeed they were, yet as Crossman went on: 'Failing to defend the pound would not mean the end of everything; we have already paid far too high a price in the effort to bolster it up . . . Defending the pound by frantic cuts and then in the end finding one has to devalue makes no sense at all.'

Still, if that debate was finally starting to break cover, albeit not in the public prints, what lay immediately ahead was another set-piece blow-up between prime minister and governor, with Cromer calling in that evening at No. 10, explaining that the reserves had lost £146 million since Callaghan's statement on the 27th, and demanding an instant wages and prices freeze in return for an undertaking from other central banks to support sterling. To which Wilson, deliberately and probably with some pleasure raising the temperature, riposted that 'we must be allowed to play the hand our own way and to follow the normal democratic processes for securing endorsement of the government's policies', starting with an appeal to the TUC in early September for voluntary restraint. 'It should be clearly understood,' he continued in more or less a rerun of his tactics during the previous November's sterling crisis, 'that if the Government were required to abandon normal methods of consultation and to take arbitrary unilateral action of a kind which no other democratic Government had ever taken, they might be forced to consider that it would be wiser to devalue sterling, to let the rate float and to appeal to the Country'. To this Cromer replied with some dignity that 'he would deplore this alternative course of action' and that 'in particular, to let the rate float would cause the maximum dislocation of the world monetary system'. The meeting ended with a brilliant Wilsonian ploy, graciously insisting that Cromer should not cancel his planned holiday in the South of France. And for Wilson himself? As ever, and without a trace of self-consciousness, the unglamorous Scillies – where he was soon being photographed lying on the sand dunes, in his shorts, and smoking a pipe.[10]

Elsewhere, some undated August 1965 snapshots: at Butlin's in Minehead, sixteen-year-old Rick Parfitt (on the holiday camp circuit with cabaret act the Highlights) meeting guitarist Francis Rossi (also on the circuit, with his group the Spectres); at the Wardour Castle summer school in Wiltshire, a first performance of Harrison Birtwistle's *Tragoedia*, the moment his musical vision crystallised; at Great Yarmouth's Windmill Theatre, a summer season for Allan Smethurst, aka the Singing Postman; on Blackpool's North Pier, Donovan topping the bill in a series of concerts; in the Yorkshire village of Tankersley, a few miles south of Barnsley, Richard Hines, younger brother of the writer Barry, training a kestrel; in a studio somewhere in London, an unhappy Tony Hancock making a series of TV commercials ('Happiness is egg shaped') in tandem with Patricia Hayes (Mrs Cravatte), to be screened the following spring; three miles off Harwich, Radio London relentlessly plugging Jonathan King's 'Everyone's Gone to the Moon'; in Bermondsey, eight-year-old Danny Baker and his sister seeing *Help!* almost fifty times between them; in Manchester, sixteen-year-old John Cooper Clarke and his art school girlfriend living 'just this side of squalor' in a once-grand decaying Victorian villa, their rented flat 'full of heavy, dark, mismatched, horrible old granny furniture', plus a two-ring Baby Belling with a grill ('we had fish fingers a lot, alternating with Findus Crispy Pancakes and Chesswood canned mushrooms on toast'); and in Notting Hill's Tavistock Crescent, a former social worker, Rhaune Laslett, organising an outdoor party for children. 'Russell Henderson's steel pan trio, including Sterling Betancourt and Ralph Sherry, were invited to perform,' notes Black music writer and activist Kwaku BBM in his account of the origins of the Notting Hill Carnival, adding that 'in a moment of spontaneity, the Pannists led a procession around the local streets'.[11] Not quite the Carnival proper, but getting there.

Other 'Sixties' moments it is possible to date more precisely, as with a mid-August cluster spread over barely twenty-four hours.

Late on Wednesday the 18th, Barbara Pym received back from Faber the typescript of her novel *An Unsuitable Attachment*, which Cape had brusquely rejected two years earlier. This rejection was less brusque, but still – despite Philip Larkin's best efforts on her behalf – a rejection. 'Rather a relief to feel that I don't have to flog myself to finish the present one,' she reflected next day, 'since probably nothing I write could be acceptable now.' No such zeitgeist problems for twenty-year-old Jacqueline du Pré, assuring herself of immortality that Thursday as she recorded, at Kingsway Hall, the Elgar Cello Concerto with Sir John Barbirolli and the London Symphony Orchestra. Nor that evening for David Warner and Glenda Jackson, as Hamlet and Ophelia respectively in the first night of Peter Hall's instantly legendary Stratford production – legendary not because the critics loved it (one describing Warner as 'much more like a redbrick undergraduate than a wronged heir apparent', another reckoning him as 'very impressed by Mr Bob Dylan', a third that the abrasive Jackson had 'her wits so much about her that it is absurd to think that she could credibly lose them'), but because of its rapport with the predominantly youthful audience. They responded in part to Hall's disillusioned reading of the play, but above all to the 24-year-old Warner himself, embodiment of that reading. 'Young enough to play Hamlet as a real student with a long scarf round his neck, he was gangling, spotty, his traces of a Midlands accent entirely lacked Gielgud's colour and elegance,' Hall's biographer, Stephen Fay, would recall. 'He was modern and classless, like a disaffected existentialist drop-out.' Long-haired rebellion, too, from the final element in this mid-August sequence, as the Stones on Friday the 20th released '(I Can't Get No) Satisfaction'. Already acclaimed by the *Mail*'s Virginia Ironside as 'great number, sung by Jagger in a deliciously dirty voice', it was now hailed by the *NME* as 'perhaps their most compulsive disc to date'.[12]

The new football season began on the 21st, with Charlton Athletic's Keith Peacock as the first-ever substitute in the Football League, after eleven minutes at Bolton Wanderers; Larkin on Monday wrote regretfully to his publisher about their Pym decision ('in all her writing I find a continual perceptive attention to detail which is a joy, and a steady background of rueful yet courageous acceptance of things which I think more relevant to life as most of us have to live it than spies coming in from the cold'); Arnold Wesker had his first critical flop with *The Four Seasons*, its opening night at the Belgrade in Coventry dismissed by the *Guardian*'s Derek Malcolm as 'a lumbering affair'; and on Wednesday evening, while Pat Scott, on holiday in Canvey, went with her family to the social club to see the children's variety show and especially enjoyed 'a dear little girl, about 2½' singing 'Hold Your Hand Out, You Naughty Boy' ('everyone loved her'), another diarist, Frederick Ward, in Manchester on business, headed off by himself to the Gaumont to watch *The Sound of Music*. 'There was a big queue waiting for any unsold seats. Just as I arrived a lady was asking if anyone wanted a single ticket. I snapped it up at once and found myself sitting with a party of ladies who were very interested in me. I had a very enjoyable evening.' Nearby, on Friday the 27th, the local paper reported that the last of Salford's 'stick men' lamplighters was about to retire (only forty gas lamps left in the city, compared to 5,000 prior to the war), before on Saturday a pop sort of day: in Maureen Cleave's 'Disc Date' in the *Evening Standard*, Ray Davies ('a long, pale, lugubrious, unco-operative face, but a rare gap-toothed smile that it is a joy to coax out of him') moving in barely a nanosecond from how 'people should realise that things like food and tea are important' to 'people look up to dictators, because really they don't want to be free'; thirteen-year-old Julia McLaughlin, in Preston, confessing herself obsessed with Sonny and Cher ('I just think they're gorgeous'), briefly No. 1 with 'I Got You Babe'; and on *The Kathy Kirby Show*, a serious thumbs-down from viewers for former pop idol Billy Fury ('not only had this "so-called artist" no singing voice but he seemed quite unable even to sing in tune, many complained, and his patter sequence was so weak, and ineffectual, as to be pitiful'). 'Fine & sunny for the first *end* of August Bank Holiday,' recorded Anthony Heap on Monday the 30th; while Mrs M. E. Salmon, of Bruce Road, Lincoln, ended the month hoping – justifiably, as it turned out – that her *cri de cœur* was about to be published by the *Daily Mail*:

> The craving for realism is leading to the state where TV plays become downright embarrassing.
>
> As the mother of five young daughters I consider child-birth a wonderful experience – *but not in public*. Recently we have been 'cheered' by the screams and moans of premature labour in

Emergency – Ward 10 with accompanying comments from 'nursing staff'.

I don't hide the facts of life from my children, but I feel that this type of performance is unnecessary and is surely inclined to frighten any young girl.[13]

Once government swung back into action at the start of September, its top priority was, in essence, to achieve sufficient concession from the unions on wages policy to persuade the Americans to cough up more dollars. But whereas Callaghan wanted, under Cromer's influence, to impose a wage freeze, Brown (a trade union man at heart) was adamant about sticking to a voluntary approach; and at Cabinet on Wednesday the 1st, when he outlined proposals, pending the full operation of Aubrey Jones's Prices and Incomes Board, for an 'early warning' system for wage claims and then heard Callaghan saying something about powers of enforcement, he exploded, 'I want to make it clear that I am only introducing these proposals on the strict understanding that this is *not* the first step to statutory wage control.' Eventually, after some bruising, eve-of-Congress haggling between Brown and the TUC's general secretary, George Woodcock, the TUC was left to decide, in Brighton on the 8th, whether it should back its leaders in giving some additional bite to a voluntary incomes policy (through an internal TUC committee to vet pay claims and settlements), in the hope of thereby forestalling a compulsory policy, backed by legislation, further down the road.

In a candid opening speech to a largely silent, sullen hall, Woodcock explained how parlous the country's external financial position had become, with the need to extend the lines of defence of sterling. 'The Government has got to get support,' he insisted. 'That is a categorical imperative: the alternatives are really frightful.' His appeal cut no ice with Clive Jenkins. Congress, declared the ferociously articulate leader of the white-collar union ASSET (Association of Supervisory Staffs, Executives, and Technicians), was being asked to accept a 'pathetically and thoroughly and dangerously wrong economic analysis'; instead, the fundamental issue was what was known abroad as the British disease – namely, under-production; and, advising delegates to reject a policy which 'simultaneously cuts your throats and castrates you', he finished by telling them that they were not free men in a free society unless they adopted a different posture. In the end, Woodcock just about prevailed, by 5.25 million votes to 3.31 million; and two days later, Callaghan was indeed able to announce that he had secured a further $1,000 million international short-term loan. Even so, in the ominous words of one newspaper headline, 'Little unanimity at Brighton'.[14]

The Royal Albert Hall during this first half of September staged a special Prom to celebrate Sir Malcolm Sargent's seventieth birthday; the National Youth Theatre's production of *Antony and Cleopatra* at the Old Vic featured Helen Mirren as Cleopatra ('starts far too self-consciously,' reckoned Bernard Levin, 'but soon warms into it'); Lindsay Anderson was in Manchester ('usual stimulating awful marvellous Northern urban landscape') preparing, with Shelagh Delaney, to shoot *The White Bus*; Pat Scott went to a cookery demonstration at Barking Assembly Hall and encountered a bevy of opportunistic OAPs ('I was disgusted by the way they behaved – pushing & fighting to get a free ½lb Bacon'); *Blue Peter*'s Petra had her puppies, with Patch the one being kept; in the *New Statesman*, an enthusiastic, four-page report by Mervyn Jones on 'The Comprehensive Revolution' included the assertion that 'if the comprehensive idea means what I take it to mean, the dominant tradition of the present-day grammar school ought not to be valued but discarded – for it is a tradition of élite education'; the same day (the 10th), the sixth form at Roger Darlington's grammar school in Manchester debated a motion 'in favour of the comprehensive principle of education being adopted throughout this country', decisively lost; two days later, at Sunday Evensong in James Allen's parish church, 'there were about 20 present and I talked about Church music and played the second side of the record of the Singing Nun which the congregation seemed to have enjoyed'; next day, while Julia McLaughlin apparently got little joy from confessing to a friend her secret passion for Cher's better half ('she doesn't like Sonny – neither does anyone else'), Anthony Heap was laying into Cecil Beaton ('I never suspected him to be capable of such rank imbecility') for having, in the diarist's scornful words, 'recently been delivering himself of a lot of drivel in disapproval of Savile Row for frowning upon the outlandish "mod" fashions affected by today's illiterate, effeminate, moronic, pop-group-aping adolescents'; the day after, an education minister, Reginald Prentice, was in Oxford to assure the Association of Preparatory Schools that although the government's object was 'to put an end to the public school system as one of the dividing forces in our society', even so it had never been their intention 'to put an end to all private education'; and on Wednesday the 15th, the evening papers revealed that the London boroughs had jointly decided on a common policy – immediately open to the charge of racial discrimination – of requiring a five-year residence qualification for anyone hoping to get a council house in Greater London, the experienced manager-cum-publicist Terry Pitt urged Davie Jones's new manager, Ralph Horton, to change his client's stage name (all too liable to be confused with the up-and-coming, Manchester-born Davy Jones, currently making a name for himself on Broadway as the Artful Dodger in Lionel Bart's *Oliver!*), and the latest issue of *Vogue* included an interview with Denmark's student prince. 'I don't get angry about much but one thing makes me sick,' Warner told Polly Devlin. 'The way people attack others about trivialities, the petty shackling of people by people – it must stop. Small mindedness bugs me. I hate people interfering in other people's lives.'[15]

The National Plan's moment was at last at hand, with Brown launching it – with no little panache – the following evening on television. A target of 25 per cent growth in national output between 1964 and 1970, working out at an annual average of 3.8 per cent; productivity to rise by an annual rate of 3.4 per cent; exports to rise by 5.2 per cent a year; manufacturers to increase investment by 7 per cent a year (compared with 2.4 per cent in 1960–64); significant limits on defence spending; the annual housing target to reach half a million by 1970; massive rises in spending on roads and education – one way and another, despite the recent discouraging mood music of sterling crises and deflationary measures, it was ambitious, even exhilarating stuff. 'The press this morning gave the National Plan a big build-up and I think the Tories are making a big mistake by mocking it and dismissing it as a Party gimmick,' reflected Tony Benn next day. 'Coming so soon after the rescue of the pound and the better prospects for the trade deficit, it looks ahead positively and I think will command a great deal of interest and support.' Of course, not everyone loved it – 'no cliché is omitted, no platitude left unstated', commented the *Spectator* (in the same issue that Hilary Spurling wrote of Mirren's 'unselfconsciously and immoderately sensual' Cleopatra) – but Benn was essentially correct: the first half of the 1960s had seen the emergence of a strong pro-planning mood, transcending narrow party politics, and the National Plan represented its apotheosis. Or as Baroness Mary Stocks had put it on *Any Questions?* the previous week, 'I think George Brown is making a most heroic attempt to develop something in the nature of a planned economy, rather than a free-for-all and the Devil-take-the-hindmost selfish'. Yet whether the Plan would survive much contact with reality was, inevitably, another question altogether.

One young American singer, approaching the end of a tour of northern folk clubs and feeling ever more homesick, had his mind elsewhere this potentially historic Thursday the 16th, as he sat at Widnes station in Cheshire and, waiting for his train, scribbled some lines for a song.[16] Paul Simon was not quite homeward bound yet, but soon, soon. And meanwhile, across industrial England, the movies and the factories . . .

5
Is That All?

In the middle weeks of September, one novel of the hour and one film of the hour. The novel was Margaret Drabble's third, *The Millstone*, as it happened the first novel to be computer typeset, thanks to the far-sighted printer Rowland Atterbury. 'A most moral wit, Miss Drabble, very intelligent and perceptive about the new intellectual middle class and its complicated moral problems in this novel about a cool girl graduate who gets pregnant inadvertently and manages to keep her head, her baby, and her independence,' the *Guardian* would note in December in its 'Books of the Year' round-up; while in September itself, at least one reviewer, Isabel Quigly, was struck by Drabble's 'remarkable sense of – and ear for – the middling middle-classes that have purposefully cut off their roots and gone their own way', with all her heroines to date, including Rosamund here, 'handsome young graduates with a pitiless eye for the stupid and the unhandsome'. Certainly there are no doubts about what type of person Rosamund (the daughter of well-off socialist parents) sees as the benighted: a sort of boyfriend is dismissed out of hand as 'a wealthy well-descended Tory accountant person'; and she has zero tolerance for her brother, who 'went and married a ghastly girl whose father was a colonel, and now he lives in Dorking and spends all his time having absolutely worthless people to dinner and playing bridge'. So far so snooty. Yet crucially, unlike the accountant and unlike the troops in Dorking, the progressive, liberal-minded, bluestocking Rosamund also, despite her apparent ineffable sense of personal superiority, suffers from guilt – specifically, the guilt that professional success is more dependent on a privileged education than it should be. Or as Simon Raven wrote not long afterwards about the 'subtle and amusing' Drabble, with particular reference to *The Millstone*, 'although she allows, in mitigation, that most talented people have to work hard to win their status, it is clear that in her gloomier mood she regards ability as another injustice, almost as a personal indulgence – as something which, so far from being rewarded with social esteem, ought to be tactfully obscured lest it provoke offence among the less fortunate'. In 1965 itself, it was two years since Michael Frayn had, very helpfully, divided the middle class into 'carnivores' and 'herbivores'; and for the moment, no one captured the latter more faithfully, more insightfully, than the still only 26-year-old novelist.[1]

The film, premiered on the same day that George Brown announced his National Plan, was *Darling*. Directed by John Schlesinger, written by Frederic Raphael and starring Julie Christie, Dirk Bogarde and Laurence Harvey, it very consciously combined morality tale with almost achingly contemporary social document, starting with the title itself. During the Profumo scandal two years earlier, a puzzled Harold Macmillan had privately reflected on an emerging social world, emphatically not his kind of world, 'where no one really knows anyone and everyone is "darling"'; one review described the film as 'set in the world of the new aristocracy, of which the advertising men and the fashion photographers form the dubious elite'; and almost everything on display was (as Schlesinger's biographer, William J. Mann, notes) new and modern, whether the fashions or the architecture or the abstract sculpture or, of course, the new sexual freedom. Yet Margaret Hinxman's assessment was surely correct. The characters, she wrote in her *Sunday Telegraph* review, 'exist in a tiny, claustrophobic world that the producers seem to have forgotten is just a pimple on the face of humanity'; and tellingly, when over half a century later an oral history project sought to explore memories of cinema-going in the 1960s, it found in its testimony from the north of England a significant degree of resentment about the Swinging London films exemplified by *Blow-Up* and *Alfie* as well as *Darling* itself. The places depicted in them, said a woman from Lancashire, 'might have been on the other side of the world to me in the 60s'. And she added: 'I'm from a group of people who started work at 15 . . . and you got married before you were 21. You had a family in your 20s. That's what you did.'[2]

It is a necessary and salutary perspective. Even so, as both *The Millstone* and *Darling* in their very different ways suggested, there did exist by the mid-1960s some kind of critical mass for a 'herbivore' culture that was nevertheless different from that of the herbivores of the immediate post-war years: still ultimately serious, and still progressive in political orientation, but at the same time more inward-looking and individualistic – or, put another way, somewhat less socially concerned, somewhat less earnest, somewhat less obsessively seeking the New Jerusalem. Crucially, one is not talking here about Sixties' youth culture, let alone counter-culture; this is for the most part a somewhat older generation, still tending to prize traditional literary culture above, say, pop music or even jazz. And indeed, in the increasingly intolerant eyes of the young, they would come quite soon to be seen as the stuffy, middle-aged irredeemables, almost as hopeless as the conventional 'carnivores'.

Who, then, by 1965 were some of this culture's acknowledged leaders or exemplars? Of the four elders from an inevitably arbitrary baker's dozen of such figures, the highest-profile was undoubtedly **Arnold Goodman**, aged fifty-two in September 1965, the year he was made a life peer by Harold Wilson. By this time he had become (as an obituarist put it) 'the totem and oracle for the great and the good'; but he had also become their all-purpose fixer, not least in his ever-resourceful capacity as chairman from that year of the Arts Council, presiding for the next seven years over a huge increase in the volume and scope of its work. The other three elders all helped, in a more day-to-day way, the herbivores to lead the good life: **Robert Harling** (fifty-five) was eight years into his twenty-eight-year editorship of *House & Garden*, immortalised in Flanders and Swann's 'Design for Living' and where (recalled one of his many female assistants, Fiona MacCarthy) his 'great achievement was to bring living people into previously bare interiors', thereby inventing 'what would soon be known as lifestyle features'; the cookery writer **Elizabeth David** (fifty-one) had not only already inspired – in some kitchens anyway, albeit far from everyone's – a post-war culinary revolution, and with almost all her books available in Penguin was continuing to do so, but from this autumn, opening at the start of November, she also had her own shop, just behind Sloane Square, for followers to make a pilgrimage to; and the developer **Geoffrey Townsend** (fifty-four) was, in collaboration with the architect Eric Lyons, the man behind Span housing, whose thirty estates built between 1948 and 1984 were for 'families with aspirations to modern design but insufficient cash to realise their dream, who were likely to want to live among grand houses in elegant, leafy neighbourhoods in affordable (with a mortgage) homes in a modernist vernacular' – the words of Juliet Gardiner, bringing up a young family from the mid-1960s on the widely acclaimed The Priory development in Blackheath, where on their part of the estate 'our fellow residents were architects, a couple of graphic designers, an academic, teachers, social workers (senior pay grade, presumably), a solicitor, a Labour MP, a couple of businessmen, an accountant, a potter and a boat designer'. Two semi-elders featured in the baker's dozen: **Iris Murdoch** (forty-six) was surely *the* contemporary novelist for the well-read herbivore, a philosopher who (wrote one obituarist) employed fiction in order 'to chart the progress of a metaphysical battle between evil and good, usually played out within the confines of a leisured upper-middle-class society'; while the Australian-born **Jocelyn Rickards** (forty-one) was the costume designer who 'mastered a look of everyday comfort and high fashion innovation', giving some of the defining British movies of the era, including *From Russia With Love* as well as *Morgan* and *Blow-Up*, their distinctive contemporary feel.

That left the remaining seven, all in their thirties. The first two were both in the world of publishing: Jonathan Cape's editorial director, **Tom Maschler** (thirty-two), 'a glamorous, perma-tanned figure with aquiline features and unruly hair, who dressed in brightly coloured shirts and sweaters at a time when publishing was stylistically and metaphorically tweedy', and whose authors by the mid-sixties included Joseph Heller, Philip Roth, Kurt Vonnegut and John Fowles, but not, of course, the less immediately thrilling Barbara Pym; and Penguin's cover art director since 1960, Milan-born **Germano Facetti** (thirty-seven), attracting a host of new and younger readers by giving the paperbacks a contemporary feel 'through a more defined and consistent use of illustration, photography and collage, supported by simple "modern" typography using the newly available typefaces Standard, Helvetica and Univers'. Next up were four intellectuals. **Karl Miller** (thirty-four), literary editor of the *New Statesman* at a time when the magazine's social as well as political and cultural prestige was way above that of the *Spectator*, gave its review pages a high seriousness, perhaps above all if William Empson was contributing; the turbo-charged **Jonathan Miller** (thirty-one), no relation, had moved on from *Beyond the Fringe*, had had a spell (with mixed results) in charge of the arts programme *Monitor*, and would soon be directing TV films for the BBC; the endlessly curious, endlessly sceptical **Robert Robinson** (thirty-seven) had already for four years been presenting BBC TV's *Points of View* and this autumn was about to start hosting *BBC-3*, final spluttering of the TV satire boom that had begun with *That Was The Week That Was*; and the Cambridge-based **George Steiner** (thirty-six) was, through his enthralling lectures and compelling essays, establishing himself as, in Eric Homberger's words, 'a polymathic European intellectual of particular severity', an intellectual whose wider reputation rose even as 'the suspicion' in Cambridge itself persisted 'that, for all his achievements, Steiner was something of a fraud'. The last was *the* playwright by autumn 1965. Perhaps at the start of the year that would still have been John Osborne; but in the wake of *The Homecoming* it was now surely **Harold Pinter** (thirty-four). 'In its image of the naked violence of family life and of the primal, atavistic power of the female, it shocked, disturbed and seemed to establish a direct line to the collective subconscious,' reflects Michael Billington about its arrival that summer in the modern repertory. Yet not everyone from an older generation of cultural heroes warmed to it, nor indeed to the changing temper of the times. 'I added to my depression by going to see the new Pinter play,' Kenneth Clark wrote in August to a friend. 'Really rather good, but sordid and heartless to a degree . . . this is part of the price we have paid for ridding ourselves of hypocrisy.'[3]

Equally arbitrary again, but it is also possible to identify by this autumn a quartet of distinctly herbivorian phenomena or reference points: a television programme, a cinema, an art book, an area of London. *Late Night Line-Up* was by now entering its second year, taking as its starting point the evening's TV fare but often going beyond, with its presenters (Joan Bakewell *primus inter pares* in most male viewers' eyes) impeccably liberal and progressive in their largely unstated assumptions; the Academy cinema in Oxford Street, run by George Hoellering with his stepson Ivo Jarosy as his right-hand man, was indisputably London's premier art house (and an immeasurable loss since its closure in 1986); 'British art is being produced with its own character, but free from provincial narrowness or thinness,' declared Bryan Robertson in his newly published *Private View* (co-authored with John Russell, and lavishly illustrated by Lord Snowdon's photographs), an unabashed celebration of the British art scene, now that London had become, noted Russell and Robertson in their preface, 'one of the world's three capitals of art'; and the local hotspot of middle-class herbivorianism was by this time ever more firmly identified as north London (including in those previously rather rundown and predominantly working-class districts such as Camden Town where the process of 'gentrification', the term only recently coined, was by now in relentless action). Viv Albertine (born 1954 into the working class) has a telling passage in *To Throw Away Unopened*, her wonderful – and wonderfully acerbic – memoir:

> Since my childhood I've loved looking into and out of windows. When I moved in with Mum again in my late twenties, she and I used to walk around the local streets in Hampstead and Swiss Cottage most evenings after dinner. I was always amazed that the inhabitants didn't close their curtains, even when it was dark. As we peered down into the kitchens I'd marvel at how some people were so confident of what they wore and how they behaved that they didn't mind anyone walking past their house seeing them. Mum explained that in the past the families living in these big houses used to employ servants, but in the 1960s, when the middle classes couldn't afford maids any more, they transformed the basements where the staff used to work into large kitchen/dining rooms. (When I visited friends' houses, I sensed their parents thought they were being subversive by turning this *servants' room* into the main living space. It was a radical idea at the time.)
>
> Those basement kitchens with large scrubbed pine tables, deliberately mismatched chairs, wine glasses and blue and white enamel bread bins looked like film sets to me, the people milling around inside like fantasy families.

'Life was not like that in our house,' she goes on about a contrast which also had its roots in the Sixties. 'We dressed in shabby old clothes (put them on as soon as we got in so we didn't wear out our nice ones), our furniture was second-hand and we had to sit on the settee (later learned to call it the sofa) swaddled in blankets to watch TV in the lounge (later learned to call it the living room) because it was so cold.' In short: 'No way we wanted to expose neighbours and random passers-by to any of that.'

It was some 140 'crow-flying' miles north of north London that in spring 1965 a survey was conducted into the audiences at the Sheffield Playhouse's production (27 April to 15 May) of *Uncle Vanya*. Two findings stood out: that almost two-thirds (65 per cent) of those theatregoers were female; and that 89 per cent were from social classes A or B or C1 – the three classes (ranging from higher executive and professional down to lower management, semi-professional, technicians and office workers) that between them comprised only 29 per cent of the national population. The survey also included more in-depth interviews with thirty-four of the Playhouse's regulars, of whom only one was working class. Asked to nominate their favourite play of the past season, they plumped by a considerable margin for C. P. Snow's *The Masters* ('there was a story to it; it was very human and it had a moral'), whereas least popular with them was Feydeau's farce *Hotel Paradiso* ('too much slapstick: vulgar . . . too ridiculous and far-fetched . . . trashy: too much sex'). As for playwrights more generally, they were given eight names and asked to appraise them, ranging from 'like very much' to 'dislike very much'. Easily coming out on top for favourability were Shaw and Shakespeare (+52 and +49 respectively); Anouilh lay third with +23, followed by Chekhov and Ibsen (each with +19); Arthur Miller managed +10; while bringing up the rear, by some way, were Osborne (-7) and Pinter (-9). Even so, Pinter still had six people putting him in the 'like very much' column, just as many as the out-and-out enthusiasts for Chekhov; and the survey concluded, mildly enough, that although 'the Regulars on the whole went for "safe" playwrights', nevertheless 'it was obvious that their tastes were not wholly against the new generation'.[4]

Were, then, these largely middlebrow theatregoers in a northern provincial city herbivores not quite up to Hampstead scratch, or, rather, were they carnivores far from simply the philistines of easy caricature? Perhaps there comes a point when the distinction between the two middle-class types starts, for all its obvious appeal, to be too blunt a tool to be especially useful. Still, this was only a year or two before I 'discovered' Forster's *Howards End*; and it seemed pretty clear to me, a middle-class adolescent starting to get a grip on the adult world, who at some fundamental level were the Schlegels and who the Wilcoxes.

'I have taken the liberty of writing to you,' Ralph Horton wrote to Ken Pitt on Friday, 17 September, 'and advising you that I have now changed Davie's name to David Bowie'; in the latest music magazines, Ewan MacColl condemned Bob Dylan as an 'anti-artist', the four Small Faces, all from the East End, revealed their parents' names (Kathleen and Bill; Stanley and Elsie; Cis and Bill; Violet and Samuel), and thirteen-year-old Julia McLaughlin found in *Music Echo* not only 'five photographs' of Sonny and Cher but 'a fabulous article', while at the same time, on the Saturday, conceding that she had 'decided to like Bob Dylan'; *The Times* that day had an artist's impression of the new Stock Exchange, an uncompromising twenty-six-storey tower block very different from the late-Victorian 'Gorgonzola Hall' it was replacing; the mother of Barry-based diarist Frank Lewis arrived by coach at Pontin's holiday camp at Bracklesham Bay near Bognor, where (she reported back) her evening meal comprised 'Soup, Chicken, Sprouts, Potatoes, Ice cream & Fruit, Biscuits & Cheese & Coffee'; and Frederick Ward in Bristol passed the evening at the musical *Lock Up Your Daughters* ('the main theme was "rape" and there was plenty of romping on the Stage but somehow it was not sexey'). 'We went to Chigwell,' noted Pat Scott in Barking on the Sunday. 'It was lovely. We picked about 1½ lb blackberries & then poodled round Chigwell, Theydon Bois etc. It was a perfect evening. The scenery is beautiful around this area – you would never think we were so near home.' Two days later, while the 100 Club saw Bowie performing for the first time under his new professional name, the sharp downturn in Arnold Wesker's fortunes was confirmed by the critics' dismal reaction to the London first night of *The Four Seasons*, typified by Alan Brien's reference to 'the pseudo-poetry, the sloppy philosophising, the blush-making rhetoric of this woman's-magazine ballet', albeit J. C. Trewin was partly mollified by the 'splendidly decorative' Diane Cilento; Mrs Lewis on Wednesday gave Frank her impressions of the camp ('it is bands & music everywhere, Dancing, cabaret show, tabletennis, rambles, bingo, sitting around, TV' – in short, 'something for everyone'); the *Listener* next day included the text of Derek Cooper's recent radio talk (on *Today*) about the British tourist industry's continuing inability to provide decent food for foreign visitors (with the accompanying headline, 'The bad food guide', directly leading two years later to Cooper's pioneering book-length *Guide* to what and where to avoid); and Jo Grimond this week was in Scarborough for his party's conference. 'Jimmy Savile was in town and very much wanted to meet Grimond, whom he greatly admired,' recorded the Liberal leader's biographer, Michael McManus, in 2001. 'Grimond was seized by an immediate and powerful aversion to such a meeting and spent several hours dashing around the assembly, desperately eluding his admirer.'[5]

Friday the 24th was a bumper day. The BBC's chairman, Lord Normanbrook, together with other top BBC figures and high-ranking civil servants, had a private viewing of Peter Watkins's not-yet-broadcast TV film, *The War Game*, about Britain after a nuclear attack – a viewing concerned less with the psychological damage it might do to viewers, more with its potential impact on public attitudes to the nuclear deterrent; Diana Griffith in Worthing was approaching the end of her first week at the local college of further education ('Shorthand & Typing for 5 hrs!! Phew!'); the Comprehensive Schools Committee, aimed at promoting the comprehensive principle throughout secondary education and with Caroline Benn as its driving force, was launched at a press conference ('everybody turned up', noted her husband Tony, 'except for the *News of the World* and the *Observer*'); the *Any Questions?* team pondered the public school question (Labour MP Dick Taverne asking 'Why should it be possible to buy for somebody who hasn't got any particular talents a pretty secure job?', and adding, 'you only have to look at the sort of advertisement that appears in *The Times*, the only recommendation that some people can offer is that they are public school', but to laughter and applause the *Sunday Mirror*'s Anne Allen flatly accusing his government of being ' "schizophrenic", they say one thing and then they send their sons to public schools'); and Enoch Powell, at the annual dinner of the Newport Conservative Association, declaring that the government decision to keep down the price of bread was 'an essentially lawless use of the power and influence of government'.[6]

'Went to Pinner for coffee – did some shopping & home to lunch when Bill suggested a sherry before lunch!!!!!!' recorded next day a surprised Grace Taylor in Ruislip, while after lunch young Diana went to Brighton to see *The Sound of Music* ('MARV. FAB. FANTAB etc!') for the second time in barely a week. On Sunday the Brent Cross flyover on the North Circular Road was opened to traffic; Celia Kent – a 21-year-old St Albans diarist who had left school prematurely and was now studying for her A levels – spent that evening 'mulling over University entrance qualifications & wondering whether to do it', before next day she 'wrote to 7 universities'; and on Tuesday in Chingford, another diarist, whose bathroom basin was broken and whose husband was 'fed up' about it, was also mulling over things. 'I am very sorry about it, but we do have less expenditure than any of my friends round here and should have a reserve fund to dip into,' reflected Judy Haines. 'We still have Brock's floor-covering upstairs and in the den, and until very recently in kitchen also. Yes, I'm sure we're careful to the point of being niggly – in some things. We were first with tele, washing machine and frig. though.'

That evening, a double-header on BBC1: first, at 9.30, a fairly bland documentary about Eton, prompting one viewer to comment about the still quite spartan way of life depicted that 'the majority of those who want to abolish the public school could not last a week in the conditions in which these boys have to live and study lessons'; then, an hour later, a follow-up discussion programme, chaired by Joan Bakewell ('has both brains and looks', noted another viewer), had three Old Etonians (Julian Amery, Jocelyn Stevens, Neal Ascherson) offering a range of views, but all – more than one viewer pointed out – having something in common, namely 'supreme self-confidence'. These programmes, however, were not the reason why 28 September earned its permanent niche in television history. 'Cathy Gale has gone,' observed next morning the *Daily Telegraph*'s 'L. L.' about the start of the third season of *The Avengers*. 'Instead there is Mrs Emma Peel, played by Diana Rigg, who wears above-the-knee length skirts and has a nice line in plastic tights when it comes to the judo stuff – never, I am given to understand, being very much "out" this season.' Why Emma Peel? Obviously, a play on 'M-Appeal' – brainwave of Marie Donaldson, an ATV press officer working on the programme. Perhaps the same press officer who came up with the pre-series description of the character as 'the youthful widow of an ace test pilot, daughter of a wealthy shipowner, and an internationally educated symbol of the jet-age female'. Coming complete with Laurie Johnson's memorable new theme tune (percussion, then brass, then strings), 'The Town of No Return' was the title of the first episode, concerning the mysterious disappearance of four special agents in a remote Norfolk village, with that whole village being taken over by fiendish impersonators; and the *Observer*'s Maurice Richardson applauded 'a fizzing start', in contrast to the *Sunday Times*'s Maurice Wiggin who, critical anyway of Emma's 'absurdly short skirts and outré headgear', labelled the whole thing an 'absurd farrago' with a 'bouillabaisse of red herrings'. Two days later, TV history again, as the *Thunderbirds* made their debut, likewise on ITV. Parker was the butler-cum-chauffeur ('Yus, m'lady'), Brains was the bespectacled genius with a stammer, but the futuristic puppet show belonged to Lady Penelope Creighton-Ward, exuding (in the words of an obituarist of her voice as well as co-creator, Sylvia Anderson) 'class, sex appeal, and that essential air of unattainability'. Emma Peel and Lady Penelope . . . Two almost instant female legends in only three days; and both of them combining, as another obituarist of Anderson put it, 'glamour with intelligence'.[7]

This was also the week of Labour's conference, with the novelist Pamela Hansford Johnson among those travelling north to watch proceedings. 'Blackpool', she wrote in her diary,

> is the most appallingly ugly place I have ever seen in my life: it appals because it looks as though the entire wit of man had been devoted to producing something so coarse, crude, lurid & witless, that it had to be seen to be believed. Better when the lights are on, because the neo-Disney monstrosities can't be seen so clearly. How one must despise the capacity of man to enjoy beautiful things if he is offered this degradation!

The hotel she was staying in was, she added, 'monstrously ugly like all of them'; dinner comprised 'boiler fowl & cold bread sauce'; and the whole town was pervaded by 'a faint smell of stale pastry'. As for politics, though, she did not deny that Wilson was 'a dazzling performer', a verdict which Crossman concurred with ('an immensely impressive performance') after his leader's main speech on the Tuesday. That speech included a delegates-pleasing passage ridiculing *Burke's Peerage* – prompting the retort from its editor, Peter Townend, that 'I thought we were out of the class-conscious age' and that 'people don't wear cloth caps and mufflers any more'. Wednesday afternoon saw an emergency debate on immigration, in the wake of the recent controversial White Paper. The three key contributions came from the backbench MP Reg Freeson and the two frontbenchers Robert Mellish and Alice Bacon. Whereas Freeson, noted Tony Benn, made 'a most rational case against the White Paper', of which he had been an outspoken liberal critic right from the start, Mellish 'was quite hysterical in his real working-class way, speaking for the Bermondsey dockers against immigrants'; while, according to Crossman, it was only Bacon who from the government's perspective 'saved' the situation, as 'in that grating voice she gave her clear, schoolmistressy, common-sense view of the White Paper, demonstrating what was in it to people who hadn't bothered to read it'. Her key passage was nicely judged to carry the day:

> I say that this country of ours ought to be able to absorb one million immigrants, but I would ask the conference to recognise that these immigrants are concentrated in those very areas where the supply of houses, schools and teachers is already inadequate. Of course we know that the immigrants did not create the shortage . . . but until the Labour government can make good these shortages, to put more on the already over-burdened services could lead to a very serious situation.

Half a century later, her biographer, Rachel Reeves, would quote approvingly not only those words, but also the judgement of another Labour eminence, Bernard Donoughue, on her subject: 'Alice understood the concerns of working-class communities . . . and was more able to carry them with her by argument rather than by lecturing them sanctimoniously on their alleged bigotry and prejudices.'

Over the week as a whole, it was the party leadership which, to its considerable relief, came out on top. Whether it was the government's support for the United States in Vietnam, or the White Paper on immigration, or the early-warning system for wage claims that was still the crux of a voluntary incomes policy, the votes all went the leadership's way, helped by the robust chairmanship of Ray Gunter. At the end of the week, one young Labour MP, Roy Hattersley, concluded that the party was now in a good position ('the pound seems safe at last and the opinion polls already promise victory'), and that 'next year there are even greater benefits to be gained from pragmatism'. Even so, most observers were probably agreed that, at this particular juncture, it was only the slenderness of Labour's parliamentary majority that was keeping the party's left wing in check. 'Ten years ago and more, the fellow-travelling element was merely the fringe: today it is dominant,' observed *The Economist* about the Labour left. 'The hallmarks of the average left-winger today, as seen in his favourite habitat of a Labour party conference, are clear. On foreign policy, violently anti-American, anti-Western and an apologist for both brands of communism, but particularly Peking. On home policy, relentlessly pursuing the class war . . .'[8]

'New buildings in Shrewsbury are as bad as they can get,' declared Ian Nairn in the October issue of *Architectural Review*, as he lamented the fate – exemplified by the new Market Hall – of 'one of the best country towns in Britain'; John Fowles on Friday the 1st was at BBC Television Centre in Wood Lane, where he met 'an earnest young man with floppy black hair and pink cheeks' called 'Melvin Bragg' ('a black leather jacket, a grey polo-necked sweater . . . on his guard against being corrupted by the gloss and swagger of the Centre'); Crossman, talking that evening to students at Manchester University and being asked about the idea of setting up special camps to house newly arrived immigrants, rejected the policy on the grounds that such camps were 'often thought of as concentration camps'; Ken Dodd's romantic ballad, 'Tears', now stood at the top of the charts, where it would stay for the rest of the month; attending on Saturday the 2nd a small party for the silver wedding of a work colleague, it was 'a shock' for Frederick Ward to discover that his own and another of the wives were wearing the same dress ('they were embarrassed but pretended not to be'); *BBC-3* began that evening – on BBC1, and up against *Match of the Day*, still on BBC2 – with one critic, Peter Black, reckoning 'the talk was dull without being serious', while 'the best sketches were Alan Bennett's Betjeman poem, nostalgic over lavatory equipment, and John Bird's impersonations, notably the fiendish dead-eyed one of Harold Wilson'; 'I do hope I can go to University,' reflected Celia Kent next day, before on Monday the 4th, even as she 'wrote to masses more Universities', came a trio of new BBC programmes: on radio at lunchtime, *The World at One*, presented by a former *Daily Mail* editor, the beetle-browed William (Bill) Hardcastle, who (in David Hendy's words) 'brought some of the urgency and heat of Fleet Street'; and on TV, first a football-themed soap – *United!*, earning a tepid RI of 51 – and then, much later than the programme (*Tonight*) it was replacing but still fronted by Cliff Michelmore, *24 Hours*, instantly condemned by the *Telegraph*'s man as 'all rather like a cup of stodgy cocoa without sugar, guaranteed not to keep you awake at night'. If *United!* was one new, twice-weekly BBC soap, then *The Newcomers*, starting next day, was another, this time about Londoners who had moved to a fictional East Anglian overspill town called Angleton: the strong, independent-minded Vivienne Cooper (played by Maggie Fitzgibbon) the linchpin; Wendy Richard winning her first fame by playing the rebellious teenager, Joyce Harker, living next door; and a more encouraging RI of 60. No transmission, though, of *The War Game* on Wednesday the 6th, which had been the due date; but for 7,500 Coventry City fans gathered that evening at their own ground, the gratifying experience of watching a 2–1 win at Cardiff City – the first closed-circuit transmission of a league match; and at the house at Hattersley, an overspill estate near Hyde outside Manchester, that Myra Hindley shared with Ian Brady, the utterly brutal killing of seventeen-year-old Edward Evans. Thanks to the courage of Hindley's brother-in-law – David Smith, also seventeen, a hapless bystander as events unfolded – Hindley and Brady were arrested next day, and Brady charged with the murder of Evans.[9]

By this time, though sadly with no place for Celia Kent, the universities were back for the autumn, including at Hull where the 27-year-old John Prescott, after eight years as a ship's steward and two years at Ruskin College in Oxford, had enlisted as an undergraduate. Early on, walking past the library, he spotted Larkin, whose work he knew a bit. 'I decided to go up to him. "Excuse me," I said, "Do you do seminars?" I thought I might go along, if he did. He looked down his nose at me – and walked on.' A different sort of discombobulation in Manchester, as Lindsay Anderson on Thursday the 7th inspected a small food-processing firm on the Trafford Industrial Estate ('awful back-attic where forlorn girls were packing frozen meat stew, spraying in gravy with a plastic hose'); Betty Allen that afternoon was in a Hansford Johnson mood as she went shopping ('got an artificial Christmas tree & some fireworks & some shirt material for John – tired out – I hate Blackpool'); the new *Radio Times* featured Tony Garnett previewing the upcoming season of *The Wednesday Play* ('although we shall not set out to offend people, we may be provocative – but out of a compassion that comes from a concern for human beings'); the press on Friday was full of ads launching a future transport classic ('Everything about the Ford Transit has been calculated – and tested – to ensure the most efficient, most profitable van operation you have ever experienced'), a boon for rock bands as much as bank robbers; Wilson formally opened the Post Office Tower, commemorated by new postage stamps and soon to feature Sir Billy Butlin's revolving restaurant on the thirty-fourth floor; next afternoon, while implements including beer bottles and a foot-long iron bar were thrown on to the pitch during the Huddersfield–Manchester City match, Old Trafford witnessed first Nobby Stiles being struck by a missile from the terraces, then mass disturbances and ejections behind the Stretford End goal, and finally, after the home team had won 2–0, and as 'a gang of jeering, banner-waving Liverpool fans crowded round the stadium's main entrance, a pint mug was tossed through the window of Matt Busby's office and the windows of Board Room and Visitors' Lounge were peppered with stones' – all of them scenes more or less unthinkable five or ten years earlier; that evening, the poet Adrian Mitchell, still temporarily doubling as the *Sun*'s TV critic, watched *BBC-3* and enjoyed 'one of Christopher Logue's classic true stories about gas-stoves, and Bill Oddie with a clever song about a one-man beat group'; three days later, Wednesday the 13th, the same paper's front-page headline was '"MURDERS" HUNT ON MOOR', accompanying a report about teams of police the previous night 'investigating a tip that one or more murdered people are buried on a desolate moor', near Penistone on the Lancashire/Yorkshire border; much less harrowing northern news, but still minorly sad, was the impending demolition (in a redevelopment scheme) of Salford's

Archie Street, shown since 1960 in the title shot of *Coronation Street*; *24 Hours* was now settling in, with one critic, Patrick Skene Catling, not missing its predecessor ('seems somehow less fascinated [i.e. than *Tonight* had been] by its own feats of originality' and 'has resolved to cut down on the whimsy'); on Thursday, at the Conservative Party conference in Brighton, Sir Edward Boyle, shadow education minister and generally viewed as no die-in-the-ditch defender of grammar schools, insisted that 'we do not believe that the time has come for the rapid and universal imposition of the comprehensive principle'; next day the *NME* ran a feature on the Small Faces ('four young, Carnaby Street-clad mods'), their debut single 'Whatcha Gonna Do About It' now peaking at No. 14; the *Mail*'s Olga Franklin interviewed the pair of recently married novelists Kingsley Amis and Elizabeth Jane Howard ('She bosses me sometimes, but I do so well out of it. Occasionally I feel I'm being fetched from the pub a bit early. But there's a delicious meal waiting . . .'); and Pat and Ted Scott returned to Barking after their four-day road trip through southern England, all faithfully recorded by Pat, sometimes but not always enthusiastically: Guildford ('lovely town'), Tuesday night at King's Arms in Arundel ('steak & mixed grill for dinner'), Bognor ('didn't care for it much'), Littlehampton ('nice but wouldn't care to stay there'), Brighton ('saw the Conservative Party conference people at the Metropole'), Lewes ('Ted liked it but I was disappointed'), Eastbourne (staying Wednesday night at 'very comfortable' Dovercourt Guest House & 'went out for dinner to Log Cabin'), coffee in Bexhill ('the most perfect home made cakes I have ever tasted'), Rye Harbour ('a queer place'), Thursday night at Folkestone ('very good' dinner at the Royal Esplanade Hotel, 'steak & kidney pudding etc'), coffee at Tenterden, lunch at Linton, through Dartford Tunnel, home by 5pm.[10]

'Radicals Comment on the Anniversary' was a headline in the latest *New Statesman* – with the anniversary being, of course, that it was a year since the general election bringing Labour to power. Overall, and perhaps inevitably given this particular line-up of left-leaning public intellectuals, it was only occasionally three cheers, more often two, and sometimes fewer:

> The overall picture is one of promise rather than achievement. *(A. J. Ayer)*

> I can't see any way in which this government has made or seriously tried to make this country more just or more lively than it was before. *(Robert Bolt)*
>
> Its connivance at the bombing and burning of people in Vietnam, plus its ignoble White Paper on immigration, has transformed Labour in a twelvemonth into merely the least of three evils. *(Brigid Brophy)*
>
> I must honestly say that I am totally confident about their intention, and therefore hopeful for their achievements. *(Edna O'Brien)*
>
> To sneer at this gallant effort is like standing on a sinking ship and sneering at the lifeboat. *(J. B. Priestley)*
>
> The really horrible thing is the Immigration Bill. We can no longer condemn South Africa for apartheid nor reproach the Germans for having supported Hitler. *(A. J. P. Taylor)*
>
> Most radicals like myself miss the more humane, wide-visioned new look we had hoped for. But while the government's activity is necessarily limited [by the economic situation], are we not merely childishly asking for idealistic words to cheer us through bleak times? *(Angus Wilson)*
>
> Wilson's government has not betrayed its promises; it has simply not carried them out. *(Leonard Woolf)*

What of the Conservative opposition, trailing by eleven points in the most recent NOP? 'In the public eye,' reflected Crossman over the weekend about that party's new leader, 'he is much colder than Harold Wilson, who has something rather warm and cosy about him compared to this calculating, driving politician'; while when the *Daily Mail*'s Anne Scott-James interviewed Edward Heath a few days earlier, she was clearly doubtful about whether he would turn out to be any more than 'a competent technocrat', concluding bleakly enough that 'behind the brisk efficiency and the safe talk there is an imagination which Mr Heath has never had time to use'. Even so, and for all Enoch Powell's negligible vote in the July leadership election, something was clearly starting to stir on the right, as Anthony King now explored at some length in the current *New Society*. Powell, he noted, had 'struck a responsive chord in the minds of many younger Conservatives already weary of the stock phrases of the fifties', and he identified in what was starting to be called 'Powellism' four key strands: a critical rather than blandly accepting attitude to the state system of social provision; a view of the trade unions which saw them as making a negative contribution to economic prosperity; hostility to any kind of incomes policy; and, perhaps above all, a deep scepticism about economic planning. Who, then, were this young generation of Tory intellectuals? King gave various names, all under forty, and they included David Howell (Conservative Political Centre), William Rees-Mogg (*Sunday Times*), Geoffrey Howe (founder of the Bow Group, now an MP) and Nigel Lawson (just named as next editor of the *Spectator*). All of them, according to King, shared 'a conviction that the new Toryism must be considerably more radical than anything known in the fifties'. Or in a nutshell: 'Their vision is, to put it crudely, of a more humane and civilised United States.'[11]

Of far more immediate concern to perhaps surprisingly many people, the vexed issue of Rhodesia, lurking on the political margins for several years, was now increasingly front and centre. 'Set fair for Unilateral Declaration of Independence' reckoned on 8 October the clerical diarist James Allen about that country's white leader, Ian Smith, adamantine in his opposition to black majority rule in anyone's lifetime, notwithstanding the clear wishes to the contrary of the British government and indeed the Commonwealth as a whole. Nine days later, as Gerald Nabarro insisted in the *News of the World* that 'Rhodesians are British to the core and among the most loyal of all Her Majesty's subjects', that 'there must be no bludgeoning or blackmailing Rhodesia into submission', and that 'we must not, in any circumstances, be led into a declaration of war against our own kith and kin, which is what sanctions, economic or military, would mean', the *Sunday Telegraph* published the results of a Gallup poll revealing that, should Smith declare UDI, there was indeed only minority support for banning trade with a 'rebel' Rhodesia or sending in British troops (30 and 29 per cent respectively). Allen was broadly on their side. 'It seems very wrong,' he wrote on the 23rd after the news that Wilson was shortly to fly out to Salisbury to try to stay Smith's hand, 'that a white minority of 200,000 should want to dominate a situation where 3 or 4 million black people are also inhabitants.' And: 'Much as one sympathises with the white people of Rhodesia, who after all are our brothers, the moral force of the argument in favour of the majority must in these days obviously prevail.' Three days later, speaking during a British Council of Churches meeting at Aberdeen, so too – with rather more impact – the Archbishop of Canterbury, Dr Michael Ramsey. 'If the British Government thought it practicable to use force for the protection of the rights of the majority of the Rhodesian people,' he declared, 'then I think that as Christians we have to say that it will be right to use force to that end.'

He was not courting mass popularity. 'This has caused a storm of indignation which reveals only too clearly that the last thing the British public wants is the use of force or sanctions in Rhodesia,' recorded Crossman. 'They are prepared to see us standing up for what is right but they wouldn't tolerate a war against fellow white men who are also British subjects.' A highly charged public flashpoint came on Saturday the 30th, later on the day that Wilson, back from fruitless talks in Salisbury, had – perhaps foolishly in a tactical sense, quite apart from the intrinsic rights and wrongs – made a broadcast promising no use of British force should UDI be declared. The occasion was *BBC-3*; the prominent Tory politician Quintin Hogg laid into Ramsey ('you don't find the Roman Catholics and the Jews commenting on public affairs'); and John Bird valiantly countered, citing how two of the archbishop's most prominent Tory critics, the right-wing backbenchers Bernard Braine and Gilbert Longden, had back at the time of Suez nine years earlier vigorously supported the use of force and sanctions. 'What's the difference between the Suez crisis and the present crisis?' asked Bird in a voice impersonating an MP at a Conservative rally. 'The difference is that in Rhodesia we'll be sending in troops to fight white men but in Suez we were sending in troops to fight bloody awful wogs.'[12]

Elsewhere, the second half of October began on Saturday the 16th with Jimmy Greaves's stunning, eight-touch, instantly legendary dribble and finish against Manchester United, to Kenneth Wolstenholme's backdrop of 'he changes direction so well . . . beautiful football . . . what a great goal'; while on the Sunday, as Crossman confessed himself torn between his parental and his socialist instincts about the education of his eight-year-old son ('if Patrick goes to the Dragon he will within a matter of months be learning Latin and Greek and forging ahead intellectually', whereas 'if he stays in the state system – in the village school and then in Banbury – he will develop at a far slower rate and his whole social life will be entirely different'), as Basingstoke's

Church Street Methodist church held a special farewell service ahead of demolition for town development, and as *Call My Bluff* made its debut (viewers praising team leaders Frank Muir and Robert Morley, observing that Muir's Marjorie Proops and Alan Simpson made 'a far better' impression than Morley's Celia Johnson and William Douglas-Home, and finding that Robin Ray in the chair was inclined to 'ramble on'), Keith McBride kept his diary up to date with the grimmest of stories: 'There has been a murder hunt going on for some days, on a report that several bodies were buried on a lonely moorland. A girl's "remains" – the BBC's word – have been found. Vast crowds of sight-seers turned up.' On Monday, social class again in Crossman's diary, speculating that, in the difficult area of ongoing pit closures, it was perhaps because his ministerial colleague Fred Lee was working class that he was 'handling the miners far more savagely than I would ever dare to do'; late that afternoon, directly after the Spinners in *Dance and Skylark* and directly before the six o'clock news that was in fact at 5.55, another debut as for five addictive minutes Eric Thompson took viewers into the world of *The Magic Roundabout* (episode one: 'Mr Rusty Meets Zebedee'); next day's *Sun* included Susan Barnes (aka Mrs Crosland) interviewing Lord Goodman ('I don't make moral judgements, and I'm very interested in people') over lunch at Claridge's ('his great bulk moves majestically across the room', in his 'unbuttoned double-breasted suit'); episode two was 'Zebedee Starts the Roundabout'; and Henry St John, in his lodgings at Acton, recorded with appropriate solemnity that 'for the first time since I came here in 1948, a holder for toilet paper was screwed to the wall of the water-closet'; on Wednesday (episode three, 'The Children Try to Win a Surprise'), Peter Blake's new show opened at the Robert Fraser Gallery ('engaging rather than engrossing' according to one critic, 'the artist as fan' according to another), as did the London Motor Show at Earls Court (the press reporting how 'thousands of first-day visitors swarmed around a stand bedecked with paper lanterns to see the first Japanese cars ever displayed there', with visionary car importer John Pride extolling in particular the virtues of Toyota's Corona saloon, cheaper than a Rover or Jaguar yet possessing 'more refinement than our bread-and-butter cars'); before next day, Thursday the 21st ('Florence Gets a Surprise'), proved to be one of the key dates in Welsh history – the official opening of Llyn Celyn, a huge reservoir just to the north of Bala that had been created, through the highly controversial flooding of what had once been the Tryweryn Valley (including the hamlet of Welsh-speaking Capel Celyn), in order to supply Liverpool with drinking water. Uniformed members of the Free Wales Army did their best to disrupt proceedings; at least 300 people (including the Archdruid of Wales) demonstrated in noisy protest; a former farmer, 65-year-old Owen Jones, whose fifty-five acres were now submerged, told an English reporter that 'like so many others I have lost my happiness'; R. S. Thomas had his inspiration for 'Reservoirs' (mourning '. . . the smashed faces / Of the farms with the stone trickle / Of their tears down the hills' side'); and Welsh nationalism would for many years take its cue from a graffito on the stone wall of a ruined cottage near Llanrhystud, Aberystwyth – painted by a young author and journalist, Meic Stephens – which bore the simple message 'Cofiwch Drywerył' ('Remember Tryweryn').[13]

Friday's *Spectator* had Stuart Hood noting in relation to *Panorama* that 'Richard Dimbleby seems less pontifical these days'; no Zebedee and co. this afternoon, but instead *Junior Points of View*, presented by Sarah Ward and Muriel Young; 'a second body, a boy's, has been found,' recorded McBride, with the diarist wondering 'if the police have stumbled on one of these orgy groups'; next day the latest issue of *London Life* included a lengthy, admiring profile by B. S. Johnson of his friends the brutalist architects and theoreticians Peter and Alison Smithson, with whom the experimental novelist clearly identified as fellow 'pioneers of the Modern Movement' battling in the face of 'reactionaries'; up in Glasgow this afternoon, the latest iteration of the Rangers–Celtic rivalry, at Hampden Park in the final of the Scottish League Cup, included protracted, drowning-out jeering by Celtic fans during the playing of the National Anthem, an ill-tempered match ('men went for men, tripping, kicking, hacking and jersey-pulling were rife') followed immediately afterwards by over a dozen arrests as Rangers supporters ran on to the pitch to attack the victorious Celtic players (doing an ill-advised lap of honour, with trophy held aloft), while as the evening unfolded not only were bricks and bottles hurled at a Rangers' supporters' bus driving through the Gorbals, but violent scenes on a steamer about to sail for Belfast eventually saw nineteen Glasgow policemen on board for the trip; down south, Pat Scott marked her fortieth birthday ('after tea Ted & I went for a drink, we drove up to Square Rigger in London Bridge'); on Sunday, a meeting of some sixty delegates from parents' protest committees and old boys' associations, as well as headmasters and school governors, all of them strongly committed to the preservation of grammar schools and as equally strongly opposed to the government's policy on comprehensives, led to the formation of a National Educational Association 'to safeguard parents' freedom of choice in secondary schooling', with Richard Pedley, headmaster of Chislehurst and Sidcup Grammar School, nominated as acting president; next day, a newly published official report on the status of the Welsh language in law and administration rejected bilingualism as both impractical and poorly supported, but recommended the 'principle of equal validity' in Wales and Monmouthshire for the Welsh and English languages; almost unprecedently, Dimbleby was missing from that evening's *Panorama*, but later on one young diarist, Avril Sandall, went to bed with her husband, where ('v. cosy') they listened on the Light Programme to *I'm Sorry, I'll Read That Again*; next day's press included reportage on a still notorious town ('Smethwick – a whiff of Alabama in the Midlands'), a survey of the TV-watching habits of 4,218 Bristol schoolchildren (average viewing time of nearly eighteen hours a week, with 'a preference for ITV, crime, comedy and record programmes'), and the latest Ministry of Labour figures for family spending, revealing that only 7 per cent of 3,244 sample families had full or partial central heating, and only 22 per cent a telephone, whereas 80 per cent had a television; in Keighley, the elderly Gladys Hague and her sister 'bought a nice plastic linen basket 39/11'; Dimbleby was now in hospital, at St Thomas', with 'a suspected gallbladder infection'; and at Buckingham Palace, this Tuesday the 26th was MBEs day. Outside the railings, scenes of mass teenage hysteria and a struggling thin blue line; inside the Palace, some eighty people due to receive honours gathered that morning in an anteroom, with a queue swiftly forming to get the autographs of the Beatles. 'Four slim young men in dark lounge suits and dark ties,' recalled one of the parental autograph hunters, newsreader Robert Dougall, himself also due to receive an MBE. 'Nothing flamboyant about their dress although Ringo Starr's suit had eight buttons down the front and George Harrison's tailor had given him epaulettes and buttoned pockets. There they stood, all very well behaved, with their longish hair and pale green faces.' Then came the march along 'a seemingly endless corridor' with 'miles of red carpet'; and as Ringo was heard to observe, 'Cyril Lord could make a fortune in this place'. Then the final wait to go up – alphabetical within the MBEs, but the Beatles due to do it as a group – and Dougall heard someone ask them if they were nervous. 'Yes, we are a bit,' answered John, 'but we'll be all right when we go into our routine.' Routine indeed . . . And when the Queen asked how long they'd been together, Paul's 'Oh, for many years' was speedily trumped by Ringo's 'Forty years'. 'Are you the one who started it?' she then naturally asked Ringo. 'No,' he replied, 'I was the last to join. I'm the little fellow.'[14]

'Fog,' wrote Judy Haines in her diary that evening, carefully underlining the ominous word. 'Rather worrying with clocks altered making the daylight ceasing one hour earlier, for John travelling home. It is also a nuisance – this hour back – making our time different from Continent; and my drying time shortened abruptly by one hour.' Fog indeed, and, in the early hours in atrocious weather conditions, a Vickers Vanguard from Edinburgh, on its third attempt to land at Heathrow, smashed into the runway before skidding in flames for almost an hour – resulting in the deaths of all thirty-six passengers and crew, and perhaps putting in perspective MCC's special meeting next day at Lord's, after members had protested about their annual subscriptions going up from £7 to £9.

On Friday, the Brunswick label released the Who's 'My Generation', Pete Townshend's anthem for youth ('the lyric is topical and loaded with teenage appeal', noted *NME*'s Derek Johnson, 'about the snooty approach of some adults to youngsters'); Frederick Ward and his wife acquired the third stove of their married life ('one of the smallest models but suitable for Darby and Joan'); Frances Partridge went to a Labour by-election meeting (for the Cities of London and Westminster seat) and was thoroughly unimpressed by Ray Gunter, 'a fat little man like a Nonconformist schoolmaster' who 'stood soapily wringing plump hands and raising insincere eyebrows while he talked either about how much his mother had loved him (and he repeated her words of wisdom) or praised the British people's power to face facts', all adding up to what she called 'a grocer's view of politics'; Veronica Lee, in Leeds, saw *Help!* ('I quite enjoyed it and it demanded nothing from me'); next day, the *Western Mail* quoted the quite recently elected students' union president at Cardiff University, Neil Kinnock, demanding funding for a new SU building and lamenting 'the fantastic rate at which large blocks of offices are going up while we have to bargain over something as necessary as this – virtually a welfare association for students'; Joe Ackerley noted that, in James Joll's review in the current *Listener* of A. J. P. Taylor's newly published (and instantly best-selling) *English History, 1914–1945*, the magazine had for the first time printed the word 'fuck'; in the football world, while newspaper readers digested the unquietly confident words ('Age does not count . . . It's what you know about football that matters . . . I know I am better than the 500 or so managers who have been sacked since the war') of 29-year-old Brian Clough, newly appointed manager of Hartlepool United (propping up the Fourth Division, but winning 3–1 at Bradford City that afternoon); B. S. Johnson was on *Observer* duty at the Den to watch Millwall play Grimsby Town on a late-October pitch 'even this early clearly showing itself a child of the father and mother of a mudpatch it later becomes'; as usual, some seven million pools punters checked the results; and late that night, less than five years after he and his wife Vivien had won £152,319 on the pools and proceeded to spend, spend, spend, the 27-year-old Yorkshire ex-miner Keith Nicholson fatally crashed his new sky-blue Jaguar on the A1 near his home at Garforth as he returned from the races at Catterick.[15]

Nothing fancy or Jag-like about a green, two-door Morris Minor registered on Monday, 1 November 1965 – still going strong ('you can guarantee it will start') in 2014, its proud owner John Davies, 84-year-old retired train driver from Aberystwyth, would tell the *Daily Telegraph*; hours after gales had wrecked three of the eight new cooling towers at Ferrybridge C power station near Pontefract, the month began on *Coronation Street* with Ken Barlow getting a letter from the GPO informing him that the new phone of his next-door neighbour Dennis Tanner would be a party line with his; the long-running story of Tony Benn and the newly designed postage stamps ended next day with Wilson categorically telling the Postmaster General that the Queen did not want her head removed ('she is a nice woman, and you absolutely charmed her into saying yes when she didn't really mean it'); 'I do not care much for Mr Heath,' reflected Vere Hodgson on the 3rd, adding that 'at the moment he has no magic'; and that evening at Manchester's Palace Theatre – a fortnight after it should have opened in Birmingham, only to fall victim to an acrimonious dispute between composer Lionel Bart and director Joan Littlewood – the lavish, much-touted musical *Twang!!* (based on the life of Robin Hood) was unveiled to what one paper called 'a cool reception' from the audience. Bart, though, remained optimistic: 'I believe this will be my biggest success since *Oliver*.'

Twang!! was not the only theatrical event this Wednesday evening, as Edward Bond's *Saved*, directed by William Gaskill, opened at the Royal Court – where it managed to evade the censorship of the Lord Chamberlain (Lord Cobbold, former governor of the Bank of England) through being a 'club production' for members of the English Stage Society. Set in working-class south London, the instantly notorious scene was when a gang of youths (the actors including Tony Selby, Dennis Waterman and Ronald Pickup) stoned to death a baby in a pram, after first daubing it with excrement. 'The waves of shock in the theatre were almost audible,' noted one observer, adding that there followed cries of 'revolting' and 'dreadful', as well as the noise of people leaving their seats. 'The most obscene, obnoxious, nauseating and revolting play I've ever seen in my life' was the seasoned verdict of Anthony Heap when he got home, and next morning a trio of critics fully agreed: *The Times*'s still anonymous drama critic (in fact Irving Wardle) did not quarrel with Bond's right to treat violent themes, but unequivocally loathed his play's 'self-admiring jokes and gloating approach to moments of brutality and erotic humiliation'; the *Daily Telegraph*'s W. A. Darlington wrote of his own 'cold disgust'; and the *Daily Express*'s Herbert Kretzmer condemned outright 'this revolting and distasteful play . . . peopled by characters who, almost without exception, are foul-mouthed, dirty-minded, illiterate and barely to be judged on any recognisable human level at all'. The odd semi-defence was entered elsewhere, but overall during the next week or so the balance of critical opinion remained distinctly negative, prompting Bond to write an indignant open letter defending himself. Perhaps he was simply too early. 'You can learn everything you need to know about playwriting by studying *Saved*,' Sarah Kane three decades later would tell Mark Ravenhill; while Ravenhill himself, born seven months after the play's first night, would recall how, coming across *Saved* in 1986 as a twenty-year-old, it not only in its small details lodged itself irrevocably in his mind ('the way the young characters offer each other sex in a totally casual way, as though they are offering cigarettes; the bitter rows over the ownership of a copy of the *Radio Times*; the uncomprehending love that the mother of the dead baby gives to Fred, leader of the stoning'), but evoked a world he immediately recognised: 'The world of listless, rootless youth, casual acts of sex and random acts of violence in south London parks . . . Here was a play that breathed exactly the same air as I did.'[16]

One of the play's fiercest critics in November 1965 itself was the *Sunday Times*'s J. W. Lambert, reckoning it went 'well past that point' when 'both life and art are irretrievably debased'; and he finished his review by arguing that it had been 'one in the eye for the theatre that the first performance of *Saved* should take place on the evening that Nell Dunn's *Up the Junction* was shown on BBC television (with Tony Selby again excellent in it, to point up the contrast), reaching out – too frenetically but with so much more warmth and truth – into this same grubby maelstrom of spiritual under-nourishment'. In the case of *Up the Junction*, directed by Ken Loach, the 'grubby maelstrom' of this most controversial, high-profile *Wednesday Play* so far was Battersea, setting for Nell Dunn's recent collection of short stories about the lives of mainly young working-class women, 'a patchwork of dead-end jobs, late shifts, dirty streets, crumbling houses, bawdy language and casual sex' (in the words of Loach's biographer, Anthony Hayward). At the very heart of the play lay the issue of abortion, still illegal, and here carried out by Winny, kindly faced family friend of unmarried, seventeen-year-old Rube:

> We watch Rube walking across a common after the procedure [wrote Clair Wills in 2023], then sweating and screaming in pain; the panic of those around her; the phone call for help. When her body quietens, we know that the foetus has been expelled. We imagine it lying somewhere just out of shot. And at the same time, we listen to the matter-of-fact voice of the doctor explaining that in his surgery he sees a woman every week looking for an abortion, that 35 women die every year of botched abortions [a slightly higher figure than official statistics], and that's not counting the many women who are

> unable to conceive afterwards. Viewers – and there were ten million of them – were forced to see *Up the Junction*'s storyline as a public health matter, and it became part of a political campaign.

'But', adds Wills, 'it was also personal. Behind the statistic of 35 deaths a year was the mother of Tony Garnett, *Up the Junction*'s story editor. She had died of septicaemia following a back-street abortion in the early 1940s, when Tony was five years old. Nineteen days later his father committed suicide.'

What did those ten million viewers make of it? The Viewing Panel awarded an RI of 58, with the audience research report highlighting four individual reactions to illustrate 'the sharp division of opinion':

> Powerful and exciting. *(Student)*
>
> Too coarse. I feel it would have been better to have left *something* to the imagination. *(Secretary)*
>
> A pity this young woman [Nell Dunn] could not have used her talent for writing on less sordid matters. *(Probation officer)*
>
> A play to make you think; it certainly succeeded in startling me out of my smug, snug middle-class wits. *(Receptionist)*

Significantly, the performances by those taking part – including Carol White as, in her obituarist's words, 'a blonde, mini-skirted floosie' – were 'often described (even by those who did not care for the play itself) as amazingly natural and realistic – "terrifyingly so," in some cases (such as the fight between husband and wife) it was said'. While in general, as one of the panel's members put it: 'Their clothes, make-up, everything, seemed just right, and only the appearance of one or two familiar faces reminded me that it *was* a play.'

Later that busy Wednesday evening, Dunn and Loach both appeared on *Late Night Line-Up*. 'A tearful Nell Dunn answered telephoned complaints from South London,' noted the *New Statesman*'s D. A. N. Jones. 'One caller, though objecting to his neighbours being portrayed as "subhuman", made the more valid criticism that the play looked like a documentary, claiming to present a cross-section of Battersea people.' Another critic, the *Sunday Times*'s Maurice Wiggin, was unimpressed by the 'uneasy compound of self-righteousness and pugnacity' of Dunn and Loach themselves. 'To hear them go on, you'd think they'd invented integrity.' As for the reviews themselves, there were not that many in Thursday's papers, with perhaps the stand-out ones being by Kenneth Eastaugh in the *Mirror* ('one of the most beautiful, and moving, and funny programmes I have seen on TV') and by Nancy Banks-Smith, just starting this week her stint on the *Sun*. Although largely praising 'a slice of South London served up steaming', she did still wonder whether it was truly suitable for television: 'It's hard for a family to watch life shown as bloody and near the bone as that. In the living-room. With the light on. It would have been less embarrassing in the cinema.' Her doubts seem to have been expressed in spades by many other viewers, as they bombarded the BBC switchboard to complain about the play's subject matter and treatment ('"working girl" play upsets viewers'); Mary Whitehouse, leader of the Clean-up TV Campaign, fired off a letter on the 4th to the health minister, Kenneth Robinson, describing the play as 'full of sexual titillation', insisting about the horror-of-abortion aspect that 'the BBC's concern with the problem was phoney', and generally accusing the corporation of being 'determined to do everything in their power to present promiscuity as normal'; while two days later, the *Daily Mail*'s headline was an expressive 'This must be just about THE LIMIT'. Yet were the majority of viewers *really* so indignant? After all, 58 was a far from nugatory RI. And in Sunday's *Observer*, the paper's TV critic Maurice Richardson reported, apparently from first-hand experience, the conversation about the play that had taken place on Thursday morning in a saloon bar somewhere in 'subtopia':

> The impressionistic production, which stressed the documentary rather than the dramatic element, and wasn't always dead easy to follow, didn't seem to have foxed them unduly. Nobody objected that it wasn't really a play at all. And there were only a few sniggers about the drawers in the dialogue. The message, that this was very much what some girls really are like, had got across. Some said it was too near the mark altogether. And of course that scarifying abortion sequence played the part of the wages of sin in melodrama, tipped the moral balance and enabled the Norns to wag their fingers.

Undeniably, then, some finger-wagging, some moral outrage. But also, as the receptionist said, 'a play to make you think'.[17]

That Thursday the 4th, the new issue of *Country Life* included an advertisement for the Spastics Society ('For a few weeks we thought our first grandchild was a spastic . . . As it turned out she wasn't . . . But we were so thankful we went off and wrote the Spastics into our wills . . .'); a double blow for Bernard Delfont, producer of *Twang!!*, as first Benedict Nightingale panned it in the *Guardian* ('this rambling, inconsequential and distressingly, intolerably, wickedly long show', not even redeemed by Barbara Windsor in her familiar 'chirrupy Cockney sparrow' persona) and then its director, Joan Littlewood, walked out, never to return; that afternoon in a cul-de-sac on Glasgow's south side, Frederick West, driving his four-ton ice-cream van, accidentally ran over and killed a three-year-old boy he had recently become friendly with; that evening, while *Man Alive* launched on BBC2 as British television's first documentary series to rely on interviewing ordinary people rather than experts in order to report on social issues, Avril Sandall in Sutton Coldfield had a 'nice evening in' – 'did ironing & washing & watched Val Doonican show' – as she waited for her partner to return home; the overnight by-election news was that the Tory majority in the Cities of London and Westminster had been severely cut; Friday's *Daily Mail* included the headline 'The Bank of England orders two computers' as well as Cecil Wilson reviewing the new film *Shakespeare Wallah*, where he was much struck by nineteen-year-old Felicity Kendall ('a round-faced little charmer with the poise of a young Vivien Leigh'); at the Civic Trust's conference to discuss Professor Sir Leslie Martin's controversial Whitehall redevelopment plan, Charles Pannell, Minister of Public Buildings and Works, declared of the condemned Foreign Office that 'whatever is said in praise of the famous skyline – the façade imposed on Scott by Palmerston – inside it is a squalid office slum, incapable of treatment to bring it up to the standards and working conditions which are reasonably expected nowadays', but John Betjeman was adamant that, quite apart from being architecturally 'a very important building', it really was 'not at all that slummy inside' – even though on his recent tour he had been accompanied by 'a very adverse civil servant' trying his hardest to show its worst side; Guy Fawkes Night in Wales featured in Penarth some 300 youths smashing the windows of shops, restaurants and hotels, and in Cardiff some 200 youths throwing bricks at firemen answering a call, perhaps fake; and David Dimbleby issued a statement revealing that his father had been suffering from cancer for over five years and that he had 'asked me to explain this because he is very strongly opposed to the idea of cancer being an unmentionable disease'. The national shock was instant, so too the praise for his dramatic lifting of an almost universal taboo, but the reaction of Barrow's elderly diarist was more measured. 'I never thought of Richard Dimbleby as a hero,' reflected Nella Last. 'Poor man, it looks as if his useful long life will soon be over.'[18]

Kenneth Williams was in Oxford on Saturday, enjoying a 'sumptuous' lunch at Lincoln College with two of the fellows. 'Conversation', however, 'was mediocre. Certainly not of the level one might expect from such academic minds. V. G. [chaplain-cum-historian Vivian Green, possible inspiration for John le Carré's George Smiley] said he liked the Beatles and I told him that he ought to know better.' That afternoon, an hour or so after Arkle at Sandown Park had put in his finest-ever performance, earning a rapturous reception in the unsaddling enclosure as he comfortably saw off Mill House to win the Gallaher Gold Cup despite carrying an extra 16 lb, Brentford's goalkeeper Chic Brodie picked up a hand grenade – fortunately dead, it turned out – thrown into his goalmouth from the away end full of Millwall fans; repeated plays of 'My Generation' spoke to seventeen-year-old Laurence Marks about the awfulness of his mum and dad's generation ('They simply don't want to understand that things, their world is changing and I ask myself, "will I be like them when I get to their age?"'); in the posh Sundays, the TV critics were not solely preoccupied by *Up the Junction*, as Richardson confessed himself 'hopelessly addicted' to *The Avengers* ('its dreamlike quality, reinforced by that clever stylisation, has a curiously hypnotic suspending effect' and 'enables you to overlook the most lunatic inconsistencies'), while Wiggin, in his farewell piece before handing over the job to Adrian Mitchell, accused BBC1's chiefs of foolishly trying to compete with ITV on the latter's terms ('ITV has long since clinched an association with the working class, who regard it as "their" programme'), adding that the channel not only risked alienating its traditional middle-class viewers, but that, anyway, 'serials like *United!* and *The Newcomers*, which seem designed to win over the ITV supporter, simply are not good enough to do the job'; on Monday the 8th, the *Daily Telegraph*'s Colin Welch wrote a lengthy piece strongly in favour of a choice-enhancing voucher system in state education ('the slum parent who cares can free his children from the oppression of their background'), royal assent was given to the abolition of the death penalty and the latest episode of *Steptoe and Son* had the old man ('Conservative junk is better quality than Labour junk') at serious political odds with Harold ('all junk is equal!'); next day, the press reported that *Stars and Garters*, its new series since early October set in the saloon bar and no longer presented by Ray Martine, was going to do an about-turn and revert to the public bar, with Rediffusion explaining that 'viewers want a roistering sort of pub sing-song, not the saloon-bar cabaret style'; the Queen's Speech dismayed Labour left-wingers by its absence of commitment to steel nationalisation, a perhaps unsurprising omission given the perilous thinness of the government's parliamentary majority, but did at least formally commit to the establishment of a public schools commission; a meeting of the Leicester Education Committee demonstrated only tepid support on the Labour side for the comprehensive principle; and Judy Haines in Chingford reflected on a domestic episode. 'He replaced faulty valve and was gone in ten minutes,' she noted about how, with the television (rented from British Relay) on the blink, an engineer had come by in the afternoon. 'How they hung about,' she went on, 'when it was our own set (not rented), always taking it away for at least a week.'[19]

'The day they buried Socialism' was the *Daily Mail*'s gleeful headline about the Queen's Speech; Peter Preston in the *Guardian* declared that it was 'now plain' that 'the integration of the private and public educational sectors will be a long and tortuous, but relatively painless, business'; *The Times* published a letter – whose signatories included Brian Abel-Smith, Edward Ardizzone and Barbara Robb – expressing 'shock' at 'the treatment of geriatric patients in certain mental hospitals, one of the evils being the practice of stripping them of their personal possessions', and declaring their intention 'to collect evidence of ill-treatment of geriatric patients in mental hospitals throughout the country, to demonstrate the need for a national investigation', in the hope that ultimately this would 'lead to the securing of effective and humane control over these hospitals by the Ministry [of Health], which seems at present to be lacking'; and the *Sun* profiled ('this attractive 55-year-old wife of a businessman') and quoted ('I object to programmes which persuade young people that immorality is normal or leave them confused on moral issues') the increasingly prominent Mary Whitehouse, whose Clean-up TV Campaign, launched a year and a half earlier, had persuaded almost half a million people to sign their manifesto. That evening, while Anthony Heap was at the Mermaid enjoying Bill Naughton's Bolton-set *Spring and Port Wine* ('richly endowed with good humour and appealing sentiment'), and while Desmond Hackett of the *Express* was filing his report on the home side's unconvincing 2–1 win at Wembley over Northern Ireland ('it is so inescapably obvious that the World Cup Willies are still very much with England'), Grace Taylor in Ruislip was looking back on not one of the great Wednesdays: 'Polished hall & part of the lounge – finished up polish on dining room. Rained on & off all day. Should have got on with the chair but didn't feel like it SO READ A BOOK!!!! Fed up to the teeth – I could scream! Oh what a life!' Next day, Thursday the 11th, was Armistice Day. But was it perhaps, forty-seven years and twenty years respectively after the two world wars, and almost a year after Churchill's death, losing some of its potency? 'Even we who remember the ritual of the first Armistice celebrations are inclined to overlook the date,' confessed Frederick Ward in his diary. 'Very few people', he added, 'wear poppies and there is no 2 minutes silence.'[20]

It was, in any case, an overshadowed Armistice Day. 'In the middle of our tutorial,' recorded Veronica Lee in Leeds about that morning's major news, by now widely expected but still a shock when it happened, 'someone rang up Tony [the tutor] to announce that Rhodesia had declared U.D.I.' That evening, Wilson broadcast to the nation, promising through economic sanctions to make life distinctly uncomfortable for the rebel regime. 'I am no lover of compulsory political listening,' observed Nancy Banks-Smith, 'but this was an extraordinarily potent performance suggesting that men really do expand to match the size of the occasion.' 'Rhodesia was a wonderful bonus,' Anthony Howard would reflect years later about the domestic political aspect for this still relatively new and untested PM. 'It enabled him to play the national leader and no one really could be against him. There were wild right-wingers in the Monday Club who were pro-Smithy and kith and kin and all that but even respectable Conservatives had to condemn it. He was on a winning streak there.' Life indeed was now difficult for his opposite number, with Cecil King spending social time with Heath ('jokes about deep-frozen smile quite unjustified') a few days after UDI and noting that he 'clearly has difficulties with his party over Rhodesia where, as he admitted, he is walking a knife-edge between the actions of the Conservatives in office and the views of the Salisbury wing of the party'. 'Salisbury' was Lord Salisbury, a strong supporter of Smith, while in the Commons the most prominent pro-Smith voice belonged to the former minister Julian Amery, fiercely opposed to sanctions and nicely described by his obituarist Patrick Cosgrave as 'his Imperialist father's son to the core'. What of public opinion as a whole? It is not easy to be absolutely sure, but a Gallup poll carried out in the week immediately before UDI revealed a significant shift of opinion over the last two and a half years, when faced by the fundamental question (irrespective of sanctions or anything else) of whether Britain was right or wrong to withhold independence:

	April 1963	*November 1965*
Right	28	60
Wrong	38	15
Don't Know	34	25

Among that 15 per cent was almost certainly a fair proportion of readers of the *Daily Mail*, with the paper's letters page noting four days after UDI not only 'a vigorous response' in its postbag, but also that 95 per cent of those letters were in support of Smith – including these three:

> Before indulging in long-distance idealism, people should ask themselves – Would they be prepared and happy to be ruled by a Negro majority? *(Richard Wise, Hightrees House, Nightingale Lane, SW12)*

If Mr Wilson considers – or allows – force to be used in Rhodesia, he will have to be prepared for a large number of Smethwicks. *(S. Hudson, Allenby Road, Swinton, Lancashire)*

Good luck to Mr Smith. At least he thinks about future generations of white people in Rhodesia, which is more than our politicians do here. Perhaps by the year 2050 WE shall have a coloured majority and a coloured Government. *(R. Usher, Melville Court, Goldhawk Road, W12)*

Admittedly three days later, with the letters still flooding in, support for Smith was now down to a 5:1 ratio, but it was hardly a major change of heart. Most of the diarists this November were relatively silent on the subject, but Vere Hodgson's thoughts on the 10th, a day before UDI, were perhaps representative of what one might arguably call 'old-fashioned' rather than nakedly racist thinking. 'He is a most attractive man . . . a wonderful war record as a pilot [in the RAF], a firm chin and an unquarrelsome manner,' she wrote about Smith. 'I am sure the Africans will get majority rule one day, but they must work for it and show they can do it. So long as they refuse to take any part in the government at all because they can't all be prime ministers immediately, I have no sympathy with them. We all have to learn our trade gradually . . .' Of course, for the really big picture, there was always the *Pontefract and Castleford Express*. 'UDI', its headline declared on the 18th, 'will not hurt local firms.'[21]

UDI was not this November's only claim to fame. Late on the evening of Saturday the 13th – after a disenchanted B. S. Johnson, coming to the end of his time as a regular football reporter, had spent a weary, bitterly cold afternoon watching a Brentford–Yeovil Town cup tie ('not violent, not even crude', but 'just unskilful and tedious, containing unbelievably little worth describing'); and about the same time that Judy Haines, trying to keep a tight rein on her teenage daughter Pam, lamented to herself 'what a battle it is with so many parents who are "sports"' – Kenneth Tynan was asked on *BBC-3* by Robert Robinson whether, as the National Theatre's literary adviser, he would permit a play in which sexual intercourse took place. 'Oh I think so, certainly,' he replied behind puffs of smoke from his cigarette, possibly vying with his fellow guest Mary McCarthy as to who could be the more liberal-minded. 'I doubt if there are very many rational people in this world,' he went on, 'to whom the word [at this point a palpable stammer] "fuck" is particularly diabolical or revolting or totally forbidden.' Although not the first time this particular four-letter word had been uttered on British television, this was the time that – as the BBC's phone lines became red-hot, and as Laurence Marks instantly predicted 'Tynan never gets invited on any television programme ever again' – viewers would always remember. 'Coventry: Is This Our Future?' was next day the big spread in the *Observer*'s colour magazine, with William Millinship calling it 'a rootless, supermarket civilisation' engaged in a 'ruthless drive after affluence', but still broadly applauding a city that had 'realised many of the dreams of the planners' and become home to 'a productive, highly-paid community that has scrapped traditional class divisions and outworn industrial habits'; Huw Wheldon, by now the BBC's controller of television programmes, told the press that he was 'surprised but not appalled' by Tynan's choice of language; and in the evening, as Ken Dodd, Johnny Hallyday, Dusty Springfield, Frank Ifield, Shirley Bassey and a female Japanese trick cyclist all did their stuff in ITV's recorded broadcast of the Royal Variety Performance, Tynan himself was at the Royal Court to chair a 'teach-in' on *Saved*, involving Bond as well as a range of critics – one of whom, Mary McCarthy, praised the infanticide scene for its 'delicate escalation'. The four-letter row hit its peak on Monday: the BBC expressing regret ('this is not a word that should be used on the air'), several dozen Tory MPs wanting action taken against the unrepentant offender, and (as Ned Sherrin, *BBC-3*'s unapologetic producer, would recall) a female teacher at a London infants' school trying to do the right thing:

> All morning they pestered her coyly to find out what 'that word' was. 'What was it now, miss?' She hedged all morning but by lunchtime her patience gave out and she submitted to the latest tease. 'What was that word, miss, on telly on Saturday? . . . What did he say?' She braced herself. 'He said, "fuck".' There was an audible groan of disappointment and one little boy muttered, 'Is that all? We thought he said "cunt"!'

The controversary certainly did not die overnight – the *Daily Express*'s William Barkley on Tuesday calling Tynan's four-letter word 'the bloodiest outrage I have ever known' – but life did move on, more or less. Later that day, the BBC's Talent Selection Group listened to a recent audition by David Bowie and the Lower Third, but were not blown away ('amateur-sounding vocalist who sings wrong notes and out of tune', according to one; 'the singer is a cockney type but not outstanding enough', reckoned another; 'a singer devoid of personality', thought a third); on Wednesday in the Commons, accusing the Labour government of having in its economic policy created 'the worst of both worlds', Iain Macleod coined the word whose golden age would arrive a decade later ('We have, not inflation on the one side and stagnation on the other, but both together, a sort of "stagflation" situation'); and in Bristol next day, the Co-operative Wholesale Society's Frederick Ward took the afternoon off, putting him in reflective mood:

> It was a welcome relief from the office atmosphere. My business life is taken up by an unending series of meetings which achieve little considering the time and expense involved. All around me I see inefficiencies. The sale room has its share of these and I ought to give more attention to them. If the remedies were obvious I would have to tackle them. As it is I am too lazy and unwilling to upset a reasonably adequate set up.

Perhaps relevantly, or perhaps not, the next page of his diary had, unusually for Ward, a newspaper cutting slipped in loose: it was Gavin Ewart's 'A Bad Moment', his timeless poem of the despair of a fifty-year-old advertising man.[22]

Anthony Crosland's week also had its moments, beginning on the Monday when the Comprehensive Schools Committee (CSC) issued its first bulletin. With Caroline Benn's name tactfully kept hidden, it detailed how, outside Wales, only London, Bristol and Coventry had so far made a substantial advance towards a fully comprehensive system; and it criticised Crosland not only for rejecting the comprehensive schemes of Liverpool, Luton and Stoke-on-Trent which did genuinely aim to produce all-through comprehensive schools, but also for accepting those of other local authorities (such as Doncaster, Cardiff, Wakefield and Middlesbrough) which in practice were, in the CSC's words, 'simply means of preserving the grammar schools as separate schools'. That evening, in the Commons, Crosland had a chat with Caroline's husband in the Tea Room. 'He was angry about the attack on him and said that all the facts were wrong,' noted Benn. 'We also discussed the public schools, where he is hoping to press on with the scheme for integrating them and feels that he is the only radical in the Government. It is all bunk but obviously the arrows of criticism have gone home and that's not a bad thing.' Two days later, on Wednesday the 17th, a lengthy story in the *Guardian* revealed that Crosland was going to receive that afternoon a petition signed by almost 14,000 Mancunians opposed to their city's proposed comprehensive schools plan. 'Premature', 'too much change' and 'too little progress' were among the objections raised in the accompanying memorandum of the Manchester Parents' Action Committee. Significantly, reported the article, 'many members are sympathetic to the principle of comprehensive education'; and among their arguments was that 'the present plan would lead to a proliferation of private schools which would place a premium on ability to pay rather than on natural ability', whereas 'a scheme carefully prepared and embodying the best aspects of the comprehensive principle might hold such promise of improved educational standards that the competitive attractiveness of private schools would be seriously diminished'. The exact chronology is slightly uncertain, but it was about this time that Crosland wrote a revealing memo for Cabinet. 'There is at present', he warned his colleagues, 'more public dissatisfaction about the differing standards of schools in the maintained sector than the difference between these schools and public schools, and about the eleven-plus examination than about the privileged education of wealthy families.' True enough, no doubt; but whatever Crosland's 'radical' claim to Benn, it hardly augured well for the political clout of the Public Schools Commission, the name of whose chairman was due shortly to be announced, along with its precise remit.[23]

For Daphne Meryon – an unstoppable force of a very distinct upper-middle-class type – Friday the 19th was the start of a long weekend, even by her strenuous standards a busy one full of purposeful activity:

> Up in good time; took Peter [her naval husband] and John Ellingham to station. Hurried through routine jobs and was at Warblington Church by 9.20 a.m. Arranged large vase of teazles and honesty and cleaned all chancel brass before Mrs St John & Mrs Geering arrived,

> but then left them to finish off. Changed on return and Bill Mansell drove me to catch 11.34. Had hamburger & coffee at Waterloo, then went fruitlessly to Pontings and back to A & N where I spent afternoon doing Christmas shopping. Met Peter in club [the United Services Club], where we had a room for the night. Bathed, changed, and taxi to Dorchester for Western Approaches reunion dinner . . .

That evening, venturing out of its usual West Country fastness, *Any Questions?* was at Dudley, its first-ever visit to the Midlands. 'Should obscene or rude words be used on television?' was, to audience laughter, a well-nigh inevitable question. Lord Boothby, seldom absent at such moments, declared that 'obscene and rude words are a good thing, and should be used as much as possible'; the educator-cum-mountaineer Jack Longland argued in roughly similar spirit that 'if there's one word that you may use and another word meaning exactly the same thing that you may not use, this seems to me wholly irrational'; Edward Boyle, predictably, was more cautious, saying that he was 'against using words calculated to offend'; and so, too, a recently elected Labour MP, Brian Walden, not only avowing that 'I myself would not deliberately set out to offend someone else's susceptibilities', but calling such behaviour 'rather an undergraduate kind of thing to do'. Not that any of this really mattered, for far more people this Friday were watching the BBC's overlapping coverage of Miss World, coming from the Lyceum Ballroom, fronted by David Jacobs (not yet seen as Freddy Grisewood's successor on *Any Questions?*), and won for the second year running by a Brit – 21-year-old Lesley Langley, the proverbial 'blue-eyed blonde', in her case from Weymouth, where until this point her life had been, she revealed, 'very dull'. Next day, Saturday, had the latest on *Twang!!* (still playing at Manchester, but its London opening date now put back to just before Christmas, with Bart admitting he needed 'that much time to get the show ready'); while Larkin that morning in Hull had, in his capacity as university librarian, a thoroughly awkward, even unsettling 'student encounter' with, he related to Monica Jones, 'a 3rd Yr Nigerian reported caught sneaking a book out':

> My staff said, yes, drop on him, no colour prejudice, he's always trying things on & being disagreeable when stopped. His professor

said, yes, he's been a disappointment, we've lent him money, bent over backwards – he hasn't told the truth, shuffled, lied – must treat him the same as everyone else. So I felt pretty sure of my mind. He turned up very punctually: I immediately taxed him with not wearing a gown, & he explained he had forgotten it, & to go back w[d] have made him late – dreadful dilemma! He had a soft, piteous perfectly-comprehensible voice, & I at once began to want to comfort him. Moving on to the offence, he explained exactly how it had happened, pure forgetfulness (like the gown), he had freely presented the book for inspection – he spoke very gently, yet eagerly, using his pink-palmed hands a certain amount, not being the slightest bit offensive. He had a broad, very black face. After about 5 minutes of this I said I couldn't ignore the report, read the Regulation out to him, and said I should fine him £3. The Finance Officer would write to him. It was awful – he sat absolutely crushed & still & silent, as if I'd told him he was to go back to Nigeria. In the end I got up & opened the door, & he got up and went out. As he passed me he said 'Good morning, sir,' leaving me feeling awful – either he has *perfected* a technique for dealing with Europeans, or he was a poor wronged black feller. O God! What do you think? It was his awful *limpness* that upset me: not a word after sentence had been passed. I wanted to rush after him & give him a fiver. But I had to do it. No good 'letting him go' when you do catch a n—, n—or not.

For Grace Taylor in Ruislip, not at all a bad Saturday ('made our first syphon of soda water & had a drink of it – jolly good it was'); and for Daphne Meryon, having stayed overnight at the United Services Club, another blockbuster of a day:

Woke to pouring rain, which continued all day. Had breakfast in Ladies Dining Room with a Captain & Mrs Lawford at next table, who had also been at last night's party. Peter and I caught 10.50 from Waterloo; I did a minimum of shopping in Market Parade and we had taxi home. I spent afternoon cooking and preparing for our dinner party, Peter helping, but both of us felt not quite our best. Peter took silver thimble round to Mrs Newell for her 25th Wedding Anniversary present (Tuesday was really the day, but I

> bought thimble in A & N yesterday). Had Serjeants and Margery Bammant to dinner; Peter met latter at station. Serjeants brought coloured slides of Valerie's wedding – rather too many – and finally took M. to station to catch 0015 train. So Peter and I rather late clearing up and getting to bed.

Another diarist, Anthony Heap, spent part of Sunday afternoon on a 'short' walk 'to see the site of the new King's Cross Coach Station' in Camley Street, due to open at the start of 1966. There, he found 'a grim, desolate thoroughfare hidden away among the gasometers behind King's Cross Station, with grimy coal depots along one side, iron girders of demolished buildings and abandoned wrecks of old cars on the other . . .' While by this time it was almost the last lap, for this weekend anyway, for the naval commander and his wife, a marathon finishing with only one possible – and thoroughly well-deserved – treat:

> Peter and I went to early service at Warblington, and Peter went to Matins as well, as he is duty sidesman. I spend part of morning cooking and preparing lunch, then went outside and cut out all old wood of '*cocktail*' rose. It was too wet after yesterday to dig shrub border. Peter and I spent afternoon giving Ena Harkness [a type of climbing rose] the same treatment despite very cold wind. Then warmed up by digging ground for broad beans, sowing seeds and covering with cloches. Judy [a daughter, away at university] phoned after lunch. I finished letter to her. Peter and I went round to see the Servowarm gas central heating fitting in a Mr & Mrs Acton's house in Denvilles [an area in Havant]. Sat in little room sewing and watched *Dr Finlay's Casebook*.[24]

Three days later, Wednesday the 24th, saw the publication of Crossman's White Paper, *The Housing Programme 1965 to 1970* – culmination of an autumn's hard toil, vividly recorded in his diary. In mid-October, setting aside 'a quiet weekend' at home in order 'to slave away at my own housing White Paper', as he sought to turn the 'voluminous mass of officialese' produced by his civil servants into something more like 'a military staff study' focused on 'what has to be done in order to achieve an annual output of half a million houses'; in late October, a meeting lasting almost two hours with builders ('ferociously hostile to any idea of collaborating with a socialist government') and building societies ('gradually began to join in the discussion'); a fortnight later, on UDI day as it happened, another meeting with those two key groups, who after the builders had 'spent most of their time complaining about the appalling difficulty of getting land', eventually fell into line; and on 18 November, formal clearance from the Cabinet for a housing policy which included not only 'new, very generous housing subsidies', but also 'a new philosophy of owner-occupation':

> It is a new thing for a Labour Government to admit that owner-occupation is a normal and natural way for people to live and that living in council houses is an exception to that rule. Of course we wooed the owner-occupier during the general election, but what the Party has never done before is to admit in public that if we give people favourable interest rates, in logic we have to make sure the land is available on which their houses can be built. And if we are going to take responsibility for providing the land, we must make the local authority feel as much concerned with owner-occupation as with providing rented accommodation.

'That is quite a shift of philosophy,' concluded Crossman, 'and that is why it is strange that we spent only eight minutes discussing the White Paper.'

In practice, once the White Paper had been published, not all observers fully perceived that philosophical shift – perhaps unsurprisingly, given that whereas in 1964 only 155,000 out of the year's 374,000 completed dwellings had been in the public sector, now the intention was that the 500,000 annual target would be undertaken equally between the public and private sectors, i.e. 250,000 each for council housing and for owner-occupation. 'SOCIALIST HOUSING' harrumphed the *Daily Telegraph* in an editorial next day, grumbling that 'all the financial inducements are to go to council house building and, for the foreseeable future, all the financial deterrents are to apply in the private sector'. Indeed:

> What confidence can there be that this perilous munificence will in fact succeed in producing more houses? Experience has shown that this result comes about from the liberation, not the restriction of private building; but high mortgage rates, regulated rents and anti-landlord legislation [a reference to the new Rent Act] will continue to impose restriction. Above all, there is still no firm guarantee that a vast proportion of the new subsidy will not go to those who could well house themselves.

Even so, the paper did somewhat grudgingly accept that there was in the White Paper 'a recognition of the importance of fostering owner-occupation as soon as the nation's economic circumstances permit'; which there certainly was, with the White Paper itself first noting 'a large and increasing demand for more houses for owner-occupation', then declaring that the housing plan needed in due course to go beyond that explicit demand 'and take account of what is probably an even larger suppressed demand for owner-occupation among the many families who cannot quite afford a mortgage on present terms'.

Yet whatever the public/private split over the coming years, was 500,000 overall completions a feasible annual target? *The Economist* shared the *Telegraph*'s doubts, emphasising that over the past six years owner-occupied houses built by private builders had 'forged ahead' of local authority building; and it argued that the new strategy of equally shared responsibility, to be furthered by the generous use of housing subsidies to relieve local authorities from the effects of high interest rates, would only have been a sound, sensible policy to adopt 'if local authorities had proved good agents in encouraging new and more productive ways of mass building of houses, but so far their record has been bleak'. Still, what no one denied was the overwhelming need for significantly more housing. Or as the *Guardian* put it in its largely positive but far from euphoric response to the White Paper: 'In Britain today some three million families still live either in slums, in near slums, or in grossly overcrowded conditions. This is a major evil which no humane and reasonably prosperous society should tolerate.'[25]

'She was interested in everything she saw – and seemed to like most things,' North Paddington School's headmaster, Tom Davies, told the press after the Queen on 25 November had paid her very first visit to a comprehensive. 'She put the staff and children at their ease more than anyone I have ever shown round. And the word comprehensive was not mentioned at all.' About the same time, there were 'grimaces' at Cabinet, recorded Barbara Castle, as Crosland 'introduced his memo on the public schools with the words, "This is a strictly insoluble problem."' Next day, a forty-eight-hour bakers' strike (in pursuit of a wage claim) continued in large parts of the country, seriously threatening bread supplies; announcements this Friday included the BBC's that they would definitely not be showing *The War Game*, with a nuclear attack on Kent now officially declared as unsuitable for general viewing, and Crossman's giving the go-ahead to Islington Council to demolish the Victorian houses on the Packington Estate and replace them with six-storey blocks of flats; Barking's new public library opened (soon afterwards to be welcomed by Pat Scott as 'really lovely – on 2 floors & very modern'); that evening, in the Marine Ballroom on Morecambe Central Pier, bandleader Alvin Atkins and his band bowed out after entertaining up to 2,000 dancers a night since 1948, to be followed on stage by a very different act, in the form of the Small Faces; on *Any Questions?*, after the team had been asked whether 'the incomes policy will ever work without enforcement by legislation', the three politicians present (Quintin Hogg, Shirley Williams and Jeremy Thorpe) all made a decent stab, but the novelist Henry Williamson simply said, 'I haven't the slightest idea what the question means'; and *New Statesman* readers pondered Seamus Heaney's review of Nell Dunn's collection of first-hand testimony, *Talking to Women* (one of them the artist Pauline Boty). 'Now and again,' he asserted, 'these nine women are simply not worth listening to'; such moments he attributed to 'genuine confusion or the calculated sort of, you know, vagueness of the Sixties language promised in the blurb'; and in short, 'some of the interviews should have been edited and shaped into a more coherent piece of writing'. Heaney's issues, though, went beyond the merely methodological. 'I am just too smugly male, too dominating and egotistical,' he admitted, 'to take to a book where the ladies protest so much. Ladies, I am sure, will like it.'[26]

'We do not say we are always right but we do have a right to be heard,' declared Mary Whitehouse on Monday the 29th at a press conference in Fleet Street, launching the National Viewers and Listeners Association (NVLA) as a more organised and properly constituted body to replace the Clean-up TV Campaign. 'If the BBC try to ridicule the views of half a million people what else will they ridicule in the same way?' Lady Violet Bonham Carter reflected the same day, of the probable next leader of the Liberal Party, that 'dear Jeremy [Thorpe] with all his gifts is not a politician in *depth*'; out in paperback in December was Penguin's reissue of *The Divided Self*, with R. D. Laing in a new preface insistent that 'the statesmen of the world who boast and threaten that they have Doomsday weapons are far more dangerous, and far more estranged from "reality", than many of the people on whom the label "psychotic" is affixed', as well as adamant that 'psychiatry could be, and some psychiatrists are, on the side of transcendence, of genuine freedom and of true human growth'; in the House of Lords on Wednesday the 1st, Lord Robbins, some two years since his famous report on higher education, fiercely attacked Crosland for having, especially in his Woolwich speech, 'proclaimed an internal separation between the autonomous universities and the rest of the system', a separation which 'can bring no pleasure of benefit to any but a few snobs at the centre and bullies at the periphery'; Crosland would have been happier to know that, the same day, his opposite number Edward Boyle was pragmatically, albeit privately, advising a fellow Conservative that, in the context of the rise of comprehensive education and the increasingly widespread abolition of academic selection via the 11-plus, 'no Conservative Government could reverse this trend without having to take far more dictatorial powers over Local Authorities than any Socialist Government has ever proposed'; also on the 1st, Crosland's colleague Charles Pannell formally rejected the Civic Trust's request for a public inquiry into the Whitehall redevelopment plan, with the minister apparently telling the deputation (led by Churchill's son-in-law politician, Duncan Sandys) that 'the concept had been well received by informed opinion'; and on Thursday, the latest *TLS* included a coolish review of David Lodge's *The British Museum Is Falling Down* ('not only contains the same kinds of jokes as *Lucky Jim* – sometimes, even, the same jokes – but also the same essential evasiveness'), *Hello,*

Dolly! opened at Drury Lane ('not a great musical', according to one critic, but 'pleasant and bright'), and Ray Gunter and George Brown between them managed to persuade the bakers to suspend their plans for further strikes. Friday was Beatles day: in the nation's record shops, the appearance of *Rubber Soul* ('a little subdued' for the taste of *Melody Maker*'s Pop Panel); and in Glasgow, the start of the group's only UK tour this year ('no riots', reported *NME*, but still 'two jam-packed houses, some fainting fits, and thunderous waves of screams that set the city's Odeon theatre trembling'). Sadly for George, as they had travelled north that morning in their Austin Princess, a bumpy stretch of road had resulted in his much-loved Gretsch guitar falling out of the boot and into the path of oncoming traffic. 'About 13 lorries went over it before our chauffeur could get near it,' he told a music journalist. 'Then one of the lorries stopped and the driver came up with the dangling remains of it and said: "Oy, is this 'ere banjo anyfink to do wiv you?"'[27]

For the second end-of-week running, the Who with 'My Generation' – zeitgeist platter of the year – were pipped to the No. 1 spot by the almost defiantly unzeitgeisty Seekers ('The Carnival Is Over'), the group which in fact, helped by its even more massive hits 'I'll Never Find Another You' and 'World of Our Own', sold more singles in 1965 than anyone else. On Saturday, after the *Guardian*'s Harry Whewell had noted that among young women (under twenty-five), and despite the coldest early winter weather for two decades, 'skimpy skirts and the obligatory white boots to go with them are everywhere', *Dr Who* featured the first appearance of a female assistant, Space Security Agent Sara Kingdom; next day, Angus Wilson in the *Observer* wrote glowingly of the comprehensive system ('its co-education, its heterogeneous communities, its interwoven streams of ability, its wide range of subjects offered'), the Keighley diarist Kenneth Preston reflected sceptically on the news that 'the Yanks' had put two more astronauts into orbit as a further step in its ambitious space programme ('none of the great questions that have faced and puzzled humanity throughout its history is likely to find an answer on the moon'), Richard Hearne as Mr Pastry continued to delight the Haines household in Chingford as he danced 'The Lancers' with an imaginary set and partner ('he was doing this many years ago when we had our first 9" console T.V., and it is just as polished a performance'), and the Beatles played for what would be the last time in Liverpool; while Monday the 6th saw three openings: at the Kasmin Gallery, of David Hockney's second solo exhibition (already acclaimed by one critic, Edwin Mullins, for the way the paintings of the 'airy spirit from Bradford', with his 'court-jesterish instincts', continued to appeal as 'a scrap-book of off-beat personal encounters'); at the County Hall, Chelmsford, of the public inquiry into whether London's third airport should be built at Stansted; and, at Hyde Magistrates' Court in Cheshire and attracting easily the most press attention, of committal proceedings against Myra Hindley and Ian Brady, charged between them with three murders. 'Myra's hair was bleached and set, her make-up immaculate,' notes Carol Ann Lee in her authoritative biography. 'She wore a monochrome flecked suit and yellow blouse, and sat with Ian, jotting down observations in a ring-bound notepad or laughing quietly over their doodles of Mrs Adamson [former Mayoress Mrs Dorothy Adamson, one of the three magistrates] and her natty little hat.' Next day saw the prosecution, in the person of William Mars-Jones (QC, and father of Adam), presenting its case. 'You will hear', he told the magistrates about Brady, 'that he had accumulated a considerable library of books about torture, the history of torture, murder, and sexual perversions, and that one of his favourite authors was the notorious Marquis de Sade.' That evening, the Beatles played at the ABC cinema in Ardwick, the 'dimly lit' area of Manchester through which, four years earlier, Brady and Hindley had walked late at night (after missing the last bus from the city centre) on their way to her gran's house in Gorton, where they became lovers.[28]

The Race Relations Act came into effect on Wednesday the 8th, England went to Madrid for a friendly against Spain and won 2–0 (a victory prompting one football correspondent, Peter Lorenzo, to declare that 'such was the manner and merit of it that I say England's World Cup horizon looks all the more sunny in this chilly city'), and the *Wednesday Play* was Dennis Potter's *Stand Up, Nigel Barton* – his first major impact in the medium he would make his own. The hero, played by Keith Barron, was a miner's son at Oxford University, nicely previewed by Tony Garnett in the *Radio Times* as 'part of the cream of the first Free Milk generation'; matters of social class deeply and uneasily permeated everything; the soundtrack featured 'We Gotta Get Out of This Place', the almost too-apposite Animals hit of earlier in the year; most critics responded positively to the strength and conviction of the writing, albeit Nancy Banks-Smith found it 'odd' that ultimately 'so little feeling came through'; and the Viewing Panel awarded an RI of 60, with some appalled by the 'bad language' and 'crude behaviour', but others praising it as 'very true to life', especially the miner father. Thursday's *TLS* had E. P. Thompson identifying Peter Laslett's otherwise widely hailed *The World We Have Lost* as an ill-starred product of the new marriage between history and sociology, a marriage involving in Laslett's case an 'unlimited contempt' for historians not reliant on statistics ('How', asked Thompson, 'are a wide range of societal and familiar relations – hatred and love – to be estimated if all literary evidence is to be eschewed?'); James Allen in rural Essex noted that his wife Bertha had 'gone out on her "meals on wheels" scheme to deal hot meals to old people who live on their own'; but on the Lancashire coast, less marital pride or pleasure. 'Usual washing & ironing – rained of course!' recorded Betty Allen. 'David on call & out until 1.30 – fourth night in a row! Felt most depressed & neglected – don't know what he'd do if I decided I wanted a night out!'[29]

'This box represents a fake revolution,' declared D. A. N. Jones in Friday's *New Statesman* about David Bailey's *Box of Pin-Ups*, unrivalled trendiest book of the year, with its stylised photographic portraits (presented loose in a cardboard box) of Nureyev, Beaton, Shrimpton, John and Paul, the Kray twins, Mick, Snowdon, Caine, P. J. Proby, et al.; Pat and Ted Scott both took the day off to go Christmas shopping in Basildon ('very nice, loads of shops'), complete with 'lunch in Happy Friar'; at the Den on Saturday afternoon, Millwall's home match with Walsall saw what one home fan, John Fitt, would remember as 'the first sign of any sort of aggravation' there, a scuffle between rival supporters finally broken up by the police; Frederick Ward in Bristol, after a conversation with a neighbour, noted that the topic of 'one-armed bandits' had arisen; 'I could not find any quality to admire, any beauty to start at, any charm to enjoy or flesh to desire,' observed Malcolm Muggeridge in the *Observer* about Bailey's 'essentially narcissistic' collection; discontent, too, from Radio 390, broadcasting that day an appeal to its listeners to protest directly to Tony Benn, following his decision as Postmaster General to prosecute the pirate radio stations; the Beatles played at Cardiff's Capitol cinema, last stop on what turned out to be their last British tour; on Monday, the *Guardian*'s Edward Greenfield reviewed the LP of Jacqueline du Pré's rendition of Elgar's Cello Concerto ('certainly the record of the year . . . the mastery, the sheer magnitude of the artistry, silences criticism') and the *Daily Mail*'s Barry Norman interviewed Potter ('a tall, red-haired and far less prickly man than one would expect from his work'); Benn's postbag was instantly bulging with some 700 letters and postcards of protest, many of which revealed how (in Benn's presumably reluctant words) 'the listeners hated the BBC because of its facetious announcers and the middle class tone of the programmes'; BBC TV's less than proletarian new offering this afternoon was *Jackanory*; a debut, too, this evening for ITV's *The Power Game*, a spin-off from *The Plane Makers* and starring Patrick Wymark as the ruthless businessman, Barbara Murray as his elegantly bejewelled, fur-clad wife; in real life that Tuesday, the stoicism of the mother of the murdered Lesley Ann Downey gave way in Hyde Magistrates' Court to understandably intense emotion ('She can sit staring at me,' she screamed at Hindley, 'and she took a little baby's life, the beast'); in Primrose Hill, the hugely talented feminist sociologist Hannah Gavron committed suicide, just one street away from where Sylvia Plath had done so almost three years earlier; while that evening, Ladbroke's issued its latest World Cup odds: Brazil the favourites at 9–4, then England at 11–2, and North Korea as rank outsiders at 500–1.[30]

Two notable items in the press on Wednesday morning. One, that the leading direct grant schools had come out strongly against being absorbed into any future comprehensive system, instead insisting that they should continue to have independent status, with admission criteria being strictly based on academic ability and aptitude; the other, that as part of its new mission statement that 'viewers will see less of noisy teenage beat shows like *Ready, Steady, Go!* and more of the "more mature" artists like Kathy Kirby, Frank Ifield, Ken Dodd and Max Bygraves', Rediffusion (London's weekday TV channel) was planning in the New Year to cut *RSG* itself from forty-three to thirty-three minutes, before in the spring replacing it 'by another show with more universal appeal'. Later on the 15th, as the day itself unfolded, Goldie the eagle managed again to evade his keepers in London Zoo and escape; the court in Hyde heard the tape recording of Lesley's last moments; and among the diarists, Diana Griffith in Worthing got the results of her typing exam ('I came bottom with 67%!!! Oh dear!'), Keith McBride reflected that the Americans had only three and a half years left if they were to hit their 1969 target for landing on the moon ('on a rational basis, they should have taken 50 years to do it, but on that basis, Columbus would never have reached America'), and Anthony Heap went to the first night of *Charlie Girl* ('ramshackle, lackadaisical, vapid and vacuous . . . simply in short, won't do'). Few of the paid critics were any kinder, least of all towards Joe Brown, deploying 'grins' (wrote Bernard Levin) 'into which, by the end of the proceedings, I yearned to shove a couple of herrings'. Perhaps they should have stayed at home, watching on BBC TV the scheduling coup of Edward Heath's party political broadcast – in Banks-Smith's words, 'a brisk canter through the politician's repertoire', comprising 'a smiling sympathy' plus 'beaming bonhomie' plus 'sober candour' – being immediately followed by another instantly famous/infamous *Wednesday Play*: Dennis Potter's *Vote, Vote, Vote for Nigel Barton*, again starring Keith Barron, with the hero by this time having left university and now fighting a parliamentary election as a Labour candidate, again a drama closely based on Potter's own experience. 'Surely, the first fact we must face is that all three parties are stuffed with aged tub-thumpers and superannuated windbags,' he declares in his speech at a big, black-tie civic dinner, the play's climactic scene. 'To most intelligent people, party politics are synonymous with claptrap. To be a candidate is to submit to a personally humiliating experience, in which the set smile freezes on your face like a grin on a corpse. Dead ideas. Dead thoughts. Dead slogans.' Again, as with a week earlier, the reviews were largely favourable, including *Punch*'s Patrick Skene Catling, not an easy man to please, announcing that 'not since John Osborne's early days has the art of invective been practised with such bitterly comic inventiveness and vehemence'; the RI of 64 was perfectly respectable; and one viewer probably nailed it when he commented that the play 'should shake people's faith in the so-called democratic principle – but I doubt whether it will!'[31]

Better fortune next day for Diana Griffith ('I got 141½/150 for one of the S/Hand tests – excellent apparently!!'); the release of Anthony Simmons's bittersweet, Thames-set feature film *Four in the Morning* saw, in her second cinema role, Judi Dench as a frustrated wife, with Kenneth Tynan acclaiming her 'suddenly breaking into a reminiscent chuckle half way through an otherwise straight line' as 'the truest moment of acting I've seen in a British film this year'; on Friday morning the prison guard gave Hindley a cup of tea laced not with sugar, but salt; and on *Any Questions?*, coming from the more familiar surrounds of Topsham, Devon, the team was asked whether Goldie – still free, and with Ladbroke's offering odds on whether he would be recaptured by Christmas – should be awarded the Distinguished Flying Cross. 'Yes, the DFC, George Medal, the lot I suppose, people seem to be awfully fond of it,' responded the writer Russell Braddon. 'As far as I'm concerned,' he went on in his famously tough-minded, Australian way, 'it's just a nuisance of a bird, rushing out, terrorising poor dogs, costing the taxpayer millions. Shouldn't that keeper be sacked, this is the second time?' For Dee Wells, there was no doubt that 'that clever bird' deserved the DFC, but not so the Conservative politician John Peyton: 'Personally, I regard Goldie as a nuisance, filling up far too much space in the newspapers, I very much wonder whether the customers are half as interested in the doings of this bird as the press seem to think.' That left another politician, Michael Foot, taking the characteristic line that it was 'better to do away with the whole honours system altogether for humans as well as birds instead of starting to bestow it on Goldie as well'. His real fierceness, though, was reserved for another question: should parents paying school fees, in order to educate their children privately, be allowed income tax relief? 'We live in a community together, we're all dependent upon one another,' he declared. 'The idea that we should all be trying to seize advantages against our neighbours – it's a disgusting, uncivilised method of living. We're all dependent upon the services of other people, in the education system above all others . . .' And he added that tax relief for fee-paying parents had the effect of 'intensifying the class system in this country, the snobbery system in this country which is bad enough already'.

Just over twenty-four hours later, at 11.15 p.m. on Saturday the 18th, three 'Afro-Asian students' were, in their own words, 'walking from a friend's house towards King's Cross station' when 'a group of young white people all of a sudden attacked us without any provocation whatsoever':

> They assaulted us [as P. I. S. M. Rahman (Trinity Hall, Cambridge), H. Saharay (UCL) and P. K. Banerjee (SOAS) continued their subsequent account in the *New Statesman*] and used abusive language to two married ladies who were accompanied by their husbands with us. We shouted for help but nobody in the street came forward. Seeing us helpless in the wilderness, they beat every one of us severely and broke into pieces a rare musical instrument which was carried by one of our companions. Two of us fell unconscious.
>
> One of us somehow managed to escape to telephone the police for help. But nobody turned up until several phone-calls were made to them. At last after half an hour the police came. But instead of helping us they remarked: 'You people are creating trouble for us in our country.' One policeman even told one of the married women to shut up when she tried to explain the incident. Being shocked and disappointed, some of us hired a taxi and went to the University College Hospital for treatment.

After noting that 'numerous incidents of this nature are taking place in various parts of London', the students concluded: 'We have come to this country with the sincere hope of receiving higher education and acquiring experiences of western civilisation. But you can imagine what meaning this higher education will have for us if we are faced with such inhuman treatment and what memory we shall carry with us when we return home. A sense of insecurity is more and more gripping our mind.'[32]

Literary news on Sunday was that in the *Observer*'s 'Books of the Year' W. H. Auden had plumped for Martin Gardner's *The Ambidextrous Universe* ('a splendid example of *haute* vulgarisation'), Kingsley Amis for *A Dedicated Man* by Elizabeth Taylor ('one of the three English writers of fiction whose books I order before publication', the other two not named), and Edna O'Brien ('I am constantly in search of fiction whose impact will see me through the middle of the night') for Saul Bellow's *Herzog* ('I have gone to that vast bible of human idiosyncrasy the way others might to an analyst or a lover'); news of almost universal interest was that, after four days of high-profile freedom, Goldie had been recaptured, this time for good – lured from his tree in Regent's Park by a succulent dead rat at the end of a 30-foot length of line. Next day, the 20th, the committal proceedings ended at Hyde, with Brady and Hindley being sent for trial; two northern education committees, those of Liverpool and Warrington, both decided to abolish their 11-plus examinations; *Jackanory*, at the start of its second week, moved up a gear, with Wendy Hiller reading 'The Squirrel, the Hare, and the Little Grey Rabbit' by Alison Uttley; and once again, in that evening's *Panaroma*, the absence of Richard Dimbleby was keenly felt by viewers, especially when James Mossman spoke directly to camera:

> What I would like to say, to Richard, because I hope he is watching, is that all of us here in *Panaroma*, both on the screen and behind it, send you our very best wishes. I know all of you do also, judging from the seven thousand letters he has received. Yesterday he told a colleague of mine who visited him that he particularly wanted us to pass on his thanks tonight, and to wish all of you a Happy Christmas from him.

No sentimentality, though, from the watching Nancy Banks-Smith. *Panorama*'s new front man, Robin Day, 'reflects', she asserted, 'the times rather better', being 'bony, well briefed, contentious and apparently continually cross'; while as for Dimbleby himself, 'for years I thought of him as the butler of the BBC and found "Gold Microphone in Waiting" pretty funny and appropriate'. 'There is', she ended almost defiantly, 'no virtue in back-pedalling about it now.'

This Monday evening was also the first night in London of Lionel Bart's *Twang!!*. For the cast (including James Booth, Bernard Bresslaw and Ronnie Corbett as well as Barbara Windsor), a night to forget, with boos at the end, only three curtain calls and a voice from the gallery shouting, 'Thank God that's over'; but for Bart, though still outwardly optimistic after the ordeal ('all we have to do now is speed it up a little and get the lines better, and we can run for at least one to two years'), the reviews next morning were akin to the nails in the coffin of a once glittering career. 'A show without a single witty line, a single memorable song, or a single arresting situation', 'I'd sooner have seen the pantomime version [i.e. of the Robin Hood story]', 'as lacking in direction, point and meaning as the average evening in a Munich beergarden', 'hit the stage of the Shaftesbury Theatre with a dull thud', while one headline said it all: 'Twang??

Thin as a bowstring.' Some of the critics did make a partial exception for the 'pert' and 'bubbly' Windsor, but certainly not Anthony Heap, describing her as 'diminutive, Jewish-cockney, common as they make 'em and one of my current pet aversions'. She and the others would largely recover, but not Bart, still only in his mid-thirties and still barely half a decade since his great triumphs with *Fings Ain't Wot They Used T'be* and *Oliver!*. 'He epitomised the start of the Sixties in Britain, which he uniquely captured in song and spirit,' Tom Vallance would reflect in his 1999 obituary, 'and he was one of the few composers to deal uncondescendingly with the working classes, transposing their life styles and vernacular to the musical stage.' Sadly, though, that moment had now more or less gone.

'Twang goes Thud' was the caption on Tuesday for Jak's *Evening Standard* cartoon; that evening, Bournemouth's education committee decided by thirty-nine votes to ten that comprehensive schools in the town were 'unnecessary and undesirable'; Frederick Ward in Bristol was at the annual dinner ('again a success') given by the Brislington Butter Factory for the Co-operative Wholesale Society's foodstuffs managers; and, almost four years after its debut, the original *Z Cars* wound up with an episode called 'That's The Way It Is', written by Alan Plater and much applauded by Banks-Smith. '"There's no flaming justice in this world," was the last line,' she noted. 'Only *Z Cars* could have used an exit line like that in a police series – and given it to a policeman.'[33] Still, it had been a series in perceptible decline for at least a year or two; and, rather like the dip in Bart's fortunes, its passing signified something larger, in essence in this case that – culturally anyway, perhaps not yet politically – the northern wind no longer blew quite as it once had.

The 22nd was in its way a day for the ages. On the political front, a Commons vote in the early hours over the Labour government's imposition of an oil embargo on Rhodesia saw the Tories horribly and embarrassingly split: fifty right-wing, Smith-sympathising MPs voting against the order; thirty liberal-minded MPs voting with Labour; the Shadow Cabinet ignominiously abstaining; and Heath himself, to quote his biographer John Campbell, 'enraged by the posturing cant by which Wilson milked the issue for credit with his own left wing, piously claiming that it was "a moral issue" and demanding Opposition backing for the Government while deliberating exacerbating Heath's troubles with his right'. That evening, Wilson announced a mini-reshuffle in his own Cabinet. The two key moves were Roy Jenkins to the Home Office and Barbara Castle to Transport. The Jenkins move seemed from the start a natural fit, especially given that back in 1959 his *The Labour Case* ahead of that year's general election had devoted its final chapter specifically to the reforms that a Labour home secretary should undertake; while tactically, from Wilson's perspective, the appointment of someone with such well-known liberal instincts was a good way of keeping on board, ahead of a likely general election in 1966, those *Guardian* readers and others who had been so dismayed by the deeply illiberal White Paper on immigration. Most of the immediate attention, though, was focused on Castle: not just a woman in a traditionally male domain, but a non-driving woman. 'We have only one family car,' she rather disingenuously explained in an interview, 'and it is my experience that the man of the house likes to drive.' Coincidentally, but somehow fittingly, it had been some six or seven hours earlier, at noon, that an experimental 70 mph speed limit had come into effect. How did it go? According to one motoring correspondent, reporting on a survey conducted that afternoon, 'continual offenders were chauffeurs driving Rolls-Royces and Bentleys'; while 'on average', he added, 'drivers in the North on the M6 were keeping to the limit much better than drivers in the South on the M1 and M4'.

There was another political event this day – arguably the most important, at least in the department of missed opportunities – as Crosland at last announced to the Commons the overall purpose and terms of reference of the long-awaited Public Schools Commission (PSC). Public schools, he declared, currently exerted a 'socially divisive influence', whereas they 'should, like other parts of the educational system, become progressively open to boys and girls irrespective of their parents' incomes'; they 'should move towards a wider range of academic attainment, so that the public school sector may increasingly play its own part in the national movement towards comprehensive education'; and 'in particular' they 'should seek to meet any unsatisfied need for boarding education among wider sections of the population'. The PSC, he noted, would not cover direct grant schools ('they must be treated as a separate problem and a separate operation'). Crosland's statement failed to impress the campaigning Public Schools Committee (its members largely drawn from Labour Party members), which at once expressed its regret for not only 'the failure to make clear the principle on which integration should take place', but also 'the lack so far of any timetable for the commission with the specific promise of legislative action from the Government if no agreement is reached'. They were probably not all that enthused either by Crosland's announcement about who would chair the PSC: namely, Sir John Newsom, after apparently five other people, including the robust historian Alan Bullock, had turned down the position. 'Probably best known for his chairmanship of the Central Advisory Council for Education (England) which published its report *Half Our Future*, in 1963,' helpfully explained *The Times* about Sir John. 'He was County Education Officer for Hertfordshire between 1940 and 1957, and is at present joint managing director of Longmans, Green, the publishers.' What Newsom had never shown was any particular interest in the public school question; 'a prestigious figurehead, but not one noted for radical views on this, or other educational issues' is Brian Simon's apt characterisation, adding that 'he was, at this time, a kind of educational Pooh Bah'; and Newsom himself, immediately after Crosland's statement, remarked to one journalist, 'I realise this is a job bristling with difficulties all round.'[34]

This Wednesday was not yet over. That evening, at the Morden Tower in Newcastle, the poet Basil Bunting gave the first public reading of *Briggflatts*; in London, Peter Hall's *Hamlet* came to the Aldwych (David Warner still in the title role, but Janet Suzman now as Ophelia, and welcomed by the *Telegraph*'s Darlington as showing 'genuine feeling', whereas 'her predecessor was just a smart deb'); and *The Wednesday Play*, directed by Ken Loach, was James O'Connor's *The Coming Out Party*, the story, set in Notting Hill, of a boy discovering that his mother was in prison and going in search of her. Lasting an hour, it started on BBC1 at 9 p.m. – some five minutes before, at St Thomas' Hospital, Richard Dimbleby, having fallen into a coma earlier in the day, died at the age of fifty-two. Probably the first in the outside world to hear the news were the viewers of *Hope and Keen*, debut outing of an ITV comedy series starring the acrobatic Scottish double act Mike Hope and Albie Keen – now cruelly interrupted, sixteen minutes in, at 9.26. A few minutes later, between programmes, BBC2 viewers were told; but BBC1 viewers were kept in the dark until the play ended at ten o'clock. After the announcement, there followed on that channel, very much Dimbleby's channel, a ninety-second silence before a special, tribute edition of *24 Hours*, including prominent roles for Cliff Michelmore, Huw Wheldon (calling Dimbleby 'the voice of the BBC on thousands of occasions, and on hundreds of occasions the voice of our nation') and the BBC wartime correspondent Frank Gillard. Among watching diarists, a clearly moved James Allen called him 'a great broadcaster and I think he had a personality which was acceptable to everybody, talking in a relaxed way', while Laurence Marks noted that 'my mum is deeply saddened by tonight's news, and it is as if she knew the man personally'. Watching especially carefully, and observing that 'with an air of theatrical royalty they used a spotlit empty chair to symbolise his loss to them', was Banks-Smith, knowing that she would almost immediately be having to file her TV column for next day's paper. In it she did semi-apologise for her disobliging remarks about Dimbleby after Monday's *Panorama*; but at this instantly historic moment, bookending 1965 after Churchill's death back in January, her eyes were on the bigger picture:

> There is something of the feeling of a royal death about this thing. As if he represented a kingdom – which he did, being virtually the voice, the shape of the BBC. As if his life spanned a period we could remember like a reign. Which it did. From Ally Pally to Telstar his life was as much as most of us can remember.
>
> When death suggests the end of an era you get this creeping and uneasy feeling. That the past was no joke. That the future will be worse.[35]

6

Baked Beans for Us

The overcrowded day of Dimbleby's death also included a press conference given by Brian Abel-Smith of the LSE and Peter Townsend of Essex University. Previewing their report *The Poor and the Poorest*, due to be published next day, they declared that at least a million children in Britain faced a 'very bleak Christmas'; while in the report itself, a continuation of a sustained campaign (Townsend's especially) to demonstrate the fallacy of the twin post-war assumptions that (in their words) 'we have abolished poverty' and that 'the differences between the living standards of the rich and poor are much smaller than they used to be', they presented the fullest yet array of evidence, based on the government's income and expenditure surveys in 1953–4 and 1960. The headline finding was that nearly seven and a half million people in the UK, some 14 per cent of the population, were living in poverty, defined as below a National Assistance standard; these seven and a half million included well over half of all retired people; many disabled people were poor; and up to two million children were living in poverty, often those in larger families, even though 41 per cent of those two million children had at least one full-time working parent. The report – spearheading what would become known for shorthand as 'the rediscovery of poverty' – made an immediate impact. 'Poverty cannot be defined by absolute standards,' insisted the *Guardian* in a supportive Christmas Eve editorial. 'It is not enough to know that no one in our prosperous society is actually starving. The seven and a half million are deprived of things the rest of us take for granted. This makes a mockery of our claims to be already a Welfare State.'

Back in the spring, Abel-Smith had presented his and Townsend's findings to a meeting at Toynbee Hall that saw in effect the start of the Child Poverty Action Group (CPAG), with the name itself emerging in the autumn as more likely than 'Family Poverty Group' to deter the right-wing press from invoking the spectre of 'scroungers'. If the CPAG had a single founder, it was undoubtedly the remarkable Harriett Wilson, a middle-aged Quaker who had fled Nazi Germany after marrying a Jew and was now, as a sociologist based at Cardiff University, the leading expert on child poverty. So it was that, two days before Christmas Day, she accompanied Abel-Smith to Downing Street, where they presented the PM not only with a copy of *The Poor and the Poorest*, but also from the CPAG a memorandum and a widely signed letter (led by the prominent social scientist Baroness Barbara Wootton) demanding larger family allowances for the poorest families. That evening on BBC TV, the latest episode of *Man Alive* was called 'Give Us This Day . . .' and neatly summarised by the *Radio Times*: 'Christmas 1965 . . . in the Welfare State. At a time of giving and plenty, a look at poverty and deprivation through the eyes of five families who cannot afford Christmas.' 'The documentary makers', note the historians of the CPAG, 'were so moved that they returned with toys and food for the families – more sympathetic to families on benefits than some of their twenty-first century successors.'[1]

For Labour's left-wingers, such as the backbencher Lena Jeger, all this was valuable grist to the mill in their attempt to get the government to step up its anti-poverty drive; and writing in the *New Statesman* just after Christmas, she expressed her general impatience, especially over the failure to introduce the promised minimum income guarantee for pensioners, as well as the lack of a review of family allowances. Also frustrated was Richard Crossman, who back in 1963 had launched his ambitious, poverty-abolishing *New Frontiers for Social Security* policy document, but then in government had to watch Douglas Houghton take overall responsibility for this area. 'We have let him', reflected Crossman in April 1965, 'implement our social security policy in a way which seems to have destroyed the whole of our strategy.' Three months later, in the context of sterling problems and public expenditure cuts, Houghton was joined in Crossman's black book by the pensions and national insurance minister, Peggy Herbison:

> Under cross-examination [i.e. at Cabinet] they got into a horrible mess and confirmed my fear that the whole strategy of our pensioneering, worked out for years before the election, had been jettisoned almost without noticing it by the Minister under the *diktat* of Douglas Houghton. The basic idea had been that we should switch as early as possible from flat-rate to earnings-related contributions and in this way pile up enormous sums in the pension fund which we could use to dynamize the existing flat-rate pension. That was cardinal. However Douglas and Peggy had turned things upside down, by first of all conceding [soon after the October 1964 election] an enormously increased flat-rate benefit financed by increased flat-rate contributions. The net result is the worst of all worlds as we can't raise the flat-rate contributions any higher without imposing an intolerable burden on the lower-paid worker. Even worse, the income guarantee which we have pledged ourselves to introduce would now be at an absurdly low level as the result of the money we have wasted on the huge initial increase of the flat-rate pension. After the Cabinet discussion I became quite sure that it was far too late to go back to the original strategy. The least damaging thing we could do was probably to abandon the income guarantee because the pittance we could offer would make a mockery of the whole concept.

So it turned out. Later in July, Callaghan announced the official postponement of the income guarantee; while eleven days before Christmas – unbeknown to backbenchers like Jeger, let alone Abel-Smith, Townsend et al. – its permanent death knell was sounded at Cabinet, with a slightly less bitter Crossman recording Herbison's 'plan for reforming social security':

> After more than a year wasted on reflection, Douglas Houghton and she [Herbison] had decided that the incomes guarantee was wholly impracticable and had to be dropped. What could be put in its place? The scheme she put forward this morning was a cheap substitute, a reformed national assistance which would be sold to the public under the new name of supplementary benefit. I am still sick at the thought of how Douglas Houghton has fragmented our major comprehensive reform and so minimized its political effect.

> Nevertheless, if you take it for what it is – a cheap substitute – this proposal of Peggy's is brilliantly worked out. Once again Douglas Houghton and James Callaghan got into a sinister combination trying to wreck it.

'Fortunately,' added Crossman, 'others praised it highly and we got it through without too much delay.'[2]

Could a pressure group like the CPAG – for all its ability to attract almost instant and often highly charged publicity, with even the *Daily Express* highlighting 'Poverty Plea to Wilson' – realistically hope to make a difference? The near-certainty of continued pressure on sterling so long as devaluation was ruled out, Labour's newly acquired middle-class supporters instinctively reluctant to see taxes raised, the trade unions at this stage seldom demanding that Labour prioritise the poverty issue – none of this helped, and neither did institutional factors, with one historian, David Vincent, plausibly attributing the scrapping of the income guarantee to a mixture of 'Treasury opposition to the expense' and the Inland Revenue being 'implacably hostile to the conflation of taxation and welfare'. Still, the CPAG – described by Townsend early in 1966 as consisting 'equally of social scientists and social workers' – was certainly not going to fail for want of trying; and nor was another recently established and equally spirited voluntary body. 'This group could be called the Disablement Income Group – or DIG,' Megan du Boisson (a 42-year-old Godalming housewife) and Berit Moore (in her mid-twenties), both of them afflicted by multiple sclerosis, had written to the *Guardian* in March 1965, outlining the need to achieve 'recognition for the *right* of disabled persons, irrespective of the reason for that disablement, to pensions from the State to enable them to live in a reasonable degree of independence and dignity *in their own homes*'. The DIG was duly launched that autumn, with du Boisson at the press conference pointedly contrasting 'a special Civil Service concept of time, in which a thousand years pass as an evening gone', compared with the plight of someone disabled by a degenerative disease, for whom 'every month or year is very precious'; within two years it would be holding its first national rally, with some 200 disabled people assembled in Whitehall, led by the wheelchair-bound du Boisson 'chic, smiling and gay in a pink dress'; and as Nicholas

Timmins puts it, 'the disabled were suddenly recognised as claimants on the benefit system in their own right'.[3]

It helped over the rest of the decade that this was still the golden age of British sociology: empirical and evidence-based, qualitative as well as quantitative, not yet jargon-ridden, and deeply committed to a better, fairer, more generous society. Dennis Marsden's *Mothers Alone: Poverty and the Fatherless Family* was one such emblematic study: published in 1969, and acclaimed by one reviewer as 'a moving, often horrifying, and above all anger-provoking account' which 'shows what poverty *means* to a fatherless family', it was based on a survey carried out by Marsden in 1965–6 of 116 unsupported mothers on National Assistance, some of them living in a relatively prosperous northern industrial town, the others in a market town in the south. 'The central fact of most of these women's existence was their financial dependence on the National Assistance Board, and what seemed to them the whims of its officers', noted another reviewer. 'Too often the Board acted so as to make an already hard life barely tolerable. The stringent earnings rule prevented women with average work skills from improving their position. Pressure on divorced and separated wives to pursue their husbands for maintenance through the courts embittered their relationships to the detriment of the children. Worst of all, the cohabitation rule effectively blocked the mothers' chances of remarriage.' A hard life indeed, full of frustration as well as greater or lesser deprivation, and again and again it is the voices of these mothers alone that come through, voices of an often real and moving eloquence about their daily struggles, whether physical or mental:

> An accident or anything like that, I'm stuck. It's the little things like that when you realize how difficult life is, £4 [to mend a broken sink] might not sound a lot to you, it didn't to me, but now it seems out of this world. I haven't a hope of saving that up.
>
> I eat all right, but all I ever eat is bread. I'm just eating toast after toast, and the doctor says he should tell me to diet, but it's no good because what can I diet? I can't eat any other sort of things. I can't afford chickens and things like that, and eggs. And if I cut down on bread I get a headache and I get desperately hungry. Well, I ask you. How could I sit down with a piece of chicken when the kids are wanting things?

Crumbs, I feel hard up for necessities. I'm not asking for luxuries, I'm not asking for cars and washers. I mean it's no good looking at a tin of salmon. It's baked beans for us, and you don't get a terrifically varied diet.

They don't have to have uniform for that [primary] school, but I've heard our Brenda talking about another girl in the class and she was saying how she was wearing this scruffy skirt that she'd had so long. Children notice things like that.

He wants these pointed toes, but I say he's got to have some shoes that last. I buy him a pair of them pointed ones, and within three weeks he wants another pair, so this last time I've got him some round-toed ones, some of them Tuf ones. I was determined he'd have something that would last. I tell him these fashions are for people who live on the Riviera.

That's one thing that's come out of this. I never used to smoke, but I've tried to give it up and I can't, and I get so crabby.

We had a dog, but it was too expensive. I feel so guilty. The children don't mention him, but sometimes they get his photo out and then the tears run down their faces.

You mind gets like a cash register after a while and as you go round the supermarket you add up as you go through. It's awful in a way.

If it's a penny cheaper, I go there. Even if it's only a halfpenny. My friend says, 'Why, it's only a halfpenny!' I say, 'A halfpenny's a lot to me.'

Well, thanks very much [after being asked whether she considered she was in poverty]. I've been labelled destitute by the National Assistance, but I don't think I consider myself in poverty yet. That's a horrible word. You think of little children with no shoes and only thin dresses and no fire. I don't think there's anybody like that in these days. If there is it's their own fault.

Really, I'm not hard up at all compared with some people. But it's hit me so hard because I'm used to having plenty of money and savings to fall back on. I feel lost now without them.

It's the little things that aggravate you. I used to have some curtains for many years, and those curtains used to get on my nerves, the colours of them, until finally I started scratching and saving, and putting a bit on one side, and I used to say to myself, 'That's my curtain money, and I'm not touching that for anything.'

> And finally, I got them curtains that I've got now. And when I'd put them up, I thought, 'Right, my curtains are as good as anybody's curtains in this street.'
>
> I hate Christmas coming. I dread it, because every time you go out you seem to be spending and spending, and I don't like them to miss anything. I like them to have all the trimmings. I tell you what. I hope you never have to do the same with your children as I've had to do with mine. Tell them that Father Christmas hasn't got any toys for our house this year. That's what I've had to do. And I've had to wait until Marks and Spencers have had their sales and then I've had to buy a doll for them and say that Father Christmas has remembered after all.[4]

'We watched Wrestling, then Thank Your Lucky Stars & David Nixon Comedy Box, & later The Arthur Haynes Show,' recorded Nella Last on New Year's Day, 1966. 'Not very good on Sat night. I can't understand the cult of the "weirdes" & "outer space" type of show, & Dixon of Dock Green has lost all "old fashion" appeal. I never think the artists look happy nowadays, it's so changed. I often wonder what the many third-to-*tenth* rate pop groups will do when their public tire of them.' Next day, disenchantment of a different kind from another diarist, Keith McBride:

> The thing that worries me is that we are now more than half-way through the '60's yet this country has made very little progress; building of office blocks, scratching of murals & driving of racing cars seem the only fields in which we lead.
>
> Our armed forces can best be described as pathetic, while no serious attempt has been made to tackle the balance of payments problem, the colour problem was left far too late (though that was a matter of the '50's, not the '60's), we have no metric system, no election reform [he had recently read a book on proportional representation], our transport is as bad as ever, & we are steadily falling behind in almost everything. Our scientists & engineers have lots of good ideas, but are hardly ever allowed to develop them.

Well, I hope there'll be a turn for the better in 1966, but I very much doubt it.

Two days later, on the afternoon of Thursday the 4th, was Richard Dimbleby's memorial service at a packed-to-the-gills Westminster Abbey, after long queues (mainly of women) had formed outside for hours earlier. Five million viewers watched at home; that evening, another six and a half million watched a recording; in his address, the Bishop of Guildford read out from one of the thousands of letters sent to Dimbleby in hospital ('My wife and children asked me to write to you and say how sorry we are that you are ill, and how much we miss you on *Panorama*. Who am I? Just an ordinary roadman from Berkshire. See you down my road one of these days . . .'); the last words of TV commentary went to Wynford Vaughan-Thomas ('We shall not easily forget him'); and among those watching and listening was Vere Hodgson. 'I don't know what we shall do without him on STATE OCCASIONS,' she lamented in her next diary entry. 'At the moment there is NO-ONE TO TAKE HIS PLACE . . . I cannot believe he has gone for ever.'[5]

The decisive political event of the first two months of the year was undoubtedly the Hull North by-election on 27 January. Labour had won it by a narrow majority (1,181) at the general election, but its vote was now threatened from the left by the Radical Alliance candidate Richard Gott, a red-bearded *Guardian* leader writer protesting against the government's support for the American war in Vietnam. It was an increasingly resonant cause. 'The Vietnam War is worsening,' noted the seventeen-year-old Gyles Brandreth, hardly a soulmate of Gott, the weekend before. 'The Americans have launched their biggest offensive – 8,000 troops have attacked a single Viet Cong stronghold with mass casualties. I went to a meeting addressed by Konni Zilliacus (Labour MP) at Petersfield Town Hall. He was convincing: I am pro-American, but what can the war hope to achieve?' With its tiny parliamentary majority, Labour was seriously worried, flooding the constituency with senior figures, including Barbara Castle ten days ahead of polling. 'Photographers at station, standing room only at meetings,' the new transport minister recorded. 'I told them categorically that, as soon as the development plan was decided for Humberside, they would have their bridge.

Speeches went down well.' The bridge in question was the future Humber Bridge, crossing the Humber Estuary: a bold and politically attractive promise, eventually coming to fulfilment in 1981, five years behind schedule and more than four times over budget. 'For nearly twenty years it was the longest single-span bridge in the world,' Castle's biographer Anne Perkins would observe in 2003, 'and it remains an object of great beauty and little economic merit, continually struggling with the debt incurred by overambitious projections for its use.'

Of course, this particular by-election had one especially notable local observer. 'Actually, my blue sympathies received something of a check by finding myself among a lot of them at lunch yesterday, under the Station Hotel,' Larkin reported to Monica Jones on the 23rd. 'I think even Jessel himself [Toby Jessel, the Conservative candidate] was there – there was a confident young chap among them, looking like a sort of imitation Christ Church man, and the atmosphere of youthful mediocrity that fairly steamed off him & his supporters didn't cheer me.' Then, two days later:

> Not much election news: saw Gott & his henchmen, ratty little bearded fellows, but on his election folder his photograph shows him *wearing my tie*, one of the ones I bought at Guernsey . . . Could almost vote for him for that. He says on his leaflet that Joan Baez & 'Donovan' support him in wanting to end the War in Vietnam! I think it will be a close thing. I'm inclined to tip McNamara [Kevin McNamara, the Labour candidate]. He's a solid, not very bright local Tech. College lecturer, orthodox Labour, lives here. Jessel is a flashy carpetbagger . . . Gott will have the mad element, true, but he will leave the solid characters who might have voted Liberal to go for McNamara. Old Larkin's Election Forecast, gained by studying the bottom of a pint pot.

One of Gott's 'henchmen' was Tariq Ali, still an Oxford undergraduate but no longer a Labour supporter. 'Many students from Hull University joined our canvassing parties, which were usually bleak expeditions to the housing estates,' he recalls. 'Some voters were sympathetic, many of them said that they did not think Labour should be supporting the Americans, but they would vote Labour nevertheless. They could not afford to let the Tories win and "your lot have no chance of winning."' So indeed it proved: a mere 253 votes for Gott, while Labour won with a handsome majority of well over 5,000, representing a 4½ per cent swing. 'Harold is sitting pretty with a majority restored to its full strength and a retained option on the date of the Election,' reflected Tony Benn next day; and on the Saturday, at an enthusiastic party rally at the Albert Hall, Wilson was in understandably confident vein: 'After fifteen months of the Labour Government's purposive economic policies, we can claim that sterling is strong, that employment is strong and that they are both strong at the same time . . .'[6]

The Labour leader was just about able to hold his PLP together, but the far left remained in 1966 as divided and disputatious as ever, perhaps even more so. Take Ralph Miliband and John Saville: together they worked closely as co-editors of the *Socialist Register*, but whereas Labour's refusal to condemn the Americans over Vietnam had caused Miliband utterly to repudiate the party, Saville (who lived in Hull) stoutly refused to endorse Gott, on the grounds that it would be folly to risk the overturn of the Labour government and the return of the Tories. 'The local Communist party was split on the issue, and the Trotskyists virulently hostile,' remembered Gott himself forty years later. 'Paul Foot, like me a former public schoolboy, described me as "a scab on the face of the working class", a characterisation that I took some years to forgive.' Meanwhile, the current issue of the *New Left Review* led with a brutal assault by its editor, Perry Anderson, on his fellow Marxist E. P. Thompson, some seven months after the author of *The Making of the English Working Class* had in his essay on 'The Peculiarities of the English' taken few prisoners, laying into Anderson and Tom Nairn for what he regarded as their overly theoretical 'Origins of the Present Crisis' (1964). Anderson himself now gave it both barrels:

> Elephantine homilies . . . reckless distortion . . . a matchless silliness . . . self-delighted pirouettes . . . constant sacrifices of accuracy and sobriety to epigrammatic 'brightness' of the kind that is appreciated on the High Table . . . vulgar Marxism . . . childish dishonesty . . . cheating at a parlour game fit for Sunday newspapers . . . mere hot air . . . uncontrollable need to caricature the

> opponent ... a hallucinating capacity to manipulate facts and to rewrite history to his own convenience ... a painfully embarrassing performance ... the tone of self-satisfied, sermonizing confidence with which he produces his solecisms ... groping in the night of his own memories ...

All this, and indeed more, in Anderson's epic take-down ('Socialism and Pseudo-Empiricism'), before the seeming afterthought of his last, conciliatory sentences. After noting that 'we are living through a sombre period', that 'the Left is weak and enfeebled', and that 'it would be tragic if, at this time, it were to be rent apart by local vendettas', he concluded: 'Thompson's stature as a great historian is not in question. Probably no-one has contributed so much, in their own field, to the historical awareness of British socialists. I trust that the debate which we have started will end by strengthening our common determination. More important battles lie ahead, in which we should be ranged together.'[7]

If all this was inevitably of minority interest, somewhat less so was George Brown's announcement in late January of his plan to set up an Industrial Reorganisation Corporation (IRC), with £150 million available in order (in his words) 'to search for opportunities to promote rationalisation schemes which can yield substantial benefits to the national economy, especially in terms of increased exports and more rapid technological advance'. This new body, he added, would be chaired by Sir Frank Kearton, who as the go-ahead chairman of Courtaulds since 1962 had pursued a ruthless, ambitious policy of going for scale and vertical integration in textiles, involving the acquisition of sixty cotton mills in the last eighteen months alone. The accompanying White Paper, after noting the emphasis placed the previous year by the National Plan on the need for more concentration and rationalisation in British industry, argued forcibly that, given the inaction since then, 'there is no evidence that we can rely on market forces alone to produce the necessary structural changes at the pace required'.

Next day, the response from the press was fairly predictable: the *Guardian* largely positive ('an experiment well worth trying'), the *Financial Times* typically cautious ('MORE QUESTIONS THAN ANSWERS'), and both *The Times* ('Size Is Not the Answer') and

Daily Telegraph ('CORPORATISM RAMPANT') essentially negative, with the latter even declaring – in spite of ministers' painstaking disavowal of any element of compulsory acquisition – that 'it needs little acumen to see that here is a thinly-disguised technique for ad lib nationalisation to be carried out at the drop of a bureaucrat's hat and beyond the reach of Parliamentary sanction'. Others were little more enthused. The *Telegraph*'s City editor reported, almost certainly accurately, 'a cool reception' in the Square Mile; the CBI warned darkly against 'nationalisation by the back door'; the Institute of Directors feared even worse, namely 'trap-door nationalisation'; ICI, in a notably strong statement, described the creation of the IRC as frankly 'undesirable', especially in the context of the White Paper confirming 'the impression that the Government intends to extend its control over industry, to interfere still more with individual initiative and to further the policy of the public ownership of the means of production'; while Sir Donald Stokes flatly stated that the problems of British industry 'can be solved only by the free flow of market forces', even though he was the man who in recent years had reorganised and rationalised Leyland Motors into what one observer called 'its present impressive and powerful shape'. Still, mainstream economic opinion was, at this particular time, probably more or less in Brown's corner. 'After all, the Governments in such committed private enterprise economies as France, Japan and even the US already exert far more direct and indirect pressure towards "industrial rationalisation" than we do', reflected the *Sunday Times*'s Peter Wilsher. 'And an IRC, dynamically led by someone of Sir Frank's calibre, should certainly be capable of making a contribution to this intractable problem, without necessarily fouling the pure waters of the market economy.'[8]

One industry where rationalisation was proceeding apace, but in the public sector, was the coal industry, prompting the National Union of Mineworkers (NUM) to hold in February a special conference. There, a youthful, uncompromising Yorkshire delegate, Barnsley district's 28-year-old Arthur Scargill, fiercely attacked the NUM's national executive, accusing it of a tame 'acceptance' of the National Coal Board's pit-closure programme and instead being concerned only with the second-order question of how to get it carried through 'with as little harm as possible to the people who are going to be affected'. About the same time, Scargill would presumably have been in sympathy with Clive Jenkins, pugnacious leader of one of the main white-collar unions, when he scribbled comments on his copy of the government's Prices and Incomes Bill. Seeking to establish on a statutory basis an early-warning system for wage claims, it had for the moment the support of the TUC, but certainly not of Jenkins, whose instant reactions included 'recipe for the destruction of the Labour Party', 'the ruin of industry', 'interestingly like General Franco's domestic arrangements', and – most starkly – 'Gauleiter powers'.

Even so, in the permanently charged field of industrial relations, the highest-profile episode of early 1966 had been, also in February, the very real threat of a national railway strike, after Aubrey Jones's National Board for Prices and Incomes had recommended no improvement on British Rail's 3½ per cent pay offer to the National Union of Railwaymen (NUR). With the strike due to start on Valentine's Day, a trio of diarists recorded what happened:

> The rail strike is still officially on, & disgustingly our department [at the Air Ministry] still hasn't any proper plans for getting people in . . . I feel that if the Government give way over this rail strike they are sunk. *(Keith McBride, 9 February)*
>
> The rail strike hasn't been called off yet . . . I have some sympathy with the railmen, as a lot of them are very low paid, & their pensions especially are miserable. *(McBride, 10 February)*
>
> I've little doubt that after all the drama and suspense and emergency arrangements for getting commuters to work by other means, it will, as happened in the case of the last threatened rail strike exactly six years ago, be called off at the last moment. That sort of fun is a thing of the past. *(Anthony Heap, 11 February)*
>
> It came through at 1 AM This morning that the Rail Strike is off – after talks at Downing St. Soapy Sam will get the Kudos whilst Brown & Sidy Green did the work. *(Florence Turtle, 12 February)*

'Green' was Sidney Greene, general secretary of the NUR, but who was the latter-day Samuel Wilberforce? Presumably Harold Wilson, no favourite of this strongly anti-Labour, 69-year-old Wimbledon Park resident. As for precisely how the dispute was settled that Friday night, Geoffrey Goodman in his obituary of Greene would identify this as the moment that saw 'the birth of what became the "beer and sandwiches" syndrome'; and supporting evidence comes from the diary of Castle (closely involved as transport secretary), as she described the NUR executive apparently camped for the night at No. 10, while a huge crowd of press and public waited outside for news:

> ... Harold suggested [after the government's latest negotiating point] they might like to retire and talk it over. It was 10 pm and we reeled into Marcia's room [i.e. Marcia Williams, Wilson's highly influential personal secretary] while they trooped off to another one, Harold promising to send them sandwiches ... His son, Giles, joined us, and we whiled away the hours chatting with George Wigg [Paymaster General], Gerald Kaufman [Labour's parliamentary press officer and close to Wilson] and Lloyd-Hughes [Trevor Lloyd-Hughes, the PM's press secretary]. Harold, with his high sense of drama, trooped us all upstairs to peep out at the crowds waiting in Downing Street. As time passed, Harold said, 'It looks hopeful. If we can't interrupt TV with a news flash soon, it would be better to go on all night.' At 11 pm Sid [i.e. Greene, much trusted by the government because of his moderation] came out looking tired but distinctly perky for him. But all he would say, solemnly and officially, was that they wanted to ask some more questions.
>
> By the time the men trooped in, bottles of beer, thick sandwiches, sausages and pies were circulating. Sid said the point that some of them wanted to know was, if the talks on 11 March [promised earlier in the evening by Wilson] revealed that the lower-paid workers ought to get more, could it be made retrospective? Harold decided the moment had come to get tough: he was sorry but there could be no more money this round. It seemed deadlock as the men trooped out again. I could only hope my instinct had been right: that the chief thing we had to do was to convince them this really was the brink and that we were prepared to go over it.
>
> Another painful wait, with Jim [Callaghan] looking in from next door. Just as hope seemed dead, out came Sid. The strike was off by thirteen votes to ten! I hugged Harold ...

So, yes, beer and sandwiches – but clearly, not just sandwiches to feed the inner man. 'The railwaymen came to No 10 for discussions and stayed late into the night,' writes Linda McDougall in her recent biography of Williams [later Lady Falkender]. 'Sandwiches were provided by the private office. They had been ordered from government hospitality and were very small and dainty. Marcia and her staff went shopping and fed the railwaymen plenty of beer and solid food. They also took over the job of delivering it to the Cabinet Room because Marcia had noticed that every time the civil servants went into the room, the talking dried up.'[9]

Whether the late-night provisions did the trick or not was irrelevant at one Gloucestershire village. Adlestrop station was opened in 1853 as part of the Cotswold Line from Wolvercote Junction to Evesham; Edward Thomas's train stopped there in June 1914; and, as part of the wide-ranging 'Beeching axe', it closed on 3 January 1966, with the station building being demolished soon afterwards. The transport future, certainly in the political-cum-popular imagination, lay elsewhere, above all with cars and planes – with even motorway service stations having their own temporary glamour, epitomised by Leicester Forest East opening this February with a silver-service experience at the Captain's Table café (design by Terence Conran, waiters in sailor suits, pianist on a baby grand) in the bridge over the M1. The car was also fundamentally changing policing. 'Mobile beat policing is not a panacea of all our ills but it is in such methods that we must find the best use of our available manpower,' wrote Colonel T. E. St Johnston, Chief Constable of Lancashire, in *The Times* in January about how the previous year, faced in the new overspill town of Kirkby by an epidemic of youthful hooliganism and a shortage of manpower to deal with it, his colleagues there had reorganised the eleven foot-patrol beats into five mobile beats, patrolled continuously night and day by a constable in a deliberately distinctive light-blue car, with a white panda band painted vertically around it. Other police forces, for example in Aberdeen, had been doing something similar for several years, but Johnston's article gave the 'mobile' approach a significant spur, with panda cars coming in generally in the course of 1966 and, in the words of one historian of the police, 'changing the face of British policing from a dominantly preventive [through the bobby on the beat] to a fire brigade mode'. Two very senior officers would reflect in the 1990s on the consequences:

> It is a super system of policing. The only thing it can't cope with is human nature. When you put a police officer in a tin box and call it a car, human nature being what it is, he doesn't get out that much . . . what happens in practice is that you send them by radio to deal with an incident and the flashing blue light's going . . . and when you arrive at an incident there's a certain amount of nervousness, wishing it wasn't you going there . . . when you arrive in your tin box and actually pull out of it, you become aggressive, or tend to . . . (*Chief Constable Wiseman, Lancashire police*)
>
> It was supposed to make more use of manpower and save increasing manpower which was costly. It was supplemented by a residential beat man . . . but gradually you found that with courses and training and courts and sickness you took the residential man in to cover the car, because it was essential to have someone on mobile duty then because there were vacant places where the policemen used to be, it still had to be dealt with. So in fact it degenerated into just a mobile control, and if it was a busy place the policeman in the car lost touch because all he was doing is what they are doing now, answering calls, and he didn't have time to chat to somebody and get to know what was going on . . . (*Superintendent Hearn, Durham County Police*)

As for the world of aviation, the signal moment came in February, as 43-year-old Freddie Laker, having resigned as managing director of British United Airways (which he had made into Britain's largest independent airline before becoming equally frustrated by the ignorance of his chairman and by the petty wrangling of the unions), launched Laker Airways. It would be, he told the press, an all-jet airline catering for the package holiday trade; he and his wife would be the sole directors; it would operate out of Gatwick; and he added: 'The inclusive holiday trade by air is about to explode. I will make possible cheaper and longer holidays by efficiency and speedier travel.'[10]

'The loosely worded brief given to Sir John Newsom's commission makes change by agreement possible,' optimistically argued in January, on another front entirely of national life, the *New Statesman*'s Kathleen Gibberd. 'This', she went on, 'is the only way: socially unjust though the public school system is, to try to remove it by a swift surgical operation would create too much havoc.' One reader, John Furness, could hardly have disagreed more vehemently:

> I do not believe that, left to themselves, or with only minimal state intervention, private schools will ever voluntarily relinquish their peculiar advantages and integrate themselves into any state system . . .
>
> There must be many of us in state education who helped to vote Wilson in partly because we thought that the modernisation of Britain must of necessity imply the sweeping away of a system in which equality is denied to the many in order that the Old Boy network may operate on behalf of the few. The Labour Party seems struck with palsy whenever it addresses itself to private education, keen to flourish the Commission but reluctant to wield the cut-throat. There seems to be a real prospect of effective action being lost for lack of resolve. How long, O Anthony, how long?

'Anthony' was, of course, Anthony Crosland, who on 17 February announced the composition of the Public Schools Commission under Newsom's chairmanship. The fourteen new names included the LSE's radical-minded David Donnison as vice-chairman; two public school headmasters (one of them, Marlborough College's John Dancy, of a reforming bent); Crosland's friend Harry Judge (headmaster of Banbury Grammar School); the almost statutory Lord Annan (provost of King's College, Cambridge); the philosopher Bernard Williams; and the influential educational economist (and Crosland confidant) John Vaizey, whose revised *Education for Tomorrow* was about to come out as a Pelican and affirm that 'it is ridiculous that some of the best schools should be available only to the rich'.

'It appears carefully but firmly weighted in favour of change' was the instant verdict of the *Guardian*'s education correspondent, Peter Preston, on the overall line-up; but as Brian Simon would point out, admittedly with the benefit of hindsight, the fact was that, with only 'one or possibly two exceptions', it 'hardly represented the social forces whose criticisms had forced (or led to) its appointment'. Indeed, in February 1966 itself, Preston was in gloomier mood less than a week later, reporting that the public schools were presenting 'what looks like an uncommonly resolute front'; that their headmasters were saying to each other that if they failed to stick together, 'we'll be picked off like the monasteries'; and that the chances were already visibly receding for 'Mr Anthony Crosland's hope that by appointing a commission to supervise the schools' integration with the State system with executive powers to arrange individual schemes, he might be able to avoid rigid, across-the-table bargaining'.

Next day, the House of Lords debated the public school question. Lord (Rab) Butler, who two decades earlier had masterminded the exclusion of the public schools from his 1944 Education Act, declared that 'any solution on the lines of free entry' would 'upset and destroy the spirit and character of the public schools'; Lord Caccia, provost of Eton, acknowledged 'the sincerity of the feeling for what in short is called social justice', but insisted that 'many who have given and are giving the service of their lives in independent schools have equally sincere convictions on independence in education and on the rights of parents to choose the kind of education which their children should have'; Baroness Dora Gaitskell, Hugh's widow, looked forward 'to the time when great names like Eton and Winchester will survive with the label "comprehensive" attached to them'; and Lord Longford, colonial secretary, in effect spoke for the government: 'There is a strong, passionate conviction that public schools as they stand today represent a wide measure of social injustice and social divisiveness . . . We all subscribe to the idea of free parental choice . . . But I do not think one can say that more than about 10 per cent of the country have freedom of parental choice now.'[11]

Crosland's main energies were – as ever, and understandably – focused on state education. 'Under the present system, with streaming in primary schools followed by selection at 11-plus, the working-class child of similar abilities to the middle-class child at the age of eight does progressively worse at primary school, has less chance of obtaining a grammar school place, and falls still farther behind from 11 onwards,' he patiently explained in January to the North of England Education Conference at Harrogate. Emphasising how the labour market was changing, as the number of unskilled jobs steadily decreased, he condemned as 'feckless prodigality', amounting to a 'frightful waste of latent talent through the sheer fact of segregation', the way in which some 75 per cent of children were artificially cut off from educational opportunity. As for those critics who maintained that Britain's traditional elite system was vital, he noted caustically that the country had long combined it with 'the slowest rate of economic growth of any advanced industrial country'. He conceded, though, there remained 'the problem of the one-class neighbourhood school'. Here, he was adamant that it was 'not, of course, a problem created by going comprehensive: four out of five secondary modern schools are neighbourhood schools' – a response which, notes one educational historian, Nirmala Rao, 'missed the point about the escape route for the bright child'. Moreover, she quotes undated notes in Crosland's papers revealing that he was well aware that the 'neighbourhood one-class school . . . clearly *is* danger on housing estates or in the old slums: therefore *must* try to draw catchment areas to minimise it'.

The local education authorities, meanwhile, continued to ponder their responses to Circular 10/65, with Conservative-run ones presumably taking account of Edward Boyle's surprisingly frank statement, in answer to a question at the same Harrogate conference, that if he were education secretary in a future Conservative government, it would be plain 'silly' to withdraw it; while Crosland himself observed that he was 'not losing any sleep' over the refuseniks, which by about this time included Surrey, Kingston, Croydon, Worcester, Portsmouth and Westmorland as well as Bournemouth, with some six months still to go (i.e. a year after the circular) before any final tally would be possible. It remained at local level, perhaps especially on the part of the oppositionists, an intensely emotive issue. Comprehensive reorganisation compared to the political system 'of Nazi Germany', comprehensive schools described as designed to 'tyrannize the minds of the young', even to 'create animal farms where all units receive such teaching as the State Commissars see fit to give' – such were the reported words in January of local councillors in Worcester. That same day, as it happened, saw Leeds education committee debating the matter, with a calmer Conservative voice belonging to Councillor Irwin Bellow:

> That change is due is not in dispute; what form that change should take, however, is arguable. Twenty years ago it was felt that the '11 plus' was going to be the answer to all our problems. It was claimed that at last we had found the solution as to how to choose those

> children who would be most likely to succeed academically. Strong educational arguments and theories were put forward in support of this contention. Today, this is all behind us, and we recognise the limitations of this form of selection. But now, today, we are listening to the same arguments on behalf of comprehensive education. It is to be the panacea for all our ills – Eureka, now we have it, the final solution! It may well be; but I do not know, and in truth Alderman Walsh [Labour's Joshua Walsh, chairman of the committee] does not know, and no-one else knows.

'So let us try it by all means,' concluded Bellow. 'But while we are trying, it is at our peril that we destroy what we know has positively been proved to be good.'[12]

On another matter altogether, homosexual law reform, most politicians, whether national or local, steered well clear; and it was a thinly attended House of Commons which this February debated the private member's bill – essentially seeking to make homosexuality legal between consenting adults – put forward by a Conservative backbencher, Humphry Berkeley, despite, as he told a journalist soon afterwards, 'a lot of unpleasant abuse and accusations'. 'Nobody', noted the watching Frances Partridge, 'said anything of the smallest interest,' though she did acknowledge that the home secretary, Roy Jenkins, strongly supportive of Berkeley, 'spoke in fine ringing tones, clearly and to the point', as he argued that, in the six years since the subject had last been debated by the Commons, 'public opinion has to a substantial extent been educated'. In the event, the reformers carried the day on this second reading, by 164 votes (including 112 Labour MPs) to 107 (comprising 97 Conservatives and 10 Labour MPs, with all but one of those 10 being trade unionists). The 48 Conservatives on Berkeley's side included Enoch Powell and Iain Macleod; Margaret Thatcher (on the reformers' side back in 1960) did not vote, nor did Wilson or Brown, with the latter that afternoon privately letting himself go to Castle and various civil servants: 'This is how Rome came down . . . Don't think teenagers are able to evaluate your liberal ideas. You will have a totally disorganized, indecent and unpleasant society. You must have rules! We've gone too damned far on sex already.' A notably different perspective came the following week from Colm Brogan, the Glaswegian, working-class, right-wing journalist and polemicist who was also a devout Roman Catholic. 'I trust that the MPs who have lent their support to Mr Humphry Berkeley's Bill do not imagine that it goes even half-way towards redressing the enormous wrongs that society inflicts on the homosexual,' he wrote to the *Daily Telegraph*:

> If it is passed into law, homosexual relationships between consenting adults will no longer be illegal, but they will still not be legitimised. A long-lasting, faithful and rewarding partnership will receive the same contemptuous and grudging tolerance as will be accorded to encounters that are merely casual, ephemeral and possibly even rather sordid. A happy and utterly respectable homosexual home will be regarded as no better than a *maison tolérée*.
>
> Justice demands that the law give to such a home exactly the same status and protection as it already gives to the bourgeois and now largely discredited institution of heterosexual marriage . . .

'To adapt George Meredith's progress report on the advance of feminism,' he ended, 'we may have passed both Cape Turk and Seraglio Point, but we are hardly half-way to reaching Cape Cod.'[13]

Things were shifting, too, on another great social issue. Back in November – against the background of a sustained campaign by the Abortion Law Reform Association, four major national women's organisations instructing their councils to press the government for action, and increasingly widespread media focus (not least *Up the Junction*) – the second reading of a bill put forward by Labour's Lord Silkin to liberalise the abortion laws had seen a provisional affirmative vote by the House of Lords. Now in February, no doubt fortified by Silkin's decision to change his bill in order to provide for a second opinion from a medical practitioner before a pregnancy could be legally terminated, the Lords voted (75–51) that a woman's inadequacy for motherhood should be grounds for a legal abortion; and this prompted not only the Bishop of Exeter, Robert Mortimer, to walk out of the chamber in protest at this erosion of the sanctity of the human foetus, but the Archbishop of Canterbury, Michael Ramsey, to declare soon afterwards that 'that seems to open the door to almost anything and to allow abortion just when it is convenient to have it'. Still, the tide of mainstream opinion and coverage was undeniably going the other way, typified later this month by the Home Service's *Focus on Abortion* documentary, highlighting the case of a Mrs Jones (not her real name) from Manchester. During her pregnancy she had had German measles; her baby son had been born blind and deaf, with a heart murmur; and now, two and a half years on, he was still unable even to sit up or to feed himself. 'The doctor at the big hospital', she recalled about what had happened during her pregnancy after her illness, 'told me all the things that could be wrong with this baby – it may be blind or deaf or be deformed or I may not carry it to full nine months or it may die after it was born . . . and then said, "But I can't do anything about it; you'll just have to hope for the best".'[14]

Two days before this poignant radio testimony, and two days after the vote on Berkeley's bill, came in the *Observer* on 13 February the most powerful and challenging of blasts by Ian Nairn. Called 'Stop the Architects Now', it signalled that the opinion-forming tide might just be about to turn against architectural modernism:

> The outstanding and appalling fact about British architecture [he began] is that it is just not good enough. It is not standing up to use or climate, either in single buildings or a whole environment.
>
> The battle of style has long been won – nearly *all* new architecture is likely to be modern – but the battle of quality has been forgotten, or never joined at all. Last year's buildings, once they have been applauded and got into the magazines, too often and too quickly look far worse than the 100-year-old speculations that they are replacing.

After noting that 'contempt' was the typical public attitude towards both architects and planners, Nairn then listed specifically the main things that in his view were wrong: 'most modern buildings in Britain weather badly'; 'an alarming tendency – far worse than that of the Victorians, who are accused of it so often – towards façade architecture', typified by the dismal rear of such well-known pedestrian precincts as Coventry and Canterbury; 'intolerable fussiness of detail', summed up by the equally dismal term 'artistic frills'; 'obsession with rectangular design, avoidance of curves and angles', with

Nairn at this point declaring that 'at worst it is the true arrogance of man stamping over the landscape in jackboots', that indeed 'it was the boasted trademark of Le Corbusier, that arch-priest of arrogance'; 'obsession with separate units', with Corbusier again the villain; 'zoning', i.e. 'separating out areas into industrial, residential, commercial, etc', in turn explaining why 'the new estates don't have corner shops, or why workers in a New Town may have to travel miles to a clean and inoffensive factory'; 'the eagerness to take up fads', such as the current one for pedestrian precincts, with Nairn noting that whereas 'clothes fashions can be discarded in a week, an architectural or planning fashion is something that humanity is lumbered with for half a century'; 'the insistence in nine cases out of 10 that "comprehensive development" means comprehensive ownership and comprehensive demolition instead of a comprehensive look at a town's problems', in effect a 'blind we-know-best arrogance' ignoring the abiding truth that 'in most town centres the mixture of styles and temperaments – irrespective of architectural quality – is essential to their character, and it simply cannot be achieved by one designer at one time in one scheme'; and finally, to complete the list, '"tidiness," "order," "organisation," "discipline," – sooner or later one of these slogans will crop up, and the basic issue becomes a fight between a set of preconceptions and what people are actually *like*, in all their frailty and diversity', with architects and planners again too often unable to accept that 'people have got to be trusted, and if they make mistakes they have got to be trusted again and again', that indeed 'anything else is aesthetic fascism'.

Summing up, Nairn identified as 'the basic fault' the fact that 'the professions have got above themselves'; and he called on the users of buildings, 'the consumers', to 'act and tell the professionals what they want, where they went wrong in their last scheme, how they might do better in their next'. Inevitably, his indictment did not pass unchallenged. A week later, the *Observer* published the hurt response of the President of the Royal Institute of British Architects (RIBA), Lord Esher (the architect and critic Lionel Brett), insisting that the real menace was neither the architect nor the planner, but instead the profit-minded developer; while a week after that, letters to the paper led with a defensive architect and a defensive town planner. Even so, it was the shortest of the half-dozen letters that packed the real punch. 'I would like to thank Ian Nairn for voicing the thoughts of so many of us regarding modern architecture,' declared M. Rollason of Birmingham. 'How heartily sick we are of straight lines and uniform angles. And now – even our little round pillar boxes have to go!'

Was there an element of insularity, even perhaps of British exceptionalism, in Nairn's polemic? Esher apparently thought so ('Nairn makes an attack on the right-angle, which he characteristically blames on a foreigner', i.e. Corbusier); and something similar was probably in play when it came earlier in February to Oxford MAs electing a new Professor of Poetry to succeed Robert Graves. In one corner, the 69-year-old very English poet Edmund Blunden, who had fought in the Great War, received the MC, written on many subjects (not least cricket), and lived in a Suffolk mill house; in the other corner, the 48-year-old American poet Robert Lowell, probably the first foreign-born candidate to stand since the poetry chair had been founded in 1708. Blunden started as favourite, with his known backers including Lord and Lady Longford, Douglas Jay, Sir Hugh Greene, Cecil King, L. P. Hartley and the heads of several colleges; but there were rumours of coachloads of Lowell supporters being marshalled from London (with voting being only in person, wearing academic dress).

The decisive day was Saturday the 5th. 'This morning the voters who entered the Sheldonian were mainly elderly; there seemed to be plenty of women in black gowns and spectacles who embraced each other,' noted the watching John Gale. 'This afternoon the voters were on the whole younger, with several pretty girls.' At 4.40, just before the football results (Arsenal 1 Burnley 1, Blackburn Rovers 1 Liverpool 4, Blackpool 0 Tottenham Hotspur 0 . . .), the outcome was announced to a small crowd gathered just outside the Sheldonian: a win for Blunden, by 477 votes to 241, after the coachloads had palpably failed to materialise for the poet whom Stephen Spender described soon afterwards, in a disappointed letter to *The Times*, as 'the most brilliant and original and serious poet of his generation'; and he referred darkly, with reference to Blunden's supporters, to 'the system of driving in bus loads of clergymen and cricketers to make this important appointment'. There followed a counter-blast from Graves in his Mallorca fastness, arguing that Blunden as a poet ('always keeps close to the English tradition') chimed far better with Oxford's 'feelings' than Lowell as a poet ('modernistic overtones'). While as for Spender's claim that Lowell was 'a poet of the intelligence, stature and eloquence to have a very great effect on the young', that in other words he would have a far greater appeal than Blunden to undergraduates, Graves insisted on the reverse from his experience in the chair. 'I have observed a gradual ebbing of the modernist tide. Oxford undergraduates believe now that the worst crime in poetry is to be boring: and modernism with its rhetorical libertarianism, obscurantism and unstable metrics can be excessively boring at times.' Even so, was it really the poetry as such that determined the outcome? Not according to John Wain, who wrote up the whole episode in a piece for *Encounter*. In it he referred, even more darkly than Spender, to 'the assorted xenophobes'; he quoted the artist and writer Wilfrid Blunt as saying 'We've got to stop this Americanisation'; and he described how, when an acquaintance had asked a don ('a burly man in an M.A. gown') hurrying towards the Sheldonian who he was going to vote for, the reply came back, 'Blunden, *of course*: he used to belong to my cricket club'.[15]

Anthony Heap, if he read poetry, would surely have been in the Blunden rather than Lowell camp. 'Little more than a monotonous series of soliloquies and silly charades,' he fulminated after going on 3 February to the Garrick for David Halliwell's *Little Malcolm and His Struggle Against the Eunuchs*, making its West End debut the week after *Twang!!* had ignominiously closed at the Shaftesbury, following forty-three performances to increasingly empty houses. 'A woefully tedious and trying piece', continued Heap, 'of pointless poppycock.' The paid critics were somewhat kinder about what the *Sunday Times*'s Harold Hobson described, perhaps with a degree of political licence, as 'a swinging Right-wing attack on what Mr Halliwell represents as the incompetent, sadistic, discontented, grant-aided, self-important, revolutionary young'; but none denied the longueurs, despite some trimming – fiercely resisted by Halliwell – since the previous year's version directed by Mike Leigh, and notwithstanding praise for the performances of John Hurt as Malcolm Scrawdyke, the would-be Hitler from Huddersfield, and Rodney Bewes as one of the insurrectionists. 'The success of *Little Malcolm* lay in its ability both to anticipate the student protests of the late 1960s and to parody the arc of any tinpot fascist movement,' recalled Michael Billington in his 2006 obituary of Halliwell. 'It was and remains a magnificent piece of writing,' added Leigh in a coda, 'and it is truly tragic that this quite brilliant and original dramatist procrastinated for the remaining 40 years of his life.'[16]

Not much especially interesting in the cinema these months, but BBC TV launched in early January three new series. 'The programme was set in a little, rural community, where everyone was happy, polite and respectable, and there was no crime,' remembered an obituarist of puppeteer and animator Bob Bura. 'If accidents did happen, it was likely to be no more than minor damage to Windy Miller's windmill, or the baker, Mickey Murphy, hurting his hand. Even then the soldiers at Pippin Fort could always help out.' *Camberwick Green*, replacing *Picture Book* in the *Watch with Mother* slot on Mondays, was the first of what became the Trumptonshire Trilogy – and it would have been *Candlewick Green* but for a typing error at the BBC. Next up, also explicitly aimed at a youthful audience, was *A Whole Scene Going*, presented by Barry Fantoni ('too old for a Beatle-cut and ought to dress more smartly', according to one viewer) and Wendy Varnals ('quite sensible', according to another) and featuring as special guests in its first outing Spike Milligan, Pete Townshend and Lulu, with the last reported as 'clearly the best-liked' by the largely adult viewing panel. By late February, those same viewers (consistently giving the programme a low RI, with an average of 47) had even gone off Varnals ('just too bright and breezy for words'), while, as for her co-presenter, 'Fantoni doesn't seem to have much personality and he looks terribly scruffy. Not the best example for the teenagers surely?' Finally, *Softly, Softly*, a spin-off from *Z Cars*, but with Barlow and Watt now promoted and moved south, to somewhere near Bristol. 'It has the same rough, abrasive realism, the same sharp, prickly dialogue, the same terse economy of style,' noted one critic after the first episode, but its initial RI of 62 suggested it would be a slow burner; and some seven weeks in, another critic was referring to it as 'the much maligned successor to *Z Cars*'.

No such problems for the second series of *Not Only . . . But Also*, with Margaret Drabble for one finding it 'hard to find praise high enough' after it had ended on 26 February. 'Surely,' she wrote in the

Daily Mail, 'no two people have ever before united so many talents so successfully, the verbal wit, the songs, the visual fantasies, the expert performances have poured forth from some seemingly inexhaustible cornucopia of comedy.' Over on the other side, *Coronation Street*, now five years old, was going through an overhaul at the hands of its new producer, Peter Eckersley, who brought in the Lancashire journalist Leslie Duxbury as a storyline writer (before later in the year joining the scriptwriting team, where he would remain until 1991). 'Over the next few months,' records TV historian Anthony Hayward about the fast-moving events on the street of early 1966, 'the petty criminal Jed Stone returned as Minnie Caldwell's lodger, Ken Barlow cheated on his first wife, Valerie, by having an affair with a newspaper reporter, David and Irma Barlow bought the corner shop, the former Borstal boy Ray Langton arrived and stole £5 from the Barlows and whisky from the Rovers Return, and Brenda Riley was appointed relief manager at the pub, causing a sensation in her low-cut blouses and short skirts.' Little of which was to the satisfaction of at least one elderly viewer. 'Another feature that has "gone off",' noted Nella Last as early as late January, adding that it 'verges on the silly nowadays, not the "amusing" silly, but the irritating "oh be your age & earn your script money"'.[17]

The unstoppable music machine revved away – Bowie's first single as Bowie ('Can't Help Thinking About Me', a commercial flop); the Spencer Davis Group topping the charts with the 'blue-eyed soul' of 'Keep on Running' (driving bass riff, innovative electric fuzz guitar); a portrait of Jagger included in a new exhibition of paintings by the admiring Cecil Beaton ('he looks like someone who has sprung out of the woods'); Jagger playing down the latest Stones single, '19th Nervous Breakdown' ('it's about a neurotic bird, that's all'); *NME* underwhelmed by 'Dedicated Follower of Fashion', Ray Davies's satiric pop at Carnaby Street et al. ('never thought I'd compare the Kinks with Herman's Hermits, but this is certainly Herman-type material, with bouncy beat and a cute novelty lyric'); Bowie pronouncing on Londoners ('the majority just don't know what life is') – but for young Stephen Donovan none of that mattered. 'In January 1966 I was off school with a football injury', he would remember almost half a century later:

At 13, it was that and the Beatles to the exclusion of all else, and so I'd be off across the road to Auntie Dinah's, where the record collection included the latest masterpiece from the Fabs, the LP *Rubber Soul*.

At 32s/6d this was beyond our means, so I would make the most of it every day by endlessly playing both sides. Listening, enraptured, I remember watching the rain hit the rooftops opposite – at least, that's when I wasn't staring at the picture on the cover, featuring the four coolest faces in the solar system.

I found the music mesmerising, but at that tender age was oblivious to how the melancholy of the songs was resonating, not just with my mood and the weather, but also with as yet undiscovered aspects of my character . . .

Today, still living nearby, I'm late getting up with a cold when the incessant rain on the window prompts me to reach for the iPod that the children bought to help me through chemotherapy three years ago. The sheer warmth of feeling emanating from these songs is difficult to describe. It takes you right out of yourself.

It is 1966 again, and all the years in between. Harking back to my young life, thoughts turn to my dear, late parents and, as the rain sheets down, I picture my mum rushing back from her early morning cleaning job to make breakfast for four children before school, then taking off again to her full-time position as school secretary. And my dad, down at the docks since 7am, unloading 600 tonnes of sugar near Canary Wharf, soaked through to the skin for 10 hours a day. What did we children know of that? Insulated from such harsh reality by such sacrifice and selflessness?

'In My Life' plays now, John's paean to love and a life remembered. These songs – how on earth did they write stuff like this in their early 20s? – together with countless other pieces of music, form more than a mere soundtrack to times gone by. It is the madeleine moment to all the days of your life come alive again; and to order, too.

Except, for all the magic, there can be no trace of hope, which invariably leaves everything tinged with a hint of sadness, lament and regret – for time misspent, perhaps, and things not said or done.

'In a sense,' he ended, 'it is the ultimate contradiction: music and memory as blessing and curse, and inextricably linked until the final chord.'[18]

Three notable arrivals and one sad exit during these months. *Blue Peter* had moved to twice weekly in September 1964, and now, in late January, the regular duo of Christopher Trace and Valerie Singleton were joined by the altogether more adventurous John Noakes – or, in Lucy Mangan's fond words, 'your beloved, daredevil uncle, with energy and enthusiasm to spare for the kind of spontaneous, crazy projects your parents could never quite bring themselves to get behind.' Some three weeks later, a young Yorkshire journalist, Michael Parkinson, entered the national stage with a double debut in the *Sunday Times*: a match report from Turf Moor of Burnley's 1–1 draw with Everton ('a game where brawn mattered more than brain, where skill perished knee-deep in mud and the aristocratic features of both teams took a mauling . . . it wasn't the sort of match you would like your grandmother to see, but for anyone seeking reaffirmation that the modern game is not played by a gang of cream puffs this was it'); and a humorous piece about sporting hero worship ('I know a man who's never got over the fact that he once sat next to someone in a train who, the night before, had been in a boozer with a bloke who said he knew Len Hutton'). But the momentous debut – zeitgeist-chasing, zeitgeist-making – came three days later, on 23 February, in the *Daily Express* (a week after Anthony Heap had switched from it to the *Daily Mail*, 'a much better paper these days'). 'I NAME THIS GIRL THE FACE OF '66' pronounced the centre-page spread, featuring two huge photographs of Twiggy, aka Lesley Hornby, a shy fifteen-year-old from Neasden, daughter of a Bolton carpenter, and poised to become the first working-class supermodel. That same day, suffering from depression and insomnia, the great political cartoonist Vicky (Victor Weisz), the man who had transformed Harold Macmillan into 'Supermac', took a fatal overdose of sleeping pills. '"Little?" he used to ask,' recalled next day one of his many admirers, Gerard Fay. '"Who says that the ordinary man is little? He is the great man of his age, whoever he may be, and Vicky is on his side."'[19]

No mention by the diarists of any of these four, but naturally they continued to record their daily lives:

Dreamed of Charles, Prince of Wales. Thought him well dressed but definitely a mental defective. Comforted him for impending visit to Geelong. *(Gladys Langford, 12 January)*

Pam very tired and worried about mock 'A' levels. Those recent stupid late nights! Can't tell 'em, that's the awful part. She worked all evening for English and Geography papers tomorrow – after which she has planned to go out! and Saturday! Sunday is left for getting back to study – not rest and Church. You just can't tell 'em. *(Judy Haines, 13 January)*

At a paper shop in Crown Passage SW1 a woman assistant expressed her disgust at someone paying 12s 6d for a copy of 'Playboy,' an American monthly magazine stated to be very grown up and to contain pictures of naked girls. *(Henry St John, 18 January)*

Pam had a miserable day at school, with hoods being banned being the last straw, 'especially Pamela Haines.' Apparently the most dashing boots pass, despite 'black shoes only' being on the list. And stockings! and socks! I'm afraid Chingford High has slipped for good. They will have to come round to hoods, which are high fashion and so cosy for this bitter weather. They are just too late instead of anticipating the trend. *(Haines, 19 January)*

Today, some unusual things happened on the train both coming & going. In the morning it was unusually crowded, & a couple of officer-type gents made a nuisance of themselves, charged through the coach & put everyone in a bad temper.

Coming back, it was even more crowded, but everyone co-operated, & made room. Between St James's Park & Victoria we got stopped for some time. Finally the guard & driver started chattering over the intercom.

'Let's try a G55 mate.'

'No, a 1-0-0 E.'

'Right.'

Train leaps forward about a yard, & comes to a shuddering halt. Fortunately, I & some others were able to hang on to our straps, as it was several people went over. The amusing thing was that because of the cross-talk comedy beforehand, most people treated it as a joke, instead of cussing. *(Keith McBride, 19 January)*

'Top of the Pops' good. 'Man from Uncle' fab. *(Diana Griffith, 27 January)*

Pinewood at 12 o'c [for *Carry on Screaming*]. Warren Beatty said 'Hallo Kenny, how's it going?' which was v. forward of him but secretly pleased me enormously. *(Kenneth Williams, 8 February)*

All to pay for the ever increasing cost of the social services, including, of course, subsidising council tenants at low rents so that they can afford cars, national assistance for black immigrants and education for their backward brats. *(Anthony Heap, on an imminent rise in the rates, 14 February)*

Ted ran Sue & I over to Ilford for shopping. We went in the new M&S. It was packed. *(Pat Scott, 19 February)*

We did a bit more in the sitting room – got the carpet down. *(Betty Allen, 19 February)*

We have just returned from the Theatre Royal and a very good evening's entertainment . . . We sat by a couple who we used to glamorise, but who we now find to be quite commonplace. The glamour was created by the fact that the woman was Malayan. She has bad teeth and her husband speaks with a broad Bristol dialect. Perhaps the Bohemian types that we place as brilliant University students are frauds. *(Frederick Ward, 19 February)*

Moved the T.V. & all the furniture round before tea – sitting room looks lovely. In there all evening – felt very posh. *(Allen, 20 February)*

There was beef soup & sliced brisket for lunch. Such a wasteful fatty piece this week, & we rested awhile. When it was fine my husband had a little walk round the paths to see if any thing green showed, but the borders were flooded. Looks as if things doing well earlier have been 'drowned'. Mrs Rowly came early, & we had a cup of tea before she started to do my hair, & then after she went we had Children's Criss Cross Quiz over our tea. Followed [by] The Archers, then Adult Criss Cross Quiz & Sherlock Holmes. We talked of the way popular programmes had deteriorated – 'downright silly' was Mrs Rowly's verdict on some. She said the later Plays were even poorer. I didn't feel well, & as usual, was glad to get to my warm bed. *(Nella Last, 24 February, the end of her final diary entry, two years before her death)*

> Brian drove me to church. The new Vicar like all new brooms is making changes. Nothing drastic but we must adjust ourselves to it, one thing we do have a more varied & interesting selection of Hymns. *(Florence Turtle, 27 February)*

The following evening, Monday the 28th, came the news that the diarists – or, anyway, some of them – had been waiting for. 'We are', recorded Ward next day, 'to have another general election on 31st March so for the next 4 weeks we shall be reading and listening to the usual abuse and catch phrases.'[20]

7
A Chance to Continue

'There was a little "set-to" at school during the "break,"' noted James Allen, schoolmaster as well as clergyman, as on St David's Day a long political month – the month that saw Biba move to its new home in Kensington Church Street – stretched ahead. 'I happened to say', went on Allen,

> that of the three political leaders who spoke on the television last night it was Harold Wilson who impressed me most. John Bowen agreed with me but Major Lawton would not have it! He said Wilson's answers were glib! Bowen told Lawton he was prejudiced and so he is! He is a big strapping man with the look of an ex-guardsman but in reality an Army Policeman who came up from the ranks to end up as a Major – he sticks to the title! He is a very nice, charming fellow but deeply and unutterably prejudiced, set in his views and ways, aged about 56. One of his daily features is to sit in the staff room for quite half-an-hour before school begins and read the 'Daily Express' from end to end in deep concentration . . .

The same day, in his mini-budget dismissed by Florence Turtle as 'Mr Callaghan's bribes or proposals to bid the electorate to return them to their nice snug jobs for another term' (mainly a reference to proposed tax rebates for homeowners' mortgages), the chancellor announced the government's intention to move to decimal coinage in 1971; that evening, Judy Haines and her daughter Pam reluctantly went ('dragged ourselves') to a Keep Fit class ('funny, killing ourselves with our antics on the floor to Ken Dodd singing "Tears"');

tears of joy next day for Diana Griffith in Worthing ('Driving TEST – 10.45am!! – PASSED!! Fantastic – man wonderful etc etc!!'); a dismal week continued for Tony Hancock, his thinly attended Scottish tour ending at Glasgow, where at least he kept the Blood Transfusion Service happy by agreeing to re-enact 'that's almost an armful' from the palmy days of *The Blood Donor*; John Lennon, newly ensconced in his mansion in Weybridge, spoke frankly to Maureen Cleave in Friday's *Evening Standard* ('Christianity will go, it will vanish and shrink . . . We're more popular than Jesus now . . . Jesus was all right but his disciples were thick and ordinary . . .'); Saturday was the final day for passengers on the Somerset & Dorset Railway, with the Locomotive Club of Great Britain running a special from Waterloo via Bournemouth; that evening in the Eurovision Song Contest in Luxembourg, the well-fancied Kenneth McKellar came only ninth, his cause not helped by a nondescript ballad ('A Man Without Love') and his decision to wear a kilt; the announcement on Monday by the pensions minister, Margaret ('Peggy') Herbison, that the National Assistance Board and the Ministry of Pensions would be merged into a new Ministry of Social Security, ending the distinction between insurance benefits and non-contributory benefits, meant in turn Supplementary Benefit (as it would be called) as of right and the abolition of the hated and humiliating 'two-book system' under which (in Harold Wilson's apt words) 'proud old people could not help showing to their neighbours that they were "on National Assistance"'; the early hours of Tuesday the 8th saw a shoot-out at Mr Smith's club in Catford, as the Charlie Richardson gang (with Frankie Fraser among those present) despatched Dickie Hart, an associate of the Krays; 'Workers Tried Under a Hanging Noose' was the *Daily Mirror*'s charged headline that morning, first public sighting of what became known as the 'Cowley noose trial', the much-exaggerated story about how, after a one-day strike, eight scabs in the repair shop at the British Motor Corporation's Oxford plant had seemingly been threatened by shop stewards with being hanged unless they agreed to change their ways; in the Commons that afternoon, Michael Foot moved a bill to abolish the Lord Chamberlain's censorship of the theatre, a purely symbolic action given Parliament's imminent dissolution; the press on Wednesday continued to bang away about nooses; and a new member of the Public Schools Commission was announced by Crosland, in the person of the CBI's director general, John Davies, though the *Guardian*'s education correspondent (Peter Preston) remained hopeful that 'the Commission still looks shrewdly weighted in favour of fairly drastic change'.[1]

'The Sun Ain't Gonna Shine Anymore' by the Walker Brothers was playing at 8.30 that evening on the juke box at the Blind Beggar pub in Whitechapel Road as Ronnie Kray strolled in and shot George Cornell, a member of the Richardson gang but not present at Catford, between the eyes. 'I'd known him since I was a kid,' recalled Kray about this instantly notorious revenge killing. 'He was from Watney Street in the East End. We knew him but we were never what you'd call friends.' Later in the evening, a marginally more peaceful confrontation in Downing Street, where Lord Cromer – governor of the Bank of England and no lover of Labour – sought to get the PM's agreement to a rise in bank rate in order to protect sterling during the election campaign. Such a move, he insisted, would be seen 'as a symbol of responsible Government'; but Wilson flatly refused, not only accusing Cromer of 'deliberate interference with politics', and of 'an attack on democracy', but declaring that, if he still went ahead, 'the history of the Bank of England which had begun with Governor Houblon would end with Governor Cromer'. A memorable evening, then, on two fronts, yet the most stirring action was in Lisbon, where Manchester United destroyed Benfica 5–1 in the European Cup, take-off moment for one footballer's pop-star fame. 'Best [still a teenager], with his long dark mop of hair, is known in these parts as "The Beatle",' reported *The Times*'s ungrudgingly admiring Geoffrey Green. 'Now he was the best of all, as he set a new, almost unexplored, beat . . . Best seemed quite suddenly to be in love with the ball, and the whole side followed his lead. Before our astonished eyes came the disintegration of a great Benfica side . . . There was Best, gliding like a dark ghost past three men, to break clear and slide the ball home – a beautiful goal.'

'MR COUSINS: SOMEONE HAS TO SAY IT' was the *Daily Mirror*'s front-page headline on Thursday the 10th, denouncing his continuing presence in the Cabinet as a 'cynical farce' given his palpable discontent with the government's prices and incomes policy; the latest opinion poll gave Labour a handsome lead (almost 14 per cent); bank rate stayed unchanged, with Cromer apparently advising his colleagues that 'to string along with the government would do sterling less harm than defying them'; Parliament was dissolved; Crossman that evening was in the Black Country, speaking at West Bromwich, where 'a decent, good-humoured meeting', with a 'pretty good' atmosphere, reassured him that Labour was no longer seen as 'soft' on immigration in a town where 'immigration is the strongest issue'; Anthony Heap recorded his intention to vote Labour 'out of gratitude' for how 'the infamous 1957 Rent Act has been superseded by the just 1965 one', i.e. the recent legislation giving security of tenure to almost all tenants in rented property, though he did add that 'I wish we had a worthier and more likeable candidate to vote for [in Holborn and St Pancras South] than the far too leftist Lena Jeger'; and *The Frost Report* began on BBC1, each week tackling a different issue, this week authority.

Those joining David Frost – and performing live, to the terror of at least the tallest of them – included Ronnie Barker ('a very funny man', thought Laurence Marks), John Cleese and Ronnie Corbett; Tom Lehrer (pre-recorded) accompanied himself on piano with his satirical song 'It Makes a Fellow Proud to Be a Soldier'; and accompanying herself on acoustic guitar, and singing 'What Did You Learn in School Today?', was the London-based young American folk singer Julie Felix. 'Singularly lacking in bite' was *The Times*'s overall view on this first outing (comprising a mixture of newspaper extracts read out by Frost, quickfire sketches and filmed inserts as well as the two songs), while another reviewer, the *Observer*'s Maurice Richardson, was struck by how the front man's 'new mild persona', very different from *TW3* days, 'diffused a gentle glow of sociability'. Perhaps the most interesting take came years later from Frost himself. 'Our contention,' he recalled in 1993 about the series generally, 'was that British society was not changing that much, either for better or for worse, and that the changes were in most cases superficial rather than fundamental, and merely added to or reinforced the long-established contradictions and paradoxes of British life. We tried to separate the apparent from the real . . .'[2]

As the sombrero-wearing (but also tie-wearing) 'El Beatle' arrived back at London Airport, and as noose-fever went into overdrive (the *Daily Mirror* labelling the Cowley militants as the 'centre of a web of conspiracy and disruption extending throughout the motor industry' and Quintin Hogg at a meeting at Oxford Town Hall declaring that 'lynch law should be suppressed with a stern hand'), the election campaign proper began on the 11th – a campaign, almost all observers agreed, that was of a peculiarly presidential nature, with the two main men broadly occupying the centre ground. 'He was more relaxed, far less like a baked potato nearing bursting point, almost sympathetic in fact', Richardson had reckoned after watching Edward Heath on TV earlier in the week. But not even his keenest admirers would ever call him a natural performer, whether on the small screen or in the flesh. Edward du Cann, who knew him better than most, put it well: 'He lacked the capacity to inspire and to enthuse his supporters, or any audience: he had stamina, determination and will, but he would not unbend and there was no friendliness. Perhaps emotion to him was a sign of weakness.' The contrast with Wilson, now at the height of his powers, was all too glaring: still a hint of the cheeky chappie, still a hint of radicalism, but increasingly avuncular, increasingly reassuring, immeasurably the superior TV performer, as he called for Labour to be given a sufficient majority to enable it to finish the economic job it had begun. As it happened, this Friday was his fiftieth birthday, marked by a lengthy profile-cum-interview by John Cole in the *Guardian*. 'Mr Wilson defends aggressively his pragmatic approach to politics,' noted Cole. 'All government, he says, is pragmatic. Equality of opportunity is more realistic than equality as an objective, because people are different. This is what Marx didn't understand, because he didn't know about people.' Or as the theory-averse PM himself explained: 'The idea of a proletariat is nonsense. I am more interested in people as individuals than in the mass. I am interested in the family, because most happiness is family happiness. I am interested in Saturdays and Sundays and Bank Holidays.' Three years earlier, he had been the Labour left's man, heir to Aneurin Bevan, when elected leader of his party; now he was the man of the hour, dominating the national stage; but Benn would wonder, soon afterwards in his diary, whether, 'since his success in the eyes of the public, encouraged by the press, is greater than is perhaps justified by his real achievements, so, when the moment comes for mistakes and failures, these two may be made to seem far greater than they are'.[3]

'Usual busy morning to usual dragging feeling!' recorded Betty Allen in Paulton-le-Fylde on the 12th; the *Telegraph* hailed 'playing of a truly superior order' at Croydon's Fairfield Halls, after Daniel Barenboim and Vladimir Ashkenazy the previous evening had performed Mozart's Concerto for Two Pianos – the performance that was intimately filmed to become a pioneer TV classic, *Double Concerto*; the return on Sunday of *Round the Horne* featured Bill Pertwee as 'Seamus Android', with the writers Barry Took and Marty Feldman targeting Eamonn Andrews's 'hysterically funny inability', in Took's subsequent words, 'to engage in simple chat without descending into gibberish – a fairly significant failing, one might think, for the host of a [TV] chat show'; that evening, the still largely unknown Pink Floyd began a series of weekly 'Spontaneous Underground' gigs at the Marquee, leaving behind their blues roots and instead moving into what a chronicler of the watching David Bowie (much impressed, especially by Syd Barrett's deliberately British accent in his vocals) calls 'extended psychedelic rock workouts, incorporating back projections and light shows'; on Monday morning, the Minister of Labour, the no-nonsense Ray Gunter, held a press conference at which, with the help of a rapidly compiled investigatory report by a senior T&G union official, he effectively neutralised the mounting hysteria about nooses and kangaroo trials; Anthony Crosland issued a circular to local education authorities, making it clear to any waverers about the comprehensive revolution that from the school year 1967–8 onwards there would be no government money for secondary school building projects which were 'incompatible with the introduction of a non-selective system of secondary education'; that evening, around one-fifth of the UK population watched *Come Dancing: The Grand Final* ('a really delightful programme which we never miss if at all possible . . . the dancing is always superb and the competitive element all adds "spice" '); in his regular Tuesday column, the *Financial Times*'s free-market, anti-intelligentsia commentator Harold Wincott, with a particularly strong following in the City and among small investors, launched a bitter attack on Wilson (' "Britain's Clever Little Man" ') and the dishonest, degenerate society he represented; that afternoon, the latest election odds from William Hill for the little man winning were 7–1 on; that evening, *Mrs Thursday* instantly became 'Top of the TV pops' as over 9.5 million homes tuned in to the first episode of Ted Willis's new comedy drama, starring Kathleen Harrison as a cockney charwoman who inherits a fortune; 'no-one except the politicians seems wildly excited', reflected Keith McBride on Wednesday the 16th about the election, but that evening the PM's meeting at the Rag Market in Birmingham had a certain buzz to it, as viewers of ITN's *8.55 News* watched him calmly responding ('our Tory friends are not in need of police protection – they are a matter for the Ministry of Health – the mental health department') to sustained heckling from the several thousand Young Conservatives among the 12,000 or so audience; 'What HAS gone wrong?' wailed the *Daily Mail* next morning about Labour's 'unprecedented, unnatural and absurd' continuing lead in the opinion polls; Anthony Heap decided for his day's leave on a day trip to Southend, where he 'lunched on roast beef and syrup pudding at the British Home Stores cafeteria', hours before Arkle completed his hat-trick of Cheltenham Gold Cup wins; 'infested by jokes that might have clicked from a computer' was the sour enough verdict of one critic, J. C. Trewin, to the second outing of *The Frost Report*, this time on holidays; 'I've got a housekeeper but I still do the cooking myself . . . rush in, peel the vegetables, put the roast in . . . all before I take off my hat', Margaret Thatcher confided to Jill Tweedie (not yet a *Guardian* columnist) in Friday's *Daily Telegraph Magazine*; 'there aren't any cons', replied a dutiful Enoch Powell on *Any Questions?* when asked about the pros and cons of joining the Common Market (a key plank of the Tory manifesto), adding that the biggest pro was 'it gives this country access to a very much greater market and it puts this country in conditions of competition in a very much greater market than we could otherwise enjoy'; about the same time, Frederick Ward thought about going to see Wilson speak in Bristol but – in what was generally a very cold spell of weather – decided against ('a lazy evening in front of the fire appealed to me'); on Saturday evening the future Slade – in the form of the reconstituted 'N Betweens, now joined by Noddy Holder on vocals – had their first gig, at Walsall Town Hall; Crossman spent the weekend in relaxed, super-confident mood ('we are heading for a Presidential victory of extraordinary proportions . . . the Tories can't find a way to break through the complacent acceptance by the electorate of super-Harold'); on Sunday morning, while on public display at the Methodist Central Hall in Westminster ahead of the summer's World Cup, the Jules Rimet trophy was stolen, seemingly for the thrill of it (it turned out) by a convicted street trader from Walworth called Sidney Cugullere, aka 'Sidney Coo' or 'Mr Crafty', but causing Laurence Marks and his father to worry that the whole tournament would be called off; Pat and Ted Scott treated themselves on Monday evening to the Unicorn in Gidea Park ('gorgeous . . . the dining room was very lush & comfortable & the food excellent'); next day an Ulster clergyman, the Revd Ian Paisley (described by the *Guardian*, in a briefish profile introducing him to mainland readers, as 'a spell-binding preacher') was refused admission to Italy after flying there in protest at the Archbishop of Canterbury's visit to the Pope; *How*, the ITV children's programme conceived and fronted by Jack Hargreaves about how things worked or ought to work, made its debut; a few hours later, just after Wilson had ended his speech at the Technical High School in Slough and the crowd were on their feet singing 'For he's a jolly good fellow', the PM was hit painfully in the eye by a stink bomb, prompting the instant Wilsonian quip that 'a boy who can bowl like that ought to be in England's cricket team'; contrasting editorials in Wednesday's *Times* were dismay about the election ('a tawdry business . . . it drags its slow length through a morass of mediocrity . . . neither Mr Wilson nor Mr Heath has sounded the note worthy of Britain even in her diminished role . . .') with, on the other hand, 'a thrill of pleasure' from the news that the BBC was making a TV series out of *The Forsyte Saga*; grim news that evening was the death, in his Edinburgh flat, of the eldest son of the Liberal leader, Jo Grimond; next day, *The Frost Report* was on sin, with the highlight (according to a kinder critic than Trewin) 'a devilish plea, by Mr John Cleese, on behalf of "the week's bad cause"'; and, also this Thursday the 24th, *Alfie*, starring Michael Caine, had its premiere.[4]

The film, with a screenplay by Bill Naughton based on his own play, was not quite 1966 at its best. 'Any bird that knows its place can be quite content,' summed up the Alfie approach to gender relations, as quoted by the film historian John Hill. 'It is quite evident,' adds Hill himself, 'that such a "place" means either sexual or domestic subordination to Alfie. The only female character apparently not bedded by Alfie in the film is "abnormal": a female doctor ("queer job for a bird, innit?") whose swept-back hair and glasses suggest repression.' None of this at the time seems to have worried most of the critics, not least Kenneth Tynan, relishing instead how 'sex is treated with a practical candour rare in the British cinema'; nor indeed Caine himself, who in a promotional interview shortly before the premiere gave his verdict on the main actresses involved, including Millicent Martin ('a very affectionate girl'), Julia Foster ('a smouldering one'), Vivien Merchant ('a very wilful woman') and Eleanor Bron ('now there's a strange girl'). While as for the parts they played: 'None of the women in the film comes near the ideal for me. For a start, a woman has to be wholly interested in me before I become interested in her.' And the film's legacy? 'It was *Alfie* that started me, and many of my generation, on the road to feminism,' recalled Fay Weldon in 2004. 'We watched it and left the cinema trembling. We saw that the indignity, emotional pain and helplessness that went with being a woman in the 1960s was monstrous and couldn't, mustn't last.'[5]

Nominations for the election had closed on the 21st, ten days ahead of voting. Of the 1,707 candidates, only eighty were women; in terms of educational background, the most striking change since the 1964 election was the increase in university-educated Labour candidates, up from 281 to 330; and the only octogenarian candidate was Labour's Emanuel (Manny) Shinwell, definitely not university-educated. Other candidates included Pat Arrowsmith (Cheltenham Ladies' College, founding member of CND, standing in Fulham for the Radical Alliance against the foreign secretary, Michael Stewart); Humphry Berkeley (in Lancaster, weeks after securing a second reading for the decriminalisation of homosexuality); Donald Dewar (hailed by the press as 'quickfire of speech and confident of manner', Labour's man in Aberdeen South seeking to overthrow Lady Tweedsmuir); Patrick Downey (uncle of one of the Moors Murderers' victims, Lesley Ann Downey, standing as an independent on a single-issue, pro-hanging platform and training all his fire on Labour's Sydney Silverman, architect of the recent abolition of capital punishment); Christopher Frere-Smith (founder six years earlier of the Keep Britain Out campaign and now standing in Marylebone against Quintin Hogg as the only independent Anti-Market candidate, declaring the issue to be 'Who rules Britain, Brussels or Westminster?'); Michael Heseltine (defeated in Coventry North in 1964, now aiming for Tavistock);

Geoffrey Howe (winner in 1964 at Bevington in Cheshire, now being asked at every public meeting whether he would support the restoration of capital punishment and gamely insisting that he would not); Jill Knight (one of only twenty-one Conservative female candidates, most of them in constituencies deemed unwinnable, though not in her case at the safe Tory seat of Birmingham Edgbaston, following two spirited but unsuccessful attempts in Northampton); Joan Lestor (narrowly defeated for Labour at Eton and Slough in 1964, now trying again, and a keen abolitionist when it came to public schools); Euan Luard (defeated in Oxford in 1964, but attempting again to become the city's first Labour MP); John Prescott (for Labour in Southport, informing electors that 'his special interest is economics and he holds strong views on the existence of underprivileged sections within the Welfare State'); Derek Robinson (shop steward at British Motor Corporation's Longbridge plant, fighting Birmingham Northfield as a Communist); Dudley Savill (Liberal candidate for Paddington South, intimately knowledgeable about the dreadful housing conditions of North Kensington, about to become first tenant welfare officer of the Notting Hill Housing Trust); and Ben Whitaker (suitably intellectual Labour candidate for Hampstead, no mention in his campaign literature of being an Old Etonian, and hoping to unseat former Conservative home secretary Henry Brooke). While among the many thousands of active supporters, a mention for just two: in West Lothian, the NUM's Lawrence Daly, once so strongly identified with the New Left, but now willing to speak often – and very effectively – for Labour's distinctly moderate, and Old Etonian, Tam Dalyell; and in the Shropshire seat of The Wrekin, sixteen-year-old Jeremy Corbyn, not only canvassing for Labour in his home constituency, but raising funds by selling tickets for a dance at the Royal Victoria Hotel in Newport – with many tickets sold, albeit few dancers turning up.[6]

Through the election campaign more broadly, observers kept a careful eye on whether, as Crossman had privately assumed after his heartening West Bromwich experience, the immigration issue had indeed been quietly parked, as was clearly the hope of both Wilson and Heath. 'It seems unlikely that immigration will bring forth political fruit for the Tories as it did in 1964' reported in the closing stages the *New Statesman*'s John Mackintosh from the West Midlands, epicentre of the issue a year and a half earlier. 'The harsh Labour immigration controls have brought the parties temporarily into line on the issue and, despite the monstrous over-bidding of the Conservative manifesto [presumably a reference to a proposed 'vetting system' by which would-be immigrants would have to state in advance how many dependants were likely to join them later], the differences are impossible legitimately to exploit.' Or, as one anonymous race relations expert had already noted about the campaign in general: 'The widespread search for the race issue has discouraged it from actually appearing. In any case, both parties have now taken an extremely tough line on immigration.' Still, whether in the West Midlands or elsewhere, the issue did not completely disappear. Peter Griffiths, who against the national tide had notoriously won Smethwick for the Conservatives in 1964, admittedly this time round prioritised other issues, but nevertheless made it clear, in a widely distributed leaflet, that he had 'ALWAYS stood firm on immigration', indeed earning loud applause at his public meetings when he declared it an issue on which he 'would not budge one inch'; in Wolverhampton South-West, Enoch Powell made a speech largely devoted to the issue in which he anticipated on current trends an immigrant population of two and a half million by the year 2000, calling it 'an appalling prospect which would render the social and human problem we have already wellnigh insoluble'; in Southall, a candidate for the far-right British National Party (BNP) made a lot of noise, backed by an immigrant-obsessed residents' association; in Shoreditch and Finsbury, it was a last hurrah for Sir Oswald Mosley, first elected an MP in 1918, and his Union Movement; and in the ultra-safe Conservative seat of South Worcestershire, the party's candidate Sir Gerald Nabarro told one journalist, Jon Akass, that 'immigration is a big issue here', adding that 'there is a terror that the constituency will be over-run by Indians and Pakistanis from the Midlands'. What, asked Akass, was his evidence that Indians and Pakistanis wanted to overrun South Worcestershire? 'Absolutely none at all,' replied the shameless, handlebar-moustachioed one. 'But fear is part of the general psychosis, isn't it?'[7]

'I wonder if the producer of the proposed serial on television would consider the pronunciation of the name *Jolyon* as Galsworthy once told me it should be pronounced: the name being a variant (in spelling) of *Julian*,' Henry Williamson semi-helpfully wrote in *The Times* on Friday the 25th; elsewhere, Thatcher in the *Finchley Press* declared that Europe with Britain in it 'could form a bloc with as much power as the USA or Russia', while Nigel Lawson in the *Spectator* acknowledged Wilson as 'the outstanding party politician of his generation'; and about this time, quite possibly this day, Wilson himself had a phone conversation with Frank Cousins in which the two men discussed post-election incomes legislation, with Cousins taking away the impression that there would be a fundamental reconsideration of the policy, in the direction of a softening or even abandonment – a promise that Wilson would later strongly deny having made and which would have involved an abandonment of the manifesto commitment to a toughening of incomes policy. Sporting highlights on Saturday were the Grand National (the much-loved Freddie runner-up for the second year in succession) and Millwall going down 6–1 at QPR amid crowd invasions and hundreds of pennies being thrown on to the pitch, with blood being drawn when one struck the away team's Len Julians on the head; the high-class gossip columnist Kenneth Rose was off that afternoon to Eton, in order to stay with his friend Giles St Aubyn, who taught there, with Rose noting in his diary his host's fears about the consequences of the imminent election ('what of course frightens him most is that the Socialists will sweep away his livelihood and main interest in life by abolishing the public schools'); the weather continuing cold, with Frederick Ward in Bristol recording that 'we are still managing to have a fire from 5 o'clock onwards' and praising his wife's 'technique' ('two quite small lumps of coal, a shovelful of coke and then a covering of coal dust and chippings'); in the early hours of Sunday, a shocking scene in Warwickshire as Solihull's oldest house, the timber-framed Silhill Hall, was summarily knocked down; more happily, in daylight, Pickles the dog doing his stuff by sniffing out the Jules Rimet trophy, found wrapped in a newspaper under a garden hedge in Beulah Hill in south-east London; on Monday, Heap changing his mind ('After carefully weighing my gratitude to Labour for the new Rent Act against my disagreement with Labour policy in nearly every other direction – especially the question of Rhodesia and Education – have finally decided to revert to my old allegiance and vote Conservative on Thursday'); next day had Silhill Hall's owner, a 28-year-old property man from Birmingham called Malcolm Ross who had only recently acquired it, explaining to the press that high winds had rendered the building unsafe ('I had a difficult decision to make and I made it . . . I fortunately already had a bulldozer to do some levelling on the site'); an increasingly cherished comedian finished that evening his series on BBC1 with an RI of 65 ('Frankie Howerd's trials and tribulations as an actor beset by union trouble made highly entertaining viewing, it was widely agreed'); Wednesday, eve of polling, was editorials time, most notably in the *Financial Times*, declaring that 'we do not regard the return of a Labour Government, with a reasonable majority, with any misgiving'; the *Daily Mail*'s Peter Black, while acknowledging the 'fiendish efficiency' of *Mrs Thursday*'s production, including a signature tune which would 'pull the teeth out of barrel organs', could barely disguise his vexation about the simple, feel-good characterisation of 'the saintly charlady and millionairess . . . the good old soul'; Judy Haines and her daughter Ione had a day out from Chingford visiting relations in Surrey's Claygate, lunching en route at Lyons, Liverpool Street ('Ione enjoyed steak pie and blackcurrant flan, I gammon grill and trifle'), while on the way back it was 'cheese and tomato rolls on Waterloo Station, watching the businessmen buy their bars of chocolate for the homeward journey, or the family'; and that evening, Keith McBride reflected that 'all the polls suggest a monster boost for Labour, but I'm not entirely convinced'.[8]

The weather over the next two days (31 March and 1 April) was a bit milder, as the diarists told – and reacted to – the unfolding political story:

> Went to vote at Lisson Grove at 9 o'c. I voted for a Mr [Arthur] Capel who is the Liberal candidate. Not a hope in hell I don't suppose. That awful Hogg will stay in, I expect – judging by all the prosperous looking idiots at the polling station. *(Kenneth Williams, Marylebone, London)*
>
> I met Richard [back from Wellington College for his Easter holidays] at Havant at 9.10, dropped him at home and reported to Conservative transport organiser. Did two runs for Emsworth House, then home to take Aunt Edie and the Barnards to the poll; Richard came too. We then took Miss Joiner, then to Mrs Newell for coffee and to see round her house. Back to committee rooms,

but no further jobs, so we went home to lunch . . . *(Daphne Meryon, Emsworth)*

Dad forced me to go to Shobrooke Village Hall to tell for his bloody party. I voted anyway – my first vote. Then I had to suffer the indignity of sitting in the Conservative chair & counting the voters, all 12 of them in 2 hours . . . I was fairly relieved when 2 o'clock arrived. I had planned to go into Exeter to help the Labour Party, but first Daddy wouldn't let me have the car because he wanted it for carrying Conservative voters. I felt so miserable & disloyal because I hadn't helped the Labour Party at all on their important election day. *(Veronica Lee, Shobrooke, Devon)*

Everyone I saw going into a polling booth I imagined to be a Tory. *(Frederick Ward, anxious Labour supporter, Downend, Gloucestershire)*

I was busy in the morning darning holes in my vest. Went to vote about 2.30 and saw a young lady there who has been at the psychology classes. I went to town after and had lunch in the Croft at Schofields [a big department store] then looked round and bought some food stuff. Listened to a programme about the 'Dead Sea Scrolls' and watched 'The Man from UNCLE' at the same time with the sound turned down. *(Elsie Johnston, middle-aged, Leeds)*

Watch Top of the Pops. Alfie, sung by Cilla Black, has broken into the charts and I can't wait to go and see the film if this is the song that opens the film. Still at number one, or top of the pops, is the Walker Brothers, who don't look like brothers at all. Their song, The Sun Ain't Gonna Shine Anymore, has been at the top for three weeks so we are told by the really odd-looking Jimmy Savile. He looks quite unlike all the other disc jockeys on Top of the Pops and I don't think I would like to run into him on a dark night. *(Laurence Marks, Finsbury Park)*

Went to Spanish Class & came home & went to bed, did not stop up for the election. Ivor [a nephew?] telephoned from Ireland, wanted to know whether Chelsea had won at Hull. *(Florence Turtle, Wimbledon Park)*

Watched the election results [the BBC's television coverage of course no longer hosted by Richard Dimbleby, but instead Cliff Michelmore]. We [i.e. she and her boyfriend] got suitably excited while Dad got more and more depressed. Thank Heavens, Mrs

[Gwyneth] Dunwoody got in [at Exeter] – the first gain of the evening. So pleased. We stayed up until about 2 when it seemed certain that the Labour Party would get a reasonable majority. *(Veronica Lee)*

There appears to be an unmistakable 'swing' over to Socialism all over the country so far reckoned at just over 3%. The computer they have on the job has been reckoning on an eventual Socialist majority in Parliament of about 106. Oxford and Cambridge for the first time in their history have both fallen to the Socialists. Wilson [in Huyton] had a majority of over 20,000. Heath's majority [in Bexley] has been cut in half of what it was last time. Several important Conservatives have fallen by the wayside such as Chataway, Julian Amery and others. Patrick Gordon Walker who was thrown out at Smethwick and afterwards at Leyton has now come roaring home at Leyton. It certainly is a gloomy day for the Conservatives . . . Kath has gone to bed and I think I shall now follow her and listen in with the transistor set. The Russians are sending up a rocket which they hope will circuit the moon. *(Kenneth Preston, listening on his main radio, Keighley)*

This morning as I make a cup of Maxwell House coffee, a slice of toast with butter and strawberry jam, I turn on my dad's transistor radio and learn that it looks certain that Harold Wilson is to remain prime minister and that he has won easily . . . I am delighted because if I could vote, I would vote for Labour, who seem to represent people like me and all those that live in our council block. *(Laurence Marks)*

Miriam had the news that Labour were right in front by 7.30 am . . . Labour won in our constituency with a 4,000 majority. This was a real surprise to me and to a lot of Downend Tories. Mim was very pleased for Mr & Mrs Wilson's sakes. She knows they are still churchgoers, and that is that. *(Frederick Ward)*

April Fool's Day – hilarious time before school with jokes! *(Betty Allen, Poulton-le-Fylde)*

Labour majority of 99 after yesterday's general election. Don't like these large majorities on either side, best results seem to be when more even. *(Gladys Hague, Keighley)*

I hate to think what will happen now that the Labour party have gone back with such a large majority. I'm afraid we are in for great changes all round and there's nothing to stop them. I imagine that

> the left-wingers of his [i.e. Wilson's] party will be forcing some of their hobby-horses such as nationalisation and a change in education systems. *(James Allen, Layer-de-la-Haye, Essex)*
>
> Labour Socialists in with a thumping majority. We must be a nation of masochists enjoying high taxation & inflation. We shall now get more nationalisation which means pricing ourselves out of the market. All the items nationalised in the 1945 Socialist Government are excessive in price & most inefficient – Coal, Electricity, Transport, Gas. I would like to get out of the country. I am ashamed of the colossal stupidity of about half the nation. *(Florence Turtle)*
>
> I am glad they [i.e. Labour] have a chance to continue for they have made a good beginning. *(Alison Uttley, Beaconsfield)*

Another writer was a far from contented little grey bunny. 'Grim election,' Larkin wrote this Friday to Monica Jones. 'Got the bastards on our necks now, good & proper. I stayed up until Exeter (lost to Labour) & then turned in, very tired, in disgust.'[9]

Once all the results were in, Labour had 121 seats more than the Conservatives, and an overall majority of 97; the Liberals had 12 seats; and the Scottish National Party (SNP) had none, as usual, but had doubled its vote – aptly described by Kenneth Roy as 'the party's first decent performance in a general election'. Winners included Dalyell, Dewar, Heseltine, Knight, Lestor, Shinwell and Whitaker; close or anyway reasonably respectable losers included Capel, Howe, Prescott and Savill; while Arrowsmith (163), Frere-Smith (445) and Robinson (1,029) secured less than 2,000 votes between them. Labour won narrowly in The Wrekin, but easily the closest result was in Peterborough, with Sir Harmar Nicholls for the Conservatives squeaking home by three votes, to the frazzled excitement of his daughter Sue, playing motel waitress Marilyn Gates in *Crossroads*. In Nelson and Colne, Silverman won comfortably, though Downey received over 5,000 votes; while in Lancaster, Berkeley's championing of homosexual decriminalisation cost him his seat, with a swing of some 6 per cent almost double the average national swing against the Conservatives. What about immigration? The bearded, fiercely anti-racist actor Andrew Faulds, with a tendency to the bombastic, convincingly defeated Griffiths in Smethwick; the BNP got almost 3,000 votes in Southall, appreciably more than Mosley's barely 1,000 in Shoreditch and Finsbury; Nabarro won in a canter in Worcestershire South, probably irrespective of his anti-immigrant rhetoric; and for the moment it looked as if the words of Brian Walden were largely justified, as on the steps of Birmingham Town Hall, after being re-elected in the densely immigrant seat of Birmingham All Saints with a swing to Labour of almost 8 per cent, he declared, 'we have buried the race issue'. As for the composition of the new House of Commons, apart from the much-changed distribution between the parties, there were two striking facts: that a total of twenty-six women MPs was actually three fewer than in 1964; and that among new Labour MPs, the working-class element was far outnumbered by professionals and/or graduates, prompting Tony Benn to observe with satisfaction on the Friday that Labour was 'in the process of transforming itself into a genuine national party'. Joyce Grenfell also noticed the trend. 'Wasn't it interesting that there were no new working class Labour candidates – all were professionals – teachers, doctors, lawyers, etc,' she wrote next day to a friend. 'This is good,' she added, 'and less likely to have chips on shoulders I'd guess.'[10]

'Alas, I cannot like Mr Wilson,' Vere Hodgson reflected a few days later. 'At first I did, that is a year or two ago. But there is just that something of the slick salesman talk about him that makes me distrust him.' But undeniably, she accepted, he was an election winner, in contrast to his opponent:

> It is Mr Wilson's handsome face, good looking at any angle, his relaxed and fatherly manner that has bewitched everyone. Poor Mr Heath has no magic to charm the voters. He is strong and forthright and improved very much in the course of the campaign. He must rely on the future to prove himself right and the Socialists wrong, and then perhaps his forceful unimaginative way of speaking may wash him up on the shore of Victory.

Gallup's polling soon after the election confirmed Hodgson's analysis. Asked why Labour had won and the Conservatives had lost, the

Birmingham, 28 March 1965: *Thank Your Lucky Stars*

Tredegar, Blaenau Gwent, 2 April 1965: J. Harvey Limited clothing factory

Overleaf: Hulme, 1965

The Gorbals, Glasgow

Hulme, 1965

Abinger Hammer, Surrey, 11 May 1965

Gleadless Valley, Sheffield, 1965

Coventry, 1965

London, c.1965

London, 1965: Julie Christie

for children...
BRAVINGTONS

Chirnside, Berwickshire, 22 September 1965: Jim Clark on open-top bus

Smethwick, 12 February 1965: Malcolm X

Manchester, 1965

1235 NA
RRARD'S
1898
CES

Halifax, 1965

main answers were respectively 'Mr Wilson' and 'Mr Heath'; while among those who had seen the two men on TV during the campaign, almost three-fifths reckoned that Wilson's appearances had increased support for Labour, whereas less than one-fifth felt that Heath's appearances had benefited his party. Was Labour's handsome majority a sign that the country as a whole was now moving permanently in a leftwards direction? 'I hope that we're going to carry on for the next fifteen or twenty years,' the left-wing Renee Short announced on *Any Questions?* on the Friday night, adding that the government would now 'go some way towards the Left and I think this is what the people want, this is why they've given us the majority that they have, and I think that the people will be well satisfied . . .' Another female Labour MP, Shirley Williams, preferred in this moment of triumph to emphasise how her party under Wilson had managed to find the sweet spot in relation to what she depicted soon afterwards in the *Spectator* as a quite rapidly changing country:

> The class structure of British society still plays a significant part in its politics. Where that structure remains largely intact, as in the most rural constituencies, the swing to Labour was small. The deferential vote counted. But in the urban, and particularly the fast-growing constituencies, its importance is decreasing. The traditional loyalties, too, are disappearing. Another decade or so may spell the end of class politics in Britain, among younger voters at least.
>
> Harold Wilson and Edward Heath have both played their part in this realignment. Wilson's great achievement has been his capacity to project himself as a national leader, attracting support well beyond Labour's normal loyalists. Heath has not yet had time to project himself beyond the traditional Conservative supporters, and to some of them was perhaps less appealing than his predecessors. But once the tradition of a ruling class dies, and it is now nearly dead, the Conservatives are wise to move to a leader who represents class mobility and not class stagnation.

Or put another way, much as Wilson might now claim to have made Labour the natural party of government, for so long the almost automatic preserve of the Tories, there was still all to play for. And indeed, on Friday, 1 April 1966, at 12 Tokenhouse Yard in the heart of a generally dismayed City of London, one young partner (John Kemp-Welch) in the prestigious stockbroking firm Cazenove & Co. wagered another young partner (Rae Lyster) '£5 that there would be a Conservative majority over all in the next general election'.[11]

A story perhaps relevant is my own memory of either election night or the day after. Which is of a Labour person – Wilson himself? – noting with satisfaction that whereas the Conservatives understood about finance, it was Labour who understood about industry. There was no doubt in his mind about which was the more important, as well as morally superior, of the two economic activities. But ultimately, and sadly, Labour was backing the wrong horse.

PART TWO

8

Chains at Cradley, Springs at West Bromwich, Leathers at Walsall

By the mid-1960s the shape of the British economy was perceptibly starting to change. Whereas in West Germany, France and Italy the manufacturing share of employment had risen between 1955 and 1966, in the UK it had fallen – from 36.1 to 34.8 per cent. By contrast, virtually half (49.8 per cent) of all employment in Britain in 1966 was in services. The other major development involved size, as an intensifying wave of mergers and takeovers (almost 6,000 firms disappearing by merger in the course of the 1960s) saw the triumph of 'big is best' and, with managerial control becoming increasingly divorced from ownership of capital, the decline of family capitalism. In 1953 (as indeed in 1930), the share of the largest 100 companies in manufacturing net output had stood at 26 per cent; by 1970 it would be up to 40 per cent. While just as strikingly, of the 100 largest manufacturing concerns back in 1948, some twenty years later over a quarter (27 per cent) had been acquired by other firms. In short, the laws of the jungle now largely applied.[1]

One such big beast was the Reed Paper Group, whose managing director was the acquisition-minded Don Ryder. In November 1965 the *Sunday Telegraph*'s Kenneth Fleet reported that it was 'bidding to extend its complex empire with a £1.8 million cash offer for Alex. Cowan and Sons, the old-established Midlothian papermakers', and he predicted accurately that there was 'unlikely to be any skirmishing'. 'Life for the small merchanting and converting company is becoming nasty and brutish and may become short,' added Fleet in Hobbesian vein. 'They have not the buying power to keep their raw material costs economic and they are meeting increasing pressure from the major groups who are moving into the speciality paper market.' One of the sales directors at Cowans, a firm imbued with a strongly moral Protestant ethic, was Alister Warren, based in the London office near Blackfriars. 'I don't recall much dinner-time conversation about the implications of the takeover,' his then fourteen-year-old son David would write many years later about the home scene in suburban Stoneleigh. 'I imagine that my father reassured my mother that things would be all right, that Reeds would still need experienced and capable managers like him. I imagine also that my mother, who was savvy and shrewd, and was by now, I think, doubting that my father really had the staying power that he claimed he had, was beginning to worry.' A year and a bit later, in April 1967, Reeds paid for a full-page advertisement in *The Times*. 'Last Tuesday 300 paper salesmen were invited to the May Fair Hotel and fired,' declared in bold the caption below the photograph; the photo itself featured about 150 of these salesmen (including Warren), all in dark suits, white shirts and ties; and the main text explained how they had been 'fired with enthusiasm' for what it called 'a pioneering concept in paper marketing'. 'Only Reed could do it,' continued the hard sell. 'The giant manufacturing capacity of the Reed Paper Group harnessed to the biggest paper merchanting operation in Europe to bring every printer in the country the new Plus Fabric and Interplus Two-Tier Range.'

Within weeks came the other sort of firing. 'My father received notification that he was being made redundant. I wonder how many others from the massed ranks of middle-aged men in that photograph received similar letters; my father was nearly 53 years old. The possibility of his getting another job was not great.' And: 'I do remember that my father wrote some sort of letter, I imagine to remonstrate, or complain, or just to get his feelings onto paper. I have no idea what the letter said, or indeed whether it was ever sent. But I do remember my father sitting at the dining-room table trying to write it, looking up from time to time, and saying "I can't, I just can't", as the tears ran down his face.' In the event he did find another job; but the best of his career, like the best of his marriage, was over.[2]

'In the 1950s and 1960s the United Kingdom had capitalist businesses, some of the very largest and most successful in the world,' writes David Edgerton in his groundbreaking *The Rise and Fall of the British Nation*.

> The important British firms were national, headquartered in London, produced largely within the United Kingdom and were closely connected to government. They were also close to finance, through interlocking directorships as well as financial relations. The term 'finance capital' did not necessarily mean banks, but rather the union of business and finance. 'The City' did not mean finance as opposed to industry, but the centre of all British business, including the industrial groups. Only very much later would an overwhelmingly financial City take over.

It is a salutary passage, and he is surely right; while to glance at the Square Mile's pink bible, the *Financial Times*, for just one day in 1966 is to get a sense of how, even though the painful and melancholy process of deindustrialisation may by now have been under way, it still had – to put it mildly – a very, very long way to go. 'Will the heavy duty diesel manufacturers – notably Ruston and Hornsby and subsidiaries of English Electric and Hawker Siddeley – merge into a single unit?' asked 'Onlooker' in his survey of 'The Week in the City'. Or of John Brown and Co.: 'Indications are that current contracts of Constructors John Brown (chemical engineering and pipelines) are on a profitable basis and that existing boiler contracts (apart from Tilbury) may produce modest profits. Shipbuilding now looks to be the only critical side of the business . . .' And of Imperial Tobacco: 'The reasons for Imp's emergence as a growth stock are encouraging for the future. It has won a larger share of the U.K. tobacco market at a time of slightly lower total consumption and it has turned the general trading division loss (£800,000 in 1964–5) into a profit – probably mainly because Golden Wonder Crisps have made the grade.' Or take the coverage of recent contracts awarded:

> Bristol shipbuilders Charles Hill and Sons has won a £500,000 order for a dredger from the Port of Bristol Authority.

> J. Stone and Co. (Deptford), a member of the Stone-Platt group, has received orders of £200,000 for its continuous-process laundering machine which made its debut at the recent laundry exhibition at Olympia.
>
> A total of 240,000 square feet of Unibank asbestos cement bulkheading is to be supplied by Universal Asbestos Manufacturing to the Great Ouse River Authority. Costing £20,000, the material is for the Ten Mile Bank, near Ely in Cambridgeshire.

And an array of latest profit figures included those for Masson Scott Thrissell (manufacturers of paper and board machinery), J. Bibby and Sons (seed-crushing and edible oils), J. Jarvis and Sons (building and civil engineering contractors), A. F. Stoddard and Co. (carpet makers), Bristol Plant Hire, and Jeremiah Ambler (fine worsted spinners).

Looking across manufacturing activity as a whole by this time, two long-term trends particularly stood out: on the one hand, the decline of textiles and clothing manufacture, which back in 1871 had accounted for 41 per cent of the industrial labour force, but by 1970 would account for only 14 per cent; on the other hand, the rise of metal- and appliance-intensive manufacturing, to the extent that (to quote the economic historian Michael Dintenfass) 'four out of every ten industrial workers (male and female) in Britain in 1965 were employed producing metals and assembling appliances', while 'engineering and the production of electrical goods claimed almost one worker in five and vehicle manufacture another 7 per cent'.[3]

Decline was not uniform in the challenging world of textiles. East of the Pennines, the wool-textile industry overall just about held firm during most of the 1960s; but in Lancashire, the world-famous cotton industry by and large continued its seemingly unstoppable decline. Not least in employment – 64,000 spinning operatives in 1960 down to 45,000 by 1965; 81,000 weaving operatives down to 65,000 – while the number of running looms, as many as 304,000 back in 1950, was now down to 113,000, even as the number of automatic looms rose only slowly. Even so, in the mid-1960s something quite dramatic was under way, centring on two contrasting individuals: Frank Kearton of Courtaulds and Joe Hyman of Viyella.

'We'd become very concerned by the way in which Lancashire was made up of a number of small firms,' recalled Kearton about how during these years his giant man-made fibres group had moved big time into the Lancashire cotton industry. 'We thought we'd try to bring together a big grouping, and formed the so-called Northern Project in which we were going to bring together the five biggest groups in Lancashire to provide a major cotton-spinning combine, much bigger than anything then existing and of considerable strength.' Kearton added that 'we'd no "Save Lancashire" attitude, as it were', that 'what we were concerned about was making Courtaulds more dynamic and more prosperous and developing its export trade'; but in truth, although a businessman to his core, he was also a patriot with a deep belief in the virtues (social as well as economic) of a strong manufacturing economy – a belief that made him the natural chairman of the Labour government's Industrial Reorganisation Corporation (IRC), poised during 1966 to begin its task of ensuring that the nation's growth industries did not fail for want of size among their key players.

Hyman was the more colourful character, remembered by one obituarist for his qualities of 'imagination, boldness, the ability to grasp the implications of new technology, strong marketing sense, and a mastery of finance that amounted to near-genius'. With backing from ICI (thwarted earlier in the decade in its attempt to take over Courtaulds), he proceeded through a quick-fire series of acquisitions to build up a formidable textile empire, prompting by April 1966 the *Sunday Times* headline, 'Can Joe Hyman Keep Up The Viyella Pace?' Steeped though his whole life had been in textiles, this deep-dyed Mancunian emphasised to the paper's Oliver Marriott that he would never be accused of sentimentality: 'I know that there are criticisms of redundancies, but this is what the country needs – a pruning and release of inessential labour . . .' And, of course, he also must have known, as must Kearton, that for all their attempts to modernise and vertically integrate the ultra-conservative cotton industry – and thereby to restore its competitiveness in relation to new rivals Pakistan and Hong Kong as well as old rivals Japan and India – the long-term odds were heavily stacked against them.[4]

If in textiles the storm was already happening, the sense in the mid-1960s in British manufacturing's 'metallic' world was rather that of clouds gathering before the storm, albeit not all the contemporary participants and observers saw those clouds quite as clearly as blessed-with-hindsight historians. Here, a rapid *tour d'horizon* must suffice: in the iron and steel industry, a steadily declining share of world steel exports (15.1 per cent in 1950; 7.9 per cent in 1960; 6.6 per cent by 1969), while in 1966, the latest development plan made effectively irrelevant by the fact that steel was no longer a sellers' market; in the motor-car industry, a continuing rise in car production (1.72 million in 1965, compared to 1.35 million five years earlier), and still in 1965 only 5 per cent import penetration (compared to 18 per cent in West Germany), but an annual output of vehicles per employee that at 5.8 was higher than in the 1950s, but markedly trailing behind the USA, France, West Germany and Italy (albeit ahead, though not for long, of Japan); in the motor-cycle industry, a ray of optimism in 1966 from one motoring correspondent, the *Observer*'s Gordon Wilkins, pointing out that whereas 'a few years ago' the industry had 'seemed to be prostrate under the victorious Japanese advance', now there existed 'booming world demand for British "heavies"', though at the same time conceding that imports of more lightweight machines still far exceeded exports; in the aircraft industry, suffering during the first half of the decade from a series of government decisions (cancellations, allied to a preference for buying American), some comfort from the UK share of world aerospace markets being mainly on an upward curve; in engineering generally, the three largest companies (Guest, Keen and Nettlefolds; Tube Investments; Vickers) all by the mid-1960s having significant, largely similar problems (relative lack of products of their own; poor marketing; too great a distance from the final consumer); and in the machine-tool sector of engineering, Britain's share of world machine-tool exports falling quite sharply during the decade, with by far the biggest company (Alfred Herbert) in palpable decline by 1966 at the latest, and *The Economist* the year before noting wryly and almost certainly accurately that 'the willingness of that industry to work old and often inefficient machine tools to senility rather than rigorously depreciate and replace has long been a complaint of the machine-tool manufacturers'.[5]

Which among the 'metals' leaves shipbuilding – the British industry, along with coal-mining, carrying a particularly heavy emotional charge, often transcending the purely economic. The figures were stark enough: back in 1950, British shipyards had launched 48 per cent of the world's ships; by 1966 this was down to a miserable 6 per cent.

The stats were even worse when done in terms of tonnes launched: during the five years 1961 to 1965 inclusive, the UK's 4.5 per cent share of the world export market saw it fifth behind Japan (a mighty 39 per cent), West Germany, Sweden and France. In March 1966, a government-appointed inquiry headed by the reliably big-picture industrialist Reay Geddes (chairman of Dunlop) issued its report on the industry. Key recommendations included the twenty-seven major yards to be regrouped into a handful of massive consortia, largely on a regional basis, in order to enable thoroughgoing modernisation and economies of scale; engine building to be similarly rationalised; and the industry's notoriously poor industrial relations to be put on a new footing, through a new wages structure, new national negotiating machinery and a serious reduction in the number of trade unions involved. Crucially, Geddes also recommended the creation of a temporary new government agency, the Shipbuilding Industry Board (SIB), in order to implement the overall restructuring as well as to provide credit of up to some £68 million. 'At a stroke of a pen shipbuilding is suddenly a growth industry,' commented one business editor, Anthony Bambridge. 'Many outsiders had supposed it to be gracefully fading along the path measured out by coal and cotton. Instead, Geddes projects a growth rate of over 10 per cent a year, twice the world rate and equal to almost anything the rest of British industry is able to achieve.' Clearly it was the industry's last chance to reverse almost terminal decline, but could it possibly work? 'The Geddes Committee has chosen to fly in the face of economic forces: never an easy and rarely a sensible thing to do,' added the sceptical Bambridge. 'If it comes off it will be a marvellous miracle. But £68 million is a lot of money to put on such a rank outsider.'[6]

Also an apparent long shot by this time was an industrial future that embraced a prosperous coal industry. Again, the figures were hard to argue against. Between 1957 and 1965, as Britain's annual petroleum consumption increased from under 21 million tons to over 60 million tons, and as the price of coal rose even as the price of oil fell, the number of producing collieries declined sharply from 822 to 504, with manpower in the industry down from just over 700,000 to barely 465,000. Importantly, the Clean Air Act of 1957 *did* contribute to coal's declining fortunes – but not by nearly so much as what was happening comparatively to prices. In November 1965 – a month after a White Paper on *Fuel Policy* had identified 180 million tons of coal as the maximum annual target by 1970, some 20 million tons less than the National Coal Board's chairman, Lord Robens, was publicly insisting upon – it fell to the Minister of Power, Fred Lee, to tell the Commons that the existing programme of pit closures was going to have to be accelerated. 'We realise that changes caused by pit closures must be upsetting and cause enormous difficulties,' he readily conceded. 'But there is no sense in men coming to mine coal in an area where the pit just cannot be run economically.' And he added solemnly that, unless the industry was radically rationalised, then there would exist within a few years the 'grave danger' of 'total collapse'.[7]

Clair Wills, in her fine 2017 survey (*Lovers and Strangers*) of the immigrant experience, writes of 'the post-war smog, the over-crowded lodging houses, the cafés selling dried eggs and spam alongside curry and Indian sweets, the bombed areas and construction sites, the prostitution rackets and greyhound race tracks and, perhaps most alien of all to us now, the networks of small engineering firms, foundries, rubber factories, family-owned mills, sweat shops and manufacturing concerns which were dotted throughout industrial cities . . .' It is a valuable corrective: for in the mid-1960s, whatever the long-term deindustrialising changes under way, it still *felt* overwhelmingly like Industrial Britain – nowhere more so than in seven 'classic' industrial areas, all with their roots essentially in the nineteenth century.

Not that, if we take the first of those areas, *The Economist* in November 1965 saw anything very positive in its traditional character. After urging the UK government 'to turn its deafest ear yet to the pleas of the old-established industries in Scotland for special treatment', it went on:

> These have been bitter years for Scotland's traditional industries. Coal has lost 31,600 people in five years: shipbuilding 12,800 workers: railways 19,300: textiles 4,300. But where were the increases? In construction, 32,200: in motor vehicles, 13,000: in the growing parts of light engineering and electrics, 23,100: in medicine and teaching,

> 32,500. Is this not progress? The sooner it can be hurried along, the better.

The paper then itemised, for example, how the Scottish shipbuilding force (responsible for roughly one-third of British shipbuilding) was now down to 33,000 workers, how Colvilles' recently opened (1962) giant steelworks and strip mill at Ravenscraig had been subject to 'devastatingly persistent labour troubles', and how Dundee's jute industry (employing 16,000 people and traditional linchpin of the city's economy) was in 'secular decline'. Certainly the overall Scottish trend was pointing to deindustrialisation: in 1958, mining and quarrying, manufacturing and construction had, taken together, been responsible for 50.4 per cent of the nation's employment, but by 1968 this would be down to 45.6 per cent; while within those totals, the general shift in male employment was decisively away from coal and towards engineering, especially in the traditional coal areas of Lanarkshire and Fife, both during the 1960s showing sharp drops in the number of mines, as pits were closed or consolidated, with increasingly few old-style 'pit villages' still left.

Even so, the industrial 'feel' undoubtedly remained – and half a century later would be remembered semi-fondly by Billy Connolly in *Made in Scotland*, a deeply evocative 2018 TV documentary about his youthful time in the Clyde shipyards. 'Men devoted to football, beer, swearing, hammering at colossal pieces of metal and being funny,' observed one reviewer about the culture portrayed, though adding that Connolly had also focused on 'sectarian bigotry and the drudgery the dockers' camaraderie was alleviating'. Perhaps fonder overall was the retrospective take on the early-to-mid-1960s from the Scottish writer Ian Jack, whether it was about the massive Singer sewing machine factory in Clydebank (a workforce of some 15,000, as 'special trains took them to and from their shifts to a station called Singer'), or the town of Paisley (which 'made carpets, cornflour and potato crisps, as well as all kinds of machinery – ships, pumps, looms – and millions of spools of the sewing thread that came from its handsome six-floored Victorian mills'), or the giant petrochemical refinery at Grangemouth on the Firth of Forth. 'You could see it flaring in the dark a dozen miles upriver,' recalled Jack. 'Many industries lit up the sky above Scotland in those days – the Ravenscraig steel mill, the Parkhead Forge, the Clyde Ironworks – though none as spectacularly. Coloured lights, flames, steam, smoke and burnished steel . . .' While for contemporary testimony, we have not only Oscar Marzaroli's justly acclaimed photographs (shipyards and steelworks especially), but also Archie Hind's powerful 1966 novel, *The Dear Green Place*, about Glasgow. 'Just as the Clyde comes into Glasgow it takes its last big loop,' he describes at one point:

> On the inside of this last loop is the old common land, the Glasgow Green, with its public bleaching green, its play parks, its People's Museum. To the west of the Green is the old hub of the city, where the old merchants once conducted their business and built some of their houses. From this spot, but slightly to the south of the modern commercial hub of the city, the river runs nearly straight on, under the bridges and railway viaducts to the docks and the famous Clyde shipyards at Govan. Mat turned away from the parapet and started to follow the river in this direction. He moved off the bridge to the north bank of the river and walked along past the fish market again. He went past the exodus of vehicles, past the long narrow streets with their shipping offices, sundriesmen, pubs, seamen's institutes, carriers' quarters, chandlers, whisky bonds and coopers' yards. He smelled the spice, rope, tallow, flour, butter, treacle, fish and beer. He could see the varnished tops of the ships' masts, their stays and rings and splices all whipped and white with paint. There were big red funnels and spidery derricks and cranes looming over the tops of warehouses. He was walking along an almost straight mile of river . . .

But the writing for industrial Scotland *was* on the wall. A few years earlier, in 1963, the journalist Henry Fairlie had visited Greenock, in the west central Lowlands, a town almost entirely dependent on the two allied heavy industries of shipbuilding and marine engineering. 'Everywhere,' he noted, 'there is evidence of its former prosperity: the grandiose town hall, with its splendid coloured ceiling, and the tower which can be seen by the ships passing in the Firth; the opulent squares in its West End, as respectable as any in Kensington . . .' Now, though, the rate of unemployment was persistently high; so, too, the rate of emigration from the town; and altogether, it was a place where 'hope' was 'dying'.[8]

If Greenock and much of industrial Scotland badly needed a more diversified economy, so, too, did large parts of the north-east – though there, perhaps more than over the border, the rapid proliferation of industrial estates was making a positive impact. 'Scores of new companies,' reported Graham Turner in his wide-ranging survey of *The North Country* (1967), had taken space on these estates, employing in the region more people (78,000 by 1965) than in either shipbuilding or steel, with every expectation of soon also surpassing coal. 'They now,' he added, 'manufacture synthetic furs at Shildon in County Durham and electronic equipment at Jarrow, and hundreds of southern executives have travelled to the North-east to work in the new factories.' Tellingly, the majority of employees in these industrial estates were female, whereas of course the overwhelming majority of jobs lost in the region's quite sharply declining coal and shipbuilding industries were those traditionally belonging to men. *Lost Shipyards of the Tyne* is the evocative title of a 2004 book; but for all the unmistakable trend across the region's industrial coast – including closures between 1962 and 1966 of Wm Gray's shipyard at Hartlepool, of T. Mitchison at Gateshead, of Short Bros at Sunderland, and of the shipyard at Blyth where HMS *Ark Royal*, the first seaplane carrier, had been launched half a century earlier – the River Tyne in that latter year still had Vickers-Armstrongs operating at High Walker, Wm Cleland & Co. at Willington Quay, R. B. Harrison & Son at Bill Quay, R. W. Hawthorn Leslie at Hebburn Quay, John Readhead & Sons at West Docks, South Shields, Ryton Marine Ltd at Davy Bank, Wallsend, and Swan Hunter & Wigham Richardson also at Wallsend.

As for the Durham coalfield, with its long-established culture of what has been called 'moderation and respectable Labourism', the miners were not responsible for its poor productivity record; instead, and making its pits prime candidates for closure, it was the mean, thin seams of the local geology that were to blame. Most of the closures at this point were in the west of the county, with the pit villages all too often just left to decay. The journalist Geoffrey Moorhouse, gathering evidence in the north-east for his 1964 survey of what he termed 'The Other England', was most shocked by all 'the human waste' in the region, including 'the handful of middle-aged men who seem to linger in pointless fashion on the streets of practically every pit village in Durham': 'They have the pitman's blue scars, but they have no pit to go down any more; they are always very helpful with directions to any motorist who has lost his way among those winding streets.' Or take his almost apocalyptic post-industrial description of a village just to the west of Bishop Auckland whose pits had become exhausted back in the 1920s:

> At Escomb, there is one of the most perfectly preserved Anglo-Saxon churches in the country. But it is not this treasure that you remember most vividly when you come away. It is the miserable necklet of cottages around the church, some empty and broken-windowed, others inhabited with shattered or missing corner stones; it is the pub with a faded sign and the general store with ageing stock in the window; it is the few rubble-strewn yards which pass for a kind of square and the load of rubbish which has been dumped over that Anglo-Saxon churchyard wall; it is that the people who remain seem to have nothing to live for but the end of the world – except that Escomb itself rather looks as if Doomsday has already been and gone . . .

Yet quite possibly, taking Durham as a whole, he exaggerated. Recent research, especially oral history, suggests that for most of the 1960s the Durham pit villages – or, at the very least, some of them – were still reasonably thriving places, with a strong sense of community. 'The Miners' Welfare Halls are remembered with affection,' observe Huw Beynon and Ray Hudson in *The Shadow of the Mine*. 'These were the places where people met as strangers and became best friends, husbands and wives. They were at the heart of social life.' While 'in the village of Murton, for example, miners used to meet in a local pub situated across the road from the pit. Known colloquially as the Back of the Shaft, it was full most evenings and, containing a meeting room and social facilities, was a place where people would go to meet.' So too in Sacriston, a pit village three miles north of Durham itself: a thriving working men's club; an extensive social infrastructure; and what John Tomaney et al. in their influential Sacriston study call 'a high level of conviviality'. Growing up elsewhere in the region (which in 1966 had an overall unemployment rate of 2.6 per cent, only 1 per cent higher than the national average) was the future political journalist Kevin Maguire (born 1960), just outside South Shields. 'In the

1960s there was not a single house on our street, Rodin Avenue in Whiteleas, a large council estate on the edge of town, without an adult in work,' he wrote in 2013. And he added that his mother, as she now recalled those days (when she herself had worked at Wright's Biscuits), was still 'able to list families house by house through their work: shipyards, miner, council, shipyards, Plessey's electronics, miner . . .'[9]

Few people, though, ever called the north-east 'lucky' – but that, in March 1967, was *The Economist*'s verdict on Yorkshire: 'When cotton went down, it was in wool. When steel was hit, it was already concentrated in special steels. Its ports never went in for shipbuilding, and its mines had big, fat, straight seams, and lots of them.' Indeed, argued the paper, that region's big economic problem was that it suffered from 'too much stability': 'The mills still dominate. There are too few companies in sectors of striking technological advance. There is too often an old-fashioned air, and some of the much vaunted independence is no more than parochialism and self-satisfaction.' While in relation specifically to the still largely flourishing Yorkshire coalfield (ninety-nine pits), *The Economist* grumbled that 'there is insufficient diversity of industry to make the mining towns other than shunned, introverted places'. And more generally, across the county:

> All Yorkshire suffers from an appalling backlog of dreary housing, quite apart from straightforward bad housing. Waste land is not confined to the coalfield. There is severe atmospheric pollution in some areas: in certain streets of Sheffield the housewives have complained that the air rots the curtains and stains the carpets (God knows what it does to the lungs). Industrial haze, heavy rainfall, and on the coast, cold winds, are frequent.

Moorhouse, particularly in relation to South Yorkshire, would not have disagreed. Writing with little affection about a 'small world founded on iron ore and coal', he likewise emphasised the severe industrial pollution – a gauge placed 200 yards from a row of blast furnaces in a semi-residential part of Rawmarsh, near Rotherham, had quite recently in the course of a year registered in the air well over 2,000 tons of solids per square mile; and as for positive attractions, spending the day in Barnsley prompted in him the thought that 'the paramount need is for someone to take these places apart completely and start afresh'.

Perspectives, though, change over time. In 2015, the closure of Kellingley colliery near Wakefield – the last deep coal mine left in Britain, half a century after 'the Big K' had opened as the largest coal mine in Europe and the pride and joy of the National Coal Board – prompted much reflection, most of it regretful (at least implicitly) about a now conclusively lost industrial past:

> Thirty years ago [wrote Martin Fletcher] there were collieries all over South Yorkshire, linked by a spider's web of railway lines. Today scarcely a trace of them remains. Their sites are covered by retail and industrial parks, warehouses and distribution centres, few of which actually manufacture anything. The 'muck heaps' have been bulldozed and turned into country parks, or housing estates for commuters on streets with names such as 'Colliers Way' or 'Engine Lane' . . .
>
> Despite the huge amounts of EU money pumped into South Yorkshire to rebuild its economy after the pit closures of the 1990s, the mining villages are mostly depressed, run-down places with shuttered shops, closed pubs and neglected colliery sports grounds. The camaraderie and community spirit borne of shared danger and hardship have largely gone. Where the 'stute – the Miners' Institute – once stood in Grimethorpe, now there is just a rubble-strewn wasteland next to an overgrown field that used to be the bowling green . . .

Four years later, when Labour's red wall turned blue, Heather Parry (born and raised in Rawmarsh) lamented how 'Thatcher's deindustrialisation of the North' had turned her region 'into one of call centres and retail parks, fragmenting community and entrenching low pay, pointless labour and mental health issues in its population'. And she went on:

> Towns like Rotherham are often referred to in the media as 'former mining towns', which fails to capture the current reality: high streets sit empty, with libraries closed and a sea of betting shops and discount booze outlets cropping up where small businesses once

were. My own great-grandmother owned a wool shop on a high street that is now all pubs and dodgy tattoo places; at the top of that road is the empty plot on which the public pool once stood. In the Sixties, Rawmarsh Baths hosted pop stars like Lulu in its hall; my mum went there as a young teen for its afternoon dances . . .

Across Yorkshire, as elsewhere, the sharpest, most painful phase of deindustrialisation had been in the early 1980s, prompting Jack Ramsay later in the decade to write his remarkable *Made in Huddersfield* about the post-industrial Pennine landscape, where many of its empty textile mills still stood. Much of it is autobiographical (born in 1961, he had grown up near Huddersfield, living for part of his childhood just yards away from Sunnybank Mills, belonging to C. & J. Hirst & Sons and closed down in 1982):

When I was young, the mill village, the ginnels, the old cindered back yard, that adventure book of the environment of my upbringing when all the chapters had still been in place, the feeling of living the distance between our house and the bus stop gave off was so thick it was palpable . . . It was all exemplified by the ever present background rumble of the mills, throbbing like the distant hum of the engine room in a ship, interwoven with the sound effects of a village going about its daily business. There was the sound of footsteps out in the street. There was the rattle of the chain from the block-and-tackle by which the bales of raw wool were hoisted to the upper storeys of the mill, so often my alarm clock on schoolday mornings, as were the mouthfuls of obscene four-letter words interspersed with the chains' coursing, from the men shouting aggressively at each other with several floors between them. There was the spasmodic revving of lorries backing into the mill yards, and the swish of their roller-concertina doors being highered or lowered . . .

The hold of the local mills over the environment, over our row of houses, was absolute. Although you accepted them without really stopping to sit down and fully realize it, you noticed every single sound or smell they gave off, particularly if something changed. When they closed for two weeks during the Huddersfield textile holiday in July, the place seemed empty, a bit lost. It was suddenly

> too quiet and sombre. The mills represented power back then. The people inside them were actually *making* things, not shuffling bits of paper about. Their places of work had majesty, you walked past them in the same frame of mind, and felt as diminutive as if you were walking past an ocean liner moored at a timber jetty. This sense of permanence the buildings could evoke to the place was amplified by their sheer size. They oozed an immovable solidity.

Ramsay's sense of loss is often moving. But he does record an illuminating encounter, from a foggy January day circa 1986 as he sat on a bus photographing a mill at the top end of the Colne Valley. 'A wizened old man asked me what the devil I was taking a picture of a mucky bloody old textile mill for. I told him I was shooting it to try and capture the look of the valley now, for a book I was writing. "Nay, lad," he said. "Thi' war evil bloody places. Thi' gave folk rickets, warped bones, an' malnutrition. Bloody sweatshops they were, an' thi' should pull the buggers down, 'cause they were full o' meanness and exploitation."'[10]

Across the Pennines, definitely nothing 'lucky' about Lancashire, given cotton's deep-lying problems. 'Its basic industries and associated traditional skills are declining and its nineteenth-century environment is becoming obsolete,' a delegate of the Lancashire and Merseyside Industrial Development Association, led by Lord Derby, explained in 1963 to Harold Macmillan. 'Behind any description of figures of obsolescence there are the human considerations,' they explained. 'No statistics and no description can illustrate the pervading squalor, the absence of amenity, and lack of ordinary facilities, in these areas.' Even so, it is notable that when soon afterwards Geoffrey Moorhouse (a Lancastrian himself) walked around the cotton towns, his predictable observations – about unemployed middle-aged men 'in mufflers and cloth caps with the pasty face and concave cheeks which byssinosis [a bronchitis-like disease resulting from bad ventilation in the mills' cardrooms] has given them'; about mills 'rotting in dereliction' – were counterbalanced by a positive passage about how some two-thirds of the 400 or so mills stripped since the late 1950s of 'their looms, their bobbins and their frames' had been converted to other purposes: 'They now turn out electronic devices and domestic appliances, plastic goods and furniture. Fifty or more are used as warehouses and dispatching centres for mail-order firms and wholesale grocers or as offices for the organization of football pools. Most of the young workers who had automatically gone into the mill after their parents on leaving school have been set to acquiring new skills.'

Champion diversifier, largely managing to counteract the decline of cotton and coal, was Wigan, where by the end of 1964 such was the beneficial impact of newer industries (food-processing, clothing, plastics, light engineering, corrugated containers) that there were fewer than a thousand unemployed, compared with some ten thousand when George Orwell had been there in 1936. Still, Blackburn was more typical: a declining population through the decade; unemployment rising from under 5 per cent in 1960 to over 10 per cent by 1967; in 1964 alone, Parkside Mill, Fountain Mill and the Malvern Mill all going; and a dawning realisation that the 1960 Cup Final was likely to be Rovers' last appearance in the big time for many years to come. But that said, across Lancashire as a whole, above all across Greater Manchester, it all still felt essentially and fundamentally industrial. A fascinated observer in the mid-1960s of a piece of waste ground in Higher Broughton called the Cliff ('where mining subsidence at Agecroft Colliery, together with the River Irwell, had eroded one side of the floodplain creating a landslide, hence its local name, the Lanny') was John Cooper Clarke:

> The road had collapsed, leaving a one-sided parade of uncharacteristically middle-class semis perched perilously close to its vertiginous edge. You could still see the partially submerged tramlines, mangled, twisted, and knotted like steel spaghetti. Below was a pestilential tangle of semi-uprooted trees, out-of-control weeds, and poisonous foliage, girders, rubble, mudslides, and at the bottom, that 'melancholy stream', the River Irwell.
>
> No other river made a greater contribution to the industrial strength of the nation than the Irwell, such was the concentration of industry along its banks. On a fifty-mile stretch, countless cotton mills, paper mills, coal mines, tanneries, slipper factories, bleach works, gas works, paint works, and dye works spewed a million gallons of grotesquely coloured effluent into its waters. There was Clayton Aniline, Tootal, Macphersons Paints in Bury, all pumping chemical-rich poison into the stream. Every day it was a different

> colour. Sometimes the rancid scum on its surface was so thick that birds could walk on it.

'God help you,' added JCC, 'if you fell in – one mouthful and you would have been dead on arrival.'[11]

'CONFIDENCE AND RECORDS IN THE POTTERIES' was a *Times* headline in December 1964. 'Stemming from recent mergers and moves to rationalize the disjointed, heterogeneous collection of backyard potbanks which constituted the Potteries, the industry has gained a new self-respect,' declared the accompanying article, after noting home and overseas sales at record levels of £3.2 million a month. 'It feels consolidated, more efficient. New techniques are spreading and new equipment is being installed. Traditional skills still play a vital role, but less so now that mechanization is a word that the pottery manufacturer can use without self-consciousness.' Nor, sixteen months later, was *The Economist* in grumpy mood as it put its spotlight on Stoke-on-Trent. 'The pottery industry [employing 55,000 workers, well over one-third of the city's total workforce] has more work than it can handle. It meets the desires – both for luxury and for utility – of increasingly prosperous householders.' And even better: 'Stoke has been transformed by the switch from coal-fired kilns to electric (or sometimes gas) ones. The pall of smeech no longer hangs over the city, and there are only a couple of dozen of the old bottle-ovens to give the visitor a notion of what it was like when there were 2,000 in the city.' A pang of regret perhaps from the local artist Leonard Brammer ('the visual poet of the Potteries'), who since the late 1920s had been creating a unique record of (to quote his obituarist again) 'the spoilt scarred industrial landscape of factory chimneys, bottle kilns, smoke and waste tips' of the Six Towns. Yet perhaps also one can, as so often, exaggerate the pace and extent of change. That was certainly the view of the *Daily Telegraph*'s fervently anti-modern 'Peter Simple' (Michael Wharton):

> There are people, I believe, who do not think Stoke-on-Trent an attractive place [he wrote in 1967]. For me this sprawling collection of towns, with its slag-heaps, Town Halls, rows of dark red brick terraced houses, rusting railway lines, with here and there – excellent

> strangeness – a grimy green field with real cows in it, has a mysterious beauty.
>
> At night, the prospect of the Vale of Etruria from Hartshill – a wide river of lamps with blast-furnaces in the midst – is one of the most romantic in England.
>
> Stoke-on-Trent, still almost undefiled by smart shop fronts and glass and concrete office blocks, would be a perfect place for a devotee of industrial relics and his like-minded bride to spend their honeymoon . . .

And he offered the characteristic suggestion – sadly enough, never a runner – that 'the whole district should be preserved for ever, just as it stands, as an Industrial National Park or Area of Outstanding man-made Strangeness'.[12]

The Economist spotlight in April 1966 was also on the West Midlands more generally, which the paper reckoned to be not only Britain's 'most prosperous' industrial area, but also the region 'where the highest proportion of workers are engaged in manufacturing'. Still, by this time there was – in part because of central government's deliberate regional policy not to allow new factories there until more struggling regions had replaced their old ones – a significant downside:

> The West Midlands has not been allowed to modernise its factories. There is no major chemical industry in the region; no big man-made fibres plant; no oil refinery. Many of the region's most modern installations are housed in old buildings that ensure their relatively inefficient use. The basic techniques of the main industry – the metal-working industry, geared to the production of passenger cars – have not in their essentials changed since 1922 . . .

Despite Birmingham, despite Coventry – those rival claimants to the title 'Motor City' – no one could doubt where the region's industrial heartland lay. 'It is crammed with boroughs which have traditional specialities of manufacture: locks at Willenhall, chains at Cradley, nails at Blackheath, springs at West Bromwich, enamels at Bilston, glass at Stourbridge, leathers at Walsall, and so on,' noted Moorhouse. 'These places are so close to each other that it is only by keeping an eye on the signs outside the post offices as you drive through the Black Country that you can be sure which town you are in . . .' The future economics journalist David Smith grew up in the 1960s in the Black Country, between Walsall and Wolverhampton:

> Everybody I knew had a father who worked in manufacturing. Many worked for Rubery Owen, which made components for cars and commercial vehicles. It employed 17,000 people, many at its factory in Darlaston, close enough for us to hear 'The Bull', a bullhorn signalling the end of a shift. Minutes later a sea of men on bikes would appear . . .
>
> Rubery Owen, with engineering interests extending beyond the motor industry, made just about everything. It manufactured stands for Twickenham and Old Trafford. Its 20 constituent companies included Conveyancer, forklift trucks, Leabank office furniture and Easiclene, which made fridges, melamine kitchen units and other domestic equipment. Rubery Owen made equipment for the aerospace industry, as well as nuts, bolts, chains, agricultural tools and equipment. It made chassis for double-decker buses and Ferguson ploughs . . .

One of Smith's most lasting memories is of the noise from the factory across the road from his school, Walsall Road. 'Think of a giant drum kit, a slow bass beat interspersed with a hi-hat, at maximum volume, and you have something like it.' 'Black dust and iron filings,' he adds, 'blew into the playground from nearby factories.' Or take the recollections of the six-years-older Brian Griffin (born 1948, future virtuoso album covers photographer of the 1980s), who grew up in the small Black Country town of Lye, quite near Stourbridge:

> It was known for its traditional brickworks and for holloware (the manufacture of galvanised metal goods). Lye was the bucket capital of the world! . . . We lived in Stocking Street, a small cul-de-sac about ninety yards long with a wall at the bottom. Of course, although it was a small street it had its factory. Everywhere there were factories; even my school was surrounded by a factory.

'Growing up in the Black Country amongst the factories, the whole world appeared to be partly made out of metal' is how Griffin puts it at one point. 'Everything you touched seemed to be iron or steel. When playing, eating, sleeping or at school, there was constant music coming from the factories. The bass would be the big forge hammers, tenors the stamping works, with the sopranos tap, tap, tapping away in the bucket and bath works. Being a churchgoer I even believed that heaven was partly made out of steel.'[13]

The overwhelming story in South Wales through the 1960s was the contraction of the coal-mining industry: a closure rate averaging some seven pits a year, a decline in employment of some 5,000 a year. In their 1980 history of 'The Fed' (the South Wales Miners' Federation), Hywel Francis and David Smith wrote eloquently of how, following each closure, there took place what they called 'the virtual collapse of a welfare scheme so that by the end of the 1960s the whole philosophy of "miners' welfare" with its emphasis on educational, sporting and cultural pursuits had for the most part given way to bingo and drinking'. Moreover:

> The period of uncertainty when a colliery was threatened with closure, followed by the inevitable closure itself and then transfer elsewhere led to a sullen bitterness not experienced since the thirties. Older miners were moved from colliery to colliery after having worked all their lives in the village pit, whilst some young miners, having worked in as many as four pits, could not take seriously an employer who promised that the next transfer would be the last. The initial transfer itself could often be traumatic enough, especially if it was from a drift mine to a colliery. The old comradeship and customs, the sheltered employment for the disabled and the familiarity of the old pit were threatened or lost with a transfer.

'Constant references to "dying valleys" and "dying villages" in themselves implied a certain inevitability', they added about the wider repercussions of mining's decline. 'It became not only difficult to encourage young men into the industry, but also to keep them in the valleys. It also proved difficult to encourage light industries into the region. The infrastructure rotted. Railway lines were pulled up, health-care problems increased, chapels closed, youth clubs became derelict and the young left.'

It was a mainly happier scene in the region's two biggest steelworks, Port Talbot (largest steelworks in Europe, employing some 18,000 men) and Llanwern (opened by the Queen in 1962). 'Once, it would have been the first thing you saw as you approached Newport by train from the east,' recalled Stephen Moss in 2014:

> The great furnaces and cooling towers belching smoke; the long blue mills which stretched for miles; 10,000 men worked here, but from the train you never saw a soul. This vast, beautiful – by night, as you passed, truly it was beautiful – industrial monstrosity seemed to run by itself, without human agency, an image of the future. And yet now it is an image of the past. Today I don't even see it from the train; lose my bearings on the approach to the Newport I thought I knew so well because I do not see it. The furnaces have been flattened, much of the 600-acre site cleared, the workforce now is little more than a thousand, reduced to processing steel rather than making it, and even they are on short time. When I was growing up in Newport in the 1960s, Llanwern steelworks was the heart of the town, directly employing around a quarter of the workforce, indirectly employing most of the rest. It belched and roared and squealed, and it provided our sustenance.

'Boom town, or . . . ?' had been the title of an article in the *South Wales Argos* on the eve of the Queen's visit. 'Rich, powerful and growing, that is the Newport of today and, say the experts, of the future', it had declared, being going on more circumspectly: 'But the opinion is clouded by two major considerations . . . that Newport could price itself into a ghost town; or with industrial prosperity as the major consideration, it could become culturally barren. Will Newport's boom continue, or is its destiny that of a 20th-century Klondike, with gloom replacing boom?'[14]

Finally, the seventh industrial heartland was . . . London. And although, like most of the others, it was a heartland with by the mid-1960s perceptible signs of decline – a manufacturing workforce of 1.43 million in 1961 down five years later to 1.29 million – the range of industrial activity remained impressive: whether making pianos and furniture in north London (Tottenham especially); or sweets in Hackney (Clarnico), Wood Green (Barrett's) and Hayes (Callard &

Bowser); or Ford cars in Dagenham (the journalist Paul Lashmar would remember from his childhood on the eastern edge of the vast factory watching at night 'the glow of hundreds of tons of red-hot pig iron waste being dumped' as well as how 'the factory's fortunes and three-shift system imposed the rhythm of life on everyone I grew up with'); and much else besides. Increasingly, in significant part for transport reasons, London's industries had shifted by this time from the inner city to the suburbs and outer areas. To take alone what is now the London Borough of Ealing: Greenford had Glaxo (baby food, pharmaceuticals), J. Lyons and Co. (tea, chocolate, coffee), Rockware Glass Syndicate (milk bottles) and British Bath (sinks, basins); Perivale famously had Hoover, not to mention Perivale Silks and A. Sanderson and Sons (the latter making wallpaper); Acton, which included the Park Royal industrial estate, had well over 300 factories, including Wilkinson Sword, T. Wall and Son (processed meat and ice cream) and the Guinness Brewery; Southall's major players featured Quaker Oats, the Associated Equipment Company (AEC) chassis works, Taylor Woodrow and Woolf's rubber factory; while Ealing itself had its industrial focus in Hanger Lane (Wolf Electric Tools, the Kiwi Polish Company, and, as makers of cod liver oil and malt extracts, Virol Limited).

Of course there were also – at the other end of London, and complementing the capital's industrial feel – the still more or less flourishing docks, where the high point of Port of London trade (as measured by volume) had been as recently as 1962–3. By 1966, though, the big and increasingly unavoidable question was how the containerisation revolution, already well under way in Rotterdam and elsewhere abroad, was going to affect London's docks, constructed in a very different age. That autumn, government gave its financial backing for the Port of London Authority's decision to build at Tilbury – twenty-five miles below London Bridge – two miles of new quay largely devoted to deep-sea container berths; and the following summer it became public knowledge that the closure of some Port of London docks (including London, Surrey Commercial and East India) was being actively considered. 'These docks are losing money because they are too far up-river for the large ships now being built for bulk cargo and roll-on services,' noted one shipping correspondent. 'They are 19th-century docks trying to handle 20th-century ships.' He did not need to add that it was the start of a threat to a whole East End way of life as well as work.

In fact, London's economic future – indeed, arguably the UK's as a whole – was already foretold. The financial press (let alone the press as a whole) largely missed it, but crucial in the 1960s was the rapid growth in the City of London of what became known as the Euromarkets: these were a series of telephone (as opposed to physical) markets, spanning the short-term Eurocurrency market through to the medium-term syndicated loans market through to the long-term Eurobond capital market – all of them markets trading in offshore US dollars, but mainly conducted by banks (including an increasing number of American banks) based in London. Half a century after the guns of August 1914 had severely impaired London as an international financial centre, these markets signified the start of the City's subsequent trajectory as a restored international financial centre, with as time went by an understandably – if unhelpfully – far greater focus on the world at large than on the problematic and relatively declining British economy. In effect, in the City's post-war story of re-internationalisation and ultimately globalisation, this pioneer development in the 1960s, actively encouraged by the Bank of England, represented Big Bang Mark I, before in the 1980s the much more publicised Big Bang Mark II, centring on the London Stock Exchange, completed the process, including the full-scale cultural Americanisation of the Square Mile. Soon after the second Big Bang came the emergence of the mighty money-making machine known as Canary Wharf – where the docks had once been. And, from around the turn of the century, to experience close-up its distinctive milieu (eerily reminiscent of Fritz Lang's *Metropolis*) has been to feel as remote as one possibly can be from the unique industrial heritage of a country which happens by an accident of geography to be attached to our new all-powerful city state.[15]

That said, back in the 1960s there was incipient globalisation across the economy, not just in the financial sector. 'Shave with Gillette, eat Kellogg's or Quaker Oats for breakfast; drink Maxwell House; do your washing with Daz or Fairy Snow; drive on Esso or Mobil, in

Goodyear tyres; cook with Brown and Poulson; write with Eversharp or Waterman's; decorate yourself with Coty or Max Factor . . .' Such was a selective list, compiled for *New Society* in 1967 by Benedict Nightingale, to mark American ownership of British industry by now accounting for almost 10 per cent of manufacturing sales, or one in seventeen British workers. And he added that US-owned companies – or what a less than welcoming *Daily Mail* liked to call 'chequebook conquistadores' – placed a higher value than UK-owned on the latest management techniques, as typified by each IBM manager being expected to spend each year an average of 2.6 weeks training and retraining. Certainly, business schools were suddenly a boom sector, with three new ones (London, Manchester and Oxford) having been established in the past year or so alone to supplement the already existing ones at Cranfield, Henley-on-Thames and Ashridge; management consultants were thriving, too, with one of them, John Tyzack, telling Anthony Sampson for the 1965 version of his *Anatomy* that it was only since the early 1960s that British industry had come to realise that 'we have got to fight in a hard, tough, competitive world', and that 'the job of management is to manage'; while when in 1965 the *Financial Times* initiated a regular column called 'World of Management', its explicit rationale was that 'over the past year the idea that industrial management should acquire a new "professional" outlook has gained ground'.[16]

Not that this new professionalism and hard-headedness suddenly meant the instant death of the old paternalism. Of course, it is all too easy in our post-paternalistic age to exaggerate and also sentimentalise it. Even so, while obviously varying between industries and between companies, it did undoubtedly exist, and not solely in the public sector. Take just a handful of examples, starting with ICI and its large plants at Billingham and Wilton. 'From the 1920s until the early 1990s, "the ICI" embraced Teesside tightly,' noted the *Financial Times* in 1998 after news broke of an imminent restructuring, likely to bring major job losses and be a heavy blow to a dependent local community. 'For decades, ICI stood for sound training, decent wages, good fringe benefits and a job for life, embellished with social clubs and outings, then a Christmas hamper and a pension.' In South Wales it was essentially the same with British Petroleum at Llandarcy, as oral testimony half a century later would recall landscaped grounds in and around the refinery, a wide array of sports teams (ranging from rugby and cricket through to archery and shooting), 'three or four people working full-time maintaining bowling greens', and the whole thing, work as well as leisure, largely run by ex-military men who invariably expected to be addressed by their military title. Roughly likewise also at Vauxhall in Luton, with its sports, its monthly dances, its theatrical shows in the staff canteen, its Vauxhall Motors Concert Orchestra, its art exhibitions, its children's parties at Christmas, its long-service gold watch presentations – and its annual Miss Spectacular beauty contest, with the winner in 1967 officiating at the Vauxhall Spectacular Sports Day, alongside Honor Blackman and Jackie Pallo.

Paternalism, too, in the much smaller-scale, more intimate world of the old City, as exemplified by the stockbroking firm Cazenove, where in a still fairly tightly knit community, based in large part on a continuing mixture of trust and deference, the older partners came into their own at Christmas, as one of them (Geoffrey Akroyd) took the messengers to the Victoria Palace for a party where much beer was consumed, while another (Philip Cazenove) would give his dealers on the country-broking side dinner at the Royal Aero Club followed by a show. Clearing banks like Barclays were altogether bigger, but Martin Vander Weyer, son of a senior figure there in the 1960s, neatly summarises the 'code of conduct' if it had ever been written down: 'Work hard, do everything by the book, never let the side down, and we'll look after you for life.'

Finally, through the pages of the summer 1966 edition of *Yorkshire Imperial*, house magazine of Yorkshire Imperial Metals Limited (based in Leeds, with additional factories in Kirkby, Smethwick, Swansea and Dundee), one enters an almost archetypally paternalistic world. A lengthy, entirely uncritical pen portrait of 'unflappable' 53-year-old manager Bernard Brown ('still enjoying a steady game of tennis or a round of golf, Mr Brown also takes a great interest in all the sporting and social life of the Smethwick factory'); lists of engagements ('Mr B. Dale (Scheme 3 Engineers) to Miss P. Dawson (Fitting Warehouse)'), weddings ('Mr B. Hubbert (Advertising) to Miss G. Latimer (Telephonists)'), births and anniversaries, with six happy couples photographed; lists and photographs of retirement presentations; an abundance of sports and social news; a selection of individual stories (the nineteen-year-old apprentice in the Dundee toolroom who already held a black belt in judo, the long-distance lorry driver whose Army son was about to go to Catterick for an officer's course, the 22-year-old 'attractive blonde' from Norway currently doing 'a first-class job as secretary to Mr J. C. Leitch, Executive, Domestic Products Export Section'); above all, a focus on veteran employees, including nine who had each recently clocked up fifty years of 'service'. Two were Swansea men (Dai Rosser choosing a bedroom suite as his gift from the company, Dai Davies opting for a fridge), while a third, George Doswell, was a warehouseman in Smethwick's Condenser Section. 'A keen sportsman at one time, with interests in football, angling and motor-cycle "scrambling", he now takes things easy and is looking forward to retirement in another 14 months.'[17] In short, a world of seemingly assured two-way loyalties.

Was old-style paternalism part of the so-called 'moral economy'? The concept – largely deriving from E. P. Thompson's seminal 1971 study of the eighteenth-century English crowd's 'popular consensus as to what were legitimate and what were illegitimate practices' – has recently been explored in relation to the difficult and bruising story of Scottish deindustrialisation, thereby enabling (write Jim Phillips, Valerie Wright and Jim Tomlinson) 'an important transition in historical interpretation out of older and arguably dead-end narratives of economic decline and trade union defeat':

> In post-Second World War Scotland there was a working-class moral economy, consisting of customs and expectations that were rooted in the worlds of employment and industry. Economic security was prioritised, along with an obligation on policy-makers and industrialists to obtain the consent of workers and communities affected when significant restructuring was proposed. The workers' moral economy co-existed with a social-democratic policy-making moral economy that accepted the state's obligation to maintain high levels of employment. This was superseded in the 1980s by a Thatcherite moral economy, emphasising the values of personal responsibility and a limited role for the state in stimulating employment provision or industrial activity. Workers in Scotland tolerated changes to industrial employment when their longer-term economic security was protected, and when their trade union and political representatives were involved in managing the restructuring.

This notion of a moral economy was inevitably most potent in the context of the nationalised coal industry, where – in the twin context of coal's crucial importance to the economy and the inherent dangers of the work – the expectation of miners was that the National Coal Board (NCB) would have a far more enlightened and humane appreciation of their situation than the much-vilified private owners had had. 'Nationalisation,' writes Ewan Gibbs in his study of how the moral economy worked in relation to post-war Scottish coal-mining, 'was understood by miners and their families as an imposition of social order which would displace liberal market logic':

> Colliery closures were a moment that tested the nationalised industry's distinctions from its privately owned predecessor. During the early years of the nationalised industry, customary measures developed during colliery closure processes to protect economic security: the observation of procedure regarding the management of closure through discussion with trade union representatives; ensuring transfers for the workforce within travel distance; the provision of transfers to appropriate jobs, especially for high-earning face-workers; the provision of either retirement or suitable positions for elderly and disabled workers. Moral economy conditions were rarely met in full, but these customs formed the basis of how pit closures were managed between the 1940s and 1970s.

For the period between the mid-1950s and mid-1960s, Gibbs particularly focuses on the Lanarkshire coalfield, where he finds that although 'economic closures were still objected to', and although indeed 'the NCB rarely met expectations in full', nevertheless 'the rundown of mining employment was broadly managed within policymakers' moral economy obligations', including the provision of alternative employment (sometimes in pits, sometimes not) within reasonable travel distance.[18] For the moment, here anyway, the moral economy broadly held; but elsewhere, a couple of mid-1960s episodes – both of them in Scotland – were suggestive of inherent strains at play in what were still, after all, only the nursery slopes of deindustrialisation.

The first revolved around the Bathgate plant established by the British Motor Corporation (BMC) in 1961 with a workforce largely drawn from West Lothian's traditional industries (coal, the railways, textiles), by this time being allowed, or even encouraged, to decline. Within a few years it was clear that the loss-making plant was suffering from significant production difficulties – difficulties that the workforce very plausibly attributed to components shortages caused by over-reliance on road deliveries from the West Midlands, at a time prior to the completion of the M6. 'The difficulty of "crossing the Shap", the high Cumbrian peak of the old A6 connecting Scotland with England, became', report Phillips et al. on the basis of local oral history, 'lodged in West Lothian memory.' Management responded by increasingly treating the workforce as casual labour; and in June 1966 a lengthy unofficial strike ensued, protesting against job insecurity (lay-offs, short-time working) as well as a large pay gap between Bathgate and BMC's plants in the West Midlands. In essence, the workforce believed that the implicit contract of 1961 – about how best to manage deindustrialisation – had been dishonoured.

The other episode featured the moral economy writ large. Told here very baldly, it was in its way a remarkable and perhaps under-publicised story: in October 1965 the long-established Glasgow shipbuilding firm Fairfields called in the receivers; but within three months – thanks partly to the active role of George Brown, partly to a visionary banging-heads-together Scottish industrialist called Iain Stewart, and partly to unsuspected reserves of adaptability from the union leaders – the new firm of Fairfield (Glasgow) Limited was fully under way, with the shipyard's 3,000 workforce having in the closing days of 1965 agreed to a complete revision of the rule book governing restrictive practices. In what became known in some circles as 'the Experiment' (celebrated in 1967 by Sean Connery's documentary film *The Bowler and the Bunnet*), the crux was tripartite cooperation between government, managers and workers, with status distinctions abandoned and all pulling in the same direction. Brown himself on New Year's Eve arrived at the Clydeside shipyard to an enthusiastic reception from the workforce, who gave him three cheers and the thumbs-up. 'What it adds up to,' declared the *Observer*'s equally enthusiastic correspondent two days later, 'is an unprecedented new deal in labour-management agreement which could, just possibly, set the pattern for a revolution in industrial relations throughout the country.' Even so, it became clear enough in the course of 1966 that, quite apart from the grave underlying problems of the shipbuilding industry at large, it would not be all plain sailing. To quote again Phillips et al.:

> Workers did not accept all changes unquestioningly. Wage rates continued to be a source of tension in the implementation of measured day working. This was predictable, given the Clydesider emphasis on protecting and enhancing earnings. There were three notable strikes in 1966 and [the first half of] 1967, the men having 'lost patience' waiting for productivity rates to increase and result in higher wages. Ken Alexander's study of the Experiment [a reference to detailed fieldwork being done by a professor from Strathclyde University, co-author of a subsequent book on Fairfield] acknowledged the frustrations facing workers as they adjusted to a new regime. The desired resource of 'mutual trust' between managers and workers was difficult to establish; adversarial relations had deep roots on the Clyde.

So they had, so they had. And, fatefully, Fairfield was too small a yard to fit into the Geddes masterplan, with its big-is-best philosophy so characteristic of the age at large.[19]

What about the world of work more generally? In 1966 there were something over twenty-four million people who were economically active in employment, of whom all but about three million were in full-time employment; and the majority of the British workforce was engaged in manual work, even as that proportion was declining from 64.2 per cent in 1951 to 54.7 per cent by 1971. What circa 1966 was their world of work like?

It could still undeniably be a grim environment. 'The conditions, for the 1960s, for a well-respected firm – they were really bad,' recalls Ian White about going in his late twenties to work in Metal Box's Manchester factory. 'The fumes used to come down from the forklifts, the diesel forklifts all day. There was no noise suppression ... You could hear the clanking when you got home, hear it til about 2 in the morning.' A far smaller firm, but also in Manchester, were the printers Cheetham & Co. 'Working conditions were Dickensian: a dismal, windowless basement room with a single strip light,' remembers Cooper Clarke about his apprentice years. 'Later we moved [from Ancoats] into the equally squalid Sedgwick Mill, a former cotton-spinning mill on Redhill Street right next to the Rochdale Canal, which housed hundreds of small firms of every description – die stampers, engravers, clothing manufacturers – all under the same roof.' But not so far away – in Standish, near Wigan – an impressed Graham Turner visited the brand-new Heinz plant. 'Even in the drizzle, the grey marble façade glitters, the giant picture windows are so clean that you could walk through them and the spotless foyer is decorated with a selection of modern sculptures and tropical plants.' While for the workers themselves, in their 'white overalls and Aertex-ventilated caps', nothing was seemingly too good: 'Each of them has a locker, and the washrooms and showers are as lavish as the foyer. In the factory, they walk about like a congress of cricket umpires. The production areas of the plant have glass curtain walling, which provides what is called "Psychological Light".' When it came to the always high-profile motor industry, another Turner – H. A. Turner, Cambridge's Montague Burton Professor of Industrial Relations, assessing the physical backdrop to that industry's notoriously problematic labour relations – was similarly inclined to emphasise the positive:

> While there are few of the gimmicks of pop industrial psychology in evidence – such as pastel-shaded walls, or the aural bombardment of 'music while you work' – the car plants are on the whole modern, clean, and well-kept. Nor are they cramped. That the standards of lighting, ventilation and heating are generally adequate is suggested by the comparatively occasional character of disputes where, say, fumes in the paint shop, or lack of heating, may be associated with exceptional operating or climatic conditions. There *is* dust in polishing shops, water splashing about in sections of the paint shops, noise and welding sparks in some body shops; but generally, car plants bear few traces of the dark, dirty mills of days past.

Thanks to the recollections of Tom Richardson, who about this time became industrial relations manager at BMC's Cowley plant in Oxford, we can get a bit more granular about the progress slowly being made:

> It was just terrible, and my immediate predecessor had stopped one of the worst things, and no one ever really believes it – was that in

> the men's lavatories, the hourly paid people's lavatories, there was no lavatory paper. And after an enormous battle he got lavatory paper put in there, you know, you didn't dare go to the lavatory unless you'd got your *Daily Mirror* with you. And – those huge lavatories – such was the opposition to that, that whoever had to give the order to have the lavatory paper holders put into the WCs there, they instructed the carpenters to put the holder on the outside of the door so that everyone going in had to estimate how much they would need before they'd started. And I took on the job, and then it took another struggle of about six months behind the scenes to get the lavatory paper holders put on the inside of the door.

'So you know,' he added, 'we're not talking [in the early 1980s] about the dark ages, we're talking about the mid-1960s and it was this sort of attitude.'[20]

Sometimes a dangerous environment, too. Take the steelworks at Consett in County Durham: in 1961 it had been the first in the UK to introduce the more efficient Linz-Donawitz steelmaking process, enabling the elimination of the open hearth, but it was still not a deeply reassuring place when, five years later, Peter Smith as a young man spent a couple of months working there, as part of a small gang keeping the site generally tidy:

> Slag from the blast-furnaces was run off into huge rail-mounted ladles shaped like inverted bells which were filled right to the top. These were propelled over the works' internal rail network to the tipping site in groups of two by small diesel engines. Much of the routine site tidying involved removing odd bits of slag from between the rails; these had been spilled out of the ladles, which swayed alarmingly in transit. Most of the very top layer of slag had solidified and cooled a bit, but we could see the red glow from still-liquid in the interior. I wondered what would happen if a swaying ladle tipped over near me – could I run away in time?

Unsurprisingly, an unskilled manual worker was (on the basis of the Registrar General's statistics for 1961) 93 per cent more likely to die from an accident (excluding motor and home accidents) than the average person; a semi-skilled manual worker was 28 per cent more likely; while within specific occupations, a coal-face worker was 422 per cent more likely, a fisherman 380 per cent and a dock labourer 268 per cent, but an engineering fitter 14 per cent less likely and a bus or train conductor 69 per cent less likely. Overall, of course, deaths through industrial accidents were gradually declining through the twentieth century: an annual average of 4,341 in 1900–9 down by the 1940s to 2,425, by the 1950s to 1,564, and by the 1960s to 1,140. Fortunately, most industrial accidents were not fatal; and when in 1965 the seventeen-year-old Tony Iommi lost part of his fingers in a Birmingham sheet metal factory, he ingeniously made prosthetic thimbles out of melted-down Fairy Liquid bottles so that he could go on playing guitar – and, in early 1968, co-founded Black Sabbath.[21]

Accidents were one thing; disease, and a generally unhealthy working environment, were another. The statistics, again on the basis of 1961 standardised mortality ratios (SMRs), were stark enough: an unskilled manual worker was 43 per cent more likely to die between the ages of fifteen and sixty-four than the average person; 85 per cent more likely to die of tuberculosis; and 94 per cent more likely to die of bronchitis. For coal miners, the killer disease remained pneumoconiosis, a respiratory disease ('miners' lung') resulting from exposure to coal dust, albeit the authors of the most detailed study conclude about the two post-war decades that the workforce tended almost as much as the NCB to prioritise high production targets – and thus high earnings for themselves – over a drastic reduction in dust levels. Elsewhere, the greatest culprit remained asbestos, as the inhaling of asbestos fibres continued to cause a range of often fatal diseases, above all mesothelioma (cancer of the lung). 'Scientists track down a killer dust disease' was the headline of a *Sunday Times* report in 1965 about a study revealing that, of seventy-six patients who had recently died from mesothelioma at the London Hospital, over half had a history of occupational exposure to asbestos, or had lived in the same house as an asbestos worker. Four years later – during which, as typical examples from just Glasgow's shipyards and building sites, Cunard insisted that asbestos be extensively used in constructing the *QEII* and the massive Red Road blocks of flats were built without adequate exhaust ventilation – new Asbestos Regulations came into force, though far from fully comprehensive; and it was not until 1999 that the use of asbestos was totally banned.

More than most causes of cancer, it was a ticking time bomb, so that between 1995 and 2017 rates of mesothelioma nearly doubled. 'I was a baby when I jumped up to greet my father,' one sufferer living on borrowed time, 51-year-old Wendy Holland, remembered in 2018 about how her father Patsy would return home to Stepney Green every night after a day's work in the Millwall Docks unloading asbestos cargoes and at once – with the deadly white dust still on his clothes and bushy hair, but oblivious to the risk – pick up his little girl and carry her on his shoulders. Another London docker was Danny Baker's father, 'Spud':

> In 2007 after a period of feeling 'a bit rough', which culminated in him turning an awful shade of yellow, with some difficulty I persuaded him to go to Lewisham hospital. I was taken to one side and told cancer had spread throughout his internal organs. He'd never been a smoker, yet the cancer had started in his lungs. A doctor, when delivering the fatal prognosis, asked me if Spud had ever worked near asbestos. I turned to him and said, 'You worked on asbestos a lot, Dad, didn't you? Bloke wants to know how much.'
>
> Typically he squirmed a bit in his seat and looked at his hands.
>
> 'Oh, don't go on about all that, boy,' he said, irked as ever that someone wanted to know our business. 'It was fucking years ago. It's not that anyway. I'm all right, it's the fucking flu, that's all.'
>
> The doctor and I exchanged a brief glance.

'And,' adds Baker, 'it was never mentioned again in the five months he had left to live.'[22]

Across industry as a whole – but especially in sectors with expensive, heavily mechanised equipment which it was not economic to leave standing idle – there was an increasing trend by the mid-1960s to shift working, up by then to almost one in five of all industrial employees. This certainly applied to the motor industry, for example at Ford, where at any one time about two-thirds of its workers were on shift systems; while across the industry, the usual pattern was that shift workers in one fortnight did five day shifts of between eight and nine hours, followed in the next fortnight by four or five night shifts of eight to ten hours. One place where shift-working had become almost a way of life was the long-established steel-making town of Scunthorpe: of its working male population of 38,000, some 19,000 were employed in steel, of whom 10,000 were on shifts (divided over twenty-four hours into 6 a.m. to 2 p.m.; 2 p.m. to 10 p.m.; 10 p.m. to 6 a.m.). The upside was material prosperity, with the visiting journalist Stephen Aris noting in 1964 'the almost total absence of the traditional back-to-backs', but instead 'in their place are tree-lined housing estates, full of children, prams, and lawnmowers' – and indeed, 'on one of these estates I was told that the birth rate [i.e. of Scunthorpe] was nearly double the national average'. The downside was obvious enough. 'Lack of sleep is the shift worker's universal complaint,' and Aris quoted one: 'I've been on shifts for 34 years, and I've never got accustomed to sleeping during the day. I might be in bed for six hours but normal sleep is almost impossible even though my wife does much of her housework at night.'[23]

As the proportions in the overall UK workforce of skilled manual and semi-skilled manual steadily declined – from 24.9 per cent and 27.2 per cent respectively in 1951 to 21.6 per cent and 20.6 per cent respectively in 1971 – it became ever more clear that the heyday of the old British 'craft' tradition was now long gone. The situation in Coventry was emblematic, with the city during the 1960s beginning, in Adrian Smith's regretful words, 'to see the loss of its most priceless asset: the reservoir of skilled engineering workers that had been built up throughout the century, and had survived a depression and two world wars'. And he goes on:

> Although Mrs Thatcher accelerated [in the 1980s] the process of deindustrialization, Coventry was in fact witnessing [in the 1960s] the demise of manufacturing industry – of *making* and not merely assembling – at the height of its prosperity. The car plants' tolerance of high unit costs in the absence of major import penetration encouraged the de-skilling of those assembly workers who had opted for high wages and regular overtime rather than seeking employment in what was already a shrinking engineering sector. Machine tool companies, most notably Alfred Herbert, experienced a loss of skilled labour to the assembly line ('the track' in Midlands parlance) . . .

De-skilling also played out in the coal-mining industry, following the widespread introduction from about the late 1950s onwards of power-loading machinery. 'By the end of the 1960s,' explain Peter Pagnamenta and Richard Overy, 'very little coal was undercut, and loaded onto conveyers':

> Instead, the much faster 'longwall' mining system was in operation in nine out of ten pits. On faces up to 200 yards long, machines traversed up and down, shearing coal away and simultaneously loading it onto the conveyor. Rather than have to stop and erect pit-props before the machines or conveyors could be moved forward, self-advancing roof supports meant work could be almost continuous over two or three shifts.
>
> In the course of these changes the old skills of the hewer, working with nothing but his own tools and his knowledge of the best way of bringing down coal, disappeared.

Graham Turner in his tour of the Wigan area visited the Tupperware as well as the Heinz factory. 'The main job of many of the workers seems to be to make sure that the machines are operating efficiently,' he noted about the latter. 'There are electronic giants which meticulously sift any stones or other extraneous objects from among the beans, eyeing each one individually, and giant kettles which mix Junior Beef Dinners, 150 gallons at a time.' While at the former, as he watched the workers 'feeding plastic balls into machines which press out the required shapes', he found himself wondering about the 'sheer boredom' they must feel. 'But,' he discovered, 'the workers themselves seem happy enough. "I used to be up to my elbows in muck," said one young man who had come from the railway. "This is grand."'

Not so grand, though, in a bakery studied in about 1964 by the sociologist W. W. Daniel. The context was that whereas 'formerly baking had been considered a semi-skilled craft carried out in demanding conditions, now it was becoming an unskilled, light routine chore'; the men working there 'were engaged on single tasks on a production line, such as transferring lumps of dough from one conveyor belt into tins on another belt'; they worked a shift system, averaging 'over 50 hours a week on the day shift and over 60 hours on the night shift'; and, to judge by a trio of vox pop, they were not happy in their work:

> There's nothing really hard about this job. It's just the tediousness of it. It does get tedious and monotonous when you've done six or seven hours of it. You're fixed to your job. You can't move away . . .
>
> You do get fed up with being stuck on one job all the time. I've been here for twelve years and I've been stuck at the front of that oven for twelve years. You never get a change or a swop round. Then, eventually you tell them that you want a change and you get put on the other oven . . .
>
> Well I think that a bakery that gets mechanised like this has, well you don't get that atmosphere that you had when everybody was more or less getting together like, round a table. You don't get the same atmosphere. I mean it's not that feeling like when everybody's mucking in sort of thing, getting everything done together. I mean you're isolated now, you're like an individual doing a certain job, like not all together. When you've got a group of men doing a job there's more fun and it's more sociable than a man working on his own. There's always something happening, some cracks or something. There's always some fun going on . . .

'Well,' he concluded, 'you miss that now.'[24]

What role did female workers – traditionally often marginalised – now play in this industrial world? Across the UK workforce as a whole, the proportion of women in it was steadily increasing, from 33 per cent in 1961 to 37 per cent by 1971, with an increasing proportion of those women (25 per cent in 1961; 33.5 per cent in 1971) working on a part-time basis. This move to part-time work was particularly marked in manufacturing industry, where the percentage of female part-time workers rose from 11.9 in 1959 to 17.7 just nine years later. 'Within manufacturing,' notes Chris Wrigley, 'the greatest number of these women worked in the metal and engineering trades, followed by the food, drink and tobacco sector.' A telling example of a larger trend comes from Merthyr Tydfil and its valley community: back in 1938, when 40 per cent of that economy was coal-producing, there were eleven men to one woman in the paid labour force; by 1965, when 40 per cent of its economy was now based on light manufacturing industry (typified by the Kayser Bondor hosiery factory), the ratio was down to two men to one woman.

The gender divide in the workplace tended to be strict. Not only did the Factories Acts continue to forbid women to work night-time shifts, but even during the day there was usually clear demarcation, for instance at the giant Fort Dunlop factory in Birmingham, where subsequent oral testimony recalled 'men milling and machining at one end of the corridor while women assembled, tested and packed at the other end'; while when Cooper Clarke, before becoming a printer's apprentice, was taken on as a starter cutter by a Manchester clothing manufacturer, Seidelbaum's, 'the workforce was almost entirely Jewish and male, apart from the machine room downstairs, which was all women'. A particularly vivid description of women at work – though not in manufacturing – came in 1966 from the 26-year-old Angela Carter, working that summer washing dishes in Bristol Zoo's café. 'As many as eight women move about continually in a space perhaps five feet wide,' she wrote soon afterwards in a *Guardian* piece ('The backroom girls'). 'They are all old and most are fat. Their feet are swollen but they move with the rhythmic precision of dancers. It is a kind of spontaneous choreography and no one gets trodden on or, at least, rarely . . .' The only man in the kitchen is Alf, working the chipping machine. 'The women make fun of him and make him the butt of various sexual jokes and allusions but, all the same, he always gets his cup of tea sugared for him and first choice of the plate of cakes for, after all, he is a man.' The stand-out female character is the 'selectively huge' Ruby ('all the fat has settled on top, like a fall of snow'), in charge of the washing-up. 'Ruby has a running feud with the chip-frying lady. They hurl dishcloths at one another and banter one another all the time. Or the chip-frying lady will threaten Ruby with a ladleful of boiling fat.' And inevitably, the day has its contrasting rhythms:

> At rush times the work is too hard for talking, but sometimes Ruby and her friend, May, will sing together, Ruby at the plates and May beside her at the cups, singing 'Promises,' but very softly, because it is forbidden to sing in the kitchen.
>
> 'She 'asn't 'ad a man for 10 years,' says Ruby, nudging May. 'Or is it 15?'

'No, 16,' says May placidly. 'The man next door, it was. But I was always good friends with his wife and she never knew, poor soul.'[25]

On 30 September 2024 the last working blast furnace at Port Talbot's steelworks was shut down and the last UK power station dependent on coal, Ratcliffe-on-Soar, ceased to generate electricity.[26] Taken together, a richly symbolic day in Britain's long retreat from once being the pre-eminent industrial economy in the entire world. We now increasingly recognise that a fateful mixture of deindustrialisation and de-skilling – both of them just starting to quicken in the 1960s – holds the key to much of recent British history. Economics, it turns out, is never solely about economics; and given the human and social consequences, even leaving aside the more contestable political, it is a tragedy that this was not appreciated rather earlier.

9

Kazam!

'Death of a street' was the title of Jeremy Seabrook's piece in *New Society* in February 1965. 'In the condemned streets in the town centre,' he began, 'the wind blows through the derelict houses, which await demolition':

> Strips of corrugated iron beat against the window frames, a zinc bath scrapes the wall on its rusty nail. The white china door handles are smashed, the fragile gas mantles flaking into a fine powder, the blue tin advertisements outside the corner shops corroded by rust, advertisements for products no longer on sale – cough cures and cordials and remedies for indigestion, forgotten now, like the people they killed or cured.

While later, after describing some of the abandoned possessions in the empty houses: 'In this street there was always such a feeling of permanency, so great a sense of following a long established and deeply rooted pattern of living, that it seems impossible for the street to have been evacuated without inflicting the cruellest blow against its inhabitants and their lives.' And at the end, 'the few old women who still gather on the doorstep':

> They have lived to see their customs and rituals fall into desuetude, their accredited beliefs spent, their received ideas suddenly used up, as though in a decade they had passed through some vertiginous and incomprehensibly accelerated lifetime, and when they handed on to their children the only life they knew, enshrined in the family

> treasures now abandoned, the children laughed and went their ways . . .
>
> The houses they were so proud of appear suddenly ugly and shameful. They have served their purpose, and there is no reason why they should stand any longer. Already the cranes and bulldozers have moved in.

So they had, so they had, as in the mid-1960s not only slum clearance, but urban redevelopment (aka 'renewal') more generally moved to peak intensity. And two months after Seabrook's heartfelt lament, a beat group with an almost parodically modern-sounding name, Unit 4 Plus 2, entered the charts with 'Concrete and Clay' – which, wearing jackets and ties, they jauntily mimed for *Top of the Pops* on the building site that was the Barbican.[1]

In London, it was not just the ongoing brutalist Barbican housing development (stretching from the late 1950s to the mid-1970s before completion) that involved serious quantities of concrete and clay, often after the dust storms of demolition. Take just a dozen or so areas where the face of the capital was palpably and rapidly changing. On the South Bank, those paeons to concrete, the Queen Elizabeth Hall and the Hayward Gallery (the so-called 'ugly sisters'), were both approaching completion, so too were the many surrounding walkways and stairways, while just down the river Denys Lasdun's National Theatre was in theory under way; in Knightsbridge, just by Hyde Park, work would begin in early 1967 on Sir Basil Spence's controversial, thirty-storey barracks for the Household Cavalry; bang in the middle of town, Richard Seifert's landmark skyscraper, Centre Point, an opportunistic triumph for the developer Harry Hyams, was completed in 1966, with Seifert recalling years later how, at the outset of the project, he had said to Hyams, 'One thing you must do is let this building as soon as you can; there's going to be a lot of architectural comment and political criticism'; further testimony to London's office boom, a goldmine for developers, was the newly completed Euston Centre, this one the baby of Joe Levy, involving the bulldozing of the attractively residential Euston Square and, along American lines, the maximisation of office space ('the buildings are alien and, to the pedestrian, unapproachable,' regretfully noted Tony Aldous a decade later, adding that 'a street with houses and shops has been replaced by huge walls of glass fenced off by traffic-scape'); Americanisation, too, in the City by the mid-1960s (London Wall's huge new office blocks, the 'Zidpark' in Upper Thames Street, the drear and bleak Paternoster Square development to the north of St Paul's, towers like Drapers' Gardens off Throgmorton Avenue and BP's Britannic House in Ropemaker Street, work starting on the new Stock Exchange), as the Square Mile became daily less intimate, less reassuringly Victorian; few areas changing faster than in heavily slum-cleared East London, whether Shoreditch (by 1965 the highest multi-storey flats per capita completed rate of any London borough), or Stepney (the Green's three Corbusian seventeen-storey towers completed by 1964) or Poplar (Ernö Goldfinger's instantly celebrated/demonised twenty-six-storey Balfron Tower completed by 1967) or Canning Town (eight high-rise towers, all for public housing, built between 1965 and 1968 alone) or Newham (the 1965 local government merger of West Ham and East Ham, resulting in a rapidly scaled-up high-rise building programme); at Elephant and Castle, a brand-new shopping centre was now the intended focus of the area's whole drastic post-war redevelopment, but in practice sadly stranded, as (in John Grindrod's words) 'budget restrictions imposed by the Ministry of Transport had reduced the promised spacious and elegant pedestrian subway system to a warren of poky tunnels less than nine feet wide'; in Deptford, a particularly ruthless clearance/high-rise policy, documented in microcosm almost half a century later on BBC TV's *The Secret History of Our Streets*; while in much of North Kensington and Paddington, site clearance from 1964, followed by continuous construction work from 1966, as the Westway (Europe's then-largest stretch of elevated motorway) started to become a reality. Or, to go further out, take Uxbridge. 'Described in *Pears' Cyclopaedia* in the 1950s as a "market town,"' remembered F. W. Nunneley in 2021 about what then happened to his home town, 'it didn't survive the onslaught of the planners. The town had many old industries, including a steam laundry, a maltings, a corn chandler, coaching inns and Harman's Brewery. By the time the redevelopment had finished, they had all gone, and in their place was a vast, featureless, wind-scoured shopping plaza with, at its centre, a small tower painted to look old, the final irony.'

Nowhere by the mid-1960s, though, could quite rival Croydon. 'Wherever you go in the centre of Croydon,' one journalist had noted as early as 1961, 'there is new building taking place: cranes, skeletons of steel, rising office blocks wreathed in mists of scaffolding, hammering on metal, the hum of cement mixers everywhere'; four years later the *Croydon Advertiser* reckoned that the town centre's skyline was getting 'more American every month'; 'the Croydon office phenomenon', declared a property correspondent in 1966, 'just goes on and on'; and the same year, this mini-Manhattan, or 'Croydonopolis' as some now dubbed it, featured in *Nairn's London*: 'Even the rebuilt deserts of central London', observed Ian Nairn, 'have nothing like this wholesale transformation of rather staid Victorian lumps into rather shoddy modern boxes.'[2]

'Within minutes of getting out of the train at Snow Hill Station I was lost, and I was lost more often than not throughout the three days I was in Birmingham,' recorded the writer Walter Allen soon after his visit there in late 1964. 'And this,' he added, 'in the city where I was born and spent the first 25 years of my life and that was, I confidently believed, the setting of my novels. They have become period pieces.' High impact, too, if less bewilderment, for the journalist Paul Barker two years later: 'As you drive along the mean road that the London motorway has decanted you onto, you suddenly see, kazam!, the tall neat drum of the Rotunda office-block, the rectangular concrete of the Bull Ring shopping centre, and the two-thirds-finished spike of the Birmingham Post Office Tower.' 'Birmingham,' he justly reflected, 'has done the biggest city-centre reshaping of any British city not granted a vast bare acreage by the Luftwaffe.' Other landmarks of the new he might have mentioned included the continuing march of the urban motorway that was the Inner Ring Road, though it would not be completely finished until 1971; John Madin's striking new home for the *Birmingham Post and Mail* (in Elain Harwood's admiring words, 'a 17-storey glazed office tower set over a low podium, in the style of Lever House, New York'); and, following the demolition of its Victorian predecessor, the almost completed New Street station, unfondly recalled half a century later as 'a concrete bewilderment, sandwiched between a car park and a shopping centre, with dank underground platforms and a warren of dismal fluorescent-lit passages', not helped by 'no daylight' and 'little natural ventilation'.

More generally, across the city and as the housing drive intensified, this was peak time for high-rise – to such an extent that in 1965 some 88 per cent of all newly built dwellings (in the public-housing sector) were in the form of high flats. As almost throughout the 1950s and 1960s, much of this new build was on the outskirts, so that by the early 1970s, of Birmingham's 464 high-rise blocks of flats, 'almost two-thirds were,' notes Richard Vinen, 'on or beyond the city's outer ring road'. Typical of these new outlying council estates were Castle Vale (built on the site of the Castle Bromwich airfield and to be much criticised for having an unduly high proportion of children living in its prominent cluster of tower blocks) and Druids Heath (as many as fourteen tower blocks). Where Birmingham was, for once, not ahead of the redevelopment curve was in slum clearance, where prior to a frenzied spurt in the late 1960s it lagged somewhat behind the major northern cities. Even so, significant clearance was under way, not least in inner-city Ladywood, with comprehensive redevelopment taking place through the decade – thereby reducing the total of dwellings in the district from 7,558 before redevelopment to only 3,609 afterwards, but transforming the amount of open space, from only two acres to nearly fifty acres. Norman Bartlam's *Ladywood Lives* includes a particularly evocative, wide-range photograph taken in October 1965 from the top of St John's Church tower. 'The great planning disaster in the making, officially known as the Ladywood Middleway, slices its way through the area,' notes the melancholy caption, 'and one of the appalling pedestrian underpasses can be seen on the left near the church roof. The blocks of flats are Wells, Truro and Brecon Towers. In the lower right the last remaining houses on Wood Street and Alston Street await the bulldozer . . .'[3]

Elsewhere in the Midlands, Leicester's clearance programme had in the mid-1960s similarly not yet peaked. But remorselessly – and in significant part determined by the construction between 1960 and 1968 of the city's inner ring road, complete with its 1,520-foot-long Southgates Underpass – the urban environment changed fundamentally. 'In the course of the last fifteen years – no more – the Old Town of Leicester has been almost entirely destroyed,' lamented the transport historian Jack Simmons in 1974:

> In the late 1950s its medieval street plan was clearly visible, and it was dominated by the industrial buildings that summarised and embodied the town's Victorian prosperity. Now nearly all this has gone: not merely the streets but their very names – Applegate Street, Blue Boar Lane, Bakehouse Lane, Red Cross Street; and almost all the chief commercial buildings, notably Everard's Brewery at the top of Castle Street, and Preston's boot factory with its double-curved front, in Bakehouse Lane. In their place we have a huge swathe of concrete, taking the traffic through the city north and south, with windy and desolate stretches, of concrete again, on either side of it . . .

Across the county border an even more wholehearted embrace of the modern. 'In a frantic bid to stop Leicester overtaking it as the major city of the East Midlands,' records Harwood, 'Nottingham gave developers a free hand to build tall offices', with the result that its central rateable value soared from £4.8 million in 1961 to £14.6 million by 1966. Height was also the name of the game in public housing, with twenty-one blocks of flats at sixteen-plus storeys built in the five years from 1963, all of them by the two biggest multi-storey contractors, Wimpey and Bison; while from 1966 work was under way, on the site of the old Victoria station, of Victoria Centre, five times bigger than Birmingham's Bull Ring and combining (Harwood again) 'a shopping centre and car parking, and 22-storey blocks of council flats'. The *coup de grâce*, carrying all before it, was Maid Marian Way. 'A no-nonsense creation of Nottingham's post-war era' is how the official 2011 picture history of it describes the brutal urban highway, constructed between 1958 and 1966, that cut through the western side of the city centre. 'Its concrete blocks and its sheer scale have all provoked strong reactions in the hearts and minds of Nottingham's people and visitors to Nottingham. As the dramatic gash in the landscape forced its way through a series of the city's most historic streets, Arthur Ling, Professor of Town Planning at Nottingham University, declared the street, in 1965, to be an "insult to Maid Marian" and added that it "must qualify as one of the ugliest in Europe."' Arguably, though, Ian Nairn had already, the year before, had the last word: 'Wreck a town, and give it a fancy name.'[4]

Just over thirty miles away was the city of true believers. 'Words like "redevelopment" and "rehousing" are dull clichés, at least to most people in this country,' reckoned Roger Ebbatson, a postgraduate student doing a thesis on Dickens, in November 1964. 'But live in a terraced house and you would think differently.' He was writing in *Darts*, the paper of Sheffield University's students' union, and he went on:

> Outside in the narrow, hilly streets you breathe the soot-impregnated air. The sky, whatever the season, is a steely grey, leaving distant perspectives vague and blurred. But the choking drabness outside is a pale reflection of life inside these houses. Go in off the street through the door with its peeling paint into a gloomy hallway, or into a cluttered living-room. Dampness and shabbiness everywhere, concentrated in the cramped kitchen, water running down the walls. The house, despite its smallness, often cold and draughty, the backyard grimy and permanently full of sodden washing.
>
> Too many people in Sheffield, for too long, have had to live under such conditions . . .
>
> But the problem has been tackled by the authorities with exciting zest and imagination. Utilising the hilly nature of the landscape, many ugly sites have been cleared and converted into open spaces near the city centre. At the same time, redevelopment has taken the form of skyscraper blocks of flats, towering across the city contours . . .
>
> The work of the City Architects' Department and the City Council is very much work in progress – there is still a large amount of work to be done. But the benefit of their work as internationally famous pioneers in housing and redevelopment is to be seen daily around us . . .

By this time that work included the huge, soon-to-be-completed Hyde Park (second stage of the Park Hill redevelopment scheme; a spectacular view over the Midland railway station; 1,317 dwellings; blocks ranging from three to eighteen storeys; three pubs, a child welfare clinic, a youth club, a tenants' meeting hall, a launderette and a working men's club); while quite apart from the ongoing Norfolk Park scheme (featuring fifteen seventeen-storey towers), a major brutalist redevelopment in the offing was Kelvin in the Upperthorpe area. With J. L. Womersley again closely involved (this time as co-architect), the hope was that these twin thirteen-storey blocks would replicate the apparent success of much-vaunted Park Hill I, where, according to Ebbatson, 'loneliness has been combatted by an original communal emphasis', in particular by how 'long open corridors on every storey provide streets without traffic', i.e. the celebrated streets-in-the-sky concept. Did this future distinguished critic of Victorian literature have any doubts about the social consequences of what he called 'an architectural city revolution'? 'Here the shattered window of a dilapidated pub stares out past a Victorian lamp-standard to a 13-storey point block,' he described a photograph included in his article. 'Behind the flats, the old terraces still remain, until they too are cleared away. The old Sheffield of the working men's pubs and clubs is gradually giving way to a more cosmopolitan, but still very characteristic, town.'[5]

'I soon discovered,' noted Richard Crossman in January 1965 after a day trip north, 'that Leeds is as proud of its policy of improving the old central areas, wherever possible, as Manchester is proud of its policy of total clearance.' The contrast was also with Bradford, albeit that city practising what Simon Gunn has characterised as 'rather a banal urban modernism, based on functionalism rather than the iconic, a modernism of office blocks, urban motorways, and car parks, not of landmark buildings', in fact 'as in so many other British cities'. Collections of historical photographs, together with their captions, make it clear that Bradford's modernism certainly included some robust clearance-cum-demolition: whether for the new, eight-storey Central Library (opened 1967) or for Wardley House (1965 tower block, including theatre, ice rink and offices) or off Otley Road ('Outside middens, gas lamps and dumped rubbish: Ripon Street prepares to disappear in 1966') or on Dudley Hill ('Wakefield Road, after whole rows of houses have been demolished to make way for the road-widening scheme which will link Bradford to the nation's motorway network') or in Victoria Square (goodbye in 1965 to the handsome Victorian premises of turf accountants Fred Truelove, to be replaced by the new Law Courts and police headquarters) or on Forster Square (the Cathedral and the General Post Office surviving, but not much else, replaced by a new shopping and office complex).

As ever, the twentieth-century monster played its part. 'This has meant pulling down most of the buildings at the core of the town,' reported *The Economist* in March 1967 about the consequences of a new inner ring road starting to be built. Or as David West would put it in 2004 – as Will Alsop's project director, planning a facelift for the northern city which by then, more than any other, had struggled to reinvent itself post-deindustrialisation – about the long-term legacy of the 1960s: 'There is an outer ring road, an inner ring road and an even more inner ring road. They cut the city centre up and leave it absolutely empty by six in the evening. Piece by piece, we hope to remove some of the roads – perhaps get Alan Titchmarsh in to help turf over a section . . .' A sceptical observer of it all, not only in Bradford, was the diarist Kenneth Preston, who lived in Keighley but on this particular Saturday in 1966 was back from a cycle ride to Skipton:

> The old 'King's Arms' pub, which must have been there for a century or two, has now been completely demolished. It will be interesting to see what is to be put in its place – surely not more offices. I wonder when some of these demolitions are going to go bankrupt. Almost everywhere these great new blocks of buildings have been put up and remain empty. In Bradford, along Manningham Lane, there is a row of shops and one only is occupied. In Colne there are eight shops unoccupied – and they have been unoccupied since built, like the Bradford ones. In Keighley the great office block in Devonshire Street is empty except for one letting. Somebody has his capital locked up in these white elephants. How long can they afford to have so much capital bringing in no return?

'If only there were a few really big financial crashes,' he concluded, 'we might perhaps see an end to this tearing down in all directions.'[6]

Simon Jenkins would have sympathised. 'The interview,' he recalled in 2024, 'did not go well':

> I was in Liverpool as a journalist being shown a model for the city's future by its proud architect, Graeme Shankland. I told him I regarded his city as the most magnificent port in Europe. He corrected me and said Liverpool was 'glaringly obsolete'. His plan, produced in 1965, was to demolish two-thirds of the city centre as

> well as much of Everton, Toxteth and Sefton. A new metropolis of towers and slabs would rise, pierced by swooping motorway overpasses and tunnels. A few historic buildings might be allowed to survive.
>
> I was horrified and said so, making a tactless reference to the RAF's 'Bomber' Harris. I was much moved by a visit I had just made with a colleague to see a similar scorched-earth project in Manchester's Hulme. We watched as Mancunians were herded on to buses with their belongings, to be dumped miles from their old homes on out-of-town estates. Many were in tears or dazed. We compared them with wartime refugees. They were to make way for Europe's biggest council estate, Hulme Crescents, its blocks bizarrely named after Georgian architects such as William Kent and Robert Adam.

'Liverpool and Manchester,' he hardly needed to add, 'were not alone.'

Of course, Manchester by the mid-1960s was not just about slum clearance and comprehensive redevelopment – the huge Piccadilly Plaza complex (including nine-storey hotel and twenty-four-storey office block) was completed in 1965, to be instantly dismissed by the visiting Graham Turner as 'gimmicky rubbish'; the Mancunian Way, a two-mile stretch of urban motorway (the so-called 'highway in the sky'), was officially opened by Harold Wilson in 1967 – but they were at the heart of the story. A seminal scene was played out in early 1965. 'They briefed me very well in the town hall and then took me to the top of a skyscraper to see the great area of slums they have cleared in the centre of the city,' recorded Crossman about his time with the mayor and his colleagues. 'A few months ago I visited the new space cleared for the university campus. This slum clearance area is five times as large and adjacent to it. It must be the largest hole ever created in a big city in the history of modern conurbations.' That was the aerial view, but two years later the great architectural writer Nikolaus Pevsner was at ground level as he drove through 'areas of total desolation' and reckoned that Manchester was 'engaged in one of the largest slum-clearance enterprises of all time'. Increasingly, the great symbol of the whole phenomenon was, as Jenkins rightly indicated, Hulme – where slum clearance had been taking place for many years but now intensified, including the destruction of its many shops, pubs and churches (altogether comprising Manchester's largest ecosystem outside the city centre), in order to make way not only for much fairly conventional redevelopment (including a lot of high-rise), but also for the great vision so bitterly remembered by Jenkins.[7]

As for Liverpool, Shankland's ambitious city centre plans (definitively formulated in late 1965) did in the event mainly fail, because of lack of financial backing, to materialise. The major exception was the largely unloved St John's Shopping Precinct, eventually completed in 1969, following the demolition of St John's Market – a fine market hall dating back to the 1820s – five years earlier. 'It was during these years that *the planners* arrived in Liverpool with grand schemes for transforming the city,' recalled Labour's Eric Heffer about the mid-1960s generally. 'We had city plan after city plan put before us. It all seemed very exciting. The bulldozers appeared and parts of the city were pulled down. The whole place became a construction site. Buildings were demolished but little was put in their place.' But if that was broadly true about the centre of the city, it was not quite the case with Liverpool as a whole. 'An urban renewal planner said that a third of the city had to be rebuilt by the end of the century,' noted one reviewer in August 1965 after watching *The Singing City*, a BBC documentary. 'There were shots of sooty brick terraces that proved the need for modernisation, and shots of modern housing developments that made the old rat-infested huddle look quite cosy.' Already the city's erection of high-rise blocks of flats had been transformed by the use of the French 'Camus' system of industrialised building, resulting in ten twenty-two-storey blocks going up by the end of the decade; while in April 1966 the City Council announced that it intended to treble its rate of clearance in the worst slums, to be accompanied by a crash programme of new housing in the city and overspill areas. During these years there were few more symbolic developments – anywhere – than 'The Piggeries' at Everton. Built in 1966 from large, pre-cast concrete panels bolted together on site, these were three identical dark-grey, fifteen-storey tower blocks, called respectively Haigh Heights, Canterbury Heights and Crosbie Heights. The derogatory local nickname was soon earned. 'The blocks went downhill right from the start,' recalled a decade later one early tenant, James Cleary. 'The park surrounding them was wrecked within 12 months, and nobody came to do anything.' Or from a 2015 oral history project, long after demolition, take the memories of 'Eddie', whose family had relocated to Huyton in 1964 before two years later deciding to move back to Everton:

> My dad wanted to be in amongst his mates. My mam went along with that; I think she was happy to move back because it was a long haul up to Huyton. Thinking about it now we should have stayed there but for some mad reason they took this flat in Canterbury Heights as an alternative to a three-bedroom house. Looking back now it was fun, but it was hard as well. You had to be tough to survive. The stairwell was full of shit and piss and you had to walk up and down it regular because the lifts never worked. It was alright for us kids; we'd have a laugh. But not for the 'ald ones. It was a hovel.

'Looking back now I wonder how the hell we survived,' he reflected about the two years there. 'But people lived in them. The community was great.'[8]

Another ambitious plan only partially fulfilled was Wilfred Burns's 1963 City Development Plan for Newcastle – in particular, the envisaged network of urban motorways, with the main exception in this case being the East Central Motorway, situated uncomfortably close to the city centre and opened in 1975. But in the fullness of time, the two big vandalistic aspects of the plan – the demolition of much of Eldon Square (to make way for a shopping centre, the vast yet claustrophobic Eldon Square mall, opened in 1976) and of the Royal Arcade (to make way by the early 1970s for the Swan House office block, forlornly isolated in the middle of a roundabout) – *did* go ahead. Already under way by the time of Burns's plan was work on the 'truly joyous' (Elain Harwood's words) Civic Centre, modelled in part on Stockholm Town Hall and officially opened in 1968 by King Olaf of Norway. Nothing joyous, alas, about Westgate House. 'Dampens my spirits whenever I step out of the railway station,' wrote Carole Souter in 2003, a few years before its belated demolition. 'Representing all that is wrong with 1960s architecture, this concrete-slabbed office block is an ugly landmark that awkwardly straddles the streets leading to the historic Grainger Town. At least we have come to realise that this type of sterile monstrosity offends not just the eye but also the soul.' Overall, taking the city centre redevelopment as a whole, it is hard to disagree with Thomas Faulkner's judicious verdict that 'most damaging' was how 'the failure of the 1963 Plan to achieve its aim of integrating the modern with the historic led to harsh juxtapositions of old and new architecture, either by default, or intentionally so, based on the modernist principle of "dynamic contrast"'.

What about beyond the city centre? The bulldozing indeed continued during the mid-1960s, so quite often did the high-rise. But often it was a long-drawn-out and sometimes inconclusive process. The *locus classicus*, sited in Newcastle's West End, was Rye Hill. A prosperous middle-class area in the nineteenth century, it had been in decline ever since, with its post-war character summed up by one local historian as not only an area that 'attracted the weak and poor', but also was 'a notoriously tough area where trouble waited around every corner'. For most of the 1960s, a comprehensive plan for Rye Hill seemed to be in the offing, but it never quite materialised; and the upshot was an almost textbook example of planning blight:

> Housewives stopped papering [wrote Jon Gower Davies in his richly suggestive 1972 account of the Rye Hill story], men stopped repointing the brickwork or painting the external woodwork. Landlords refused to do repairs or to make improvements, especially as grants were refused – 'until the Plan comes'. The Planning Department busied itself with colouring maps [here he added the footnote, '"Ten maps for every brick," said one local wit'], drawing up critical paths, and working out a phased programme for work implementation.
>
> All the while, Rye Hill crumbled. Derelict houses, rubbish dumped on the open allotments, increasing multi-occupation, fleeing owners: the whole area gradually acquired the aura of the dustbin with, it seemed, no one or no one organization capable of doing anything about it.

'It was scarcely surprising,' added Davies about these years (1960–68) of 'accelerating decay' in what was for tenants of the many multi-occupied properties 'the worst housing conditions in the city', that 'the local citizenry came to regard the Corporation's claim for proficiency and wisdom with a certain amount of scepticism'.[9]

Finally, in this big-city tour, Glasgow – whose plans, noted *The Economist* in November 1965, for 'physically rebuilding itself . . . are both much larger and further advanced than those of any other city'. 'These aims', the paper added, 'go far beyond slum clearance'; and it cited as evidence 'a £21 million inner ring motorway [northern section already under construction, work to start shortly on the western section] to steer unnecessary traffic from the central business and shopping area', with the route planned to go through most of the city's twenty-nine CDAs, i.e. comprehensive development areas. As for the new public housing, no one could dispute Glasgow's claim to be the high-rise king, certainly in Britain and arguably even in Europe: of all completions between 1961 and 1968, nearly three-quarters were in the form of high flats, with its proportion of seriously high tower blocks (over twenty storeys) three times that of London, eighteen times that of Birmingham. Nor by any means were all these towers (more than 160 of them by 1969) in the inner city. 'Beyond the CDA zone, there was a startling and awesome sight,' writes Miles Horsey [later Glendinning] of the visuals by 1970, as seen from the centre. 'Away into the far distance, groups of colossal multi-storey blocks were rising – twenty, twenty-five, thirty storeys high – not in planned slum redevelopments but planted haphazardly on gap-sites anywhere in the suburbs, on pockets of waste ground, corners of golf-courses, redeveloped prefab-sites . . .' Nearer the centre, two new estates, both of them in the Springburn CDA north of the Clyde, would come to have an emblematic quality rivalling those of the Gorbals, itself still continuing to be redeveloped on largely high-rise lines. One was Sighthill, where – in part through slum clearance, in part on reclaimed chemical waste ground – ten twenty-storey slab blocks were built between 1964 and 1969; the other was Red Road, built over the same period, with the first of its eight blocks (each of twenty-seven or more storeys) opened in October 1966, and in due course housing some 4,000 people decanted from Glasgow's slums.

What lay ahead? That same autumn, a new survey of the city's central area found that 48 per cent of property there was obsolescent; that over a quarter of the obsolescent buildings were houses; and that they were mainly within the designated CDAs. In short, a recipe for continuing drastic urban renewal – or, as the distinguished local architect Jack Coia had dramatically put it about the CDAs and the inner ring road, at a conference held a few months earlier by the Glasgow Institute of Architects to discuss Glasgow's rebuilding, and presumably as he held up a city map: 'Take this wee piece of paper and burn twenty-nine holes with your cigarette in it, and cut a circle round it, and what's left of that is what will be left of Glasgow.' What he did not say – did not need to say – was that a whole working-class world, a way of life, was in the process of being destroyed. A world that, in a virtuoso passage set on the cusp of the mid-1960s, Andrew O'Hagan has evoked:

> There were ads in corner shops for Capstan Full Strength; there were public baths in Collins Street. There were numerous pawnbrokers. Boys were playing at marbles on the corner of McAslin Street, Kearney's Bar was open in Castle Street, and the Co-Operative Society in Parliamentary Road was well attended. Vans were busy with flittings. Irn-Bru was being drunk. There were broken windows, boarded-up shops, footballs bouncing off gable ends. The Casino Picture House was showing several films a day. Black police vans scuttled past like creepy-crawlies. The Sun Foundry in Kennedy Street was belting out smoke. The chains in the swing park were all twisted up. Rattray's Cycles was open in Murray Street and the Rottenrow Maternity Hospital did tea for visitors at 10 a.m. Rag and bone men appeared with balloons for 'any old rags'. Girls stoated about in their mother's high heels, kids with squints or harelips, cowlicks or NHS specs. The boys wore woollen tank-tops and grey shorts; the girls had pinafores and ragged cardigans. They did handstands. They played in the Middens. They knew the lamplighters. They had buns from the City Bakery. They drank bottles of milk and Virol. On lucky days when the sun was out they had picnics up at the Necropolis . . .[10]

Sadly, and inevitably, not just the obvious major conurbations. In Aberdeen, the massive slab blocks of the slums-cleared Gallowgate and Castlehill redevelopments being built to complement the new point blocks in the suburbs; in Bath, 'the practice becoming marked', to quote from Adam Fergusson's 1973 *The Sack of Bath*, 'of separating the less spectacular expanses of period architecture from the centre, and then mopping them up quickly as soon as their relevance to the totality had gone', typified by the 1963 destruction of Charles Street; in Blackburn, locals by this time starting to get used to daily life without either the old open market (closed in November 1964) or the fine Italian market hall and its splendid clock tower (both demolished the following month), with instead a new shopping precinct – white, clinical, unsentimental – starting to be built on their site, as well as a new tower block extension to the Town Hall; in Bolton, it was Graeme Shankland again to the fore, with a two-stage plan (1964–5) largely geared to the car and the shopper, while admittedly making a conscious effort to keep the character of the town centre; in Bootle, major plans afoot by June 1965 ('a vast new office quarter . . . a £5,000,000 traffic-free shopping centre . . . sweeping arrangements for car parking in the town centre . . . big housing developments . . .', with the *Liverpool Echo* reporting it all under the headline 'Big Redevelopment Plans Will Provide Bootle With a New Image'); in Bristol, demolition jobs in 1965–6 included the Toll House at Bedminster Down (the City Engineer declining to reprieve), the 1894 Methodist church at Fishponds (making way for a supermarket), and the last part of the fine early eighteenth-century St James's Square (to enable the completion of the Inner Circuit Road), while going up on the hillside at Kingsdown, to replace the cleared Georgian houses, were three fourteen-storey slab blocks; in Chesterfield, a case of unnecessary, reinforced 'obsolescence' and 'blight' as a result of the local council failing to act on its 1962 decision to designate the market place as a CDA where the Victorian market hall, and accompanying open trading area, would all be replaced by a new, enclosed building; in Coventry, icon of early post-war idealistic reconstruction, a later generation of planners was now, in Adrian Smith's words, 'busy creating a new urban landscape in which car finally triumphed over community'; in Dundee, not just a huge wave of new high-rise blocks, but the comprehensive development of the city centre, earning the retrospective despair of Gavin Stamp ('the small-scale buildings which gave interest and character to the High Street and Nethergate were eliminated', while 'the Overgate, the ancient western route from the High Street out of the city, was entirely obliterated from the map in favour of the

Overgate Centre, a blandly overweening and nasty new shopping centre which opened in 1967'); in Edinburgh, where the first stage of the enormous Leith Fort redevelopment (including two twenty-one-storey point blocks) was now complete, and where the City Engineer was set on building an inner ring road to motorway standards, perhaps the two worst areas of destructive philistinism were between the New Town and Calton Hill (the Georgian terraces on the western side of Leith Street cleared for an undistinguished shopping precinct called the St James's Centre) and on the other side of the Old Town (George Square losing most of its Georgian character as the university put up instead its own buildings); in Elland, the process of demolishing the centre's buildings (far from all of them derelict) and putting up in their place blocks of flats and offices earned the town clerk an MBE (or 'making a bugger of Elland', as some locals thought); 'a bleak row of shops has taken the place of St Michael's demolished nave in the city centre,' lamented Geoffrey Moorhouse in 1964 about Gloucester, where 'the same drastic surgery' also applied to secular buildings, including 'some of the few remaining half-timbered houses' being 'chopped down to make way for the redevelopment of the Westgate area alongside the cathedral'; 'a horrifying sight,' declared Ian Nairn in March 1967 of Gosport, adding that 'photographs can't convey the desert that has been built in place of the Georgian town'; 'poor, shattered place,' wrote Nairn two years earlier of Gravesend, regretting bitterly how 'the most individual town on the Thames estuary' was 'now being transformed from a tough, close-knit pattern of cottages to a drab architect's exercise in slabs of flats'; in Hull, most distinctive development in these years was Orchard Park, a cluster of low-rise 'villages' incongruously combined with eleven 'gap-site' towers, four of them of twenty storeys or more; 'the thing the alderman is proudest of is his council's response to its slums,' reported Moorhouse from Jarrow after a conversation with one of the unemployed marchers of 1936, who anticipated their complete disappearance within five years; in Kirkby, increasingly notorious overspill town from Liverpool, fourteen blocks of at least eight storeys (accommodating 6,500 families) had already been built by August 1965, with more under construction or planned; similar in Motherwell, notably its Muirhouse Area development, featuring ten eighteen-storey point blocks built for public housing by Wimpey from 1964; slum clearance (including of the area around George Street to build the windswept St Peter's Shopping Centre) and demolition (including in 1967 of the Theatre Royal in Horsedge Street, originally the Working Men's Hall) were well under way in Oldham; kingpin of Preston's mid-1960s redevelopment was the St George's Shopping Centre (obliterating the heart of the medieval town plan but acclaimed by the *Sunday Times* on its 1964 opening for having transformed 'a 4½-acre tangle of mean alleys and sagging warehouses' into a shopping centre fit for the late twentieth century, 'with its half-mile of shop windows, its circular, two-tier central piazza, its winter-warmed escalators and its Venetian tessellated pavements'); 'high above are the five great tower blocks which Wimpey have clamped down in the middle of the town,' noted Richard Crossman in autumn 1965 about walking around Rochdale's rundown Deeplish area, and soon there would be two more – altogether, the so-called 'Seven Sentinels' or 'Seven Sisters', each of seventeen or twenty-one storeys, totalling some 760 flats, and instantly dominating the centre of the town; in St Helens, the start by this time of roads being (to quote Trevor Rowley) 'ruthlessly pushed into the heart of the town centre, accompanied by unlovely multi-storey car parks'; in Salford, the Ellor Street redevelopment in the city's centre moving on by April 1965 from thoroughgoing slum clearance to the first three soaring blocks of flats (Walter Greenwood Court, Eddie Colman Court, John Lester Court) being occupied by tenants, with many more blocks to follow and the *Salford City Reporter* acclaiming 'a Salford for the Space Age'; in the centre of Stockport, recalls Paul Morley from his childhood, 'the finicky patterns and controlling precision of massed Victorian brick began to be replaced with pale grey sixties concrete, fussiness within a basic form of functionalism'; near Stoke-on-Trent, in Etruria, the old Wedgwood factory, built by Josiah in 1769, was demolished in September 1965; in 'enormously overcrowded' Wigan, noted Crossman about the same Lancashire visit that he went to Rochdale, 'the council has undertaken an enormous building programme', including 'an enormous cube of flats of very poor quality' that he had just opened; in Wisbech, road plans were likely to condemn the town to, reckoned the *Architectural Review* in November 1966, 'a virtual death sentence' in terms of its 'shape and quality'; and in Worcester, which 'used to be the sort of place that means bread and butter to the British Travel Association, with a cathedral and row upon row of tipsy half-timbering and demure Georgiana in the city centre,' wrote a saddened Moorhouse in November 1964, 'now it looks as if a lot of bombs have been dropped there . . .'[11]

10

Heart-weary with It All

The whole process had started before the mid-1960s and would continue after them; but these were arguably the epicentre years of what in our modern urban history can pardonably be called The Great Dislocation, or The Great Upheaval. How, then, was the human experience? To try to answer this, a series of key questions. Did people want to move from their condemned houses and streets? If they did (or were given no choice but to move), where did they want to move to – and to what type of housing? What was slum clearance like for those going through it? Once moved, were they happy in their new environment, particularly if it was high-rise? While in relation to urban redevelopment more generally, especially city-centre and town-centre redevelopment, was this something that people welcomed in advance? And, once it had happened, what did they make of it?

'Giant Tower Flats Replace Terrace Houses of Old Everton' was the *Liverpool Echo*'s headline in October 1965; and after noting that Everton was one of the city's areas 'where the change is daring, drastic and sometimes painful,' the reporter added that 'there are many of its old residents who are sad and bitter at the thought of leaving the cosy companionship of its streets'. A year later, in a letter to the *Manchester Evening News* about slum clearance in Ardwick, Mrs May Bish of Wythenshawe amplified the point:

> While young people may be glad of the chance to move to a new area with the luxury of a bath and hot water, when you're old these things count for little compared with the place where their roots and old friends are . . . We younger folks are apt to say, 'They're old,

> they've had their day; progress must go on; the future belongs to the young.' But one day we'll all be old and I wonder how we would feel being uprooted and moved away from old neighbours . . .'[1]

Certainly it seems to have been a general trend that, among people living in slum or 'twilight' areas, older people welcomed much less than younger people the prospect of moving, especially if it meant moving away from their neighbourhood. But can one generalise beyond that? Fortunately, over and above qualitative evidence, we have the evidence of as many as ten attitudinal surveys conducted between 1962 and 1967.

Inevitably, results varied. Eight designated slum-clearance areas surveyed in Leeds in May–July 1962 had over four-fifths of dwellers wanting to move not just to different living accommodation, but out of their immediate districts; the same year in St Mary's, Oldham, home to some of the town's worst housing, three-quarters of respondents wanted to stay in the area after redevelopment; in Birmingham's increasingly rundown Sparkbrook, a winter 1964 survey had most English residents wanting to move, but West Indian immigrants fairly evenly divided; about the same time, the majority of residents living in 'inner-urban twilight zones' in Cambridge and Reading revealed themselves as 'reluctant' to move, with almost half 'positively anxious to stay'; in summer 1965 it was back to Leeds, but this time accompanied by Batley and York, showing overall that people living in slum areas wanted to move, but not people in the more gently decaying twilight areas; an autumn 1965 survey of Sunderland's Millfield area, much of which was due to be cleared in the next five years, found almost half to be satisfied with their living conditions and not wanting to move; also in the north-east, in Newcastle's Rye Hill, some two-thirds in January 1966 declared they wanted to leave; later in the year, opinion was fairly even in a twilight area of Peterborough, while a Liverpool study of people living in 'unfit' inner-city dwellings not dissimilarly found half wanting to be rehoused within the area and half wanting to move well away; and finally, in a survey begun in October 1966 of Nottingham's St Ann's district, due for imminent comprehensive redevelopment, some two-thirds welcomed that prospect, with nearly one half saying they would like to leave the area altogether. So, a mixed picture – with no clear, unambiguous expression of the people's will. Even so, the evidence from the 1965 Batley, Leeds and York survey is probably about right, suggesting that (in the words of a subsequent overview of the slum clearance literature) 'a typical pattern of response in a poor condition inner city area would be between one quarter and one third of households in favour of staying put, one quarter to one third in favour of a change of accommodation within the same locality, and between one third and one half of households in favour of a complete change of both houses and locality'.[2]

We can dig a bit deeper, and hear some voices. The Sunderland survey of autumn 1965 had been undertaken by Norman Dennis, a remarkable sociologist who was the son of a Sunderland tram driver, lived in the city's Millfield area and was hitherto best known for his co-written *Coal Is Our Life* (1956), a classic community study of Featherstone in West Yorkshire. Although the main thrust of what became *People and Planning* (1970) concerned downsides of slum clearance, he did not exclude the voices of those who for entirely understandable reasons welcomed the prospect:

> Every wall is damp – not just one. The rain comes in: it's penetrating damp, there is no cement left at all between the bricks. The downcomers are all cracked and leaking. The place is deteriorating at the back – the cement, the brick, the wood, it is all a bit musky now. My husband has had two heart attacks, yet he has got to use the stairs; we have no option but to be up and down stairs for water all the time.
>
> When you have been out of the house a couple of days it is all foisty when you come back in. You can't kill the smell with Dettol or anything. The floor is all rotten with woodworm. I would gan out tomorrow. It's been unlucky to me this house! I'd only been here two years. We blamed the house when we lost the bairn – we lost a bairn y'knaa. Three months. Pneumonia. Dampness. I wish they'd pull it all down this week. The daughter is full of caad – she gets a cold once every month. We had a few floor boards replaced, but only after we've had the Health Inspector in four or five times. Which estate would we prefer? Just put 'Any'!

For some the problem could be simply the wrong type of neighbours. 'Oh yes, they are friendly,' conceded one respondent, before going on: 'A lot of the neighbours sit around the doorsteps from morning till night.

I can't stand them. They just sit and gossip all day long.' 'Friendly – but I don't want to be friendly with them!' explained another. 'They are the type who run into debt. I have known lots of people in trouble because they didn't keep neighbours out of their houses.' Or as a third unarguably put it: 'We were warned by the previous tenant that they are very nosy. They are watching behind the curtains when you go out and when you come back. Just like Coronation Street.'

Yet at least as many wanted to stay put, certainly in their neighbourhood and often in their house:

> I've always lived here and I dread leaving.
>
> I was bred and born down here.
>
> I've been here a long time and I'm used to it.
>
> It's home. I wouldn't like to live anywhere else. It's my life.
>
> I'm used to it. I've been in this area for sixty-odd years.
>
> I love it here. I never feel lonely; somehow I can feel the presence of both my mother and sister, both of whom lived here until they died.
>
> If it's a crap night at the Willow Pond, in five minutes you can walk to the Buffs in Rutland Street or to the Mountain Daisy or the Railway or the Millfield Club.
>
> It would be all right for me [i.e. to move], I would get my own transport. But me Dad can't walk and he can only get as far as the Buffs. If you put him out to Town End Farm you might just as well shoot him up in a rocket and let him orbit in outer space.
>
> Work? Just right! Shops? Couldn't get any better than this for anything like that! School? Just out of the backdoor! Church? Just down the street! Pubs and clubs? All around us! Town centre? Only a thruppenny bus ride!
>
> Everything is handy. Shops, entertainment, and church. I just like it around here, that's all.
>
> When you are getting on in years you can't be bothered shifting.
>
> We are getting on in years. We'd say, 'Leave them up'.
>
> When you get on you don't want to be disturbed.

'If they'd only let us stay,' said perhaps the most poignant voice. 'No one wants to go. We are not young, he [her husband] will only last five years. That's what he says, "If they'd only let us stay."'

On a key aspect of any new dwelling, whether going there voluntarily or in effect being forced, Dennis's interviewees seemingly spoke with one mind:

> Flats! They say it's just like going into hospital when you go. We know two or three who want to be out. You've only got to set fire to one of them and they're all gone.
>
> I would die if I had to go into a flat.
>
> I am against flats. Once you're locked in, you're locked in. Here you can walk out of the front or into your own backyard.
>
> I don't believe in flats or maisonettes. My mother moved to a flat. It didn't work, having to climb stairs. There was somebody above her with kiddies. There was always rows over not taking turns cleaning the stairs.
>
> If you have an argument or a fight with your wife it ought to be private. In a flat everybody in the building hears – it becomes everybody's fight.
>
> Your privacy has gone in flats. You can't have a noisy party. You don't know who you're going to get next to you. If I got someone on either side of me I don't like here, it wouldn't matter to us. I wouldn't have to pass them on the stairs every day.
>
> I wouldn't dare go into the sky scrapers: I'm frightened of heights and people are careless of cigarettes – I don't want to burn to death. They are gorgeous inside, but more like dolls' houses, you are too much fastened in.

Or as a verse published in the *Sunderland Echo* in June 1966 nicely expressed the widespread sentiment:

> We are proud of our trim little palace,
> We've worked hard to make it just that.
> Can the council be cruel and callous
> And force us to fret in a flat?

These Wearsiders were far from alone – well *before*, of course, the Ronan Point disaster of May 1968. 'Nearly all the households emphatically wanted a house or a bungalow,' noted Joan Ash in 1963 about the slum-dwellers of St Mary's, Oldham. '"I'd rather have a tent on the moors than a flat," said one woman.' And Ash added: 'Almost half the housewives who wanted to stay in St Mary's were not prepared to remain if they had to live in a flat or maisonette, and given the alternative of a multi-storey dwelling in the area and a house elsewhere they preferred the house elsewhere. Generally, the alternatives of a flat in St Mary's and a house elsewhere were equally undesirable to most respondents.' Two years later, the Batley/Leeds/York survey revealed only 12 per cent of households expressing a preference for a flat, with furthermore most of those specifically wanting a low-rise development; in November 1966 a *New Society* article arguing against high-rise cited the latest Rowntree Trust Housing Study, indicating that over 80 per cent of households wishing to move had expressed a preference for a house as against a flat; and the following year the GLC found that three-quarters of their applicants hoped for a house and a garden. By this time, Ernö Goldfinger's Balfron Tower was going up in Poplar. 'As a teenager, I watched it going up at the end of my street,' recalled Joe Connolly in 2013. 'My family and our neighbours dreaded the prospect of being sent there under the slum clearance scheme. We called it "the Barracks" and it became a symbol of the threat to our community.' And he continued: 'We wanted houses; no one wanted a flat, especially in Goldfinger's gruesome tower. Where would children play? What happens when the lifts break down? Who would be looking out when criminals came by?' This at a time, not to labour the point, when only 9 per cent of the GLC's housing output was in house-and-garden form, compared to 65 per cent being in high flats.[3]

Uncertainty, apprehension, fatalism – these were perhaps the governing emotions as an area awaited clearance. Certainly, Dennis's witnesses suggested all three:

> It all depends when we gaan where they put waa. When they pull it down you got to go where they say. There is that many people mixed up! You can't pick and choose. They dinnit seem to bother. They seem to mix the good'uns with the bad'uns.
>
> We hope we'll get amongst nice clean people – but we won't! We'll be put among dirty people to give them an example!
>
> If I couldn't get where I wanted to be, the bairns would be a drawback, because I'd be tied with them on some estate well out of

the way. Here, if I want to go out I have the family all round. There I couldn't get out on a night with me husband. We'd have to take the children all over with us.

We are hoping they won't put us in a flat. But you are only allowed one refusal now. Saw it in the *Echo* a couple of months ago.

The Corporation takes no notice of the opinion of people like us.

You could sign a petition, but what's the use? You can't go up against the Law.

I like this house and don't want to leave it, but I know it has to come down on account of the others. When I get a council house I won't have the room I have here. There is room for family gatherings. But there is nothing else for it but slum clearance . . .

It was perhaps unsurprising, then, that when the proposed 'action plan' for north-west Sunderland (a working population of 20,000) was revealed through a pamphlet and an exhibition, with comments invited, a mere thirty-six observations were submitted. Dennis's explanation for this apparent apathy emphasised class: 'The working-class family has a low expectation that it will be influential in any negotiations. The middle-class group is likely to be more knowledgeable about and active in the pursuit of opportunities for self-protection.' He also stressed 'the sheer magnitude', to those about to be affected, of what was involved:

Slum-clearance means a total change in circumstances, the possible ramifications of which may be too complex to grasp and too obscure to be contemplated. One reaction to this state of affairs is analogous to that which arises when war breaks out. The pattern of the future will be completely disrupted. All the known irritations of workaday life will be at any rate halted. Another reaction is analogous to the state of shock; the residents' state of mind can be that of stunned disbelief.

It was somewhat similar in Nottingham's St Ann's district. There, the young writer and incipient community activist Ray Gosling was largely responsible for setting up in April 1966 the St Ann's Tenants and Residents Association (SATRA), whose first meeting saw hardly any of the 500 present expressing satisfaction with the council's redevelopment proposals. But for Gosling himself, it proved – for a time anyway – a sobering experience, including one particularly salutary episode in February 1967:

> It was the first piece of paper in anyone's letterbox about the future. We appealed on the leaflet for people to write to authority: let their landlord and the council know their opinions, and also to get in touch with us to build a people's organisation. I'd expected an avalanche of mail. That didn't happen. I was heartbroken. We'd debated and agreed, and written and paid the printer, trudged and distributed these leaflets to every home: delivered 15,000 handbills by hand ourselves over one snowy weekend – and the response was two.

'Few honest poor will ever admit to a stranger that they live in a slum,' reflected Gosling years later. 'It's like naming names, pointing a finger. The consciousness of what was happening, many people pushed back into their subconscious.'[4]

All this was compounded by the slum-clearance process itself: often extremely lengthy and stop-start, with for the poor toads under the harrow far too much about it that was cruel, threatening and seemingly arbitrary – as well as just plain horrible and deeply inconvenient. It was not as if only a small number of lives were, across the post-war years, being turned fundamentally upside down. The best overall figures we have are for England and Wales, where between 1955 and 1985, according to Jim Yelling's authoritative overview, 'some 1.48 million houses were demolished or closed as a result of slum clearance, displacing more than 3.66 million people'; and he identifies the peak period as 1965–74, led by Greater Manchester, West Yorkshire and the West Midlands. The hollowing out could be dramatic: in Glasgow, for instance, the population of the Gorbals decreased from 23,428 in 1961 to 7,445 by 1971, in Anderston from 21,457 to 9,265 and in Kingston from 19,508 to a mere 1,189 – a decrease of 94 per cent. 'Seen Out' was the title of a heartfelt 1973 poem by the Glaswegian poet Maurice Lindsay:

> Over small print in papers,
> arguments at public inquiries,
> a demolition squad moves in;

coloured helmets swarming up to
patched roofs, unpicking rafters . . .
now and then a tenement
fights back, stumps snarling
chokes of dust, menacing
what once had been a passing street.
Machines bring all stone
down to its own level.

Or take Norman Dennis's equally heartfelt description of how the long-drawn-out process tended, because of the consequences of planning blight, to play out in practice:

> Modernisation is abandoned. Maintenance is held at the lowest level compatible with comfort and self-respect. Interior decorations are allowed to deteriorate. Eventually spring cleaning may be regarded as not worth the trouble. Public spaces are neglected. Pavements are patched rather than renewed. Streets remain cobbled while all other town roads are asphalted. In design and efficiency all such items as lamp standards fall behind. The decay of the physical environment and changes in the area's social composition adversely affect the area's morale. People are ashamed when their friends visit them.
>
> It is only as the scheduled time of demolition approaches that the accumulation of such grievances leads to protest. The protest now, however, is based on the desire to accelerate demolition. Conditions for many families have become intolerable.

'Slum-clearance may be, therefore, to some extent a self-fulfilling prophecy,' he concluded. 'In some areas the descent to slumdom can be traced directly to a single cause: the slum-clearance proposals themselves.'[5]

We are fortunate, for what has become a shamefully semi-forgotten story, to have no shortage of vivid, first-hand testimony. 'I understand that eight houses situated behind the Empire Theatre are being demolished to make space for a car park,' Karen (no surname given) wrote to the *Sunderland Echo* in August 1965. 'A simple sentence,' she went on, 'but what heartache lies behind it!':

> Nearly all the residents in this block have lived there for over 50 years; they are for the most part very old, and the younger residents of this small street help to make their lives a little easier. The uprooting at their age is bad enough, but some of the places suggested for them are ridiculous and disgusting. One person was sent to view a place and upon arrival found not only a house but old furniture, a mouldy meal on the table, and to complete the picture, a 'gusunder' complete . . . Others are being sent so far away that there is little hope of them finding themselves able to get into the town, due to age, and others having to take places that are centrally heated, when their main comfort in life is their coal fires.

Elsewhere, for Manchester and Salford in the mid-sixties, we have the devastating visual record of Shirley Baker's photographs – never pre-arranged and deeply authentic – but it is also worth quoting further from May Bish's November 1966 letter about slum clearance in Ardwick, highlighting not only the young/old contrast, but also praising two women, Major A. Seward and Capt. J. Welsh, based at the local Salvation Army centre: 'All the area around their centre is being demolished and for months they have worked without pause helping old people, regardless of their religious beliefs, to their new homes,' she testified. 'They've collected the keys for the new home from the Town Hall, scrubbed the place out, laid oilcloth, made curtains, and where needed have obtained furniture, repaired, cleaned, and polished and painted. They've done absolute wonders to help these elderly people in their time of stress and trouble . . .' Stress indeed, and she described older people's 'worry at the thought of moving and hearing of the death of old neighbours who braved it out to overspill areas then only lived a few weeks'. Earlier that year, in nearby Bolton, the local paper's George Riley had evoked (under the headline '"Survivors" wait in dust and dirt') the scene in the town's Vernon Street area, which 'once rang with the laughter of children at play and echoed to the bustle of life in an everyone-knows-everyone-else "Coronation Street" world of tight-packed terraced houses':

> Now the days are hideous with the endless thunder of bulldozers, the eternal bonfires of crackling, smoking timbers, the clank of

sledge-hammers and the noisy cascades of crumbling old bricks into lorry after lorry, as one by one the houses are swept away under a clearance order.

But even in the midst of the battlefield-like desolation, life still goes on for a handful of 'survivors' who wait for their turn to follow the hundreds of others who have already moved to new homes in other parts of the town. Here and there in the rows of gaunt, windowless, doorless, roofless shells that once were homes, a wisp of smoke curls from a chimney over the still-curtained windows to proclaim that someone still waits for the word to move on and begin a new life.

Seventy-nine-years-old Mrs Mary Elizabeth Redshaw, a rheumatism-plagued widow who lives alone at 41 Ainscow Street, huddled over the fire in the black-leaded grate of her tiny home and said: 'It's disgraceful. They should never have started knocking the houses down until they had found us all somewhere else to live. No one has told me when I will be leaving or where I will be going. But what's going to happen to me in the meantime if I'm suddenly taken ill? I'm the only one living on this side of the street. Once I could have knocked on the wall for help from a neighbour. Now no one would hear me.'

Across the street at No. 54, 62-years-old widower Mr John Best lives alone with only a budgerigar for company. He pointed at a bulldozer toppling a load of old bricks into a lorry in a cloud of thick dust, and said: 'I suffer from chronic bronchitis – and I have to breathe this kind of air all day long seven days a week. It's not right to make people live in these conditions.'

Next-door neighbours Mr and Mrs James Robinson and sons Allan, aged 12, and Brian, aged eight, own their own house. They have already turned down the offer of another home at Deane. Said Mrs Robinson: 'It was filthy and on a hillside, much worse than this one. But we should never have been left here like this. The dust and the smoke get in the house and every time we come in we tramp mud and brick-dust all over the carpets.'

At No. 5 Mortfield Street, 62-years-old Mr Richard Farnworth and his wife Alice, aged 65, who has to sleep downstairs because of her health, wait for news of when they will be leaving the 11s 4d-a-week cottage which has been their home for 30 years. Mrs

> Farnworth said: 'I'm fed up with it. It's impossible to keep the place clean. I've just got heart-weary with it all.'

A few weeks later, a letter to the *Bolton Evening News* described how, as the remaining residents in and around Ainscow Street waited to be offered a new dwelling, 'houses are being demolished, stripped and burned, all the week through'. In short: 'The place looks like Berlin 1945. Glass and rubble fills the streets: litter of all kind lies about . . .' Or, moving on to Leicester, take this testimony from an oral history of the city's Walnut Street area:

> We all got a letter – compulsory purchase. It was dead out of the blue, we didn't know much about it at all, only just a little bit in the *Mercury* my husband read out – it was all going to be redeveloped at the Infirmary. Fair enough, we'd sat and watched them pull all the other side of New Bridge Street down but we still didn't think they were going to touch us because we saw them build part of the new Infirmary, the boiler house and that, and then they started putting these flats up and they put these temporary wooden shops up in Walnut Street, I mean we never dreamt that they were going to take us over as well. We thought we were safe this side of New Bridge Street 'cos, I mean, they'd half built those flats before we got the letter. We all thought, oh it'll never happen to us. I felt really ill, I did feel ill . . . I just couldn't believe it.

In Birmingham's Ladywood district, no sharper-eyed critic of the whole wretched process than Canon Norman Power, of the local St John's Church. 'Half-demolished buildings (one shop – still there – has been half-demolished for eight years) become centres of petty crime,' he wrote in his aptly titled *The Forgotten People*, published in 1965. 'Here tramps and vagrants sleep. Here gangs of youths and girls come and go. Here stolen property is dumped for convenient collection later. The whole district has deteriorated.' Power also complained bitterly of how 'nearly the *worst* property is not yet destroyed': 'Increasingly it is used as "temporary accommodation" for problem families. In overwhelming numbers such families cannot be helped. They make life horrible for many decent families left behind, and there are many wonderful people still struggling to maintain vestiges of civilisation in streets like this.' For London, we have as witness the young Michael Collins, who some forty years later would remember how during the mid-to-late Sixties, and even into the Seventies, it had all unfolded at the Elephant and Castle:

> The bulldozers moved in. The new world they brought would be a grey world, but not the grey of age, soot and grime that it promised to replace. In the meantime we waited. We watched. If there had been any indication that the planners might sweep a finger over The Street, doubtless a riot would have ensued . . . Over the years, rumours would circulate that these houses were next in line for a demolition job, and immediately the women, for it was mostly the women, would be tanked up on something like Dunkirk spirit, ready to batten down the hatches, pile up the sandbags, evacuate the kids and prepare for invasion. More than only bricks and mortar, they were protecting their past, as well as their present and their future.

It was worst, emphasises Collins, for the old, especially those living alone. 'They dreaded the rumble of the distant bulldozer that began to make its way into the neighbourhood, almost as much as they once feared the doodlebugs and bombs. Louder and closer it got, and one day, with the merest of warnings, and no say in where they might end up, their home could be a target.' The final witness is a diarist, Barking's Pat Scott, starting with a visit from a public health officer:

> Evidently we bought our house too late to qualify for Market Value & we shall only get Site Value – approx. £200–300. The Compulsory Purchase order will come in March . . . We seem to have a fair chance of getting accommodation where we want it – the houses aren't coming down yet & they [i.e. the council] will have plenty of time to find somewhere. *(25 January 1966)*
>
> Ted had letter from District Valuer & we have to name a price we want for the house. *(9 February 1966)*
>
> We wrote to Valuer & asked £1150. *(14 February 1966)*
>
> The District Valuer came at 11. He was very nice & very businesslike. He knew everything about the house & purchase & will let Barking Council know about the price. (*23 February 1966*)

We had letter from Housing Dept. to ask what accommodation we have & need. *(1 March 1966)*

I was going over to see Nance Cooper but it was too wet. It's possible we could get her house – it may be better than waiting for a couple of years & then having to take anywhere. I'm not sure about it but Ted thinks it may be best. St Awdry's Rd is very handy for trains buses shops etc & the house has a bathroom although only an outside toilet. There are four rooms downstairs. Anyway I'll go and see it . . . *(19 April 1966)*

It's awfully dull & needs a lot of repair but it has possibilities. *(20 April 1966)*

We had a letter from Mr Tweedy. The Council haven't bought Nance Cooper's house yet so they can't do anything about our request for it. *(3 May 1966)*

Quite a few people over the road got letters today about moving & Rene told us the Days have been offered Nance Cooper's house but turned it down so we still have a chance. *(14 June 1966)*

There are only 12 people left on the other side now. *(29 June 1966)*

Today we had a letter from Mr Tweedy – offering us our house, Nance Cooper's, 130 St Awdry's Road. They will give us the key to view as soon as decorations are done. I don't know how I feel – glad to be away from here with all the empty houses over the road – but terribly sad to leave this house. 8 people over the road were offered a place this morning. *(30 June 1966)*

I still feel all tangled up inside. Dad went over to have a look & he thinks most of the decorations are done. So maybe it won't be long before we move . . . *(1 July 1966)*

We started packing this evening just in case we hear soon. *(4 July 1966)*

No letter but I left work at 3 & looked round shops in Ilford to price bedroom suites. There's very little under £100 so we must think again. *(6 July 1966)*

In the evening I sorted out & packed my winter skirt & suits. *(7 July 1966)*

Letter – seeing Mr Tweedy Monday at 10.30. Hectic day. Did lots of packing. Ted did cupboard under the stairs. We went over to Winches & bought Mahogany Wardrobe & Dressing Table.

Absolutely first class condition. Also two chairs – covered in red loose covers. *(9 July 1966)*

Went to Housing Office. We were given the keys of 130 St Awdry's Rd to view. The house isn't as good as we had hoped but better than a flat so we took it at a rent of approx £3-2-0 per week. I felt rather upset at having to decide so quickly (we only had a couple of hours to make up our mind) but it will all be O.K. . . . We went over there in the evening & showed the children. They seem to like it. *(11 July 1966)*

My mouth is full of ulcers – I feel really queer. I didn't have any sleep last night – it seems to be upsetting me more than I thought. *(12 July 1966)*

The diary then goes virtually blank for the next ten days, but on the 22nd: 'We have been much too busy to write this up but today we moved to 130 St Awdry's rd . . . I didn't have the scene I thought I would have. When I saw our house empty I didn't mind leaving. I have been crying all the week but I feel quite O.K. now.'[6] Taken altogether, it could have been worse; and for many, many people it surely was.

'Inveterate class contempt for slum clearance families is virtually inevitable among other local authority tenants' was the striking first sentence of James Tucker's 'From the Slums' chapter in his 1966 book *Honourable Estates*. 'There are two main ways of getting a council house: one is via the waiting list; the other through slum demolition and rehousing by the authority. Time on the waiting list is frequently spoken of as a pedigree.' Even so, he noted about those families without that pedigree:

Whatever social difficulties they may suffer the simple, enormous improvement in the physical setting of their lives makes all other considerations subordinate. I know there are families who ask to go back to the slums; but I never found one . . .

Where discontents are mentioned, they are usually preceded by a blanket proviso: 'Well, it's better than the slums.' The wife of a shot blaster in a two-bedroom maisonette at Raeburn Road, Gleadless Valley, Sheffield, said: 'I was four months pregnant before I would tell my neighbour. I hardly ever see her.' They had

> come from Pittsmoor, an old district of the city. Had she found any class difficulties? 'Well, some of them are a bit snobbish about the bins.' The bins? 'If my bin is full and instead of leaving stuff wrapped up on the floor I put it in somebody else's bin they put it back in mine. Yes, they're a bit snobbish about the bins. But it's very nice here.'

A study conducted in 1966/7, re-interviewing thirty-two of the Batley/Leeds/York families who had been originally interviewed in 1965, broadly concurred with Tucker's overall impressions. Some two-thirds of the families had been moved from 'slum' areas; the others had come from 'twilight' areas; and they were now asked how the move had gone and whether they were happy to be living on a council estate further away from the centre of the town or city, i.e. as opposed to paying rent to a private landlord in a more inner-urban area. The study's conclusion was that – while not denying 'there had been some initial difficulties and problems in settling down nor that some people still had reservations about the new environment', with loneliness perhaps the main issue cited – 'for most there had been all-round benefits and it had been the means to a general improvement in the standard of living':

> For younger people it had resulted in a better family life while older people at last felt they had achieved the advantages and rewards due to them years ago. The significance that was attached to improved living conditions is perhaps best illustrated by quoting comments that respondents made themselves; after a rather testing period when her husband was trying to find new employment and the whole family was living with relations one Leeds mother said that the move had changed their life completely and had 'put them back on their feet'. Another Leeds widow who had been nervous in her previous home and frightened of going out (the house opened immediately on to the street) claimed that 'moving had made all the difference to her'.

And, asked if they would like to leave their new dwelling and/or district, only six out of the thirty-two respondents said that they would.

There is, however, a crucial qualifier – namely, that although almost half (fifteen) of those thirty-two were now living in flats, only one of them was not on either the ground or the first floor. Might the survey's conclusions have been different if more of them had been located appreciably higher up?

As ever, the qualitative evidence is mixed. 'Most tenants seem stimulated by these quite new environmental conditions and have settled down to one main mutual complaint – about the vandals (mainly non-resident) who play hell with the lifts, break glass and have also been known to attempt to set fire to the lift motor room,' claimed the *Architects' Journal* in April 1965 about life in the newly built twenty-one-storey blocks in Leith Fort, Edinburgh; in Everton Heights, declared the *Liverpool Echo* later in the year, 'tenants of the new sky-scraper blocks of flats are discovering the advantages their homes offer, and there are few who would rush to come down to earth again'; while Tucker in his tour of council estates found tenants liking their high-rise, with the middle-aged wife of a Liverpool stoker unanswerably telling him, 'You've got the comfort'. Still, most of the evidence went the other way. Reporting in October 1966 on the recently completed Mardyke House, a thirteen-storey block just off the Old Kent Road, the *Guardian*'s Tony Geraghty wrote vividly of suffering mothers ('the isolation of living above 100ft with children whose hunger for play space and company makes some of them long wistfully for the happier times in Guinness Buildings, the creaking place from which they moved'); about the same time, the *Wythenshawe Express* ran a story about children in new high-rise flats resentful of how 'the old folks tend to make them scapegoats – by blaming them for such irritations as damaged lifts, broken windows and noise'; and the *Daily Telegraph* the following spring quoted a concerned London social worker: 'These children grow up like prisoners in concrete boxes in the sky, cut off and with nowhere to work out their energy in a harmless way. They turn to violence and destruction. The evidence is there, and if something is not done quickly we will have a new race of thugs and hooligans on our hands.' Among observers, no one was more down on the whole phenomenon than Norman Power, as he gazed balefully at Ladywood's new tower blocks, named provokingly after cathedral cities (Truro, Lincoln, Canterbury, Salisbury, Wells, Brecon, Durham) because they were intended to be the new cathedrals of the sky. He depicted them as, in reality, miserable places full of 'uprooted' people: 'Insecure, they fall back on their new homes as refuges; they go out little, the "telly" dominates their home lives. They show their carpets, curtains and furniture with great pride, but there is little social life, and less cultural or spiritual life. There is much loneliness, especially among old people.' And, he added, 'people in the new flats are saying that they would give up all the amenities for the little gardens they left'.

Perhaps the fullest journalistic exploration of the experiences of this new generation of high-rise dwellers came in the *Sunday Times*'s colour magazine in April 1966. 'People sometimes panic when the lifts stick at Hyde Park South, the biggest block in the vast complex of workers' flats which dominate Sheffield,' wrote Peter Dunn. 'An old lady, just out of hospital and with her leg in plaster, once got stuck in the lift for two hours. It is a favourite story among the Cliff Dwellers. "I was in bed," said one, "and I heard the alarm go at about 11 p.m. and it didn't go off again until about 1 a.m." The Cliff Dwellers hate the lifts and, for those who have moved in from cosier and perhaps slummier areas, it is only a short step to hating the flats themselves.' In addition to identifying 'inadequate schools and almost total lack of playing space for children' as two further serious problems, Dunn also quoted some of the residents themselves:

> You get no real friendships. You've got to go out on the deck and it's not like standing on the doorstep. There's a social club and we've joined it. It's like a holiday camp. *(Doreen Jackson, married to a fitter, mother of a six-year-old)*
>
> My great point about these flats is when you come home from work it's aired up. When you get up on a winter's morning you're not stood wondering whether to get out of bed. You can walk around, perhaps half-dressed, it's so warm. *(George Bennett, railway lorry driver)*
>
> We didn't like it here at first, but now we wouldn't move; you're safer up here: you're not on the roads. We've got cracks in our walls, but we've to be in six months before anything's done, and we can't paper until it *is* done. It's not altered me being here; I'm still rough and ready. *(Sheila Beckingham, twenty-six, penknife whetter)*

I don't like the flats; there's too many people together. They've tried to make it nice but I think they've put some terrible people up; they've tried to mix rough people with decent people. We went on holiday, and all my window was smashed at the side of the door. I think this building's all right but I think it's been shoved up personally. There's been damp coming into the hall, both bedrooms and toilet; no one's done anything about it. Well, they're *supposed* to. *(Maureen Burns, twenty-four)*

I really think they ought to have put all the old ones together. Young ones won't be bothered these days. But I don't get lonely. I don't brood. I do a jig-saw ... I don't think people have owt to grumble at. They see it before they come in and they don't have to take it. Where we came from we had a back yard and all we could see was bins. *(May Wilson, sixty-eight)*

Summarised rather than quoted were Terence and Patricia, twenty-seven and twenty-two, with a four-year-old son. 'They bitterly regret ever having moved into the flat. They complain about the keeping-up-with-the-Joneses atmosphere as well as the structural failings of the building – doors that don't fit, damp, lack of soundproofing.' Why, Dunn asked a housing expert from Sheffield University, were the Corporation so apparently indifferent to these practical issues, such as the malfunctioning lifts? 'They feel a sense of material achievement and don't really want to know much about that sort of thing ... There's a kind of pride involved. People don't like to admit their faults.' But perhaps the ultimate explanation for this lack of responsiveness to the concerns of the cliff-dwellers lay in a glancing remark by the same expert: 'No middle-class person would want to live there.'

What feels like a particularly balanced, trustworthy assessment comes from a caretaker in Wigan quoted by Graham Turner. Since 1961 he had been responsible, living on the ground floor, for the newly built Douglas House block of flats, 120 in all, and he began by telling Turner that the Corporation had, to his mind, been at fault for the way they had moved people into the flats:

They didn't pull a whole street down and put them all in together. They pulled three houses down here, three somewhere else and then mixed the people up. Here, of course, they can't stand on the

> doorstep and have a chat – those corridors [described by Turner as having 'the tawdriness of municipal flats everywhere'] are very lonely. I start at eight and up till lunch-time, you never hear a soul. It's just the same between two and four in the afternoon.
>
> Mind you, there's a lot of advantages. You've got your own baths and toilets, something you've never been used to, and it's all under-floor heating, but of course these places are no use to children, they can't play in the corridors because they echo so. By and large, the people in here don't neighbour a great deal. They don't depend on each other like they did. The difference between the old days and now is the money.
>
> In the old days, if my mother was ill, the neighbours would send me to school, give me a basin of gruel, even mop the doorstep over to keep you decent. In a block of flats, it's not like a street. If there's one change, how shall I put it, it's meanness. Most of them wouldn't put themselves out to do anything for the place.

'Life in Douglas House is apparently warmer and quieter than it was in some of the old mill rows,' concluded Turner himself, 'but it has clearly lost a good deal along with the noise.'[7]

Something indeed, and three statistical surveys we have for the mid-1960s all suggest strictly modified enthusiasm on the part of this generation of high-rise dwellers. The first, undertaken in 1965 for the Ministry of Housing, found 27 out of 41 residents on the Ebor Gardens Estate in Leeds wanting to move, 43 out of 60 on the Loughborough Estate in Lambeth and 41 out of 53 on the Everton Heights Estate in Liverpool, with 'better for the children' the reason most often given; when asked if they liked the appearance of their estate, the percentages for positive responses were respectively 23, 21 and 0; or as Joan Ash, summarising the report, very mildly put it in relation to most families in those high-rise blocks, 'they did probably have to make more adjustments, to live with more care and more strain, than the people living in houses'. So, too, in a similar study in St Mary's, Oldham, where only 11 per cent had wanted flats in the first place and barely half, having moved in, pronounced themselves 'satisfied', with the main reason for willingness to stay on being the ability to continue to live in the central area of the town. The third survey, carried out in 1967, was of the residents of a new fifteen-storey block in Cardiff's badly rundown Butetown area. Most having gone there reluctantly in 1964 following slum clearance, almost 85 per cent were still wanting to live somewhere else, with 30 per cent wanting to move out of their flats immediately; and there was a familiar litany of complaints, including lack of play facilities for children, fear of children falling from heights, problems with the lifts, lack of anywhere to dry clothes, 'hospital atmosphere' of the entrance halls, nosy neighbours undermining privacy, even fellow residents dropping rubbish out of windows . . . In October 1966 a major three-year research programme began at Glasgow University into the social aspects of living in high flats. One of the researchers was Pearl Jephcott, and in 1968 she would tell the *Guardian* that (in her paraphrased words) 'first impressions are that families in high blocks suffer from the same or a worse lack of social life as people brought together on large new housing estates built on more traditional lines'.[8]

It is important not to exaggerate. High-rise living may have turned into something of a nightmare in the 1970s and beyond, but in the 1960s it was still for quite a few – though clearly not everyone – a dream fulfilled, certainly by comparison with the demolished slums of yesteryear. 'Getting a house within Glencairn was a real prize,' recalled Jack Daly in 2011 as Motherwell's seventeen-storey block, completed in 1964, was demolished. 'When we walked in everything was brand new – a fresh coat of paint, there were tiles on the floor, new bathrooms and kitchens and under-floor heating. All that was nothing like where we had come from.' Another Scottish child of the 1960s was the future Labour politician Patricia Ferguson, an eight-year-old when in 1966 her family left their Glasgow tenement (the four of them sharing two rooms) and moved into the first of the Red Road blocks (their flat comprising three bedrooms, a lounge, a big kitchen and, most wonderful of all, a bathroom). 'We had lots of space and fabulous views,' she remembered in 2010. 'When people moved there, this was the future, this was hope.' But, of course, there and elsewhere, once the vandalism kicked in, once the drugs kicked in, once above all the heroin kicked in (mainly from the 1980s), it was hope against hope, then finally hope abandoned.[9]

Unfortunately, our testimony is rather less rich (in the mid-1960s anyway) for the whole related area of city centre and town centre redevelopment, with its almost invariable emphasis on cars and shopping. In part this may have been because of a prevailing apathy-cum-fatalism ahead of redevelopment, perhaps especially in places like Newcastle lacking a strong middle class. 'In the mid-1960s Wilf Burns and the rest of us did everything we could to attract public participation,' claimed fellow planner Kenneth Galley in 1974, 'but people were just not interested.' Two groups, though, who almost invariably did make their voices heard were market traders and small shopkeepers – for instance in Leicester in 1963, when market stall-holders insisted that any scheme had to 'ensure the preservation of the individual character of the market area as an area of private businesses operated by persons whose lives are centred in the city'; or in Liverpool two years later, when the proposed massive extension of Marks & Spencer had Kenneth Jones, managing director of Whitty's sports outfitters in Basnett Street, demanding that the council 'consider whether the people in Liverpool prefer one huge store or 20 or 30 smaller shops'. A larger question remains: *if* there was a broader popular mood about the prospect of this sort of redevelopment, what was it? The evidence is patchy, but in 1964 a survey of shoppers in Bolton found only 30 per cent giving the existing town centre their unqualified approval, with instead the majority finding fault with some mixture of traffic congestion, parking difficulties, architecture, layout, shortage of cafés and lack of large department stores; while in early 1967 the *Daily Mirror*, after proclaiming that provincial cities were 'booming sky-high with vigorous young ideas, dynamic modern industries and go-getting leadership', asked readers to enter a 'Boom City' competition and submit their own thoughts:

> Top planning is creating beautiful estates serving all sections of the community. *(L. Sidebottom, Sheffield)*
>
> There are bonny babies, well-groomed teenagers, well-planned housing estates, new industries, enticing modern shops, an airport open to the world. There's an ever-expanding university, two of the most modern and best-equipped hospitals in the country, acres of moor to wander over within sight of the bustling traffic, and a dazzling night life. *(Frank Nichols, Newcastle)*

What makes any city the greatest? A modern, far-seeing council, a modern active local press – and most of all, the people . . . In Leicester, we don't think and wait, we think and do. *(A. R. Walmall, Leicester)*

Couldn't be 'swinging' if it wanted to be, with control from the university stopping even popular chain stores from building. As for the undergrads – ugh! *(Elizabeth Still, Cambridge)*

My city is supersonic. New precincts to shop in. New art galleries . . . New flats and flowers . . . We are a city with new ideas. *(Mr McHugh, Coventry)*

Ours is the city of the future . . . The sky is forever lit up [by chemical plants]. Fabulous apartment blocks and excellent new estates are developing fast. *(Robert Jones, Middlesbrough)*

'Manchester is GO!' proclaimed 21-year-old Gill Maxted, winning the top prize of £100. 'Around me I see new buildings going up-up-up – flats, laboratories, incising the skyline with that sharp, stark beauty of an age of precision.' Of course, we know that not everyone, particularly older people, felt the same way; but to deny the existence of an appetite for change, for modernity, would be, well, preservationist folly.

It is a moot point, though, how far that appetite extended in Blackburn. Admittedly, when in November 1964 the old market opened for the last time, ahead of a new, ultra-modern market opening on a new site, 'there were', reported the *Lancashire Evening Telegraph*, 'no last-minute protests, no last useless fight against the march of progress'. Still, as William Atkinson, selling fish at the market for the previous seventeen years, remarked: 'The new market will be better, but I think I shall miss the old place.' The focus now turned to the 116-year-old market hall clock tower, due for demolition despite the stubborn campaign of one councillor, Kenneth Culshaw. Support came in a letter to the paper from 'sentimental sense', calling for it to be cleaned up and preserved:

Think how our old people would appreciate this small portion of their Blackburn preserved . . . It is so much a part of Blackburn, a land mark, and if the stone work was cleaned it would be most attractive.

> I am all in favour generally of the modernisation, yet I can't help but feel that if the tower is pulled down the heart of Blackburn is destroyed.
>
> I have never written to the Press before, but have done so now because so many people are of the same opinion as myself . . .

But all in vain, for on the penultimate day of the year:

> While hundreds of shoppers stopped to stand and stare at the stone sentinel they have looked at thousands of times over the years, a lone demolition man went in for the kill and brought the tower down in a heap of dust and rubble.
>
> At the controls of a tall crane, he swung a huge bludgeon against the stone-work, and slowly, reluctantly, the tower gave up its ghost . . .
>
> Slowly the tower shook at each merciless blow of progress, and finally collapsed, until only the four pillars between which thousands had walked into the market hall remained, with a twisted mass of rubble, smashed wood and broken glass between the arches.

'I'm heartbroken,' declared Culshaw. 'Most people I have spoken to in the last few days have come round to my view and believe the tower and clock should have stayed put. They still look up to it and are missing it very much.'[10]

As for the new shopping centres, it is quite hard to detect overwhelming enthusiasm. 'A scene of concrete emptiness' was a description in November 1965 of the first-floor piazza of Manchester's Piccadilly Plaza, where overall, almost a year after completion, half the sites were still unlet; it was a similar story at the Merrion Centre in Leeds, where in 1966, two years after opening, tenants were seeking rent reductions as compensation for their 'disappointing trading experience' and 'substantial losses'; around the same time, Birmingham's Bull Ring was doing well on Saturdays, but operating far below peak capacity during the week; while in London, noted in April 1966 the *Guardian*'s Elizabeth Gundrey in her monthly 'Consumer's Column', the 'much-vaunted' Elephant and Castle shopping centre, just over a year old, was struggling: 'More than a third of the shops are still empty; the two-storey car park is not used to capacity. It is now planned to spend more millions on equipping the centre for fashion parades, car previews, and athletic displays; more circuses than bread.' She also pondered more generally why 'the now fashionable shopping centre concept' was seemingly proving a case of white elephantiasis:

> A lot of the planners' passion for big shopping centres is based on the belief that before long everyone will shop by car. I doubt it; and I hope not. I doubt it because an increasing percentage of the population is elderly or frankly old, and getting more so; and I cannot foresee a day when roads are solid with dear old ladies pelting along at all of 10 miles an hour on the crown of the road. Nor can I see shoppers finding it convenient to shop by car when (as is inevitable) this involves manhandling the goods across acres of car park. Long live the 'little man around the corner' on whom a call is so effortless by comparison.

Indeed, when it came to shopping, the forces of a deeply entrenched conservatism remained strong. Evidence from both Birmingham and Leeds suggested a marked continuing preference for markets over malls; while a survey by Gallup in 1968 revealed not only that just one in six housewives went shopping by car, but that fully one-third still went shopping every day and preferred to make many small purchases rather than a large one. In short, in the words of the report's accompanying headline, 'Super Shops Do Not Attract Housewives'.

Ultimately, in this whole charged area of urban redevelopment and responses to it, it all depended – on personal experience, on stage of life, on temperament, on so much else. Yet to dip into the diary of Gordon Bentley, or, rather, what he himself called his 'odd jottings and gleanings', is suggestive of a perhaps not wholly atypical English sensibility. He had been born in January 1935; and by May 1965 he was living at 27 Spath Road, Didsbury, Manchester 20:

> I like Didsbury 'village' with its quiet streets lined with small terraced houses that are really cottages, their diminutive gardens, with roses and the occasional almond tree. I like the numerous little corner shops there where one can buy practically anything at all hours of the day and night, even on Sundays. It is all so cosy and

> somehow solid and peaceful, yet it is just round the corner from one of the busy city main roads.

Bentley also reflected on how he liked the part of Didsbury with its 'quiet roads lined with big trees and big solid old houses whence one can hear on summer evenings the sound of music from the BBC Third Programme or the strains of a late night string quartet from the Home Service'. Six months later, it was distressing news from Oxfordshire that got him jotting:

> Now they are going to move Banbury Cross because it is in the way of traffic. How English! . . . Many cathedrals are islands in a sea of car-parks, market halls no longer preside over markets because these impede the flow of road transport, elm trees interfere with telephone cables and therefore have to go, pigeons foul buildings and have to be dealt with – of course in most English cities buildings have replaced trees so what else can the pigeons foul?

Still, just occasionally he did give an approving nod to the modern – provided it was the right sort of modern. 'Now we have dustbins with rubber lids,' he had recorded that June; and he deemed them 'a great improvement on the old metal ones because they don't make any noise and they don't jam'.[11]

11

Quite Magnificent Schemes

Setting aside the vagaries of public opinion – consulted or otherwise, mute or otherwise – what about all those well-intentioned 'activators'? The politicians, the planners, the architects, the commentariat – what responsibility did *they* bear for the profound urban disturbance now reaching its peak? As they looked about them, did they have qualms? And how did they see the future?

Ultimately, and often for the most understandable of reasons, it was the numbers game which continued – especially when it came to housing – to exert for politicians the decisive pull. A key figure was Sir Keith Joseph, who at his party's 1963 conference had fired the starting-gun for a fierce bidding war by setting an annual target for 1965–70 of 400,000 housing completions. 'I was just a "more" man,' he would recall guiltily in 1987 about his time as housing minister. 'I used to go to bed at night counting the number of [slum] houses I'd destroyed and the number of planning approvals that had been given . . . Just *more*.' Labour in the 1964 election had promised to match that target; and in March 1966 it upped the ante by pledging a target of 500,000 houses per year by 1969/70. 'In housing, the effort was to really get the numbers up, and to get everybody involved in it,' remembered years later the Labour politician J. Dickson Mabon about his time (1964–7) as minister in charge of the Scottish Development Department, a role which included for rural parts of the country taking 'the good-natured lairds who usually ran the County Councils, to actually see their slums, before they recognised that they had some'. 'Because I was selfish,' he added, 'I wanted numbers, I wanted ten, twenty, a hundred from anywhere, to add to my numbers . . .'[1]

Inevitably, of course, 'numbers' often in practice meant high-rise, not least given the understandable desire of inner-city local authorities to use new high-density housing to try to stem the drift to the suburbs of the economically active, even perhaps to hold communities together amid the often chaotic dispersal of slum clearance. Could it have been different? In 2017 there appeared in the press a striking letter from Ann Carlton:

> Research indicating that conventionally built terraces could be built at similar densities to tower blocks and be as cost-effective, as well as being best for tenants, was available 50 years ago. I was then the Labour Party official responsible for housing and local government policy and had already seen in Liverpool the adverse effects on families of high-rise living.
>
> Horrified by the Labour government's advocacy of tower blocks I tried to persuade Dick Crossman MP, who was then [until August 1966] minister for housing and local government, to look at the research, re-consider policies on slum clearance, stop advocating industrialised building methods and support conventionally built terraces instead. I was wasting my time. He was not interested and his minister of state, Bob Mellish MP, was completely sold on pre-cast concrete and tower blocks.

'How I wish,' she hardly needed to add, 'they had listened.'

There is a compelling photograph of Crossman taken in November 1965. He is at the Royal Festival Hall – so emblematic of the post-war New Jerusalem dream – and the occasion is the opening of the 'Tomorrow's Lambeth Today' exhibition; in front of him is what looks like a Lego construction, but is in fact a model of the borough's planned Clarence Avenue development, featuring three high-rise blocks largely surrounded by trees; and he is staring intently, even gravely, at the highest of the blocks. Rather like the Webbs and Soviet Russia, it is as if he and those accompanying him (local Labour MP, two male local councillors, councillor's wife, architect) are seeing before them a future civilisation, and apparently endorsing it without even the hint of a question mark. Yet perhaps it is somewhat all too easy to be dismissive in hindsight. Reading Crossman's diary for the mid-1960s, what emerges again and again is a sense of powerlessness, of a huge and complicated world way beyond the power of any one individual really to grapple with. It is that awareness that helps to make him such a good diarist. One such moment of seeming helplessness occurred in September 1965 as, 'in appalling Lancashire weather – sheets of rain, driving wind', he inspected housing in Rochdale:

> There is an area in the centre called Deeplish where we have been doing a special sociological study. This is a part of the town which is now going downhill, but the quality of its housing is good enough to prevent it being certified as a slum. It is therefore being classified as an improvement area and our survey was designed to find out how people actually live, how they work and what they want done to their homes in an area of this kind. I spent the morning holding a seminar with the people engaged on the study and the local officials, and despite what they told me I was shocked and surprised when I actually walked round Deeplish. This is a so-called improvement area and its houses have been given thirty more years of life; yet they are little dwellings, each with a tiny courtyard behind, the tin bath hanging on the wall of the courtyard and two steps across it to the toilet in a shed. Upstairs in the houses there was a fairly stenchy smell, beds unmade in each house I visited and blankets with no sheets. It's a primitive, dismal life in Deeplish . . .

A moment of explicit helplessness had occurred a few months earlier on a visit to Newcastle – specifically, in relation to Eldon Square ('a beautiful Georgian square which they are going to destroy for a new shopping centre'). 'I am passionately opposed to this,' he recorded, 'and I blew up our regional staff in Newcastle and told them they were vandals for giving my consent. But I knew that it was already a *fait accompli*, and when I get back I shall be forced to draft the directive letter saying they should have permission.' Nor did it help that his permanent secretary, near the end of her lengthy tenure, was the fearsome Dame Evelyn Sharp (or 'the Dame' as she liked to be known), unrivalled for her ability to manipulate and outmanoeuvre her ministers, with Crossman (to judge by his diary) no exception. 'She was the civil servant who presided over some of the most hideous and unsympathetic urban developments of the past 50 years,' noted Tristram Hunt in 2002 when, in a *New Statesman* feature on 'My

Worst Briton', he nominated her. 'With an unbridled faith in the power of Whitehall,' he went on in an assessment that perhaps should have made more of a nod to her undoubted positive aspects and contribution, 'she sanctioned the mass destruction of historic street housing in favour of bleak modernist developments. Described as having "no aesthetic sense whatsoever", Dame Evelyn was typical of an arrogant bureaucratic elite who severed our architectural bonds with the past, destroyed the civic fabric and delivered the British city over to the automobile.'[2]

Seemingly in the champion class of hubristic, forward-thinking, hot-for-certainties arrogance was the Labour local politician Alderman Dennis Thomas ('Mr Redevelopment'), starting in May 1965 his seventh year as chairman of Birmingham City Council's Public Works Committee when he spoke to the *Birmingham Evening Mail*. The Bull Ring Centre and the Rotunda begun and completed during his tenure, the Inner Ring Road taking shape, multi-storey flats towering higher and higher – these were just the baby steps:

> What we have done so far in Birmingham will be dwarfed by the things to come. Earlier this week I had the pleasure of giving details of the £8 million Civic Centre plan, but there are other quite magnificent schemes to be announced. There is, for instance, what is going to happen at the other end of the Inner Ring Road, at the new University of Aston. There will be halls of residence and other quite exciting developments. Another thing I want to see completed if I can is the full redevelopment of Colmore Circus into the finest island site in the city.

While as for flats, 'I hope more developers will include blocks of them in their plans for the centre.' Or in sum: 'Others have held this office a little longer than I, but I do not think anyone has seen more achieved in his time.' Thomas would have fitted in well in Glasgow, where, as *The Economist* nicely put it later in the year, 'rehabilitation' was 'a word apparently unknown to the city council'.

All the same, there was the odd dissenter among the ranks of local politicians – one of them a Conservative councillor in Manchester, Thomas Baron, who in early 1966 attacked the city's policy of high-rise flats and proposed that certain housing projects containing high flats should be rejected. 'There is no difference between the tenants of our houses and those who buy their own,' he argued. 'The only difference is that our tenants cannot afford to pay the price of private enterprise, but they are no different in their need. They should be treated the same as any other house owner and given the sort of accommodation that most people want to live in.' To which his fellow Conservative, Alderman Sir Richard Hooper, countered: 'I have never heard anyone suggest that the whole of the cleared sites should be occupied by cottages, which are the most desirable type of accommodation, but you know you cannot do it in the centre of a congested area.' And he added reassuringly that 'there are many tenants of high blocks who like them once they move in'. Predictably, Baron's proposal was defeated, by 106–21. Another contrarian, this time in London, was a Labour councillor in Islington, Harry Brack, fierce opponent of his colleagues' plan to demolish the early Victorian Packington Estate ('the swansong of Regency taste before the railways and industry hit the borough'), now council-owned, and to build instead six-storey blocks of flats ('barracks for the workers'). For much of 1965, helped by Crossman's apparent opposition to the scheme and despite being expelled by his own party, it looked like he was going to win; but in the end the minister gave way – to be instantly condemned by the *Architects' Journal* for 'a shocking decision', albeit explained by how the council had ruthlessly been 'decanting families' and deliberately allowing Packington Street to fall into a state of 'dereliction': 'Children played in the empty houses, lead was stolen, windows broken, rain poured in.'[3]

Inevitably, there was often a strong element of 'boosterism' involved, perhaps especially in the north, where some leading local figures were just starting to think about the challenges that might lie ahead for their particular city or town in a post-industrial future. Few more assiduous boosterers than Blackburn's Alderman George Eddie, chairman of the Civil Development Committee and the key man behind the town's Master Plan. In November 1964, 'with great pleasure and thrill in my heart', he performed the opening ceremony at the new market, before that evening hosting a big celebratory dinner at the Windsor Hall:

> Our citizens have been waking up to the fact that the new Blackburn is at last really being born . . . Most of the people of this town, now

> they have seen it, like the reality. They are growing more and more excited about it and are eagerly looking forward to the vast changes that the future is going to bring . . . We have reached the stage where everybody wants the new Blackburn.

The following June it was the turn of a Manchester councillor, Andrew O'Toole, promising to the National Council of Women that through its new housing policy (essentially one of comprehensive redevelopment and tower blocks) Manchester would again be 'one of the great cities'; while later that month, the big redevelopment plans being announced for Bootle could hardly have been a more conscious attempt to improve the town's image, with Alderman Joseph Kelly, Labour leader of the council, declaring, 'I have never agreed with the ridicule or the theatre jokes about Bootle.' Or take Sheffield, where the Queen Mother's opening in June 1966 of the Hyde Park redevelopment scheme was marked by a positively self-congratulatory official brochure. Not only had the scheme, together with its Park Hill predecessor, 'had a far-reaching effect on architectural thought throughout the world', but

> the completion of Hyde Park must give a feeling of great satisfaction to those stalwarts of the City Council whose original ideas have now been brought to fruition; such personalities as the former Aldermen C. W. Gascoigne and P. J. M. Turner, Alderman Albert Smith and Alderman Harold Lambert, who throughout have given encouragement to the Architects and the Builders . . .

Still, it was all relative to Croydon, where one man, the American-style boss Sir James Marshall, presided until the mid-sixties over the Americanisation of Croydon's skyline, as the office boom turned into a veritable high-rise 'concrete renaissance' (or, as David Bowie would put it less flatteringly, 'concrete hell'). His underlying credo was simple: 'I believe in Croydon. I have always seen it as potentially the most important area of Greater London.' He certainly made Croydon better known; and when Bootle's town clerk, Arthur Taylor, talked to the press in 1965 about the redevelopment plans, he quite naturally boasted that 'the office quarter, in its conception, is second only to that of Croydon'.[4]

How much corruption was there? 'I spent the evening with Karl Cohen at one of his typical Jewish suppers,' recorded Crossman in June 1966 about a visit to Leeds:

> Afterwards, in came people from all the big construction firms, Wimpey, Parkinson, etc. What a power Karl Cohen as chairman of the Leeds housing committee holds over these big contractors. If he wasn't a strictly honourable man, which he is, he could be so easily corrupted, because he is personally disposing of millions of pounds'-worth of contracts and this is particularly open to corruption now that 70 per cent of his building is industrialized.

It is a tricky question to gauge. 'The contractors,' argue Miles Glendinning and Stefan Muthesius in their authoritative account of high-rise social housing in the post-war period, 'succeeded not because they bullied or bribed weak councils into adopting policies against their best interests, but because they gave politically strong councils what they required: high blocks, built reliably, quickly and in large numbers.' Similarly, in his study of the essentially pragmatic public-private partnerships that transformed city and town centres during the 1960s, almost invariably involving new shopping complexes, Alistair Kefford takes the line that the balance of power lay not with the councils but with the developers, with the latter not the former being far more likely to have to be persuaded to stick with the particular partnership. One historian, Barnabas Calder, has focused on the long and painful birth of the ultimately unsuccessful Anderston Centre in Glasgow; and he quotes the regretful 1967 words of the deputy city chamberlain to the town clerk about how 'numerous meetings were held between the developers and Corporation officials between March 1964 and March 1966 at which, on almost every occasion, some effort was made to wring some concession from the Corporation and to whittle away the original agreement'.

Even so, when it comes to possible corruption among local politicians, the shadow of the ambitious and highly productive Yorkshire architect John Poulson cannot but loom big. 'His business was large and its impact on post-war urban Britain was considerable, with over 240 planned projects,' notes Peter Jones in his overview of 'The Poulson Affair', with those projects (peaking in 1965–6, with fifty-nine planned commissions in progress) including many schools, colleges, hospitals and swimming baths as well as a range of shopping and town centre developments, with a strong geographical bias towards the north and north-east; while as for his backhanders, the legal proceedings after his downfall in the early 1970s directly implicated local politicians in various places, but especially the West Riding and Durham (notably Andrew Cunningham in the latter). Also corrupt, though less directly connected to Poulson, was Battersea's Sidney Spowle, Labour chairman in the mid-1960s of Wandsworth's housing committee – in which capacity, as the key driving force in the area's redevelopment, he took the bribes that would lead in 1971 to a six-year prison sentence for corruption. He remained unrepentant on release, recalling the deprivations of his own childhood (unsafe multiple occupation, shared outdoor toilets, no running water or central heating) and insisting that for its residents the new, system-built, high-rise housing he had presided over was 'heaven'. 'Now they have a separate kitchen, separate toilets,' he explained. 'It was unheard of in the old days there. You went down the end of the garden . . .'[5]

Poulson's name (and indeed Spowle's, though only as a bit player) would always be linked to that of T. Dan Smith, aka 'Mr Newcastle', *the* local-cum-regional politician of the era. In all of Smith's roles – whether as leader of Newcastle City Council until 1964, or as chairman from soon afterwards of the Northern Economic Planning Council, or as chairman of Peterlee and Aycliffe New Town Development Corporation, or perhaps most particularly running his own public relations company – he was deeply venal, seeing no conflict between the creation of a better world and the strengthening of his bank balance. Undeniably there was an idealistic element, not least when it came to pushing for high architectural standards, as he made clear in April 1965 with his presumably less-than-popular contribution to a discussion at RIBA on urban renewal. 'Architects weren't facing up to the job they had to do, he said,' ran the report:

> They must recognise that the public were their clients and they must be prepared to speak out against bad architecture and to hell with maintaining a united professional front. All that industrialised building meant in the present context was more mess more quickly. The architectural profession, he said, was still in the nineteenth

century and he didn't think much of their chances of reaching the twenty-first.

Almost a year later, in March 1966, the words of praise flowed thick as Newcastle University bestowed an honorary degree. 'His caring and unselfish activities over the past decade,' pronounced the Public Orator, 'have been devoted to banishing forever the spectre of economic depression from Tyneside and building here a regional civilisation of unique and genuine character. He succeeds the great city planners of early nineteenth century Newcastle and marches not unworthily in the footsteps of Clayton, Dobson and Grainger . . .'

Also receiving an honorary degree that day was Bob Dylan's friend, Alderman Theresa Russell ('always on the side of the angels'); and a third was 'architectural visionary' Wilfred Burns, recruited by Smith in 1960 as the city's first chief planning officer:

> The revolutionary principles of city centre planning which he evolved in collaboration with the Newcastle Planning Department long foreshadowed the findings of the Buchanan Report [on traffic in cities]. They have received unstinting praise both here and abroad, and they have made the City a Mecca for experts in this field from all over the world.
>
> Firmly thrusting aside the uninformed objections of carping spirits who failed abysmally to grasp that the splendid symmetry of Eldon Square must be sacrificed to preserve the subtler charm of Percy Street, Mr Burns has pursued his charted course with Messianic fervour, and his erstwhile critics can do little but cower beneath the glittering if somewhat faceless edifices that now rear above them . . .
>
> To him planning is not a matter merely of bricks and mortar or even of the more modern techniques of automated construction. It is a matter of service to man and his needs, and to man conceived with a lively and imaginative sympathy.

Burns himself the following year set out his convictions in *Newcastle: A Study in Replanning*, declaring that in the past seven years he had sought to create 'an atmosphere of a capital that knows its job, that wishes to lead, is prepared to think big'. 'The ball is now rolling fast in Newcastle upon Tyne,' he concluded at the end of his treatise, while also quoting from *Revelation*: 'And I saw the holy city, new Jerusalem, coming down out of heaven from God, prepared as a bride adorned for her husband . . .'

What was the Smith/Burns legacy? In 2024, responding to Simon Jenkins's claim that Smith 'began to demolish the city's Georgian Grainger Town', John Griffiths (author of a recent doctoral thesis offering an admirably nuanced treatment of Smith's career as a whole) argued instead that Smith was 'actually the saviour of Georgian Newcastle': 'One of his earliest actions on becoming council leader in 1959 was to revoke planning permission for a bank to construct a modern office block on Grey Street, in the heart of Grainger Town. The 1963 city development plan drawn up by Wilfred Burns under Smith's leadership pioneered the concept of conservation districts to protect historic areas of the city from inappropriate development.' It is a fair point, and indeed 'Keep the Best of the Old' featured as a section in Burns's treatise. Even so, taking Newcastle's redevelopment as a whole, the balance sheet is surely the other way. Inadequately selective slum clearance, so that 'areas which were very far from slums like much of Shieldfield were unnecessarily demolished under the guise of slum clearance in order to facilitate road programmes'; old slums replaced by 'new expensive slums', when 'good traditional council houses could have been built more cheaply'; tower blocks preferred not because of high subsidies or because of supposed land-saving properties, but instead because of their visual impact; 'attractive Victorian and Georgian squares' destroyed 'to make way for motorways which cut off ordinary access from the east end to the city centre'; and a city 'so carved up by radial road schemes that in some major areas (e.g. Scotswood Road) the places where people live are fitted around the roads, rather than the other way on' – such was David Byrne's persuasive assessment a year after Smith's death in 1993. Or to quote the title (but without the question mark) of John Pendlebury's similarly critical 2001 overview of the conservation aspect in the Newcastle of the 1960s: 'Alas Smith and Burns'.[6]

Burns is one of those 'architect-planners' identified by the architectural historian Otto Saumarez Smith as key figures in the radical urban renewal of the era. Another is Graeme Shankland, whom Saumarez Smith himself defended in 2024 from the Jenkins onslaught: 'There are certainly aspects of Shankland's Liverpool plan, not least the urban motorway, that was swept up in the neophilia of the 1960s, but Shankland was not influenced by Le Corbusier, who he was vocally critical of. His professed influences were current Swedish architecture, William Morris, and contemporary sociologists, many of whom were his friends. Shankland prophetically envisioned Liverpool as a tourist destination . . .' In that city he worked closely with a further architect-planner, Walter Bor, whose 1965 report on high buildings not only, noted the *Architects' Journal*, argued that 'high buildings are often the result of a desire for prestige and an indecent love of building high', but altogether had 'a strong preservationist bias'. Still, destruction there certainly was at this time; and Gavin Stamp, a less forgiving architectural historian than Saumarez Smith, wrote poignantly of the trails of destruction of Georgian Liverpool (not all of it slum housing) both in the university area around Abercromby Square and in the area around Sir Giles Gilbert Scott's Anglican cathedral – all of this quite apart from how 'whole areas of terraced housing in inner suburbs, like Everton, were wiped out, their inhabitants being decanted to new council estates on the periphery'.

For a final (and perhaps reasonably typical) architect-planner, take Percy Johnson-Marshall, who in 1966, looking back on a career largely spent in Coventry and London, produced his magisterial survey-cum-treatise, *Rebuilding Cities*. 'Planners and architects, as the chief designers of our physical environment, should never forget that the most important thing about a city or town is the people,' he declared in the first sentence of his chapter on 'The City of the Twenty-first Century'; he insisted on 'drastic controls on the motor vehicle'; zoning areas for particular purposes needed to be used 'flexibly'; houses, not flats, were the right place for large families; the question of whether or not to demolish, especially in areas where 'finely designed streets and squares and terraces and buildings have been allowed to fall into decay', demanded 'high skill in expert advice and civilized judgment from community leaders'; while in sum: 'Every large city needs a rich diversity of activity, and hence of opportunity leading to endless possibilities of fulfilment of personality – that vital human need which seems today so much neglected.'[7]

As for out-and-out architects, it is tempting to concentrate on the big names – whether Basil Spence (Hyde Park Cavalry Barracks) or Ernö Goldfinger (Balfron Tower) or Peter and Alison Smithson (the brutalist Robin Hood Gardens by now under way) or Richard Seifert (Centre Point) – but the real challenge is to unpick the governing assumptions of the profession as a whole. 'I was sworn at by the masters and told, "You will fail if you do another classical scheme",' the defiantly anti-modernist Quinlan Terry would tell Lynn Barber in 2004 about his time in the early 1960s as a student at the Architectural Association. 'Architects,' he added, 'are worse than theologians at disagreeing with one another, and they really believe passionately in their modernism.' A particularly suggestive analysis of what British architects of the 1960s believed to be their purpose came in 1969 from Alan Lipman (architectural writer-turned-sociologist), examining nine addresses delivered at RIBA between 1965 and 1967 by 'well known' practitioners under the title 'An architect's approach to architecture'. In the broad context of architects now working for a much wider range of clients than had traditionally been the case, he reached three main conclusions: first, that their approach was increasingly functional and technocratic, following the inter-war modernist precepts of Walter Gropius; second, that – to compensate for this lack of 'artistic' autonomy – they conceived themselves as social engineers, hoping to create environments that would help to improve human behaviour; and third – crucially – that there often remained in practice a huge social and imaginative distance between themselves and their ultimate clients, the public. Lipman in his analysis did not mention the 'a' word, but perhaps he should have, for it is hard to avoid the feeling that there was in the profession a certain residual arrogance. 'Portsmouth is a pretty nondescript city, and at least we have now built something which will make people stop and stare' was how Owen Luder in 1967 would publicly defend his recently completed – and soon to be notorious – Tricorn shopping centre. 'It is not streamlined or slick because it is not intended to be. If you have done your job properly, you will be ten years ahead and the public will not have caught up.'[8]

If post-war architects have in retrospect generally received a poor press, perhaps not always entirely fairly, that of planners has arguably been even worse. Few dissented when Margaret Thatcher in 1987 bluntly accused them of having 'cut the heart out of our cities':

> They swept aside the familiar city centres that had grown up over the centuries. They replaced them with a wedge of tower blocks and linking expressways, interspersed with token patches of grass and a few windswept piazzas, where pedestrians fear to tread . . . they simply set the municipal bulldozer to work. What folly, what incredible folly . . .

Historians have largely agreed, typified by Simon Gunn's close reading of what happened between the mid-1950s and mid-1960s to Bradford – a modernist transformation masterminded by the 'aloof' and 'autocratic' town planning officer, Stanley Wardley, that saw the guts starting to be ripped out of a once-great Victorian industrial city. Not only did his plan, notes Gunn, 'contain little sense of different communities or social needs', but 'the model of space and time deployed was equally rudimentary':

> Bradford was perceived from the planners' eye view, as suggested both by the miniature replica of the redeveloped city that stood in Wardley's office and by the predilection for aerial views of construction, utilized by both the planning authorities and the popular press in their reportage of urban transformation. In the latter case, helicopter-eye views of works in the city centre were favoured, allowing for a stark 'before' and 'after' perspective on progress. Temporality further entered into proceedings in the form of abstract ideas of efficiency and rationality. A continuous leitmotif in the development plan was how long it took people and goods to move from one zone or activity to another – from factory to warehouse, bus station to office, and home to work. The plan was innocent of people's actual, complex relationships to place, space, and time and to the way that these were used in practice. It dealt in clock time, not lived time . . .

Or take the critique of another historian, Clara Greed, arguing convincingly that planners – an almost entirely male cohort – largely ignored, until the mid-1960s and indeed even beyond, the everyday concerns and practicalities of women, whether relating to work or to shopping or to family life. Nor were contemporary estimates necessarily kinder. In a radio talk in March 1965 on 'The planners and the planned', the veteran planner Max Lock was careful not explicitly to blame his colleagues for the fact that 'the gap between planner and planned has become so wide that people have come to think of planning more as a mystique than a technique', instead arguing that 'the planning officers in County Hall are usually so burdened and obsessed with the problems of their administrative machine that they have little or no time to cultivate the citizen's interest and win his approval'; but his warning near the end that 'under the pressure of the present unprecedented wave of town-centre redevelopment it is easy to forget that we are dealing with the most sensitive elements of community life' was a clear implied rebuke. While when later that spring Peter Willmott was appointed 'consultant sociologist' for Ipswich and Northampton, it was apparently the first time that a sociologist was to be involved at the crucial decision-making stages of the process, prompting his wife Phyllis to call it 'the beginning of what we must hope will be a fruitful association of sociologist and the planners'.

Probably the two most detailed studies we have of planners in action during the mid-to-late 1960s are those of Norman Dennis in Sunderland and Jon Gower Davies in Newcastle. For Dennis, a particular bugbear was how town planners too often fell back on what he called the 'benefit of posterity' argument, i.e. insisting that 'the quality of a town's housing stock is an important part of its "image" and the image of a town in this sense influences to a significant degree the location decisions of industrialists'; while as for planners in day-to-day action, he noted (and included chapter and verse) about how 'whatever the intention, the effect of certain statements by planning officers is to engender a sense of helplessness'. As for Davies, planning in his intensely local experience amounted to nothing less than 'an all-out effort to abolish the past and manufacture the future' – a process by which planners 'accord unto themselves the role of the voice of that future'. Just occasionally, though, the planner (Davies's 'evangelistic bureaucrat', wedded to bold concepts of 'progress') has struck back. One such moment occurred in the *TLS* in 2021, after a contributor, Gillian Tindall, had referred to the 'wrecking' in the early-to-mid-1960s of the urban landscape:

> If by that comment she means the advent of new blocks of flats, this was the outcome of a valiant effort, unfortunately never attempted

> since on such a scale, to provide decent housing conditions and a civilized environment for hundreds of thousands of folk living in the slum conditions of the large conurbations [responded Jim Humberstone, a town planner back in the day]. For these people, their own indoor toilet (i.e. not shared and out in the yard), proper space, heating and hot water on tap, all of which would be provided in their new flats, was something of a dream come true. Sadly this aspect of the 'wreckage', which was a considerable social and political achievement, may not have registered in any positive way with the likes of Tony Armstrong-Jones [aka Lord Snowdon] and Sir John Betjeman. What had happened clearly offended their aesthetic sensibilities (oh calamity).

'Bearing in mind, however, who they were and where they'd come from,' he concluded, 'would one expect otherwise?'[9]

The larger mood music still predominantly favoured those wanting rationalist, modern-minded urban renewal on a radical scale. The press certainly helped, to judge by Patrick Dunleavy's analysis of attitudes in three very different papers to the question of increased levels of high-rise housing provision: in *The Times*, between 1960 and 1964, almost twice as much of its coverage was pro as anti; in the *Newham Recorder*, between 1965 and 1967, similar proportions; and in the *Municipal Journal*, tracking local government, overwhelmingly 'pro' percentages up to 1967. The housing historian Peter Shapely has tracked 'boosterism' in the local press, particularly in the north-west, as typified by the *Manchester Evening News* in October 1965 hailing Manchester's ambitious redevelopment scheme for Hulme V as a 'fascinating concept that should make proud not only the planners but the citizens', with the accompanying headline 'A Touch of Bloomsbury'; while earlier that year, in March, even an instinctively anti-modernist paper like the *Daily Telegraph* had, on its news pages, an 'architectural reporter' acclaiming Battersea Council's new eighty-acre estate going up in the Winstanley Road–York Road area near Clapham Junction: the end of 'dreary rows of Victorian houses', the architects 'by building high' able to provide more open space around the buildings, 'boldly modelled' blocks varying in height from four to twenty-two storeys, construction speeded up 'by using factory building methods' . . . No complaints presumably from the

New Statesman's Edward Hyams, who in June 1965 (the same month that Bristol City Council's press officer noted of the redevelopment of Georgian Kingsdown that 'the picturesque is seldom comfortable and rarely convenient') considered the claim that 'tall buildings of flats require – in access, in open space, preferably parkland, about them, in car parks, etc – as much land as would be required to house the same number of people horizontally, i.e. suburb-wise'. His answer was unambiguous: 'I do not believe it; I think that the strength of argument and figures lie on the high-density side. I also think that high-density housing is socially much more desirable if we are ever to re-create, as we must, a true community of people.' Even so, he did feel morally compelled to add a rider: 'There remains the social and psychological problem. The Englishman's ideal is supposed to be a house inside a fenced garden.' 'But surely,' he concluded reassuringly, 'this is a matter of education.'

Arguably there was no more articulate or influential cheerleader than the architectural writer Reyner Banham, who in November 1965 reflected proudly in *New Society* that 'insofar as there is a Corbusian school of mass housing in the world, it is because the LCC (by now the GLC) has built half of it', in other words through its widely renowned Architect's Department. And, in similar vein, he highlighted the current Handley Street development in Battersea, featuring two twenty-one-storey towers as well as clusters of four-storey maisonette blocks; praised the 'exposed concrete' of the former as an uncompromising exercise in the 'domesticated Brutalist style'; was gratified by the absence of 'well-grown suburban cedars and acacias to provide instant landscaping and cover mistakes'; and more generally, heaped scorn not only on 'the chintzy, plastic-laminated cultural aspirations of Greater London Councillors who tend to find exposed concrete rather "low class"', but also on 'whatever anxieties sociologists and others may be working up about mixed high and low flatted developments'.

Yet Banham by this time was not entirely in celebratory mode. Yes, he duly noted, 'the tide of architectural taste has flowed in a Corbusian direction steadily for the last 15 years or so'; however, he could not help but accept, 'a reaction is inevitable and probably imminent'.[10]

He called it right. 'The period of dim-witted adulation of Le Corbusier is over,' announced David Usborne in June 1966 in a televised debate by architectural students on the future of architecture; two landmark housing developments under way in London by this time, Patrick Hodgkinson's Brunswick Centre near Russell Square and Kate Macintosh's Dawson's Heights in Southwark, achieved high density without tower blocks, without sacrificing an essentially humanist approach; while only weeks after Banham's gloomy prediction, the pages of the *Architects' Journal* were lit up by a *cri de cœur* from architect-planner Derek Abbot:

> Nothing less than a nation-wide programme of repair and rehabilitation, supervised by dedicated and experienced architects and surveyors, can save our architectural heritage from hasty destruction. Throughout the Inner London boroughs, acres of fine, eighteenth-century and early nineteenth-century terraces are threatened with destruction for one or more of the following reasons:
>
> 1 Unnecessary road-widening schemes and urban motorway proposals, aggressively pursued by the GLC Department of Highways and Transportation.
> 2 Philistine councillors who, acting on hasty and ill-considered advice, are not prepared to rehabilitate areas and buildings of historic, townscape and cultural value, because they consider it is not an 'economic proposition'.
> 3 The obsession of the present Government and many planners in obtaining housing gain; often resulting in the destruction of amenity areas.
> 4 The fact that some planners are obsessed by a belief that *any* building over a hundred years old is automatically a slum.

Other mid-sixties dissenting voices from the modernist orthodoxy deserve to be remembered. Earlier in 1965 the architectural journalist Kenneth Browne laid into Norwich's recent redevelopment ('a disgrace . . . outstandingly bad are the brutish chunk of the Norwich Union offices in All Saints Green, and a nearby high-rise office block known as "the glass tower" . . .'); that autumn, Mark Girouard was appalled by the prospect of 'planning on the grand scale' that, in order to create 'an international centre' complete with hotels, a sports centre and a trade exhibition hall, would see the virtual flattening of the Covent Garden area once the market moved to Nine Elms; in Birmingham, the university's David Eversley was a resolute, long-standing critic of the inner city's transformation into a bleak, car-dominated environment ('the benefits to the ordinary citizen so far are pretty meagre,' he declared in 1964); in Liverpool, the leader of the Liberals on the City Council, Cyril Carr, came out strongly in May 1966 against the prevailing high-rise policy, condemning outright 'the deplorable social consequences of multi-storey flats, especially for children and old people, and the effects on individuals and the community when people are uprooted from their own areas'; while among economists, the pioneer was Lionel Needleman, whose *The Economics of Housing* (1965) influentially applied (in Glen O'Hara's words) 'cost-benefit analysis to the question of renovation as against clearance', demonstrating with helpful clarity that 'the longer a house might last if it was repaired, and the higher the interest rates a council or private developer would have to pay if it borrowed to build a new house, the more it was worth spending on repairing a dwelling in the short term'.

Then, of course, there was the indomitable Ian Nairn, by now writing regularly in the *Observer*, where typically, in December 1965 in the context of ambitious plans afoot for Stockton-on-Tees, he turned caustically on the fashionable catch-phrase 'comprehensive development': 'Abolish all the awkward separate ownerships, get things into one tidy parcel: then we can make a Unified Plan and everything will be marvellous. Maybe. The difficulty with abstract ideas like this is that they ignore the fact that towns are as various as people. Some places are well served by being developed in large chunks and some aren't. Stockton-on-Tees is, emphatically, one of the latter . . .' A few months earlier, his new book, *Your England Revisited*, had found a particularly appreciative reviewer:

> The sad thing is that local authorities and even ministries (in particular, the Ministry of Transport) treat old towns and villages as though they were all the same and without heart, soul and way of life but just 'cases', for exploitation by rule of thumb methods – road widening here, new estates there, 'slum clearance' somewhere else . . .

> For all the attention that is now given to Bath [site of an ongoing controversy about threats to its character], none is given to a more live and in its way equally exciting town, such as industrial Halifax or Huddersfield. It is only by using our eyes and hearts we will save what is left. That is what Ian Nairn says and so does his humble disciple –
> John Betjeman

'Have you come to admire, as K[enneth] Clark and I have, some of the work of Sir [George] Gilbert [Scott], including St Pancras station, which is to be pulled down?' Betjeman wrote to the leading architectural historian John Summerson in June 1966. 'Would you be prepared to write an appreciative article on it? You count and I don't.'[11] He was wrong, for already – and over the next decade – no one would do more, especially through his flair for television, to create and fortify a new conservationist quasi-consensus.

Two developments in July 1966 were particularly suggestive of change in the offing. The first came on the 8th, when Duncan Sandys, the Conservative politician who as housing minister back in 1957 had been largely responsible for founding the Civic Trust, now took the opportunity of having come first in the ballot for private members' bills to enable a first reading for the Civic Amenities Bill, potentially allowing whole areas of historical merit (as opposed to just individual buildings) to be protected. Sandys in this initiative owed much to Lord (Wayland) Kennet, a junior minister at housing passionate about the cause. 'A town centre is not just a machine for making money,' Kennet told a meeting of developers and local authorities a fortnight later. 'It is a living organism, economic and cultural, and the fine old buildings in it are among the most valuable of its cells.' That was on the 22nd, the day *The Times* ran an important article by its excellent Midland correspondent, Brian Priestley, about how on his patch, especially in Birmingham, 'more and more local government people' were in agreement with the Town and Country Planning Association that extra grants from central government would be better spent on houses than flats. Not, he emphasised, that it was solely a question of value for money: 'There is also the fact that high flats are arguably not suitable for families with children.' And he went on:

> Flats have the virtue that they can cram a great many people into a small acreage. In some authorities there is the feeling that one can do almost as well with low-rise housing – a mixture of houses and low flats or maisonettes, with an occasional high tower to improve the view.
>
> It is a matter for argument, but at least all the signs are that the pendulum is swinging away from the council flat. Birmingham is building proportionately fewer flats. The Warley Labour Party has just decided to cut the height of a new flatted development from 22 storeys to eight.

'Not many ordinary people,' concluded Priestley, 'are likely to regret the change.'[12]

Yet the reality was that the building of many unpopular and poor-quality high-rise blocks, preceded by whole swathes of indiscriminate slum clearance and accompanied by the destruction of much Georgian and Victorian heritage, still lay ahead. 'Maybe future generations will curse us,' Robert (Bob) Mellish, Crossman's no. 2 at housing, conceded publicly in June 1966 when asked about high blocks of flats, before adding, 'but if we don't build higher and faster those on the housing lists will curse us too.' Crucially, plans continued to be laid for giant new housing estates, of which the much-cited exemplar – notwithstanding other contenders such as the Ferrier estate in south-east London, or the Broadwater Farm estate in north London, or the Chelmsley Wood estate near Birmingham – would in time undeniably be the Aylesbury Estate in Southwark, the vast medium-rise development, justifiably characterised by Simon Jenkins as 'high-density, low-cost, "system-built" slab', that became the largest council estate in Europe. Responsibility was shared, but the main architect seems to have been the Austrian-born Hans Peter Trenton; some sixty acres, largely comprising rundown terraces and tenement blocks, were cleared to make way for the construction of some 2,700 flats housing up to 10,000 people; and the ruling Labour group, giving its approval to the scheme in 1966, had few if any doubts about the rightness of what it was doing:

> The council's optimism [wrote Thom Gorst in 1977] lay in a number of features of the design: the new scheme was to include shops, a school and a community centre – it was to be an entire

> neighbourhood. In addition, all the dwellings on the estate were to be heated by a 'district' heating system, in which a huge central boiler provided all the hot water; the flats were to be grouped around courtyards, to give them a sense of identifying with a particular space; each flat was to have its own garage, in a secure zone at the base of each block; pedestrians were to be kept away from traffic by providing 'pedways' at third-floor level, and the shops would be situated on these pedways; finally, next to the estate there was going to be a brand new park – the only new so-called 'Metropolitan park' to be built in London this century.[13]

Streets in the sky, in this case eleven miles' worth of streets: as with Sheffield's much-vaunted Park Hill, what could possibly go wrong?

Standing back from it all, it sometimes seems we are still only just starting – half a century later – to grasp the enormity of what happened. In January 2025, after the *TLS*'s reviewer (Robert Bevan) of Simon Jenkins's history of British architecture had complained about the 'much-told . . . modernism-bashing', the author riposted in take-no-prisoners mode:

> I only wish it was much told. Public discussion of architecture might be less tone-deaf as a result. The reality is that, after a richly diverse history, this British profession attempted in the three decades after the last war to rebuild the nation's cities and public housing in the totalitarian terms of the modern movement. This led to community destruction, human misery and economic ruin on a staggering scale, from which many northern cities have never recovered. As a journalist at the time, I reported on the millions who were evicted from working-class homes that were being flattened in numbers far exceeding those razed during the Blitz. Billions in public money were squandered on barely habitable estates, good only for subsequent demolition . . . History has never done justice to this scandal.

The same day, the *Guardian*'s Scotland editor, Libby Brooks, highlighted the palpable decline of Glasgow city centre, as the city prepared to celebrate its 850th anniversary. And she quoted the director of Glasgow City Heritage Trust. 'This stretches much further back than the pandemic or austerity,' stated Niall Murphy. 'It's the legacy of deindustrialisation and depopulation in the 1960s and 70s. You get these border zones, and particularly to the south of the city centre, like the area around Bridge Street, where the urban clearance of the notorious Gorbals moved out 90,000 people. We have these grand buildings, built to last, that don't have a purpose any more.'

Again and again, one comes back to zeitgeist, including the deeply entrenched prejudice against all things Victorian felt by so many elderly, working-class Labour politicians (national and local) who had known urban squalor in their own childhoods. Just two final examples. 'I want,' declared Edward Heath during the 1964 election, an election largely fought on competing 'modernisation' credentials, 'to see the guts torn out of our older industrial cities and new civic centres and shopping areas built there, the older houses torn down and new ones in their place.' Ten months later, in August 1965, *Sheffield Forward*, journal of the Sheffield Trades and Labour Council, ran a euphoric overview piece about the city's redevelopment housing projects, with the latest, the huge Kelvin development (due to comprise a total of almost a thousand dwellings in thirteen-storey blocks), in the pipeline. 'In total, you have an endeavour unmatched for enterprise and originality of design,' it boasted. 'Viewed by a new generation, it provides a new conception of living . . . This is the city of the innovators, of the imaginative planners and skilled builders, directed by a Party who are building the future along lines commensurate with a new society, whose values are completely different from those which went before . . .'[14]

And, whether to individuals or communities, the psychic cost of the great upheaval? What, weighing the losses against the gains, was the ultimate human price of this unflinching and unsentimental pursuit of the modern? Half a century or more after the famous Jackie and Bridie song ('Don't want to go to Kirkby, or Skelmersdale or Speke / Don't want to go from all we know, in Back Buchanan Street'), Jeff Young, in his deeply evocative portrait (*Ghost Town*, 2020) of the lost Liverpool of his childhood and adolescence, puts almost all the emphasis, as a kind of writerly cousin of the film director Terence

Davies (above all, *Of Time and the City*), on the loss; and he describes his ageing grandfather, after all the scorched-earth slum clearance, walking around with 'a map inside his heart of the city he had lived in all his life':

> He couldn't hear the bulldozers, couldn't see the houses falling. He would walk along the desolate wasteland streets, his inner compass guiding him past the ghosts of vanished terraced houses, corner shops, alehouses, the butcher's and the baker's. There was nothing to the left, nothing to the right, nothing on any of the four horizons except for debris and rubble. The cobbled streets still framed the emptiness, but there was no one left to walk through the frames, no photographer to capture the city as it once was. Just grandad walking through a city which is no longer there.

There is and was another perspective. 'I like the modernity in Glasgow,' the great Scottish poet Edwin Morgan reflected in the 1980s. 'I like to think of Glasgow as being a place that is quite willing to renew itself in a fairly devastating sort of way.' And indeed, back in the 1960s, the closing lines of the title poem to his collection *The Second Life* (1968) had, while not denying the downside of modernisation, nevertheless accepted – even welcomed – the necessity of change:

> A great place and its people are not renewed lightly.
> The caked layers of grime
> grow warm, like homely coats.
> But yet they will be dislodged
> and men will still be warm.
> The old coats are discarded.
> The old ice is loosed.
> The old seeds are awake.
>
> Slip out of darkness, it is time.

Arguments on both sides, naturally, yet in the end I find it hard to side with Morgan. And, back to Sheffield, a last word goes to the rather chilling message contained in a July 1965 photograph of a window in that city's new and monumental, top-of-the-hill Hyde Park development:

WARNING
NOTICE
NO ANIMALS
CATS OR DOGS
TO BE KEPT IN
THESE FLATS[15]

12

I Can't Put My Finger on It

'"SIT-IN" STRIKE AT GIANT MILL: Five hundred coloured workers demand better pay, bonuses' was near the end of May 1965 the front-page headline of the *Lancashire Evening Post*. The strike, viewed by many at the time as Britain's first 'racial' strike, was at Courtauld's Red Scar rayon mill, a ten-minute bus ride from the centre of Preston; most of the strikers were Indians and Pakistanis; and a few weeks later, after the nineteen-day strike was over, the industrial reporter John Torode explained for *New Society* readers its background. Noting the complaint of the strikers that they had not been consulted about a new terms-of-work agreement reached between the company and the Transport and General Workers' Union (T&G), he went on to give the bigger picture:

> Money is good, but conditions in the four departments affected by the strike are pretty ghastly. For just over £18 gross on a 42-hour week, men mind a bank of spindles on which rayon is bound automatically. Their job is to service the machines and catch any emergency. The noise and stink of chemicals are bad and the heat overwhelming, though ventilation has recently been improved. The strikers claim that the machine-minders here are 98 per cent immigrant.
>
> Traditionally one man has worked one machine (a bank of 102 spindles). Under the new agreement they work one and a half machines for an extra 10s a week. It was this agreement which caused the explosion.

In charge of the company's labour relations was 'a tough, no-nonsense ex-RAF officer', Robert Law. 'They are gentle folk, on the whole, and are good workers when they wish to work,' he told the press at the outset; but when, later on, he was asked by Torode whether more should have been done about 'the social training' of immigrant workers who had mainly come from remote villages in the Himalayas, he replied flatly that 'the social life of employees is not company business. We do nothing at all about it.' Crucially, the strikers received little or no support from the T&G's factory branch, with the senior shop steward, Robert Roberts, informing Torode that the immigrant workers lacked the requisite industrial discipline: 'This is the worst kind of plant these people could be working in. Everything must be done to rigid specifications. In an emergency you must move men around fast. English workers understand this.' Torode himself contended that it was 'lack of sympathetic contact', not discrimination, that had been 'at the root of the strike'; but Ray Challinor, a technical college lecturer from Westhoughton who joined the strike committee, was less inclined to underplay the racial divide. 'There have been coloured workers at Courtaulds for up to 12 years,' he noted. 'But for one minor exception, there has not been promotion for coloured workers, yet unskilled white workers are doing skilled jobs simply because of the colour of their skin. Courtaulds is simply a black industrial ghetto.' While even less softly-softly was a Prestonian writing to the local paper and calling himself 'Long View English': 'The best thing that Courtaulds could do would be to give all the coloured workers a one-way ticket to Pakistan. This should be applied throughout the country.'[1]

Some six months later, in late November 1965, almost 600 workers, the great majority of them Sikhs who had migrated from the Punjab, went on strike at Woolf's, a smallish factory in Southall largely supplying rubber accessories for the motor industry. 'Unpleasant, dirty and laborious' was how Peter Marsh, the closest chronicler of the strike, described the work they did; the dispute largely arose from what the men regarded as unjustified sackings; and again, support from the T&G was nugatory, culminating in the regional secretary refusing to blacklist firms continuing to deal with Woolf's. The reason given was that this would 'put a lot of people out of work in a few days' – but the result, almost seven weeks in, was to give the strikers little alternative but to return to work. Perhaps the most revealing aspect of the episode was, in the absence of strike pay from the union, the wider solidarity revealed. 'Indian landlords are foregoing their rents for the duration of the strike,' reported the *Guardian* shortly before Christmas. 'Shops and restaurants are allowing long lines of credit. A strike fund has raised £300 from all classes among the area's 10,000 Indians.' And, the paper added pointedly, 'this demonstration that it is possible to mobilise a whole immigrant community will not be lost on politicians'.

It was a dispute that attracted widespread attention. 'Sad! Mad! Bad! . . . This Strike That Exists on Tick' ran the *Daily Mail*'s headline for a piece by Rhona Churchill on 5 January, a week before the strike ended:

> Exactly five weeks ago [she began], a turbanned Sikh, a peasant from the Punjab, cried: 'Everybody out' . . . cried it in Hindustani, Punjabi, Bengali, and Assamere. And 500 Indians obeyed him. Most of the pickets can neither read nor write. Most speak no English. Most had to be introduced to piped water, flush lavatories and dustbins when they came here from one to five years ago . . .

There followed some detail about the strong community support, before solemn reiteration of the inevitable overall message: 'But it is a sad, mad, bad strike. Whatever the apparent complaints and demands, the root cause is a total failure of these people to become integrated into our society.' She did not quote different views; but after the strike was over, another journalist, Colin McGlashan, revealed what one white resident, fearful of the unity displayed by Southall's Indian workers, had said to him: 'They're taking over; already they're the biggest landlords in the town.'[2]

Few doubted in the mid-1960s where the political hot spot of immigration and race relations lay. It was not in London, even though such boroughs as Brent (7.4), Hackney (7.1), Lambeth (6.7) and Haringey (5.6) had, according to the 1966 sample census, higher percentages of West Indians, Indians and Pakistanis in their total populations than anywhere else; nor was it in Bradford (4.2), or Slough (4.7), or even High Wycombe (4.9). 'At that period, I felt Birmingham and the West Midlands generally, and the Black Country, was a very mean-spirited place,' recalled Stuart Hall many years later about coming to Birmingham in 1964 – just weeks before that autumn's election made Smethwick a household name – in order to head the new Centre for Contemporary Cultural Studies:

> I was just married and looking for a house. And I can honestly say, this is the first time [after leaving Jamaica for England in 1951] that I personally encountered people who said, 'We don't take any blacks here' . . . People shouted at us in the street when we were going around trying to find places, myself and my white wife. She was the particular object of vile remarks about mixed race couples, and so on. So, I had a very bad introduction to the West Midlands, I must say. And I have always thought, it may be wrong, but I've always thought that I could understand that Powellism would have come out of the West Midlands. I thought one could hear a particular kind of resentment, deep resentment, almost as if we'd been left behind by England and now we were going to be left behind in relation to race, permanently left behind. And that's a historical resentment, latched on to race, the symbol signifying its isolation. So, that was a very troubling experience.

The proportions were not so spectacular – 4.2 per cent in Birmingham, 4.8 in Wolverhampton, 3.6 in Warley, 3.1 in Walsall, while in the West Midlands as a whole it was 3.3, compared to 3.2 in Greater London, 1.8 in West Yorkshire and 1.2 for England and Wales overall – but the reality was hard to deny. In May 1966 three young, moderate Conservatives (including Kenneth Clarke) published a pamphlet, under the auspices of the Birmingham Bow Group, arguing that discrimination against non-white immigrants existed in all sections of society in Birmingham and the Black Country; and, they noted, 'it is particularly alarming that so many educated and respectable people in the West Midlands regard it as fashionable and usual to hold extremely anti-coloured views'.[3]

Certainly, turning to Birmingham specifically, there was no shortage of evidence of racial prejudice and discrimination. Take the personnel manager of a small firm where thirty-three of the fifty-six workers were Pakistanis. 'Some of the Pakistanis have been here 12 or 14 years, but they are still called Wogs by other people,' he told *The Times* in January 1965 (for its controversially titled series of reports on 'The Dark Million'). 'They don't accept them as they accept a white man. They say they are only Wogs.' And he went on:

> White men wouldn't tolerate them being on a level with them. One man has been doing a skilled job for 18 months, but he only gets the official labourer's rate. Unofficially, he is paid £8 to £9 more. The other workers don't know about it. If they did know we should have trouble. Even though he was educated up to their standard, I don't think they would tolerate it, because he is coloured.
>
> The average pay of the ordinary labouring Pakistani is £13 to £14 a week. We pay £25 to £30 to Pakistanis doing more skilled work. They are getting the difference slipped to them on the side. White men doing a similar job get over £30. I think this is general. I have spoken to one or two coming from other factories.

Similarly, in the context of his research into crime and race relations in Birmingham – research revealing that of indictable offences recorded and solved in 1966, only 4 per cent were committed by West Indians, Pakistanis and Indians – John Lambert concluded that 'the police share commonly and widely held views about coloured immigrants and the colour problem which are detrimental to good policing and which augur badly for an improvement in the general tenor of race relations'. While when it came to Roy Jenkins stressing, as a liberal-minded home secretary from late 1965 (and also a Birmingham MP), the need for 'coloured' police and magistrates, the response of the chairman of Birmingham magistrates spoke volumes: 'I am sure that the magistrates would have no prejudice against coloured magistrates, but it is a question of whether the public, that is the criminal public, is ready for them.'

By almost unanimous consent, though, the front line was housing. 'The council's policy towards immigrants is in dispute: does it operate, in practice, a system of segregating coloured immigrants into revamped old property, rather than new houses; or not?' was the question posed in November 1966 by *New Society*'s Paul Barker in his 'Kazam!' piece on Birmingham. 'The fact is that two-thirds of white families taken off the top of the 38,000 waiting list go into postwar housing. The proportion of coloured families who do is a tiny percentage; and this comes on top of the five-year residents rule which makes it very hard for an immigrant to get on the list in the first place. There are seemingly good reasons produced in each case (household standards; the need to keep the housing list under some sort of control), but together they add up to unhelpfulness.' Soon afterwards, John Rex and Robert Moore published their *Race, Community, and Conflict*, an important, pioneering study that focused on one of the city's 'twilight' zones, Sparkbrook, and in particular the housing aspect. One reviewer, Paul Foot, rightly praised the book for its detailed description of 'the dreary ritual of the immigrant's search for housing: the denial of council houses; the discrimination of private landlords; the buying at high mortgage rates of "twilight" lodging houses; the crowding of tenants; indifferent landlordism; squalor, depression, decay; and finally the cynical response of the local authority'. 'The Birmingham Corporation Act, 1965,' he went on, 'simply tightened up restrictions on lodging houses. These restrictions tend to be applied sparingly to "twilight areas," ruthlessly in decent suburbia. This is the politics of the ghetto.'

Strikingly, and perhaps unexpectedly, of the 192 white respondents in the Rex and Moore survey, only seventeen (mainly women) cited immigrants as a problem as such or made out-and-out racist remarks ('They ought to be sent home . . . shot . . . put in concentration camps . . .'); but at the same time almost half the respondents gave 'coloureds' an unfavourable mention in relation to day-to-day social problems. 'From these data,' reflected the authors in moderately hopeful vein, 'we may conclude that statements about race and colour arise not simply from wrong thinking or "prejudice-in-the-head", but from an appraisal of an actual situation as seen by the locals. Pre-existing racial stereotypes may help people to identify people with particular problems, but the housing situation, which dominates the thinking of our respondents, also helps to reinforce the stereotypes. We would not say that a large proportion of the English are prejudiced in a psychological sense.'[4]

Nothing hopeful, though, about the tone of John Sanders, chairman of the Birmingham Immigration Control Association and himself an estate duty and company finance consultant with an upmarket address in Sutton Coldfield. 'More than a million unassimilable people . . .

multi-racial, largely unskilled, illiterate immigrants . . . vast economic burdens on our overstrained economy . . . ineradicable social problems . . . this huge alien population . . . already the day is gone when a Briton returned from a foreign land can walk our streets feeling that he is again among his "ain folk"' – all this and more in his pamphlet *Immigration: The Incredible Folly*, some 25,000 copies of which were distributed on its publication in summer 1965. That was, of course, the summer of the Dutch auction between the main parties, culminating in August in the Labour government's hardline White Paper on immigration. Among its defenders was the young MP for Sparkbrook, Roy Hattersley, arguing in the *New Statesman* that for 'the creation of a society in which all ethnic groups can live in peace, harmony and equality', it was necessary to accept that this was 'a goal that can only be achieved if something is done to assuage the fears and prejudices that abound in the areas to which the immigrants have come'; and he added that those prejudices were 'the product of a fear that chronically inadequate welfare and social services will become intolerably scarce if shared with newcomers'.

Perhaps more surprisingly, the magazine's same issue also featured a revealing letter from E. Collins of 30 Beaconsfield Road, Balsall Heath, Birmingham 12:

> I live in this street of about 60 houses of a good residential type; there are seven different nationalities in this street, and if you look out of the front room window for a few minutes you would see 10 non-English to one English pass by. That I suggest is a bit overbearing! I have twice got the police to have GO HOME BLACKS notices painted on hoardings in the city removed.
>
> I fear that those who write and talk about this subject most are themselves living in all-white districts; to show their sincerity they should move to a multi-racial district. Some of us older citizens expected that the slums of this city and other unsatisfactory housing would have been swept away years ago – but now with overwhelming immigration we have a filthy, festering sore which will not be cleared up in 10 years. It is sensible and humane to call a halt . . .

Also calling for a halt on immigration were the Conservatives on Birmingham City Council. 'Birmingham is at present facing a huge task in providing decent housing conditions for overcrowded and inadequately-housed citizens,' they had declared earlier in the year in the local *Evening Mail*. 'We maintain it is folly and is unjust to allow the housing problem in the city to be aggravated because of circumstances which can largely be prevented.' The same page had an emotional letter from Mrs V. Arnold of Perry Barr, relating how, following a roadside accident, the life of her twenty-year-old daughter had been saved by the prompt action of 'a coloured bus driver', 35-year-old Sinclair Simmons. 'My family thank God,' she wrote, 'for at least one immigrant.'[5]

The Hattersley/Collins letters in August 1965 coincided with disturbances in Wolverhampton that made the national press. On four consecutive nights, the Low Hill council housing estate saw what the local *Express & Star* called 'squabbles between white and coloured people', with the worst night being Friday the 13th, as a long-running feud in Broome Road between the 'coloured' occupants of No. 59 and the white occupants of No. 61 came to a head. Some 150 white people, armed with bricks, bottles and sticks, stood outside the house occupied by Jamaican immigrants, chanted, 'Come out and fight you black bastards', and even started attacking the house, until the police eventually intervened, amid shouts of 'We want to get at the blacks'. Next morning, at the special court proceedings, the police conceded there had been 'a certain amount of race hatred' involved. Meanwhile, in nearby Wednesfield, two other stories were emerging. The first concerned the Wolverhampton building firm William Whittingham imposing, via the estate agents Skelding and Boucher, a ban on people of colour buying houses on the new Lyndale Park Estate – in order, stated one of the firm's directors, 'to protect our clients' interests now and in the future'; and five housewives already living on the estate told the paper that they were fully supportive, having bought their houses only after being reassured that the estate was to be 'kept white'. The other story was at the three high-rise blocks of council flats at Lakefield Road, where more than 100 tenants attended an open-air meeting to protest at having an Indian as a neighbour, after two young housewives, Mrs Pamela Twyford and Mrs Patricia Bellingham, had organised a petition to keep the flats all-white. 'Mrs Twyford said she objected to the smell of Indian cooking. She added: "Now we shall be having lovely all-night parties." Both women said they would object to their own children playing with coloured children. Mrs Twyford said 97 people had now signed the petition for a colour bar. She had only had six refusals so far.'[6]

As for Wolverhampton itself, Shirin Hirsch argues in her *In the Shadow of Enoch Powell* that racial tensions, although far from unknown in earlier years, only really began to intensify from the mid-1960s. A key moment occurred in May 1965 when, replying to questions by a Conservative councillor, the Labour chairman of the town council's health committee disclosed that, out of 3,300 births in 1964 to Wolverhampton residents, as many as 793 – or 24 per cent – had been to 'coloured mothers'. Councillor Peter Farmer, chairman of the Wolverhampton South-West Conservative Association, responded immediately by not only declaring publicly that 'there should be no further immigration in our area if the local traditional culture is to be preserved', but drawing the figures to the attention of his MP, Enoch Powell – who in turn, after pondering for a fortnight or so, made a statement on national immigration policy, describing the prospect of the continuation of the previous year's inflow of 75,000 Commonwealth immigrants as 'almost inconceivable', in that by 1985 this would mean an extra 1.5 million, quite apart from natural increase. 'This,' notes his biographer Simon Heffer, 'was the first recorded instance of Powell using the tactic that would mark out most of his future speeches on this issue: spelling out not just the consequences of a year's immigration, but the effect of it were it to continue at the same rate over a given period.'

Inevitably, because of the Powell connection, Wolverhampton would find itself ever more in the spotlight, even before Powell's defining 'rivers of blood' speech in 1968. In *Housing on Trial*, her invaluable 1967 study of immigrants and local government, Elizabeth Burney interviewed a Mr Rhodes, chairman of the Claregate and Blakely District Residents Association and himself living in 'a small 1930-ish semi-detached house in north-west Wolverhampton':

> I come from Dudley and twelve years ago we moved to Wolverhampton – Whitmore Reans. It was a lovely street until the coloureds moved in and we had to go. I lost a lot of money on that house. We came here two years ago and I started the residents' association last year: we've got 300 members and a good renewal rate.

> The aim is to keep up the amenities – that means stopping the neighbourhood going downhill. It *will* go down of course, but we may delay it. Oh, it means agreeing to maintain our gardens, and lobbying the council to mend the pavement. Keeping out coloureds? No, we couldn't do it. They're bound to come. Other associations have tried, but they've failed because people turn round and say 'You give me so much or I'll sell to coloureds'.
>
> I've got strong personal views you know, but they're my own views . . . You can't live in the same street as them. If you've got a daughter she can't go out . . . And if they're next door the other side of the wall it's a thousand times worse. You see them every time you walk down the path, you smell their food, the mice start coming . . . You may say what's the difference except skin, but I tell you they *are* different in ways we don't understand. You don't know what's going on in their heads. But I can tell you they breed on purpose; they plan to outnumber us . . . People are moving out of Wolverhampton as fast as they can. They don't want to but they're forced out.

'Maybe only a minority of Wolverhampton people would express themselves as strongly as this,' reckoned Burney. 'But open disapproval of coloured people is often evident, typified by the woman who glared across at some turbanned Sikhs talking loudly in their own language in the park and burst out angrily to her friend: "If only they would *conform*!" '[7]

For obvious reasons, no spotlight was fiercer at this stage than that trained on Smethwick. Take three episodes in spring 1965 alone. In April, when Richard Crossman reluctantly allowed a visit to his ministry from an all-female delegation, after he had refused to permit a government loan to the local council to enable it to buy up houses in Marshall Street and thereby 'keep the coloured people out', the result was that 'the five complaining ladies of Marshall Street . . . were hysterical and shouted at me a good deal'; similarly making headlines was the insistence in early May of Councillor Ernest Gould, Conservative chair of the housing management committee, that the newly opened fifteen-storey block of ninety council flats off Windmill Lane would be for whites only, in order 'to avoid recurrence of the former troubles when a coloured family was given a flat in Price Street'; and in late

May the story was about how Midland Motor Cylinder's new factory on the Middlemore Industrial Estate was to have separate entrances and toilets for Indian and white workers.

That autumn, 'Smethwick – a whiff of Alabama in the Midlands' was the title of Jean Stead's piece in the *Guardian*. She focused partly on Don Finney, leading local backer of Peter Griffiths in the previous year's general election, but now running the English Rights Association and wanting all non-white immigrants sent home ('I am doing for England what Martin Luther King is doing for the Negroes in America – what is wrong in that?'); partly on one of his strongest supporters, Ken Bunche, running a whites-only youth club ('the coloureds will take over Smethwick soon if we let them'); and partly on the white housewives of Marshall Street. 'They've become arrogant,' one of them complained about her immigrant neighbours. 'I don't speak to them because if I did they look at you with a sort of contempt. Because we don't speak to them, they say we operate a colour bar.' Even so, according to Stead:

> Because their children know each other at school, one or two of the white housewives have been drawn willy-nilly into the struggling lives of their immigrant neighbours. One told how an Indian woman had cried on her shoulder for two hours because her daughter had died, and another one had asked her to speak to her husband and tell him she could not stand any more children. Two white wives had sent for an ambulance when a West Indian woman had to go to hospital to have her baby.

'In almost any other place, these would have been beginnings of lasting neighbourliness,' added Stead. 'In Smethwick, they were bound to be stillborn – the local racialists are making sure of that.' Admittedly, Griffiths did lose his seat in the 1966 election, but James Mossman's *Panorama* report that year on Smethwick suggested that little had changed in daily life. It featured a newly arrived Indian immigrant, fitted with a hidden microphone, being denied entry into a barber's and being told by a church to leave for fear of offending white churchgoers; while Mossman himself heard directly the views of white residents. 'They should live in a district by themselves. They're not clean.' And: 'They're a nuisance when you've got to walk past them in the street, they won't move. They're a nuisance at work.' And most damningly of all: 'They're content with Kitekat and dog food, instead of ordinary meat.'

Wolverhampton and Smethwick were and are generally considered to be part of the Black Country; so too the 'iron town', Dudley, where John Sibley had taught for eleven years before moving to Birmingham's College of Commerce. His 1965 letter to the *New Statesman* offered a revealing window into a world not exactly unique, but nevertheless very much a world of its own:

> Black Country people in behaviour (and speech) are in many ways nearer to Elizabeth I than II. They live in villages (industrial villages) where everyone is related, knows everyone's family history for hundreds of years, and where the people of the next village are referred to as 'foreigners'. To dump large numbers of actual foreigners among these estimable and warm-hearted, but undeniably rough and clannish, people is bound to cause trouble, however necessary it may be. A century ago there were riots in Birmingham over the influx of Irish with different accents and religion. How much more difficult, then, to integrate people who, unfortunately, can be *seen* to be different, and whose different skin make a few of them, interspersed in a crowd, much more numerous than they are. And one mustn't forget these people's real worries – strong notably among the lower middle-class, who perhaps have bought a terrace-house and fear the very genuine depreciation (and consequent immobility) if some kind of immigrants appear next door. I have been in India and prefer many Indian and Pakistani sanitary habits to the insanitary habits of my countryman, but the same won't apply to a householder who finds the Asians next door preferring the convenient hole-in-the-ground of the yard drain to the unfamiliar privy indoors.[8]

A sequence between early 1965 and late summer 1966, in roughly chronological order. 'Officially there is no colour bar in unions,' the personnel manager of a west London firm telling *The Times*. 'But you get pressure from the shop floor. They have sent for their trade union officials and said that there were far too many here. Then they do a bargain – the same as with wages. They say, "Get the proportion of coloured down to 10 per cent", but really expect to get 20 per cent.' 'If,' the manager adding, 'you took on coloured, and white people were unemployed, you would get pressure building up. We would want to employ white people anyway. They are much easier.' A more positive story in the West Indian magazine *Flamingo*: 200 bus drivers and conductors walking out of the Midland Red depot in Wolverhampton after a West Indian colleague, Beresford Thelwall, was unfairly docked a day's wages. Mildenhall Rural District Council, in west Suffolk, refusing to allow non-white workers into the area as part of the London overspill scheme (Councillor George Willis: 'I'm getting tired of the do-gooders'), until reluctantly backing down (eighteen-year-old bricklayer Dave Clark: 'I don't mind them coming, if they leave me alone'). At QPR, chants of 'Zulu, Zulu, Zulu' after the Loftus Road crowd spot Workington's black winger, Peter Foley. Local residents and businesses complaining in the *Middlesex County Times* of 'the appalling and revolting smell' from an Indian restaurant in Southall's The Crescent. *The Times* printing a letter from N. Willbourne, 7 Prideaux Place, WC1:

> The ordinary English citizen is getting tired of the continual harping of theorists who express emotional sentiments about colour bar and racialism.
>
> It cannot be too often repeated that immigration has nothing to do with colour: any immigrants who bring their own moral and cultural standards which are lower than our own into an already overcrowded island are going to cause trouble. If some of the theorists who live in Kensington or the Hampstead Garden Suburb would walk through the Caledonian Road or other parts of Islington with their eyes open, and read the local newspapers for these areas with an open mind, they might begin to understand the problems which are worrying the natives of these areas. 'Justice and common humanity' is only a sanctimonious phrase when it is applied to one set of people; and the natives of these islands have the prior rights.

In the *New Statesman*, this eight days later from Michael Lipton:

And did offensive coloured feet
Walk about England's pastures white?
And were constituents annoyed
By gramophones played late at night?

Did countenances black and brown –
Busmen and nurses – take our jobs?
And were the holy voices heard:
'Send 'em all home, the n—slobs?

Bring yellow feathers, voter's gold!
Bring me my pledges, in disgrace!
Bring me my crook! O clouds, unfold!
Bring me my Gallup poll on Race!

I shall not cease from selling cheap
The slime on which my rivals stand
Till we have built Johannesburg
In England's green and pleasant land.

Reviewing Paul Foot's new Penguin, *Immigration and Race in British Politics*, the impeccably liberal Shirley Williams first quoting Foot's admission that he was 'inexperienced about the effects of immigration from a working-class angle' and then reflecting for herself: 'It is ignorance of these effects that so cripples the attempt to work out policies for good race relations in Britain. At best, we are well-intentioned gropers in the dark.' In Flintshire, a building company justifying in the local press why they had returned the deposit of the black electrician from Liverpool trying to buy a house on a new estate near his workplace in Broughton: 'We had to ask ourselves if prospective buyers would be prepared to live on the same estate as coloured people . . . If we allowed coloured people in, there might be twenty or thirty families within no time. Then how would we stand?' In the London Electricity Board's Brixton depot, the men refusing to work with a sixteen-year-old black apprentice ('You have to remember that we go into people's homes and many residents might object if a coloured man went along to carry out work'). In Handsworth, Birmingham, the headmistress of Grove Primary School (420 children, only 79 of them white), Miss

Edith Wilkes, reflecting that 'it is extremely unfair to send new teachers from college to a school like this, but the truth is that experienced teachers don't want to work in immigrant areas'. At the Old Bailey, John Platts-Mills QC defending a black man accused of murdering his wife, but failing to get the composition of the jury changed from all-white, not helped by all of the reserve jurors being similarly all-white. On the front cover of *Nova*, the picture of a young black girl in a party dress, set against a white background and the headline, 'You may think I look cute but would you live next door to my mummy and daddy?' Labour's Alderman Harry Watton publicly laying down the law on housing ('Birmingham people must come first . . . I am not in favour of any form of priority for immigrant families . . . Surely, those who come from outside are lucky if they only have to wait five years?'). Philip Larkin explaining to Monica Jones why he felt below par ('I think there's a lot of infection about these days, upsetting one's insides: with all these foreigners about, one is never completely well, as when abroad'). Billy Graham, about to launch his Greater London Crusade, highlighting at a press conference the UK's colour bar after a colleague, the Revd Howard Jones, was asked to move from his flat in Drayton Gardens ('he has never been asked to do that in the United States'). A junior master at an inner-city boys' comprehensive giving the low-down to *New Society*: 'The "coloured boys" are often seriously classed together as troublemakers, and even held responsible for the falling standards of the school. I tackled this view once in a heated staffroom argument, but it was earnestly defended. There is a frightening emotional logic about race prejudice, utterly irrational, and set inexorably deep.' And this still entirely typical small ad in the *Brixton Advertiser*: 'TO LET. Tastefully furnished single bed-sitting room in superior residential property, Brownhill Road, Catford. Own hand basin and cooking facilities, constant hot water. Europeans only. – Ring Bex 7056 or Crayford 26155.'[9]

A mixed picture – some light, but more darkness – is confirmed by a clutch of memories. Graham Clark (born 1953) recalls the moment in 1965 when an Anglo-Indian family came to live in wholly monocultural Ham, near Richmond:

> The people who lived nearby were initially curious and came to stand outside the gate on the day that the 'brown people' moved

> in. This could have been seen as a slightly menacing scene, but the Dad was an outgoing, friendly man who saw the small crowd as a welcoming committee and warmly invited everyone into the house, shouting to his wife to 'put the kettle on'! Everyone came in and were soon chatting away like old friends! This new family didn't see that they were different and after a very short while, neither did their visitors and the village.

Which is not to say that the family's two children were not 'subjected to racist jibes on an almost daily basis' – but 'they were mostly just childish name calling and were usually settled with a little scuffle!' A largely positive recollection, too, from the fiercely left-wing trade unionist Alan Thornett, about how at the Cowley car plant it was the increasingly strong shop stewards movement that by 1967 got management to agree to open all jobs to black workers: 'There was initial hostility from many of the white workers and stoppages on some of the tracks with groups of white workers using all the worst racist arguments to refuse to work with blacks. Fryer [his colleague Bob Fryer] made no concessions to this pressure and every revolt was faced down.' Definitely mixed emotions for Norwell Roberts: undoubtedly a proud moment for him, and of considerable symbolic significance, when in March 1967 he (still known as Norwell Gumbs) started his training at Hendon as the Met's first black recruit; but the attendant publicity provoked a pile of letters that 'were downright racist, with the ugly words "n—" and "black bastard" appearing in many of them, and the correspondents making threats to my life if they ever encountered me on the beat.' Moreover, he adds, 'I have no doubt that some of those letters came from within the Met; some of the anonymous writers threatened to resign if I was posted to their station.' For some, inevitably, out-and-out negative memories. Sandra Knight, whose family had moved from Trinidad to Shepherd's Bush early in the decade, remembers without affection how the supposedly progressive Holland Park School was divided into high-flying H-forms and low-flying P-forms, with 'very, very few black kids' permitted into the former; for Diane Abbott, starting in September 1965 at Harrow County School for Girls, humiliation came early as her English teacher accused her of copying an essay ('she couldn't believe that a little chubby black girl with her pebble lenses and her plaits could have written that essay'); and in Derby, at the Queen's Hotel in Crompton Street, Anton Rippon (born 1944) watched as the landlord Ted Taylor, 'a nice enough chap', took instant action after spotting a mixed-race couple in his lounge:

> Seeing that someone else had served them, Ted was round from the bar in a flash. The couple were sitting at the next table to us and he told them to leave, or at least to move into the [public] bar. The worst aspect of all of this was the resigned look on the black man's face. He accepted the ruling without question and they picked up their drinks and shuffled back through to the bar to finish them before, a few moments later, leaving. I felt terribly uncomfortable at the time and, in retrospect, always wish that we'd also got up and left in protest.

One mixed-race couple in the mid-1960s, living in Bristol and recently married, were the Bullimores: Tony, the future miraculously rescued yachtsman, and Lalel, who had arrived from Jamaica in 1963. His mother, living in Southend-on-Sea, accused him of having thrown away his life and never forgave him; Lalel got used to overhearing on the street words like 'disgusting' and 'slut'; but in October 1966 they set up the rapidly celebrated Bamboo Club – in his justifiably proud words three decades later, 'a magnet for black entertainers' (including Bob Marley) and attracting 'a clientele of all colours'.[10]

Yet ultimately, if we are to gauge the extent of racial prejudice and discrimination in mid-sixties Britain, we need to look at contemporary attempts to estimate that extent: not just qualitative-cum-impressionistic, but also the more systematic surveys with a significant quantitative element.

'This problem of colour' was the title in August 1965 of Tony Bushby's investigation for the *Loughborough Monitor* of the situation in that very 'middle England' sort of town (and home to Larkin's mother), where so far only a 'few hundred coloured immigrants' had settled. Against a background of three young white students, all of them outsiders, agreeing unanimously that Loughborough *did* have a colour bar in the sense that there was a complete absence of integration, and of almost all his white, long-term resident interviewees insisting that 'Oh, of course I have nothing against a coloured person – a person's skin doesn't make them good or bad', he tried to dig a bit deeper with the latter group, starting with John the trade unionist who had 'worked in the same factory as many coloured people for several years'. Would he want to mix with them socially?:

> I do not know why I would not want to mix socially with the coloured chaps, but I just do not. I have nothing against them. I mean there is the odd one who I don't like, but then there are lots of white people I don't like for one reason or another, so that doesn't count. It is just that there is something there – I can't put my finger on it, but it's there all the time – something I can't get rid of, tells me not to mix.
>
> Do you think this is a right attitude to have? – Now who can tell, mate? It's what I feel and you can't alter that, can you?
>
> Well, would you like to feel different, to go out and mix? – Look, I have said what my views are and that is that, things are OK as they are, I lead my life, they lead theirs, and we are all happy.

Bushby's next three interviewees were all women:

> If a daughter of mine wanted to marry a coloured man I think both my husband and I would try and forget the fact that he had a different colour and try and decide if he was right for our daughter as we would if a white person asked to marry her. I think we would be able to do that, I hope we would anyway, yet if I am perfectly honest I suppose I would like to think my daughter would marry a white person. *(Housewife in her late twenties)*
>
> What do you think about these people – do you know their names or what the man does for his living? – No, I don't know much about them. The chap at the corner shop says they're Pakistanis. The woman wears some lovely dresses; I must say they look very nice. I once spoke to her – no, I have spoken to her more than once when we have been shopping in the same shop. Just to say 'Hello' and that, nothing more. I mean, we haven't much in common, have we?
>
> But surely she has, she being a housewife, a mother with a working husband like yourself? – No, you don't see what I mean. It's just that we haven't anything in common, have we? They are different, aren't

they – but don't go thinking because I say that, that I am against coloured people – I am not. There are good and bad in every country, but folks get on best with their own, I think. *(Housewife on a bus)*

Everyone has the same fears, I believe, and I also believe that sex is behind a lot of these fears. I am dead serious here. You see, girls are brought up from being small children to regard living, marrying or what have you, with a coloured man as wrong.

You can't get away from this; it's something that's there. Women don't want coloured men living near them because, although they know they won't, they fear they might be tempted to associate with a coloured man. Of course, the men, I think, are all frightened underneath that their women friends might leave them for a coloured man. *(Publican's wife)*

Mr J. H., who 'has lived in the town for more years than he likes to remember', was given the last word for the natives: 'I think we in Loughborough should not be criticised because we do not mix socially with coloured people a great deal. It doesn't mean we do not like them or have anything against them, but just that we are used to people we have known for a long time – and, after all, are you a great friend of all your neighbours?'

In Bradford in 1966 for his book on the north, the journalist Graham Turner was struck by how much less visibly difficult race relations were there compared to the Midlands. After noting that 'roughly eight out of ten night-shift workers in Bradford are now Pakistanis' and that 'they make up twenty per cent of the male textile work-force', he explained further: 'The Pakistanis are generally not competing for work which white men (or women) want; in many cases, they are not living in houses (or areas) which Bradfordians would choose; and they are not, despite the high proportion of bachelors, competing for the local women, because as the immigrant population has built up, Bradford has become the Mecca for prostitutes and near-prostitutes from all over the North of England.' Still, it was all relative, and in the city's areas of increasingly dense immigrant presence he soon heard grumbles from white residents:

There's just five of us whites left. We're hemmed in. There are some African kids on the end there, the mother goes to work, she's had five kids while she's been here. They have 'em every year – and she takes lodgers as well. The kids thumb their noses at me. The family is Jamaican, of course . . . The Paks, they're not bad, if only they'd keep their windows clean. This used to be a residential square, but now it's just a muck-tub. I'd like to sell this, but they won't give you the price because it's the Pak area . . . They're up and down stairs all night long. They'll be ten or twelve in that house down there – they eat and cook in the cellar. The worst is, there's nothing, only wogs, passing all t'time on a Sunday – it gets on your nerves. I'm nervous of going to bed. *(Woman, 'stout and comfortably dressed in a flowered pinafore', Peel Square)*

We've been here two years now, and it's beginning to drive the wife crackers. Wednesday afternoon, she had a drink, there were so many Pakistanis in here by 10 she started crying. At two in the morning I was still trying to comfort her. This last month, at least ninety per cent of my customers have been Paks. I've about six whites apart from the girls, you get them of course. The whites have just drifted away . . . There are some Paks now who get white women to work for them. They take the money off them and send it home. The Jamaicans are the ponces mainly, though they all work from one particular place. There's that feller in the Zodiac always in the betting shops, he hasn't worked for eight years. How does he do it? Filth, that's it. Mind you, they're good spenders, I'm not saying they're not . . . *(Publican, 'broad Lancashire accent', Lumb Lane)*

We never did like their habits – half of them don't work, and they're definite liars throughout, though they're often polite. Mind, they're not all bad. You can't blame them throughout . . . I'd go to them for help in some cases – if there was fighting. I'd call the Indians out of the back room first of all, because they know the language. We're not fond of Jamaicans here. The Paks are generally that little bit afraid of us, but the Jamaicans would take the English down if they could. *(The publican's wife, 'thin, bony, heavily powdered')*

Turner left the pub with some relief, before soon coming across 'a work-worn little man who was obviously delighted to talk, and to air his grievances'. '"They're all right," he said, "they're good and bad, like you are. I don't exactly dislike 'em, but there's more ner them than you. You don't get public assistance like them. There's that many of 'em as far as housing is concerned. They go into a little house, you can't get on to the floor for little beds. I know they've got to be somewhere, but there's just too many."'[11]

Turning now to the more quantitative and/or systematic, and starting with a trio of small or smallish surveys. In late 1964, after Labour in the election had narrowly lost the Slough constituency, in a contest which many observers compared to Smethwick because of the racial element, a survey there of the opinions of the 'host community' about immigrants produced 314 replies. Predictably, quite a lot of don't knows, but plenty of definite opinions one way or the other:

Well behaved: 238	Troublesome: 29
Industrious: 132	Lazy: 138
Quiet: 170	Noisy: 86
Anxious to 'fit in' to the community: 123	Deliberately trying to live by themselves: 139
Honest: 216	Dishonest: 19
Clean: 147	Dirty: 99
Polite and courteous: 199	Ill-mannered and rude: 62

About the same time, a small-scale survey of West Indians and Africans living in North Kensington, Brixton and Islington found thirteen out of nineteen reckoning that the police were unfair in their attitudes, typified by the view of a 27-year-old labourer from British Guiana that 'sometimes the police don't believe the coloured man, because they think he's not so good as the white man'. The third of the trio was soon afterwards, as *Flamingo*'s John Ross went into a dozen pubs in London, the Home Counties and the Midlands, and in only one was refused service – though sometimes not without 'a hurried, whispered conference between barman and landlord'. Ross in his report emphasised that much depended on circumstances, including time of week, and he quoted a couple of licensees:

> There is no colour bar here. What happens is this. We have a very nice lounge upstairs; open on Friday, Saturday and Sunday. I control this lounge while my husband looks after the downstairs customers. Now the upstairs lounge is always very busy at weekends and it is

true that I discourage coloured boys from coming in: I generally ask them if they wouldn't mind going downstairs. The reason is that while I don't look for trouble, there always seems a greater possibility of a misunderstanding with coloured boys. If I have any trouble, I can talk to my own people more easily ... *(Mrs Grant, Admiral Nelson, Leicester)*

We don't have a colour bar: I prefer to call it a behaviour bar ... If one or two coloured fellows come in quietly, O.K. What I don't like is a gang of six or seven coming in. They do tend to go around in gangs like that, you know, and if my white customers see half-a-dozen coloured faces in one corner of the bar they simply don't come in. They say to me, 'We'll see you later.' But I know they won't. *(W. P. Twomey, Beaconsfield Arms, High Wycombe)*

And the pub that had refused to serve Ross unless he left the saloon bar and retreated to the public bar? 'I am not prepared', said H. C. Hawes of the Dartmouth Arms in Forest Hill, 'to discuss this matter with the Press.'[12]

Next, to complement Rex and Moore on Sparkbrook, a quartet of local surveys. *How Colour Prejudiced is Britain?* asked the Congregationalist minister Clifford Hill in his 1965 book, based on fieldwork (probably a year or two earlier) in Tottenham, Islington and Edmonton. He found the most prejudice in the first two areas – in Tottenham 25 per cent objecting to the notion of working with a 'coloured' person, 53 per cent objecting to having 'coloured' neighbours; in Islington, 23 per cent and 50 per cent respectively – whereas in Edmonton, with a much less dense immigrant population, the figures were 17 per cent and 45 per cent. Other information provided was that on shop display boards in Tottenham in summer 1964 advertising rental accommodation, 33 per cent said 'No Coloured', many in the form of 'SORRY, No Coloured' or 'REGRET, No Coloured'. Hill also noted how his inquiry had 'brought to light the existence of a considerable body of prejudice against the employment of coloured people in the retail trades', i.e. as sales assistants; and, he added, 'the vast majority of retail shops, including most of the large West End London stores, will not even try to find out what the effect of coloured sales assistants would be'.

The focus of Anthony Richmond's fieldwork, largely carried out in 1965, was the St Paul's-Montpelier area in Bristol, where 'racially and ethnically the population was extremely heterogeneous'. Among his findings were that 'without prompting, 31 per cent of the white inhabitants said that the factor which they disliked most about the district was the presence of coloured immigrants'; that this was 'the single most frequent expression of dislike'; that only 29 per cent of the 'native-born' disagreed with the statement that 'immigrants usually cling together and don't really want to be friendly with English people'; that when asked about ways in which immigrants were thought to be different, the most cited was 'food habits and cooking', followed by 'standard of living' and 'family customs', with 'crime and bad behaviour' only in sixth place; and that when faced by the proposition that 'in general immigrants take more out of the welfare state than they put into it', 70 per cent agreed, whereas only (relatively speaking) 33 per cent agreed that 'coloured people are taking jobs our people should have' and 32 per cent that 'coloured people are inferior to white people'. As for age and gender, Richmond found that the most instances of 'spontaneous antipathy' came in his sample from the women over forty-five. Or in his own words (exclamation mark included), 'it would not be altogether an exaggeration to suggest that the wagging tongues of older women gossiping with each other probably set the tone of prejudice against the coloured immigrants in the area!'

Another social scientist, Daniel Lawrence, chose Nottingham – a troubled city in 1958, but generally reckoned to be more tolerant than, say, Birmingham – for his study of race relations, undertaken in 1966/7 and drawing overall a fairly downbeat picture. Half his indigenous respondents who were dissatisfied with the area where they lived blamed the newcomers (typical comment: 'There's too many coloureds round here . . . This area's known as the jungle'); 61 per cent opposed equal treatment in allocation of council housing ('It's our bloody country so we should get first chance'); 67 per cent wanted priority over jobs ('It's obvious – we belong here – they don't'); and 74 per cent did not rule out a repeat of the city's 1958 racial disturbances ('It's brewing all the time – look at the flow of Asians coming now'). 'If nothing else,' concluded Lawrence himself mildly enough, 'this investigation seems to have demonstrated that Nottingham does not enjoy harmonious race relations. Similarly, it does not seem that its inhabitants are unusually tolerant towards coloured people.' Roughly the same conclusion was reached by the fourth local study – of Liverpool, done in 1967 by a Liverpool Council of Voluntary Service working party, and finding that most of the overt hostility was less in the immigrant parts, but more in the almost exclusively white 'downtown' areas. This discovery, about a city which had long enjoyed a reputation for non-discrimination, provoked in the authors of the report what they could only call 'a deep sense of unease'.

A local study with a difference – and a particularly valuable, trustworthy study – was Dennis Brooks's *Race and Labour in London Transport*, its fieldwork done between mid-1965 and mid-1967. 'I concluded that the industrial absorption of immigrants is a slow process,' he wrote. 'The majority of natives accepted that the immigrants were a permanent part of the workforce, but this acceptance was often grudging, a recognition of reality as it was perceived. Many probably wished it were otherwise.' Indians and Pakistanis, he added, 'appeared to provoke relatively little antagonism', but at the same time only 'minimal acceptance'; whereas '*some* West Indians' were '*fully* accepted by their native workmates', while others inspired 'marked antipathy'. Much of his study concerned bus workers, and he asked them whether there was hostility in their garage towards Commonwealth immigrants: to which 50 per cent of natives answered in the affirmative, as did 53 per cent of the immigrants themselves. Brooks also let the contrasting voices come through about what the two categories thought of each other:

> I talk to some and ignore others because they ignore me. Some are gentlemen. *(White driver)*
>
> There are a few awkward ones, but we mostly get on pretty good. It's best to miss the awkward ones – the older ones, those who've put in twenty years and all that . . . the younger ones are better. *(West Indian driver)*
>
> There tends to be segregation in the canteen: between coloured and white crews. The coloureds make no effort to overcome this. They tend to prefer to sit with their coloured friends. *(White driver)*
>
> If one of us is behind [on the road] he is ignored. If one of them is behind they help him out. *(Pakistani conductor)*

> If they weren't here we would get a better wage. *(White busman)*
>
> I thought it might be difficult as he [the driver] didn't want to change his conductor. I decided I had to get round him. I saw him reading the racing page so I talked to him about horses; we get on O.K. now. *(West Indian conductor)*
>
> They are too arrogant and too slow. They have a chip on their shoulders – they think we don't like them. They treat us with contempt – but it is our country. *(White female conductor)*
>
> When the inspectors book you for running early or late they ask you 'why?' If you say something in your favour, they don't write it down; if it will incriminate you, they do write it down. I find that a white crew gets away with more than a coloured crew . . . *(West Indian driver)*
>
> Bus driving is different from all other driving: you have passengers to think of and the coloured immigrants don't. *(White driver)*

What about the potentially thorny issue, still academic, of immigrants being promoted to the inspector grade? Most of the native busmen were convinced there would be serious objections, with 'I don't know why, but it would be wrong' the most frequently given explanation. One, though, did elaborate: 'Coloureds stick together like flies. They'd be out to catch the locals and look after their own.' And, of course, what did those 'coloureds' working on the capital's buses make of the actual passengers?

> You get insults left, right and centre. I'm not bothered now – 'bastard' is just a national name. *(Conductor)*
>
> A lot call you names, especially if you have to go past a stop to pull in. They call you names, but I laugh at them – it saves a 'punch-up'. *(Driver)*
>
> I tried to help one old woman off with her shopping – 'take your black hands off me'. *(Female conductor)*

'When I was at home,' she reflected about coming from Jamaica, 'I never thought the English were any different: I had not expected any problem over colour.'[13]

That still leaves the two most ambitious attitudinal surveys, both of them largely conducted in the winter of 1966/7. The first, commissioned by the Survey of Race Relations in Britain and carried out by Mark Abrams's Research Services Ltd, focused on five particular areas – the London boroughs of Lambeth and Ealing (which included Southall) and the three county boroughs of Wolverhampton, Nottingham and Bradford – known to have relatively high proportions of Commonwealth immigrants; the second, part-commissioned by the Race Relations Board and mainly employing the think tank Political and Economic Planning (PEP), focused on six other places – Brent, Islington, Slough, West Bromwich, Keighley, Sheffield – which also had higher than average immigrant populations. The findings of the first did not emerge until in 1969 the Institute of Race Relations published its capacious *Colour and Citizenship: A Report on British Race Relations*, edited by Jim Rose; but the findings of the second were revealed much sooner, in spring 1967 when PEP published its report, turned the following year into a Penguin Special.

Overall, the five-borough survey, involving some 2,500 white respondents, came out on the moderately optimistic side. Or as Abrams himself put it:

> Over one-third of all white adults interviewed expressed views with no trace, or practically no trace, of hostility to coloured people; and almost another two-fifths of the sample seemed to be strongly disposed in the direction of tolerance.
>
> At the other extreme there emerged 10 per cent of the white population whose antipathy to coloured people was almost unconditional; standing near to this one-tenth of the white population there was another one-sixth who, while they were strongly prejudiced-inclined, were still prepared to make exceptions and who presumably, having once made some exceptions, could move either in the direction of more exceptions (i.e. towards tolerance) or fewer exceptions (i.e. towards unconditional hostility) . . .

Other, more granular findings included that women were 'slightly more tolerant' than men; that the highest levels of 'extreme prejudice' were among the middle-aged, especially skilled workers and their wives and in the lower middle class; that 'people whose full-time education extended beyond the minimum school-leaving age were less prejudiced than others'; that Conservative voters were more prejudiced than

Labour supporters; that the survey produced 'little evidence to support the view that people who have travelled overseas are less prejudiced than those who have never been abroad'; and that those of the sample who had revealed themselves (by their responses to various statements) to have 'consistently authoritarian' views were 'substantially more colour prejudiced than the non-authoritarians'. None of these findings were without value – far from it – but at least one sociologist, Daniel Lawrence, would cast significant doubt on Abrams's definitions of 'prejudice' and 'tolerance', arguing that they were too arbitrary. Even so, the five boroughs still supplied plenty of less debatable grist to the historical mill: for instance, an overwhelming majority considering the British to be superior to Africans and Asians, but with far fewer thinking the same in relation to Europeans and Americans; at least 60 per cent believing that West Indians, Indians and Pakistanis took 'more out of the country than they put into it'; and, when asked to explain why they had agreed with the statement that immigrants should 'adopt a more English way of life', most finding it difficult if not impossible to get beyond the assertion that 'they should live the way we do'. Abrams returned in his conclusion to the irreconcilable 'highly prejudiced'. The 'most important' of his findings, he advised those attempting to improve race relations, was that 'while they must not ignore the views of the 10 per cent minority', nevertheless they 'should see them for what they are – irrational "solutions" to personality inadequacies which would persist without regard to the policies adopted'.

The PEP report was more investigative, finding that in all sorts of areas of daily life – whether going to the hairdresser or obtaining motor insurance, whether seeking hotel accommodation or hire-purchase facilities – significant levels of racial discrimination existed. But its principal focus was, as clearly demonstrated by the subsequent Penguin Special (written by W. W. Daniel), on the two crucial aspects that had been so glaringly omitted from the provisions of the 1965 Race Relations Act: housing and employment.

In the former, almost certainly the most frequently exercised racial discrimination was in the private letting sector, and landlords in the six selected places were candid enough:

> I've nothing against them but you've got to think of the neighbourhood. Nobody wants this to become little Jamaica, do they?

> Well, they aren't very clean and also they're noisy. All their friends come round. I don't think it's good for the children either to have them around.
>
> This isn't that sort of neighbourhood.
>
> I discussed this with my wife. She said she doesn't go for them much and anyway it would look bad with the neighbours. And, come to think of it, give me a good reason why we should?
>
> They cause trouble, don't they?

Confirmation of widespread prejudice came from three carefully chosen 'testers' – white Englishman, white Hungarian immigrant, West Indian – each approaching the same sixty landlords to apply for accommodation. On no fewer than thirty-eight occasions, the West Indian was told that the accommodation was already taken, whereas both other applicants were told it was vacant; on four occasions the West Indian was asked for higher rent than the others; three times the Hungarian as well as the West Indian was discriminated against; but on fifteen occasions (i.e. one-quarter of the times) there was no discrimination and all three applicants were given the same information. Meanwhile, a similar exercise with accommodation bureaux and estate agents found racial discrimination occurring at least two-thirds of the time, with one explaining:

> Once they're in, they're there for ever. Landlords are worried about overcrowding. Also they are under pressure from their neighbours – people don't want coloured people living in their street, let alone their own building. As soon as one house or flat is let to coloured people, it's looked on as the first hole in the dyke. People think it's only a matter of time before the area becomes a slum. For this reason I'd say it's virtually impossible to get an unfurnished flat for, say, a Jamaican or a Pakistani.

When it came to discrimination in the provision of council housing, the report provided no comparable 'situation tests', but it did emphasise how housing officials were often expected not only not to allow immigrants on the waiting list too quickly, but also in the fullness of time not to provide them with the better accommodation. As for actual house buying, the situation tests were back in action, with racial discrimination in evidence from twenty-seven out of the forty-two estate agents approached: most typically, either the West Indian alone was not invited to leave his address, or the West Indian alone was told that a mortgage would be impossible or was given different information about terms. A trio of estate agents explained the situation as they saw it:

> To begin with, people are reluctant to sell to them. They are under pressure from their neighbours and so forth. Secondly there are great difficulties in getting mortgages: either they are asked for higher deposits, or the interest rates are higher – or they aren't given loans at all. That's the way the building societies do it.
>
> We face two problems. First, the lack of property available to them and secondly the virtual impossibility of getting a reasonable mortgage without asking a high deposit or a high interest rate.
>
> It's important to remember that estate agents are only go-betweens. If we seem to discriminate it's because we are acting on behalf of vendors and are also responsible, in a way, for putting forward the viewpoint of building societies or the council.

None of which was much comfort to the survey's West Indian, Pakistani and Indian informants refused a mortgage:

> I was told by the agent 'They have totally shut down on your people, Mr Khan.' He said that all the building societies were doing so.
>
> I saw the mortgage broker and he said it was very hard to get a mortgage for coloured people.
>
> The agents refuse to give Pakistanis mortgages. They refused to sell us houses unless we pay cash.
>
> I approached a broker for a mortgage. The broker agreed to get it for me. He wrote me confirming it, then he said later I couldn't get it. So I asked him why and his reply was 'probably because you are coloured.'

'I had almost £1,500 for down payment on a house of £4,000,' recalled another. 'I had a stable job. The house was in good condition. My application was not successful. I know white people don't have all this trouble. We earn more money. We are hard-working. But they don't trust us.'

Situation tests, too, in the equally charged area of employment, and here the starkest, most impactful of revelations. In only *one* of the forty firms tested was the non-white tester told that a vacancy existed or offered a job, whereas the no-better-qualified English tester had fifteen offers and the equally no-better-qualified Hungarian tester had ten. In another set of situation tests, involving applications to employment bureaux to apply for accountancy posts, the three applicants each of the fifteen times comprised a white English tester, a West Indian with similar qualifications and a West Indian with higher qualifications. Result: the West Indian with comparable qualifications to the Englishman was told there were no vacancies ten times; the West Indian with superior qualifications was told this four times; and the Englishman only once. Unsurprisingly, across the employment piece as a whole, immigrant testimony evoked a sense of almost fatalistic frustration:

> It was six of us [applying to a steel company]. I was the only coloured. Three of them came before me. The man called me first and before I could even talk he told me there were no jobs. So I went outside and a little while after three of the men came out with jobs. I didn't wait for the others.
>
> Applied to a sponge factory for any kind of work, on recommendation of white friend working there. When the manager saw I was coloured he said 'Sorry, no vacancies.' There was a sign up outside saying all types of jobs going.
>
> Telephoned an engineering firm to inquire about a job as a machine operator. Was told there were jobs going and to come round. When I arrived ten minutes later and they saw I was coloured they said all the jobs were gone.
>
> Saw a card for a tailor's presser in a window. Went in and the receptionist took all my particulars. Then a man came out who may have been the foreman. As he saw me he said 'Sorry, full up.' If there was no job the girl would have told me in the beginning.
>
> Applied to a public office for a job. I was given a job behind the scenes and not allowed to mix with the public. It was said in my

> presence that the public did not like coloured people. So I was not given a clerical officer's job although I am a graduate and am better educated than my superiors.

A contentious issue, difficult to be sure about, was how much discriminatory pressure employers were under from the unions. The report argued that, however non-discriminatory official national policy might have been, the fact was that attitudes further down the food chain meant that in practice 'a very substantial proportion of coloured workers' did experience real racial discrimination in the workplace. 'I am a very strong union man,' explained one interviewee:

> I've been a union man for thirty years – it's almost my way of life in a way. But even within unions there is a tendency to ignore what you don't want to see. This is only natural and I'm not blaming anyone. What I am trying to say is that it's all very well to condemn discrimination – I condemn it – but you've got to work with them to get it all in perspective. A lot of very reasonable people have strong feelings about coloured immigrants – and they have good reasons for them too. A lot of it can be put down to emotionalism sometimes – but they are real problems and you're a bloody fool if you say they aren't. Union members are people, you know. You don't turn into a bloody angel just because you join a union.

It is unclear whether he was a local union official, but other interviewees certainly were:

> It's often very difficult to put across to them [the immigrant workers] what the union is about. They don't seem to be able to grasp its meaning. Either that or they join because they think it's some sort of protection racket. They are so used to being exploited by their own people that when you go round to collect their dues they think you're charging them protection money.
>
> I have found that when I tackle them about non-payment of dues, they resent it and think I'm chasing them because they're coloured. This is a point I've heard several times – but who likes parting with money anyway?

They join, they pay up and they think it ends there. They don't come to meetings, they seem to want to stand apart.

Members do get annoyed with them, of course they do. The feeling is 'why should we do everything for them if they won't help themselves?'. I must admit I understand that view at times.

In the end, though, it largely came down to the attitude of employers. Take a quickfire baker's dozen slices of testimony:

They never stick at anything. They move around – they're a sort of floating population. They don't seem to be very interested in permanency. I think a lot of their problems stem from this – employers have learned not to trust them.

They're all very casual – even off-hand. They seem unable to grasp the important things in life.

It takes a long time to get through to them, you know. They're not very quick at picking things up. You have to explain everything four or five times. Some are plain thick.

They have very little ambition. Oh, they'll work hard on piecework but they don't want to better themselves job-wise.

They're lazy. It's the tropical sun, it's in their blood. That makes them that way.

They are lazy, arrogant, shifty, difficult and dirty. You can only get a day's work out of them if you stand over them.

They are lazy, bone lazy. One Jamaican told me yesterday that he wouldn't move the barrels because it made his watch vibrate. They always have an excuse.

Some can stink – I mean really stink. Workers object to being alongside them – it leads to all sorts of friction.

I told one lot that cleanliness was next to Godliness. This upset them more than ever. They were Hindus. They accused me of trying to convert them.

They spit all over the place.

They're always up to something, particularly the Jamaicans. If it isn't pilfering it's peddling dirty pictures. They're on to everything.

The only time they're sharp is when they're thinking up the latest dodge. Apart from that they're either asleep or looking for sex.

While as for promotion, 'we have some coloured foremen over coloured workers but I doubt if it would be on if they had whites under them'.[14]

Finally, attitudes *across* Britain, not just in the more immigrant-populated parts of the country. The key source is Gallup, which in its polls regularly asked people (overwhelmingly white) about whether their feelings in relation to other races were becoming more favourable or less favourable. In May 1959, 'more favourable' enjoyed a 5 per cent advantage over 'less favourable'; by August 1964, this was down to 3 per cent; by November 1965, 'less favourable' was 4 per cent ahead; and by August 1967, eight months *before* Powell's rivers-of-blood speech, this had widened considerably to 15 percentage points. Admittedly, at least 80 per cent invariably denied that there was 'a colour problem' in the district where they lived; but the overall direction of travel, in this highly emotive area, was unmistakable and one-way.[15]

13

It Hurts You Deep Inside

The April 1966 sample census revealed that West Indians remained the dominant immigrant group (an estimated 454,100 resident in England and Wales), followed by Indians and Pakistanis (343,300). The balance between these two main groups, though, was shifting, in large part because of the application of the 1962 Commonwealth Immigrants Act, with the systematic use of employment vouchers pushing the emphasis towards immigrants from the subcontinent with either a job already assured or possessing a more skilled or qualified background. Accordingly, from when the Act came into force in July 1962, through to 1967, net arrivals of Indians and Pakistanis totalled 160,190, compared to 59,060 from the Caribbean. The fastest-growing single element were Pakistanis: net arrivals of only 17,120 between 1955 and 1960, but then 114,510 between 1961 and 1967, with the great majority heading north – to a mixed reception from what would one day be called the red wall.[1]

Predictably, the West Indian experience was still in the mid-1960s the more publicised than the Asian. Take this cluster of contemporary snapshots, starting with *The Colony*, Philip Donnellan's celebrated documentary, shown on BBC television in June 1964, that allowed West Indian immigrants in Birmingham to speak for themselves. 'When coloured people go to an English dance, the English boys don't ask for a dance,' explained a girl (whose brother suffered hostility if he spoke to white women at work). 'Sometimes I think some of them would like to but it's what their friends would say that matters, not what they really feel. Some of them speak to you in the street with their friends, you know.' Another interviewee, Rudolph, a crane driver at the Austin works at Longbridge, attributed his previous occupation – professional boxer – directly to racial prejudice: 'I just wanted to beat somebody's brain out because I had a pretty rough time here. Hatred brought about by intolerance, my experience in Birmingham here as a Jamaican.' Rudolph presumably did not pull his punches, but perhaps another Jamaican interviewee did, reflecting that 'sometimes we think we shouldn't blame the people, because it's we who have come to this country and trouble them', and adding wistfully that 'if we had not come we would be none the wiser, we would still have the good image of England, thinking that they are what they are not'. By general consent, the star of the programme was the highly articulate railway signalman, Stan Crooke:

> Seeing me working here, you would look and say, 'Well, that chap looks perfectly happy. He's working amongst English people. How come they say there is no integration in this country?' I may have a different story to tell. I know quite a few men working in the same job as I, we work together, we may travel on the same train together; on the train we discuss things appertaining to the job. We get into the station and the moment we arrive at the station, all contact ends. We don't even walk ten yards together on the station platform. So this matter of integration is very very difficult. Apparently both of us, in this case my fellow work mate and myself, are finding it difficult to bridge a gap which apparently doesn't exist.

'The West Indian,' he reckoned, 'no longer consider himself a Jamaican, a Trinidadian, Barbadian, Kittian, Antiguan. We are all subtly but inexorably considering ourselves as all coloured people.'

The mainstream press at this stage still gave relatively little space to West Indian voices, which made a magazine like *Flamingo* all the more valuable. Later in 1964, Eric McAlpine told from the inside what it was like for 'the West Indian living in a single room in one of the big cities':

> On average he pays between £3 5s and £3 10s for his accommodation. The room is alleged to be furnished; no irony could be greater. There are two very ancient blankets, probably army surplus at the end of the war and we don't know which war.

> A pair of sheets and a pillow case. Ragged curtains changed yearly if you are lucky. No utensils. No heat. The furniture, such as it is, might have been in the Ark with Noah.
>
> There is a bath, shared. There is also a kitchen but in most instances the kitchen is situated on the landing outside the room. 'God help you fe cook the two patayta out dey during winter.' And there is a toilet without toilet paper.
>
> If you have an English landlord, chances are that you must be in on time; if allowed visitors, they've got to come on a certain day of the week and leave at a certain time. And, brother, if you're an ideal bachelor, beware of the peeping tom landlady when your sweet, sweet West Indian girl friend comes to visit you.

Soon afterwards, the magazine's John Ross wrote an open letter to Millie, the young Jamaican singer whose 'My Boy Lollipop' had been a huge recent hit; he criticised her for talking too much and too openly to the press, including about her Uncle Wilbert as an Obeah-man, called by the white interviewer a 'witch-doctor'. Most readers, but not all, backed his criticism:

> If this don't tell Millie guard her tongue in future I don't know what will. I can assure you that many Jamaicans I know agree with Mr Ross. *(Mrs Dorothy Gordon, London N1)*
>
> Millie has been letting us down before the English people. *(M. Henry, London SW8)*
>
> She really talks too much – and she's from nowhere. *(K. A. Brown and C. T. James, Birmingham 11)*
>
> In my candid opinion, Millie's critics – who, regrettably, are her own people – are probably not bold enough to voice out their real grievance: the allegation that Millie prefers white company to coloured. But surely our little pop queen still enjoys the right to choose any company she likes – white, black, pink or indigo. *(Akin Elegbe, London NW2)*

More generally, noted McAlpine, of the estimated 8,000 West Indians living in Wolverhampton, not a single one was employed by either the Post Office or the council.

'There is certainly far more prejudice among the English working class than among the middle classes,' Orlando Patterson, a young Jamaican novelist who also lectured at the London School of Economics, told Home Service listeners in September 1965. 'I don't think that among the working classes there is ever a complete acceptance; there might be a great deal of conviviality, but there is this deeply rooted instinctive feeling of an innate superiority.' And also, the rather older Trinidadian novelist Samuel Selvon might have added, it was often a gaping ignorance deriving from that sense of superiority, not just among the working class. At one point in his 1965 novel *The Housing Lark*, as he starts to introduce his cast of central characters (a motley group of young West Indians in London), he breaks off abruptly to address the presumably white reader:

> To go into more detail – tell you where he come from originally, whether he six foot tall or five foot six, whether he have big eyes and a small nose – what difference it make to you? All you interested in is that he black – to English people every black man look the same. And to tell you he come from Trinidad and not Jamaica – them two places a thousand miles apart – won't matter to you, because to Englishers the West Indies is the West Indies, and if a man say he come from Tobago or St Lucia or Grenada, you none the wiser.

Or as the patients at a hospital in Wakefield would ask Barbara Nnaemeka when in 1966 she arrived there from Barbados to train as a nurse, 'Do they still wear grass skirts in your country?', 'Do they still swing in trees in your country?', 'Do they still live in tree houses in your country, luv?' Selvon's characters, in the words of the critic Sukhdev Sandhu, 'give as good as they get': very different in feel to this unknown West Indian writing home:

> I bin in the country six munths now and I am fine. The man at the employment ofice send me to a job. So I working. Life in Jamaica and England is not one. Things have them ups and douns but the thing that friten me very much in London is the loneliness. You dont know any body in this town. Even the black people them is not talking to no strangr just like the white people. I bin in thes

> building now going four long, long monts and I dont no the naim of al the people in the building. the same thing at me workplace. you talk to an Inglish man Munth after mont but you dont ask him for is naim Him not telling you either. The house them close to one other but you no know the nam of you neybour. You don't know if them like you or them hate you. If i be ten yeers in this country i wont know the proper name of ten Englishmen.

'Sometime,' ended this unfinished, unsent letter on sixpenny airmail paper (and discovered by Donald Hinds for his often heartbreaking 1966 book *Journey to an Illusion*), 'I really want to know what it is that is going on in ther heart . . .'

Nnaemeka's was retrospective testimony, and others add to the picture of an often hard and discouraging immigrant life. 'In the school, I remember his name, this kid, it was Colin Flood – I'll never forget him – he called me a wog, but because I didn't know what a wog was, I just kind of went quiet,' recalls Jimmy Ellis (arrived in 1963 from Jamaica, aged twelve). And:

> We had a schoolteacher called Mr Kay – he did maths, but he wasn't very good at it. I'd say, 'Oh, I don't quite understand that, sir', and he'd go, 'Blah, blah, blah!' and move on. But if ever the white kids didn't understand anything and put their hands up, he would then go next to them and help them to resolve it. But he would never come next to one of us lads. He'd stay at the blackboard and discuss it. So straight away I started to think, 'Hmmm.' Because racism wasn't even a word to me then.

Doreen Phillips came to London from Guyana in 1964 and, a young mother with two small children, began an evening shift in a sweet factory:

> The Blacks were on one side, the Whites were on one side. We sort of got all the worst bits to do, the sweeping up and things. We were packing sweets, they were packing the sweets, handling the things, but all the dirty jobs the Blacks were doing. Then they would use remarks like 'What's smelling like that?', you know, them sorts of things because they used to say Black people stink.

Yet of course, despite all this, many West Indians decided to stay and to try to improve their lot, above all to move from being a renter to an owner-occupier. Perhaps typical were the working-class St Vincent parents of Michael McMillan, coming to Britain in the 1960s. 'The front room,' their son describes with a shudder of embarrassment about the aesthetics, 'was a contradictory space, where the efficacy of the display was sometimes more important than the authenticity of the objects, such as artificial flowers, plastic pineapple ice buckets, floral patterned carpet and wallpaper that never matched, and pictures of the scantily clad "Tina" next to *The Last Supper* . . .' The memory is quoted by Clair Wills in *Lovers and Strangers*; and as she comments, 'after the ignominious struggles in rented rooms and overcrowded flats, the simple fact of having a good room in which to relax and entertain visitors spelled respectability. It was an accomplishment in itself. It said, we have arrived, and it said it loudly.'[2]

Rex and Moore's Sparkbrook survey and Lawrence's Nottingham survey get us consistently the closest up to the immigrant experience in the mid-1960s – the former mainly through illuminating case studies, the latter mainly through direct quotation. Among the Sparkbrook West Indians, three case studies particularly stand out:

> Mr and Mrs N. were born in Barbados and St Kitts respectively, though they came to England from Curaçao, Mr N. two years ahead of his wife and family. They have three daughters and Mrs N. has a married son and daughter by a previous husband in the West Indies. They live on a whole floor of a house divided into two flats, theirs being very well kept and brightly furnished, with new furniture. Mr N. took charge whenever we called. His daughters (and, by implication, his wife) were told to sit down properly and keep quiet. Mr N. does all the talking and he knows all the answers. He works at a car factory and as a spare-time insurance agent. He believes that West Indians who try to do well in England must work hard and behave themselves. He said that he has no trouble with jobs or accommodation and is quite happy here. The family are stalwart members of the parish church which provides their only associational activity. They intend to settle permanently in England. Mrs N. minds babies for working West Indian mothers. There is a great demand for baby-minders among West Indian women and this is usually done by the

older woman, either unable to work or with large families of their own. The children of working mothers in the West Indies would be cared for by the grandmother, aunts or sisters, but these are seldom readily available in England.

Sid lives with his mother, his sister and her baby in Sparkbrook. They came from Barbados and appear to be a very tight-knit family group, although neither Sid's mother or sister are married. They pay £6 a week to a Kittician landlord who lives next door and whom they accuse of snooping on them. They live in two rooms, although they rent the whole of a small terraced house, Sid sleeps in one room and his mother and sister in the other, which also serves as a sitting-room. They do not use the other rooms except for storing furniture and luggage, as they intend to move as soon as possible. The landlord forbids the use of electric fires so they normally use a paraffin stove; but sometimes they lock the doors, draw the curtains and bring out an electric fire from under the bed. Sid's main problem is to find a woman, but he is not very articulate and a little unused to social gatherings, coming as he does from a very poor, low-status peasant community in Barbados. So he has little success socially. He watches a lot of television, his friends call once or twice a week, and sometimes they go out for a drive in a car . . . This family's main concern is to stay together and find good living accommodation, though they live in far better physical conditions than many of their fellow-countrymen. They take little interest in affairs outside their home but are vaguely resentful of the way West Indians are treated in England.

Daniel C. came from St Kitts two years ago. He was a blacksmith at home, but is content to have a labouring job in a factory near his lodgings. He lives in one room and spends a lot of time in pubs and cafés, where we often saw him in the evening. He likes England and does not want to go back to St Kitts, though he says he misses the cheap fruit. He had a woman and some children in St Kitts. The children are still there but his woman is now married in England, 'without telling me'. Daniel would like an English girl. West Indian woman are crafty and put on airs in England, but really they are no good, he says. So far, he has had no luck with English girls. Two white 'business girls' asked for his room one night, so he shut them in there and went to stay with a friend, but he would not take any money from the girls; 'Prostitutes' money doesn't do you any good'. So Daniel, in his late thirties or early forties, and only a couple of inches over five feet tall, lives on his own, cheerfully hoping that one day the right girl will turn up. Meanwhile, he has more or less 'adopted' a family of seven little Irish girls. 'They are my friends now.' He first met them in previous lodgings and was glad to find them again in his present street; they, too, seem to have adopted him.

From Nottingham, the specifically West Indian testimony largely concerned motives for coming to England and questions of identity, first for themselves and then, looking to the future, for their children:

> Well I left Jamaica because I saw the advertisements in the 'Gleaner'. I left to better my position. That was the chief reason.
>
> Well I knew I'd find it hard to get an office job here – I had a nice job at home – but I wanted to have the experience.
>
> I had a chance to go to America once – but I didn't go. And when I wanted to, it was easier to come to Britain – and I thought London's streets was paved with gold.
>
> Before I thought of myself as British but now I think of myself as Jamaican. Now you see we are a nation and anyway when you get here you find that they think that if you are black you cannot be British.
>
> Well to be honest when I was in Jamaica the teaching we got about Britain gives us she's got a motherly feeling towards us. Now that I'm here it's different and I'm proud to be a Jamaican.
>
> They'll [the children] feel English at first but as they grow up they'll come to think of themselves as Jamaicans. Even now they say things to my kid at school to make her feel like this. The parents will worry in case they get upset about things later.
>
> The parents will not be able to do much about it. You have to learn the hard way.

'Well I feel sorry for them,' said another parent. 'I know they is silly. I tries to tell them pretty often that you cannot be British really – not unless your skin is white.'[3]

Lawrence also asked some of Nottingham's Indian and Pakistani immigrants why they had come to England and, again, looking ahead, how parents would feel if children born and raised in England started thinking of themselves as English:

> To seek employment. I was unemployed in Pakistan.
>
> It was difficult to support my family on the land I had. I wanted to better my prospects.
>
> Nobody wants to leave one's country. But the financial situation forced us to leave. We have come here to earn money.
>
> To learn about life. I wanted to know the people who had reached such a position that the sun never set on the British Empire.
>
> The parents would feel that they were living in exile. They would feel that coming here had been an 'expensive' affair.
>
> They will think it a disaster. Their children will learn all the bad habits of English children and their parents will be sorry they came here.

'It will happen in only one out of 10,000 cases,' predicted another. 'It cannot happen. If it did the parents would be most unhappy.'

Over in Sparkbrook, the Asian case studies seem to have focused on Pakistanis only, including a particularly suggestive trio of examples:

> A. K. comes from Campbellpore, where he worked on the family farm, six years ago. He has worked for short periods in Bradford, Sheffield, Cardiff and Smethwick but left all these jobs as he objected to paying bribes to avoid the dirtiest and heaviest jobs. He now lives with his brother in Sparkbrook and works at a motor-car factory where he says there is no bribery. He does not much like English workers but thinks that his present Managing Director is a 'good man'. A. K. speaks very poor English and seldom goes out. He spends a lot of time reading his Qoran and is deeply religious (which his brother takes as a sign of his mental simplicity). When we first met A. K., he was sitting in his room playing a small harmonium-like instrument and singing to himself. He is quite happy in England now, but yearns for his wife. He will not bring her to England as he believes it would be impossible to maintain Purdah here. It would not be good for his wife to see English ways (kissing in public). England is a morally corrupt country with thousands of divorces to prove it. A. K. was deeply

> shocked to learn that one of us was nearly thirty years old and unmarried.
>
> G. H. is a Rawalpindi Pathan. He arrived in 1956 and lived with his brother, who supported him during the three months it took him to find a job. By choice they later separated. Now G. H. lives in one room in a friend's house. In this room he has a bed, a chest of drawers, a wardrobe, paraffin stove, and all his belongings. G. H.'s first (and so far only) job is as a driver for the Fire Brigade and Ambulance Department in Birmingham, a job requiring no little skill. G. H. is very class-conscious and sees most of the Pakistani immigrants as low, rather dirty, unintelligent peasants and 'domestic servant class'. In spite of this he is very much in demand among the immigrants around him for advice on passport matters and reading letters, which services he appeared to perform free of charge ('they are only simple-minded people').
>
> Abram K. we first met in an Irish pub. He explained to us that Islam always adapts to the culture in which it finds itself. Soon it would give way on drinking. Thus he saw himself in the 'Black Horse' as in the vanguard of theological reform. His wife he kept in strict Purdah and she has not been out of the house for two and a half years. She was, however, the only Pakistani woman we were able to interview at length. Mrs K. has four children, a boy of fifteen (by Abram's first wife), two girls of three and two, and a baby. She keeps the family room spotlessly clean and the children well dressed. She has no visitors, no women to chat with. Mrs K. would prefer to be back in Pakistan and would prefer her husband not to drink. She wants her daughters to be brought up as strict Muslims . . . Abram works in a factory and owns his house. He has a number of kinsmen, brothers, and brothers-in-law here in Sparkbrook and has no intention of returning to Pakistan permanently.

'This is in spite of strong pressure from his wife,' added Rex and Moore. 'The only reason Abram gives for not returning to Pakistan permanently is: "No pubs".'[4]

Undeniably, the contrast drawn by the authors between Sparkbrook's West Indian and Pakistani communities was a sharp one. In the case of the former, they highlighted the absence of 'any kind of commercial middle class', with 'few West Indian landlords and only a handful of shopkeepers in back streets, who had an insignificant share even of West Indian trade'; a relatively thin formal associational life; parties which, though sometimes noisy and drunken and featuring the odd white prostitute, were more often than not 'marked by the petty-bourgeois respectability which pervades so much of West Indian life', as exemplified by 'the shiny radiogram found in so many West Indian homes'; and in general, 'a largely English culture pattern' – or as they also put it, 'the young men meet and talk about sex and motor cars', while 'the older people discuss housing and their children'. Whereas:

> The Pakistanis are fewer in numbers than the West Indians in Sparkbrook, but their impact on the area is far greater because of the role which they play as landlords and shopkeepers. Moreover, whereas the West Indians so largely share English culture and affiliate themselves to its institutions, the Pakistanis have a culture and institutions of their own, so that their presence is doubly visible. They are seen not only as coloured but as culturally foreign.
>
> On the Stratford Road [Sparkbrook's main road] there are, mixed up amongst the English shops, some dozen Pakistani-owned stores and several Pakistani-owned cafes. The clientele of these shops and cafes is predominantly Pakistani, but includes also a strong minority of West Indians and a few English and Irish. In a very striking way these shops and cafes declare the Pakistani presence, for they not only have their shop signs in Urdu or Bengali, and sell Oriental spices; they also serve as social centres. In the New World Stores, for instance, a Pakistani may bath and eat, meet his friends and pick up news of Pakistani community activities. Thus the Pakistani has a supporting social world in the High Street . . .
>
> The typical Pakistani migrant is a peasant-turned-worker, who has left his wife, if he has one, at home. He will suffer the trials and tribulations of the city for a period of five or more years but intends to return home at least for a time. He seeks a temporary home to establish himself as a worker, but in the great majority of cases does not aim at assimilation.

Crucially, and far more than their West Indian counterparts, Pakistani immigrants were in practice part of a whole Pakistani ecosystem – not just shops, but also wholesalers, banks and newspapers, all underpinned by the active and interventionist Pakistani Welfare Association. Rex and Moore's key insight here from their fieldwork was that the Pakistani 'spirit of commercial enterprise' was *not* 'linked with an individualist ethic', that 'the successful entrepreneur was seen as having obligations to his kinsmen': 'If he had a house, his fellow-villagers and kinsmen could reside there for a nominal rent. And if he had a successful business he felt that he had an obligation to do charitable works which was felt more immediately and carried out more conscientiously than might be the case with a pious Christian businessman.'[5]

By some way the largest concentration of Pakistanis was in Bradford, but there were also significant clusters in Birmingham (including, of course, Sparkbrook), Nottingham, Coventry, Leicester, Sheffield and Glasgow; Bradford by 1967 had 51 Pakistani grocers and butchers, 16 Pakistani cafés, 5 Pakistani banks, and an almost implausible 50 Pakistani schools of motoring, while by the same time Balsall Heath in Birmingham had 60 Pakistani shops or cafés, and 100 retail grocers and 25 wholesale stores served Glasgow's 7,000 Pakistanis; the great majority of Pakistani workers had jobs in textiles, in heavy engineering, and in transport; and to take the Oxford example of Pakistanis working at the Cowley car plant, they tended to stick (increasingly as owner-occupiers) to the city's more rundown housing areas, especially in east Oxford, whereas their West Indian counterparts were more able-cum-willing to move to new or newish council estates on the periphery, especially Blackbird Leys.[6]

A quartet of Pakistani immigrant lives adds some flesh. Mohammed Bashir would look back wryly three decades later about his coming to England as a 24-year-old in March 1965, having been working happily enough as a telephone clerk in Karachi:

> My cousin wanted to go to England. He applied for a voucher from Lily Mill [in Oldham] and asked me to send my details and photo. At that time the Ministry of Labour used to issue vouchers due to the demand for workers in textile mills. I sent the details and I received a letter. I went to my village and told everyone. They were pleased to hear that I was going to England. It was considered a good move as many people who went to England provided their family in Pakistan with a better lifestyle. When I

went to get a visa a friend asked me what I was going to do in England. I said naturally for employment. He jokingly said 'The Queen of England is not inviting you, don't go leaving this job. There will only be a labourer's job there.' He told me that I did not have enough command of the English language and it was going to be a problem so 'do not go and ruin your life'. 'You have more chances here for promotion,' he said. I did not like his advice. At that time I felt that he was jealous of me going to England. Later I realised that he was right . . .

During the early years I worked at a number of mills. When I first arrived my cousin told me that my skin colour was very dark so I had to wait until it got lighter. I waited for two weeks. Then I went to the mill. I got work as a waft carrier in the mill. I'd never done any physical work in Pakistan. I was very tired. I had problems moving the trolley. The chargehand helped me with that. I thought there would be a lot of machinery in factories to do the physical work. I heard the stories that in England you only need to press buttons to do work. I found that I had to do everything. I did not have any experience of operating lifts. I also had a language problem. My shift was 7.30 to 5.00 pm. In Pakistan I used to have a job with status . . .

By contrast, no regrets from the upwardly mobile, super-motivated Salik ur Rahman, interviewed by Graham Turner as part of his Bradford foray in 1966. Thirty-five years old, living in Bradford (by now in some comfort in a 'well-kept terraced house' out of the city centre) since 1957, a former secretary of the Pak Social Club, working as a weaver at S. L. Upton but sometimes also doing an evening shift for another firm, he saw no signs of any colour bar. 'We have so many English friends, we have English neighbours both sides,' he told Turner. 'Sometimes we go on holidays with them. I have toured Britain, but most to Wales, not my own, but English friends' car. Racial harmony – this is up to us. If we make trouble with the neighbour, well . . . If anybody think about own respect, will not do anything wrong.' Faruk Miah, leaving Sylhet (in what is now Bangladesh) in 1962 and coming to London's East End, where for the next quarter of a century he worked as a machinist in the same Brick Lane sweatshop, was another motivated man:

> When I started to earn money in this country I didn't let my mum struggle. I used to send money every month. My governor was a good man, a Jew, and he helped me to learn my work and to make good money. I used to bring work home to earn extra money. When I joined the factory I used to earn £7 a week, and another £25 from overtime – because that was not taxed. That was more than enough for me. Rent was £1 a week and a packet of cigarettes, which I could manage for two days, was less than a pound. So I was able to make property in my country and spend money on my children . . .

Last of the quartet is Mohammed Manzoor, a senior clerk at the Karachi Development Authority who, a recently married man in his early thirties, arrived alone in England in the perishing cold of January 1963 and went straight to a scribbled address in Chesham, where he became one of thirty-two Pakistanis living in a seven-bedroom house. 'It was soon explained to my father,' relates his son Sarfraz, 'that they slept in shifts; some of the men worked nights and others during the day.' No TV in the house, but of an evening the men not working would 'gather together and listen [on an old twin-track tape recorder] to old Hindi film songs in the living room'. And: 'When they were feeling especially homesick they would take a coach to Southall where, on Sunday afternoons, the cinema would play Indian films. The theatre would be full of lonely Asian men who had travelled from across the south-east to see these films.'[7]

Indian immigrants – coming largely from the Punjab (mainly Sikh) and Gujarat (mainly Hindu) – had a somewhat less northern orientation than the Pakistanis, with the main concentrations being in Greater London, Birmingham, Wolverhampton, Coventry, Slough and Gravesend. Their background tended to be unskilled and their most common occupation as immigrants was as factory workers, though there was also a significant minority of the more professionally qualified. A near-contemporary study of Sikhs living in Gravesend ('Gravesindia') brings out their seemingly tireless work ethic ('Generally in the evening I was restless because we Jats are unhappy unless we are working hard – so I started this grocery delivery business in my spare time'); their strongly mutual-aid approach in response to increasing local hostility by the mid-1960s; and how, after whole families had arrived in the beat-the-ban flurry of the early 1960s, the Punjabi women were able to regain their traditional power, which in cultural terms meant a firm separation from the English, typified by daughters being made to keep their hair braided and legs covered. One Sikh, probably not living in Gravesend, was profiled in *The Times* in 1965 under the headline 'THE SIKH – 12 JOBS IN 18 MONTHS – IS A MANUAL MISFIT'. 'I cannot adjust to manual work,' confessed Mr S., who had just spent his first day as a bus conductor. 'He is very slim, and since he arrived has lost two stones in weight through work and worry,' noted the reporter. 'The biggest blow is that all the testimonials and certificates he has carefully kept from earliest schooldays are of no use in finding him a white-collar job here.' While, when it came to talking about England, 'his eyes clouded and his jaw tightened' as he spoke through clenched teeth: 'It hurts you deep inside. They sometimes call you a black bastard. Even the children do. I do not understand how children can speak like this. Where do they get it? Their parents? I pretend not to notice.'

Another Indian talking to the press that year was Chanan Kohli, a de facto community leader, holding down a white-collar job in a Loughborough engineering firm as well as running an Indian food shop:

> I am well educated. I have degrees in English and History. I have a good job but in this town there are Indian men who also have degrees and are qualified professional men. Because of a colour bar they cannot get a job they are qualified for, so they work as labourers or the equivalent in factories.
>
> This is all wrong. People must see that. There is also the other problem – the working man who is Indian or Pakistani. He is not well educated but is able to do a good day's work. Yet he is not getting equal rights. He has no hope of owning a home of his own. He has no security. He feels sure that he could lose his job any time because he is coloured and I know this fear is well founded. He is also afraid of physical violence. There have been incidents in this town, let me assure you of that.
>
> The police have been unable to help although they have always done their best. The trouble is that when one of our people reports something that has been done to him the police ask for names or a

description. Many of my people are not well educated and do not speak English well. They cannot give names or descriptions so the police are not able to do very much.

The *Loughborough Monitor*'s Tony Bushby asked him what he thought was the cause of the trouble:

> Simply accommodation. Our people are living in overcrowded houses. This is bad. White people criticise us for this and I do not blame them for doing so. It is wrong that people should live like that and our people are the first to agree, but they are forced into doing so . . .
>
> I do feel that the Town Council could help us in two ways, firstly by helping the coloured people get proper accommodation and secondly by helping us financially to get a centre of our own where we can mix with our own and cause no offence or trouble to anyone.
>
> There is a public house not far from here which a lot of my people once used. Now they go there no longer. The man behind the bar said one night, 'Get out, I am not washing any glasses that you black so-and-so's have drunk out of', so they went, causing no trouble.

Finally, what did he think of the latest restrictions (in the Labour government's White Paper that August) on immigration? 'I think they are right,' Kohli replied. 'The people of India and Pakistan have no idea what conditions are really like here. They think that it is a plentiful land. It is, but not for coloureds. They would all be better off back in their own countries.'[8]

So much comes back to that eternal gap between expectations and realities. It is true that, taken as a whole, Indian and Pakistani immigrants were significantly less disappointed by their experience than were West Indians, with the PEP report revealing that only 16 per cent of the latter group had found nothing disappointing, compared to 41 per cent 'among Asians and Indians'. 'I was a labourer in Pakistan and here I am a labourer too but the difference is that I am well paid,' said one. 'So I am quite happy.' Even so, in Lawrence's Nottingham sample, while 36 per cent of Pakistanis may have 'found Britain as expected', only 14 per cent of Indians did so – and a mere 3 per cent of West Indians, with instead 88 per cent recording their surprise at the prejudice and discrimination they had faced or witnessed. While across the three Nottingham groups, the oral testimony spoke for itself:

> Well at school we's told we's British and England is your mother country. So we thought we'd be treated nice here. So you get a shock when you come and they don't like coloureds.
>
> I thought the people of Britain would be good and full of affection. Some did treat us well at first but as more and more of us came here they grew less friendly and now most of them are against us.
>
> We heard there was a lot of wealth here and everything was automatic. But after working a full day of hard work we have to cook for ourselves. We thought English people were Sahibs but we found them just like common people.
>
> Some is good – but some is not. But the main trouble with English people is that they don't speak their mind broad enough. That's why I'm more with the Americans – they tell you straight. When an American is not with you he will tell you point blank and then you can keep out of his way. But an Englishman cannot do that. He may even offer you a cup of tea and not be with you. But some are real nasty in the way they live as well. If they offered me a cup of tea I wouldn't take it.
>
> They hypocrites.
>
> Some are good but some are rotten. But the majority you just don't know how you stand with them.
>
> People from the lower classes they're very hostile. But white collar people – whatever they feel they won't show it – they are very careful what they say. But you can still tell what their feelings are.
>
> Boy these English people are no good!
>
> The English people are not friendly. They are so cold. I think they are uncertain about themselves. They do not look you straight in the eye. When a man looks you in the eye you have a chance to find his favour. But when he looks down on you – he don't recognise you – you haven't a chance.
>
> They don't like us – well some are O.K. – but a lot of them are rotten.
>
> If you keep quiet you're all right. But if you don't you've had it.

One notable immigrant – leaving the Punjab in 1958 and settling in Wolverhampton, where he worked in a foundry – was the already middle-aged Madho Ram. Soon after arriving, he started a long, first-person poem (*Mera England da Safr*, 'My Passage to England'), eventually completed in 1970. It takes the reader through 'the newly arrived immigrant's new environment of working in a factory, his standing among his friends, new romance in the pubs, the family reunion and finally his emergence as a responsible and somewhat troubled Punjabi householder', notes Darshan Tatla. 'Its narrator weaves in a poignant and romantic tale about a man's separation from his wife and family in the Punjab as he sets out to Britain. In between, he tackles the themes of kin pressures to call other members of the family, particularly his in-laws, and his moral dilemmas.' Near the end, as he takes stock, come six unforgettable lines of lament:

> For my kids' future I have settled in England
> For such life I left my parents alone
> For money I had to forgo my morals
> What a bargain I had
> Oh god, my kids, how are they growing!
> Shorn of religion, without culture, and no sense of home![9]

There were, of course, the minimisers – among them, perhaps surprisingly, the great West Indian writer C. L. R. James, who since the 1930s had lived for many years first in the USA and then in England. 'What now astonishes me,' he declared publicly in late 1964, 'is the small amount of racial prejudice today in Britain and the exaggerated claims that are being made in describing it . . .'

> It is Smethwick and the special areas where there are special racial problems which continually fill the newspapers and are constantly on the lips of propagandists. The general impression that these give is quite false, so false that I have heard a person well established in public activity against racialism say that there is no difference between Birmingham, Warwickshire, and Birmingham, Alabama . . . But the situation in Britain bears no relation whatever, no possible relation, to what is taking place in the United States . . .

'There is one permanent and very British characteristic – empiricism,' he argued about the prevailing attitude to immigrants; and accordingly, 'I do not believe there is any danger of racialism in Britain becoming a pervasive feature in the democratic process.' Another minimiser was the sociologist Ruth Glass. 'There has been so much fallacious arithmetic of vast colour problems, alleged to be directly determined by the number of coloured people here, that this is now widely believed to be true,' she wrote to *The Times* in August 1965, protesting against the White Paper. 'In fact, though there are difficulties and tensions in some areas, coloured people have on the whole been accepted and dispersed in British society with remarkable speed.' Among historians, John Davis in his magisterial survey of London in the 1960s/1970s has emphasised, partly on the basis of fieldwork in Willesden and Brixton, that immigration was not most people's most pressing daily concern, even in two of the capital's main Black reception areas. 'Race could never shape the politics of inner London – let alone the rest of Britain – as it shaped the politics of South Africa or the US South,' he reflects. While as for Britain as a whole, a Gallup poll conducted during the March 1966 general election revealed not only that a mere 5 per cent of voters considered immigration to be the most urgent problem facing the country, but that even in specific 'colour problem' areas those voters prioritising the immigration issue peaked at 11 per cent in Birmingham. Davis, then, is surely right when he concludes that 'instead the race question was itself refracted by other issues'.[10]

And yet . . . It is hard, indeed impossible, to gainsay the cumulative evidence of considerable racial prejudice and discrimination in the Britain of the mid-1960s, culminating in PEP's devastating 1967 report. Where did it come from? Over the three or so decades after the war, two of the closest observers of race relations were the sociologist Michael Banton and the anthropologist Kenneth Little. For both, the explanation for the largely unfriendly and rejecting reception was essentially cultural – deep-lying cultural, with Banton fond of quoting from George Santayana's 1922 *Soliloquies in England*: 'The Englishman is no missionary, no conqueror. He prefers the country to the town and home to foreign parts. He is rather glad and relieved if only natives will remain natives and strangers strangers, and at a comfortable distance from himself.' He also quoted a more recent visitor, the American sociologist George C. Homans: 'Any society rests on a set of unstated assumptions, British society more than most: that is, indeed, its strength.' The crux here for Banton was the words 'unstated assumptions'; and at the core of his argument was that British society, more than most societies, relied on *implicit* norms of conduct. As a result: 'It is hard, very hard, for a stranger to become British. Feeling that the object is virtually unattainable, and in any case scarcely desirable, Britons do not encourage him to try.' This, he reckoned, applied in private relations even to an Englishman of theoretically liberal assumptions about equality of treatment (for instance, in relation to employment), such was that Englishman's – and presumably Englishwoman's as well – desire to avoid embarrassment caused by misunderstanding:

> The Englishman cannot be sure that the coloured man will recognise or accept the former's intention of extending to him only a limited acceptance. He cannot be sure, if he is kind to a colonial immigrant, whether that man will appreciate the limits of his gesture and not take advantage of his kindness. He does not want to be suddenly confronted with an inordinate demand for help, financial or otherwise, which is all too possible when the immigrants have such difficulty in finding work and housing. Consequently, where he suspects that the coloured man may not be familiar with the social norms to which he is accustomed, the Briton is inclined to refrain from entering into relations with him.

'British behaviour towards coloured people,' concluded Banton, 'is characterized not by aggressiveness but by avoidance of them in relationships which might get out of hand. It is a response not to dark skin colour as a biological fact but to its social significance.'

The so-called 'stranger hypothesis' also found support from Little, while throwing in a twist of social class. In a 1967 overview for the American journal *Dædalus*, he spent several pages describing the habits and customs of Asian and West Indian immigrants 'because', he explained, 'from the local people's point of view these immigrants are not "British"':

> Not only their racial appearance but their different styles of life, dress, and behavior mark them as foreigners. For many British

> people, 'foreigner' denotes a category of person who has no place in one's own society. Although he is not to be treated with hostility, it is considered best to regard him with suspicion and to keep out of his way. This aversion to and avoidance of outsiders does not operate only in relation to colored immigrants. In recent years, xenophobia has included opposition to Polish, Italian, and other Europeans brought into the United Kingdom to work under government schemes . . . Although hostility is displayed toward the colored immigrant, almost identical complaints have been made at various times about the Jews and even about the Welsh, the Scots, and the Irish. In each case there has been an unfavourable stereotype of the 'intruders'; the only difference is that the colored individual apparently represents the furthest removed type of stranger. The darker the color, the more likely the exclusion.

Later, he elaborated on the cultural divergence – a divergence, he would probably have conceded, based on perception as well as reality:

> Immigrant individuals and families have entered a society with standards of life and education materially and technically much in advance of their own. Adaptation is also rendered difficult by the different sets of expectations on both sides and by the conflict between much of the newcomers' behavior and the bourgeois values of the host society. The latter include such things as a settled home life based on legal marriage, a degree of companionship between man and wife, an absence of extramarital relations, a tidy house, punctuality in personal as well as business dealings, and restraint and impersonality in most social relationships outside the sphere of kinship and close friendship. Their lack of conformity to these norms marks immigrants as foreigners, and their darker complexion and other physical characteristics enhance their unlikeness.

While as for class, added Little, 'most of the recent immigrants lack education, work in manual and unskilled occupations, and occupy the more dilapidated and less respectable parts of the town – all criteria, in British eyes, of low social status'.[11]

This is not to deny that there *could* be a logical, hard-headed element in the mix. A good example is the contrast between Bradford and Birmingham: both of them cities with a fast-growing immigrant presence, but in Bradford far less palpable prejudice, helped by considerably less pressure on housing. While in general there were the arguments, starting to be heard increasingly, about pressure on wages and pressure on public services, the latter often involving some tenuous assumptions about future immigrant numbers. Yet ultimately, we are not talking about reason, certainly not reason alone. For one historian, Kieran Connell (author of *Multicultural Britain*, scoring highly for its archivally driven, non-London focus), an emblematic moment was the television interview in 1965 between an ATV reporter (Kenneth Hill) and an unnamed shopkeeper ('white, middle-aged, with a thin face, thick-rimmed spectacles and black hair slicked back') in Birmingham's immigrant-rich Balsall Heath area. How had he felt when he first noticed immigrants arriving?

> Prejudiced against them coming in to the country.
>
> You didn't warm to them? – No, I did not.
>
> Why not? – Well I don't hold with coloured people coming into this country and taking jobs off our own countrypeople . . .
>
> What about your shop, are they good for business here? – Oh, they're good for business, they spend money, they don't quibble over the price or anything like that.
>
> And how do you correlate that with your feelings . . . you're prejudiced against them and yet you take money off them . . . ? – Well you have to live with the problem don't you . . . the quicker they move out of this district the better . . . it will take the degrade out of Balsall Heath, won't it, because it's got a bad name at the moment. When you speak to someone and they ask you where you come from and you say 'Balsall Heath', they say 'Oh, blackie district'.
>
> Yes . . . is it only the immigrants . . . I mean, are there other problems, there's vice is there not? – There's plenty of vice, oh yes, lots of vice. You can see them walking down here every day . . . soliciting.
>
> And the vice, has this got anything to do with the immigrants do you think? – I should imagine so, yes. They attract it.

'With his emphasis on the arrival of black and Asian immigrants as the chief cause of the problems that face the area, and his hope that the immigrant population would one day be forced out – no matter what the economic cost to his own livelihood – his was in many ways,' Connell reflects about the shopkeeper, 'a textbook example of the perverse, hypocritical logic of racism as it habitually functioned in the dilapidated, inner-city geographies of 1960s Britain.'

Was there yet a culture of loss negatively affecting race relations, especially in areas where the painful and even cruel process of de-industrialisation was by now under way? Over the coming decades, the incomparable chronicler of that culture would be Jeremy Seabrook, especially once he got to know Blackburn in the late 1960s; while as Clair Wills has noted about the letters of support that flooded into Enoch Powell's office after his 'rivers of blood' speech in April 1968, 'the overwhelming focus was on cultural rather than economic losses', with very many of the writers going out of their way to insist that they were not 'racialist' and did not believe that non-white races were biologically inferior. 'Instead they feared for British culture and traditions which could not survive under the pressure of so many newcomers, who brought with them alien ways of behaving.' The culture of loss would have a long, long lifespan, still seemingly ('I Want My Country Back') far from exhausted. 'Watching the televised debate, I realised why Nick Clegg has difficulty with a 70-year-old like me who grew up in Hackney in the 1950s,' Edward Thomas wrote to the *Guardian* after a duel in 2014 between the Lib Dem leader and UKIP's Nigel Farage about the European Union:

> There the local population lived contentedly enough in a mono-cultural society in a cockney setting reflected by Broadway market round the corner, cinemas in Mare Street and a straightforward English way of life.
>
> Mr Clegg made great play of how he wants us to live in the present rather than the past. The problem is that the elements he cited in his wish were all foisted on us. We never asked for mass immigration. We never asked for multiculturalism. We never asked for diversity . . . I do not want mass immigration. I do not want multiculturalism. I do not want diversity . . .

'Rather,' Thomas ended, 'I wish to be allowed to continue to live my life immersed in my own culture, with all its foibles and its faults as well as its joys, and not immersed in a melting pot of other people's cultures, no matter how beneficial that is perceived to be for my own culture.'[12]

During summer 1966 a study was made of five schools in Handsworth – that part of Birmingham where more than one-third of the city's 'coloured school leavers' came from. Focusing equally on boys and girls, it found that whereas 81 per cent of the 'coloured students' wanted to stay in school for an extra year, only 36 per cent of the 'English students' wanted to do so; while as for wanting to go on to further education, the contrast was an even sharper 10 per cent to 1 per cent. A wholly different story, though, when it came to what the school leavers then *actually* found themselves doing:

	'English boys' (%)	*'Coloured boys'* (%)
'Skilled occupations'	7	0
Jobs in 'recognised skilled crafts'	50	27
Unskilled jobs in factories	43	72

Malorie Blackman's father was as aware as anyone of the potential mismatch between aspiration and reality, of indeed the fixed odds at work. Joe and Ruby had come from Barbados, settling initially in Clapham and later in Beckenham; he drove buses (though back home he had been a master craftsman carpenter), she worked in a factory as a machinist; Malorie, their third child, was born in 1962; and he would get angry if, even at an early age, she spoke with a Bajan accent or used Bajan idioms: '"Speak proper English," he would say. "The only way you'll get anywhere in this country is if you speak proper English."' Blackman subsequently came to regret the larger denial of her heritage ('All requests for stories from and about Barbados were waved aside by both my parents . . . It feels like a part of me has been lost for good'), while fully accepting that they had acted with the best of intentions. 'My dad used to say that as a Black person in the UK, I'd have to work twice as hard and know twice as much to get half as far.' And, she reflected in 2022: 'It's the same for so many people from an immigrant background or immigrant heritage. There's an innate sense that no one is going to give us anything so we must work hard and expend blood, sweat and tears to set foot on life's ladder.'[13]

14
Absolutely Nothing Old Hat

July 1966, a warm summer's evening and almost the end of term at the Leys School in Cambridge, as 'our very own homegrown school "pop" group, harmlessly enough named "The Saints",' gave a concert on the cricket field and seventeen-year-old Christopher Hitchens had a belated epiphany:

> Boys and masters sat or stood as they would have done for a cricket match, the more senior in comfy seats in the pavilion, the others on benches, the rest on the grass. After taking us through a fairly tame Buddy Holly-style repertoire, the respectable 'Saints' switched to a passably potent and twanging version of 'House of the Rising Sun.' The amplifiers must have been good and the night was soft and still. At any rate, the sound must have carried because very suddenly, and very quietly, the cricket ground of our exclusive private school was overrun by a huge crowd of boys (and even girls) from the town. They had heard the strains of rock, even of mild rock, and they knew about Eric Burdon and The Animals, and they also knew by now that there was nothing much their parents or the police could do about it, or about them. They crossed a social and geographic boundary that they had never transgressed before, and suddenly found it to be delightfully easy. Nonetheless, they were civil and quiet and curious, which meant that even my most awful contemporaries were embarrassingly polite and broadminded in return (as well as nervously aware of being surprised and outnumbered). There was even some mild fraternization before the school authorities saw the way things might go and pulled the plugs that had

animated the drums and guitars. Then, but too late, the traditional police constables made their appearance.

As one who had already been employing the town against the school for all kinds of private and public purposes, I was still rather slow to see what had just happened to old Britain in front of my very eyes. The first thought I had was derived from my traditional and classical half: surely this was like those other 'animals' of the forest who had been shyly drawn to sit, forgetting their own wildness, when Orpheus began to pluck his lute? It was quite some while later that I thought, no, you sentimental fool, what you were seeing, and hearing, was the opening of 'The Sixties.'[1]

Ah yes, 'The Sixties' . . . Undeniably, Mr Jones, something was happening by the middle years of that much-mythologised decade – something far from confined to sex and drugs and rock 'n' roll. A freewheelin' moment demands a freewheelin', mid-sixties playlist.

Multi-flavoured Golden Wonder crisps displacing Smith's plain (farewell those grudging portions of salt wrapped in blue wax paper); farewell, too, to watch committees, staunch local guardians of public morality; British Midland Airways formed to take Brummies on package holidays abroad; some half a million women on the Pill ('This makes me the boss,' nineteen-year-old girl in Newcastle with Cathy McGowan hairstyle); divorce rates increasing (23,900 divorces in England and Wales in 1960; 37,800 in 1965), central heating increasing, the rise of the 'patio' garden (no need now to grow fruit and veg); Carnaby Street becoming iconic Carnaby Street, poised to be London's second-most-visited tourist attraction after Buckingham Palace; a majority approving of professional sport on Sundays, also of other places of entertainment having the same hours as on weekdays; Anglican communicants down from 2.6 million in 1960 to 2.3 million in 1965; one-third of new marriages now civil marriages; 'a kind of heaven in the sheer precision of a geometric Vidal Sassoon haircut and a minimalist Mary Quant striped gym slip' (Fiona MacCarthy); at an alternative bookshop in Nottingham, the cat called Chairman Miaow; rising illegitimacy rates (70,000 illegitimate babies born in 1967); 8.4 million women in employment by 1965 (34.6 per cent of total working population), with married women as proportion of female workforce reaching 54 per cent (41 per cent back in 1950); 1964 'the best year for 45 rpm singles ever', before soon afterwards 'stereo became the norm, and the 33 long player the hot format' (Jon Savage); infant baptisms on a steadily downwards trend; an NOP survey in 1965 revealing that almost three-quarters of the public, including even a majority of Catholics, wished to see abortion legal in at least some cases; Richard West (1965) on the rise and rise, especially in northern cities, of 'the "big clubs," often converted cinemas, where a thousand or more people gather to drink, watch strip-tease and listen to ripe comedians'; Mervyn Jones (1966) on how 'long hair [on men] now found among all social classes', albeit 'rather more in evidence in the streets of Bermondsey than of Mayfair'; Jane Ridley (1965) on 'Britain Eats Foreign' ('In the supermarkets, the delicatessen counter now stocks sausage from a dozen countries, big jars of black olives, and dishes of ready-mixed salad niçoise . . . Even the food department in Woolworths now sells several dozen kinds of Continental sausage and cheese, while the corner grocer offers salami as well as pork sausage-meat, tinned guavas as well as pineapple . . .'); both Gallup and NOP finding in autumn 1965 almost two-thirds of adults approving the decriminalisation of homosexual acts between consenting adults; a 1966 survey conducted among 200 buyers for fashion stores finding that the demand was for 'lighter colours, simpler styles, unbroken lines', while what they did not want were 'frumpish styles, bows and frills, drapes, sleeveless dresses and dull, old-fashioned colours'; Church of England confirmations per 1,000 of population aged twelve to twenty dropping from 24.7 in 1962 to 17.7 by 1967 (male), from 36.7 to 27.6 (female); an NOP survey in 1965 showing that 88 per cent agreed that it was better for a child to live with one divorced parent than with two unhappily married parents, that 80 per cent agreed that 'divorce should always be possible if both husband and wife want it,' and that 62 per cent did *not* agree that 'nobody should be able to get a divorce if they have children under 16'; the number of known heroin addicts rising from 62 in 1958 to 670 by 1966; in Cardiff in 1967, cannabis involved in all but one of fifty-five court cases for drug offences, with the accused far likelier to be shop assistants than students; no car more iconic of modernity than the Mini Cooper; newspapers by 1966 starting to send reporters to football matches to report on crowd behaviour, not just the actual game; 'Nobody wants billiard tables these days' (1965 headline in *Pontefract and Castleford Express*); the increasing retail muscle of 'the C2 commuters who drink lager instead of beer, smoke tipped instead of plain, eat plain chocolate instead of milk'; tufted carpet synonymous with Cyril Lord; cinema admissions in 1965 less than half those in 1958, TV licences up to 13.5 million (4.6 million in 1955); pubs reluctantly installing fruit machines; pubs less reluctantly rebranding themselves with illuminated Perspex signs; the Walker Jubilee Club, a working men's club in Newcastle, acclaimed as 'one of the most swinging and scintillating places in the Britain of the Sixties' after a refurbishment involving a 'new look of gloss and glamour, style and sophistication'; Ian Jack's first sweetcorn ('at a Reo Stakis steakhouse in Ingram Street, Glasgow, 1966 – served deep-fried (of course) as part of Chicken Maryland'); the remorseless decline of the hat (going going gone the bowler, the homburg, the derby, the cloth cap); Deborah Hough (later Moggach) at 'achingly hip and trendy' Camden School ('at lunchtime we danced in the hall to the latest Beatles records and ate yoghurt, which seemed very cutting edge'); Jimmy Hill's Sky-Blue revolution at Coventry City (own radio station, branded trains to away matches, hospitality suites, more seats, less standing); heyday of the Mod ('What I loved about the Mods was the fact that they were largely working-class kids, who a generation previously would have been whacked around the head for worrying about how their hair looked' – Paul Smith, 2024); lights coming on at the end of the Saturday morning ABC Minors session at the Regent cinema in Crosby, Liverpool – mad rush for the exit, even as National Anthem starting – door barred by ex-servicemen demanding respect ('I fought in the war for the likes of you lot') – Ringo-style retort from massed chorus of youthful voices ('I bet you're sorry you won!'); AA patrols no longer required to salute; members of the Privy Council going to normal meetings at Buckingham Palace no longer required to wear morning dress; closure in 1966 of the last branch of Boots Booklovers Library, its decline attributed to 'a new generation of readers who would not choose to be called "Booklovers"'; in 1966 in the top year of a primary school, only one child in a class of about thirty saying he knew his local parson; 'I used to enjoy my regular visit to the cinema but lately the films have been full of sex and violence – all with X-certificates' (1966 letter to *News of the World* from Mrs Ada Johnson, OAP in Manchester); opening in 1965 of Danish Food Centre in Manchester; a fish-and-chips shop in Horsham, Sussex, introducing small wooden forks in early 1966 and declaring that 'the days of eating chips with fingers out of paper bags are over'; first sighting that summer of badges with slogans like 'Tolkien is Hobbit-forming' and 'Gandalf for President' and 'Frodo Lives'; the fireplace, especially in suburban homes, 'removed, boarded up or simply ignored and the TV moved to centre stage'; allotment plots in England and Wales down by 1964 to 729,000 (1.3 million at the end of the war); picture rails, seen as dust traps, removed en masse from Victorian and Edwardian houses; Anthony Sampson's 1965 assessment of how 'between the leisurely atmosphere of Ascot, with its careful status distinctions between Royal Enclosure, Silver Ring and Heath, and the noise, fumes and thousands of classless young men in sweaters and girls in tight trousers at Brands Hatch, there is the gulf of a social revolution'; by 1967, on an average Sunday, only 15 per cent of the English attending religious worship; Boots from 1965 at last consenting to sell condoms; 'They're getting shorter, shorter and shorter – all eyes will be rivetted on the legs and feet' (*News of the World*, fashion page headline, March 1965); the City just starting to relax (soft colours and striped shirts on the floor of the Stock Exchange, a few women in trousers, first-name usage); in 1965 at Birmingham University, Richard Hoggart's eye-opening experience at the reception desk of the campus's health centre ('I noticed a box of what looked like packeted pills on the right-hand side. Were those packets of The Pill, which I'd heard of but never seen? Yes, said the nurse-receptionist. Are they available to anyone? Not quite; they have to be having a serious relationship. How do you discover it's serious? We take their word for it . . .'); vandalised Cardiff hotel after 1965 Wales–England rugby match (chandeliers ripped down, 5,000 glasses broken, male striptease, people urinating in the lounge); Lord Chamberlain's Office struggling to hold the line over theatre censorship; recorded crime increasing by 121 per cent between 1957 and 1967; the man from the Pru no longer calling weekly to collect payments; women working at the Pru just about allowed to wear trousers, so long as with matching jackets; 'one girl was fucked by 38 blokes in her fortnight' (Butlins worker talking to journalist Paul Ferris in 1966); Turkish baths ('the staff mostly turn a blind eye to much of the midnight prowling'), news cinemas ('it is a common practice for queer customers to get up frequently and go to the lavatory'), big railway stations ('the main termini on the Southern Region are by far the most popular'), the part of Hampstead Heath near the Bull and Bush ('even on a January night with snow falling a few hardy habitues can be seen searching for alfresco partners') – all of them integral features of London's gay scene; Fitzrovia's Greek restaurants daring to put tables on the pavement; arrival of open-plan offices (theoretically less hierarchical); arrival, too, of the hot drinks vending machine, retreat of the tea trolley, erosion of the fixed tea break; *Où Est Le Garlic?* (title of Len Deighton cookbook, 1965); 'Do you see lesbians in Battersea? – Oh yes, there's lots in Battersea now' (Nell Dunn interviewing factory worker Kathy Collier, 1964); cheekbones 'highlighted', eyes 'blackened', lips 'whitened', curls 'ironed, often singed' (Anne Sebba, remembering the 'dolly birds'); membership of Methodist youth clubs down from peak of 114,000 in 1962 to under 90,000 three years later; 'I wanted to have my hair as long as I could get away with and used to dread the inevitable day, just as my hair was just growing nicely over my collar, when Dad would issue his terrible command that I had to get it cut' (Ian Mole, Sunderland); all-figure codes replacing in 1965 the venerable mixed telephone numbers, most famously Scotland Yard's WHItehall 1212; 'emboldened by photographs of the new model Twiggy, one evening, secretly, I shortened all my skirts' (Alexandra Pringle, born 1953); at an Ipswich state secondary school in summer 1965, 'everyone laughed so much that he had to stop talking' (after the head telling his 800 boys and 600 girls that, following 'complaints from influential people about pupils walking hand-in-hand while wearing the school uniform', the practice was henceforth banned); and Virginia Ironside half a century later remembering the Sixties as 'an endless round of miserable promiscuity', when as a young woman living in London and writing about pop music 'it often seemed easier and, believe it or not, more polite, to sleep with a man than to chuck him out of your flat'.[2]

Explanations of the phenomenon that was (or was not) 'the Sixties' often prioritise those terrible twins, the Pill and youth culture. Yet, in part because of problems of access for much of the decade, the fact was that a survey in 1970 of single women found that only 9 per cent had ever used the Pill; while despite the obvious and striking circumstantial evidence relating to Britain's youth – by 1965, over 7 million teenagers in England and Wales, compared to less than 6 million in 1955; end of National Service; hourly rate of pay for juveniles in manufacturing industries increasing by 77 per cent between 1956 and 1966, compared to 62 per cent for adult male workers; student numbers in full-time higher education rising from 82,000 in 1954 to 118,000 in 1962 to 457,000 by 1970 – it is crystal clear in retrospect that something was under way of far more fundamental importance than youth culture, for all its increasingly high visibility. Across demographics, and notwithstanding the necessary qualifiers about significant and largely underestimated pockets of poverty, the defining fact of the decade was not just affluence, but an affluence ever more focused on domestic consumption. The bald figures of possession (whether owned or rented) tell the overwhelming story:

Percentage of households	*1955*	*1975*
TV	35	96
Refrigerator	8	85
Washing machine	18	70
Telephone	19	52

'Our highly industrialised society is geared to the ever-growing production of a vast range of consumer goods, most of which help to simplify domestic management,' reflected Alva Myrdal and Viola Klein in 1966 as they prepared a new edition of *Women's Two Roles*. 'At the same time, they act as a spur for married women to seek gainful employment in order to increase the family income and be able to purchase these consumer goods.' It was, in short, 'a spiral effect': 'More household gadgets set more women free for employment, and more wives in paid employment increase the need – and provide the cash – for more and better domestic appliances.' Can one, though, go further? 'There is no doubt,' argues one historian (Jeffrey Weeks, in his level-headed account of what he calls 'the permissive moment'), that 'the prolonged [economic] boom depended in part upon a switch in moral attitudes away from traditional bourgeois virtues of self-denial and saving ("prudence") towards a compulsion to spend'. 'And', he adds, 'these general moral characteristics – "saving", "spending" – have for long held strong sexual connotations.' John Fowles might well have agreed, as in September 1964 he pondered why, despite the success of *The Collector* at last making him his own master, he was failing to feel any happier:

> These last two or three years have seen a strong conservative-fascist-selfish swing in the West; the decline of the intellectual approach to life and the rise of the visual; the predominance of what its defenders call an amoral (healthily free), pragmatic attitude to living – enjoy it while you can, buy as many pleasures as the affluent society and you yourself can afford – and its attackers call immoral (blindly uncommitted to anything but selfishness). So I feel what many must have felt in the 1930s, a being swept on in the direction I do not want to go.

'The usual metaphor is of being swept in a sea-current,' he went on, before a presumably unconscious nod to the bard of Minnesota: 'But this is more like a current of wind. I walk one way, and the world blows the other.'[3]

So what exactly *was* blowing in the wind? Here, a key insight comes from another historian, Callum Brown, who in his work over several decades, largely on religion and secularisation, has very helpfully emphasised, not least in relation to 'the Sixties', the crucial importance of 'discourse' – or, in other words, changes in cultural experiences and representations, neatly summed up by Brown as a 'turn to the self', which were over and above everyday material change or continuity.[4]

But before turning to some of the main sites of discourse, and their changing message and signals during the decade, a couple of almost random examples. The first derives from a study of the representation of women and girls in post-war secondary school English course books. 'The 1960s saw the emergence of a change in style,' notes Eleanor Wright. 'Readings became longer and language exercises became fewer. Pictures which had been infrequent and for ornamental purposes became an integral part of the material; use was made of a wider range of material including writing from the social sciences, children's writing and contemporary writing for children instead of or in addition to the classics of English letters; material was organised on a thematic basis.' Altogether, she continues, it was a trend which 'reflected a change from prescription to encouragement; from transmission of knowledge to development of understanding; from a detached academic style with emphasis on correctness to a direct energetic style whose aim was to involve children in personal language use'. The other example utilises pioneering analysis by Abigail Wills of the detailed progress reports written on the 795 teenage male delinquents who passed through the High Beech probation home in Nutfield, Surrey, between 1950 and 1970:

> In the 1950s, the project of reforming male delinquents centred around the notion of *mens sana in corpore sano* (a healthy mind in a healthy body), which involved ideals such as strength of character, emotional independence, restrained heterosexuality and disciplined work ethic. These ideals were underlain by a holistic understanding of society: the task of reform was conceived in terms of the reclamation of delinquents 'for the nation'. As the 1960s progressed, the project of reform did not alter in its fundamentals. Self-control, fortitude and hard work remained the three principal facets of the successfully reformed character. However, the contours of normative masculinity were softened considerably. Ideals of reform were recast within a vision of national society that was fragmented and problematic; reform came increasingly to be understood primarily in terms of its benefit to the individual.

In these progress reports, she further explains, 'the 1960s saw a significant increase in the positive use of terms associated with a more "emotionally attuned" masculinity, such as "friendly", "sensitive", "considerate" and "thoughtful"'. And, most daringly, 'there was also a greater acceptance and understanding of the need that some boys had for open demonstrations of affection'.

In the national press, the stormtroopers pointing the way to a more socially liberal future – and acclimatising their readers to the possibilities of that future – comprised a quartet of female journalists. 'In those early years (she was 40 in 1968) she wasn't a feminist, but she cleverly and with great charm removed enough bars of the gilded cage so that those who came after her could slip through more easily,' recalled Yvonne Roberts many years later about the *Observer*'s justly celebrated columnist Katharine Whitehorn. 'It wasn't just that she depicted a different kind of woman, gin drinking, "cups in the study, books in the kitchen", she also demonstrated how a woman working alone in a sea of men could make them think again. Where exactly is a woman's place?' Across in the *Guardian*, the regular 'Mainly for Women' page – nicely described by Fiona MacCarthy as 'an onslaught on old-time suburban female values from within' – owed almost everything to Mary Stott's editorial drive as she commandeered a wide range of women's voices, often youthful, often unknown. 'You are in mid-flight – the generation trying to conquer the "back-to-work" problems', she semi-apologised in 1962 to the middle-aged Phyllis Willmott, explaining why she had turned her down for a particular piece, in favour of someone much younger. 'Miss Jones is at the beginning of her career, which she finds enthralling, and also is contemplating matrimony. It seems to me that the attitudes of *her* generation are the most interesting and important of all.' Stott was probably the inspiration for Susanne Puddefoot, from March 1966 the first editor of the Women's Page in *The Times* where (in her obituarist's words) 'she enlivened the familiar home, food, beauty and fashion elements with hard-hitting, campaigning features on economic equality, immigration, medicine, nutrition, crime, marriage and many other topics where women needed a voice'. 'Women in our society are the victims of frightening ambivalence,' she herself declared in April 1967, introducing a Women's Page special for Budget Day. 'At once over- and under-valued, worshipped and feared, used and discounted, we are told by husbands and employers alike that we are a luxury ill-afforded without the sacrifice of our income and our independence to their will. Yet truly the woman always pays.' This was not typical *Times* fodder. The fourth of the quartet was, inevitably, the *Daily Mirror*'s Marjorie Proops. Her absolute heyday (in the form of her 'Dear Marje' column) was still to come, but already in the mid-sixties she was making waves. 'Nine out of ten women,' she announced, 'would rather have a man who would surreptitiously caress their thighs under a night-club table than a good rugged chap who'll slap them heartily on the back at a Saturday football game – even though they suspect that their night-clubber will be caressing another girl tomorrow and the good rugged chap would never look at any other girl.' The article was headed 'But then – men simply do not understand what it is about a man that appeals to a woman'; a reader (a married woman in Altrincham who acted as a voluntary youth worker) complained to the Press Council that this gave young people wholly the wrong impression about normal standards of behaviour; and the Press Council in early 1967 rejected her complaint.[5]

Among magazines, two titles arguably stand out, both of them creations of the mid-sixties. *Jackie* was launched by D. C. Thomson in January 1964; its first editor was Gordon Small, remembered as 'a bearded, Scottish, former RAF aero engine fitter who had a paternal concern for the "wee lassies"'; and it has a fair claim (albeit competing with *Honey*) to be the first modern teen girl magazine, or in Zoe Williams's words 'the first magazine explicitly to recognise youth as a distinct state, girls as something other than smaller versions of their mothers'. What was also pioneering was not so much its treatment of sex as such – the agony advice column seldom if ever broached issues more risqué than the etiquette of kissing – but rather what Callum Brown has termed 'the disappearance [compared to *Boyfriend*, 1960–65] of discourses on domesticity, separate spheres, and women's limited career ambitions': 'The home hardly featured at all in the strips. Discourses on feminine identity were now conveyed by everything other than family, domestic routine, virtue, religion or "respectability."' From March 1965 its adult counterpart was surely IPC's *Nova*. 'Our new kind of woman has a wide range of interests, an enquiring mind and an independent outlook – not to mention that her numbers are multiplying,' declared early publicity material; in 1992, long after it had folded and almost become a lost legend, Linda Grant would remember fondly how its 'flamboyant, audacious coverlines announced the existence of male impotence, the sexual needs of widows, homosexuality and abortion long before they were legalised, bigamy, racism – every issue that the social legislation of the period was about to liberalise, and many, such as pornography, compulsive eating and breast implants, that were not discussed until a decade later'; while at the time, in 1967, Stuart Hall at the Centre for Contemporary Cultural Studies offered a rather more critical perspective into how this 'new, emancipated, fashionable, sophisticated, trendy' magazine fitted into what he called 'this loosening up of social attitudes', an analysis starting with *Nova*'s undeniably striking fashion spreads:

> The clothes are extremely expensive, though a mixture of Courrèges and Quant rather than Dior, but every now and then, just to establish the link, the accessory will be militantly inexpensive and fiercely pop. Interspersed with these glossy layouts are articles, sometimes of a serious purpose – serious in that manner which is part of the new journalism, tough without being too committed, sceptical, hard-hitting but somehow neutral in stance: but the *Nova* message is carried in full spate, and quite unambiguously, 'in the margins'. The women imaged in its pages are liberated all right, but their liberation is a limited affair – they have entered the world of men (and, to judge by *Nova*'s readers, the men have entered theirs), but only as the most clued-up, switched-on consumption objects of all.

What about men's magazines themselves? *King* (1964), *Penthouse* (1965), *Mayfair* (1966) – all hit the top shelves in these years, with *Penthouse* introducing itself through a million mailshots featuring naked women. Arguably, very arguably, liberating in its way for men; but although these magazines talked a good game when it came to female emancipation – *Mayfair*'s first cover story celebrating a 'new breed' of 'sexual suffragettes' eager 'to go to bed with whom they want, whenever they want' – it was always clear in the new pornography where ultimately the power lay. 'I could never think of myself as being equal to men,' confessed one of *Penthouse*'s earliest 'Pets', Bambi Lynn-Davies. 'A girl naturally hasn't the rights that a man has and wouldn't be happy if she did. A man earns his place in the world and his aggressiveness and responsibilities put him into a different category altogether . . . Girls who work competitively with men because of a particular ambition – not out of necessity – are terribly unhappy. Their ambition is a sort of escapism; a kind of fleeing from life and the natural responsibilities of their sex. Women in government are the worst offenders . . .'[6]

Which new books peculiarly caught 'the liberal hour' and made a significant impact? Leaving aside Margaret Drabble's *The Millstone*, four candidates (inevitably among others) have particularly strong claims. Containing the first detailed description of sex to appear in the Welsh language – sex, to boot, between a minister and a member of his congregation (a middle-aged woman whose mother lies dying upstairs) – John Rowland's 1965 novel *Ienctid yw 'Mhechod* (*Youth Is My Sin*) caused Welsh dovecots to flutter in a way reminding many of the more famous *Lady Chatterley* controversy five years before; then, in autumn 1966, the vain legal attempt by the Tory MP and moral diehard Sir Cyril Black to prevent the UK distribution of Hubert Selby Jr's allegedly obscene novel *Last Exit to Brooklyn* only had the effect of helping to normalise the literature of drug-taking, sexual transgression, etc; and early in 1967 R. D. Laing's Penguin Original, *The Politics of Experience*, was described by David Storey as conveying a view of society in which the 'really sick' were 'the bank managers, the schoolteachers, the parents, the wielders of power, the working class, the bourgeoisie, the army, the one-uppers: those, that is, who feel obliged to make it work and even derive advantage from it; those who are merely a function of the roles they play and little else', with Storey adding admiringly that Laing himself was 'the only polemicist of any substance writing in this country at the moment'. The fourth book had appeared (in 1964) before any of the other three. This was *Generation X*: a book largely comprising interviews with notably eloquent, outspoken teenagers, and compiled by Jane Deverson and Charles Hamblett (young and middle-aged journalists respectively), that for a few years enjoyed a considerable vogue as it circulated around sixth-form rooms and elsewhere, before disappearing almost entirely. 'Old people are ridiculous, anyway, so phoney, everything they do is false,' declared one interviewee. Another reported on how 'Sheila at school slept with her boyfriend and everyone looked up to her, there's a sort of mystique to it.' While according to the most disenchanted of them all: 'I find my parents humdrum and I feel I've grown out of their ways and the ones of small-town existence. I don't think any two people can really get on together in a state of permanent legal bondage. My ideal of a woman comes from poetry and films and is therefore unreal and rather infantile. Blame it on education.'[7]

Across the cultural range in these mid-sixties years, the sense of an opening up, of new possibilities, was palpable. In the theatre, the explicit treatment of homosexuality in John Osborne's *A Patriot for Me* provoking in summer 1965 a much-publicised confrontation between the playwright and the Lord Chamberlain (Lord Cobbold), resulting in a significant erosion of the latter's authority to continue censoring theatrical productions; V. S. Pritchett the same summer describing Frank Marcus's *The Killing of Sister George* as 'a breath of fresh air in the West End'; three commercially successful films – *The Knack . . . and How to Get It* (1965), *Alfie* (1966), *Georgy Girl* (1966) – all helping to cement and largely celebrate an image of permissive, 'swinging' London; Lindsay Anderson's *The White Bus* (1967), largely shot in Salford in October 1965 and based on a short story by Shelagh Delaney, representing (in Selina Todd's words) 'those in authority as out of touch with most people's lives', as 'speeches by civic leaders and scenes of hymn singing were juxtaposed with young people dancing on desks in offices, of the main character screaming'; few boutiques more influential, more celebrated, more Jagger-endorsed than Granny Takes a Trip, opening on the King's Road in 1966; that autumn, two years after Alan Blaikley and Ken Howard had sourced the title for the Honeycombs' hit 'Have I The Right?' from the closing paragraph of the classic lesbian novel *The Well of Loneliness* ('Acknowledge us, oh God, before the whole world. Give us also the right to our existence!'), the same songwriting duo opting for a certain direct simplicity for the new, distinctly suggestive Dave Dee, Dozy, Beaky, Mick & Tich number, 'Bend It'; Dusty Springfield's voice, remembered by Ali Smith as 'a combination of energised, exhilarated, sure and insecure'; *Disc & Music Echo*'s Penny Valentine ('Britain's most influential reviewer of new pop singles . . . lived up to the dolly-bird perfection of her improbably glamorous byline . . . loved soul music, and campaigned on behalf of the likes of Aretha Franklin and Marvin Gaye when they were still on the margins of popularity . . . she was writing for the kids who bought and danced to the records, not for Tin Pan Alley . . . probably the first woman to write about pop music as though it really mattered'), as recalled by Richard Williams; old-style, romance-oriented, boy-girl lyrics in the Beatles canon dropping from 83 per cent of their 1965 output to 40 per cent in 1966 and only 5 per cent in 1967; a new social commentary edge to the Stones' lyrics, whether reacting to America-style consumerism ('Satisfaction', 'Get Off of My Cloud') or hypocritical anti-drugs messages ('Mother's Little Helper') or sneering at ostentatiously-slumming-it bluebloods ('19th Nervous Breakdown', 'Under My Thumb'); edge, too, but different, to their 'Let's Spend the Night Together', entering the charts in early 1967; and as if in conscious, salutary riposte, a seventeen-year-old girl having her say a few weeks later in *Tit-Bits*: 'When will the older generation stop ramming sex down teenagers' throats? First it was our clothes, particularly miniskirts, that were disgusting. Now it's our pop songs. I don't run out for a couple of pep pills or dive into bed with anybody just because a song mentions this. Half the time I don't even hear the words of a song, let alone worry about how immoral they are.' 'To which,' Peter Doggett very reasonably comments in his judicious survey (*Growing Up*) of sex in the Sixties, 'adults might reply that these lyrics were helping to mould a culture that took pre-marital or casual sex for granted'.[8]

Broadcasting, of course, was integral to all this – and here, just a few mid-sixties examples, far from exhaustive. 'You could almost hear the corsets coming off as listeners woke up to the 1950s being over,' recalls Andy Medhurst about *Round the Horne*, featuring scripts by Barry Took and Marty Feldman that were 'insanely inventive, crackling with a love of language and delirious with the delighted knowledge that by deploying Polari, and other coded queer terminologies, things could be said in a nationally popular Sunday lunchtime radio series that would have been utterly taboo if expressed in mundane speech'; *This Week* ran Bryan Magee's pioneering documentaries on male homosexuals (1964) and lesbians (1965), the basis for his 1966 book *One in Twenty*; one of BBC's many controversial Wednesday Plays was the gay-themed *Horror of Darkness* (1965), starring Nicol Williamson and Glenda Jackson; with its 'frequent black American and female guests and the gay presenter Michael Aldred', *Ready, Steady, Go!* provided (in Jon Savage's words) 'a vision of a more pluralistic world to come'; BBC2's *Marriage Today* series in 1964 included interviews with Sussex University students ('as self-consciously modern as their architecture'), one calling marriage 'an increasingly unworkable concept', another bluntly saying it had 'no future'; two years later, an edition ('Living in Sin?') of *Man Alive* had the cohabiting Ted and Joan, both married to other partners, defiantly refusing to be stymied by archaic divorce laws ('You've got to make a life for yourself'); while in 1965 – the same year that the early morning radio talk *Lift Up Your Hearts* was replaced by the more questioning-cum-sociological *Ten to Eight* ('finding out what Christianity means to ordinary people') – BBC TV programmes included, as markers of a new religious pluralism, *Is Britain Pagan?* and *The Folklore of Christendom*, the latter billed as 'an agnostic's investigation into Christian beliefs in life after death'. Cumulatively, all these and much else undoubtedly made an impact, at the very least by exposing millions of viewers and listeners to attitudes and ways of life they were personally unfamiliar with. 'I can still remember the change in atmosphere in my mildly conservative Scottish rural home as the new programmes came blasting in,' reflected Andrew Marr in 2022. 'Huddling down in front of the telly was no longer an entirely comfortable family experience.'[9]

To stimulate 'an atmosphere of healthy scepticism', to aim at 'the maximum liberty of expression' and 'to question authority rather than to accept it' – such, declared director general Sir Hugh Carleton Greene in a 1963 speech, were the BBC's aims. Overall, very broadly speaking, it would be, despite stumbles and even retreats on the way, mission accomplished. 'With a great deal of heart-searching and a good deal of hesitation, marching and counter-marching,' reckoned Stuart Hall in 1967, 'the BBC is beginning to see its role as that of reflecting and exploring the diversity of social experiences, rather than performing the rite of handing on the Tablets of Stone.' Not everyone, to put it mildly, was happy. 'Cheap and trivial and largely responsible for the vast increase in sex and violent crimes and for the general very heavy decline in morality of all kinds' was Lord Reith's unsparing private summary in 1966 of what had once been so much his organisation; while the current DG was, by a country mile, enemy no. 1 in the eyes of Mary Whitehouse, prompting Greene in 1967 to reflect defiantly rather than ruefully about how 'she has chosen to pick on me as a sort of Antichrist engaged in a conspiracy to undermine the morals of the nation'.

Tellingly, the Shropshire teacher's views, and increasingly high-profile campaign to 'clean up' television, did not go unchallenged by some other viewers – notably by Avril Fox, a middle-aged Labour councillor in Harlow who in 1965, infuriated by Whitehouse's claim that she 'spoke for the women of Britain', initiated and led what became known as the Cosmo Group. Its purpose, she told *The Times* next year, was to defend and fortify the BBC against 'the puritanical protesters with their shrill voices'. 'I am,' she added, 'deeply opposed to a minority group trying to impose its own values on everyone else.

I think that the citizens of our country should have a chance to grow up and make their own judgements.' How was Cosmo getting on? 'To some extent it seems appropriate,' noted the paper itself, 'that Harlow – which Mrs Fox praises as "a new classless town, there are no 'posh' areas here, we are starting from scratch" – should have given birth to Cosmo and attracted membership that includes a General, one or two Wing Commanders ("for some reason the RAF is particularly anti-Whitehouse"), clergymen, writers, housewives and an amorphous group of people described as "lower-to-upper middle". "So far though," Mrs Fox comments, "we haven't touched the working class." '[10]

What, amid the swirling cultural currents, was the message coming from the Church of England? The short answer is that it was by this time, in the wake of the best-selling *Honest to God* (1963) by the Bishop of Woolwich (John Robinson), an increasingly liberal one, on the whole with the encouragement of Michael Ramsey, Archbishop of Canterbury. A key moment occurred in the House of Lords in May 1966: following a debate on the decriminalisation of male homosexuality, seven bishops, Ramsey among them, voted in favour – and none voted against. While two months later, a working group that Ramsey had set up three years before finally issued its report, *Putting Asunder*, on divorce reform, recommending that 'the doctrine of breakdown of marriage should be comprehensively substituted for the doctrine of matrimonial offence as the basis of all divorce'. Such a shift of emphasis, argued the group, chimed 'better with social realities' and reflected divorce 'for what it essentially is . . . a defeat for both'. Plenty of twists and turns lay ahead, but in essence the road was now clear, a major obstacle removed, for what would become the 1969 Divorce Reform Act, creating a single ground for divorce – the irretrievable breakdown of a marriage – and introducing, at least in part, the crucial concept of the no-fault divorce.

Two historians, Callum Brown and Sam Brewitt-Taylor respectively, have argued powerfully that two other major, related things were going on by the mid-sixties. In *The Battle for Christian Britain* (2019), Brown tells a richly documented story about how the sudden, unexpected collapse of the Christian-dominated Public Morality Council (PMC), together with the increasing unwillingness of local authorities 'to impose moral puritanism upon the people through the licensing system for public venues' (including pubs, restaurants, dance halls, theatres, cinemas, coffee shops, plus also advertising), amounted to a large-scale, if not yet universal, dismantling of Christian Britain. Traditionally, the PMC had been especially active in London, viewed of course by many Christians as prime hotbed of immorality; the organisation had been dominated since the 1940s by George Tomlinson, a prominent Methodist preacher; but his illness and then death in 1964 changed everything, as his successor, Edward Oliver, proved no match for Ramsey, who was determined to draw a clear line between private and public morality, with only the latter a subject for the state and the courts. As for the erosion of a morality-heavy licensing system, Brown's case studies of local authorities (in London, Blackpool, Sheffield, Glasgow and Isle of Lewis) do reveal significant variations, but even so an overall picture where, in Brown's uncompromising words, 'the will to personal autonomy, widespread loss of personal faith and increased migration drove a vibrant nexus of popular music, drink, drugs and sexual revolutions'.

Brewitt-Taylor's complementary focus, in his suggestively titled *Christian Radicalism in the Church of England and the Invention of the British Sixties* (2018), is on increasingly prominent elements within the Church of England at large, not just at the highest level. His often striking chapter titles – among them, 'Christian Radicalism and the Hope of Transcending "Religion"', 'Christian Radicalism and the Hope of Escaping Human Authority', 'Christian Radicalism and the Hope of a Revolution of Love' – convey alone the often highly charged territory he is staking out. Somewhere near the heart of his argument is that Christian radicalism not only played a major part in helping to undermine traditional Christian authority, but also involved by the mid-sixties an acceptance – both tacit and explicit – that modern 'Sixties' Britain had become a predominantly secular society:

> When leading Christian radicals interpreted the new 'secular age' as necessarily involving the collapse of human authority, they played a significant role in the wider invention of Britain's secular modernity as intrinsically anti-authoritarian, a crucial development which made British secularity markedly different from the authoritarian secularity practised in Khrushchev's Soviet Union. Similarly, when

> leading Anglican radicals interpreted 'secularization' as necessarily involving the collapse of fixed sexual codes, they played an important role in the construction of the 1960s as the decade of 'sexual revolution'. When they interpreted 'secularization' as necessitating a search for new spiritualities, they played a contributory role in the early stages of the making of the British counter-culture . . .

In short, claims Brewitt-Taylor far from implausibly, Christian radicals made 'substantial contributions' to 'the outcomes as well as to the existence of Britain's moral revolution'.[11]

These years also saw the coming of age of the liberal, progressive-minded, single-issue pressure group – the start, indeed, of identity politics. The Abortion Law Reform Association, the Campaign Against Racial Discrimination, the Campaign for Homosexual Equality, the Child Poverty Action Group, the Disablement Income Group, the Homosexual Law Reform Society, the National Association for the Welfare of Children in Hospital, the National Council for the Unmarried Mother and her Child, the National Council of Civil Liberties: these were just some of them. There was, of course, always work to do. 'The social and professional barriers which restrict the opportunities open to many non-Christians are still real, and only by outspoken onslaughts can they be broken down,' reflected Baroness (Barbara) Wootton in 1967. 'It was for instance not until the formation of the Agnostics Adoption Society in 1965 that the formidable opposition which faced a confessed agnostic who wished to adopt a child began to crumble.' Or take the Conservation Society, a pressure group formed in 1966 whose concerns transcended the single issue of the harmful environmental impact of excessive consumption and population growth, but nevertheless had that concern at its core. In truth it was not always impeccably liberal, campaigning for instance on the strict maintenance of immigration controls; but it was one of the earliest Green organisations, so perhaps ultimately on the right side of history.

Among the fullest contemporary pictures we have of one of these pressure groups is John Barr's March 1967 profile (in *New Society*) of the Abortion Law Reform Association (ALRA). Founded in the 1930s, it had after the war 'lost much of its drive' and 'become less a pressure group, more a social club' – until, in the wake of the thalidomide tragedy of the early 1960s, there took place 'a takeover by younger, vigorous people'. 'We became,' an ALRA officer told him, 'a fighting organisation rather than a mild middle-class wine-and-cheese party.' Even so, reckoned Barr himself: 'ALRA remains essentially a "Hampstead" group of professional men who can spare the time for its work and the otherwise unemployed wives they can afford to support. Although ALRA's membership is tiny, because of the calibre of its membership (considerable overlap with Fabians and humanist groups) its influence is out of all proportion to numbers . . .'[12] Few words more loaded than 'calibre', but clearly individuals mattered. Who then, more broadly, were the influencers and enablers of the social revolution, whether actual or incipient or merely putative, known as 'the Sixties'? Excluding some of those already substantively mentioned (in earlier chapters or earlier *Tales*), here is a gallery, of course subjective and arbitrary.

Leo Abse was the crusading, independent-minded Labour MP for Pontypool who not only steered the Commons through the decriminalisation of homosexual acts between consenting adults ('I was able to ride the storm because they were too ashamed to talk about it,' he recalled of his socially very conservative constituents), but was also an ardent champion of family planning, legal abortion and divorce law reform; **Kingsley Amis** was moving quite sharply to the right politically, but remained a social liberal, declaring in 1965 that 'our collective morality is based on an unwholesome mixture of envy and guilt, and for its repressive purposes, as for most such, the values of Christianity will come naturally and neatly to hand'; described by Frances Partridge as 'a small restless white-haired man', **Lord ('Boofy') Arran** was Abse's equivalent in the Lords, and on being thanked by the floral painter Dicky Chopping for his efforts on behalf of homosexual law reform, he replied brusquely, 'So you think I did right? I've LOATHED every minute of it'; **David Attenborough** as controller of BBC2 (1965–8) ensured that the new channel's values, unstated but palpable, were liberal, civilised and outward-looking; **Michael Baron** was among the parents of autistic children (still by the 1960s generally labelled as 'mentally retarded') who in 1962 founded what soon became called the National Society for Autistic Children, leading three years later to the creation of the Sybil Elgar School, named after the inspiring teacher; **Canon George (G. B.) Bentley**, a year before contributing significantly to *Putting Asunder*, wrote in 1965 – for the Mothers' Union, incongruously enough – *God and Venus: An Essay on Sex*, proclaiming that 'it is probably healthier to think of sex as fun than to treat it as sacred' and winning himself some tabloid attention; no more charismatic or perceptive pop artist than **Pauline Boty**, celebrant of female sexual pleasure, interrogator of male sexual gaze; **Margaret Bramall**, a single mother herself, ran from 1962 the National Council for the Unmarried Mother and her Child, with her personal situation doing much to 'sharpen her campaigning edge and fuel the energy, courage and tenacity of her commitment to what remained a deeply unpopular cause'; tenacity, too, from **Helen Brook**, founder in 1961 of the Brook Advisory Centre for the explicit purpose of giving contraception to unmarried women, six years later unilaterally taking the controversial decision to admit girls under sixteen to the Centre, and adamant throughout that far from encouraging promiscuity and abortion, her overwhelming twin purpose was for women to be in control of their own fertility and, in her own words, 'the prevention of the unwanted child'; **Gwen Bryson** became in 1965 the first female junior school headteacher in Ipswich and, after being offered the job, overheard one rejected applicant saying to another, 'A bloody woman has been appointed'; **John Calder** was the go-to man when it came to publishing (through his firm Calder & Boyars) the avant-garde and the shocking, including *Last Exit*; 'a folk poet, a holy sceptic and an iconoclastic theologian', the great song- and hymn-writer **Sydney Carter**'s most controversial composition – 'Friday Morning' (1960), where the thief next to Jesus on the cross tells him, 'It's God they ought to crucify, instead of you and me' – came at the start of his most prolific decade; **Eustace Chesser**, **Martin Cole** and **Alex Comfort** were not just alphabetically adjacent, with the first a leading Harley Street abortionist as well as a prominent, unflagging campaigner for frank sex education, the second a Birmingham-based geneticist who opened the first abortion clinic in the city and shortly before wrote in the *Birmingham Daily Post* in August 1965 that 'we must do away with the taboo on sex, dispense with the titillation of substitutes and lose some of our fear of the real thing', while the third would win his greatest fame in 1972 as author of *The Joy of Sex*, but for many years before had been making waves as 'a poet, novelist, doctor, biologist, gerontologist, anarchist, scientific humanist, public intellectual, and activist in the pacifist and anti-nuclear movements'; another doctor with forceful views (and close to R. D. Laing) was **Dr David Cooper**, a South African with a memorably bearded appearance who in March 1965 wrote for *New Society* about the logic behind the 'anti-hospital' for mental patients that he was running near St Albans ('As cabbages exist comfortably enough, at least until they go into the soup, many patients choose to collude with the illusions of their keepers, and this interplay of illusion and collusion is the basic social fantasy system upon which the structure of the conventional mental hospital is erected: it is plainly a totally alienated structure'); up in East Lancashire, king of the counter-culture was the experimental, modern-minded poet, editor and anthologist **Dave Cunliffe**, acclaimed by the *Guardian* in 1964 as Blackburn's very own 'beat poet', albeit Cunliffe himself describing the Blackburn scene generally as being 'stone cold dead'; in 1962, four years after founding VSO (Voluntary Service Overseas), **Alec and Mora Dickson** initiated CSV (Community Service Volunteers), again just the ticket for idealistic public schoolboys to discover how most of the rest of the world, or in this case the rest of Britain, actually lived; **Peter Diggory** was the pivotal gynaecologist backing abortion law reform, including making a 'stunning' speech at the 1966 Family Planning Association conference on abortion in Britain where he 'compared the rich women getting safe private operations with the poor women admitted to an NHS hospital whose neighbours had injected soap, whisky or even toothpaste into the uterus'; few more tireless campaigners for gay rights than the writer **Maureen Duffy**, who earlier in the decade had become one of the pioneer public figures to come out as lesbian and whose 1966 novel *The Microcosm* was 'an avant-garde mosaic of voices from London lesbian venue Gateways'; more behind the scenes, the literary critic and editor **A. E. (Tony) Dyson** was active throughout the decade in the Homosexual Law Reform Society (HLRS) and the Albany Trust, remembered for how his 'careful and courageous handling of the campaign during these years was instrumental in ensuring that it did not arouse animosity and become counter-productive'; still by the mid-1960s the only woman with a major salon in Mayfair, the hair stylist **Rose Evansky** pioneered for women's hair the use of the hand-held blow dryer (no longer 'the torment of sitting for an hour or more with hair doused in chemicals under a fixed hood of hot air'); 'Barry doesn't so much know what is in – he decides it,' adjudicated the *Daily Mirror* in 1967 about *Private Eye*'s satirical cartoonist (and much else) **Barry Fantoni**; 'calamitous' is Richard Davenport-Hines's adjective for the prescribing practices (heroin, cocaine, methadone) of the high-profile **Lady (Isabella) Frankau**, psychiatrist and so-called 'junkies' doctor'; the Labour government's Lord Chancellor, **Gerald Gardiner**, who back in 1960 had defended Penguin Books in the *Lady Chatterley* trial, had deep-rooted reforming instincts, not least in relation to divorce law, in a Cabinet not always over-endowed with such instincts; **Patrick Garnett** of the architects Garnett Cloughley Blakemore was crucial to the firm's biggest hits between 1965 and 1968, including the Top of the Tower restaurant at the top of the Post Office Tower, the acrylic-glass-and-stainless-steel Albrizzi furniture showroom on Sloane Square and the Chelsea Drug Store on King's Road with its 'electric Kool-Aid interiors'; 'rather like a Rotary Club', quietly but firmly replied **Antony Grey** (at the day-to-day heart, as the HLRS's secretary, of the campaign to decriminalise homosexuality) when asked at a Rotary dinner what homosexuals were really like; 'the connected fixer' is Jonathon Green's admiring epithet for **Jim Haynes**, the American who had opened in Edinburgh the inspirational Paperback Book Shop and would open in Covent Garden the Arts Lab as well as being intimately involved with the start of *International Times* (usually known as *IT*); **David Hockney** 'reassured postwar Britain that it was OK to take pleasure in beauty and freedom' (Ben Eastham); *English for Maturity* (1961), *English for the Rejected* (1964), *The Exploring Word* (1967) – these were hugely influential books by **David Holbrook** aimed at liberating the teaching of English, so that 'rather than being put through a series of grammar and comprehension exercises based on inert extracts from dull authors', children instead would be 'encouraged to explore the relationship between language and feeling, and, above all, to write for themselves' (Tom Deveson); even by Haynes's standards, no better connected, more inspiriting creator-cum-energiser of London's emerging, countercultural underground scene than the mercurial, often grinning, ex-scientist **John ('Hoppy') Hopkins**, nicely evoked by Joe Boyd for how 'in his purple Mini he dashed from one end of the city to the other, dropping off film, convening conspiratorial meetings, joining girls for afternoon assignations, scoring dope and bestowing favours';

no purple Minis for **Allan Horsfall** ('a resolutely uncharismatic man of shining integrity'), the National Coal Board clerk who, from his miner's cottage in Atherton, Greater Manchester, formed in 1964 the North West Committee for Homosexual Law Reform, instantly effective at lobbying often reluctant northern Labour MPs, albeit at personal cost, including being 'shunned in local gay bars by people who feared he would bring the police down on them'; Biba steadily growing under the so far unerring hands of **Barbara Hulanicki** ('we created a framework for our customers to discover themselves') and her husband **Stephen Fitz-Simon**; emerging during the first half of 1966 as definite editor of *Private Eye* – its reach still limited by WH Smith's obdurate refusal to sell it – was **Richard Ingrams**, who before deciding whether to attack a particular MP would ask the question 'How did he vote on the pooves?', with a vote in favour of homosexual law reform indicating that the politician was 'fundamentally' all right; Parish and People, an organisation pursuing what it called an 'open and militant approach' to furthering the Church of England's 'reform and renewal', was the primary vehicle for **Eric James**, a radical Christian who had left school at fourteen to work in London's docks and was by this time its vigorous director (two decades before he provided the initial impetus for the *Faith in the City* attack on the Thatcher government); **Dr David Kerr**, Labour MP for Wandsworth Central, was one of the very few parliamentarians willing publicly to support 'abortion on demand'; ever more influence as the decade went on, especially after the paperback came out in 1966, for **Sheila Kitzinger**'s *The Experience of Childbirth*, in which she demanded the prioritisation not of controlling obstetricians, but instead the mothers themselves, backed up by the pragmatic hands-on experience of their midwives; **Elizabeth Lane** became in 1965 the first female High Court judge ('in court she concealed, under a stern and even intimidating exterior, a warm, kindly, and understanding approach to the problems of families in the throes of separation and divorce'); extravagant costumes, expensive blonde wigs, gruff voice leaving no doubts about gender, strictly no jokes about homosexuality, the flamboyant **Danny La Rue**, often on TV and approaching the zenith of his career, 'made drag acts respectable in Britain and introduced them to a mass audience'; not just the moral reactionary of tedious stereotype, **Lord (Frank) Longford** chaired Labour's committee on crime whose 1964 policy report directly paved the way to the 1967 Criminal Justice Act, introducing the parole system and generally, as his biographer puts it, 'the high point of Longford's attempts to bring a more humane approach to punishment and rehabilitation'; 'really the first written text of the British women's liberation movement' is Elizabeth Wilson's description of the article in *New Left Review* in late 1966 by an English literature lecturer based at Leeds, **Juliet Mitchell**, in which, having asked forcibly why socialism to date had done so little for feminism, she envisaged a much more hopeful, less rigid future ('couples living together or not living together, long-term unions with children, single parents bringing up children, children socialised by conventional rather than biological parents, extended kin groups, etc . . .'); barrister and writer **John Mortimer**, the liberal's liberal, was ever-prominent in the campaign to abolish theatre censorship; **Andrew Loog Oldham** ('egotistical, talented, insulting, outrageous and likeable almost in spite of himself') oversaw the Rolling Stones, founded the Immediate record label, and declined to manage Marianne Faithfull on the grounds that 'her talents are not diversified enough'; coming from a progressive Anglo-Catholic standpoint, the Woolwich Polytechnic lecturer **Valerie Pitt** had what an obituarist called 'a long and turbulent relationship of disloyal faithfulness' with the Church of England and would in June 1967 initiate at the Church Assembly a resolution calling for the ordination of women; **Nancy Raphael** was the Family Planning Association's honorary secretary who eventually guided that conservative-minded body to reluctantly accepting the case for providing contraceptive advice to unmarried as well as married women; the 'vivacious, pretty and stylish' **Elisabeth Rivers-Bulkeley** was a stockbroker with a mission – 'writing a series of articles in the *Daily Telegraph* about investment from a woman's point of view, undertaking lectures on investment around the UK and appearing on numerous television and radio programmes' – but because of her sex was not yet allowed to become a member of the London Stock Exchange; 'a buyer of junk around his native south London', **Tommy Roberts** 'knew where to pick up a Life Guard's tunic or a kaftan, even a penny-farthing bicycle, with which to stock his place', with his first boutique, Kleptomania, opening in 1966 just round the corner from Carnaby Street; the Hungarian-born **Egon Ronay**, of the eponymous annual *Guide*, would in later years often be credited with having, alongside Elizabeth David, made food habits more adventurous, but in his own view, noted a 2010 obituarist, 'the greatest single change had come through the emergence of a new class in the 1960s – "pop stars, advertising people, photographers and so on" – who found ways of making money without the benefit of a public school education' and whose 'great love of eating out meant that food began to be a topic of conversation in its own right, an interest that was increasingly reflected in newspapers and magazines'; ITV's *Candid Camera*, creation in 1960 of the inveterate, sometimes cruel, prankster and practical joker **Jonathan Routh**, seemed by 1967 less daringly anarchic and anti-authoritarian as it finished its run, but by then had had its effect; **William Scholl** gave his name to the Finnish-designed wooden sandal reputedly owned in the mid-1960s by half of all British women, a sandal that 'with its organic connotations and clip-clop sound became associated with a simpler way of life'; if there was a single key figure behind the very systematic Humanist challenge to the often illiberal assumptions of what still thought of itself as Christian Britain, it was arguably **Madeleine Simms**, in Callum Brown's words 'a leading organiser of the Abortion Law Reform Association, an active author in the *Humanist* as well as the medical and social science press, a member of the Voluntary Euthanasia Society and a campaigner and researcher on family planning and teenage pregnancy'; youthful and dynamic, with a seemingly endless ability to attract publicity, **Nicholas Stacey** was compelled by the mid-sixties to concede, following the clear failure of his ambitious plans as rector of Woolwich to revitalise religious life, that institutional religion's only hope was to become both more secular and more radical, as he now called on clergymen to get involved in housing and other social projects, to teach in comprehensives, and to perform 'sacramental duties' within 'every office, factory, and street'; *The King of Carnaby Street* is the entirely justified title of Jeremy Reed's biography of **John Stephen** – eight shops (mainly menswear) to his name there by 1965, supplying the Mod subculture with 'an indelible look', dressing the Stones for the cover of *Aftermath*, in 1966 inaugurating floral shirts and ties, it was Stephen who, to quote Richard Davenport-Hines's graphic words, 'quelled the violent repulsion at seeing an Englishman in pink'; when the Lords in 1965 debated homosexual law reform, no one was more outspoken in favour of change than the Bishop of

Southwark, **Mervyn Stockwood**; pet dislikes of the increasingly prominent psychiatrist **Anthony Storr** were authoritarian doctors who sent patients to hospital by compulsion, similar doctors who prescribed treatment (such as pre-frontal leucotomies) by which brain tissue was surgically destroyed, and anyone who insisted that cannabis was more harmful than tobacco and alcohol; **Mary Tisdall** in her weekly column (under the pen-name Mary Redcliffe) in the *Northern Echo* covered, notes her son Simon, such 'taboo subjects' as 'the pill and making contraception available to young women, sex education in school (then largely non-existent), divorce (almost unobtainable), NHS treatment of expectant mothers (poor) and discrimination against women (ubiquitous)', while a harrowing radio piece in 1964 about a woman who had had an illegal backstreet abortion 'helped spur national debate', three years ahead of the change in the law; at the National Marriage Guidance Council, it was **John Wallis** who played the key role in shifting focus away from guidance aimed at saving marriages and towards counselling aimed at individual fulfilment; under the gifted leadership of **Colin Ward**, the magazine *Anarchy* would in later years be hailed by Ken Worpole for the way its articles 'amounted to a vibrant re-description of contemporary British life as a patchwork of voluntary action, informal education and social endeavour, with a strong sense of locality'; 'lively and vivacious, theatrical in manner, passionate and sometimes unpredictable', **Gina Ware** ran London's first openly lesbian nightclub, the Gateways in Chelsea, making it women-only in 1967, the year that a *Man Alive* documentary about lesbians remarked that 'there they can dance, drink, flirt and discuss their problems'; and in December 1965 the pioneering social scientist **Barbara Wootton** – see the magnificent biography by Ann Oakley for the astonishing range of her indomitably public-spirited, reform-minded activities – became the first woman Deputy Speaker of the House of Lords, sitting on the Woolsack itself for the first time in February 1966.[13]

That still leaves a trio, but now in reverse alphabetical order.

John Lennon, Keith Richards, Charlie Watts, Eric Burdon – all these, and many others, had a background as art students. 'Art colleges were meant to train students to become graphic designers,' reflects David Simonelli, 'but they also served as educational halfway houses for later adolescents who clearly had brains and talent, but refused to conform to the dictates of the school system – almost a job description for the average British rock 'n' roll musician.' In the case of the Who's main man, **Pete Townshend**, it was Ealing Art College, whose head tutor was Roy Ascot, passionate about the new movement called cybernetics. 'Essentially [Simonelli again], it was about how a machine could become, in the hands of an artist, an organic thing, a tool of the artist's vision as useful as his own limbs and digits, and just as reflective of his own ideas. Townshend used these ideas throughout his career, always obsessed with technology and the possibilities it raised for expressing his ideas. The destruction of his guitar was frightening and exhilarating precisely because Townshend was destroying a part of himself . . .' The man himself elaborated in his May 1965 interview with Maureen Cleave:

> If I can't get the sound I want out of a guitar, I bang it against the amplifier. If I still can't get it, I drop it on the floor out of frustration. When I get the feed-back noise, it sounds like a bomber, so I put my own little flying to it, swinging my arms around; then [Keith] Moon can bang the drums and the audience thinks of guns and smashing people up. We're catering for their suppressed aggression.

The interview coincided with the Who's second single, 'Anyway, Anyhow, Anywhere', acclaimed by the group itself, noted Cleave, as 'the first true POP ART single', while soon afterwards Townshend attempted to define for *Melody Maker* readers what pop art actually was: 'It is re-representing something the public is familiar with, in a different form. Like clothes. Union Jacks are supposed to be flown, we have a jacket made of one. Keith Moon, our drummer, has a jersey with the RAF insignia on it. I have a white jacket, covered in medals. We stand for pop art clothes, pop art music and pop art behaviour . . .' Any broader context or purpose? Here he looked ahead to their next single:

> Not only is the number pop-art, the lyrics are 'young and rebellious.' It's anti middle-age, anti boss-class and anti young marrieds! I've nothing against these people really – just making a positive statement. The big social revolution that has taken place in the last

> five years is that youth, and not age, has become important. Their message is: 'I'm important now I'm young, but I won't be when I'm over 21.' Even London's streets are making a massive anti-establishment statement, every Saturday night. This is what we are trying to do in our music, protest against 'showbiz' stuff, clear the hit-parade of stodge!

'My Generation', hitting the charts that autumn, was indeed the ultimate Who moment as well as Mod moment, 'with Roger Daltrey's speed-freak affected stutter and Pete Townshend's windmilling power-chords, turning the song into a two minutes' compacted delirious expression of Mod philosophy'. And Jeremy Reed goes on:

> 'My Generation', with its aggressive charged-up incitement to live optimally within the unrepeatable moment spoke directly through its lyrics to the kids who John Stephen dressed . . . Riding high on a shock wave to No 2 in the charts, the record's commercial spin-off for Stephen was immediate in terms of a generation starting to consolidate its own definition of itself, based in part on the clothes he had singularly created . . . The heady mix of Pete Townshend's subversive lyrics, combined with Roger Daltrey's rushed vocal attack, together with the percussive meltdown of Keith Moon's drumming, and John Entwistle's cavernously descending bass chords, had The Who appear through this song to power the whole scooter-led Carnaby Street ethos forward into the mid-sixties orange sunshine optimism of a generation flagrantly proud of its disaffection from the past.

More great (if not quite so epoch-defining) moments lay ahead, including a year later 'I'm a Boy', in Jon Savage's words 'an extraordinary record which had as its subject the angst of a young boy dressed by his mother as a girl – helpfully described by bassist John Entwistle as "almost a queer song" in the pop press of the time.' Back in summer 1965, the twenty-year-old Townshend had been asked some searching questions by *NME*. Hobbies? 'Scalextric car racing, painting, making pop art montages.' Favourite colour? 'Any that shouts!' Favourite clothes? 'New or very old.' Personal ambition? 'Just not to let what happens to me get me down.' Professional ambition? 'To be a recognised composer/arranger. Die young.'[14]

Of course, with even the best-known influencers and enablers, one can easily exaggerate how well known they really were. 'She's fabulous,' one respondent said to a Mass Observation survey in autumn 1966 seeking to find out how much people knew about famous names in the news. 'Not many people would give up their lives for Chinese children the way she does.' The famous name being asked about was **Mary Quant** – fashion designer, certainly not Christian missionary, and overall known by about one person in two, well behind such names as Tommy Steele (known to 97 per cent), Edward Heath (85 per cent) and Bobby Moore (73 per cent), but way ahead of foreign secretary Michael Stewart (a name accurately identified by only 26 per cent). Quant, with her signature Vidal Sassoon bob, was in the news partly because she had just received the OBE (or, as the *Daily Mail*'s headline put it when the award was announced, 'Miss Kooky OBE'), partly because she had recently branched out into cosmetics, featuring a strong personal message amid profusely illustrated advertising: 'Nothing fussy, no unnecessary bits and pieces, absolutely **nothing** old hat – just the essentials for today's look (and the **newest** ideas). And when the look changes so will my cosmetics. Newies will happen <u>all</u> the time – so watch it!' The honour was a big thing for both Quant and her partner-cum-husband Alexander Plunket Greene. 'We're both thrilled,' he told the press. 'Don't forget that when we started [in 1955 in Chelsea, with their first Bazaar shop] the whole fashion trade laughed at us, and went on laughing right up until two years ago.' Quant herself, the daughter of teachers who had instilled a stern work ethic, was not shy of explaining what she was about. In her 1966 autobiography, *Quant By Quant*, she described women's fashion as 'a tool to compete in life outside the home'; while in spring 1967 she spoke freely to Maureen Cleave:

> She [Quant] is delighted with the way fashion has developed: hair that looks like hair, shoes that can be walked in. 'People are no longer horse-hair imitations of themselves,' she said. 'Ordinary people in England used to look so plain, so ugly. Now ordinary people are good-looking: the lorry driver, the window cleaner – I think they

all look beautiful. I myself am fairly ordinary – fairly plain, fairly pretty: but if I am ingenious, I can be very attractive.'

But did she think fashion was *important*? 'Of course not,' said Miss Quant, for whom the wood has never been obscured by the trees. 'What I think is that people who look well are more at ease with themselves, better able to concentrate on other things. It's the small things that hold you up – the little blister on your heel.'

But what was the point of fashion, where was it all leading? 'Sex,' said Miss Quant promptly.

But surely people were going to arrive at sex in any case, without all the frills and provocation and the linen drooping sexily between the legs? 'Of course they are,' she said. 'But it's a pity to miss all the extra things. You see, I've never understood why one shouldn't have one's cake and eat it. I don't see why you can't have everything.'

How exactly did she change how women dressed? 'She was the first with the Leather Look, with the shiny PVC look,' noted the *Mail* in its 'Miss Kooky' story, while according to Karen Dacre, writing in 2021 on the occasion of Sadie Frost's film *Quant*, she did so in nine specific ways: by possibly inventing, but certainly popularising, the mini-skirt, 'thigh-skimming symbol of optimism and youthful rebellion'; by focusing, dynamically and flexibly, on clothes for the young working girl; by popularising tights instead of stockings; by more or less inventing the dress pocket, which 'emerged as an emblem of modernity, as well as the perfect place to stash a lipstick and the bus fare home'; by being far ahead of the curve with gender-fluid clothing, especially through her use of knitwear; by popularising the American concept of 'house wear', especially through her launch in the late sixties of adult-sized babygrows ('somewhere between a tracksuit and a dressing gown, this was the original adult onesie'); by pioneering the fine-knit, skinny-rib sweater, which 'served as the perfect pairing with her signature pinafore and became the foundation of a look that was emulated across the globe'; by turning flat shoes into the glamorous option; and by pioneering waterproof mascara ('not only could women run for the bus in one of her skirts and do a day's work on their feet in her shoes, but they could also shed a tear in her mascara and still look good'). Quant's achievements were also remembered at a major V&A retrospective in 2019 (four years before her death), including particularly perceptive commentary from the show's co-curator, Jenny Lister: 'She used clothes to demonstrate that change was coming. Fashion was no longer about couture, it was about expressing individuality . . . She expressed the way in which women's lives were parting from traditional stereotypes. Her clothes provided a language to express the empowerment of women at a time when words like sexism had barely been invented.' And, perhaps most tellingly of all, not just about Quant but about the decade she won her greatest fame: 'She did not want to grow up, the clothes wanted to keep childhood going, but that became a new kind of sexiness, defined by her.'[15]

Finally, it is hard not to come back to **R. D. Laing**. Apart from a handful of fellow psychiatrists, few knew him better in the early-to-mid sixties than the American writer Clancy Sigal, one of his patients. 'Smoking a thin cigar, he leans forward intently in his cracked leather chair and examines me through half-lidded eyes,' he recalled about their first session, in 'a dark shaded consulting room on the ground floor of 21 Wimpole Street, London W1':

> 'What are ye fookin' around wi' all that neurotic shit for, Clancy?' he says in a Scottish accent I am to learn he can put on or off at will. 'Tummy aches and faintin' spells is crybaby stuff. Ye've got the makings of a good schizophrenic. Lucky ye've come to the right place.'
>
> For all its Sartrean chatter, ontological insecurity, being-for-itself, etc. – Laing's message was starkly simple: doctors must stop treating mental patients as objects to be done things to, and have the courage to meet patients as equals in an 'I-thou encounter' . . . Laing's ascendent star was perfectly timed. Antonin Artaud's 'madness is truth' was all the rage, as was David Mercer's *A Suitable Case For Treatment*. The feminist playwright Jane Arden went around chanting, 'We are all mad. If you are a woman then you are mad.'
>
> Laing's early writing spoke, poetically, from his troubled gut to growing audiences of the disenchanted and mentally unbalanced. He preached that the root of the thing that sickened us was the emotional dysfunction within families encoded in the parents' 'double bind' ('Go away but tell me you love me'), and loveless (or overbearingly loving) contradictory communication that drove kids

> literally mad. In this sense, love itself was the ticking time-bomb of all personal relationships. One struggled to free oneself from the chains of love in order to find a selfhood that might exist only on the other side of madness . . .

'Whether or not his contributions to psychiatry prove of lasting importance, his very being is the stuff of legend,' concluded Elspeth Barker in her review of John Clay's excellent 1996 biography. 'Avatar of the Sixties, melancholy psychopomp leading lost souls only to a greater darkness, humanitarian and innovator, archetypal Scotsman – Laing may be seen from many angles, but he undoubtedly has his place in the strange firmament of twentieth-century icons.'[16]

15

White Shirt! Black Shoes and Socks!

Historians juggle all the time with the competing balls of change and continuity, but the juggling feels especially fraught when it comes to the 1960s. Two things, though, do seem reasonably clear: that in all sorts of ways, by the mid-sixties, a certain framework was being laid for a social revolution in the decades to come, heading in the direction of individualism, of greater acceptance of diversity, of greater gender equality, of greater questioning of authority, of the claims of emotion and personal authenticity enjoying an increasing sovereignty over those of impersonal reason or traditional moral authority; but that at the same time – in the quotidian, in people's everyday lives, in places far away from the King's Road in Chelsea or Carnaby Street in the West End – actual social and cultural change on the ground was, relatively speaking, only just starting to happen, and perhaps in some places not even that. Or as Pete McQuay, my sardonic northern friend at university in the early 1970s, once remarked, 'I can tell you this, David, the Sixties never happened in Blackburn.'

It seemed an old country to David Lodge. 'It takes a bit of getting used to, England,' he wrote in 1965 after returning from a year in America:

> You have to reacquire the taste for it: for the change that sprains your wrist as the bus conductor pours it into your hand. For five different shops to buy five different kinds of food. For politeness when it is least needed ('*Please* tear off,' it says on the tab inside the matchbox). For the National Health Service (I've been limping about on a verruca for months, determined to wait for free

> treatment. 'Most people do it themselves,' said my doctor. 'Just take a razor-blade . . .'). For pedestrians who prance out at oncoming cars like bull-fighters, arching their backs as you brush past them. For houses all identical on the outside, all with different electrical sockets on the inside. Tiny, tiny houses, like cosily furnished hen-coops.

'And in one such hen-coop,' he ended, 'I lie on my bed, my nose streaming, my throat itching, my eyes watering – with, in short, the common English cold. Back.'

A clutch of memoirists, all of them children or young adults at the time, flesh out this sense of stasis, of life being led in a seemingly unchanging pattern and rhythm. 'It was freezing in the morning, not only in the dead of deadly winter but as far into the year as tentatively brightening May and then again by the darker part of September,' recalls Paul Morley about growing up in Reddish, near Stockport:

> A coal fire needed to be quickly built as soon as we woke up, around seven, firmly twisted copies of the *Daily Express*, my dad's favourite newspaper, laid on top of a few pieces of coal when we didn't have Zip firelighters, which was mostly the case. A few damp matches would be struck before there was any sort of ignition. The coal would splutter into life behind the cheap buckled metal fire guard and above piles of soft grey ash from the day before and even the day before that, pathetic little flames forcing themselves into flickering motion soon gaining in confidence and alerting the icy grey room where we were gathered to the benefit of warmth. After early-morning fire duty, perhaps scooping up in a small battered shovel some of the old ash from coal and *Daily Express* and crushed unknown objects that all ended up mushroom-coloured, my mum would make tea.
>
> My dad took a big dollop of milk and three teaspoons of sugar, probably craving enough energy to get out of the door and head for work and an unnamed occupation which was never clearly described to me, but which, from odd clues I've picked up, consisted of hours of paperwork, boredom and irritation in an office. If there was some sort of ladder of seniority, from what I could gather he was at the bottom with no chance of ever being a boss.

Chilly, too, in Jeanette Winterson's Accrington. 'I got myself up for school every day. My mother left me a bowl of cornflakes and the milk in a flask. We had no fridge and most of the year we had no need of one – the house was cold, the North was cold, and when we bought food we ate it.' In the town itself, she remembers Accrington Market ('stalls stacked with dirty potatoes and fat cabbages . . . stalls selling household cleaners out of vats – no packaging, you took your own bottles for bleach and your own tubs for caustic soda . . . a stall that sold nothing but whelks and crabs and eels'), the rag-and-bone man's rummage and junk shop under the viaduct ('pre-war prams with wheels the size of millstones and canvas hoods on steel frames . . . hundreds of chairs, most with a leg missing . . . rusty canary cages and balding stuffed animals, knitted blankets and trolleys on castors . . . tin baths and washboards, clothes mangles and bedpans'), and the ubiquitous corner shop ('bread shops and pie shops and vegetable shops and shops that sold sweets in jars'), sometimes occupying people's front rooms while they lived upstairs. 'A two-up, two-down terraced house with the miracle of an inside toilet and a tin bath, but no running hot water' was the Black Country childhood home for Brian Griffin, son of a horizontal borer who worked in a factory all his life and went to the pub every night of the week. 'A bath would mean kettles of hot water being poured in the tin bath until it was about 8 cms deep. I was lucky as I always bathed first with Mom, then Dad following afterwards using the same water.' The family had a smallholding, with calves, pigs and chickens, so 'quite often I would come home to see a pig's head steaming as it cooked on the stove'. High drama compared to 'reasonably well-to-do though not ostentatiously so' Harpenden in the Home Counties, where Martin Newell's grandparents lived and to which he returned in 1966 after two years abroad with his Army father:

> It was the kind of place that Monty Python might have satirised for its sheer respectable ordinariness. On weekday mornings, the London side of Harpenden Station was packed with bowler-hatted men carrying newspapers and umbrellas. Sainsbury's had its distinctive black-and-white mosaic floors and smelled of clean sawdust and fresh bacon. Woolworths had wooden floors, girls in green coats and smelled of cheap cosmetics and pic'n'mix sweets. Everything about the town was as I'd remembered it from two years earlier.

So, too, in its unchangingness – and barely yet even a candidate for the incipient trend just starting to be known as 'gentrification' – that subsequent metaphor, Islington in north London. 'Going there was like visiting the nineteenth century,' recalled in 2006 the poet Hugo Williams about moving there in 1966:

> A marvellous poetical gloom hung over its grimy terraces and squares, untouched by Swinging London going on at the foot of the hill. Net curtains ruled, except where some bohemian family like my own had braved the wilderness. Street after street was painted in the London & Manchester Insurance Company's glum and ghostly 'Gossamer Green'. To collect a bunch of rusty house keys from the one estate agent was to explore an almost Dickensian London – all gas and lino and layers of landlord's paint, with only the occasional bit of electricity run in across a ceiling to a dangling light bulb, privies and pigeon coops in the gardens. Coalmen, fish-sellers and rag-and-bone men were likewise still in place. It was an education for me and a love affair. All now gone.

Also on the move in 1966 was the family of the five-year-old Michael Collins, to a street in thoroughly white, working-class Elephant and Castle. Just out of reach of the surrounding demolition-and-redevelopment area, and always known as 'The Street', it was, remembered Collins in 2004, 'a long blind alley of a road, with a pub on its corner, and plugged at the other end by the rear wall of a boys' school':

> The houses in The Street were old. Over the years tenants installed inside toilets, sometimes bathrooms, and a kitchen where the scullery had been. For decades, a man turned up regularly, dressed in black, like Shadrach from *Billy Liar*. He looked like he might be collecting bodies, but he collected the rent from every household. A man walked the street offering to sharpen knives; another sometimes called out for 'rag 'n' bone'. These characters were more suited to another era, but like the tipsters, quacks and sarsaparilla sellers on the market they remained until the 1970s. There were Sunday roasts, and Sunday tea, always with prawns, winkles, cockles. A hairdresser living in The Street did the sets, perms and colours of

other women; another neighbour, a dressmaker, was always in and out of houses doing alterations. Kids went swimming at the municipal baths or watched relatives box there as part of a family night out. The pattern was sometimes shattered by mothers almost coming to blows defending their children . . .

The Street began to represent both a haven and a time capsule harbouring the rituals, the routines, the culture that had been the lifeblood of the neighbourhood and the area at large for so long. As the walls came tumbling down all around, as rubble settled and dust rose, it was as though the time capsule itself was being buried underground. But the future would have to wait, whether it was housing estates as wide as their accompanying tower blocks were tall, or the influx of interlopers.

The final sentence of Collins's evocation, perhaps especially the third word, packs an undeniable punch: 'Homes, heritage, homogeneity, the holy trinity of the neighbourhood and the wider community, were the territory that was now being protected, defended even.'[1]

'I grew up with no telly, no phone, no car, no inside bathroom,' noted Billy Bragg in 2002 about his Barking childhood. How badly, asked his interviewer, would he need to have to pee in the middle of the night in order to persuade him to visit the outdoor loo? 'Very badly. You really didn't wanna go unless you had to. We all cheered when the dunny came down.' The fact was that in 1967 at least a quarter of homes still lacked either a bath or a shower, an indoor WC or a sink with hot and cold water taps; while when it came to domestic appliances, still almost two-fifths of households lacked a washing machine, over half lacked a fridge, only a small minority had a freezer, and dishwashers were almost unknown. What more generally were interiors like? The child psychologists John and Elizabeth Newson conducted in the mid-sixties many interviews with working-class mothers living in inner Nottingham's small, red-brick terrace houses:

The back kitchen is the heart of the terrace house [they wrote in their 1968 classic, *Four Years in an Urban Community*]. Here the family lives its life. Here meals are eaten, first steps taken, quarrels fought out, decisions made. The baby watches his world from the pram in the corner; the toddler pursues his own schemes under

> the table, or enjoys his 'five minutes' love' on his mother's lap in the easy chair; this is the base for the child's early forays into the world outside, the first goal of children breathless from school; here 'missus next door' drops in for 'a bit of a natter'; here father stumps in heavy-footed from work, and relaxes at the cloth-spread table-end over his tea and the *Evening Post*. Here, too, is the television set, always a good indication of the family's true living room. The mother who is not at work must spend more than half her waking life in this room, or in and out of the tiny lean-to scullery beyond it; if she is doing 'homework' – machining or lace-work, perhaps – she will probably find space for this too in the cheerful clutter of the kitchen.

By contrast, 'the front room is still, in most cases, the "best" room, and therefore kept for special occasions', though the Newsons added that 'in some of the poorer homes the front room may be no more than a store room and passage-way: left unfurnished, unheated and often uncleaned, it becomes a depository for pram and pushchair, bicycles, handcart, and the discarded junk of the whole family.' No junk in the front room of the Dyers, living similarly in a two-up, two-down but on the edge of Cheltenham. Barely ever used, apart from alternate Boxing Days, it was in effect, recalls their only child Geoff, 'a trophy or show room', conveying the message that 'we had more space than we needed, at least until we had to move to somewhere larger, because of a lack of space':

> I ventured in there sometimes, always feeling like an intruder, conscious of the contained force of its redundancy. It was obviously nicer than the room we did use and had a better view through the small sash window (of the daisy-flecked front lawn), but, because of its unused-ness there was no point staying in it (nothing to do there) and so its strange negative power was reinforced, the tradition of non-use carried on even by me. It was also amplified or presided over by the things *in* the room. The armchairs and sofa comprising the brown three-piece suite had no real purpose in life; sitting there, waiting to be sat in, they had the effect of making the room seem crowded with emptiness. Robbed of the function for which they were manufactured, they had no choice but to adapt, to assume the

plumped aspect of comfy altars. But the real altar, the place of intensified redundancy, was the cocktail cabinet . . .

What about American-style open plan? 'Our attitude', the chief architect of Wates Limited told a journalist in 1965, 'is that where space is confined it is better to make use of the space in open form – to have one room 20ft by 10ft than two 10ft by 10ft.' Logical perhaps – but, discovered the journalist, far from popular. 'We have built open plan houses and still do where we can sell them,' said Wimpey, 'but most people want a separate dining-room, a separate sitting-room and a separate kitchen.' Costain noted that 'most of the houses built by our companies are in the North where open plan design is particularly out of favour'. And a last word went to A. J. Waite: 'We like the idea of open plan houses, but we find that most people are not very keen, so most of our houses are traditional.'[2]

Continuities ran deep in food. Back in 1947 a Gallup poll had found that the 'Perfect Meal', regardless of cost, comprised sherry, tomato soup, sole, roast chicken, roast potatoes, peas, sprouts and trifle; fifteen years later the results were identical, except the trifle had given way to fruit salad with cream. Even so, John Barr, writing in *New Society* in early 1965, did detect certain shifts: a growing preference for clear rather than thick soup; traditionally popular foods with 'strong flavours and smells' – such as cabbage or game and rabbit or mutton – on the decline; and being superseded by much less flavoursome fodder like fish fingers or battery-raised chickens. Much depended on class, and he cited a recent survey of favourite menus of housewives in middle-class Hendon compared to housewives in working-class Shepherd's Bush. Over a third of housewives in the former indicated a preference for 'exotic Continental dishes', whereas 96 per cent in the latter favoured 'plain English dishes'; while in terms of individual items, there was agreement over the desirability of peas, Hendon had greater enthusiasm for smoked salmon, Hendon also favoured roast duck to Shepherd's Bush's roast beef, Shepherd's Bush was some eight times as keen on roast potatoes, and the charms of apple pie were largely lost on Hendon. Regional differences mattered, too, with Barr noting that Londoners consumed 35 per cent more poultry, 32 per cent more green vegetables, 31 per cent more fresh fruit and 25 per cent more coffee than the national average. After a foray to Bolton in 1964, Katharine Whitehorn revealed how her moussaka, 'though nice', had been 'made with potato, and it suddenly made me realise just how little you can take aubergines for granted out of town'; while a year later, in Wigan, Graham Turner came across a pork butcher apparently selling up to two tons of black puddings a week, also some 60,000 pies and 18,000 potato cakes, and with tripe and pig's trotters as much in demand as ever.

In 1968, in his book *British Tastes*, based to a large extent on mid-sixties evidence, David Elliston Allen produced a comprehensive report into the likes and dislikes of the regional consumer, building on his own experience in market research. To take some examples almost at random: in London and the south-east, 'Indian and Chinese food has less of the out-of-the-ordinary connotations than it has in the provinces'; in East Anglia, 'they stuff themselves with fish-and-chips and their diet has traditionally leant rather heavily on pigs'; in the West Country, 'cream, like fruit, seems to have taken on an almost magical aura, poured into and over as much as possible like a kind of sacred libation', including even over kidney beans; Wales the region which 'eats easily the most canned meat, a great deal of canned salmon and canned peaches, pears and pineapples, and drinks all the canned milk and cream it can afford'; the Midland diet 'remarkable only for a rather stodgy unimaginativeness', including 'great hunks of meat, lavish helpings of peas and cabbage, apple pies by the plateful, interminable quantities of tasteless shop bread'; across the north as a whole, 'large quantities of chips' and 'the most lard'; in the north-west, 'a weakness for obscurer flavours in products like jellies', but an aversion to raspberries and Blue Stilton; in Yorkshire, 'home-baked food devoured in great volume', while packet cake mixes were met with 'exceptionally stiff resistance'; in the north-east, 'an astonishing capacity (and presumably liking) for canned peas, a quite exceptional demand for corned beef, and by far the heaviest consumption in the country of brown bread, which here accounts for some 10 per cent of all bread eaten – compared with only about 5 per cent everywhere else in Britain'; and north of the border, 'the Scots eat almost as many cakes as anyone, but, not content with this, they also gorge themselves on fantastic amounts of Scotch pancakes and scones . . . they also eat far more chocolate biscuits than the English, treating them as an integral part of the meal'.

'The End of Difference?' was the questioning title of Allen's final chapter. He thought it unlikely. 'The fact is that over long periods of years – over decades, certainly, and probably over far lengthier periods still – basic tastes remain the same, and with them the particular likes and dislikes of one part of the country compared with another.' Accordingly, he went on: 'In many fields even the brands retain their respective positions long undisturbed, the producers keeping their promotional energies roughly in permanent proportion and having the sense not to tempt providence by introducing newness to a contentedly somnolent public.'[3]

Conservative attitudes, too, when it came to money. When in spring 1966 the main banks introduced a system of banker's cards in order to facilitate customers being able 'to pay by cheque at shops, garages, hotels, restaurants, travel or ticket agencies, in fact almost anywhere – without query or delay', those places all too often pulled a long, doubtful face. 'On May 8, on returning from a weekend abroad, I took my son and daughter-in-law to dine at a West End restaurant,' Mrs N. W. Alexander, of Hutton Buscel near Scarborough, recounted to *The Times*. 'I had my Midland Bank "Credit Card" cheque refused by a very apologetic manager, who said he was forbidden to accept a cheque of any kind. No amount of explanation would persuade him to change his mind and we all had to turn out our pockets and handbags in order to pay the bill.' Later that month it was the turn of Richard Jones of Cringleford near Norwich. 'Last evening I tried to pay for a meal on a train with a cheque backed by a Lloyds Bank "Banker's Card"; it was not accepted. I was told that if the conductor takes a cheque he must replace it with cash from his own pocket.' Ah yes, cash . . . 'Working-class sixties Liverpool was a patriarchal cash economy,' recalls Stephen McGann, whose father worked in a copper factory. 'Dad got paid every Thursday in a small brown packet and provided mum with "housekeeping" – the money necessary to fulfil her wifely duties.' A key aspect of that working-class economy, as Avram Taylor has shown in detail in relation to Tyneside, remained the role of the 'doorstep' credit agent, especially in the north and especially for older people, often unaware of cheaper forms of credit (such as through a bank loan) and reluctant anyway to break with the habits of a lifetime. He quotes the memories of a

Mrs Hughes – living in Forest Hall in North Tyneside, married to a panel beater – as evidence of how 'up until the 1970s the old credit firms were still very embedded within working-class communities':

> You would get a ticket and you would go to a wholesaler and buy something and, after that, a guy would come round once a week. I mean, you had a really good relationship with these people, if you paid you did, I don't know what it was like if you didn't pay. They were great friends. You used to wait for them coming for a cup of tea, and they'd run you to whatever wholesalers . . . And they'd always want you to have more and more all the time. They were always happy for you to do that . . .

Eventually, in the early 1970s, she made the break. 'Thomas left the company, the guy who collected, and we didn't like the next fellow. So we just didn't bother getting any more. It was that simple.'

Getting about remained, for most people, a slow business. Of course, car ownership was rapidly increasing – almost 13 million motor vehicles in Britain by 1965, compared to 4.4 million in 1950 – yet it was still the fact that only some 47 per cent of journeys were being taken by car, while 'as late as 1968', as Simon Gunn points out, 'more than half of urban households did not own a car'. Birmingham, 'motor city' itself, is a striking case in point: barely two-fifths of households with a car even by 1972; 'in the least privileged neighbourhoods,' notes Richard Vinen, 'this figure was 20 per cent'; and, that same year, just 8 per cent of women living in council houses possessed a driving licence. Instead, through the 1960s in Birmingham, the majority – inevitably, women, children and the elderly above all – relied heavily on public transport, which for most meant the buses. With slum clearance and redevelopment under way or about to get under way, these were the last classic years of the city's much-used No. 8 bus route, aka 'The Inner Circle' – or sometimes the 'Workman's Special', because of all the factories (such as Lucas, Ansells Brewery, HP Sauce, B.S.A. and Bulpits) on or near the route, while 'several of the areas through which the buses travelled had smaller factories and workshops, almost jostling side by side with the very houses lived in by the factory workers'. 'People would jump on the No. 8 to go to the nearest shops, to go to the local cinema or even the next pub down the road,' further recall the authors of its definitive history. 'It was the bus service for the real "Brummie", who didn't have to go "into town" to find food, entertainment or work.' And within each distinctive area the No. 8 passed through – whether, travelling clockwise, Ladywood or Hockley or Nechells or Saltley or Bordesley or Small Heath or Sparkbrook – a still largely tight-knit, head-down world of its own.[4]

Many, many other continuities and entrenched habits-cum-assumptions. More than 70 per cent of men smoking, more than 40 per cent of women smoking, and the boilermakers' leader Ted Hill casually holding an untipped cigarette in his right hand as he was about to be formally inducted in 1967 into the House of Lords; David Hessayon's series of 'no-nonsense, populist Expert guides' to gardening, 'jam-packed with information', becoming bestsellers; the bowler still *de rigueur* in the City of London; Saturday morning cinema for children still flourishing (no Saturday morning TV programmes for children until 1968); Sundays still Sundays, albeit the odd sign of some loosening; still a plethora, especially in London, of Lyons teashops; in the valleys of South Wales, still dozens of Bracchis ('the little Italian cafés with their hot pies, steaming espresso machines, bottled sweets and home-made ice-cream'); Burton's for men's suits up to a certain point on the socio-economic scale, Moss Bros above that point; early closing on one weekday afternoon no longer compulsory but still often followed; many stores in London's West End closing for the weekend at Saturday lunchtime; Graham Turner's pork butcher in Wigan discovering his customers' innate aversion to change ('When for the sake of efficiency he bought and introduced a machine which sliced up lard and wrapped it in packets, the sales of lard fell away steadily, so he reverted to cutting it from a slab with a "home-made" tag prominently displayed, and sales promptly recovered'); Viv Albertine's mother saving all year for Christmas pale-blue Co-op stamps ('then you'd go with the full book of stamps to the shop, and in return they'd give you a Christmas hamper with a packet of loose tea, chocolate biscuits, fresh dates, a bottle of R. White's lemonade and a round fruit cake with a layer of thick yellow marzipan on top'); in the West Midlands, door-to-door traders ('tatters') leaving plastic bags containing children's picture books on door knockers in exchange for old clothes and rags, though by now banned from leaving goldfish; and, as remembered by Morrissey, 'still the old and weathered Manchester where people carry deep bowls to ice-cream vans, and load them with scoops, or carry dinner-plates to fish and chip shops where their supper is dumped onto their own trusted china which is then covered by a tea towel for the walk home . . .'[5]

A notably suggestive slice of quotidian life comes from the sociologist Otto Newman, investigating in winter 1966 betting shops in London's East End, but first placing them in their physical context:

> Strikingly obvious is the coexistence, rather than the conflict, between the old and the new – the intermingling of sparkling launderettes and of male boutiques with the traditional East End 'caff' – dark, dank, reeking of stale tea-leaves and of slop; the supermodern chainstore and the chaotic second-hand dealer; the miniskirted factory-girl, still wearing her curlers barely concealed under her headscarf; the shining, underslung, supersprung pram, being pushed by mother wearing her scruffy bedroom slippers . . .

Betting shops themselves may have been a recent innovation (at least in their current, now legalised form), but Newman discovered quickly that the prevailing culture within them would have been familiar long before:

> Each betting shop has its hard core of supporters, loyal, steadfast, ranging elsewhere briefly to break their luck, to avoid the embarrassment of a long streak of winning bets, or to gain new insights by exchange of opinion with a different set of students of form. Within their own betting shop they are known and addressed by their first names, or even more often their nicknames; their foibles, preferences, idiosyncrasies are known and taken account of, their moments of glory, their splendid exploits are fully recalled in surroundings familiar; their near-misses given a sympathetic ear, their prestige firmly established and regularly reinforced by new deeds of valour – the successful bet, irrespective of volume of winnings, made in face of overwhelming odds, in defiance of expert opinion, the result of personal courage and of firm resolve. Their honour, prestige, self-respect will be revalidated by withstanding without flinching within the range of public scrutiny the assault of sustained losing runs, by display of the appropriate mixture

> between elation and restraint at their moments of triumph. Each subtle nuance of action and reaction will undergo the litmus test of judgement by equals, will serve, not as on first impact one might be inclined to assume, to divide the wheat from the chaff, to separate the leaders from the mass in competitive encounter, but rather to sustain common values, to confirm the image of what man ought to be like – resolute, independent yet cooperative, humorous, modest, indifferent in the face of danger and adversity.

'We find only very slight evidence of value preferences representing the middle-class way-of-life and almost total correspondence with the values postulated in respect of traditional community life in our working-class sample,' he concluded about his study of one particular betting shop. 'We must, on the basis of our material, reject the hypothesis claiming embourgeoisement of the working-classes as premature or possibly even as ill-conceived.'

A world similarly in football of working-class continuities. The reassuring click-clack of the turnstiles, the crowd at least nine-tenths male, Bovril the main drink available, wooden rattles whizzing round, the man walking round the cinder track as he repeatedly shouted 'Peanu-uts, tanner a bag!' – these are some of Ian Mole's memories of going to Roker Park to watch Sunderland. Other aspects in general of the football experience included the small proportion of available seating (an average of around 12 per cent at English League clubs), the absence of shirt advertising, the muddiness of the pitch for most of the season, the brain-damaging heaviness of the leather ball, and (though not for much longer) the lack of fan segregation in the crowd. Almost invariably, the ground itself still had a hemmed-in, utterly urban setting; while Arthur Hopcraft's classic *The Football Man* (1968) included this passage on what he called 'the privileged places of working-class communion', i.e. the standing terraces behind the goals:

> They are hideously uncomfortable. The steps are as greasy as a school playground lavatory in the rain. The air is rancid with beer and onions and belching and worse. The language is a gross purple of obscenity. When the crowd surges at a shot or a collision near a corner flag, a man or a boy, and sometimes a girl, can be lifted off the

> ground in the crush as if by some massive, soft-sided crane grab and dangled about for minutes on end, perhaps never getting back to within four or five steps of the spot from which the monster made its bite. In this incomparable entanglement of bodies and emotions lies the heart of the fan's commitment to football.

No place of working-class communion more privileged than Liverpool's Kop end, where the 20,000 packed like sardines sometimes included the future writer Michael Elliott. Unsurprisingly, the great 'half-time ritual' would linger in his memory: 'It involved a rolled-up *Liverpool Echo* and warm rivulets of piss would be cascading down the terraces within minutes.'[6]

Places of working-class communion, too, were, in their own distinctive way, the almost three and a half thousand working men's clubs (WMCs) affiliated to the Club and Institute Union. Perhaps reasonably typical was the one in Middlesbrough glimpsed on a Saturday evening ('when husbands and wives went in together and sat next to one another all evening without saying much') by the young Paul Vallely:

> After the bingo, which everyone called Housie-Housie, there would be a turn on. 'Quality turns, you know,' my Gran would say as she got ready to go, taking her rollers out, patting her buoyed-up hair under her hairnet, taking off her pinny and pulling on a pale blue cardigan or a powder-pink one that always looked as if it belonged to someone else. 'Some of them go on to be famous after they've been at our club, you know.'
>
> And when the turn – it might be a comedian or even a juggler, but most likely a singer – went off to take a mid-act break there would be pie and peas. Pork pie with marrowfat peas that had been soaked overnight and were sometimes a day-glo green, depending on whether someone had put in too many of those bicarb tablets.

The humour on offer tended to be unreconstructed. Graham Turner related how one Saturday night in 1965 at Greasbrough Social Club near Rotherham, 'he thinks a polythene bag is a Greek prostitute' and 'he thinks a Gentile is a man who buys things retail' were typical quips from the comedian on display; while a few years later, in Oldham, Clancy Sigal watched as 'the act builds to his patter, a mixture of ethnic slurs and what he calls "mucky", a seemingly inexhaustible cast of transvestite butlers, phallic Black Panthers, ineptly circumcising rabbis, farting policemen, effeminate cabinet ministers (by name) and slow-witted Irish animal buggerers' – as 'all around me women are laughing as hard as men, teenagers joining in as eagerly as their dads'. Generally, the link between the WMCs of the 1960s and a once hugely popular form of entertainment was palpable. 'The working men's club,' Alan Brien explained in 1966 to *New Statesman* readers after visiting one in Sunderland, 'is the East End pub music-hall of 50 years ago with its programmes of comedians, singers, impressionists, jugglers, advertised each week in the local paper.' The closest analysis we have of WMCs comes from the historian Laurence Saywood, who shows how in the musical entertainment provided they did embrace modernity to at least some degree, especially in the form of guitar-led groups, while at the same time largely sticking to more traditional, more music hall-variety forms, often 'Vicwardian' in their pre-1914 origins and often participatory, not least as an assortment of acts were each given their 'turn' on stage; and he quotes a beat group, called Get Rich, telling the *Daily Mirror* in 1966 of their frustration about how on the WMC circuit it was almost invariably the familiar that trumped everything: 'Audiences there only want to hear Beatles' music or the stuff they can sing along to.'

While the long-established WMCs mildly reinvented themselves, the 1960s also saw the emergence of a wave of privately owned, profit-oriented, well-appointed and often very large 'cabaret' clubs, aimed predominantly though not exclusively at that legendary figure 'the affluent worker' and most famously epitomised by Batley Variety Club, opening in March 1967. Concentrated particularly in Yorkshire and Lancashire, these clubs (also known as 'theatre', 'variety' and 'proprietary' clubs) were, noted the veteran comedian Max Wall, 'the halls over again', with audiences 'like the old crowds in the music halls'. Bernard Manning's Embassy Club in Manchester was one such; while across the city, recorded Richard West after a visit in 1965, these clubs majored on drink, striptease and comedy, as well as presumably music. 'The club comedians avoid four-letter words, but their jokes are scarcely fit for family ears. For instance one mordant, white-faced man specialises in humour about the sexual life of lepers, syphilitics and hunchbacks.' And he quoted verbatim the patter of a comedian at the College Theatre Club in Moss Side ('where many immigrants live'):

> I went abroad the other day – to Denmark Road. There was a guy there who said if we got rid of the Pakistanis we'd have four hours more sunshine each day . . . I met another Englishman and said 'snap' . . . I saw six Jamaicans carrying a coffin. I said what are you doing. He said 'Blackberrying' . . . Then I met the Mayor of Moss Side. He's an Irishman. He has a shamrock in his turban . . . Did you hear about the Pakistani who married a Scotch girl? They had a baby and called it Pacamac . . .

The authoritative overview of these 'cabaret' clubs is that of the cultural historian Dave Russell, who argues that they 'provided a method of engaging fully with 1960s consumerism, a way of "being modern" and experiencing activities previously associated with more privileged social groups, but without losing contact with pre-existing practices and habits'. Yes, modernity with the sophisticated interiors (like the dragon's tooth ceiling at the Stockton Fiesta) and the scantily clad waitresses and the scampi-in-a-basket to eat and the opportunity for American-style casino gambling and on a good night the stars from stage and screen; but at the same time, the music safely mainstream, the sexual display 'safely diffused', the gambling carefully regulated – and in general what he calls, with a surely spot-on phrase, 'a quiet permissiveness'.[7]

Russell in turn approvingly quotes Dominic Sandbrook's argument for the place of 'familiar' mainstream within the popular musical culture of the time, specifically his claim that 'show tunes, light classical music, jazz and cabaret music all thrived during the sixties, appealing to middle-aged listeners because of their association with affluence, sophistication, glamour and romance'. For all the far greater noise, then and later, about rock and pop music, plus assured recognition for blues and folk, this has to be right, with no doubt nostalgia to be added to the ingredients. Take, for instance, that household name, Max Jaffa. Whether for many years leading the Palm Court Orchestra on radio's long-running *Grand Hotel* (where he chose the music and guest singers), or appearing with his orchestra at Scarborough's Spa Grand Hall (twenty-seven successive summer seasons), he stuck unabashed to a light classical and popular repertoire, ranging from Schubert to Rodgers & Hammerstein. 'When he was accused of playing a "dated" repertoire,' noted an obituarist, 'he replied that it was just because the repertoire was dated that people wanted to hear it.' Or take the continuing popularity of brass band music, with one estimate being that though the number of bands had declined from the late-Victorian peak of some 40,000, there were still at least 2,000 amateur civilian bands (including works bands) as well as almost 800 Salvation Army bands and some 250 armed forces bands. 'Besses o' th' Band players are expected to be smart and well groomed on all jobs,' insisted a notice in the rehearsal room of a well-known Lancashire band, recent victors at the national open championship at Manchester's Belle Vue. 'White shirt! Black shoes and socks!' While as Eric Ball, editor of the weekly *British Bandsman*, observed in 1966: 'Bands are very conservative indeed. If contest organisers didn't insist on it, many of them probably wouldn't play any new music at all.'

Almost certainly, no one told the old-fashioned, pub-style pianist Mrs Mills what she was going to play. *Everybody's Welcome at Mrs Mills' Party*, *It's Party Time*, *Mrs Mills' Party*, *Let's Have Another Party* – these were the titles of some of her mid-sixties albums, while as the sleeve notes to her *Look Mum, No Hands* nicely put it in 1967: '"swinging" grandparents can recapture the days of their youth ... "with-it" parents will feel nostalgic ... "switched-on" teensters will want to dance ... So, Mum, organise a jolly family get-together or party, spin this record on the turntable, and watch everyone join in the fun.' Laurence Saywood notes that her choice of singalong numbers was 'eclectic, providing a mixture of inter-war popular song and jazz standards with songs from the turn-of-the-century music form'; and, as further explaining the broad appeal of this reassuringly homely figure, never one to stint on the puddings, he quotes a writer for *The Stage* pointing to 'her obvious sincerity, and her sound sense to be herself', and a *Sunday Mirror* reader, Mrs J. M. Place of Yorkshire, unfavourably comparing (in the paper's 'Be Your Own TV Critic' column) the 'glamour boy efforts' of pianist Russ Conway (a staple on *The Billy Cotton Band Show*) to her much more relatable 'natural performance'.[8]

Homeliness, too, from the easy-going, almost defiantly non-trendy Irish singer Val Doonican. His *Times* obituary in 2015 would be sneery enough – the 'middle-of-the-road neverland of perpetual middle-agedom' that was *The Val Doonican Show*, where he was 'romantic without being seductive, tender without being passionate, and successful without being ambitious', until viewers were 'finally beaten into soporific submission by his trademark final ballad performed while swinging in a rocking chair' – but for millions of families he was from 1965 at the very heart of their weekend TV viewing. In the mid-sixties themselves, he had five Top 10 hits (including 'Elusive Butterfly' and 'If the Whole World Stopped Loving'); he was loved for his relaxed charm as much as for his patterned sweaters and cardigans; and just occasionally he would break out into 'Paddy McGinty's Goat' or 'Delaney's Donkey'. None of Doonican's hits, though, quite matched the commercial triumph of Ken Dodd's 'Tears', in the Top 10 from mid-September 1965 through to early January 1966, including five weeks at No. 1. Admittedly he was already well known as a toothy comedian, but that alone hardly explained the astonishing popularity of this lachrymose number firmly in the tradition of the Victorian sentimental ballad. 'I don't like "Tears", but my Mum does,' Sandie Shaw told *Disc Weekly*, adding that 'she goes mad over it'. Yet was the younger generation as a whole really so averse? For shortly before, but also in October 1965 (the record's peak month), the same magazine had sought out opinions from people aged between fourteen and twenty-five. 'The kind of artist who appeals to everybody, no matter what their age is,' reckoned Brenda Ousley (twenty) of Yorkshire, adding she was 'very glad he made number one'; Maureen Walsh (sixteen) attributed the hit to Dodd performing his vocal 'with great feeling'; 'it's great to see this kind of record doing so well,' declared Gordon Davies (twenty-five); and according to fifteen-year-old Michael Coombes, 'we need more of these records'.

Indeed, one can even exaggerate the relative popularity of the Beatles. Their longest-lasting single in the UK charts would turn out to be 'She Loves You', with twenty-four weeks in 1963 – two weeks fewer than Jim Reeves's 'I Love You Because' the following year; while taking the 1960s as a whole, the Beatles had 219 weeks (the equivalent of over four full years) with a single in the charts – but Cliff Richard, admittedly starting earlier, had 315 (equivalent of six full years). And a February 1967 piece by the music critic and academic Wilfrid Mellers, teasingly entitled 'Sixties' and arguing that the traditional 'vast gap between the serious and the popular arts' was now closing (in part because of the Beatles and Bob Dylan), included a highly telling detail. Whereas his university students had all loved *Revolver* since its release the previous summer, the LP 'was dismissed by a class in a large, industrially-centred school with the ominous words: "Aw, no, sir, we don't like that; it's all *chinky*."' No disturbing chinkiness on the soundtrack of the 1965 film *The Sound of Music* – at No. 1 in the album charts for a remarkable sixty-nine weeks.[9] The hills were alive, but not invariably with the sound of the Fab Four, huge cultural phenomenon though they undoubtedly were.

The film itself played in cinemas across Britain for month after month. As it happened, October 1965 was not only the month of 'Tears', but also when *The Sound of Music* became, in its seventh month, Wales's longest-running film, with a feature in the *Western Mail* revealing it to be not unusual for cinema-goers in Cardiff to have seen it at least thirty times. 'It's a family story,' reflected a cinema manager there. 'It's got a universal appeal. It's an acceptable story with a little bit of humour affecting members of a family, and a large family at that. It has a romantic angle and, of course, there is the wonderful music.' Devotees in Cardiff and elsewhere would not have been watching it in a multiplex, for as Ian Mole recalls of growing up in Sunderland, 'most cinemas were a decent size with a large stalls as well as a circle':

> The back row of the stalls and circle were of course where younger couples would sit, hoping for a snog when the lights went down. You also got a full programme, i.e. adverts, maybe a cartoon, Pathé News, a B-film and then the main feature. Pathé News lasted about ten minutes and was a resumé of recent big news stories around the world. I don't remember them being in anything but black and white and the commentary was always in one of those posh BBC voices that dominated the media back then. There wasn't anything really heavy in them but you'd see the Queen and Prince Philip riding an elephant in Kenya or something like that.

As an expression of mainstream cinematic taste in the mid-sixties it is hard – with the possible exception of the Bond films – to avoid the claims of the *Carry On* comedies, by now in or entering their commercial heyday, including *Carry On Cleo* (1964) and *Carry On Doctor*

(1967). 'A cocktail of dreadful puns, sexual innuendo and scatological jokes delivered by characters drawn with a very broad brush and regardless of what became known as political correctness' was how a 2009 obituary of their producer Peter Rogers would accurately describe their essential character; while regular if not invariable members of the troupe included Kenneth Williams, Joan Sims, Charles Hawtrey, Sid James, Kenneth Connor, Hattie Jacques and, years before she became a national treasure on *EastEnders*, Barbara Windsor. Inevitably, a raft of academic critics have pointed to some of *Carry On*'s worst, most irredeemable aspects – Marion Jordan, for instance, noting how 'sexual desirability (however much parodied) is most commonly female, sexual desire and potency most commonly male'; how gay men are depicted as 'effeminate' and 'bereft of sexuality'; how 'the most objectionably cruel of the stereotypes of the unattractive woman is that of the aging (or in some other way non-pin-up) spinster, aping a coy girlishness in the hope of catching a man' – but perhaps just as interesting is Roger Lewis's less censorious take, emphasising how 'sex in the *Carry Ons* was always unmistakeably off-putting, despite Swinging London ostensibly being somewhere in the background', an off-puttingness typified by Bernard Bresslaw being 'accompanied everywhere by a battleaxe of a mother-in-law'. Or in short, 'nothing much ever happened' – ultimately puritan films, one might fairly argue, for an ultimately puritan grin-and-bear-it country, even two decades after the end of the war. The films, adds Lewis, 'portray an England full of restrictions, with the cheerful inhabitants enduring an existence of delayed or cancelled gratifications. They drive rusty cars. They go on day trips to paddle in the English Channel. They eat pork-pie picnics. They go on no-frills, self-catering weekends where Hattie Jacques is queuing for the turbo-toilet.'[10]

In the world of armchair Britain, and despite rumours to the contrary, not all that much changed in its underlying habits and preferences. 'For most viewers the liberating influence of Hugh Greene meant little,' the notably unsentimental, clear-eyed TV critic Milton Shulman would argue some years later. 'They watched the BBC for *Grandstand*, *The Black and White Minstrel Show*, *Top of the Pops*, *Come Dancing*, *The Billy Cotton Band Show*, *Dr Finlay's Casebook*, *Perry Mason*, *Dr Who*, *Dick van Dyke*, *Rolf Harris*, *Val Doonican*, and they were contented enough.' A quick sample of what one might call viewer norms suggests he was right.

On *Not So Much a Programme* and then *BBC-3*, the most popular figure was the stammering, resolutely non-intellectual Patrick Campbell, receiving a flood of appreciative letters which, in his own words, 'thanked me, sincerely, for the breath of fresh air that I intruded into overly pompous and opinionated argument'; *Come Dancing*, introduced by Peter West and Judith Chalmers, would not have been *Come Dancing* without, at the end of each programme, what one critic described as 'schoolboy cheers from victor to vanquished, vanquished to victor'; 'she was a motherly, sometimes bracing teacher, guiding her flock towards greater economy, efficiency and gentle adventure,' notes an obituarist about the homely and very popular television cook Zena Skinner; 'Come in, come in, it's nice to see you / How's yoursel', you're looking grand . . .' was Andy Stewart's invariable sung introduction, as he welcomed viewers to the White Heather Club; an intrinsic part of the appeal of the comedian Eric Sykes lay in how, to quote Stephen Dixon, 'there was about him an air of faded, working-class gentility and stifling respectability, of best suits on Sundays and highly polished boots, of boiled ham and limp lettuce salads and the best tea-set specially got out for visitors'; on *Crossroads*, the introduction of a storyline about a single mother working at the motel proved hugely controversial among viewers; and when in 1966 an edition of *Man Alive* focused on the effects of lengthy imprisonment, almost half the Viewing Panel professed themselves 'irritated' by the programme's treatment, seen as 'unjustifiably sympathetic towards the prisoners and their relatives', with one viewer especially vexed by how those relatives 'seemed to think they were entitled to hold a grievance against society'.

For hitting a particular sweet spot, there was perhaps nothing quite so surefire – or so emblematic – as *The Good Old Days*. Calling it 'a cheerful parody of music hall', and 'one of those essays in nostalgia in which the BBC specialises', *Punch*'s Bernard Hollowood was struck in 1964 (eleven years into its run, nineteen years before it finally ended) how by contemporary standards 'the inevitable Can-Can seems absurdly modest, gymnastically unsuggestive', while 'the patter and cross-talk seem as pure as the driven snow after a few séances with *TW3* and Lenny Bruce-type comedians'. Recorded each week at the City Varieties in Leeds, a surviving nineteenth-century music hall, *The Good Old Days* did what it said on the tin, as an unabashed celebration of an old-style participatory culture. 'All performers were presented in period-correct costume as well as the filmed audience that had gathered inside the music hall, with Leonard Sachs guiding proceedings as the verbose and alliterative chairman,' notes Saywood, adding that 'the participation of the filmed audience was an essential element in reconstructing an idealised atmosphere of Edwardian communal conviviality, not only for the performers but also for the TV viewer'. Or as *Radio Times* put it not long after Hollowood's observations, 'not only do the audience look so much like authentic Edwardians, they obviously feel like Edwardians as they join in the choruses, heckle the chairman, provide the gaiety and gusto and warmth in which Variety flourishes'. In 1963 the waiting list for a chance to sit in the Leeds audience was some 2,000; by the end of 1967 it was up to 14,000; and a sales manager would hardly have been alone, among the ten million or so regular viewers, when he told audience research that what he loved about the programme was its 'atmosphere of shared hilarity and enjoyment'.[11] The good old days . . .

A sense of the reassuring, the familiar, from the press, too. 'There was a time when Saturday night would not have been Saturday night without the pink 'un, the green 'un, the buff 'un or even the white 'un: the late evening special edition which told you how your team had got on,' recalled David McKie wistfully in 2004; but the great day was Sunday, with the three most popular titles – the *News of the World*, the *People* and the *Sunday Mirror* – having between them close to forty-five million readers. 'It looks very much the same and reads very much the same in the mid-twentieth century,' commented Francis Williams in 1965 on the *News of the World*, 'as it did in the mid-nineteenth: the symbol of an immutable editorial conviction that the British liked their Sundays bloody, violent, adulterous, and concerned with what went on in public parks . . .'; and he quoted some typical headlines ('Songs They Sang At a Strip Show', 'Kisses On The Sunshine Cruise', 'His Fatal Friday Night Out', 'A Girl of 14 Tried Blackmail'). By contrast, the *People* 'specialises particularly in exposures', currently the ill-treatment of dogs, though Williams noted that both papers liked royal stories, with the *News of the World* currently running 'My Life With Princess Grace' (by the nanny), the *People* running 'The Royal Teenagers', to be followed of course by 'The Royal Toddlers'. As for the *Sunday Mirror*, he acknowledged it was a bit more serious, while also pointing out that it specialised in gossip columns, jokes and cartoons, not to mention features like 'The Men Women Prefer' and 'The Women Men Prefer'. Scotland had its own high-circulation Sunday paper, the *Sunday Post*: faithfully read during the week from beginning to end, unquestioningly trusted, of intense respectability combined with the popular touch, and once described as representing 'a blinkered romanticism of Scotland Past: a Scotland of quaintness, kindness, and community intimacy, where political thoughts or aspirations are taboo'.

Across the national daily press, the startling rise of television had as yet only barely dented overall circulation figures: 15.59 million in 1965 compared to 16.03 million in 1960, with the two most popular papers, the *Daily Mirror* and the *Daily Express*, selling just over 5 million and just under 4 million copies respectively. Each had a rock-solid, seemingly unchanging cartoon for the ages. Barry Appleby's the Gambols (the happily married suburban couple George and Gaye) had started in the *Express* in 1950 and would run almost entirely untroubled for virtually half a century – 'there was,' reflected Appleby's obituarist, 'no violence in their lives, no social stress, and sex was something which took place out of sight'. Quite a contrast with the *Mirror*'s thoroughly working-class Andy Capp (created and drawn by Reg Smythe), certainly in the relative levels of rumbustiousness. Even so, that sense of cultural continuity was at least as strong:

> Andy [wrote the *New Statesman*'s D. A. N. Jones in 1965] likes his wife treated with respect. Merely praise another woman and Andy will throttle you; rewarded with Flo's kiss in the smoke-room, Andy growls: 'Watch it!' . . . At least Florrie can be sure that his advances, like his rare compliments ('The girl's got guts. Worth her weight in beer. I *love* yer'), don't spring from politeness or a sense of duty . . . He is a one-man watch committee for the by-laws of masculine behaviour . . .

'It's alleged that Andy is out-of-date in our foambacked era,' added Jones. 'Not so. Every true locality maintains a Capp, appalling yet enviable with his happy, patient wife and the shamelessness with which he accepts situations, like being barred from pubs, which most would consider a disgrace. If he weren't so recognisable, he wouldn't be funny.'[12]

The middle-class Gambols were still much likelier than the Capps to take a foreign holiday. The figures for 1967 were revealing: just 7 per cent of the population travelling abroad that year; while of those holidaymakers venturing across the Channel, more than one-third belonged to socio-economic group AB, which of course was a far smaller group than the working-class C1s and C2s. Between them, the C1s and C2s amounted to some 22 million people, but in 1966 (and probably not much different the next year) barely 1.5 million of them took a foreign holiday. Almost certainly the explanation is part cultural, part economic (inclusive package holidays were still relatively expensive, something over twice the average weekly wage for a fortnight in the Spanish sun). Which in the mid-sixties meant, in short, that even though the package holiday abroad was in every sense poised to take off, for the time being the distinctive joys and traditions of the British seaside holiday could more or less remain unthreatened and intact.

Those traditions by now firmly included holiday camps. The best known were Butlin's and Pontin's; but in these years, Tim Lott's father (a greengrocer) and mother preferred to go just slightly inland in order to avoid 'the hobbledehoys, or real working class', opting instead for places, mainly in Devon, calling themselves 'Country Clubs' or 'Halls', though in truth they were fractionally upmarket, and fractionally less regimented, holiday camps:

> The pattern of each of the country clubs was much the same – bluecoats, or greencoats, or greycoats, urging participation from the wake-up call announced through the barking PA. *Roll out of bed in the morning / with a great big smile and a good, good morning*. Jack and Jean [his parents] were treated as hybrids of adult and child, as evidenced by the signs on the toilets, 'Lads and Lasses', and the gamesmasterish invocations to 'have a go'. We swam in unheated pools, secretly pissed in by children and stuffed with chlorine. There were card rooms and snooker halls, ping-pong tables, rooms full of dartboards and communal televisions. There were egg and spoon races, tugs-of-war, treasure troves, day trips, beetle drives, paper chases, crazy golf and gorgeous granny competitions . . .
>
> In the evenings the main meal would be slightly continental – perhaps paella, or cannelloni, or curry with raisins – and the wine was rosé or Asti Spumante or Liebfraumilch. Then Jeff [Tim's brother] and I went to bed in monitored chalets, little more than beach huts with beds, Goblin Teasmades and nylon sheets that

> issued tiny electric shocks. After nightfall, ballroom dancing and novelty competitions – lookalikes, knobbly knees, fancy dress.

Many years later, Lott came across a photograph engraved in copperplate 'A Souvenir of Our Holiday Torbay Chalet Hotel', showing his mother and two other guests 'dressed up in pyjamas and nylon nighties, holding candles, for the theme of "Wee Willie Winkie" ':

> A showgirl stands off to the left and Rory Blackwell, a bluecoat, to the right. His face screwed up in a showman's smirk. A three-piece show-band is in the background in jackets and ties, playing 'Spanish Fly' or 'Que Sera Sera' or 'Volare'. Later they will accompany the ritual singsong that ends the evening: 'Run Rabbit Run' and 'Lily of Laguna' and 'Hello, Hello, Who's Your Lady Friend' and 'Ta Ra Ra Boom De Ay' and 'I've Got Sixpence' and 'Mairzy Dotes' and 'How Much is that Doggy in the Window?'

Familiar numbers indeed; and, of course, 'always the evening will close with "Goodnight, Campers" sung to the tune of "Goodnight, Sweetheart".'

Seaside resorts themselves – whether Morecambe with its Alhambra, Floral Hall and Winter Gardens, or Littlehampton with its miniature steam railway and Billy Smart's Fun Fair and upmarket Beach Hotel, or Weymouth with its legendary sand sculptures by Fred Darrington – continued to hold their own, albeit with the business of their often famously strict landladies (guests booted out after breakfast and told not to come back until high tea at 5 p.m.) starting to be eroded by significant rises in self-catering (up from 18 per cent of main holidays in 1955 to 25 per cent in 1965) and caravanning (up from 8 to 13 per cent). No resort more celebrated and/or denigrated than Blackpool, to which Graham Turner devoted a full chapter in his northern panorama. Over 5,000 hotels and cafés; 120 fish-and-chip shops; up to 95,000 people entertained each day during the season in theatres, cinemas, ballrooms and bingo halls; 232 donkeys – he naturally delighted in the impressive stats of 'a holiday factory', while at the same time observing that Blackpool itself was 'an extraordinarily staid and puritan town' (for instance, 'only two pubs with singing licences in the whole place, and local vigilantes keep a sharp eye on the shops for things like suggestive ashtrays'). That 'high moral tone', he argued, made commercial sense, given 'its traditional clientèle, the Lancashire and Yorkshire mill-workers, have always deported themselves in a remarkably restrained way on their holidays'. Or take the reflections – a somewhat different take, but ultimately complementary – of Blackpool's premier historian, John Walton, as he examines the photographer Alfred Gregory's 'wonderful collection of spontaneous shots of holidaymakers enjoying themselves on and around the beach in the 1960s, in which local teens and twenties no doubt mingle with the holidaymakers':

> It illustrates the emergence of a distinctively dressed new youth culture, and of public manners which had the power to shock an earlier generation. Mini-skirts, girls ostentatiously smoking and passionate kissing on the beach among the crowds in broad daylight were novel extensions of the licence Blackpool granted to young wage-earners, but there is something innocent about the horseplay and endearing about curlers as beachwear which are on display here.

A much younger photographer, Colin Jones, was also in Blackpool, spending a week in 1966 at a boarding house (full board, including a tea of Spam, marrowfat peas and an ice-cream scoop of mashed potato, for 25/- per night; up to 104 guests sharing one bath between them; the stark written warning, 'Any Disturbance and You Will be Asked to Leave the Premises On One Minute's Notice'). Looking around, and taking his photographs, he saw what seemed to him in retrospect, returning to the resort thirty-five years later to take more photographs, an almost wholly unreconstructed world: 'When the blokes booked in they used to share a single bed so they had more money for the booze. But there was no bed-hopping. The women didn't drink: they were very modest, but the blokes used to go out and get amazingly pissed, and then sleep it off in a deckchair on the pier.' Whereas, 'these days [2001] the women seem to drink more than the men. It can be quite hairy on a Saturday night behind the Tower. When I went back, it was the gangs of pissed women that I found the most intimidating.'[13]

16

Whipped at the Cart's Tail

'The repression was difficult to confront – like finding your way down a foggy street,' recalled Derek Jarman (born 1942) about being a young gay man before decriminalisation (though not in Scotland) in July 1967. 'In the sixties, we were to be open but illegal. This did not make it easy to form relationships and led to fumbling, furtive sex.' 'Heterosoc', he added, 'kept its tabs on me; my parents were still alive. Would they murder me, exile me, what *would* they do if they found their son was a "pervert"? There were few young people in the bars, only the old who had come to terms with their *fate*.' Similarly, the music critic Patrick O'Connor remembered the advice he had received in 1965, aged sixteen, from 'one of the first queer men I ever met': 'Don't dress like that; don't look ostentatious or kinky; you'll never meet anybody.' Or as O'Connor himself reflected:

> The permissive society had not yet begun. In the background, if one was aware of the language of clothes, there were tiny details. Thin, almost transparent black socks seemed popular among the slightly older homos. But these people – living out a life using sign language, discreet dress codes, waiting for the release of being safe behind a locked door – seemed to feel almost as affronted by dandified clothes as the grey suburbanites were. They all united to affect shock or to deride someone like Quentin Crisp, who had been dressing as he liked, using make-up and flouting convention for decades.

Standing back at the time from the issue, and even allowing for the odd 'stately homo' exception, Bryan Magee was surely right. 'They cannot sit on a park bench kissing each other,' he wrote in his 1966 book *One in Twenty* based on his two recent TV documentaries, 'or walk down a street hand in hand, or embrace on a railway platform, or any of a thousand things that heterosexuals take for granted.'

We can drill down a bit further about prevailing attitudes. 'The predominant attitude', reckoned Magee, 'is one of disapproval, but also of interest':

> There are lots of jokes about homosexuals – many forms of popular entertainment now contain camp figures as stock characters. In offices the secretaries are as likely as anyone else to giggle and gossip about a man's being homosexual. So there is a general interest in the subject, and a general disposition both to joke about it and be shocked by it – the two of course being related to each other – all of which rest on an acknowledgement of its existence.

Undeniably there were strong levels of prejudice, with indeed Magee himself observing how 'the homosexual is all the time running up against absolutely built-in assumptions on the part of other people, totally and unthinkingly accepted by them'. 'The element of homosexuality aroused a good deal of distaste,' noted BBC audience research in March 1965 about viewer reaction to John Hopkins's Wednesday Play, *Horror of Darkness* ('after the day's activities we need to relax, not to have to see and hear other people's depravities,' declared one viewer, though another grudgingly commented, 'I suppose these twisted people are fascinating in an awful sort of way'); three months later, 'too much time, effort and money are wasted on sympathy for criminals, homosexuals and the like' was the blanket view of S. H. Perry of Shevington in a letter to the *Lancashire Evening Post*; 'he wants homosexuals imprisoned,' recorded the elderly Gladys Langford next year after a conversation with a Mr Caulker, although she for her part took a more relaxed view ('I think they prevent adding to overpopulation'); and at auctioneers Christie's in 1967, the young Brian Sewell resigned after an office enemy had effectively blocked his application for promotion with the damning words, 'We've got one homosexual on the board; we don't need another.' Or take, as quantitative evidence, the opinion poll in autumn 1965. Yes, two different polls each found that almost two-thirds (63 per cent) of those asked were in favour of the decriminalisation of homosexual acts between consenting adults; but when one of the polls (NOP) asked for responses to the proposition that 'homosexuals are in need of medical or psychological treatment', a staggering 93 per cent agreed.

Yet perhaps this was not so surprising, given that earlier in the year a Home Service discussion about 'The Male Homosexual' had featured a presumably well-intentioned psychiatrist (who worked mainly in northern hospitals) talking confidently about the great value of aversion therapy:

> Many homosexuals are excited by the sight of the naked male body. One can see many magazines on book-stalls which cater for this interest. You can take this stimulus which, say, is the picture of a naked male, show it to the patient, and he will, of course, experience the sexual pleasure to which he has been accustomed. At the same time, you bring in the aversion, which is usually either a forced and sudden vomiting or else an unpleasant electric shock. Going on principles of learning, and particularly of conditioned reflexes, the two will tend to become associated, and, after a course of treatment of this sort the patient, rather than being attracted towards the stimulus will tend, in fact, to be driven away from it. Correspondingly, though this is more difficult, it may be possible to associate pleasurable feelings with the stimulus of the female body. There are certain drugs which may be used here, but I think the biggest thing of all is the sheer relief of the unpleasant stimulus fading away. It is at that point that behaviour therapists would then bring in the female picture, or some form of female stimulus, hoping that the pleasant feeling of relief would then be associated with this.

Over the years, horrifying accounts would emerge of what aversion therapy meant in practice for the unfortunate patient. Here, just one. In 1964, aged eighteen, the future radio DJ Peter Price reluctantly took the advice of his adored adoptive mother and went to see his GP about possible treatment, in turn leading to a referral to a psychiatric hospital in Chester:

> Peter [the journalist Beverley D'Silva revealed in 1996] will never forget his first interview with the psychiatrist. 'He asked me if I

realised how revolting homosexuality was, how vile and revolting anal and oral sex were. He used the grossest terms. He wanted to make me feel disgusted.' Peter claims that nothing was explained about the treatment he was to undergo (contrary to recommended practice). 'If I'd known what they were going to do to me, I would never have gone in.'

He was shut up in a room containing a bed but no windows or furniture. He was given a crate of Guinness, his favourite drink, and a pile of erotic photographs of men. 'I can't imagine how I was supposed to be turned on by those – they were just pictures of men in rather baggy bathing costumes.' Not such awful treatment, he thought – until, that is, the 'real horror' started. Price was injected with a drug (probably Antabuse, although he doesn't know for sure), and felt violently sick. He asked for a bucket but was told to be sick in the bed. An hour later, he was given another injection, which made him vomit again. An hour later, another injection. And another and another. This continued for 72 hours. There was no lavatory in Peter's room. He was told to defecate in the bed.

'I felt dirty, grotty, filthy,' he says, his sentences becoming staccato as he revisits the painful memory. 'I was petrified. This was the lunatic asylum, a loony bin. There was screaming through the night, other patients would come in and whisper in my ear or piss on my bed. I couldn't concentrate on pictures of men's bodies. I could only think of getting out.'

When the doctors told him about the next phase of his treatment – a further two days of therapy, this time electric shocks – Peter hastily discharged himself . . .

So, three days only of treatment – but, reckoned Price, destroying thirty years of his life. 'I feel that something was messed around in my head . . . I've only had two relationships, of just three years each. It makes me very sad. I'm a caring, loyal person . . . But I have a self-destruct button. A trigger goes off in me and I push people away.'[1]

By contrast, lesbians passed to a remarkable extent under the radar. 'Our society deals with lesbianism,' reflected Magee, 'by pretending that it does not exist'; and he noted how when he had made his programme specifically focusing on lesbians, 'the great majority of people who asked me what I was working on were visibly pulled up in their tracks when I told them, and made an embarrassed joke, or changed the subject' – altogether, an embarrassment so pronounced that 'even quite sophisticated people found difficulty in actually uttering the word "lesbian"'. Or take the experience of Olive Stevenson (born 1930). 'At that time, it was far from easy to acknowledge myself as a lesbian and, although I never denied it, I did not formally "come out",' she recalled about lesbian relationships in the 1960s. 'A kind of social denial was then common; such relationships amongst middle-class women were often tacitly acknowledged by those close to the people concerned. But nothing was ever said.' Not that there was *no* out-and-out prejudice. Lesbians, according to a *Tit-Bits* feature in 1964, were unusually numerous in women's prisons, treated there as either 'butches' or 'femmes' (sometimes 'fems'); and the magazine's expert pronounced: 'In all lesbian relationships, no matter how innocent, danger and corruption lurk. Jealousies lead to fights and worse.' Particularly revealing was the experience of Joe Orton, when in March 1967 he went to the theatre at Wimbledon for a matinee performance of *The Killing of Sister George*:

> The pianist began playing a selection of popular songs of the past fifty years. The audience brightened considerably. There was a buzz of anticipation in the air. A lot more women came in. 'I don't suppose they'll understand what the play is about,' I said to Kenneth [Halliwell]. 'Don't you believe it,' he said. 'They'll know very well what it's about.' He was right. It became clear, from the opening scenes, that they understood and weren't amused . . . There were hardly any laughs. The lesbianism seemed to stun them. Though I'd thought it was a second-rate play in the West End, light and offenceless, Wimbledon wasn't up to it. Glumly they sat. At the end of the first act, the tea-trays were passed around and the piano began to play; this was the part the audience enjoyed. The second act began. There are two scenes in this act. When the curtain came down on the first scene half the audience thought it was the end of the act and the aisles of the theatre were suddenly crowded with old men and women hobbling out into the foyer. Suddenly the curtain shot up on the second scene and, to murmurs of irritation and surprise, the audience slunk back to its seats. During the third

act, alarm grew at the (to them) uncontrolled sexual perversion and (to me) flat unimaginative dialogue.

Finally, 'at the moment where Sister George orders her companion to drink the bathwater, a couple of old ladies rose and stumbled out'.[2]

In general, and despite what was happening in pop music, in fashion, on TV, on stage and screen – the private silences about anything to do with the subject of sex remained deep and often unbreachable. 'I simply could not afford for anyone to find out anything about my situation, let alone my parents,' remembers Janet Street-Porter about finding out as an eighteen-year-old, just as she was about to sit her A levels, that she was pregnant. 'As we had never discussed sex at all, the idea of mentioning casually over breakfast that I was expecting a child seemed ludicrous. Apart from anything else, we didn't talk much at mealtimes, let alone about anything of an intimate or personal nature.' Two summers later, in 1967, the decriminalising Sexual Offences Act was in the process of being passed. 'I know I was alert by then to the word "homosexual" as it appeared in headlines, and disturbed by this bold-faced naming of a deepening preoccupation of my own,' recalls Alan Hollinghurst about his thirteen-year-old self. 'I can see my father's *Times* and my mother's *Mail* raised on either side of the fireplace, and catch still the slight discomfort in the air, though I can't recall their saying anything about the great question in my presence – a wholly typical reticence, and a great relief to me.' Perhaps no Englishman was more archetypal of his time than the England football manager. 'I'm a very emotional person but my feelings are always tied up inside,' Alf Ramsey would later say. 'Maybe it is a mistake to be like this but I cannot govern it.'[3]

Unsurprisingly, then, the state of sex education left something to be desired, with the Newsom Report on secondary education noting in 1963 manifest deficiencies, not helped by excessively nervous parental-cum-teacher attitudes as well as a failure of leadership from local education authorities. Moreover, 'although the 1960s saw a boom in publishing sex-instruction manuals – so that no major publisher was without its sex-education textbook – most of these were either totally inadequate or endorsed a very conservative view of sex':

> Even the most liberal texts [continues Jeffrey Weeks] tended to endorse a 'stages' view of sexual development, which was either to be happily resolved in heterosexual monogamy or unhappily resolved in sadness and isolation. Homosexuals, as a 1967 textbook designed for teachers put it, must be regarded compassionately for many 'are suffering from psychological disturbance' and none of them 'can ever find the happiness of raising their own family'. An examination of 42 books on sex education conducted for the National Secular Society in 1970 found most of them were obscure in style, inaccurate in content, and badly written. Nearly all of them were moralistic, particularly about non-marital sex; and some of them were positively dangerous. One text suggested that 'your eggs won't get fertilised until you are quite grown up and have a husband'. Another advised that it was morally and *legally* wrong to have sex before marriage . . .

A few months after Street-Porter's unwelcome discovery, BBC1 showed a documentary called *The Young Adults*, about the sexual behaviour of teenagers. 'The film started with the customary pop music and some sinister hints of teenage drug-taking, road-hoggishness, violence and debauchery,' wrote one critic, 'but was quickly taken over by a good-tempered, reasonable panel of teenagers gently chiding their parents and teachers for the coy backwardness of sex education for the young.'

The occasion for the programme was the publication that week in July 1965 of Michael Schofield's *The Sexual Behaviour of Young People* – a survey, largely conducted in 1962–3, which in the reviewer's words revealed there was 'more virginity, fidelity and romantic idealism among teenagers than they are given credit for'. The figures themselves for the sample (a total of 1,873 interviews) revealed that 70 per cent of teenage boys, and 84 per cent of teenage girls, had not experienced premarital intercourse; while as for promiscuity, only 12 per cent of the boys had had more than one partner in the previous year. Even so, attitudes among the young undoubtedly did shift significantly in the course of the decade. Our clearest evidence comes from a survey of grammar-school sixth-formers (both sexes) conducted first in 1963, then in 1970. What, they were asked each time, was their opinion about premarital sexual intercourse?

	Always wrong (%)	*Usually wrong (%)*	*Sometimes wrong (%)*	*Never wrong (%)*	*Undecided (%)*
1963					
Boys	28.6	27.6	20.5	10.2	13.1
Girls	55.8	25.2	6.6	2.4	10.0
1970					
Boys	10.3	12.8	30.4	33.7	12.8
Girls	14.5	19.5	30.0	17.7	18.2

Significantly, though, the same 1963/70 survey showed no comparable change when it came to attitudes to promiscuity, still condoned only by a small minority.

What about the population as a whole? The decade's sole thoroughgoing survey of sexual behaviour and mores – though only of people up to the age of forty-five – comes late, with Geoffrey Gorer's conducted in 1969. Based on a sample of almost 2,000, he found that almost half of men, and well over three-quarters of women, were either virgins when they married or had had sex only with their future spouse; that 'the great majority of the younger English married men and women still put a very high value on marital fidelity'; and that only one in twelve of the married sample had had an extra-marital affair. The strong probability is that these findings would have been even more suggestive of a sexually conservative society if the survey had been undertaken a few years earlier. 'All my male friends were still going out with nice girls and, believe it or not, it was still a big thing to marry a virgin,' a male interviewee in the north-west remarked many years later about the mid-sixties to the oral historian Elizabeth Roberts; while, when Graham Turner travelled more generally around the north in 1965, he was forcibly struck by how 'particularly among older working-class people – though the feeling is by no means confined to them – there still exists a conviction that sex is a dirty thing and that the flesh is both unsightly and wicked'. A trio of his anecdotes spoke volumes: the woman working at one of Sheffield's railway stations who 'told me proudly that she had been married for thirty years and that she had never "seen" her husband and he had never "seen" her'; the friend in Darlington who 'told me that when women became pregnant – even after marriage – they described it as "falling wrong" '; and the charwoman in Cheshire who, 'telling the story of a couple who had had to get married because the girl was having a baby, commented "I don't know how they can – it's bad enough when you're married." '[4]

Marriage itself remained an astonishingly ubiquitous institution – to the extent that, in the mid-sixties, some 95 per cent of men and 96 per cent of women had married by the age of forty-five. Moreover, the normative pressure not only to get married, but to *stay* married, was still great. *Woman's Own*'s agony aunt 'Mary Grant' was asked by a wife in 1965 whether she should forgive her husband who had been 'cold' with her and then confessed he had been having an affair. 'I just can't forget the hurt of those few weeks.' But the advice could hardly have been brisker: 'Just as your husband pulled himself together for the sake of your marriage, it's your turn to do the same.' Divorce rates, it is true, were on the rise – from 38 for every 10,000 married women aged under fifty in 1955, to 42 in 1961, to 71 in 1968 – but these were still small numbers. And while it is also true that an October 1965 poll showed an increasingly broad tolerance for the concept of divorce as such, the same poll found a majority agreeing that they would 'tend to have a poor opinion' of someone who had been the guilty party in a divorce involving adultery (52 per cent) or desertion (62 per cent) or cruelty (86 per cent). This disapproval could even apply in the world of showbiz, as Kenneth More found after leaving his second wife to live with Angela Douglas. The social ostracism culminated in October 1963 with the first night of a West End play – final curtain coming down; dressing room all ready with a hired butler plus three cases of champagne, canapés and smoked salmon sandwiches; total absence of the promised guests – and did not really lift until 1967, as More restored his fortunes as Young Jolyon, role close to the bone, in *The Forsyte Saga*. Painful, too, for the children. Robin Douglas-Home's 1964 novel *Hot for Certainties* features early on a prep school dormitory, where the central character (in his first term, and whose parents are about to get divorced) naively asks why one particular boy is seemingly exempt from the customary rude remarks about the parental photographs on the bedside lockers. 'The answer came in a kind of sacrilegious whisper: "Because they're DIVORCED" . . . From then on he blushed whenever the word "divorce" was mentioned.'[5]

No scene in a novel would ever speak to me more strongly than that, when I read it a year or two later. My own parents had divorced early in the decade; and I spent much of the rest of it going to extraordinarily devious lengths to try to ensure that, at my successive boarding schools, as few people as possible knew about it.

'You didn't plan in those days like you do now,' one of Elizabeth's Roberts's interviewees from north-west England – 'Mrs Wallington', married in 1946, three children – told her in the 1990s. 'You didn't say, "I'm getting married and having three children," or "I'm getting married and I don't want any kiddies." You just took what came along.' If that was often the case in the early post-war years, so to a perhaps surprising extent it seems to have been in the mid-sixties. When in 1965 the sociologist John Peel questioned 20 per cent of all those who got married in Hull that year, he found that 'the majority wanted two children, no couple wanted more than four children – yet all couples accepted that they will have more children than they want'. Around the same time, fatalism, too (plus crossed fingers) from Veronica Lee, studying at Leeds University:

> Rick [her boyfriend] did find the courage to get a package of condoms but we both felt embarrassed by them. I didn't like the smell and he complained of a loss of sensation. So, in the end, we relied on that most unsatisfactory method – withdrawal. I don't know how Rick felt but it led to a lot of anxiety from me, fearing that he wouldn't be able to pull out in time. And then there were occasions when passion got the better of both of us and Rick wouldn't bother to pull out. I knew all the time we were playing with fire.
>
> My period had a very irregular and long cycle, anything from five to eight weeks. That gave me a lot of worrying time. Each month I was sure I must be pregnant and became more and more worried as each day passed with no sign of the arrival of my period. I spent a lot of time planning how I was going to tell people and thinking of the many people I would disappoint and upset. And, although it was one way of ensuring I wouldn't have to do sociology again, the

> alternative suddenly seemed far worse. Dick [her father] had always threatened me, when he thought I was being too clever for my own good, with the spectre of Gossards factory in Exeter. This factory made bras and according to repute only the worst kind of woman worked there. I knew it was what I deserved but how I dreaded it . . .
>
> In my third year I did pluck up courage to go to student health to talk about my irregular and painful periods but the doctor was fairly dismissive and said all would be solved by having a baby. This was not the answer I wanted to hear.

Notwithstanding the best efforts of Helen Brook, contraceptive advice generally remained patchy. For the most part, the 530 or so Family Planning Association clinics seem to have enforced, until 1967 anyway, their long-standing policy of refusing to see the young unmarried; while it was not until that year that the Family Planning Act enabled local authorities to give – though sometimes more in theory than in practice – birth-control advice regardless of marital status, and on social as well as medical grounds.[6]

What about the fabled Pill? 'We heard vague rumours about this wonder pill,' recalled Lee, 'but we knew unmarried women would never get it prescribed for them' – as indeed largely remained the case until 1967. Moreover, even among married women there was far from universal take-up during the years after it first came on the market in 1961, so that by 1967/8 still barely a quarter of married women had ever used it: partly no doubt because it was relatively expensive, but perhaps just as much because of what one might call an instinctive cultural resistance, especially (as Gorer discovered in 1969) among the northern working class. There, both men and women tended to view it as somehow unnatural; they were often surprisingly relaxed about taking their chance and continuing to rely on withdrawal; and, of course, men wanted to stay in charge. Two other things did not help. 'An alarmingly high proportion of men have found their ardour decreasing in relation to their wives' increasing desire,' noted Marjorie Proops in early 1967, in the context of increasingly widespread warnings-cum-rumours that the Pill could directly cause male impotence. The second factor, on rather firmer empirical ground, was the often palpable effect upon the users themselves; and Roberts quotes another interviewee, 'Mrs Hunter', who until the birth in 1965 of her third child had relied on coitus interruptus, but then gone on the Pill. 'I went enormous,' she remembered. 'I went fat, big round fat face, and headaches. I was in a terrible state, and the doctor took me off.'

She decided to trust to luck; but not long afterwards, and by now living with a new partner, the inevitable happened. Whereupon: 'He said, "I don't want it." And I was so wrapped up in him at the time that I did what he wanted.' Agreeing to the termination, her GP sent her to the hospital, where a traumatic interview ensued. 'He [the doctor] made me feel like a loose woman. I was in tears. He said, "OK. If we get rid of this, how do I know you are not going to be in next year for the same thing?" I was so upset that I nearly threw myself under a bus when I came out. I cried all the way home on the bus.' Despite this, the termination did happen. 'At the time I was glad I was having it done. But I think that anyone who has had a pregnancy terminated always looks back and thinks, "Would it have been a boy or the girl I always wanted?"' Estimates varied about how many abortions were taking place prior to the 1967 legislation – whether in NHS hospitals or private clinics or, probably by far the most numerous, shady hole-in-the-corner back-street rooms – but the total may lie somewhere between Lord Silkin's 1966 claim of 100,000 and the more conservative NOP estimate the same year of 31,000.

Where estimates seldom vary, in retrospective accounts, is about the physical and often psychological horrors involved. 'An abortion is the most *unspeakable* experience you could have in your life,' remembered Carmen Callil; while for Amanda Brooke-Dales, it was 'all deeply unpleasant', leaving her 'stuffed full of gauze' and, in the fullness of time when she was unable to have children, 'rather wondering whether I'd done something horrible to myself'. At the grislier end of the physical spectrum (albeit living to fight another day, unlike those thirty or so women who died each year as the result of criminal abortions) was Janet Bull's teenage experience that secretive summer of 1965:

> I stumbled through my A-levels in a daze [recalls Janet Street-Porter]. Through a friend we [i.e. she and her lover Rex] found out about a woman in Camden Town who would deal with the situation

> for £25 cash. I arranged to see her one Friday after school when my parents had gone away . . .
>
> I took the tube to Chalk Farm and walked up Malden Road, stopping on a corner to ring the bell to a flat above a shop. A blonde woman let me in, took the cash and showed me into her kitchen. Shaking with fear, I took my knickers off and sat on a towel on her kitchen table, leaning back with my legs apart. She stuck a syringe of something (soapy water, I don't know) up me, seemed to scrape something around a bit, which was painful, and then told me to go home and I would have a miscarriage in an hour so, just like a heavy period. I barely made it back on the Central Line to Perivale before the cramps started – they were terrible. I spent hours sitting on the lavatory losing a lot of blood. Luckily my parents and sister were away for the weekend. It was pretty disgusting, but all I felt was a tremendous sense of relief. Providing I hadn't totally fucked up my A-levels I would still be going to the AA [Architectural Association] in September . . .

Her abortion cost six times as much Rube's abortion, so central that autumn to Ken Loach's adaptation of Nell Dunn's *Up the Junction*, watched by ten million viewers. 'At one point,' observes Clair Wills, 'Rube tries to explain why she wants to end the pregnancy but Winny, the kindly-faced family friend who will carry out the abortion, cuts her off: "Oh, there's no need to explain. How can you ever explain anything? It's the most bloody difficult thing in the world." '[7]

Of course, the great majority of pregnancies went to term, some in happier circumstances than others. 'Mum', recalls Ken Livingstone about his sister's teenage pregnancy in 1965, 'went on endlessly about what the neighbours would think and the shame Linda had brought on us.' As often as not in such situations, the parental pressure to marry – and quickly – proved effective. 'Saturday, 10 April, 1965,' remembers Reina James:

> I'm a bride. But not a princess bride in a cloud of veil lace, more like a baby-pink silk balloon with fat legs poking out at one end and a fat face at the other. My hair is so stiff you could bang me on

a gong, my shoes are baby-pink satin, warping and creaking under the weight, and as for the dress, the camouflaging dress: we could have held the wedding in it.

I'd made the announcement on a Sunday visit home. My mother was drinking Guinness and I was leaning on the Aga with a mug of tea. I think the conversation started:

'I'm pregnant.'

'Oh, Christ . . .'

My mum had never toed the line. She'd been a bold girl, a dancer, a round-the-world traveller, drawn to the unorthodox and always on the side of the underdog. Even so, I was only 17 and the times they might have been a'changing somewhere, but not in Surrey they weren't, not just yet . . .

She didn't hang around. In a matter of days, I was booked in with a posh dressmaker and an even posher obstetrician who grinned over my raised knees and said – he really did – 'Good child-bearing hips, my girl.' A hotel was arranged for the function and everything else taken care of without a word to us, the groom [a sixth-former at a nearby grammar school] and me. We were led to the scaffold, dazed, compliant and, in my case, nauseous.

'It never occurred to me,' adds James, 'to be brazen and co-habit and not a single soul suggested it as a possibility.'

Even so, the illegitimacy rate was rising, from 1955's 10.3 extra-marital births per 1,000 single, divorced and widowed women (aged fifteen to forty-four), to 1960's 14.7, to 1965's 21.2; and not infrequently, in the case of an unwelcomely pregnant teenage girl, the parents would insist that she and the male perpetrator were far too young (and/or unsuitable) to get married – and that the only realistic alternative was adoption, usually via a mother-and-baby home. Each year, reckoned Dennis Marsden in his 1969 study of *Mothers Alone* based on mid-sixties fieldwork, roughly one-quarter of illegitimate children were adopted, almost certainly often against the mother's wishes. Some of these mother-and-baby homes were run by local authorities, but most by the Church of England, including the one in East Finchley where in 1963 the sixteen-year-old Cindy Downs was almost forcibly taken by her parents three months before she was due:

> There, among 30 young women – some as young as 14 – Cindy gave birth [related the journalist David Cohen in 2002] to a little girl weighing six pounds, with fair hair and blue eyes. She called her Kerrie. 'She was perfect,' recalls Cindy. 'I pleaded with the matron and welfare officer to keep her but they said if I didn't sign her over, I would be chucked onto the street and the baby would be taken into care. I would lose her anyway.'
>
> The regime was so Dickensian the mothers dubbed it Colditz. Each mother was given a daily rota of duties to perform: scrub baths, clean toilets, make beds, lay breakfast. At fixed points, 6am, 10am, 2pm, 6pm, 10pm and 2am – they were allowed to feed their babies and change them. For the rest of the daytime, their babies were placed in prams and left in the garden with a nursing sister.
>
> Cindy would watch in dread as, one by one, the other birth mothers had to hand over their babies. Eventually, the day arrived when it was Cindy's turn. She recalls it vividly: 'I spent all morning playing with Kerrie and taking photographs until, at 2pm, I was told to take her up to the nursery to prepare for the handover. This involved feeding and changing her and also preparing a bottle of milk for the journey.
>
> The sister kept coming in, asking, "Have you finished yet?" I kept dragging it out, saying that she wouldn't take the bottle. I was crying, telling Kerrie I loved her and that one day I would find her. I found myself repeating my name, over and over, as if to imprint it on her mind so that later she might wonder: why do I know this name? She lay in my arms, watching my face and smiling up at me. Later, that became important – I didn't have much of her life but I did have her first smile.'
>
> After half a dozen calls, the matron grew impatient, forcing Cindy down the stairs. 'Three steps from the bottom, I just froze. By now I was crying hysterically, tears falling onto Kerrie's face. The matron wrenched the baby from me and disappeared into her office, locking the door and leaving me standing there totally distraught.'
>
> A few hours later Cindy's father picked her up. They travelled home on the bus – he talked about the weather – and the baby was never discussed again.

Many comparable stories would subsequently emerge, leading to the founding in 2010 of the Movement for Adoption Apology, seeking a government apology to all those coerced or forced, between the 1950s and 1970s, into giving up their children for adoption. Obviously, each individual set of circumstances was unique – but ultimately, this was a cruel phenomenon, a scandal even, owing almost everything to unforgiving, deeply entrenched attitudes.

'It was just this poor girl, and these babies were so beautiful, and she was giving it away,' remembers Liz Currie (born 1945) about a fellow inmate at a Church of England home in Wiltshire for unmarried mothers. 'It wasn't because she wanted to, it was because society said well, this was what you had to do because nobody would accept you if you were, you know, if you were an unmarried mother, so that's what used to happen.' While as for those single mothers who were looking after their own babies, and often were dependent on National Assistance, Marsden found that they tended to encounter, especially if they were working-class mothers, marked hostility from neighbours and even friends. Double standards were hard to shift. 'The unmarried mother', reflected the National Council for the Unmarried Mother and her Child in its 1967 annual report, 'remains a symbol of our fears and guilt about ourselves and our children. She illustrates the hypocrisy of a society which condemns her, as her predicament may be the inevitable result of the more permissive code of sexual behaviour which the public in fact now accepts while still preserving a different standard of morality for men and women.' A last word goes to Gladys Langford and her wide-ranging conversation the year before with Mr Caulker: 'He wants unmarried mothers to receive still more from state & charities. I want them whipped at the cart's tail . . .'[8]

'She never married and was proud to be financially independent,' noted an obituary of Fay Kramrisch, much-respected teacher at Fairfax Upper School in Bradford, 'so it caused her not a little frustration that to apply for a mortgage in the 1960s she needed the signature of her uncle as a male guarantor.' Or take the experience of the young Polly Toynbee, starting work in 1968: 'With my first paycheck from the *Observer* I tried to buy a washing machine on hire purchase, but was refused without a signature from a husband or a father.' More generally, moreover, a wife's income continued to be treated by the Inland

Revenue as belonging to her husband; while in the social-security system, the governing assumption remained the Beveridge one that the woman was dependent upon her man. What about the increasing sociological norm that marriages were becoming ever more 'companionate', a partnership of roughly equals rather than two people living in largely separate spheres with the husband calling almost all the shots? Geoffrey Gorer, in his detailed 1969 survey, asking much the same questions he had back in 1950, did indeed point in his findings to 'the greatly increased emphasis on doing things together'; but at the same time he reflected that 'symmetrical marriage' was 'difficult to achieve if the husband "gives" his wife a housekeeping allowance and keeps her in ignorance about his total income' – still the situation, he found, in more than one in six marriages. As for the major purchases of domestic goods (cookers, fridges, washing machines), a large-scale 1967 survey revealed that sole responsibility rested with the wife in only one-third of families.[9]

Nor in three other key areas was change, in all probability, all that rapid. 'I took the mechanics of being married extraordinarily seriously and was determined to be a good wife,' recalls Veronica Lee about getting married in early 1967 to her boyfriend from recently completed student days. 'I bought a notebook and wrote down every single item of expenditure in it; there was going to be no extravagance from me. I planned menus. I borrowed books from the library on how to run a home. I undertook every task, from shopping to cooking to going to the launderette, and I expected nothing from Rick . . . At first I was happy to do all this because I thought that was what good wives did.' A second area was the husband's most inalienable right. By this time, the novelist Penelope Mortimer would remember about her husband John, what he demanded from life was 'a succession of accessible girlfriends':

> He felt that our marriage would be perfectly satisfactory if I could understand this and give him my blessing, but I couldn't. Actual sexual infidelity was the least of it, provided I wasn't expected to sympathise, but I furiously resented hints and confessions, implausible excuses, furtive muttering on the 'phone, a flowering of Carnaby Street shirts and medallions. I despised him for needing my sympathy as much as for the minor and clumsily conducted affairs . . .

Then, of course, there was domestic violence. 'The working-class north of England was a routinely brutal world' is how Jeanette Winterson puts it about growing up in Accrington and keeping her eyes open. 'Men hit women – or as D. H. Lawrence called it, gave them "a dab" – to keep them in their place.' Elsewhere in the north-west, one of Elizabeth Roberts's interviewees, 'Mrs Gerrard', was asked what in particular her mother had tended in the 1960s to have to see her doctor about:

> Near enough the same thing; black eyes and being strangled.
>
> Did she ever take you children away to avoid seeing him? – No, because he never came home before the pubs shut. And we were in bed, so she would probably think that we didn't hear it anyhow, but we did.
>
> Did she ever consider leaving him? – Yes, but she had nowhere to go. My nana couldn't put her up, she didn't have enough room.
>
> Did you say anything to him or ever interfere at all? – Yes. Well one night he had come in and it weren't like it usually was, it was really quiet. And I remember standing at the top of the landing screaming, and I jumped back into bed and my sister said, 'Aw, what'd you do that for? He'll kill you now.' I were really frightened of my dad. And he come up and told me off.

'And,' she added, 'my mum said, the morning after, that if I hadn't screamed . . . he was strangling her and it had all gone black.'

No one person can be wholly representative of an era or a society; yet to read the description by Tim Lott (born 1956) of his mother Jean (born 1931), living in suburban Southall, makes it hard not to feel that she was in her way peculiarly emblematic of many millions of other women, leading a life in which, as he writes, 'the pattern of existence was traditional and conservative, a life more accurately reflected in "The Gambols" than *Cathy Come Home*':

> Jean was a Daz housewife, a Gibbs SR mum, worried about the cleanliness of clothes and the neatness of home and children. She took pains to be bright and optimistic. She left money matters to Jack, since she considered herself *innumerative*. She stuck to what she sensed she was good at. With pinny and novelty oven glove,

> she prepared dinner every day for Jeff [older brother] and me. We walked home from Lady Margaret Primary School at midday, to be met with skinless sausages, fried luncheon meat, liver sausage, boiled potatoes, bubble and squeak or leftovers from the previous night's tea.
>
> Jean did not consider that her function was to hold opinions, or hanker for a larger life. Her particular job – apart from child-rearing and hygiene – was to keep the threads of the family together. It was she who would remember birthdays, who would carefully pick a card from Forbuoys in Allenby Road, one with a soft toy or a sunset on the front. The sentimental rhymes were carefully and seriously examined for relevance. The love they spoke of, in copperplate decorated with fluffed clouds, was the solvent for all ills, all disadvantage. This, I imagine, was her great and deepest belief . . .
>
> Perhaps she would add a poem of her own, agonizing to get the rhyme and meter right. Her job, her role, was to maintain relationships, to smooth wrinkles and resolve quarrels. There was an almost complete myopia for anything outside the family.

'Her chores were completed without complaint or resentment, with, in fact, pride,' emphasises Lott. 'Jean did not consider herself a drudge and never seemed to be sapped of her childlike brio, her slightly taut "perkiness", by the endless round of tasks.' Lott also looks ahead a few years, to the time of his adolescence. 'The women's movement – *women's lib* – did not register, let alone find a place in domestic conversation. If brought up, it would be left to one of the men to suggest, artfully, that he was thoroughly in favour of bra-burning. And that was as far as it went.'[10]

Slow change, too, notwithstanding an outraged former miner, in what was still arguably the country's favourite leisure pursuit outside the home. 'God strike me dead, but the introduction of women to clubs and pubs is terrible,' the indignant Welshman declared to a Sunday paper in 1966. 'It's two drinks and two packets of fags and the kids going without. If my grandmother could come back and see the women drinking in the Swansea pubs she'd go mad.' Certainly, any possible fears of a female takeover were misplaced. Two recent historians of working men's clubs are agreed that, despite their increasing physical presence, women remained largely marginalised, above all when it came to running the clubs; Michael Wolfers, writing at the time (1967) about the north, noted how 'you see mixed crowds in the pub but they split into two groups with the men taking one end of the table, the women the other, and two distinct conversations being held'; and someone who had recently moved to the north-east from more socially liberal Reading told Graham Turner about his great disappointment with the pubs: 'They're just not built for women up here he said. There just are nothing like enough where you can take your wife. In most of them, you see the women standing in clusters while the men stand at the bar.' Some younger northern women, though, were less willing to play the game. 'In the mid-60s, my friend and I fought our way to the bar and ordered pints,' recalled Irene Fergie in 2020 about venturing into 'The Phil', the famously ornate Victorian pub opposite the Liverpool Philharmonic Hall. 'We were politely told that if we wanted to drink from pint pots then we would have to get our boyfriends to buy them for us. We left.'

Still, at least they had the option, whereas another popular leisure activity was in effect virtually barred to women: the playing of football, ever since the Football Association back in 1921 had forbidden women's teams from playing on FA pitches or utilising FA officials. As it happened, the first real signs of a grassroots movement to counter the ban came now, in summer 1966 on the back of female enthusiasm for the World Cup, as almost overnight seven women's clubs were formed in the Southampton area, mainly office-based teams using rudimentary pitches and facilities on Southampton Common. Three years later the Women's Football Association (WFA) was formed; two years later the FA at last rescinded its ban; but it would be a long, long time before the women's game emerged fully out of the shadows. 'So many wasted years,' reflects football historian John Williams about the largely sorry story, 'and so much sporting opportunity blighted by small-minded and bigoted men.'[11]

It was not exactly a level playing field in other, more fundamental ways. *Jobs for the Girls* is the title of Ysenda Maxtone Graham's excellent, highly sympathetic survey, mainly covering the 1950s to the 1970s and based on a wide range of oral testimony – a survey which, for all its considerable human interest and appeal, makes ultimately for depressing reading. To take just some of her findings: she is struck by how 'that vital passport to industrial mobility, the maths O level, was mysteriously off the menu at both the very lowest-aspiring state schools in the country and at the poshest private schools'; by how, listening to stories about those girls' private schools, she 'lost count of the women who said to me, vaguely, "Our school didn't really do A levels" ', which in practice meant that 'there was a one-year sixth form that you could stay on for, doing a bit of French and history of art, just to keep you quiet and occupied till seventeen', whereas 'at private boys' schools, the only boys who didn't stay on for the whole sixth form were the complete "thickos", considered almost "backward" '; by how at secondary moderns, most girls left almost as soon as they turned fifteen, with no academic qualifications and heading straight for the workplace ('You just gorron with it' in the words of a woman in Sunderland who had gone immediately to work in a department store); by how, when she asked, 'did you have any careers advice at school?', the most common reply was 'there might have been a few leaflets put out on a table' or 'there was a little-used room with a few dusty pamphlets'; and by how, even at better schools, the limited, puritanical ethos of the female teachers – 'so desperate not to allow their girls to become in any way arrogant that they went a long way in the other direction, ladling them with self-doubt and reminding them again and again that they must never boast or "blow their own trumpet" ' – meant that 'for girls with only mild ambition, or vague dreams, or whose spark of ambition ignited only when they were in their late teens, it could be too late'. Or as she concludes, grimly enough, 'for the millions of shy, self-effacing girls who kept their heads down and did what they were told, it was all too easy for their potential to be snuffed out early'.

For those who did manage to keep themselves on what Maxtone Graham calls 'the achievers' track', the possibility of higher education loomed large. 'The sixth-form spends its second year in a state of continual excitement,' one headmistress told the *Observer* in 1962. 'We urge a philosophical outlook, but the strain of waiting for the offer of a place is terrific, with the suspense mounting as the months pass by.' Certainly there was no abundance of supply: in the mid-fifties, just over 25 per cent of university places had been allocated to women; by 1965 this proportion was still under 30 per cent. That same year, as some 15,000 women (compared to 38,000 men) entered university, as many as 26,000 went to teacher training colleges, well over double the intake for men. 'The academic reputation of these colleges was not always high,' observes the historian Carol Dyhouse, 'and they have been seen as a cheap form of higher education for women.' While at university itself, the classic, much-quoted Oxbridge experience belonged to Ann Oakley, who despite the distraction of getting married while still an undergraduate naturally hoped, as the daughter of the great social scientist Richard Titmuss, for a First when she took her finals in summer 1965. 'On learning that I had "only" got a second-class degree, I wrote on the back of an envelope, which I've kept: "People who don't get Firsts have babies" – a First might have provided a passport to a masculine career path, a justification to do different.' The pressures were perhaps different at the new 'plateglass' universities, with Kathleen Ollerenshaw, author in 1967 of *The Girls' Schools*, noting their particular appeal to 'bright and lively girls who have good brains but do not see themselves devoting their lives to academic study'. And famously, it was Sussex above all that attracted upper-middle-class female entrants, almost invariably to read arts subjects, and indeed to such an extent, reckons Dyhouse, that 'the "dollybird" was effectively part of the branding image of the new university'.

Perhaps the fullest account we have of the broader female experience comes from Mary Ingham, reflecting on her own at Liverpool University (1965–8) and that of her contemporaries more generally. Although far from denying aspects of liberation, and ways in which the women were treated as equals of the men, she also casts a darker hue. 'Universities', she notes, 'still discriminated in their job hierarchies, and girls weren't expected to talk much in tutorials'; 'male students lived where they pleased, or could find room', whereas 'girls had to stay in halls of residence or lodgings until their third year', often with strict rules about being in by a certain time in the evening; and far too often, when it came to sex, 'college girls were so much fruit, ripe for picking, to be discarded, unfeelingly and insensitively once appetite was satisfied'. Or as Ingham also puts it about a typical hitherto relatively innocent first-year student suddenly feeling defenceless and all at sea, 'badly articulated protests that she didn't know him very well (the only way she could express what felt "wrong" about the situation) sounded feeble and ineffectual in the alcohol-blurred gloom into which she had allowed herself to be led'.[12]

Nor on the whole was it much better in the workplace. 'The spirit of Fleet Street is still as ineradicably masculine as the old-style men's club,' declared the *Daily Express*'s Ann Leslie in 1966 (but not in the *Express*). 'The solid core remains untouched by the vague ambi-sexuality that has crept over other publishing media . . . It stays as solidly male as beer and sawdust and battered sheepskin jackets.' As in Fleet Street, so in office life at large, at a time when, as the economy started its shift from manufacturing to services and new executive positions mushroomed, there was a huge increase in women working in offices, especially as secretaries. Sartorial rules could be strict (definitely no trousers or short skirts at the stockbrokers Cazenove), while in offices where greater leeway was given the decade saw the introduction of the so-called 'modesty board', covering that section of the desk where female legs were dangerously visible. That, though, was about the only precaution taken against the pervasive sexism of office life, as so eloquently documented in *Jobs for the Girls*. The imperious shouting by male bosses of female first names, the publisher George Weidenfeld throwing an inkwell at his secretary, Hyde Park 'awash with bosses meeting up with their secretaries beside the Serpentine', the latest edition of the *Secretarial Duties* textbook warning a would-be secretary to be 'silent in matters such as her own personal troubles, office gossip and her employer's affairs and business', almost ubiquitous bottom-pinching, even in some cases the tacit threat of the sack if sexual advances were refused – such was the prevailing culture, on the whole to be silently put up with. 'There was a feeling among the women,' reflects Maxtone Graham on the basis of her many interviews, 'of slight pity for the rather desperate, lunging men. "I just thought, 'Silly old bod,'" said Cicely McCulloch, when the retired Army major for whom she was working as a secretary at an animal charity in Bedford Square in 1966 stood behind her desk and tickled the back of her neck. Cicely just looked across the room at the other secretary and they both grimaced at each other.'[13]

Of course, in this era of marriage becoming overwhelmingly the social norm, not every wife was encouraged by her husband to enter the workplace. 'Strong patriarchal structures persisted, linked to the idea of men as breadwinners – something that retained a deep meaning in these places,' reflect Huw Beynon and Ray Hudson about traditional mining communities in the economically challenged 1980s.

'Many men found it morally unacceptable to be financially dependent upon their wives.' Undoubtedly, such assumptions would have been even stronger, even less shiftable, two decades earlier. Or take two well-established authors, both of them perhaps surprisingly unreconstructed in this particular area. 'The house was a comfortable home, thanks to my mother, who worked an endless shift of cleaning, washing and ironing, shopping and cooking for a family of six,' recalls Michael Chaplin (born 1951) about his Newcastle childhood:

> This began at 6 in the morning and finally ended after 11 at night, when Sid [the novelist Sid Chaplin] put the cover on his typewriter at the end of another evening stint. Rene's day involved the preparation of four cooked meals, ending with late supper featuring anything from lamb barley stew to fried egg sandwiches. Rene had been a shop girl, but her working life outside the home ended the day she married. Despite his liberal values, Sid never countenanced his wife going to work: it was a misplaced point of honour of his Durham mining culture that a man's labour provided for the family and the woman's job was to care for it. The redoubtable Rene accepted this and like many women of her generation found other ways to use her intellect and character.

The other author, whose wife similarly possessed much intellect and character, was the sociologist Peter Willmott. Here the gender divide was appreciably less extreme, yet Phyllis's diary entry from autumn 1965 is still revealing:

> Petie gave me a little 'pep talk' this morning before going to work! I explained I felt a bit at sea – not sure where I was going from now on, wondering a bit whether I ought to take on more of a 'proper job' with the boys so nearly grown. Feelings of guilt and parasitism etc. Petie, he says, would rather, ideally, I did less not more. He says he wants support from me in carrying his own load of responsibilities and although he likes me to have my own interests and sees I need them, he wants me not to get more pressed and so on . . .

Inasmuch as one can generalise, the findings of Elizabeth Roberts from her oral history of families in Barrow, Lancaster and Preston feel fairly representative: that men in this period had a range of views, none of them dominating the others, about the desirability of married women working for wages outside the home – but that 'there was, however, one commonly held assumption: male wages would exceed those of the female'. And the women themselves? Maxtone Graham is struck by how, when in her interviews she asked about going back to work after having a baby, the reply very often was, 'It didn't even occur to me'; while in her contribution in 1965 to a Women's Institute scrapbook, this testimony from a member living in the Gloucestershire village of Woodmancote would surely have had many other wives (not just WI members) nodding in recognition:

> My husband prefers me to stay at home, so that in the evenings I can relax with him instead of doing the household chores. In the winter we enjoy doing crosswords and reading. I like cooking and gardening. I can try out new recipes and grow more unusual flowers, things which I could not do if I went out to work. My sons come home at irregular hours and I consider it a duty and a pleasure to have a warm house and a meal ready for them and my husband, and I know they appreciate it.

'I also have time,' she added, 'to talk with my neighbours and friends, besides taking part in village affairs . . .'[14]

Even so, the broader trend was going the other way. In 1965 a large-scale official survey (overseen and analysed by Audrey Hunt) revealed that almost half of mothers with children aged five to fifteen were doing paid work (though only 15 per cent of mothers with under-threes); while in terms of female attitudes, over two-thirds of the women surveyed had no problem with the statement that 'a woman and her family both benefit if she does a job', with fewer than one-fifth thinking that mothers with school-age children 'ought' to stay at home. These figures are cited by Helen McCarthy, whose survey (*Double Lives*) of working motherhood in modern Britain gives us a full and objective account of a subject traditionally freighted with emotion and misunderstanding. She also notes that it was 'a different story when it came to mothers with very young children; here, attitudes were far less tolerant, with over three-quarters of Hunt's sample agreeing that women with children below school age should stay at home to look after them'. And she elucidates some of the problems continuing by the 1960s to face the working mother, including animosity from full-time workers (most working mothers were part-timers), ambivalence shading into hostility from male-dominated trade unions anxious to maintain pay differentials between the sexes, and nursery schools existing by 1965 for only 3 per cent of three- and four-year-olds. McCarthy's judicious overall conclusion about working mothers in this period deserves to be quoted in full. After describing 'the post-war model of working motherhood' as resting on 'women's acceptance of a bargain which opened up new employment opportunities without disturbing wider inequalities in the labour market and at home', she goes on:

> Women settled for jobs which were less skilled and lower paid than the ones they had done before becoming mothers, and they continued to accept primary responsibility for childcare and housework. Most married women took this deal because it delivered a higher standard of living and better prospects for their children, and a slice of financial independence and psychological fulfilment for themselves. For women without male breadwinners, this deal was never on the table. Lone mothers found themselves standing outside looking in on the home-centred post-war family, just like other groups who failed to conform to its norms, including older unmarried women, women in same-sex partnerships and many of the migrant mothers who sought to make new lives in Britain in these decades. Finally, the post-war ideal made little room for mothers who wished to pursue continuous careers offering progression and high earnings rather than 'little jobs' to be picked up and put down.

'This group', she acknowledges, 'formed a small, privileged minority of working mothers, but they voiced a dilemma which dogged middle-class women for the rest of the century: how easily could professional ambition be reconciled with the demands of family life?'[15]

Assumptions about who was going to rise to the top remained heavily gendered. To take just one example, Sarah Aiston's examination of career advertisements and articles in Liverpool University's student newspaper, the *Guild Gazette*, which reveals an overwhelming emphasis, through the 1960s and even beyond, on male graduates. An ad placed by Unilever in November 1963, featuring one 'Peter Salt', could hardly have been blokier or, according to Aiston, more typical:

> **Line of work.** Marketing. I approve those things they squeeze between television programmes when people hurry to the kitchen for a glass of milk.
> **But what would you really rather do?** Nothing. I don't mean not to do *anything*. There just isn't anything else I'd rather do.
> **Driving Force.** The usual one. A hungry wife. Two hungry children. A hungry cat and a hungry dog. Besides I get hungry too.
> **Most paradoxical quality.** I'm lazy. I can watch my wife mow the lawn without a qualm of conscience. Yet at the office I work hard.
> **The terrible temptation.** About 5 feet 6. Blonde. Blue eyes. Luckily I married her.
> **Unfounded fear.** Being old and broke. But I have a good job with a future and a good salary.
> **Personal panacea.** Work when I'm upset at home. Home when I'm upset at work. The local when I'm upset at both.
> **Greatest satisfaction.** Joining Unilever after I went down. A man's choice of career is one of the biggest decisions in his life, and his greatest satisfaction is being able to look back and know that he chose the right direction . . .

Or take a range of stats from the mid-sixties: only 1 per cent of working women becoming managers in establishments with more than twenty-five employees; women comprising only 13 per cent of managers of large establishments; university medical schools sticking to a quota system of 80 per cent men to 20 per cent women; solicitors some 98 per cent men, 2 per cent women; among those classified as 'higher professionals' generally, fewer than one-tenth being women, and of those almost 70 per cent employed as 'clerks'; the ranks of chartered surveyors, accountants, auctioneers, estate agents, and electrical and mechanical engineers almost entirely bereft of women (in each case, less than 1 per cent); female members of the Institute of Directors numbering only one in forty . . .

Albert Memorial, London, 11 June 1965: Allen Ginsberg centre and front

Birmingham, 1965

Westminster Hospital, 14 January 1966: matron's daily conference

Hulme, 1966

arettes

T. Dan Smith (chairman of the Northern Economic Planning Council), 1966

Glasgow, 1966: Red Road

Regent Street, London, 3 July 1966

Carnaby Street, London

Hull docks

Marine Gardens, Skegness

Brighton, 1966

Harold Wilson travelling to Nottingham, 6 November 1965

Claudia Street, Liverpool, July 1966

XLV
89

Wembley Stadium, 30 July 1966: Herr Dienst awards England's third goal

Two particularly important worlds still largely male-dominated were the City and politics. The Stock Exchange remained a male fortress, even after the very well-qualified Muriel Bailey had promised not to stray onto the dealing floor if she was made a member; at the Bank of England, the top positions stayed a male monopoly, even after the aptly named Aphra Maunsell had made the front page of *The Times* in 1967 by being appointed as deputy chief of Establishments; and that same year, when Barclays launched its graduate recruitment programme, no woman was even interviewed, let alone accepted. While at Westminster, there were barely two dozen female MPs following the 1966 election – three fewer than in 1964, and representing just 4 per cent of all MPs. The most prominent of those was, by some way, the high-powered, strikingly red-haired, sometimes flirtatious Barbara Castle, recently interviewed by Susan Barnes after becoming transport minister. Barnes in the course of her profile mulled over the traditional assumption that it was impossible for a female politician to be both tough *and* feminine. 'Can't she? Tigresses can fight tooth and nail, but no one ever suggested they weren't profoundly female creatures . . . Men are considerably less dismayed by aggressive women when they are clearly and unmistakeably women – and decorative as well. Mrs Castle is.'[16]

That was in early 1966, a few months after IPC – owner of both *Woman* and *Woman's Own* – had appointed a new editorial director, Clive Irving, with a brief to make women's magazines more contemporary, more representative of a woman's life in modern Britain. 'The idea that a woman's magazine has to place a genteel filter between a subject and its reader must be hopelessly out of date at a time when any other medium can open up any issue for adult discussion,' he told an industry paper, citing issues like 'the morality of living on the HP', the Pill, sexual impotence, 'the strain of living with a successful husband', and of course 'the Other Woman' as the sort of taboo-breaking areas that it was time to venture into, and not just in the problems page. 'Women's magazines', in short, 'have been wearing their skirts too long.' Over the next year or so, *Woman* and *Woman's Own* – the two market leaders, traditionally very conservative in their approach – did become significantly more progressive, especially (for all its obsession with slimming) *Woman's Own*; but in both cases, they found themselves too far ahead of their readers, sales fell, and (as the historian of women's magazines, Cynthia White, would note soon afterwards) 'both magazines reverted to a policy of "quiet evolution"'.

The key figure at *Woman* was Barbara Buss (later Boxall), no-nonsense editor from 1964 and insistent that each issue included not only a 'womb-trembler' feature, but also a 'triumph over tragedy'. Although banning trouser suits in the office, and invariably arriving herself with hat and gloves, she *did* allow a certain broadening of focus; yet 'as someone who religiously cooked a Sunday roast every week, she also firmly believed that dressmaking, cooking and knitting still had their role to play – and she ensured that assistant editors were familiar with how to make a lemon soufflé or bath a baby'. 'One edition', adds her obituarist, 'might easily include: "Her baby was a prisoner", "Dreamy evening knitting", and "Teenage marriages". A feature on an up-and-coming singer – Barbra Streisand – was once considered too cutting edge.' Buss herself talked to White, probably in about 1968. 'Affluence is giving women the freedom to be persons in their own right through increased leisure,' she said. 'Some women are still only interested in their homes and families, but today this role is dynamic. A woman has to grow with her children and keep in step with her husband too.' 'She sees it', commented White, 'as *Woman*'s task to keep pace with this development, even to keep a little ahead of it. But the criterion of what the magazine can include is still whether or not it is accepted in the population at large. *Woman* can talk about abortion when it is a common topic of conversation and not before.'[17]

One way and another, in this whole area in the mid-sixties, underlying assumptions and patterns of behaviour looked back at least as much as they looked forward: Harry Corbett only allowed to introduce the character of Soo on promising that she and Sooty would keep their paws off each other; female newsreaders almost entirely absent from the screen; 'she has those important physical prerequisites (both of them),' the critic Francis Hope writing appreciatively of Honor Blackman in *The Avengers*, grateful also that on the whole she wasn't becoming 'that all-time drag, a talking dumb blonde'; Joan Bakewell learning to take sexual harassment ('a quick squeeze, a salacious leer, an unlooked-for pinch, a remark on one's cleavage, speculation about one's sex life') for granted ('a matter of routine'); directing the teenage Hayley Mills in *The Family Way*, Roy Boulting – thrice married, six children, thirty-two years her senior – taking the opportunity to seduce her, hit her and turn her against her parents before marrying her; an outbreak of thrush requiring for the young Sheila Rowbotham 'a trip to Whitechapel VD clinic, where building workers leered at you as you went in', while once inside 'you were assumed to be either a prostitute or the wronged wife of a man who had caught the clap from prostitutes'; 'silly moo' as almost the least of Alf Garnett's insults to his wife; fathers calling intelligent daughters 'sparky', to avoid the dreaded 'clever'; the young Sue Johnston rushing into relationships just to conform ('It was the first thing your aunty or cousins would ask: have you got a boyfriend? Is it serious?'); 'girls don't get raped unless they want it' (line from *The Knack*); 'I always say, make a married women laugh, and you're halfway there with her' (line from *Alfie*); Action Man (launched at British Toy Fair, January 1966); 'some general practitioners are requiring written consent of the husband before prescribing oral contraceptives to women patients' (Renee Short, House of Commons, June 1966); the 5 foot 2 inch man, after admitting a series of indecent assaults ('to prove my virility') on taller women, receiving from the judge no more than a mild verbal rap on the knuckles and told to focus his attention on shorter girls; and the memories of Anne Robinson:

> I can hardly think of a girlfriend at this time who wasn't subjected to a rape or an attempted rape. The usual method of dealing with it was to say not a word. Rape was something that happened if you were stupid enough to allow the opportunity to arise. Being pawed, being leered at, the size of your breasts being remarked upon, your bum being patted was, well, normal.
>
> My friend Olivia, who had just graduated from the LSE and was due to be married, innocently went to her doctor to ask for some birth-control advice. The doctor examined her and declared her vagina was altogether too tiny. He advised her to go to John Bell and Croyden – the large chemist in Wigmore Street off Harley Street – and invest in a vibrator. She was, he ordered, to bring it back to the surgery and he would instruct her. The vibrator was bought and the instruction had begun before it dawned on Olivia that the doctor was actually a dirty old man.[18]

17

Not a Guitar in Sight

Of course, youth culture, including pop culture, demands almost by royal decree pride of place in any account of 'the Sixties'. Certainly, the music mattered to many adolescents, the indispensable backdrop to an emerging sense of personal identity; and among them, Michael Williams in Sunderland, in his mid-teens by 1964 as, probably like plenty of other grammar school boys, he transferred his allegiance from the Beatles to the Stones, Manfred Mann and the Animals:

> I'd watch *Top of the Pops* on Thursdays and take the bus into town at lunch-time on Friday to spend my pocket money on an outstanding new record, like the Animals' 'House of the Rising Sun', the Moody Blues' 'Go Now', the Righteous Brothers' 'You've Lost that Lovin' Feeling' or Them's 'Baby Please Don't Go' (with 'Gloria' on the B-side). I acquired a musical education from teenage Norman Jopling's articles in *Record Mirror* about 'great unknowns' among American R&B singers. In late 1963 I picked up Marvin Gaye's 'Can I Get a Witness' and Martha and the Vandellas' 'Heatwave' on Radio Luxembourg, like signals from a distant planet. On Saturday mornings I'd call at Graham Mole's home in Elmwood Road behind the Royal Infirmary and we'd set off on a tour of grimy junk shops in Chester Road, Hylton Road and High Street East in search of obscure American records and hits from the late 1950s and early 1960s. Sometimes Ian Wall would join us. We'd go back to Graham's home to play and swap our acquisitions. On my own I'd rifle through discounted records in Atkinsons in Athenaeum Street or White's Market. I was a terrible music snob. I bought the

> Kingsmen's 'Louie Louie' and sneered at the Kinks' cover. I brought the Jaynetts' 'Sally Go Round the Roses' to play in our Music class. I was primed for Bob Dylan's 'Subterranean Homesick Blues' and the Byrds' 'Mr Tambourine Man', blown away by their effortless cool when they performed on *RSG* in August 1965.

Above all, it was that sense of *being young*, of belonging to a different generation from one's parents. 'I had a very smart, skimpy little King's Road beige dress, which I loved with a fetishist passion: over it I wore a full-length dark brown suede coat with a fake fur collar which made me feel like Julie Christie,' remembers Margaret Drabble. 'The streets belonged to the young. We stopped trying to look like our mothers, discarded our twinsets and two-piece suits, and celebrated our youth.'

An earlyish recognition that something fundamental was going on came in August 1964, when the conservative-minded Oxford sociologist Bryan Wilson wrote two lengthy articles for the *Daily Telegraph* on 'War of the Generations', arguing that 'as the security of community, family and class distinctions have been eroded so the age-group has become the focus of identification for the young'. And, naturally enough, he concluded that 'the circumstance is not one which is conducive to their socialisation and civilisation, to their acquisition of those values which will sustain them in a routine work-a-day world when youth has gone'. No quarrel there from Roger Mortimer, to judge by his letters to his teenage daughter Jane, attending a sixth-form college (St Clare's) in Oxford:

> You will soon be grown up and presumably will then be regarding pop music with the same bored nausea as other adults. *(17 January 1965)*
>
> I enclose a small present for some of the peculiar meals you cooked in the holidays. I will give you another when you stop putting all that stuff on your eyes that makes you look as if you were in a No. 3 touring company of the Black and White Minstrels. *(4 October 1965)*
>
> I enjoyed seeing you last week but I would rather you did not wear a long discarded jersey, clearly from a male wardrobe. I trust you are working hard and not looking too farouche. If there is one type of adolescent that gives me quite a severe pain it is the male or

> female to whom the label of 'student' is unmistakeably attached. Undergraduate, OK, but 'student', never. It makes me think of spotty young socialists at the London School of Economics. Avoid, therefore, if you can the cult of ugliness so distressingly fashionable with the young. *(5 November 1965)*

Mortimer by this time was racing correspondent for the *Sunday Times*, but as a young man he had been a regular officer in the Coldstream Guards and had been captured unconscious at Dunkirk, all his men having been killed, before five years followed as a prisoner of war.[1] From that particular generation, a certain understandable intolerance perhaps.

And yet ... Roberts's north-western oral history shows parents usually determining the choice of their children's (especially their daughters') occupation; young people were not only getting married in ever-greater numbers, but (especially men) at an ever-younger age; membership of the Young Conservatives was roughly four times that of Labour's Young Socialists; drugs were much written and talked about, but as late as 1968 a nationwide police survey found whole parts of the country that had barely experienced cannabis use; a series of sociological surveys of young people published between 1964 and 1966 broadly revealed an underlying continuity between adolescence and adulthood, limited sexual experience and no fundamental grievances against the traditional dictates of family, work and society; while when asked by NOP whether a minimum age of twenty-one should remain the case for credit purchases, home ownership and marriage without parental consent, two out of three sixteen- to twenty-year-olds agreed that it should. That last piece of data was cited by the report in 1967 by the Latey Committee on the Age of Majority – a report which in fact recommended that the age of majority *should* come down to eighteen, largely on the grounds that 'we have had impressive evidence that the young are usually quite capable of conducting their own affairs with sense and honesty'. Stock horror images of teenagers – 'pop fans screaming at airports, gangs roaming the streets, and long-haired rebels being rude to their headmasters' – were, insisted the report, almost entirely misleading; and it called on the press to write more about the 'enterprising, responsible and vigorous people about whom we have had so much evidence'.[2]

The probability is that, taken overall, childhood's conditioning in the sixties was not so different from what it had been in the legendarily conformist fifties. 'We didn't know or use terms like "autistic spectrum", "Asperger's" or "Attention Deficit Disorder",' reflects Viv Albertine about the lack of allowances made for people, 'especially children', who were somewhat different from the norm. 'Even being "artistic" was considered a defect. Teachers, parents, classmates and the medical profession thought children who didn't conform were just difficult, annoying misfits.' Education *was* starting to become a bit more progressive, a bit more child-centred; but one former teacher at Risinghill – the Islington co-ed comprehensive under Michael Duane's leadership closed down in 1965 for being excessively progressive – undoubtedly spoke for many teachers in general when after the closure she talked to Leila Berg:

> I'm an old-fashioned teacher. A child has to do as it's told for me. I go to great lengths to understand it; to know the background; but beyond that I don't think it's kind to the child to go. I shut my door and get on with things my own way. I know the background well – I've taught in this particular district twenty years. No, I don't know their families. I know perhaps two of their parents. The background of these children is exceptionally difficult. But they have to know before they go into the world what their limitations are. The world is a hard place. Many of them are going to find things very difficult next year, when they are not going to be allowed to do as they like. I believe a child *likes* discipline, knowing that if it oversteps the mark it is a calculated risk. I don't think children are capable of deciding for themselves the difference between right and wrong . . .

Corporal punishment remained in the mid-sixties the rule rather than the exception, to such an extent that when one day at a secondary school in Cambuslang (a working-class town on the outskirts of Glasgow) an indignant teacher shouted 'Stop it! Stop it! I'll call the police!', as the head was dishing out six strokes apiece to several boys, the protest was considered so unusual that it made the newspapers. And, of course, especially at boarding institutions, there was still no shortage of physical and/or sexual and/or mental abuse. 'From 1963 to 1968 I was at a prep school in Kent called Grenham House,' wrote Louis de Bernières to *The Times* half a century after he had left:

> The smallest boys, one as young as six, were accommodated in a private house called Sheltwood. Here the deputy headmaster, Jack Lidgate, would slipper us so severely that the imprint would be left as a dark bruise that lasted for days. He liked to show his fondness for us by sitting us on his knee with his hands up our shorts.
>
> The headmaster was called Denys Jeston. When he beat us, he would move the furniture so that he could get a good run up. After punishment we were supposed to say 'Thank you, sir.' We would have neat, bloody, parallel wounds across our backsides, in shades of yellow, black, blue and green that took weeks to heal. He could admire his handiwork during compulsory naked bathing in the pool. He was most concerned to make sure that the cracks in our backsides were properly dried afterwards, so he took on that task himself.
>
> Throughout the school there was a culture of extreme physical and mental cruelty. One six-year-old developed a stammer so bad that he could hardly speak. Boys were ganged up on and beaten up. I still remember the names of the bullies. I remember having to switch off all my emotions on the first day of every term, and the difficulty of trying to switch them on again on the first day of every holiday.
>
> Years later I sat in the attic of my parents' house and taught myself how to cry. My parents thought they were doing their best for me in paying for all this, and I decided not to speak out until they were dead. Even so, I have never quite managed to forgive them.

Then as now, the great majority of children lived at home, and a helpful guide to parental behaviour is the study made by John and Elizabeth Newson of 700 children in Nottingham born in the late 1950s. Class differences were there from the start; and by the time the children were seven in the mid-sixties, the contrast was stark between middle-class parents (seldom smacking and mainly seeking to use 'democratically-based, highly verbal means of control') and working-class parents (using 'highly authoritarian, mainly non-verbal means of control, in which words are used to threaten and bamboozle the child into obedience'). Still, even the most democratic parental methods could hit an impasse. 'There was an awful moment when I was 16,' recalls Gordon Brown (born 1951). 'It was the school prize-giving, and my father (a Church of Scotland minister) was giving the speech, and my mother was presenting the prizes, and I was getting the Dux (top dog) prize. We had a row I'll never forget, because they were determined I'd get my hair cut, and I refused! It was supposed to be a nice occasion, and we were fighting each other.' 'Did you get a haircut?' asks the interviewer. 'Err,' and one can almost hear the reluctance as he replies, 'I did.'

A trio of further childhoods remembered. 'Because I was born 1955 in Saltcoats [on the north Ayrshire coast], I spent my childhood years in what was called, even at the time, the swinging sixties,' Janice Galloway has written:

> I was there, and Saltcoats never swung. My circumscribed upbringing stressed the importance of three things with little swing about them: the important of knowing one's place; the social obligation to develop self-doubt and openness to shame; a sidelong appreciation of human absurdity to make the other two bearable.
>
> Several refrains recurred in my childhood as reinforcement. 1) Who do you think you are? Princess Bloody Margaret/The Queen of Sheba? 2) I suppose you think you're special with your nose in a book? and 3) Who asked your opinion, short arse?
>
> Having only just survived the ghastly privations and fears of the second world war, large families where a high rate of infant mortality was the norm, life-endangering work and stoutly defended class divisions, most people (certainly most children of said survivors) believed the refrains no more open to question than the laws of physics. The survival skill of knowing one's place in a hard world was paramount. And one's place was wee.
>
> Teaching your children not to want 'too much' (sometimes to want anything) was for the ultimate good of all . . .

'Turns out,' she adds about years later reading a lot about child development, 'that the inculcation of multiple guilt complexes, a tendency to depression and a fierce rein on self-expression was a shit way to bring anyone up.' Nothing rose-tinted either from Paul Morley, born two years later, about growing up in Reddish, near Stockport:

> I remember the time when I was no more than a boy, immersed and acceptant in a world that was still made out of steam, church and tradition, which contained immovable ceremonies, duties, routines, unseen stumbling blocks, and the non-stop demands, restrictions, instructions and occasional ferocity, even danger, of adults, who could be kind but were essentially in superior unforgiving control. Adults who promised a future made up of more of where you were and what there was around you because of the way they seemed so stuck inside their own thorough and unchangeable fate. There was too a coldness and darkness, a heavy atmosphere in the house where I lived, that seemed to repel the very idea that you could change who you were and where you were because something outside immensely anchored Reddish might make it through some unreal, invisible opening and into the clear spaces inside your mind.

But for the most part – albeit noting the zero counselling from the school staff, and sheer lack of emotional intelligence, when the father of one of his best friends and classmates died suddenly in 1965 – a happier picture from Ian Mole (born 1954), above all his evocative chapter about the joys of trainspotting in the last days of steam:

> I'd travel alone from my home in Sunderland across country to Carlisle at the age of 12 and then proceed to try and sneak around engine-sheds full of potentially lethal machinery. When we were 13 a friend and I travelled to Edinburgh twice in a week and had a great time. Far from the bespectacled wimps of popular belief, a lot of the other kids we'd meet were right little hard cases and all-round scallywags. They'd of course be from all over the country and it was good to meet kids from exotic places like Skipton, Birmingham or wherever and exchange tales.

'I treasure those times we all had together in those days,' he ends. 'In the mornings our mams would see us off, having knocked up a load of sandwiches etc to keep us going, and we'd arrive back late in the day scruffy, happy and home from the hunt.'[3]

Happy or unhappy childhood, most children left school soon after they turned fifteen and entered the workplace; for whereas in the United States some 50 per cent of eighteen-year-olds went to university, and potentially got involved in a flourishing, often politically angry youth culture, in Britain the proportion, even by the end of the 1960s, was less than 6 per cent. How can one briefly characterise that adult world they were going into? Yes, undeniably, a world of increasing affluence, even if there was still rather more poverty than the 'never had it so good' cliché tended to assume; and, yes, almost as undeniably, a world of increasing individualism, fuelled in significant part by that affluence. Yet in so many ways it was also a world – to an extent sometimes seriously underestimated both then and later – of deeply grounded certainties. Certainties of order and authority, certainties of place (in both senses), certainties of behaviour and ethos – these were certainties that for most people transcended questions of 'good' or 'bad', but instead just *were*.

Some suggestive snapshots of order and authority. 'I find myself looking back at the way that bosses used to talk to workers, for instance, and loathing that time; the way teachers scowled and pushed, and sometimes punched or pulled hair, and loathe that equally,' reflected in 2014 the *Big Issue*'s John Bird about the post-war sweep of the 1950s through to the 1970s. 'Children could be beaten on public transport by their parents without anyone turning a blind eye. Wives could be chastised and onlookers would look on. Dogs kicked, cats chased: you name it, it was done in those gone times.' The memories of Jenni Russell (born 1960) have an overlap with Bird's, but are essentially more benign:

> As children in the 60s, we knew about funny men, but were told they were rare. Adults in general, and women in particular, were people to be turned to and trusted. They were also there to stop us doing things we shouldn't, whether that was running out across a road, or hitting another child. As children in London we were frequently out by ourselves, but we felt that the adult world was constantly checking on us. Any passing grownup could say hello, or tell us how to behave, and frequently did. It seemed that adults

> in general had shared beliefs about what we could and couldn't do, and they tended to back one another up.

Or take this recollection by Anton Rippon, of how in Derby in the sixties 'all town-centre pubs catered for a middle-aged, or older, market':

> Couples who fancied a night out in town, away from their own neighbourhood, would travel in on Corporation petrol or trolley buses, enjoy a few drinks – usually pints of bitter or mild for the man, port and lemon for the woman – and then do the reverse journey without any fear of being mugged on the way home, even on the darkest night. Any youngsters even talking too loudly (in the opinion of older pub-goers) would soon be put in their place . . .

Or this memory from Alan Dobson about working in 1964 for a large insurance company in Norwich. 'On a particularly hot day I removed my jacket, revealing braces,' he wrote in 2024. 'I was told by my head of department to put my jacket back on. I queried this and it was referred to the personnel department. An hour later, back came the ruling that I could continue exposing my braces as long as I could not be seen by members of the public.' More often than not, of course, authority was not challenged – sometimes with devastating consequences. *The Sleep Room* (2025) is the title of Jon Stock's detailed exposure of the life and career of the psychiatrist Dr William Sargant, archetypal male consultant of the era who through the 1950s and 1960s, based at the Royal Waterloo Hospital for Children and Women, 'administered ECT [electroconvulsive therapy] and other experimental treatments to patients who were put into deep sleep, or continuous narcosis, for up to three months, and sometimes longer'. One of those patients was fourteen-year-old Celia Imrie, suffering from anorexia nervosa:

> She recounts [noted Blake Morrison in his review] being forced to drink such large doses of chlorpromazine – the first antipsychotic – that she dribbled, shook uncontrollably and found her hair in clumps on her pillow. She was injected daily with enough insulin to make her drowsy, weak, sweaty and near comatose. She remembers other

> women around her having huge rubber plugs jammed between their teeth before the high-voltage electricity of ECT was sent through their temples, and their bodies 'shuddered and jerked' with the 'scent of burning hair and flesh'. Sometimes a patient would reappear on the ward with their head thickly bandaged, scarcely able to walk after being lobotomised. Amid the moans, screams and stale stench of sleep, Imrie recalls the nurses reporting her own resistance to the drugs to Sargant, to which he ominously responded: 'Every dog has his breaking point'.

While in Imrie's own words, 'the Great Man was very grand when he came on his ward rounds', as 'the other doctors and nurses all bowed and scraped . . . He was brusque and cold, and he never talked directly to you. Instead he issued orders over your head, talking about "this one" and "that one". But that was preferable to making eye contact with this proud, incorrigible man with his hard, dark eyes.' And the legacy for Imrie herself? 'Sargant continues to cast a long shadow over me, 60 years later. Even today, I can still see his face so clearly; his ape-like features. And sometimes I go to the depths of despair for no real reason.'[4]

Then, there was knowing one's place, with its accompanying sense of certainty, for the watchguards anyway. 'When I, as a 17-year-old art student, began wearing cords in the mid-1960s,' recalled Peter Betts years later, 'my father, a blunt Yorkshireman born in 1898, exclaimed: "Corduroy trousers? What are you wearing them for? Them's workhouse clothes!"' Or when about the same time, or slightly later, the young Ian Jack (born 1945) went with a girl for a weekend at a hotel on Islay, they found 'a dining room as quiet as the grave':

> Dinner was spaghetti on toast, followed by fish and then steak. It was much better than it sounds, and I asked the waitress what kind of fish it had been. 'Trout, sir,' she said, and from far away across the room I heard a Glasgow matron telling her husband in an outraged stage whisper, 'Imagine! They come to a hotel like this and don't know what a trout is!'

Two sharp contemporary observers of social class in action were David Frost and Antony Jay (future co-writer of *Yes Minister*). 'In the factory, there are still the different levels,' they observed in their 1967 book on the English (*To England With Love*). 'One man has his lunch in the executive dining room. The second has his lunch in the staff canteen. And the third does not have lunch at all. He brings his dinner with him.' So, too, with the justice system, where 'one only has to visit a few courts and hear the suave, confident, upper-class accents of Bench and Bar, and the hesitant, ungrammatical, regional accents of the dock, to appreciate that the most important function of our courts is to teach the lower class a lesson'. While in general, they reckoned:

> Movement between the classes might be a little easier than it was, but they are still quite separate and any attempt to fuse them meets with resistance and uproar. Nothing, for example, has quite so stirred the English recently as the suggestion that all their children, regardless of class and wealth, should go to comprehensive schools. And nothing has stirred them less than the fact that it was not thought necessary for Prince Charles to pass an entrance examination before going to Cambridge University . . .

A more academic study was Margaret Stacey's, as between 1966 and 1968 she re-examined the Banbury area (site of a previous study by her). If some of her respondents were a little confused at times about how exactly, sociologically speaking, to categorise themselves, they had no doubt in their minds about who was too high up to speak to them, or who was too low down to be spoken to – with the most extreme example being a colonel's wife, who admitted to the existence of only three other families in her village. What about the tension, though, between class loyalty and individualism? A much more recent sociologist, Mike Savage, argues, on the basis of an analysis of studies in and around the 1960s of male manual work cultures, that those two elements could be complementary rather than necessarily at loggerheads; and he coins the term 'rugged individualism', reflecting how class identities would often be as dependent on an individual as a collective basis. For him, a key pointer occurred in Huw Beynon's study towards the end of the decade of car workers at Ford's Halewood plant, including the shop stewards. 'They followed fashion, wore smart clothes and exemplified the new pop culture sweeping Britain,' notes Savage. 'They were profoundly concerned to emphasise their individuality.' Even so, and here he quotes Beynon himself: 'The stewards weren't interested in promotion, in becoming "dedicated Ford men". For them to take the white coat at Halewood would be to join the other side. "I couldn't do that. Leave the lads? Not in this firm anyway. They're a crowd of gangsters here."' 'Here', comments Savage, 'we have the kernel of the notion, which slips through the net constructed by the sociologists of the 1960s, which is that individualism need not be at odds with a form of class awareness.'[5]

Naturally, 'place' for most people primarily meant physical, geographical place; and undoubtedly, the British of the mid-1960s, in whichever city or town or village they lived, were citizens of somewhere, not nowhere, with a strong sense of local identity and, very often, a relative or even total indifference to the world outside their own particular patch. 'Still quite an insular town, its traffic continually interrupted by the closing of railway level-crossing gates as grain, hops, malt and then the finished product, beer, were moved back and forth to the Bass, Ind Coope and Marston's breweries that dominated life there' is how Rippon recalls Burton upon Trent, where he worked in the *Derby Evening Telegraph*'s office. 'By and large,' he goes on,

> I found Burtonians far less sophisticated than even Derbeians. Our office cleaner had hardly ever left the town; she had certainly never seen the sea, for instance. And she was fairly typical. One of our newspaper sellers, Wally Bridge, was married in Burton but spent his honeymoon in Derby – for the afternoon. After the reception, Wally and his bride, Molly, hopped on a Trent bus and spent the rest of the day travelling down the A38 before returning home; that was a big enough adventure for them.

A similarly self-contained world of its own in Dunfermline, where 'until the 1970s,' remembered Ian Jack, its town centre 'held banks, the law court, the local newspaper office, four cinemas, a dance hall, a centre of local government, hotels and inns, a grand post office, two bus stations (the two railway stations were further off), several newspaper criers (Edinburgh's *Evening News* and its *Dispatch*, Dundee's *Telegraph*), magnificently appointed public toilets and libraries, large churches, cafes, public baths'. While 'as to shops: a bookseller, various tailors, greengrocers, licensed grocers, haberdashers, confectioners, butchers, bakers, milliners, electricians, ironmongers. All of these had a loyal clientele – people who would, say, disparage the mutton pies of Allen's in favour of Stephens's.' Nothing more 'intensely local', added Jack, than the town's football team, Dunfermline Athletic. 'The town's solicitors and owners of small businesses held the shares, and the players met most days for lunch in the City Hotel, where the proprietor was the team dietician. You would see them shopping in the high street and gripping a billiard cue at Joe Maloco's snooker hall or a glass in the East Port Bar. They took the bus . . .' Or from the north-east – where, on a visit to Teesside in October 1965, Richard Crossman was struck by 'how localized interests are in this country!' – take South Shields, evoked by Robert Colls many years and much change later as 'intensely communitarian', making 'degraded environments and hostile economic relationships not only habitable but hospitable'. Less than seven miles from there to Sunderland, where Alan Brien's visit in 1966 prompted a bravura passage, published in the *New Statesman* a week before the World Cup Final:

> It is a democratic land where no one is insolent because no one is condescending, where the poor who are mainly the old and the sick are buoyed up with strong and tender family ties and good neighbours, where the majority live modestly but well, while a few are making their fortunes turning comforts into necessities. In the evening, even in July, the people who clog the town in the day vanish as the sun begins to slant down and you can scorch along the main streets at 8 p.m. without seeing another car. Life is in the pubs, in the clubs, by the telly, with an iron-tasting beer served in a glass like a flowerpot. It is a gregarious, family, matey world full of nest warmth and communal solidarity. It has many of the qualities of the England of the past which have vanished in our atomised South.[6]

Although Brien had grown up in Sunderland, he had barely been back in the past ten years, and it feels essentially like an outsider's take. No doubt somewhat sentimental, too. But it *does* convey some underlying reality, ultimately one of psychological stability rooted in place; and it is hard to read his final sentence, declaring that Sunderland 'has many of the qualities which a social-democratic England of the future will need to develop', without a certain pang of regret.

That said, Brien perhaps underplays the obstinate streak of puritanism – and sometimes more than streak – which continued to anchor many people's daily lives. As ever, impossible to quantify, but such was certainly the view of the penetrating American sociologist Edward Shils, who in 1964 – eleven years after his wonderful essay with Michael Young on the meaning of the Coronation – contributed to a collection on *Labour's New Frontiers*. In his piece, hopefully called 'Britain Awake!', he characterised British society as possessing a fatal 'constriction of spirit', thereby leading to a national character 'frowning on enthusiasm, distrusting spontaneity and regarding soundness and steadiness as the highest of human virtues'. And inevitably, he contended, such 'puritanical suppression of feeling and imagination' amounted in effect to 'a restraint on aspiration', to a narrowness of conception about the 'possibilities of life'. Shils's reflections should perhaps have been accompanied by the cartoons of 'Larry', whose 'Man' lived happily and unambitiously in the middle of suburbia. The middle-aged cartoonist's real name was Terence Parkes: born in Birmingham, the son of a welding foreman in a car factory, now living in Solihull. 'The Midlands has no glamour,' he told an interviewer in 1965, before going on in his Brummie accent: 'But there's an imperturbability about the place. People in these parts aren't easily led or roused or impressed . . . This bloke I draw wouldn't know what love is about, but he's reliable.'

A trio of filial reminiscences help to flesh out the picture. 'The magic of numbers guided his life,' writes the historian Frank Mort about his father, working during the 1960s as a cost accountant for ICI, first at Runcorn, then at Buxton:

> It formed the basis of the rule by which he lived. I believe that it was a source of continuing disappointment to him that neither my brother nor I ever shared this infatuation. For he made sure that these financial principles influenced our family life. Every second Wednesday evening my father and my mother would sit down at the opened top of his bureau to audit the domestic budget, with its columns for mortgage payments, bills, car, clothing, holidays, entertainment and 'sundries'. My mother had her own allowance paid out of this fund, and there was also an entry marked 'children's pocket money' . . . We grew up despising his tabulations. We also

> grew up believing that my father lacked generosity of spirit and that he was mean.

Or take – though written with more affection – Geoff Dyer's Cheltenham recollections:

> Many times, when I asked my dad if I could have something that had taken my fancy in a shop, he responded, 'You don't want that.' To which I wanted to reply, 'But I *do*.' And then after a while, I stopped wanting things. The constant calculation of cost was redundant since the result was always and inevitably that everything cost too much. Nothing was ever reckoned to be cheap. My dad's reaction to any price quoted by shop assistants was always a stunned '*How* much!' I don't recall him ever exclaiming with delight, '*That's* cheap!' Even before the massive injection of cash into the Premiership, his judgement about the transfer fees for or wages paid to any footballer was absolute and uncompromising: 'No one is worth that much.' The key word in these and other exchanges is 'much' and it illustrates how much emphasis was placed on its opposite: how little we wanted, how readily we could make do with less . . . The spirit of wartime and post-war rationing – themselves built on the thin and therefore, in this context, extraordinarily fertile soil of the 1930s – had been internalised to the extent that it continued without the need for vouchers or any kind of external monitoring. Rationing, in my dad's consciousness, never went away . . .

In sum, 'the idea of pleasure or indulgence played no part in my father's make-up'. John Cleese completes the trio, including this description of what was involved in going out for a meal with his parents (living in Weston-super-Mare):

> The main criteria for choosing our restaurant would be its state of cleanliness, the temperature of the plates and the food, and the size of the portions (not too big); but the *taste* of the food would play no part in the selection process. Thus my parents' favoured restaurant was the Copper Kettle because here the napkins and tablecloths were 'spotless', the plates 'lovely and warm', and the food 'sizzling

> hot' and not 'oily' or 'rich' or 'spicy' (especially garlicky). The highest praise for food (other than hotness) was 'plain' . . .

In 1965, by now an established comedian, Cleese went to Weston to spend Christmas with them. There, the days passed with excruciating slowness, until 'one morning, in a desperate attempt to enliven the hours till television-time, I suggested that we might go and see a film that afternoon':

> It was as though I had proposed that we invade Poland. Father was instantly at the window, peering towards the Quantock Hills, noting clouds, comparing his observations with the newspapers' weather forecast, remembering the car was low on petrol, checking that our raincoats had not been stolen overnight, and starting to make a list of things we would need to take with us. Mother, meanwhile, stood in the middle of the room, her eyes staring, repeating, 'Well, will we go before tea, or after tea? Will we go *before* tea or *after* tea?' I got them both seated again, but there was fear in their eyes and they could take nothing in. I tried to calm them by talking to them about the happy times we'd had at the cinema in the past, but when I ran out of these – after about twenty seconds – they were still looking as though they had seen a ghost. They had had a perfectly good, workable schedule for the day – not to do much until, at seven o'clock, we started to watch television, and then bed at ten. Now their plans lay in ruins.[7]

It makes for painful reading; but it does tell an essential historical truth about something that was still seemingly ineradicable in the British psyche.

More generally, was it still 'respectable Britain', still 'moral Britain'? Surely on the whole the former, if only to judge by beards. 'It was a full beard, befitting a geologist who had spent time in the field without a mirror,' recalls Susan Treagus about meeting in 1966 her future husband. 'It was regarded with suspicion by Scottish farmers; one even offered to shear him with his sheep. At the time, beards were associated with artists and revolutionaries. My aunts, on first meeting Jack, summed him up as "very nice, considering he has a beard".' A similar sort of concern this decade among the Blackheath branch of the Wives' Fellowship. 'Some Wives were reprimanded by some Senior Wives for wearing pearls to morning meetings – "they should not be worn before 1pm",' records the history. 'There was an occasion when a working wife produced a bought cake for an afternoon meeting tea. This caused great consternation, added to which the member wore trousers – unheard of at that time.' But 'moral Britain' still? A harder call, given not only that crime was rising quite sharply through the decade, but so too was the incidence of illegitimacy, reaching 8.5 per cent in 1968 (compared to 4.7 per cent in 1955). Nor is it at all empirically clear that Mary Whitehouse was justified in claiming a vast 'silent majority' existed in sympathy with her campaign to restore 'moral values', above all to the BBC. After all, pointed out the sceptics then and later, one of her most hated programmes, *Till Death Us Do Part*, attracted huge viewing figures, so much so that by a sample week in 1968 almost half of all TV sets in Britain were switched on to it. Yet it is striking to read an October 1966 memo sent by BBC's head of TV drama, the experienced and pragmatic Sydney Newman, to all drama producers, directors and story editors, in which he called for less violence ('knives are flashing too readily'), for the exercise of 'every care' when it came to 'references to sexual parts, underclothes, contraceptive devices, portrayal of near nudity, the physical handling of someone with sex in mind, couples in bed', and for a similar circumspection, too, in relation to language: 'Religious people, and this is still a Christian country, take offence at blasphemy. Exclamations or curses like "Jesus", words like "bloody" and so on are offensive, and obscenities like "arse", etc put people off in their hundreds of thousands . . .'[8]

Yet, was it really 'still a Christian country'? Undoubtedly the overall trends in formal religious observance were downwards, with national surveys through the decade of church attendance showing respondents increasingly answering 'less often than monthly' and 'never'. Or to cite some specific places at specific times: whether in Liverpool (four wards) in 1964 or Kirkby Stephen in 1965 or Swindon in 1966 or Hemel Hempstead in 1967, church attendance amounted to less than 20 per cent of the population, sometimes appreciably less. Even so, a nationwide NOP survey in 1965 revealed indeed that less than a quarter of Church of England respondents had attended church within the previous three months, yet (among all respondents) only

5 per cent of men, and 2 per cent of women, were 'willing to say that they were atheists, agnostics or of no religion'; while in answer to the actual question, 'Is Britain a Christian country?', almost 80 per cent replied in the affirmative, including a slight bias (84 per cent) to northerners. The process of secularisation, of a somewhat looser and more relaxed society, was unstoppable, of course it was; but it was not all a straight, unbroken line. 'At a Liverpool parish church,' remembers Linda Grant about the 1960s, 'a friend's mother attempted to christen her new baby Sue. The vicar forbade it. No diminutives were permitted in the Church of England . . .' And in its rather cherishable way, an advertisement (presumably not a spoof) placed in the *Church Times* in 1967 spoke volumes. 'Old-fashioned vicar,' it began, 'seeks colleague. Left-hand fast bowler preferred. Good golf handicap an asset but not essential. Fine church with good musical tradition . . .'[9]

Bob Dylan's historic, radically counter-cultural British tour – Bristol, Cardiff, Birmingham, Liverpool, Leicester, Sheffield, Manchester, Glasgow, Edinburgh, Newcastle, London – naturally dominates my generation's collective memory (or imagined memory) of May 1966. But over those two and a half weeks, the 10th to the 27th, an arbitrary (and thus truly scientific) dip into the flourishing local press evokes something of a slow-moving, deeply conservative world a thousand miles away.

In roughly chronological order . . . At Hamish Watt's farm near Keith, members of Strathbogie Junior Agricultural Club taking part in a stock-judging contest ('the judging was of a herd of 60 Ayrshire dairy cows'); the *Haltwhistle Echo* reporting that for the fifth time Haltwhistle rural council had refused a pub's application for 'a "one-armed bandit" fruit machine' and quoting Councillor J. Armstrong ('I think we are guardians of public morals'); the *Clitheroe Advertiser*'s country diarist ('Naturalist') blaming the despoiling of the surrounding countryside by visiting urbanites on the cult of self-expression and wanting culprits set to work in stone quarries (where in breaking stones 'they could have all the exercise and self-expression they need free of charge'); the *Fraserburgh Herald*'s 'Round and About' columnist noting that the local police 'have still two very old, and supposedly very effective, crime deterrents in the form of two birch rods'; the *Gourock Times* recording with satisfaction how at the recent fifty-eighth annual inspection of 3rd Gourock Boys Brigade, 'not a guitar was in sight nor a transistor, or any long-haired specimens (well, perhaps a few)'; a rally in Brechin's Masonic Hall – including speeches, tea and cake, music and presentation of long-service medals – to mark the golden jubilee year of the National Savings Movement; Cowal Floral Art Club's annual exhibition, at Dunoon Masonic Hall, with Miss J. M. Bennett ('When the Red, Red Robin . . .'), Mrs Allison ('Sweet Memories'), Mrs Cooper ('Blues and Bones'), and Mrs Cassels ('The Nut Brown Maid') judged the top four in the 'Title of a Song' section; a concert party from Bonnyrigg WRI (Women's Rural Institute) providing the entertainment at the May meeting of the Rosewell WRI ('the visitors delighted with their singing of songs from the "Sound of Music" . . . Mrs Hogg won the competition for the best paper hat . . . Mrs Flockhart was placed first in the contest for a supper dish'); an advertisement placed in the *Littlehampton Gazette* by Bells of 150/152 The Street, Rustington ('The Misses Campbell wish to announce that, contrary to all rumours, they have **NO** intention of disposing of their business and will continue to serve all their customers with the greatest attention and civility'); a story in the *Pontypridd Observer* about a local couple, Mr and Mrs David Rees (her name not given), due shortly to celebrate their sixty-third wedding anniversary, with Mrs Rees in reflective mode ('Life was sweeter in the old days . . . I have seen many changes in the town; new buildings are going up but I prefer the old ones . . . Even the food today has changed; everything is artificial . . .'); Tenbury Sports Club holding its annual barbecue ('Miss Margaret Morris ran the "guessing the number of sweets in the jar" section, won by Mr Tony Davies, while Mr P. Waterfield won the half tea-service competition'); Leighton Angling Club's dinner at the Bossard Hall ('as much a treat for the "angling widows",' reckoning the *North Bucks Times*, 'as a celebration for the anglers themselves'); the *Dewsbury Reporter* running a full page of local cricket scores and reports ('Dewsbury Just Scrape A Win', 'Batley's Batsmen Lacked Confidence'), with no first names given, unless to distinguish between two Smiths on the same side; 1,800 entries for Aberystwyth Agricultural Show and many prizes awarded (Best Bull: Messrs M. Tomlinson and Sons, of Home Farm, Llanerchydol, Mont., with a young Hereford bull, 'Sarn Wagner'; Welsh Mountain Pony (stallion): Lieut.-Col. E. W. Williams-Wynn, Abergele; Child's First Pony, shown off leading rein by a child born in or after 1956: Misses Susan and Diana Vaughan, Newport; Old English Game, clay, wheaton or partridge (female): George Harris, Manselton; Rhubarb Jam: Mrs M. E. Evans, Llanafan); at Pewsey, monthly meeting of the Marlborough branch of the Guild of Ringers (more than thirty members attending, plus visitors 'welcomed from as far afield as Shrivenham'); at the Albert Hall, Llandrindod Wells, an evening of 'Old Time Music Hall', with local amateur acts including The Twins (Misses Gwen and Coris Pal of Pantydwr, doing 'Two little girls in blue'), The Intemperate Seven, and Mr Eric Williams of Ledbury ('Comedy Unlimited' and 'Magic and Mirth'); Mrs Sarah Davies celebrating her 100th birthday and telling the *Llanelli Star* that she attributed her longevity to the contented mind provided by knitting ('the only day I don't knit is Sunday because I don't like to . . . I spend the whole day reading the *Star* . . . the *Star* is the only paper I read'); near Felixstowe, a rogation service ('parishioners were conveyed in a farm cart around the fields and meadows of Friston Hall, when the crops and meadowlands were blessed'); near Wantage, in Hanney Village Hall, the May meeting of Hanney Women's Institute ('some outstanding entries for the competition for a hat representing a song title and the winner was Mrs Stephens' "Button and Bows" '); members of Andover Operatic Society deciding on *The Mikado* as their next production ('the producer, Mrs Jeffreys, emphasises that this production will be "trad," to use the modern idiom'); at the Ilkley Baptist Church Women's Meeting, Mrs G. H. Whittaker speaking about the dangers of a 'luke-warmness' towards God, resulting in 'a crumbling of the Christian's moral values in life, wrong attitudes towards parents, and every other moral weakness'; in a marquee on the County Show Field, and in front of 'large congregations' over a day and a half, the annual Montgomeryshire Welsh Congregational Preaching Festival, with the four preachers coming from Cardiff, Llanelli, Llangennech and Penrhyndeudraeth; the *Peterborough Standard*'s fashion columnist, Pamela Rae, advising on leather shoes for the summer ('for the real avant garde there are shoes which look almost identical with those your mothers and grandmothers buy – strong lace ups with clunky heels, often punched or decorated on the vamp'); at four different venues, including Leith Links, all sixteen bowling clubs in the Leith and District Bowling Club Association competing for the Dresner Trophy; and at the Victoria Hall in Glossop, marking the town's centenary, the centenary carnival queen dance. The finalists to be carnival queen were six local girls aged between nineteen and twenty-two; the judges were looking for 'grace, charm, deportment, personality and diction'; and one of the judges was BBC TV's Stuart Hall. The winner was twenty-year-old Kathleen Harrison ('works at Sterling Coating of Manchester . . . likes driving and enjoys watching fashion shows . . . plays tennis and table tennis'). And after her name was announced: 'Kathleen walked to the end of the room, where a flowing royal blue velvet cloak lined with white satin was draped over her shoulders. She sat on a throne as Stuart Hall placed the sparkling, shining coronet on her head, and the white satin sash around her shoulders.'

That was on the Friday evening that Dylan ended his tour – world tour as well as British tour – at the Royal Albert Hall. His new single, 'Rainy Day Women Nos. 12 and 35', currently lay at 10 in the charts; but 'Sandy', in her 'Teenage Column' in that day's *Holyhead & Anglesey Mail*, was thoroughly unimpressed by the call for everyone to get stoned: 'The latest Dylan song does not appeal to me: a load of tripe with the title having nothing to do with the song. It would be much better if it was an instrumental without any words.'[10]

PART THREE

18

Turn It Down!

'I don't like the scramble for meat at Sainsbury's Supermarket,' reflected Judy Haines on 1 April 1966 about going shopping in Chingford. 'One would think,' she added in an entry which made no mention of the previous day's general election, 'they are giving it away.' 'THE PROBLEM: FINDING ONE TO KEEP YOU AWAKE' was James Thomas's take next day in the *Daily Express* on late-night TV shows, though he was happy to make an exception for *Late Night Line-Up*, 'distinguished by the presence of TV's new first lady, Joan Bakewell, who can best be described as "The Thinking Man's Pin-Up"' (thereby anticipating Frank Muir's 'crumpet' tag); while in Sunday's *News of the World*, a reader in Devon shared his recent experience at a local swimming pool:

> A young girl wearing a striking blue bikini entered the pool. She had a beehive hairstyle and her face was covered with all kinds of make-up, mascara included. After she had been swimming a while she looked a real sight. Her hair resembled that of a horse's mane and most of her make-up had spilled down her face – she looked a horrible mess! When will these glamour girls learn? *(Private N. Lane, Seaton Barracks, Crown Hill)*

On Monday, at a performance of *Peer Gynt* at Bristol's Theatre Royal, Frederick Ward was impressed but also worried by how many intently watching young people there were ('I should think some of the macabre scenes must have upset the more impressionable ones'); *The Money Programme*, presented by William Davis, had its first run-out on BBC2 on Tuesday; on Wednesday evening – as Enoch Powell told City of London Young Conservatives that he was in favour of full-scale, across-the-board denationalisation of state industries ('above all, the persuasiveness and the inspiration of capitalist free enterprise would be immensely enhanced if its adherents can liberate themselves from the racket of nationalisation'); as BBC1's latest Wednesday Play (*Pity About The Abbey*, co-written by John Betjeman and Stewart Farrar) won an RI of 64 (well above the Wednesday Play's current average of 53) with its story of a group of youngsters foiling the attempt by Whitehall planners to demolish Westminster Abbey 'in order to make way for more Government offices and a new one-way traffic system'; as Laurence Marks went up to the West End to see *Alfie* ('the story is one I can identify with . . . fabbo . . . Eleanor Bron is to die for') – the Beatles were back in the studio for the first recording session (starting with 'Tomorrow Never Knows') of what became *Revolver*; and next morning, Thursday the 7th, the newly reshuffled Cabinet – no major changes at the top, but the fluent and ambitious 38-year-old Richard Marsh replacing Fred Lee as Minister of Power – met for the first time since the election. Top of the agenda was the Queen's Speech, due in a fortnight, and in particular the already delayed renationalisation of steel, unpopular with the public but a totemic issue for Labour's left. 'It looked as though a well-organized postponement lobby was going to get its way,' recorded Crossman, 'when Dick Marsh came in with his first intervention as a Cabinet Minister. He clearly intends to be vigorous, young and dynamic. He told the Cabinet bluntly that he was going to push his Steel Bill through in the first session and at once the notion of postponement faded away.'[1]

This particular Maundy Thursday, the *TLS* focused not on religion, but instead on 'New Ways in History', including contributions from three notable historians. In an introductory overview, the young Keith Thomas welcomed the increasing number of British historians who, no longer 'content to grub away in the old empirical tradition', were turning 'to see what help can be derived from the new sciences of society which have sprung up elsewhere', such as sociology, social anthropology, demography and social psychology – but at the same time could not resist pointing out that 'in so doing they are decades behind their colleagues in other countries', not least the *Annales* school in France; Eric Hobsbawm warned that the current publishing boom in history could lead to 'debasement through over-production', indeed that 'already there are cases of young historians who have been tempted to write too fast and too much on big broad subjects which are rarely tackled with full success before a man's fortieth year'; and E. P. Thompson's 'History From Below' called on historians of the working class to continue broadening their ambitions, to avoid 'a prodigious proliferation of pretentious jargon', and if possible to 'remain somewhat disestablished, with an extra-mural audience still partly in mind'. It was Thomas's piece which especially fluttered the dovecots, not least with its full-frontal attack on A. J. P. Taylor's recently published history of England between 1914 and 1945 as 'a brilliant swansong for the dying concept of real history as past politics, and social history as an undemanding subsidiary' – an attack which failed to change the view of an irritated Taylor that 'sociology is history with the history left out'. Overall, across the issue's contributors, the possibility of women's history as a new sort of history barely featured. But probably all were agreed on the centrality of social class; and this evening, as it happened, saw on the subject of that peculiarly British obsession one of the great television moments, featuring three comedians of distinctly different heights as well as accents:

> JOHN CLEESE: I look down on him [Ronnie Barker] because I am Upper Class.
>
> BARKER: I look up to him [Cleese] because he is Upper Class, but I look down on him [Ronnie Corbett] because he is Lower Class. I am Middle Class.
>
> CORBETT: I know my place. I look up to them both. But I don't look up to him [Barker] as much as I look up to him [Cleese], because he has got innate breeding.
>
> CLEESE: I have got innate breeding, but I have not got any money. So sometimes I look up [bobbing down] to him [Barker].
>
> BARKER: I still look up to him [Cleese] because although I have money, I am vulgar. But I am not as vulgar as him [Corbett] so I still look down on him.
>
> CORBETT: I know my place. I look up to them both; but while I am poor, I am honest, industrious and trustworthy. Had I the inclination, I could look down on them. But I don't.

BARKER: We all know our place, but what do we get out of it?
CLEESE: I get a feeling of superiority over them.
BARKER: I get a feeling of inferiority from him [Cleese], but a feeling of superiority over him [Corbett].
CORBETT: I get a pain in the back of my neck.

'Class' was the subject of this latest *The Frost Report*; the immortal sketch was written by John Law; and Frost, previewing the programme in the *Radio Times*, had pointedly quoted from a recent *Sunday Times* profile of himself about how 'it still seems unbelievable – at least in the mind of some contemporaries – that the son of an evangelical Methodist minister, a grammar school boy who played *soccer* and didn't have the right accent, could do so well (and better) in the predominantly upper middle-class world of the Soho satirists'.[2]

The *NME* on Good Friday acclaimed the Rolling Stones for having, on their new fourteen-track LP *Aftermath*, 'produced the finest value for money ever', with particular praise ('an hypnotic tempo is maintained throughout') for 'Under My Thumb'; a high RI of 73 for BBC1's teatime offering, *Hey Presto, It's Rolf* ('we all think Rolf Harris is "smashing" and his programme really super entertainment', though another viewer did find him 'just too, too, determinedly matey'); the warmest Easter Sunday since 1952 saw Mrs Alice Gamble from Kettering complaining in the *News of the World* that supermarkets were 'a temptation' to shoplifters ('I don't like the way they tempt the honest shopper by too many cheap offers'), Evelyn Waugh dying at home in Combe Florey soon after attending Easter Mass ('died of snobbery' as Cecil Beaton's instant verdict), Anthony Heap crossing the river to attend the Easter Parade in Battersea Park ('starts half an hour late, is very slow moving, and not as good as usual'), and Mods and Rockers on the evening train back from Brighton giving the railway staff a hard time ('all the way along the line we were stopping and starting because of hooligans pulling the communication cord'); while next day, a waistcoated Charlie Chaplin took a nostalgic, hat-doffing walk along the Old Kent Road, Britain's first safari park opened at Longleat ('Luvaduck, no,' replied Lord Bath when asked whether he would act as host to the paying visitors, 'I find it hard enough to talk to my friends'), the eighth annual CND march ended as usual with a rally in Trafalgar Square (the teenage Hitchens brothers among those having walked, with Christopher recalling 'various folk-moaners like Julie Felix' singing to the crowd), and Ray Davies gave a revealing, palpably sincere interview to *Melody Maker*:

> I hope England doesn't change. I'm writing a song now called 'You Ain't What You Used To Be' which expresses what I feel. I hope we don't get swallowed up by America and Europe. I'm really proud of being British . . . I don't care if a bloke votes Labour or Conservative as long as he appreciates what we've got here. We have so much that is great, compared with other countries, and people just don't realize it.

In short, 'I want to keep writing very English songs'.[3]

'Gentrification' was not yet a term in common currency, but that was the subject of BBC2's *Six Sides of a Square*, a six-part documentary series about Gibson Square in Islington, with the final episode on Tuesday the 12th earning an RI of 78 and demonstrating 'the impossibly wide gulf between the middle-class "invaders" and the needy poor, whose homes they were taking over'; almost certainly an absorbed audience too next evening at the National Film Theatre, where Peter Watkins's controversial, highly charged *The War Game* (described by Tynan after a press preview as 'a mosaic of stunned and shattered faces') was shown for members only; and on Thursday the coldest April day since 1950, including 'blizzard' conditions in Florence Turtle's Wimbledon Park and snow generally in London, discouraging backdrop for Judy Haines's evening treat:

> Stood for nearly 20 minutes at Allen's waiting for 38. Couldn't shelter in shop from sleet since advertisement board for new shops and flats obscures the view of oncoming bus. Should have walked to the 'Albert,' where I could have sheltered in shops and saved 4d fare.
>
> Finally got nicely seated by engine and enjoyed uninterrupted ride.
>
> Wore boots and needed them to wade through puddles en route Festival Hall. They looked good with red dress.
>
> Arrived a couple of minutes before John and we ate and drank in warmth and comfort.

> Leonard Bernstein's conducting and Mahler's 7th Symphony was received with wild applause. It is clever but doesn't stir me. A lovely evening out.

'In a decade dominated by youth, London has burst into bloom,' declared *Time* next day, even as the city shivered and froze in what Heap bleakly noted as 'the coldest April weather of the century'. 'It swings; it is the scene,' continued the magazine. 'This spring, as never before in modern times, London is Switched On.' Nothing too swinging that evening in Edward Heath's flat in Albany, where the Conservative leader summarily informed Powell that the price of staying in the Shadow Cabinet was to stick to party policy in his public pronouncements; front-page news on Saturday was the story of how a Liverpool supporter called Peter O'Sullivan, a bricklayer from Burton upon Trent, had – without telling his wife – given their seven-month-old daughter Paula the additional names of fifteen of the club's players and officials ('I was very upset,' said his wife, 'but I've got over it now'); the palmiest days of the Amateur Cup Final at Wembley were long gone, but 40,000 were still at Wembley that afternoon to see Wealdstone defeat Hendon 3–1; although *Ready, Steady, Go!* had been temporarily reprieved, *BBC-3* bowed out that evening, with Nancy Banks-Smith reflecting that it 'will be, as they say, sadly missed'; 'THE MURDER TRIAL OF THE CENTURY' was the *News of the World*'s huge front-page headline on Sunday morning ('After weeks of preparation the scene is finally set for the murder trial that is gripping the world more than any other in our time – the Case of the Bodies on the Moor'); and that evening, altogether more reassuringly, *Dr Finlay's Casebook* was opened for the 100th time. 'It is still gentle, unpretentious, and faithful,' commented an only semi-appreciative Banks-Smith. 'It's also eternally restricted to being gentle, unpretentious and faithful.'[4]

Away from the small screen this mid-April, a film, a musical and two plays. The film (admittedly evolving out of the TV play) was *Morgan – A Suitable Case for Treatment*, written by David Mercer, directed by Karel Reisz and starring David Warner as (in Dilys Powell's words) 'a proletarian artist who is crazy nor' nor' east, i.e. when he finds his wife [Vanessa Redgrave] has divorced him'. Most reviewers (including Powell herself) were positive, with Richard Mallett observing that 'the secret' of its treatment of Morgan's mental illness 'is that one's laughter is sympathetic, related to character'; though one critic – the *Sun*'s Ann Pacey – was worried that 'its blend of fantasy and reality does get a little out of hand', while John Coleman was blunter in the *New Statesman*: yes, 'chic, funny, jumpy', but 'I can see it dying a modish death in a year'. The musical was Anthony Heap's delight (not). 'At long last we come to the First Night of the much ballyhooed musical "Funny Girl" starring the over publicised Barbra Streisand at the Prince of Wales,' he recorded on the 13th. 'And are we dumbfounded? NO!' And, after calling it 'the most mediocre of musicals', he appraised 'the allegedly "fabulous"' Streisand: 'I am impressed by neither her talent as a comedienne nor her ability as a singer. She isn't really funny and she hasn't much of a voice. Nor for that matter is she strongly endowed with charm or personality much less attractiveness. In short, she doesn't appeal to, or "register" with, me at all.' Next evening it was the turn of Noël Coward, starring at the Queen's in his own *A Song at Twilight*. 'It is a most courageous piece of play-writing for Mr Coward to present himself as an old man, fading, possibly faded, sick, sub-alcoholic, talking about a love life which has passed,' reflected Gerard Fay. 'Particularly courageous,' he added, 'as one of the major affairs is a homosexual one.' Most reviews, however, were respectful rather than enthusiastic; Joyce Grenfell, present on the first night along with Princess Margaret and Edward Heath among others, privately noted that 'the subject calls for depth and depth is the one thing Noël doesn't have'; while Richard Huggett, biographer of 'Binkie' Beaumont (the play's dedicatee), shrewdly reflects that the revelation of a play's central character being a homosexual had by this time largely lost its 'shock value'. Indeed, another sign of gradually shifting mores had come earlier in the week, in the shape of a warm review in the *Daily Telegraph* – of all papers – of the newly rewritten and retooled production of Joe Orton's hitherto disastrous *Loot*, now playing (no longer with Kenneth Williams) at the Manchester University Theatre. 'Bizarre humour isn't to everyone's taste,' conceded the paper's Eric Shorter, but he himself found all the goings-on – involving 'coffins and corpses and heaps of stolen bank-notes which are frenziedly required to change places from time to time' – unashamedly 'very funny'; and he applauded 'the furious, formalised wit of the dialogue to carry the grisly joke from one absurdity to another'. Admittedly the police were in the stalls that first night, just in case the performance exceeded what the Lord Chamberlain had permitted after scrutinising the script, but no one was too fussed; while, ironically, the reviewer who complained about Orton's 'culpable dishonesty', making 'macabre jokes intended to shock' that were in reality just 'cheap gimmicks', was not the man from the *Telegraph*, but the *Guardian*'s Ann Shearer.[5]

'Building operatives on internal jobs seem to be incapable of working these days without a portable radio blaring away all the time,' grumbled Heap on Monday the 18th. 'The men renovating the flat below us prior to new tenants moving in have the radio playing from the moment they arrive at 8.0 am till when they leave about 6.0 pm. Likewise the men converting our old office [at Finsbury Town Hall] into the new computer room have one playing all day.' Nearby, at Euston station, the full passenger service began that day of electric trains to both Manchester and Liverpool; next day, Keith McBride noted that 'the famous "Moors" trial has opened', speculating whether it was a case of 'one of those witchcraft sects one hears about'; that evening at Anfield, in a European Cup Winners' Cup semi-final played in torrential rain, a disallowed Celtic goal three minutes from the end resulted in ambulancemen crouching behind a fence as a fusillade of beer bottles rained over their heads, a mass pitch invasion and more than a hundred spectators injured, with twenty-one taken to hospital; press coverage on Wednesday morning of the trial of Hindley and Brady at Chester Assizes included double-page spreads in the *Mirror*, *Sketch* and *Express*, whole-page spreads in the *Sun* ('Woman lured brother-in-law to watch axe murder'), *Mail* ('Left Luggage led to Graves') and *Telegraph* ('Children's Secret Fate'), while even *The Times* devoted a half-page spread; *Punch* had its editor, Bernard Hollowood, laying into Enoch Powell for his 'primitive economic notions' and advising the post-election Conservative leadership instead to 'look to France and Sweden for their models' – the former for showing how 'long-range planning can be introduced without destroying short-term enterprise', the latter for having 'evolved a paternalist state – with the finest welfare services in the world – while allowing 95 per cent of industrial activity to remain free from rigid state control'; the BBC later in the day decided that the details being revealed at Chester were so shocking for viewers that it would wait until the verdicts before continuing to cover the trial; and the working-class writer Jack Common reported to an old friend from Newcastle days about what was happening to his local in Newport Pagnell:

> The Bull has been reprieved from drastic re-building for 4 years. But there is to be some re-modelling, putting in of soft lights, curtains and electric fires. Reg [the landlord] is putting up a terrific fight to keep his cellar (Watney 'experts' forced to admit that on results it is first-class) and his 'drawn from the wood.' But Vera [Reg's wife] has weakened, thinking of her feet on the passage (who can blame her except that Reg has feet he'd gladly swap for hers any day) so I'm afraid that by next winter it is going to be press-button Special Pale Ale for ordinary and Red Barrel keg – my lovely I.P.A. will become a memory like draught Bass.[6]

Back in the 1930s, Common had been friendly with George Orwell; and that regular at the Moon Under Water would surely have sympathised about the price of progress.

'Would Mr Harold Wilson please do something about the weather?' ran *in toto* the letter in *The Times* on Thursday morning from Lord Drogheda, managing director of the *Financial Times* and chairman of the Royal Opera House; 'what an advertisement for the British sporting spirit,' declared an editorial in the *Sun* on the violence at Anfield, 'if we end with football pitches enclosed in protective wire cages'; the Queen (on her fortieth birthday) delivered her speech at the State Opening of Parliament – the first time it had been televised; the speech itself revealed that, from the government's perspective, there was (in *The Times*'s words) 'no provisional timing yet for the controversial early warning Bill to underpin the prices and incomes policy, and the delay will allow further consultations between Mr Brown and the group of sceptical trade union leaders and MPs'; while after attending a meeting of Labour MPs (many of them first-timers) which followed the Queen's Speech, Barbara Castle reflected that 'from the truculent tone of some interventions on Vietnam, etc., it is clear the Party is in a different mood from the last Parliament'. A week after *Time*'s already much-publicised take on the capital, what about swinging London? 'You wouldn't know the place, honest,' wrote James Cameron in a nicely judged take-down in next day's *New Statesman*. 'Not, that is, if you live in Acton or Edmonton or Balham or Tooting, and do not buy your gear at Hung On You and are not entertained by Miss Leslie Carron and eat at Le Rêve and fulfil your sex-life under a Mary Poppins chimney-pot off the King's Road.'

An apposite moment for the publication of Ian Nairn's instant classic, *Nairn's London*, with E. S. Turner's review in the same issue describing his approach as 'more idiosyncratic than iconoclastic . . . he simply wishes to see atmosphere and character cherished'; Wilson this Friday, addressing the Scottish TUC in Aberdeen, demanded an 'end to bloody-mindedness on both sides of industry'; in the Commons, Ray Gunter's new Parliamentary Secretary at the Ministry of Labour, Shirley Williams, made her maiden ministerial speech and spoke optimistically about how the government intended to 'advance towards the principle of equal pay', in other words of women in relation to men, a principle she described as one 'of justice'; Pat Scott and her daughter went to East Ham on Saturday ('we paid another 3 months for the T.V. but we will have to think about buying a set – the rental seems to go up instead of down . . . we want to change to BBC2 & it means 8 months rental as deposit'); the final episode of a four-part *Dr Who* story called 'The Celestial Toymaker' provoked a fourth-successive poor RI (43 this time, lowest yet) and the majority reaction of viewers that it was 'fantasy gone mad', though some found it a welcome change from 'the more obvious horrors like Daleks and monsters'; 'all one's carefully proposed arguments about capital punishment being wrong drain away on reading about this sort of filth,' admitted Kenneth Williams about what he called 'the "Moors Case"'; and under the headline 'After four days of the Moors Trial . . . Even The Ghouls Stayed Away', the *People*'s Ken Gardner reported from the epicentre itself about local reaction:

> Before the case began, it was predicted that Chester would be invaded by gawpers who would overcrowd the few hotels and overspill into private houses doing a lively trade in bed and breakfast. In fact, people have tended to boycott the city this week and in some cases traders have reported a drop in their takings. The horrifying nature of the allegations produces in pubs and elsewhere a kind of vocal numbness when anybody tries to raise the subject . . .[7]

The *Daily Worker* became the *Morning Star* on Monday the 25th; 'good plain cook – won't argue about the menu' was reputedly the reaction of Morgan Grenfell's Lord Harcourt to the news that the current deputy-governor, Leslie O'Brien, would be succeeding Lord Cromer at the Bank of England, after the City had been worried about rumours of Sir Eric Roll, far too cerebral for its taste, coming over from the Department of Economic Affairs; Betty Allen in Lancashire 'decided to find out about gas central heating'; and on BBC1 a special edition of *Look*, as part of National Nature Week, focused on wildlife in the London area and had Peter Scott joined by the Duke of Edinburgh, helping to achieve an RI of 86 and particular applause for the prince from a watching machinist ('with his very plain speaking and his sense of humour he was at his very best'). A controversy running by this time, in the context of *Sunday Times* serialisation ahead of book publication, concerned the propriety of Churchill's physician, Lord Moran, revealing intimate details about his patient's physical and mental decline, with *The Times* on Tuesday printing a furious denunciation by Churchill's son Randolph, who warned that 'eminent people' would, with their doctors, henceforth have to follow the example of the royal family, who 'have found it necessary to enter into covenants with their domestic staffs inhibiting them from writing anything they learn when in service'; that evening, while Princess Margaret and Lord Snowdon were at the Empire in Leicester Square for the premiere of *Doctor Zhivago* (one critic, Dan Jacobson, struck by Julie Christie having 'quite the prettiest nose I've seen on the screen since Ingrid Bergman's'), Frederick Ward was at Bristol's Theatre Royal for *Man and Superman*, featuring a 'first-class performance' from Paul Eddington; and Michael Foot in the Commons was laying into the foreign secretary, Michael Stewart, for even thinking about bowing to American pressure and sending troops to Vietnam – 'an evil and shameful war which is being fought for the wrong reasons and can never be brought to a successful conclusion'.[8]

Less than three months to go until the World Cup, and at a press conference on Wednesday about the choice of commemorative postage stamps, their designer, David Caplan, caused a stir by giving away, in Tony Benn's rueful words, 'the fact that the Foreign Office had banned the first choice because it contained the North Korean flag'; in the Commons that day, Wilson announced that, following mass resignations (including from the distinguished Cambridge criminologist Leon Radzinowicz), the Royal Commission on the Penal System, set up in April 1964, would no longer continue its work – an announcement provoking an impassioned reaction from the Conservative MP Tom Iremonger, whose own experience of being a member of the Commission had convinced him that the dissenters cared more for the criminal than for the victim of crime; that evening, a new criminal potentially came to light, as *Coronation Street* ended with Ena Sharples and Minnie Caldwell being stopped outside the Pick-a-Snip Supermarket by the manager, who told Ena that she had failed to pay for some of the items in her bag; next day saw Philip Larkin in York for a conference, where to his dismay the star speaker was F. R. Leavis ('what a ghastly little man! . . . really a typical Oxbridge don, cocky, smart, full of petty cattiness . . . stupid little sod, the ideas rattling in him like peas . . . I've not met a *sillier* man for many a long day'); Phyllis Willmott in Highgate noted that she was, a couple of months after two of her friends (Mavis Nicholson and Margot Jefferys), 'at last' going on 'The Pill'; and the latest *Country Life* had Cedric Venables mulling over 'Cricket Prospects at The Schools':

> Eton have hopes of a good XI . . . Experience will be lacking at Harrow . . . If Winchester can find reliable openers for batting and bowling they should have few worries . . . For Charterhouse this will be a year of building with an eye to the future . . . Radley's prospects are not obviously good . . . If some of the eight old colours can make runs, the prospect at Cheltenham should be bright . . . By contrast Haileybury and I.S.C. will be strong in batting and looking for bowlers . . .

Venables then covered the prospects of sixteen other schools; all of them, like the first seven, were public schools; and presumably none of his readers batted an eyelid about that definite article, including that capital 'T', before 'Schools'.

'We are not sitting on our backsides,' declared Mrs Ethel Chipchase at Weymouth on Friday at the annual conference of representatives of trade unions catering for women workers. Inevitably, the subject was equal pay, and she warned the government that 'if something is not done within the next few months we shall be at the barricades getting something done about it'. Or as Miss J. French of the Amalgamated Engineering Union (AEU) put it, in the context of millions of women working a full week for a half-week's pay, 'How much longer are we to wait until we can say that women are not regarded as a reservoir of cheap labour?' As ever, the end of the week meant chart action, and this week had another woman who knew her own mind, Dusty Springfield, perched on top with 'You Don't Have To Say You Love Me'; the press on Saturday revealed that only one in seven cars currently on the road were fitted with seat belts (not yet compulsory); and that afternoon, after the match was over at the local football ground in Hayes Lane, it fell to a fiercely determined nineteen-year-old wannabe to crown the eight Bromley May Queens: Anne Sutton (Bickley), Christine Baker (Hayes Common), Carol Sharp (Pickhurst Park), Linda Dutton (Sundridge Park), Rosemary Reynolds (Bromley), Jacqueline Mann (Shortlands), Yvonne Lomax (Bromley Common), Sandra Cousins (Southborough) – they had all processed down Bromley High Street, accompanied by their attendants and two musical bands (Bromley Boys' Brigade and 1st St Mary Cray Girls Life Brigade) before now, in front of some 500 people, having their crowning moment from the nerveless hands of David Bowie.[9]

May itself began on Sunday with what Oxford's deputy chief constable described as 'the worst May morning in my experience'. 'We have always considered it a light-hearted occasion with a few harmless undergraduate pranks,' he went on, 'but it has now become vicious; the excuse for every type of hooliganism.' Elsewhere, on the warmest May Day since 1940, Wilson told the Merseyside May Day meeting at Kirkby (in his Huyton constituency) that job-defending restrictive practices were in fact job-endangering and compared them in their counter-productive futility to the Maginot Line; Benn at Bristol's May Day meeting was disappointed that 'only about 350 people turned up' to listen to Lord Longford (a junior member of the Cabinet as Lord Privy Seal); and Veronica Lee in Leeds watched the May Day march. 'It was quite amusing. Cliff Slaughter attempting to direct operations. Communists & Trotskyists but not many of them all trying to make the workers politically conscious. Most of them (workers) were enjoying the Sunday sun & lying in the park or playing bowls.' No marches that afternoon at Wembley's Empire Pool, but instead an *NME* Poll-winners Concert whose line-up included the Small Faces, the Spencer

Davis Group, Roy Orbison, the Walker Brothers, the Yardbirds, Alan Price, the Shadows, Cliff Richard, Herman's Hermits, Dave Dee (not forgetting Dozy, Beaky, Mick & Tich), Dusty Springfield, the Who, the Rolling Stones and, dressed in beetle-black, the Beatles – in fact, as it turned out, their last-ever official UK gig. 'When their set ended,' recalled the *NME*'s Derek Johnson, MC for the event, 'the Beatles did a quick bow and then, to avoid the huge amount of fans, they raced to their cars and drove off.'

Next morning, the front page of *The Times* was, as usual, news-free and included not only announcements of births, marriages and deaths, but also the familiar enticing array of 'Personal'. To take just five:

> MRS. TZUMAIO (formerly Miss Sophie Selby-Lowndes) has cancelled all her engagements for Whitsun.
>
> ANOUCHKA, this summer will be very long and lonely without you. – D.
>
> ALICE IN WONDERLAND. – Jonathan Miller is looking for an enormous corridor – at least 100 feet long – in an 18th or 19th century house for use in the BBC T.V. production of Lewis Carroll's famous story. He also wants a large antiquated Victorian kitchen, complete with black-leaded stove, perhaps an old pump, rows of house-bells, &c. Also wanted one very sinister, cranky, indoor swimming pool, very old and very peculiar for the 'Pool of Tears' scene. – If you can help, please write to Tony Palmer, E.515, BBC T.V., White City, London, W.12.
>
> WELL-EDUCATED Public School girl, aged 18¾, fluent French, excellent with children over 5 years old, willing to help mother travelling abroad during August; Protestant families only; fare and pocket money required. – Mrs. Sullavan, The Dingle, Whaley Bridge, via Stockport, Cheshire.
>
> MONKEY ISLAND needs girls as general assistants, aged 18 to 27, ex-public school or similar background; driving useful, handy for London and seldom a dull moment! – Telephone Maidenhead 20849.

Main item for the Cabinet was Tuesday's Budget, with Callaghan's proposed centrepiece, largely the work of his Hungarian-born economic adviser Nicholas Kaldor, being the introduction of a

Selective Employment Tax (SET) aimed at the service sector and in effect discriminating in favour of manufacturing. Crossman noted general 'bewilderment and consternation' round the table, while according to Castle 'there was a lot of uneasiness about the new tax but, with the enthusiastic support of Roy Jenkins and Tony Crosland, Jim got away with it'. That evening, a bewildered and indignant Ena was taken to the supermarket manager's office, accused of failing to pay for two tins of salmon (4s. 6d. each), escorted by PC Russell to the police station, and charged with intention to shoplift; next morning, Tuesday the 3rd, the front page of *The Times* was news-full (including a photograph of Callaghan at work on his Budget), with not a public schoolboy in want of a job – and willing to do anything legal – to be seen; the signatories to a letter inside from Cambridge University condemning the US's escalation of bombing of North Vietnam included T. Eagleton, John H. Goldthorpe, Joan Robinson and Raymond Williams; the press had their first look at the Post Office Tower, where up on the twenty-seventh floor the restaurant was already in action, with cooks 'preparing steak and kidney pies for the staff and the scores of workmen putting finishing touches to the interior of the building'; Florence Turtle visited a friend in hospital in Balham ('he said the food was absolutely awful & that most of it went into the pig swill'); and Callaghan delivered his Budget, with the City predictably down on it from the start. 'Puritan in tone, neo-Marxist in economic intent', and introducing into British economic policy 'a wholly false antithesis between "productive" and "non-productive" activities': such was the *Banker*'s description of the SET as seen through the City's eyes – and there would clearly be little sympathy from that quarter should sterling hit another period of turbulence.[10]

Next day, Castle told MPs of her intention to make the fitting of seat belts compulsory on all new cars and vans; Turtle in Wimbledon Park 'went to Painting class & had a chat with Miss Cardwell the teacher who said so many children in her class who cannot read she has to coach them in her lunch time'; Ena was found guilty and fined £2, though in giving her an absolute discharge the magistrates accepted that the offence had been out of character; sixteen-year-old Peter Shilton made his debut for Leicester City (a clean sheet at home to Everton); Hannah Gavron's *The Captive Wife*, a pioneering study of the problems of young housewives with young children, was published on Thursday, almost five months after her suicide; *The Times*'s parliamentary correspondent found himself that afternoon applauding Margaret Thatcher's demolition job on SET ('with her blonde curls a constant bobbing reminder of the prospective increase in hairdressing charges, she attacked the whole structure of the tax with incisive feminine logic'); Turtle got home in the evening to find her brother 'wrapped in front of a Football match between Liverpool & Borussia of Dortmund at Hampden Park', prompting after two weary hours the timeless reflection, 'Cannot think how men can get so excited about men kicking a ball about'; and Vere Hodgson, a faithful *Telegraph* reader, noted of its newly revamped rival that she would buy a copy and take a look ('I never used to think their presentation of news was particularly good. It had no Come Hither look'). She also mulled over immigration, 'one of the fundamental problems of the country': 'No-one will face it and it was pushed under the mat at the Election by everyone. But there will be trouble for the next generation, for these kindly people breed rapidly. I like them well enough. And though there are black sheep among them, there are far more among the whites!'

On Friday, 6 May – two and a half weeks and much sensationalist press coverage after it had begun – 'the Moors trial' ended with guilty verdicts for Brady and Hindley, each sentenced to life imprisonment for what Mr Justice Fenton Atkinson called 'calculated, cool, cold-blooded murders'. 'Absolute sadists, Ian Brady and Myra Hindley,' wrote Judy Haines in her diary, Laurence Marks struggled to understand their motivation ('What did the children do to these two that made them want to take their lives?'), and Florence Turtle called it 'a great pity' that 'capital punishment has been done away with'. The Sunday papers inevitably had their say: at one end of the spectrum, a thoughtful attempt by the *Observer*'s Maurice Richardson to understand the background and psychology of the two murderers (Brady with his 'hopeless start' in the Gorbals and 'probably drawing something sinister in the chromosomal lottery', Hindley 'profoundly affected' when 'at thirteen she saw a boy drown in a canal'); at the spectrum's other end, Percy Howard in the *Sunday Express* blaming the murders on 'the smart teachers' who 'gave Brady his first lesson in despising the ordinary conventional people around him as unthinking cabbages' and who 'suggested to him that right and wrong are only relative terms – and that, so far as sex is concerned, they should not be used at all', with Howard broadening out his analysis to blame 'the leaders of the Permissive Revolution'. Whatever their causes, these were murders – and murderers – destined to remain lodged in the national memory bank for many years. 'Icon of homicidal infamy' would be the headline to the *Independent*'s obituary of Hindley when she died in 2002; 'Burn in hell Brady' the *Daily Mirror*'s front-page headline when he died in 2017; and a few days after that, the *Big Issue*'s John Bird recalled how back at the time of the guilty verdicts he had been 'a 20-year-old, non-reconstituted "hang them high but let the family tear their eyeballs out first" sort of fellow'. 'Maybe we have become nicer,' he reflected about the continuing absence of capital punishment since those days and also about his own liberal, humanitarian journey. 'But I still can't help thinking,' he went on, 'that wouldn't it have been great if the ending of the death sentence had happened after the Moors Murderers, so we could have seen those particular two off to their maker half a century ago. Rather than wake up one day in the 21st century and realise that that piece of shit had been allowed to have a life where his victims and their families got death and a life sentence of sadness and suffering.'[11]

If the Moors Murders verdict was undeniably a 'Sixties' moment, so too was the publication of John Fowles's *The Magus*. 'On a Greek island where he has gone to teach, Nicholas Urfe, the novel's cynical and unsympathetic protagonist, is bewitched and beguiled by a manipulative Prospero-like figure [Conchis] and a young woman of apparently unfathomable mystery with whom Urfe falls in love' would be the part-summary of the plot of a very long novel (617 pages) by one of the author's obituarists almost forty years later; while in early May 1966, one of the first reviewers was Angus Wilson, acknowledging Fowles's 'remarkable abilities', regretting how it was the type of novel in which 'a general peppering of pretentious cultural or metaphysical or mystic talk spoils the entertainment and floats over the surface of any of the human profundities it appears to be exploring', and predicting a box-office hit in the film version – an overall verdict prompting Fowles in his diary characteristically to dismiss Wilson as 'the hermaphroditic voice of the traditional (twentieth-century) English novel chastising the new'. Such was Fowles's instant standing on the back of *The Collector* three years earlier that, in the space of a week, almost all the other main outlets ran substantial reviews, sometimes but not always by prestigious reviewers:

> Intellectually flamboyant . . . a deliciously toothsome celebration of wanton story-telling . . . immensely seductive and brilliantly entertaining. *(Frederic Raphael)*
>
> A major work of mounting tensions in which a human mind is the guinea-pig. *(John Moynihan)*
>
> The narrative skill and power of invention, the sense conveyed of an obsession having been run dry to the last drop of titillating juice, must command our admiration. *(Anonymous reviewer,* The Times*)*
>
> A stunner. *(Iain Hamilton)*
>
> The power of the book is considerable, but the naturalistic skill serves less a story than a ritual intolerably prolonged. *(Anthony Burgess)*
>
> What a pathetic longing, that the whole world should revolve in order that the masochistic fancies of youth might be indulged and expiated . . . A silly book and an unhealthy one. *(Marghanita Laski, writing anonymously in the* TLS*)*
>
> An odd, readable mixture of Romantic Agony and contemporary: an overgrown, over-indulged fantasy. *(Christopher Salvesen)*
>
> Overembellished, powerful, sometimes pretentious. *(Christopher Wordsworth)*
>
> Has an intellectual vulgarity. It tackles all of psychology, mythology, history, mysticism, art with an idiotic abandon . . . Should never have seen the light of day. *(Bill Byrom)*

That last review was in the *Spectator*, but across the aisle the *New Statesman*'s Penelope Mortimer, one of the novel's few female reviewers, was little kinder, with her reaction mainly characterised by 'bewilderment' and 'irritation' – caused, she explained, 'not because one feels one cannot understand what is there, but because one cannot understand that there is nothing there'. 'All vinegar' was Fowles's response to her review, while more generally he reflected: 'Various sorts of in-between reviews; a few good . . . I don't really care now, reviews hurt far less than they should; and in a way it seems healthier, in a sick culture, to be rejected than approved.' What no one could have quite predicted was the novel's huge popularity among younger, university-educated readers and indeed its, for a time, almost cult-like status. Not that that made Fowles himself particularly happy. 'I now know the generation whose mind it most attracts,' he wrote in his foreword to the 1977 revised version. 'And that it must always substantially remain a novel of adolescence written by a retarded adolescent.'[12]

Back in the more humdrum, everyday world, serious industrial strife was looming – specifically, the refusal of the National Union of Seamen (NUS), despite Ray Gunter's face-to-face plea to them on Saturday the 7th, to call off their national strike, planned to start on 16 May in pursuit of a pay increase equivalent to a 17 per cent rise in earnings, clearly a breach of the government's current incomes policy; in the Sunday papers, while Tynan semi-hailed Joseph Losey's *Modesty Blaise* as 'a triumph of inventive obsolescence, with instant rust built into its modish glitter', a letter in the *News of the World* from a Pontypridd reader, J. L. Morgan, noted he was struck by how often 'darling' was used on TV, radio and films, wondered whether in real life British couples ever called each other by that word, and answered categorically 'No fear!'; Benn, as Postmaster General, spent his morning trying but failing to get the upcoming rematch between Cassius Clay (now calling himself Muhammad Ali, but still generally known as Clay) and Henry Cooper shown live on BBC or ITV, in the inconvenient context of Viewsport being the fight's part-promoter; the Lords on Tuesday gave second readings to both Lord Silkin's Abortion Bill (legalising abortion) and Lord Arran's Sexual Offences Bill (decriminalising homosexual acts between consenting adults), despite Lord Kilmuir, a former Lord Chancellor, warning in relation to the latter that 'it is becoming more evident to more people every day that we are rolling more quickly down the slope of the permissive society' and that 'unless we stop it, the position may indeed be serious'; that evening, ten months after the sensational events at the Newport Folk Festival, Bob Dylan brought his electric revolution to England, with Bristol's Colston Hall (Frederick Ward sadly not present) full of shouts of 'Turn it down!' from the dismayed folk purists; Wilson on Wednesday, addressing the Parliamentary Press Gallery, again attacked 'restrictive practices', calling instead for a 'new spirit of anti-amateurism'; Dylan that evening, after a lengthy, moody wait earlier in the day at the Aust Ferry terminal to cross the Severn (the bridge not yet completed), played at Cardiff's Capitol Theatre, with the 26-year-old Angela Carter (first novel about to be published) acclaiming him as not just 'the first ever all-electronic, all existential rock and roll singer', but 'a prophet of chaos'; next morning, the Cabinet's sole item was the rapidly approaching seamen's strike – 'the discussion,' recorded Castle, 'wandered all over the place for an hour and then ended with the inevitable conclusion: we must stand firm'; Heap spent his evening at the Empire in Leicester Square (*Doctor Zhivago* 'pictorially brilliant but dramatically dire'), Dylan his at the Odeon in Birmingham (the disgruntled audience sarcastically told, 'If you want some folk music, I'll play you some folk music', before a defiantly electric 'Baby, Let Me Follow You Down'); Nancy Banks-Smith on Friday took marked exception to the claim of a fellow critic, the *Mail*'s Peter Black, that *The Frost Report* was the funniest show on TV, instead calling it 'push-button, trans-Atlantic humour, deep-frozen jokes, plastic-wrapped, pre-packaged, to keep all the dirt out and all the artificial flavouring in', or in short 'a kind of comedy, as a battery broiler is a kind of chicken'; the disputatious musicologist (and avid Spurs supporter) Hans Keller offered in the *New Statesman* his prediction that 'our World Cup hopes, such as they are, depend on Greaves the genius, and Bobby Charlton the steadier master'; Wilson had the NUS's leaders in at No. 10, but got no joy from them, as they (in Philip Ziegler's words) 'abused the employers and berated Wilson for supporting the capitalist against the working man'; later on, Turtle 'cooked rather a full dinner – liver, bacon, sausages, carrots, cauliflower, potatoes & fruit salad (partly fresh) & custard – seemed to be over the stove rather a long time', and another diarist, Keith McBride, watched on TV the seamen's leader, Bill Hogarth ('a lovely scouse accent & looked very tough . . . the clever interviewer couldn't upset him in the least'); Geoffrey Goodman, the *Sun*'s well-informed industrial editor, stated unambiguously on Saturday that 'nothing can now prevent the strike of the National Union of Seamen from midnight tomorrow'; Everton overcame Sheffield Wednesday 3–2 in the Cup Final, where just before the final whistle the blues' combative Scottish midfielder Jimmy Gabriel spent a full twenty-eight seconds on the ball, most of them near the opposition corner flag – virtuoso skill, but the birth of a wretched tactic; Dylan that evening at the

Odeon in Liverpool, backed as usual by the Hawks, made Merseybeat seem like the proverbial vicar's tea party with his raw, elemental version of 'Just Like Tom Thumb's Blues'; in Sunday's *News of the World*, the customary letter of complaint about the modern world came from W. A. Hewitson of West Kirby, Cheshire ('Our bad habits grow worse. Is there anything more distasteful than hair-combing in public? Yet people do on the bus, in shops, and in the street. How can one brush off the offenders?'); at Ilford, in front of a large crowd, first-class cricket was played for the first time on a Sunday ('a pleasant family scene,' reported *The Times*'s John Woodcock, 'mother being there with the best of them to see whether it was all worth while'); in Derbyshire the recently elected chairman of Clay Cross Urban District Council explained to the press his refusal to wear the gold chain of office ('Council chains and the pomp and ceremony of local government and parliament,' declared 34-year-old Dennis Skinner, 'are outdated and a waste of time'); on ITV that evening the *London Palladium* show starred Liza Minnelli, David Nixon and the Hollies; and, while clutching their 17s. 6d. tickets announcing 'an Evening with America's Greatest Folk Singer, BOB DYLAN', the folkies at Leicester's De Montfort Hall listened in the now customary reverential silence to Dylan's acoustic first half, before the equally customary mood of betrayal set in during the electric second half. Not everyone, though, missed the bigger picture. 'Dylan's protest songs achieved their aim and started people thinking much more about the wrong things that were going on – and not only in America,' wrote one of those present, David Sandison, in the *Leicester Chronicle*. 'But Bob Dylan is through with shouting and protesting. He has grown up and out of the missionary zeal that was so much a feature of his early career. Perhaps those who spoiled the De Montfort Hall concert will also mature in time and realise that their prejudice is almost as great as the prejudices Dylan used to campaign against.'[13]

A rather different American visitor was the veteran American naturalist and writer Edwin Way Teale, who with his wife Nellie, and travelling for much of the time in a 'compact' blue Vauxhall, undertook a swing through much of Britain between roughly late March and early July. 'The harsh, stony fields of Cornwall', so much less attractive than 'softer, more fertile Devon', where 'the country cottages appeared to have grown where they stood'; 'the sprawling pile of Dartmoor Prison' looming up out of the mist 'less stark and grim than we had expected'; 'like all English woodlands' the Forest of Dean 'more open, less shaggy, more parklike than American forests'; buying at Dymock in Gloucestershire 'fruit at a florist's shop, pencils in a wool shop, and bakery goods and a small bag of Devonshire clotted cream toffees at a grocery store called the Daffodil'; unfamiliar food during the early weeks, including steak and kidney pie, finnan haddock (for breakfast), elvers (for lunch), steamed whelks, Dorset knobs, devils on horseback; in the New Forest, home for thousands of years to the native red squirrel, 'the balance of nature' now severely upset by 'the introduction of American gray squirrels'; in open country almost everywhere this spring, being 'thrilled by the aerial displays of the lapwings'; staying in an 'immense hotel' in Tunbridge Wells, noticing that fellow guests 'usually stepped aside and waited until we reached a landing on the stairs', and attributing this to English politeness 'until, one morning, an elderly gentleman smilingly volunteered, "You know, they say it is unlucky to pass on the stairs"'; in Leominster, beside an antique shop named The Den of Antiquity, buying 'a quart of milk for a wayside lunch from a deliveryman wearing a huge leather pouch weighted down with small change, the large and heavy small change of England'; the Black Country, where 'the houses were darkened by that universal pigment of the region, the black soot of the burning coal', and where 'piles of industrial waste ran in low, saw-toothed ranges below the chimneys'; after much ear-straining in vain elsewhere, a nightingale at last heard, in a wood near the Six Day Inn, north of the Suffolk village of Elveden; stopping at a bakery in Spilsby in Lincolnshire for a loaf of its celebrated plum bread, being impressed by 'the extreme politeness' of server as well as customer ahead of him, involving 'a dozen or more thank-yous and pleases until all the purchases were made'; in Knutsford, no longer Mrs Gaskell's 'leisurely' Cranford, the town 'swarming with Saturday shoppers'; in the Dewsbury region, 'a seemingly unending pall of smoke and mist', as 'huddled together along the way, grim under the sunless sky, stone houses rose dingy with soot'; also in Yorkshire, a sleepless night in a hotel room overlooking

Huddersfield railway station ('a metallic blaring of loudspeakers ... the clash of couplings'); across the border, driving into Inveraray, the burghal motto, *Semper tibi pendiat halac*, or 'May you always have a catch of herring'; finally, flying back home from London Airport, a glimpse from the air of 'the convoluted west coast of England, the rocky offshore islands ringed with the white lace of breaking water' ... *Springtime in Britain* was not one of the great travel books; but it had its charm, its odd unexpected insight – and its implicit reminder that there was far from only one '1966'.

'The impression made by the British countryside is one of lived-in beauty, of a land long associated with man,' Teale reflected at one point about what he had seen over the three or four months. 'Its scenery is not overwhelming or inspiring. It holds no Alps, no Sahara, no Grand Canyon ... The English countryside is essentially companionable country. A "green and pleasant land" are words that return again and again to the traveler's mind.' Unsurprisingly, on the book's eventual publication in 1971, one reviewer, Beverley Nichols, noted how, for all the occasional disagreeable urban interlude, 'hardly a blemish mars the Elysian perfection of the picture which unfolded before him', or in short 'a rhapsodic account of his 12,000 mile journey'. Yet just to glance at contemporary press accounts that spring, between March and May while Teale's hired Vauxhall was doing its stuff, is quickly to sense a harder, non-Elysian edge to rural life: 'keen regret' the reaction of the National Farmers' Union (NFU) when the agriculture minister, Fred Peart, unveiled the government's annual farm price review (small increases in guaranteed prices for milk, beef, sheep and potatoes, no change for cereals, oats, rye and sugar beet, reduction for eggs as well as the lime subsidy and the ploughing-up grant); in the context of particular concern about DDT, dieldrin and aldrin, local councils across the country to operate a scheme, devised by the Association of Public Analysts, to test by gas chromatographs samples of almost every type of food in order to determine the level of pesticide residue; scientists in the Ministry of Agriculture remaining baffled by the plague of poison-resistant rats in West Scotland and on the borders of Montgomeryshire and Shropshire ('farmers are losing animal feeding stuffs and grain worth thousands of pounds each year'); farmers also waging war against moles and molehills, with chemists across the country reporting a sharp increase in demand for strychnine crystals (to dip earthworms in, with the treated worms then left to poison the mole runs); the annual report of the government's Fishery Research Department revealing marine scientists to be well on the way, through experimental work at the fisheries laboratory at Lowestoft, to finding out how to enable fish farming on the same sort of intense scale as already used to produce beef and poultry; during the biennial conference of the National Union of Agricultural Workers, at Weston-super-Mare, the very left-wing Joan Maynard, secretary of the Thirsk branch of the union, fiercely attacking ministers, especially Richard Crossman, for failing to do anything about the 'pernicious evil' of tied farm cottages; and in Scotland, the attempts of the Highlands and Islands Development Board to bring industry to the more remote islands and stop the drain of young people coming up against the stubborn refusal of the islanders themselves, typified by the Lewismen, to make the necessary adjustment – '"the croft," they say, is their "way of life, and that is final."'

By this time, having started in early April, ITV had its first rural soap. Made by Anglia Television, and created by the husband-and-wife team Betty Paul and Peter Lambda, *Weavers Green* was set in a Norfolk village, centred on the veterinary practice at the Old Forge (facing the village green), had plenty of location shots, and during its run included appearances by Wendy Richard (barmaid) and Kate O'Mara (young vet). That run, though, was sadly short. High ratings for the weekday, peak-time episode were offset by low ones in the weekend, children's slot; by June the refusal of ITV's 'Big Four' (ATV, Granada, Rediffusion, ABC) to give it a second regular weekday slot led to Anglia deciding to discontinue; and by the end of September after forty-nine episodes, not all that long after one critic, Mary Crozier, had reckoned 'this serial is better than some and certainly streets ahead of the puerile *Crossroads*', it was all over. Tellingly, and perhaps to its ultimate disadvantage, *Weavers Green* 'did not', notes Anthony Hayward, 'idealise country life, with Paul and Lambda portraying the difficulties both for those new to rural life and others who wanted to escape it'.

The journalist Harry Whewell would presumably not have had it otherwise, to judge by his *Guardian* piece about the experience of being in a North Wales milk bar early one Wednesday evening, in fact the evening before the soap's launch:

> The one I was driven into – by lashing rain and a hungry four-year-old son – was done out in a bilious shade of acid yellow flaking emulsion paint. It boasted several assorted strips of rotting lino, a score of bentwood chairs, five tables covered in plastic paper with cigarette burns all round the edges, an advertisement for the local cinema, and nothing else at all that I could see except a back room where they presumably kept the milk. I had been served with a cup of traditional Welsh milk bar tea; it had the inevitable raft of leaves floating on the top. My son was consuming the only solid food available – a lukewarm sausage garnished with cold fried onions and pushed into a roll of sweetish bread.

Whewell then broadened into a more general critique of the still entrenched dour puritanism outside the big cities:

> In many rural parts of these isles, there is a curious equivocal attitude to visitors. The local inhabitants seize eagerly on the opportunity to make money from holidaymakers but still find it impossible to do more than the bare minimum for them. Publicans order in extra beer and two more tins of crisps and perhaps some meat pies and feel that they have done all that can be expected. A farmer decides that he will let off one of his fields as a caravan park so he erects some chemical closets, lays down a cinder path, nails a notice on the gate, and waits for the money to roll in. The idea of serving proper meals in the pub or of landscaping the caravan site with trees and gardens and then letting it with a good restaurant occurs to few.

'Nowhere,' went on Whewell (based in Manchester but with a holiday cottage on Anglesey), 'is this view of tourism more widespread or deep rooted than in North Wales':

> Moreover, to add to the chill, the nineteenth century hangs heavy in the air. Not only in the gaunt, grey Ebenezer chapels and the shops called Manchester House and Medical Hall, and the licensing hours, but also in the unspoken ever-present feeling that enjoyment should neither be indulged in nor indulged. If people from outside will persist in pursuing it, then no one should encourage them by creating a favourable environment. I think the saddest sight I have

seen this year was on a recent wet Sunday evening in a shuttered and silent Conway. I heard the sound of music through the driving rain, and following it I found four youth hostellers listening to a transistor radio in a public lavatory.[14]

19
Moaning Minnies

'MR SKINNER, chairman of the Clay Cross urban council in Derbyshire, deserves a round of applause for declining to wear his chain of office because he feels that it is old-fashioned and apt to promote self-importance,' declared *The Times* on Monday, 16 May; Barbara Castle was 'delighted and astonished', at a meeting of the Cabinet's Home Affairs Committee, to win her battle to extend until September 1967 the experimental 70 mph speed limit, reflecting that 'the ease with which Roy [Jenkins] capitulated indicates, I think, that public opinion is firming on this issue'; Wilson that evening in a TV broadcast about the seamen's strike, starting that day, insisted that to have accepted their demands would have been to 'breach the dykes of our prices and incomes policy', a policy crucial to 'our hopes of solving our national economic problems on a basis of maintaining full employment', and he called the seamen's action 'a strike against the state – against the community'; Dylan was at Sheffield's Gaumont Theatre; next morning, the 17th, James Allen was at the Bishop of Chelmsford's house for a conference of rural deans, with lunch afterwards to which wives were invited ('a mixed lot and I am afraid a good many of them looked frumpish'); early that afternoon, upstairs in his transport café at Leamington Spa, and beset by debt, 38-year-old Randolph Turpin, who back in 1951 had defeated Sugar Ray Robinson to become Britain's first black world champion boxer, shot himself dead; Mary Whitehouse was in the picturesque Worcestershire village of Chaddesley Corbett, speaking to the local Women's Fellowship ('to my way of thinking, sexual intercourse is a very private thing in the lives of men and women – we don't want it to be turned into a pornographic peep show'); Keith McBride in his diary looked to Wilson 'to produce one of his lightning solutions', given that already 'things are getting pretty bunged up in the docks'; on BBC1 this evening, *Comedy Playhouse*'s offering was 'The Bishop Rides Again', an almost Trollopian comedy of ecclesiastical rivalries set in the fictional diocese of St Oggs, starring Derek Nimmo as the bashful young curate (Mervyn Noote), and pilot for what became *All Gas and Gaiters*; comedy, too, on BBC2, where *Show of the Week* featured a wide range of sketches from Roy Hudd, including singing 'I likes to be a Peeping Tom', a take-off of that East Anglian phenomenon the Singing Postman (real name Allan Smethurst, best known for his recent minor hit, 'Hev Yew Gotta Loight, Boy?'); and at Manchester's Free Trade Hall, a resonant sequence plays out. With Dylan and the Hawks about to go into their final number, a loud accusatory voice cries out, 'Judas!'; Dylan snarls back, 'I don't believe you'; a magnificent, thunderous, uncompromisingly defiant version of 'Like a Rolling Stone' follows; then, to Dylan's perhaps sardonic 'Thank you', somewhat muted applause; and just as it dies down, at arguably this ultimate musical acme (in retrospect anyway) of a whole counter-culture, the rather tinny sound of . . . the National Anthem starting up.[1]

'It looks horrible from the outside, but we are not here for things which look pretty but which work,' Portsmouth's Lord Mayor, Alderman Frank Lines, told the assembled traders, developers and city councillors on Wednesday as he opened the first stage – the wholesale fruit and vegetable market, on the first floor – of the Tricorn shopping centre, as designed by the severely brutalist architect Owen Luder; next day the Cabinet had, in Castle's words, 'an unhappy discussion' about the seamen's strike, eventually agreeing to, if need be, proclaim a state of emergency the following Monday; that afternoon, Benn as Postmaster General, together with Sir Billy Butlin (responsible for the restaurant), formally opened the Post Office Tower to the public, with Benn jokingly offering a revised definition of a cockney ('someone born within sight of the new Post Office Tower'); the crowded private view that evening at the V&A of the forthcoming Aubrey Beardsley exhibition, far more crowded than it would have been ten years earlier, prompted one art critic to remark that 'suddenly whimsy and charm are again in demand'; Dylan played at Glasgow's Odeon

('Folk fans walk out on Dylan' the predictable headline); next day, in his regular column in the *Leeds Weekly Citizen*, Bernard Ingham accused the seamen, and indeed 'all the unions fighting the incomes policy', of 'conspiring to set back the progressive forces which were unleashed at the General Election'; the revolving restaurant opened on the Tower's thirty-fourth floor, featuring on the menu 'Le Rump-steak' at 25s. 6d.; appropriately for a Friday, Larkin in Hull completed 'Friday Night at the Royal Station Hotel', last word on late-afternoon gloom once the travelling salesmen had departed, leaving behind only full ashtrays; Dylan was at the ABC Theatre in Edinburgh ('second night of cat calls,' reported the *Scottish Daily Mail* with evident satisfaction); and McBride noted that 'the seamen's strike goes on, but no one seems terribly worried'.

Saturday the 21st was, apart from Dylan at the Newcastle Odeon, big-fight day: the Cooper–Clay (Ali) rematch, this time at Highbury football stadium. 'Well, did you hear the fight – not very good really,' Larkin wrote next day to Monica Jones, having, like most people, listened to it rather than watched it. 'It sounded as if Clay just went a few rounds to please the crowd, then finished it in that unsatisfactory way' – a reference to the fight ending in the sixth round, after Cooper's eye had been, as so often in his career, badly cut. 'Funny Cooper sh^{d} be so keen,' added Larkin, 'on boxing – if I had a wooden leg I shouldn't skate.' In Ali's corner, and supplying him with a bodyguard, was the hustler Michael X (real name Michael de Freitas), self-appointed successor to Malcolm X; afterwards, Ali gave him his blood-bespattered shorts, which were duly paraded up and down Ladbroke Grove. Over the weekend, more than 9,000 people paid to ascend the 620-feet Tower (4s. for adults, 2s. for children); Noël Coward told a Sunday paper that he regarded the existing law on homosexuality as 'very stupid, quite barbarous', adding that even if it was repealed 'that won't change much here . . . it takes more than a few outspoken books and plays and speeches in Parliament to uproot moral prejudice from the Anglo-Saxons'; that afternoon, with Joe Boyd producing at Sound Techniques in Chelsea, the Incredible String Band recorded the whole of their first album; next day, in his first speech on race relations since going to the Home Office, and defining integration 'not as a flattening process of assimilation, but as equal opportunity, accompanied by cultural diversity, in an atmosphere of tolerance', Jenkins hinted that he intended to extend the Race Relations Act in order to outlaw the colour bar in employment; after Gunter's latest meetings with both shipowners and seamen had proved in vain, a state of emergency was duly proclaimed; Tuesday not a great day for two diarists ('once Empire Day, now Commonwealth Day – no gaiety left,' lamented elderly Gladys Langford; 'don't feel up to Keep Fit,' noted Judy Haines, though adding that Ione had gone with a friend, 'and they got their leotards'); at a mayoral dinner in Clitheroe, the Midland Bank's regional manager, L. F. Smith, blaming current social and economic ills on the post-war welfare state ('like the athlete out of training we ran to seed, became selfish, seeking personal gain with a complete disregard for the needs of those less fortunate than ourselves'); but perhaps some cheer from the box with a trial pilot of the latest BBC sitcom, *Beggar My Neighbour*, with the contrasting neighbours being the affluent working-class Dutts (Reg Varney and Pat Coombs) and the poverty-stricken executives the Garveys (Peter Jones and June Whitfield).

Next day, Wednesday the 25th, five prisoners opportunistically made their getaway from a coach taking them back to Parkhurst Prison from Winchester Assizes, among them John McVicar, on the run for the rest of the summer; that evening's *Coronation Street* included the first appearance of Bet Lynch (Julie Goodyear), prompting the comment from Annie Walker behind the bar, 'Goodness knows, I've always shunned snobbishness, but there are limits to how far one can condescend'; and the *Wednesday Play* was, when it came to the Viewing Panel, a classic of its kind: *Toddler on the Run*, based on a novella by Shena Mackay, producing an RI of 41:

> Negative, nasty and incredibly depressing. *(Teacher)*
>
> The inevitable recourse to sex. Nasty bit in the bookshop, I *hated* the jokes about mental illness and dwarves. *(Personnel officer)*
>
> When the end arrived I looked back on it and found nothing. *(Housewife)*
>
> I'm afraid there'll be more than Toddler 'on the run' if the standard of plays does not improve. *(Design engineer)*

Of course, not every *Wednesday Play* got such a dusty reaction; and indeed, broadsheet reviewers during 1966 were now finding reasons, often to do with being stylistically innovative, to praise them. Yet it remains counter-intuitive that by this time the series was averaging a weekly audience of some nine million viewers, almost double compared to a year earlier.[2] Perhaps it was the increasing whiff of notoriety that was the attraction – or, put another way, a brief walk on the wild side before Ovaltine and bed.

On Thursday the 26th, Gunter took decisive action, appointing a judge, Lord Pearson, to head a court of inquiry into the Merchant Navy dispute, with a brief to produce in the next fortnight an interim report that could seek to resolve the situation. The latest figures showed 605 ships strikebound and almost 17,000 men on strike, both of them totals which would only rise as individual ships reached a British port; while according to Peter Jenkins, the *Guardian*'s well-informed labour correspondent, the fact remained that the NUS's general secretary, Bill Hogarth, had 'so far proved easy prey for the militants who last weekend frightened him off peace moves'. One of those militants was undoubtedly Jim Slater: a hard-drinking Geordie, and left-wing but never a Communist fellow traveller, he had still been an able seaman deck scrubber when becoming a leader of the National Seamen's Reform Movement and leading his first strike in 1960, two years before being elected to the NUS's national executive. As for the broad rank and file, the *New Society*'s Jeremy Bugler focused, on the day Pearson was appointed, on the Victoria and Albert Docks in London, where the previous week the union branch had pickets on twenty-five dock gates:

> The strike pay is not enough to house and feed the seaman, let alone his family. The cheapest seamen's lodgings would leave small or no change out of the £3 [i.e. weekly strike pay]. The Flying Angel in Victoria Dock charges 10s a night for lodging; bed and breakfast is 12s 6d at the Red Ensign Club in Dock Street; bed alone costs 7s 6d at the Queen Victoria's Seamen's Rest in East India Dock Road, and 12s 6d at the British Sailor's Society hostel – known as the 'Stack of Bricks' – in Salmon Lane.

Importantly, and helping to explain why the strike remained solid throughout its duration, it was a dispute not solely about pay and hours. 'The real reason for the strike is a resentment by the lower deck of the Merchant Navy that their conditions are still largely dictated by the Merchant Shipping Act, 1894,' another observer, David Hawarth, had already noted even before it began. 'The NUS wants to be on a par with other unions in not having its actions circumscribed by statute. The union is particularly anxious to get the penal clauses of the Act altered. These provide for punishments for any indiscipline at sea – which can include industrial action by seamen.' Would Pearson (abetted by Stephen Brown, president-elect of the CBI, Joe O'Hagan, chairman of the TUC, and Hugh Clegg, a respected academic expert on industrial relations) do the trick? 'The findings of courts of inquiry,' Peter Jenkins pointed out non-committally, 'carry a good deal of authority usually, but are not binding on any of the parties.'

The larger politics of the situation were tricky for Wilson and co. The demands of the seamen may have seemed a direct threat to the government's stated policy on incomes, but the awkward fact was that generous settlements had recently been reached with judges, doctors and civil servants – none of them groups exactly on the breadline. 'We listen to George Brown, telling us to resist to the death,' Crossman had noted after Cabinet the previous week. 'We listen to James Callaghan telling us to resist to the death . . . We are committed to it although in the general public mind and even more in the minds of our back-benchers it seems outrageous for a Labour government to quarrel with the seamen and defeat them after all those lavish increases to professional people.' Unsurprisingly, Labour's left was particularly indignant, with Foot declaring in the Commons on the 24th that 'many of us believe that the seamen have an extremely powerful case which has not been fully taken into account'. While at Cabinet on the 26th itself, Crossman remained deeply uneasy, though now more on the grounds of strategy than principle – an uneasiness not helped by drawing an analogy. 'On both the Rhodesian crisis and the seamen's strike the P.M. has taken personal control and played them by ear from moment to moment. He has never worked out a strategy for winning in Rhodesia and I don't think before the seamen's strike started it had ever occurred to him to plan how he would win it.'

Moreover, the evidence from Gallup was indeed that, following the start of the strike, the sympathies of the public were more on the side of the seamen (48 per cent) than the employers (14 per cent) – for all Florence Turtle grumbling about how 'this everlasting whining for more & more pay infuriates me' and how, when 'the leader was bleating about an attack on the sacred right to collective bargaining', what he really meant was 'their sacred right to collective blackmailing'. Tellingly, and arguably to an unusual extent, the broad thrust of public sentiment at this point was out of step with that of the press. The right-wing papers naturally had, with the partial exception of the *Sunday Times*, little to say in favour of the strikers and their cause; but nor did the *Sun*, the *Guardian* and, crucially, the *Daily Mirror*:

> The seamen are demanding feather-bedding for their industry [declared its front-page editorial, 'Calling All Seamen', on the day the strike began]. What they are saying, quite simply, is this: 'If the shipowners cannot afford to pay us the money and give us the conditions we want – well, the government must pay up.' Which means you.
>
> An island nation can be expected to shed a voluntary tear on behalf of its seafarers. But these salty strikers would be naive to rely upon public sympathy in this particular, this headstrong, this stubborn dispute. It would not be possible to plot, or conceive as an exercise in sophisticated sabotage, a graver body blow against all the people of Britain in 1966 than this blunt and impatient holdup.
>
> The seamen have refused to think again. But they would be foolish to underestimate the landlubbers. Britain has lived on rations before, but never before as the result of internecine economic warfare.

'We must learn, in Britain in 1966, that there are saner ways to a square deal,' concluded the *Mirror*, 'than a strike which dynamites the welfare and prospects of the nation.'[3]

Ten days after that rebuke in vain, on the evening of Thursday the 26th, Dylan was at the Royal Albert Hall for the first of two shows, including dedicating 'Like a Rolling Stone' to the Taj Mahal; next evening, the farewell show of his entire world tour, he told his audience that 'this is not English music you are listening to' and that 'you can take it or leave it'; the Troggs as this week ended were at No. 2 with 'Wild Thing', just behind the Stones with 'Paint It, Black'; 'wholesome' rather than sexy, that indeed she was 'the Doris Day of Boreham Wood', was Diana Rigg's implausible tabloid claim on the Saturday; and the National Association of Head Teachers assembled at Worthing for their Whit weekend conference, with H. G. Barlow, headmaster of Kings Norton Secondary Modern School in Birmingham, declaring in his presidential address that it was the teachers' task to present 'the old-fashioned virtues of honesty, truth, and hard work' as a 'salutary counterblast to the forces that are at present pulling our young people the wrong way'. An unimpressed participant was A. S. Neill, founder and head of famously progressive Summerhill. 'I found the conf. just deadly dull,' he reported soon afterwards to a more kindred spirit. 'The new heads talked mainly about O's and A levels. Apart from a brilliant talk by Duane [Michael Duane, the head at the centre of the recent Risinghill controversy] I didn't once hear co-education, freedom, sex mentioned in three days. It might have been a gathering of prep school heads.'

'There have been thousands of cars at the seaside today causing traffic blockages on the way home,' noted James Allen on Whit Sunday, adding that 'something drastic will have to be done to deal with this serious situation ... many new roads I'm afraid'; 'the A.A. estimated there were 11 million cars on the road today', just as solemnly recorded Frederick Ward on Whit Monday; the new issue of *Manchester Sketch*, a recently started glossy monthly sub-titled *Social, Sporting and Industrial Life of Manchester*, had its showbiz correspondent observing that 'the tills are alive with "The Sound of Music" still playing at the Gaumont Theatre, Oxford Street'; one press story at the start of June was about the BBC planning to devote an ambitious fifty hours of TV coverage to the World Cup, with its head of outside broadcasting, Peter Dimmock, commenting that 'for once football-mad husbands will decide the evening's viewing'; another story was about the English Speaking Union refusing to send on an American debating tour one of the two undergraduates put forward by the Oxford Union, a decision endorsed by the other undergraduate, Douglas Hogg (son of Quintin), on the grounds that 'he [Stephen Marks] is extremely Left Wing and not the kind of chap to send'; 'Pam offered to do my shopping and obtain pink stamps from Victor Value', gratefully noted Judy Haines, also on this Wednesday the 1st; and that evening, at a packed Earl's Court Arena, Billy Graham opened his much-publicised Greater London Crusade. Some 19,000, with a preponderance of the young, were present; at one point, in his uncompromisingly evangelical message, he cited a 'world leader' who had expressed doubts about whether the civilised world would make it to 1975; at the end of it, between 450 and 1,000 (press reports varied) came forward to 'make a decision for Christ'; and according to one watcher, taking stock of the whole occasion, 'the audience were clearly slightly embarrassed. Not by the religious aspect, but by the trimmings – the gift-wrapped prayers and the Hollywood-style choir.'[4]

The news on Thursday was that ITV was planning to devote only sixteen hours to the World Cup, concentrating mainly on England, the sole home nation to have qualified (by dint of being the host country); in the summer game, the West Indies series began at Old Trafford, with Bill Frindall making his BBC debut as scorer-cum-statistician on *Test Match Special*; as Pearson continued to deliberate, and as Benn reflected that 'the strike is not making any great difference to ordinary life', the Treasury, in the words of one economic commentator, 'went out of its way (surely not hoping to shame the strikers into a sense of national responsibility?) to emphasise how much speculation had cost it in gold during the latter half of May'; 'the strike goes on,' noted McBride on Friday, '& there are signs of trouble, with seamen "blacking" ships, & so on'; Grace Taylor on Saturday morning 'had coffee in Pinner', where she 'bought the new "Busy Lizzie" and did the shopping'; later in the day, a standing ovation for Bertrand Russell, who told delegates at a meeting of the Vietnam Solidarity Campaign, held in the Mahatma Gandhi Hall, that 'Britain has been made into a bully's lackey, and a brutal and heartless bully at that'; 'I heard enough of the Test to gather that England cocked it up against the n——s,' Larkin wrote to Monica Jones; and that evening *The Likely Lads* were back, still on BBC2 and rapidly becoming a critics' favourite. 'A creative achievement as genuine as *Three Men in a Boat*,' reckoned Maurice Wiggin about Ian La Frenais and Dick Clement's two central characters, Bob and Terry. 'The happy fact is that they are rooted in life, true to life and to themselves; and life will not let them down. They have *growth* within them.'

'22nd day of strike and is now a serious business,' noted Keighley's Gladys Hague on Sunday, while that afternoon the NUS itself staged a major rally in Trafalgar Square, prompting *The Times*'s labour correspondent to contrast 'the difference between the mild if resolute tones of Mr William Hogarth, general secretary, and the demagogic cries of Mr Gordon Norris, the union's outstanding communist', as they spoke to a crowd of some 2,000 in which 'Communist banners were prominent and Young Socialists swarmed'; next day, as one diarist, Phyllis Willmott, recorded her encounter with a junior minister at a recent party ('Bill Rodgers made some remark about how marvellous it is, with Labour in power, to find so many of the civil servants "are friends" '), another, Betty Allen on the Lancashire coast, was back home following a week away with her sister in Derbyshire: 'Great big wash – always is after a holiday! Got it all ironed & did a lot of shopping. Children back at school & I enjoyed the quiet! Did quite a lot of gardening at night. I love my little home.' What was the cultural highlight this evening of Monday the 6th? On paper it had to be the first night, at the Old Vic, of *A Bond Honoured*, John Osborne's adaptation of an obscure seventeenth-century Spanish play. Despite starring roles for Robert Stephens and Maggie Smith, the critics for the most part loathed it, typified by Peter Lewis's verdict in the *Mail* that 'for me it smells of pretentious bunkum'.

Yet even if they had loved it, the event for the history books lay elsewhere: on BBC1, at 7.30, the start of the first series, following its successful pilot the previous summer, of Johnny Speight's *Till Death Us Do Part*. Alf Ramsey was now Alf Garnett, still played by Warren Mitchell; his wife ('Else') was now played by Dandy Nichols; and their daughter Rita and son-in-law Mike were still played by Una Stubbs and Anthony Booth. Reviewers' responses were largely but not wholly positive: 'noisy, honestly vulgar and at times hilarious,' according to *The Times*'s anonymous critic; 'as Cockney in its warmth and humour as the sound of Bow Bells', with Alf 'the embodiment of inbuilt prejudice who finds his traditions and beliefs so easily bruised by the brash cynicism of his son-in-law' (Patrick Kavanagh); 'outrageously funny . . . this gale of false sentiment, injured pride, mountainous prejudice and wheedling grievances' (Peter Black); 'too raucous, too sustained a note of invective' (Philip Purser); 'of course it was vulgar; but it was alive' (Maurice Wiggin). And Nancy Banks-Smith? 'It is family life fortissimo,' she declared appreciatively:

> Warren Mitchell, a magnificent Tory dad going on about 'Arold Wilson who, he insists, made a bomb out of betting on the Election.

> A shapeless, much shut-up mum generally referred to as 'you silly old mare.' And a daughter and son-in-law very with-it but noticeably without it, which is why they're living with the in-laws. It's a quick-on-the-draw fluctuating family gunfight. With any two taking sides against any other two in the ritual war dance of home life.

'It's not Steptoe, but it's not at all bad, either,' she concluded. 'And it will pass summer Mondays very nicely and noisily until something better comes along.'[5]

'That TV film was a blot on respectable people in Moss Side,' declared 'Fed up' in Tuesday's *Manchester Evening News*, following a recent Granada documentary (*This England*) on life in that largely rundown part of Manchester. 'The area where I live is not at all like that . . . Will I ever be able to sell my house if ever I want to leave after the way those people painted it?' On the same letters page, L. H. of Prestwich saw a bigger picture:

> Television has this fetish about depicting the North as a seamy, sooty squalid place, full of tumbledown houses, dirty streets, people on one long booze and living on a diet of fish and chips . . .
>
> We've got our grime, our depressing districts and lots of earthiness, but what about the new North? The smart, attractive housing estates? The new skyline in Manchester? The new breed of get-ahead young people whose hopes and dreams stretch beyond betting shops and punch-ups?

Next day, the publication of Pearson's report – insisting that the NUS's executive council 'was not justified in using the strike weapon without further attempts to resolve the position, because there was nothing to call for the use of this very drastic and dangerous remedy', but recommending that the shipowners bring forward from 1968 to 1967 the introduction of the forty-hour week that had become the strikers' main rallying call – saw Hogarth et al. rejecting it outright as a basis for negotiation; that evening, the Conservative Party, having discovered that their leader had been referred to in the opening episode of *Till Death Us Do Part* as a 'grammar school twit', formally asked to see Speight's script; by Thursday the temperature was at last rising (to as high as 84°F (29°C) in Southampton, to 77° (25°) in London) and some kind of summer was under way, appropriate backdrop for the Kinks' newly released 'Sunny Afternoon' and just the thing for sixteen-year-old Julie Walters, growing up in Smethwick, to acquire her first, much-longed-for suntan as she 'sat out on a kitchen chair, head back, eyes closed, revising for my [GCE] geography exam'; *The Frost Report* that evening was the last of the series – a series, reckoned *The Times*, 'for most of its time cleverly and pointedly funny', with 'the solemn Mr John Cleese' now established as 'an irresistible provoker of mirth', but Banks-Smith still hostile, calling it 'safe' and 'vulgarised' satire and accusing Frost of having 'sold out the satiric movement for rather more than thirty shillings'; Donovan, living in a flat in Maida Vale, found himself in the early hours of Friday morning being very forcibly busted by the drug squad for being in possession of cannabis (Indian hemp), first but far from last of Norman ('Nobby') Pilcher's pop-star busts; in the *Daily Express*, after Osborne in the previous day or two had hurled his customary abuse at the theatre critics, Herbert Kretzmer made his unabashed riposte ('I . . . take a taxi to Fleet Street, write down my responses in about 400 words and 45 minutes. I don't need more time . . . If you don't like it, Johnny baby, well that's show business'); and on that evening's *Any Questions?*, Margaret Thatcher pronounced not only on the requirements to become an MP ('It would probably be better if we had a good deal less theory and a good deal more practical knowledge. At the moment the place is full of lecturers . . .'), but on whether the BBC was right to devote so many peak viewing hours to the World Cup ('Well, I think it's going to be a good idea because all the members of the House of Commons and all the members of the House of Lords who are male members, will be watching the football match, and we, then, the women can get on and do the job in their absence, and I think that's very much better'). Even less enthusiasm from fellow panellist Jeremy Thorpe: 'I don't know whether this is on television or sound, but it would bore me on whatever medium it was on.'[6]

On Monday the 13th, against a background of sterling once again looking distinctly fragile, the world's leading central banks announced their latest support operation, though with stern accompanying words about how 'Britain's pressing economic need remains to secure a major reduction in the size of wage increases'; on the same day in the Commons, back from its Whitsun recess, one of Labour's most left-wing MPs, Eric Heffer, hitherto a leading champion of the striking seamen, called it 'regrettable' that they had not accepted Pearson as a basis for negotiation; watching the second episode of *Till Death Us Do Part*, notable for its 'pathos, affection and humanity', had Banks-Smith also noting caustically how the first a week earlier had 'exploded surprisingly like a stink bomb among people with finer feelings than my own'; and Anthony Heap mulled over changing habits in relation to Pilcher-acceptable weed:

> One noticeable result of medical research findings in recent years as to heavy cigarette smoking being one of the main causes of lung cancer has been the increasing popularity of small and medium size cigars, which are, apparently, not deemed so harmful as cigarettes.
>
> Judging by the numerous advertisements that now appear in newspapers and magazines, there seem to be almost as many different brands of popular sized cigars as cigarettes and their smoking is certainly no longer confined to 'bloated capitalists' and plutocrats. I enjoy a small Hamlet (11d each) myself occasionally in addition to my average of ten cigarettes (Kent) a week, and I'm not being scared into giving up that modest consumption.

The *Daily Mirror* that Tuesday had its most celebrated columnist, 'Cassandra' (William Connor), beginning a three-part investigation into Pilcher-unacceptable drug-taking, this part majoring on 'the amoral negativeness' of a seventeen-year-old girl addict who he called 'Baby Doll' and was 'on "purple hearts" or "bennies" or "goof balls" or "co-pilots"'; in the context of the just released 'Paperback Writer' only entering the charts at No. 2 (behind Frank Sinatra's 'Strangers in the Night'), the *Sun*'s Mike Nevard had a pop at the Beatles (losing touch with their fans, virtually no live appearances since Christmas, seldom on TV) which ended almost wistfully ('I once liked their humour. Their music. Their songs. Some of the best of the era, they were. And they could write many more. If they came down to earth . . .'); in the Cabinet 'a bitter discussion' (Castle's adjective) on the seamen's strike had Crossman concluding that 'Harold is out to smash the seamen's union'; the PM was presumably cheered this Tuesday by the dockers, supposed to be staging a one-day strike in support of the seamen, in fact taking only very patchy action, in part because the leaders of their main union, the Transport and General Workers', strongly opposed widening the strike; Benn that evening, after chatting over the general state of political play with a handful of colleagues (including Peter Shore, Gerald Kaufman and Judith Hart as well as Crossman), concluded for his part that 'it would be foolish to say that Harold is finished but the magic has definitely gone'; and an industrious diarist travelled to Earl's Court ('the huge hall packed out') to hear Billy Graham. 'I can't say I felt impelled by his pleading to join the thousand or so who went forward at the end to receive advice from the cohort of "counsellors" in attendance and dedicate themselves to more active pursuit of Christian ideals,' recorded Heap. Even so: 'He's a good man and he's obviously doing a good job. And if he can help to purify the decadent cesspool that is London today the best of transatlantic luck to him!'[7]

One port where the dockers did show a strong spirit of solidarity with the striking seamen was Hull; and 'it was no coincidence', to quote Paul Foot's account of the strike written fairly soon afterwards, 'that the best statement of the seamen's case and exposé of the Pearson Report, the pamphlet *Not Wanted on Voyage*, which sold 23,000 copies, was produced by the Hull seamen'. The main authors of the pamphlet, again according to Foot (though this time several decades later), were the branch chairman, Charlie Hodgkin, and a young liner steward (until going to Hull University the previous autumn), John Prescott – who would himself recall, in his 2008 autobiography, 'I pulled it together and was mainly responsible for it'. The pamphlet, a robust as well as valuably detailed piece of work, declared of Pearson that 'the job of the inquiry was to discredit the seamen's case, and to deliver up the sailor for sacrifice on the altar of George Brown's Incomes Policy'; made much of the 'huge increases' for MPs and ministers as well as judges, doctors and top civil servants ('It becomes hard to accept that all these professions can get increases well above the norm, on already comfortable salaries, while the lower earning groups as in the cases of railwaymen, busmen, and seamen, are forced to run the gauntlet of "threats to the State" and massive press campaigns for the merest fraction above the norm on a basically low wage'); and, after calling for 'a socialist incomes policy, which controls and plans all forms of income', ended with a strong sense of history:

> There is a wealth of evidence we could produce to show that behind the government, in its resistance to our just demands, stand the international banks, the financial powers which direct the government's anti-wage policy. The goodwill of the bankers, the ill-will of the working class. How familiar a story that is of Labour governments when we cast our minds back to Ramsay MacDonald and his 1929–1931 government. It was the trade unions then who stiffened the Labour party against the attacks on unemployment pay. They must rally to the same cause in the different circumstances of today. We have tried to show in this report why the hostility to our modest claim has been so fierce. The unholy alliance of Labour government, Tory opposition, press, shipowners and international bankers is both frightening and politically very revealing.

Alas for Prescott and other opponents of that formidable alliance, the unions as a whole failed to rally to the seamen's cause; while as for public opinion more generally, the NUS's blanket rejection of Pearson was a decisive moment. 'In the seamen's dispute, are your sympathies mainly with the men, or mainly with the employers?' Gallup had asked in early June, with 43 per cent coming down on the side of the men and only 18 per cent the employers. Not all that long after Pearson, however, some 72 per cent of Gallup's respondents felt that the seamen should accept the compromise on offer.[8] In the 1960s, very few unions on strike were supported for as long (some three weeks) by majority public opinion as the seamen were; but as ever, that public goodwill was ultimately finite.

With foreign exchange losses beginning to mount, governor Cromer, shortly to step down, sent to Callaghan on 15 June his final, portentously worded warning ('I have no doubt that if devaluation of sterling were to come about serious antagonism would be generated world wide against this country for jeopardising the international payments system through failing to pursue domestic policies of a type acknowledged universally by individual countries and the international institutions as appropriate to a situation which has been clear for all to see'); Betty Allen went to the flicks ('I took the children to see

"The Greatest Story Ever Told" at the Rialto & thought it was stupendous'); 'inane, asinine, witless and tasteless' was the Heap verdict on Terence Frisby's *There's a Girl in My Soup* at the Globe, a tug-of-love triangle, starring Donald Sinden, which in the event would become for a time the longest-running comedy in the West End; next day, Thursday, Andrew Alexander made his debut, in the *Telegraph*, as a parliamentary sketch writer ('it is difficult to see their lordships, collectively at least, being riotously successful as television personalities,' he commented on the vote by the Lords in favour of televising their proceedings); Osbert Lancaster's pocket cartoon in the *Express* had Maudie at the races saying to her very mini-skirted daughter, 'Tell me, dear child, which particular horse did you put your skirt on?'; the full-page ad in the *TLS* for a striking subterranean retail development in Oxford's Broad Street included a celebratory text by James Morris, careful to reassure readers that 'downstairs Blackwell's is the calmest and most gentlemanly of bookshops'; and the second Test began at Lord's. A so-so day for England, but a wretched one for Larkin, accompanied as usual by Monica Jones – to whom he wrote over a week later about a clearly preoccupying 'ghastly incident', sadly without quite revealing what it was. 'It really put me off the place – I would quite willingly have left and not gone back – I've never been treated with such insolence. If that's the MCC they can keep it. That, added to tiredness & hayfever, spoiled it thoroughly. I don't know if I was sulky, but I felt wretched & raging.' Presumably unconnected to the incident, but perhaps not helping his mood, was the Test debut this day of Basil D'Oliveira, six years after leaving apartheid South Africa to try his luck in England. 'He is moving at the moment on some Elysian field, playing for England at Lord's, not many years after being an underprivileged person in Capetown,' reflected *The Times*'s John Woodcock later in the match; while on the day itself, as at lunchtime the skies darkened, his team-mate Ken Barrington – kindest of men – turned to him and said, with reference to D'Oliviera's newly awarded cap, 'If they don't bowl another ball, this is yours for keeps'.[9]

This Thursday evening, at BBC Television Centre in White City, the Beatles made their only ever live appearance on *Top of the Pops* (introduced by Pete Murray and miming to 'Rain' and 'Paperback Writer'), while just down the road, at Earl's Court, it was Cliff Richard's big coming-out moment as, at 'Youth Night' in Billy Graham's crusade, he gave his personal testimony about why Christianity was relevant to young people's way of life and sang 'It's No Secret'. What would he and his audience – 25,000 packed in, with 5,000 left outside – have made of current parliamentary events? The day before, David Steel had presented in the Commons his bill to legalise abortion; today, the main topic in the Lords had been the third reading of the Earl of Arran's Sexual Offences Bill, duly passed but with an appreciably smaller majority (78–60) than most had expected. Lord Kilmuir reiterated his opposition ('I am convinced it will be one of the most serious blows at our moral standards that has taken place this century'), while the Earl of Dudley (not to be confused, he insisted, with the pro-bill Lord Dudley) could hardly have been blunter: 'I wish to make it quite clear I am wholly against this Bill. Homosexuals are the most disgusting people in the world. I loathe them. Prison is much too good for them.' Now it remained for the Commons, where Humphry Berkeley's liberalising bill had been aborted by the spring election, to take up the cause again; and the Archbishop of Canterbury, Dr Ramsey, joined with Arran in 'begging the Government to facilitate the passage of this Bill by accepting it as its own'. Yet in practice, Wilson, conscious no doubt of the social conservatism of Labour's working-class base, prioritised more bread-and-butter issues – including this particular day, following his party's pre-election promise, the publication of the Ministry of Social Security Bill, involving the end of National Assistance (and its attached stigma through a separate book), to be replaced by a new system of supplementary benefits (more generous than the old National Assistance scales) under a rationalised overall structure to be operated by Peggy Herbison's new ministry. Good, but not good enough, was the view of the *Guardian*. 'The recasting of State pensions into a new national superannuation scheme, a major plank of Labour policy for almost a decade, has been deferred until later in the lifetime of this Parliament,' it complained. 'This has been done in order to give priority to the schemes for earnings-related sickness and unemployment benefits which, it is felt, will contribute more directly to economic growth. But the Bill also fails to do anything to meet the problem of child poverty – which surely cannot wait until 1970.'[10]

Against a seriously deteriorating balance-of-payments situation, Wilson on Friday called in the seamen's leaders to No. 10, but they continued to refuse to negotiate; Tom Graveney, the day after his thirty-ninth birthday, made his stirring comeback innings at Lord's; 'I loathe C. & A.s,' noted Veronica Lee after going to the one in Leeds ('to try on a dress you have to go into a pen with all these other sweaty old women & undress in front of them'); 'I've never gone for traditional folk songs, I can't see how medieval songs can apply to present-day life,' the Singing Postman told *Melody Maker*; and on Saturday evening (after an unlucky run-out for D'Oliveira earlier in the day), the New Moon Carnival of Poetry in the Round took place at a semi-empty Royal Albert Hall, with (according to the *Daily Mail*'s reporter) an audience comprising 'mainly scruffily dressed students' who 'howled with laughter as four-letter words were bandied about by beatnik poets'. Among those present was the seriously unimpressed theatre director Charles Marowitz:

> We sat [he recalled almost a quarter of a century later] swilling boredom for over two hours. Spike Milligan, having an off night, read witty doggerel and clowned about. Then followed a small parade of poetic contenders . . . Then Robert Graves, Odysseus-like, his white hair flaming like the Greek god he no longer was . . . The poems were small helpings of taut privacy loosed in that Buddha-bellied hall where sound systems crackled and crude *kibitzers* blew raspberries and tried to grab the limelight . . . More interruptions, assorted cat-calls and wisecracks . . . Then followed an assembly line of poets, versifiers and rhymesters, dilly Dylans, maudlin Audens, half-spent Spenders and idiot Eliots. Bland, snotty-nosed Stevie Smith chanting light lyrics in the voice of a Tibetan priestess ready to give up the ghost; Adrian Mitchell, his Vietnam convictions now strained and unconvincing, taking refuge in aggression, reading fiery political verse which flashed like a firework and faded just as quickly . . .

The evening ended dramatically enough, with the recollection almost forty years later coming from the poet Hugo Williams, present with his heavily pregnant French wife, Hermine, as together they witnessed a happening:

> 'The Moth', as it was called, 'would evolve in the chrysalis of Albert's Dome, a spaceship of poetic discovery, with Godo Iommi as Pied Piper. It would issue forth with flares on a continuous exploration across London to the river and thence on a raft to oblivion'. The Moth's birth was a painful one. Electric cellos produced a murderous scream. Tinfoil fell from above. Totems were set up, surrounded by forbidden areas of coloured cardboard. A girl danced an epileptic fit. Poems in German and Spanish were yelled over the cellos. Suddenly Vanessa Redgrave stepped onstage, dressed in a Cuban combat jacket. Silence should have fallen for the star, but the torment continued. People danced on. Miss Redgrave stood there, lank and livid, changing hips impatiently. Eventually, despite the noise, she began to sing: stark, striving marches of 'Cuba Libra'.

A last word went to the Albert Hall's manager, Christopher Hopper, who after it was all over – and huge quantities of debris as well as much else cleared away – told the press that he had found the whole thing 'disgusting'.

Still, there was a new poet on the block. Next day, the *Observer* review of Seamus Heaney's first collection, *Death of a Naturalist*, was only moderately positive ('neat and intelligent' if 'strangely featureless'), but other reviewers around this time were generally more welcoming, culminating in Alan Ross heralding 'a book of enormous promise: highly individual, deep-rooted, closely worked and evocative'. For one troubled comedian, the days of promise were long gone. Even so, almost seven and a half million homes tuned in to ITV that Sunday evening to watch Tony Hancock compere his first *The Blackpool Show*, with guests including Matt Munro, Marian Montgomery, Ray Alan with Lord Charles, and Deryck Guyler. Critics were largely kind (Peter Black relieved that Hancock in his patter was still 'the truculent, conceited, yearning, booby philosopher'), but the strain on his nerves was palpably showing. Strain, too, this Sunday, if of a different sort, for the government's economic adviser. 'Disenchantment with the government and with Harold very much on the up,' reflected Alec Cairncross. 'Rhodesia, the seamen's strike, Vietnam, the deficit – all go on as before,' he added, 'while the rest of the world begins to think that we just don't care for anything but frivolity. The whole country is going to be badly infected with a deeper sense of frustration than ever and without any sense that a different government would change things for the better.'[11]

In the early hours of Monday, Hugo and Hermine Williams were in an ambulance heading for Paddington:

> At St Mary's, someone tried to stop me entering the maternity ward until I said I had a letter from the chief obstetrician saying I could stay until the baby was born – a rarity in 1966. It was time for the bath-enema-shave routine so Hermine sent me out to have breakfast in the station. I came back an hour later with a copy of the *Daily Mail* containing a picture of her sitting at the feet of Vanessa Redgrave in the Albert Hall two nights earlier. She wasn't interested. Nurses were giving her a hard time, pulling her about during contractions, asking her questions, until she had to blurt out, 'I am having a contraction NOW'.

Their daughter, Murphy, was born by the time Wilson, in what Ben Pimlott calls 'icy tones', made a statement in the Commons declaring that the NUS's refusal to negotiate post-Pearson had been because 'a few individuals' had 'brought pressure to bear' on 'a select few' in its executive council, who in turn had been able 'to dominate the majority of that otherwise sturdy union'; and he added, in the statement's most notorious passage, that these pressures had been the work of 'a tightly knit group of politically motivated men'. 'Everything,' comments Pimlott, 'was wrong with this statement':

> Heavy with innuendo – refusing to call a Communist a Communist – it was evidently based on information derived from the security services, and thus made clear to NUS members, and trade unionists in general, that during a strike a Labour government was prepared to authorise the tapping of telephones. It accused 'a few individuals' of intimidation, without naming them, and others of submitting weakly to intimidation, without naming them either. It implied that the seamen, many of whom had suffered hardship because of the strike, were at best innocent dupes of their own leaders. It suggested, fatuously, that 'political motivation' was something to be ashamed of, as if a political motivation had never entered the Prime Minister's head . . .

Quite apart from widespread 'consternation' (Crossman's word) among Labour backbenchers, certainly those on the left, not to mention a disgusted John Prescott watching in the gallery, Wilson's colleagues were, for the most part, deeply unimpressed. 'I couldn't find anyone in the Cabinet who thought it very clever,' recorded Castle; or as Benn reflected after Peter Shore had rung him to say that he thought the statement 'completely bonkers': 'I think I share that view. Indeed, I am beginning to wonder whether Harold Wilson is not becoming like Lloyd George. We shall have to see.'

The Cabinet on Tuesday the 21st discussed both Wilson's statement ('I asked if we could be given more details of the conspiracy,' noted Castle, 'to which Harold replied ponderously that there were some things that were better not revealed') and the delayed post-election reintroduction by Brown of his Prices and Incomes Bill (involving a potential element of government compulsion and predictably dismissed by Cousins, adamant for the rights of free collective bargaining, as 'complete poppycock'); the fierce rivalry between two pirate-radio operators, Oliver Smedley and Reg Calvert, ended with the former shooting the latter dead; Larkin, by now back in Hull, wrote to Monica Jones about the final two days of the drawn Test ('those two black bastards,' i.e. Gary Sobers and his cousin David Holford, taking the game away from England; how, when Holford completed his century, 'old flag-carrier came on the pitch & marched all over the shop, waving his flag, while his black rabbit companions swarmed round the batsman'; and bemoaning generally how England 'let 'em get off the hook'); Benn at a buffet supper at No. 10 listened to Wilson saying that the public 'are not interested in politics and want to play tennis and clean their cars and leave things to the Government', before voicing his dissent; next day, *The Times* claimed that the microwave 'is already proving a real money-spinner in snack bars, pubs, hotels, restaurants, cinemas, hospitals, and even in office boardrooms where it provides speedy meals for executives in a hurry'; Lindsay Anderson was in Chichester, rehearsing a festival production of *The Cherry Orchard* ('I've landed myself right in the middle-class middlebrow area of English theatre, where people work exclusively in the realm of effect, of technique . . . It is all thin and meaningless; a sort of conjuring trick . . .'); on Thursday the Cabinet returned to prices and incomes (Cousins threatening to resign, Callaghan pleading with him, Wilson flattering him); the Queen Mother officially opened Sheffield's ambitious Hyde Park development, rising above the much-lauded Park Hill; *Adam Adamant Lives!*, starring Gerald Harper and with *Goldfinger*-style theme tune sung by Kathy Kirby, made its BBC1 debut, but to a poor RI of 46 from viewers ('ham from start to finish . . . as far as I am concerned, the sooner Adam Adamant ceases to live, the better!'); Michael Foot in Friday's *Tribune* laid into the government ('no glimmer of a changed strategy, an enlarged vision, since the election . . . the Cabinet never sat down to consider how an intelligent and intelligible incomes policy could have been operated . . . pathetic acceptance of the Tory legacy in defence and foreign policy . . .'); and the man from *The Times* was present for the first day of Eton v. Winchester: 'The enchanting background to this match, with tall trees fringing the vast expanse of turf under a sky that Constable might have copyrighted, never varies . . .'[12]

A low point for the *Guardian* on Saturday the 25th, as an almost evidence-free article by a junior reporter, R. W. Shakespeare, slavishly followed the Wilson line about Communist influence prolonging the seamen's strike; Cliff Richard in a *Daily Mail* interview laid down the moral law ('I do believe that sex outside marriage is a sin . . . I don't believe in divorce . . . I think you commit adultery if you marry again while your first wife is still alive'); that afternoon, while Heap visited the Beardsley exhibition ('neither fascinates nor beguiles me'), the favourites Brazil limbered up for their World Cup defence with a hard-fought 1–1 draw with Scotland at Hampden Park (Pelé so oppressively marked by Billy Bremner that at the end he refused to swap shirts); over the weekend, at a conference in Nottingham on 'workers control' run by the left-wing Centre for Socialist Education, main speaker was John Prescott; 'The Plot Behind The Strike' was the title of the *Observer*'s attempt on Sunday to show, again with precious little evidence, that the NUS executive had made a deal with unnamed radicals, in essence for outside forces to control the strike in return for delivering sympathetic action by other unions; nineteen-year-old Sally Jones, after spending most of her pregnancy in a hostel for unmarried mothers, gave birth in the delivery room of a west London hospital ('I don't really remember any negative remarks about my being an unmarried mother, though I was very definitely always referred to as Mrs Hunt'); Crossman reflected gloomily on the dismal political vibe ('it is not only the Parliamentary Party – Fleet Street is geared up to a campaign against the Government, and the weeklies like the *Spectator*, *New Statesman* and *Tribune* are joining in'); on Monday, opening at Northampton the main centre for his bank's new credit card, the chairman of Barclays, John Thomson, declared, 'I firmly believe that we are moving towards a cashless society'; and that evening saw the fourth episode ('Intolerance') of *Till Death Us Do Part* – an episode, according to Banks-Smith, 'riskily brave and outrageous':

> Alf in full Anglo-Saxon flood about coons, Sambos and all savages east of Calais, was damned by his son-in-law's 'look at yer 'ooter nose, it's a right kosher conk.'
>
> 'Jewish! I ain't Jewish.'
>
> 'It's a dead give-away waving yer 'ands abaht like that.'
>
> Bottled racial prejudice exploded in laughter. A relief comparable only to reaching the sweet sanctuary of a lavatory after over-long self-control.

The Times's anonymous reviewer was perhaps more doubtful. It was indeed an episode which 'demanded that Mr Warren Mitchell displayed a ripe series of ignorant prejudices on every subject from football to coloured people', before it then 'hilariously exploded the lot'. Even so: 'It left behind an uncomfortable feeling that Mr Mitchell had provided a portrait drawn from life and not a flight into fantasy.'[13]

Wilson's Tuesday morning message to the Cabinet was that the NUS executive was at last apparently moving towards a settlement, before he went to the Commons that afternoon and named eight key Communists (including the unofficial dockers' leader Jack Dash) who for their own political ends had been exploiting the seamen's grievances. 'It made me sick and reminded me of McCarthyism,' recorded Benn. 'The Left attacked him almost unanimously with powerful speeches by Michael Foot, Eric Heffer and Ian Mikardo.' Elsewhere, a happier C&A experience for Pat Scott in Ilford than for Veronica Lee in Leeds, as she bought her daughter a PVC mac ('black & white – very mod – but only 10/- so it doesn't matter if it does look weird – and it does'); while Kenneth Tynan sent the impresario William Donaldson (who five years earlier had co-produced *Beyond the Fringe* in the West End) his detailed thoughts about a putative show where the fundamental idea was 'to use artistic means to achieve erotic stimulation', and in which 'nothing that is merely funny or merely beautiful should be admitted: it must also be sexy'. His list of possible items included 'a pseudo-drag stripper' as an opener, vaudeville routines, a ballet based on the paintings of Clovis Trouille ('his fantastic visions of begartered nuns, girls with bats on their cunts and fleur-de-lys on their behinds, novices doing the splits, circus performers who are half-girl and half-horse, would make the ideal erotic ballet'), various tableaux 'representing national erotic obsessions', a solo strip number by Dailly Holliday ('a buxom Negress, built for wrestling . . . she is Black Supremacy incarnate'), and 'erotic sketches by wellknown writers' (various names mentioned, including 'of course John Osborne'). Crucially, insisted Tynan, none of the company, including the male comics, needed to be English ('English comics tend to be coy and domesticated in matters of sex, unlike their French and American-burlesque equivalents'). As for the title:

> I made a long list of possibilities, including such outside chances as THE CONSENTING ADULTS SHOW, LET ME COUNT THE WAYS, HOW COME, etc, etc; but I've since found a beauty. I showed you [at their meeting in early June] a painting by Trouille of a reclining girl displaying her bottom, with the caption: 'Oh Calcutta!' While in Paris I discovered that this is a pun – 'Quel cul t'as!', meaning 'What an arse you have!' I therefore suggest calling the show 'Oh Calcutta!', subtitled 'An International Erotic Revue' and using the Trouille painting as a poster. Those who get the joke will get it, and those who don't will be intrigued. Anyway, it's unforgettable.

It was never going to be a show destined for Frederick Ward's eyes at the Theatre Royal, Bristol. 'The seamen's strike is now in its sixth week and it is surprising how little inconvenience it has so far caused,' the Co-operative Wholesale Society manager noted more prosaically this Tuesday evening. 'We have had goods diverted to other parts but this has involved us in little expense.'

Wednesday the 29th was launch date for Barclaycard, Britain's first home-grown credit card (prompting Laurence Marks to mull hopefully that 'if I had one, I could go and buy my second hand saxophone and pay it off'), but *Punch*'s TV critic preferred to celebrate older, less plastic values. 'Before that warmth, that determined philistinism, that patent enjoyment of the whole thing, even my snobbery collapses,' wrote Monica Furlong about the genial host ('Wakey, wakey!') of *The Billy Cotton Band Show*, now ten years old. 'He is never masterly with-it, never coldly fashionable, simply a showman with a giant appetite for life and a proper sentimentality.' American bombs had fallen that night on the populous suburbs of Hanoi, signifying a new phase of the Vietnam War, and Wilson responded by issuing a statement dissociating the British government from that action. 'Heath criticised him for it and the Left was less than generous,' noted Benn. 'Very few people realised the immense significance of this act of dissociation. From now on, things will never be the same . . .' The day's other big news, even bigger in a domestic context, was the NUS's decision, announced in the afternoon, to call off the strike – undeniably, Wilson's best political moment since the election. 'He said to me triumphantly, "So the strike is over. I know some of you didn't agree with my statement yesterday, but it did the trick",' recorded a more sceptical Castle, who privately reflected: 'We shall never be able to prove whether it did or didn't, but the effect on the Left will be enduring.' Most people were probably happy enough that the lengthy strike was over, without having caused too much inconvenience to their everyday lives, but one theatre-loving diarist could not resist a grumble. 'None of the drama promised at the outset has materialised,' complained Heap. 'No food shortages. No use by the Government of its emergency powers to bring the navy into action. It merely developed into an ineffectual bore and no one will be sorry to see the curtain fall on so dismal a flop.'[14]

'Why do Wimbledon players indulge in the irritating habit of bouncing the ball so much before serving?' wondered S. Hickman of Eastbourne in next day's *Daily Mail*, adding that 'I cannot remember this in the old days'; in a significant straw in the wind about plans to demolish and redevelop much of Whitehall, a Treasury official noted that Reginald (Reg) Prentice, the new minister for Public Buildings and Works, was 'inclined to sympathise with the preservationist line generally'; 'I have very little time for those people who are considered to be downtrodden – it's their own fault and I hold them in contempt,' pronounced Ray Davies in July's *Beat Instrumental*; almost forty years after joining the Bank of England as a clerk straight from school, Leslie O'Brien on Friday the 1st took up the reins at the Old Lady; having the previous year refused radiotherapy so as not to lose her unborn child, the artist Pauline Boty died of cancer; the publication of the government bill to nationalise the thirteen major steel companies, cutting compensation to shareholders by more than £80 million compared to earlier proposals, was condemned by the industry as a 'clear breach of faith' and caused an instant slump in share prices; 'alas,' commented Alison Uttley on the women's final next day at Wimbledon, 'Miss Bueno beaten by Mrs Billie Moffat King, a conceited brat'; nearly 100,000 people were at Wembley Stadium for the culminating event of Graham's Greater London Crusade; and Dennis Dee, smallholder at Willow Cottage in Winestead, East Yorkshire, summed up his Saturday: 'Put about a 100 sprout plants in the garden. Had a game of cricket with the boys, Simon using his new cricket bat. Went for a drink to "Crooked Billet".'[15]

Sunday's big event was political. It had been on the cards for weeks, indeed months, so few insiders were surprised when Frank Cousins that morning went to No. 10 and handed to Wilson personally his letter of resignation. 'The letter of an exceptionally angry, as well as disappointed, man' is how Cousins's biographer, Geoffrey Goodman, rightly describes it: not only an outright attack on the about-to-be-published Prices and Incomes Bill ('meaningless') and the government's wages policy generally ('fundamentally wrong in its conception and approach'), but effectively accusing Wilson of bad faith: 'Just before the general election you gave me to understand that you would help to break down the shibboleth of a belief that what we needed to secure economic recovery was sufficient power in the hands of the Government to compel the unions to accept, without question, the decisions of the National Board for Prices and Incomes. Unfortunately you did not maintain that view . . .' Cousins lingered at No. 10 long enough to have an 'abrasive' half-hour's conversation with the PM, whom he charged with consistently, since October 1964, 'siding with the Right wing of the Cabinet', whereas Cousins had been given the impression, before Labour came to power, that (in Goodman's words) 'a Wilson-Cousins partnership would be a major characteristic of the Government'. What, asked Wilson, was now his alternative policy? To which Cousins replied: all wage increases to be linked to increased productivity; a price freeze; introduction of import quota restrictions; and government to launch a major campaign for industrial modernisation. Taken as a whole, this was hardly a Luddite programme; but Wilson in his own response insisted that an overall, centrally administered price freeze was impracticable, while also making it clear that he could not bow to Cousins's central demand that the key part of Brown's Prices and Incomes Bill be instantly dropped. Accordingly, the best-known, most powerful trade unionist of the era now left politics after an ultimately ill-starred venture. Some years later, Goodman would ask Cousins why he had become disenchanted with the functioning of government, and whether that disenchantment was with democracy itself. 'No, not with government as such, certainly not with democracy,' he answered. 'Only with the limitations of the *people* in government, with their refusal, their reluctance, call it what you like, to use the instruments of change at their disposal.'

'At 5.30,' the new Minister of Technology recorded that Sunday, 'the news flash came over the radio and within a few minutes the front garden was jam-packed with photographers and reporters and BBC and ITV crews.' Anthony Wedgwood Benn (called at this time 'Wedgy' by his colleagues, partly to distinguish him from Tony Crosland and also another minister, Tony Greenwood) at last had a seat in the Cabinet, to join his fellow diarists there; and if he was, as Wilson recalled, 'more than a little overcome by the magnitude of the job', at least he had the PM's helpful advice that he 'should go easy on publicity until he had mastered the intricacies of this large and expanding ministry'. About the same time that the cameras came to Holland Park, Judy Haines in Chingford left her husband at home to watch the cricket on TV (a Cavaliers match) and walked to evensong ('Rev. Collinson isn't very profound but he doesn't annoy me'); Noël Coward this evening went with three young men (including Julian Pettifer) on 'a pub-crawl' through what seemed to him the 'much simpler and happier world' of the East End ('nobody gets roaring drunk, a great many of both sexes were extremely attractive, and nearby was the river and the docks and freight boats lit up and the feel of the sea'); Dee in East Yorkshire looked back on a frustrating day in which he 'went to Burton Constable to see a blood horse, too old'; and Crossman gloomed about how an afternoon's cogitation had convinced him that 'we are drifting on to the rocks' and that 'very soon we shall be faced with the choice between devaluation or intensive deflation'.

On Monday, 4 July the publication of large-scale gold losses during June duly weakened market confidence, as a conventional wisdom began to set in that the seamen's strike may have been settled but not before causing serious economic damage, with all eyes now waiting for the appearance in nine days' time of the latest trade figures; the key part of Brown's Prices and Incomes Bill was published, against the background of the markets anticipating serious difficulty with the unions following Cousins's resignation; the drink flowed freely at the Dorchester, as the architect and builder John Poulson gave lunch to Reggie Maudling, their first meeting. That evening, a couple of hours after the latest episode ('Two Toilets? . . . That's Posh') of *Till Death Us Do Part*, Samuel Beckett's *Eh Joe?* written specifically for TV, was shown on BBC2, with Jack MacGowran as Joe and Sîan Phillips as The Voice; Tuesday the 5th was a special day for Diana Griffith at college in Worthing ('Rained all day! Last day!! OKAY – I guess – laugh really!'); on a free vote, the Commons voted by 244 (including Margaret Thatcher) to 100 to allow Leo Abse to introduce his Sexual Offences Bill liberalising the homosexual law, though not without the most prominent opponent, Louth Tory MP Sir Cyril Osborne, declaring that he had 'more confidence in the northern common sense of the Prime Minister than to believe that he will give parliamentary time for this and have the odium of this dirty Bill tied to his party'; and Dee summed things up: 'Lots of warm sunshine while noon, then dull. England lost the 3rd test today at Nottingham. Wendy went to a strawberry tea at Holmpton. Nothing else of great importance to report.'[16]

Something else had been going on this early part of the week: the Queen's two-day visit to Northern Ireland, primarily to open the new bridge in Belfast named after her. 'The atmosphere of the Troubles has been growing: there have been stabbings, shootings and bomb-throwings,' Seamus Heaney observed in the current *New Statesman*. 'Life goes on, yet people are reluctant to dismiss the possibility of an explosion. A kind of doublethink operates; something is rotten, but maybe if we wait it will fester to death.' While according to the *Guardian*'s man in Belfast, Brian MacArthur, writing three days before the visit and utilising a recent academic survey of political and religious opinion in five towns, 'there may be at least 200,000 potential supporters in Northern Ireland of the militant anti-Stormont and anti-Roman Catholic policies of the Rev. Ian Paisley, self-styled moderator of the Free Presbyterian Church and leader of Ulster's Protestant extremists'. That Friday evening, at Castle Wellan deep in rural County Down, some 2,000 Protestants and Orangemen marched behind the union flag borne by Paisley. 'To hear Mr Paisley is a startling experience for an observer from England,' noted MacArthur. 'He speaks with the genuine voice of the demagogue. He is a big, burly man with a hoarse voice which occasionally cracks. Shouts of "Amen" and "Hallelujah" punctuate his speeches, which are delivered with an old-style biblical flavour . . .'

The Queen's visit itself had its two notable incidents within a few minutes of each other on Monday afternoon: as she and Prince Philip were driving in procession on their way to a garden party at Hillsborough, official residence in Belfast of Lord Erskine, Governor of Northern Ireland, first a beer bottle (which missed) was thrown at them, then the Queen's car was hit by a 12-inch concrete block, hurled from a building above and denting the bonnet. That evening, MacArthur watched as up to 10,000 Orangemen marched behind Paisley along the Shankhill Road, past walls dubbed with slogans like 'Kick the Pope' and 'No surrender here', and with Paisley firmly blaming the Catholics for the day's incidents. 'Certainly, it is difficult here tonight to describe what is happening, but it is alarming and frightening,' reflected MacArthur. 'The more one stays in this city, the more one sympathises with the underdogs, the Roman Catholics. If Mr Paisley has his way, there could well – and this is no exaggeration – be a religious war here quite soon.'

Next day, the royal visit proceeded smoothly enough (visiting the town hall in Lisburn, County Antrim, opening playing fields and the social sciences building at Queen's University, Upper Malone), before in the afternoon the Queen flew back to London – arriving at Buckingham Palace in time first to have a leave-taking meeting with Cousins (who received a regretful negative answer after he'd asked her whether the dress she was wearing and her shoes had been made in Britain) and then to hold a meeting of the Privy Council, where Benn made affirmation as a new minister and kissed hands upon appointment. 'Afterwards,' he recorded, 'she made a few remarks to us and as I shook hands with her she said, "I'm sure you'll miss your stamps." I replied, "Yes indeed I shall. But I shall never forget your kindness and encouragement in helping me to tackle them." She gave me a rather puzzled smile and I bowed and went out backwards.'[17]

'I understand that the 16.20 train from Paddington to Oxford is a multiple-unit diesel train which may be uncomfortable and on which no seats can be reserved,' noted on Wednesday an internal memo at the Bank of England about Maurice Parsons' travel arrangements later in the week. 'The Deputy Governor would, therefore, prefer to travel by car . . .'; 'Mini skirts and maxi girls' ran a *Guardian* headline on Thursday, attached to a mildly disapproving piece by Pippa Phemister about 'the carry-on of the King's Road', which she dubbed 'Chelsea's village street' and where 'its village girls all parade there flaunting fashions that will shock their elders and inflame the local youths', not least with 'an uninterrupted view of their burnished, never-ending legs'; 'good solid stuff, competently put together but derivative' was the *TLS*'s take on Melvyn Bragg's novel *The Second Inheritance*; visiting London, the French premier, Georges Pompidou, strongly hinted to Callaghan that, if the UK was to try again to enter the Common Market, devaluation would be better done sooner rather than later; the Post Office's 'Dial a Disc' service began its first trial in Leeds ('seven records will be selected each week from current popularity ratings and a different record will be played each day during the cheap rate period, 6 p.m. to 6 a.m. on weekdays and all day on Sunday'); presumably among those seven was 'Sunny Afternoon', as the Kinks this evening appeared on *Top of the Pops* for a lip-synching celebration of its rise to the very top; on Friday, in the wake of two nights of pitched battles between youths from Cardiff and Caerphilly, the *Rhondda Fach Leader* called on parents to make their teenage children 'realise how senseless and dangerous these outbreaks of mass hysteria are', adding that otherwise 'the Courts will have to mete out condign punishment to teenagers who act like gangsters and hoodlums'; moonlighting from his day job as a labour reporter on the *Guardian*, as usual employing the pseudonym 'Albion', and since the seamen's strike ever more disenchanted with trade unionism, Bernard Ingham in the *Leeds Weekly Citizen* shed no tears about the resignation of Cousins, brusquely dismissed as a 'prima donna'; O'Brien this Friday personally warned Wilson that continuing attacks on sterling and exchange losses were once more threatening the parity of the pound; in the context of a West Indian guard at Marylebone station, Asquith Xavier, applying for a transfer to Euston and being informed by his station master that, on instructions from Euston head office, he could not be transferred because of his colour, British Railways issued a statement on Saturday insisting that they 'have no colour bar and employ coloured staff throughout the system', but conceding that 'there is some staff resistance at Euston to the employment of coloured workers'; and that evening Judy Haines, on holiday in Devon with her husband John, daughter Pamela and Pamela's Finnish pen-friend Marri, had a reminder of the generation gap far away from the King's Road, far away from Caerphilly:

> The Mayflower has good food and there was a table d'hote meal for 6/6d each. Pamela, however, was not to be persuaded and ordered sweetcorn as hors d'oeuvres for herself and prawn cocktail for Marri (who had been eating toffees and said she wasn't hungry).
>
> Waitress suggested we wait for them for our second course, which was Dover sole. Pam fancied scampi at 10/6d (Marri the same) and didn't clear her plate! She would have eaten some pudding, though. Marri refused pudding, however, and it went for Pam, too. Their turn to wait. What an unpleasant meal with the milling crowds from Birmingham passing to and fro. And £1 more than need have been.

A contrast in Sunday's papers: in the *Observer*, a thoughtful, taboo-breaking editorial calling for sterling's devaluation ('wisely used, devaluation can become a springboard for further advance'); in the popular press, the dramatic headline 'Hancock's Wife in Coma', after an unsuccessful suicide attempt via a bottle of barbiturates. 'Vietnam is becoming more nightmarish every day,' the historical novelist J. G. Farrell wrote to a friend that day; Crossman reflected on the new technology minister ('up till now he has shown no great administrative grasp and the maximum power of alienating people and so not getting his way'); and Hancock that night managed, zombie-like, to get through his fourth *The Blackpool Show*, this time with his guests including Frankie Howerd and Lenny the Lion. Monday the 11th, yet another bad day for the pound, was also the day on which Callaghan may or may not (accounts differ) have told Brown that he was now in favour of devaluation; Crossman dined that evening in the Commons with four leading left-wing Labour backbenchers (Eric Heffer, Ben Whitaker, Tom Driberg, Hugh Jenkins), discovering that they 'seemed entirely obsessed with Vietnam and unaware of the economic crisis into which we were drifting'; while on BBC1, *Till Death Us Do Part* had to make way for – at last – the opening match of the World Cup.[18]

It was a year since 'World Cup Willie' had been unveiled as the tournament's merchandising mascot; there had been the drama of the stolen trophy; Laurence Marks had bet a work colleague back in the spring that England were not going to win it and thereby stood to lose the not inconsiderable sum of £2 12s.; the England squad itself, under the firm, unwavering guidance of Alf Ramsey, had finished all their training and preparation at Shropshire's Lilleshall Hall, a few hundred yards from Yew Tree House, family home of Jeremy Corbyn; and *World Cup Grandstand*'s preview on BBC1 the previous afternoon had won an appreciative RI of 71. 'A great help to viewers (like me) who don't know too much about the teams and "lay out" for the World Cup,' said a housewife. 'I feel really interested now.' Among the pundits during recent days weighing up England's chances was John Arlott, reckoning that England could make it to the semi-finals, but 'thereafter the players might be revealed as conclusively short of the touch of a genius'; while Hans Keller thought 'the odds are still against our fantasy coming true' and remained adamant that 'it certainly won't without the type of effective improvisation and determined off-chance-hunting of which Greaves is capable'. For this first match, England v. Uruguay, viewers had a choice of BBC or ITV, but listeners had to wait until the second half for commentary on the Light Programme. One viewer was Alison Uttley. 'Brilliant! Fascinating!' she wrote in her diary – probably a minority perspective after a drab, goalless draw, with Marks's father commenting that 'England could play until the weekend and wouldn't score a goal'. At the stadium itself, John Cleese, having splashed out on tickets for all the Wembley matches, watched with increasing disappointment. And soon afterwards, partly because England's underwhelming performance had left him convinced that the very furthest they could hope to get to was the semis, and partly because he was feeling guilty about leaving it too long before returning to Ibiza to work on a film script (*The Rise and Rise of Michael Rimmer*) with Graham Chapman, he did what he himself would remember ruefully almost half a century later as 'a very silly thing': 'I gave my Cup Final ticket to Bill Oddie.'[19]

'Big majority for comprehensives' was the *Sunday Times*'s headline the day before the Uruguay match, reporting that, with just a matter of days to go before the one-year deadline set by Crosland back in July 1965, 'all but a few' local education authorities had agreed to his request to draw up plans for ending the 11-plus and establishing comprehensive schools. It remained doubtful whether this super-majority reflected a high degree of parental engagement – 'not one person wrote to you from the parents' point of view', noted an 'appalled' correspondent to the *Gateshead Post* in April about that local education authority's adoption of a plan – but even so the drift of public opinion since Circular 10/65 was unmistakable, certainly to judge by Gallup's most recent surveys. Whereas the previous December only 40 per cent said that they thought comprehensive schools were a good idea and should be extended, by March 1966 this was up to 50 per cent, as opposed to 18 per cent disliking the idea, 18 per cent saying they didn't know and 14 per cent admitting they hadn't heard of comprehensive schools. Then in April, in another Gallup poll, 55 per cent said they approved of comprehensive education, compared to 21 per cent disapproving and 24 per cent not knowing, with this time the wholly ignorant left out of the tallies. Though impossible to be sure, Pat Scott after her experience later that spring might easily have taken the majority view. 'We had a letter about Susan's 11 plus today,' she recorded in early May. 'She hasn't passed. She was awfully disappointed. Much more than we would expect. Later – when she had stopped crying – we went to Ilford to get her slacks, but couldn't see any she liked.'[20]

The odds, given her working-class background, were probably always against Susan getting to Oxbridge. There, the big news had been in May, when the Franks Commission on Oxford University, chaired by Lord Franks, reported in favour of generally broadening the admissions system as well as abolishing closed scholarships and awards – an approach almost instantly condemned by Max Beloff (the university's Gladstone Professor of Government and Public Administration) as the wrong-headed, egalitarian, standards-lowering consequence of 'inverted snobbery', though in truth Franks had been at pains to argue that there was no conflict between social justice and the pursuit of excellence. Latest Oxford undergraduate admissions figures, cited by the report, revealed significant, though perhaps not startling, progress since the war: 41.3 per cent coming in 1965 from out-and-out private ('public') schools, compared to 62.0 per cent in 1938; and 40.2 per cent from maintained schools (entirely controlled by local education authorities), compared to 19.2 per cent in 1938. That left, among the meaningful percentages, the direct grant schools. Here, the great majority of Oxford admissions were from direct grants which were members of the Headmasters' Conference (HMC) – in other words, schools at least as much on the fee-paying side of the divide as the non-fee-paying; and from direct grants as a whole, the increase since 1938 was from 12.6 to 17.1 per cent. As for Cambridge University, admission figures published in the *New Statesman* in June showed that the traditional bias towards the richer and the privately educated had also far from disappeared:

	Cambridge Entrants (%)	*All School Leavers (%)*
School		
Independents	45	5
Direct grant	18	2
LEA maintained	37	93
Father's Income		
£1,000 and over	75	12
Under £1,000	25	88
Father's Occupation		
Non-manual	91	30
Manual	9	70

Putting a more human face on all this was the latest evidence from the longitudinal study of 5,362 boys and girls born in England, Wales and Scotland in the first week of March 1946. By now, the majority of that cohort who would graduate from university had already begun their studies; and a new survey got responses from 368 of the 382 who had indeed started, the great majority of them not at Oxbridge. Why, they were asked, had they not even applied there?

> Both socially and intellectually unacceptable.
>
> Uncertainty of success because of mediocre ability.
>
> Wanted a course with a modern bias, not merely classical literature.
>
> College system too rigid; too old and set in their ways; do not like their attitude generally – especially preference for ex-public school boys.

'It seems,' concluded an LSE analysis of all the responses, 'that it is the system by which candidates come to be put forward through the schools and the complementary self-selection which weighs against those from the maintained schools . . . Until this system alters it is hard to see any major change coming about.'[21]

The summer's most important new work of sociology had a broader remit: an account of why, in such a blatantly unequal society, the working class remained largely quiescent. The answer, according to W. G. (Garry) Runciman in *Relative Deprivation and Social Justice*, was the abiding narrowness of what he called that class's 'reference group'; and at the heart of his case was an ambitious 1962 survey in which manual workers were asked whether they thought there were 'any other sorts of people doing noticeably better' economically than themselves. Barely half answered 'yes' – and, even more strikingly, less than a quarter, when asked who those 'other sorts of people' were, referred to non-manual occupations. Or in other words, as David Marquand (former politics lecturer at Sussex, now a Labour MP) put it in his *Observer* review, 'manual workers compare themselves economically with other manual workers, not with white-collar workers and still less with businessmen or professional people'.

Runciman's book more or less coincided with the publication in June of a Pelican edition of *Education and the Working Class*, by Brian Jackson and Dennis Marsden, which since 1962 had won considerable acclaim and now in paperback proceeded, in the second half of 1966, to sell about 15,000 copies, before rising by 1973 to over 100,000 copies sold in total. 'The old dilemma', they reflected gloomily at the end of the revised 1966 edition, 'remained unresolved.' Namely: 'Working-class life – listen to the voices – has strengths we cannot afford to lose; middle-class life transmits within it the high culture of our society, that must be opened freely to all. *That* is the problem the planners must solve.' Nor, they went on, would this problem disappear 'even if comprehensives take over from grammar schools, and public schools associate with the state system':

> If we decide to send a percentage of state children to public schools, then most will come, of course, from middle-class homes, but a smaller number will come from the vast working class. It will take us right back to square one of the 'scholarship boy' problem. And no one looking at comprehensive schools will think that the battle is over. Progress is certainly made, but often the surface signs – Latin mottos, gowned prefects, first boat on the river, the race for Oxbridge awards – remind us that even here a training in middle-class deportment is still hopelessly mixed up with the transmission of that culture which matters. Comprehensive schools don't abolish grammar schools – they enclose them. And it is now clearer to see that the old purpose of education – the training of a ruling élite – has not collapsed under the new purpose – the training of enough able people to man our technological society. More and more – as Eton builds its science blocks – the two are allies, putting the same people into the same places at the same price.[22]

On 12 July, the day after England's anti-climactic start to the World Cup, the Cabinet was told by Callaghan that he would need to make cuts to public-sector expenditure of at least £500 million. After both Crosland and Crossman had raised immediate objections – the latter declaring that 'we came into office as socialists and the essence of a socialist policy is a shift from private to public expenditure' – Callaghan went, to judge by Crossman's account, into a spiral of self-pity, saying that 'he didn't know how we were going to get out of the mess', that 'we had totally failed to reach our objectives', that 'we were drifting into devaluation in the worst possible conditions', and that 'he didn't know how he could retain his position as Chancellor'. Eventually, as

Roy Jenkins would recall, 'Wilson hushed him up and brought the meeting to an end rather like a policeman trying to get a blanket around a nude streaker.' Wilson himself, at a dinner that evening for the visiting Australian premier, blamed the continued heavy selling of the pound on 'the defeatist cries, the moaning minnies, the wet editorials – yes, the Sundays as well – of those who will seek any opportunity to sell Britain short at home or abroad'. Away from Westminster, a trio of diarists recorded their respective Tuesdays, with between them that familiar mix of the public and the private:

> Sterling still under pressure. We are hearing once more talk of devaluation. Now our bad situation is being blamed on the Seamen's strike and the price of copper. There is always an excuse. The British Motor Corporation and Jaguar are to amalgamate. I wonder how long it will be before there will be only one make of car in the world. *(Kenneth Preston)*
>
> Usual sort of day. David home for dinner. Did some shopping. Fed up with my family – had a row with the children about their dreadful untidiness. So went down to have a gossip with Edna Rixon, then called to see Mrs Fletcher, & came home feeling a different woman – doesn't take much to make me happy! *(Betty Allen)*
>
> Dead boring day, 3 letters *all* day. Home at 4.00. Wash hair & did sewing . . . B. [her husband Brian] home 7.30, watch W. Cup, Brazil v. exciting. *(Avril Sandall, the day after starting work, via an agency, at the Egg Marketing Board in Woolwich)*

Brazil that evening beat Bulgaria 2–0 at Goodison Park, but at a heavy price. 'Some of the Bulgarian tackling was merciless,' noted one reporter; Dobromir Zhechev 'spent much of the game thrusting his chin into Pelé's face'; and the great Brazilian, the world's best footballer, finished the match with a seriously injured ankle. But a different kind of man-marking at St Pancras station, where also this evening a London-Midland spokesman publicly admitted that it was not just at Euston that a colour bar operated – with, at both stations, the driving force behind the bar coming not from above but from the white workers via their local departmental committee, the railway equivalent of a shop stewards' committee. As so often in these employment situations, it came down to gradation: exclusion from the more responsible, better-paid jobs; but, for instance at Euston, no problem if it was cleaning out carriages or labouring (sometimes dangerously) on the line. And the national union, in this case the NUR, doing little or nothing to redress a glaring injustice.[23]

Dennis Dee was at Beverley Market on Wednesday ('sold 8 pigs @ £7'); at Sussex University it was graduation day for Douglas Jay's glamorous twins, Helen and Catherine, while also present was the PM, receiving an honorary degree. The impact of the seamen's strike on the latest trade figures was predictably grim, with the deficit doubling in June to £55 million; Wilson, back in London late that afternoon and increasingly fearful of conspiracies to undermine him, had a thoroughly edgy encounter with Brown (strongly pro-devaluation) and Callaghan (hovering and havering); next morning, with Wilson himself still firmly anti-devaluation, the Cabinet agreed that bank rate should go up that afternoon from 6 to 7 per cent, to be followed almost immediately by Wilson making in the Commons what would be essentially a holding statement to try to stem pressure on the pound; the statement itself – 'fell limply on an unimpressed audience', according to Castle – did little more than affirm that the government would in due course be taking further steps to restrain internal demand and to cut back on government expenditure overseas, prompting Cairncross to reflect that 'it all smacked of panic because it was obvious that the government was caught unprepared and would have to work out new measures'; while that evening a packed-out chamber saw a debate on the second reading of Brown's Prices and Incomes Bill. This included not only a major set-piece speech by Cousins ('I will not have wage restraint whoever wraps it up and brings it to me in whatever kind of parcel') – a speech during which a watching Conservative backbencher whispered to a Labour backbencher standing next to him, 'Look how avidly Enoch supports what Frank is saying' – but also a credo-defining maiden speech by Michael Heseltine ('I do not believe that behind the closed doors of human motivation considerations of national interest weigh in the balance . . . Businessmen will respond to one thing, and one thing only – the opportunity to increase their salaries, their profits, and the capital value of their companies . . .'). Through the day, voting had been going on in the Carmarthen by-election, with the eventual declaration of the result, in the early hours of Friday morning, producing scenes of wild enthusiasm from a crowd of some 2,000, as Gwynfor Evans, a 54-year-old market gardener, defeated Labour to become Plaid Cymru's first MP. 'There is no British nation, there is a British state,' he liked to say; and against the background of what one Welsh historian calls 'the upsurge of vitality within Welsh language culture', this was a hugely symbolic moment.

If Wilson's interim statement had been intended to calm the markets, it did not work out as – amid feverish rumours of imminent devaluation – the pound on Friday the 15th had its worst day of this entire sterling crisis, accompanied by heavy falls on the Stock Exchange. Early that evening – after sending Callaghan a firmly worded letter outlining sterling's losses and declaring that only 'strong', rapidly taken action could restore international confidence in the currency – the Bank of England's O'Brien was at No. 10, emphasising in person to Wilson and Callaghan that 'it would be quite wrong to produce a package which was regarded overseas as being half-baked' and reaffirming his implacable opposition to the devaluation option, declaring that it would be regarded by 'overseas countries' as 'the Socialist Government's "recipe" for dealing with a situation which in fact demanded unpleasant internal measures'. After he had left, Wilson and Callaghan agreed between them to advance the date of revealing the measures, originally intended for the last week in July, to Wednesday the 20th, the day after the PM was due back from his imminent trip to Moscow to visit the Russian Trade Fair and to discuss Vietnam.[24]

Away from sterling's travails, and speculations like Kenneth Preston's that 'the Socialists appear to be in some disarray about what is to be done in the present economic situation', there were two announcements this Friday: one by Leslie Leppington, British Railways divisional manager, that henceforth, following negotiations with local leaders of the NUR, no grade would be closed to 'coloured workers' anywhere in the London division, including at Euston station and St Pancras goods station; the other, by the Multiple Shops Federation, whose members included Marks & Spencer, Woolworths, Sainsbury's, Boots and Tesco, that it would not give discounts or commissions to those operating credit cards like American Express and Barclaycard – in effect, an embargo on their use at their stores. 'A survey showed that the 310 members argued that the cost to the retailer of allowing the commission and administering the scheme could be met only by higher prices,' noted a summary of the announcement. 'This would mean that shoppers who did not use credit cards would be paying more.' That evening, as brows furrowed in Downing Street, it was back to the World Cup: at a 'dripping' White City (with Wembley saving itself for England's next match), a narrow win for Uruguay over France; and at Goodison, a far more memorable encounter as over 50,000 Merseysiders watched Hungary against Pelé-less Brazil. '"Hun-ga-ry! Hun-ga-ry!" came the roar,' wrote *The Times*'s Geoffrey Green, never knowingly guilty of lack of colour and verve in his match reports. 'It might have been "Liv-er-pool" or "Ev-er-ton!" And soon also to it was added "Ee-ay-addyo!" That is the way of an English crowd, standing neutral but now firmly behind the supposed under-dogs.' Hungary won 3–1, and everyone knew that the chances of Brazil – winners of the World Cup in 1958 and 1962 – making it to the quarter-finals now rested on the recovery of Pelé's ankle.

Saturday the 16th began with a question for Marjorie Proops from a young woman: 'If a girl has intercourse, and then has nothing more to do with boys for a year, can she have become a virgin again?' To which the *Daily Mirror*'s agony aunt answered briskly: 'Afraid not. She's had *that*.' On the political front, Brown was full of angry talk, whether to Benn in the morning as they attended the Durham Miners' Gala or in the evening as in his official flat in Carlton House Terrace he harangued O'Brien, of how he intended to resign if the government chose deflation over devaluation; 'talk of an extra 60,000 unemployed is being openly spoken of for the winter months,' noted Preston, with it now official that measures would be announced the following Wednesday; Dee 'did a lot of mowing in Bottomley's field'; Gladys Langford was taken by friends to the V&A's Beardsley exhibition ('found most exhibits erotic & illustrations of Lysistrata most obscene'); while for Larkin, a very Larkin sort of moment. 'I despatched a reprimand to the stationmaster concerning his rotten station,' he reported to Monica Jones from his mother's house in Loughborough. 'Coming back from London [where he had bought a pair of trousers at Simpson's] I said to the ticket collector that I must pay a fee for leaving my car there all day: "Oh, don't bother about that," he said. Slack sod. No wonder the railways are out at elbows. He sounded as if I were making *an unreasonable demand*.' On the bill that evening at the Keele Folk Festival was the Shropshire farm labourer Fred Jordan, who whether on stage (singing the folk songs, including 'John Barleycorn', he had learned from his father) or off it (living in a one-up-one-down cottage in Aston Munslow), 'retained', his obituarist recalled, 'the values, lifestyle and the outward trappings of the pre-war rural worker'; while at the California Ballroom in Dunstable, it was a different sort of scene for Laurence Marks and three male friends ('although there are a lot of girls dancing, most of the boys just stand in front of the stage and watch the Small Faces play'). And at Wembley, it was England's second match: an ultimately comfortable 2–0 win over Mexico, made memorable by the Bobby Charlton goal that broke the deadlock – a run from the centre circle, a thunderbolt into the top corner, relief all round. Or at least, relief in the home country. 'It was remarkable that the crowd found the spirit to sing so enthusiastically,' reflected the *Observer*'s football correspondent Hugh McIlvanney, a Scot to his bones, after what in truth had been another rather laboured display, including Jimmy Greaves again drawing a blank. 'Either Wembley audiences have changed fundamentally,' he added, 'or there should be dope tests for spectators.'[25]

Hancock, increasingly reliant on cue cards, stumbling on Sunday through *The Blackpool Show*; Dee hard at work on Monday ('turned all the hay – want some dry weather for a few days now'); and through it all, with Wilson away in Moscow, almost endless behind-the-scenes intrigue and manoeuvring, as a pro-devaluation cabal gathered traction. Its main members were Brown, Crossman, Jenkins, Castle, Crosland and Benn, all of them heavy hitters now in favour of floating the pound – but, crucially, a cabal not including Callaghan, back to an unambiguously anti-devaluation position after a blazing weekend row with Brown. A flavour of the prevailing mood, one at times of almost outright panic and emptiness, comes through in Castle's Monday late-evening exchange with a semi-drunk Brown, as she tried to steer him away from his almost obsessive talk of resigning:

BROWN: I've had an agonizing weekend thinking this out. Now the agony is over.

CASTLE: Oh God, this fissiparous movement of ours.

BROWN *(waving an arm, as he sat on the table edge)*: Don't use your long words at me.

CASTLE: You'd destroy this Government.

BROWN: Oh no, I shan't do that. I shall resign silently. No resignation speech. I'll just fade out of the picture.

CASTLE: But there's no need to resign. We shall have thirteen votes in Cabinet.

BROWN: But you can't sack the PM.

CASTLE: No one's going to sack him. He'll have to accept the majority view. He always collects the voices.

BROWN *(frantically)*: He can't do that. He won't do that. Look [*pulling telegrams out of his pocket*] this is what I sent him yesterday and here is his reply. He won't budge. He can't budge.

CASTLE: Why?

BROWN: Because he is too deeply committed to [Lyndon] Johnson. God knows what he has said to him. Back in 1964 he stopped me going to Washington. He went himself. What did he pledge? I don't know: that we wouldn't devalue and full support in the Far East? But both those have got to go.

By this time, the situation was arguably more nuanced than a simple devalue-or-deflate choice. 'During the course of the talks,' reckoned Crossman at about the same time as that Socratic dialogue, 'it had become clearer and clearer to me that the scale of the package required to float the pound was not very different from that required to save it. So the issue is not what package of cuts we should have but what should be the strategy behind the cuts, what would make it worth imposing them.'[26]

London on Tuesday the 19th was, recalled one of the unfolding drama's participants, Roy Jenkins, 'sunk in a trough of physical dismalness, with leaden skies and pouring rain'. 'I went at noon,' he continued, 'to greet King Hussein on the platform at Victoria Station. The Prime Minister, unlike the Queen, did not turn up, although he was back from Moscow. Michael Stewart and I were there from the Government, with various other plumed dignitaries. As the rain poured down around the assembled splendour, I could not avoid the thought that this looked like the last act in a dreary imperial charade.' The day's central event started at 5 p.m. – a Cabinet meeting, lasting almost five hours, for which our fullest, most vivid eyewitness to its defining passage is Castle:

> Dick [Crossman] was the first to jump in with the case for devaluation. Roy Jenkins followed, quietly but convincingly. Douglas Jay would have none of it: there was nothing irretrievably wrong with the economy and devaluation had solved nothing in 1949. Crosland swung the argument back our way and it looked as though we were winning it. George [Brown] weighed in with a passionate recapping of what he had said last night . . . But then one after another the 'do nothing yet' brigade mowed us down. I made an impassioned speech on political lines: 'Devaluation would be new because it would mark our freedom from monetary obligations to countries, *i.e.* the USA, who want political obligations in return – obligations which prevented us from finding our new role in the world. When Gerald Gardiner [Lord Chancellor] came down against us to say nothing of Tony Greenwood [Minister of Overseas Development], while Cledwyn Hughes [Welsh Secretary] called for really tough cuts to put the country on its feet, including cuts in the social services, I knew that we had lost.

The eventual vote was 17-6. 'The devaluationists,' comments Pimlott, 'saw it as a tragic, honourable defeat brought about by Wilson's characteristic finessing, using all the weapons of patronage, intimidation and appeals to loyalty open to him. The issue, they believed, would not go away . . .'

Meanwhile, ignorant of all this, the outside world continued to wait. 'Mr Wilson is to announce really granite tough measures in the Commons tomorrow afternoon,' recorded Vere Hodgson in Shropshire. 'Of course, we would all do our bit as we did in the war if we knew what to do,' she went on, 'but there is so much welfare about and so many people have things for nothing who could afford to pay for them that it seems useless to try to help.' The World Cup waited for no one, with two especially piquant encounters that evening. Ayresome Park saw one of the all-time shocks, as the crowd favourites, North Korea, sent Italy packing as Pak Doo-ik scored the only goal of the match. '"KO-RE-A, KO-RE-A," drowned the fading cries of "IT-AL-IA, IT-AL-IA,"' reported David Lacey, 'and when the game ended one would have thought that Middlesbrough had won the FA Cup'; while Arthur Hopcraft's enduring memory of the 'hysterical acclaim' after it was over would be of 'a tall British sailor lugging two Koreans off the pitch, one under each arm, like prizes'. Different emotions at Goodison Park, where despite the master's return Brazil went down 3–1 to Portugal, with Pelé himself suffering such brutal, unpunished treatment (England's George McCabe the ineffectual referee) that he spent much of the game limping with his right knee heavily bandaged. 'It may have been an illusion created by the television pictures, still in black and white, but the industrial gloom of northern England seemed completely the wrong stage for him and his compatriots, as incongruous as staging *Look Back in Anger* in the sunshine of Copacabana beach,' remembered Richard Williams in 2022 after Pelé's death. 'Brazil, with one win and two defeats, went out of the competition and Pelé vowed never to play in a World Cup again.'[27]

'It's impossible to raise ever so diffidently the question of another channel without someone calling for a university of the air or something equally depressing, as if we had just been marking time with *Coronation Street*, for the return of the fabulous era of the nightschool and the mechanics' institute lantern lecture,' wrote Keith Waterhouse in next day's *Punch*, though he did concede that 'the ghastly word "telly", which once conjured up a whitish flickering vision of awful drab families in Dagenham munching Mars bars and neglecting bingo, has entered the mock-cockney vocabulary of Kensington mums who no longer pretend that they have got it for the au pair girl'; no qualms this day from the *FT*'s TV critic, T. C. (Cuthbert) Worsley, declaring, 'Goodness, how I am enjoying the World Cup!'; qualms aplenty at No. 10 where the Cabinet met for four hours to finalise the package of measures (Wilson his 'dreary, competent self', according to Crossman, as Brown sat 'sulking on the other side of the table'); and at 2.15, barely an hour after the 'desultory' meeting had ended and barely an hour before Wilson was due in the Commons to announce the measures, Brown sent in his letter of resignation. The PM himself sounded understandably 'jaded' as, with Brown conspicuously absent from the front bench, he detailed the package. And 'when, at last, he sat down,' observed one political correspondent, Matthew Coady, 'there was a feeling that life could somehow never be quite the same for Mr Wilson. The measures, in a sense, marked the end of an era, their announcement the end of a myth. His days as a great party chief, as a British prime minister, are still without number. His life as a political superman is over.'

As for the measures themselves, adding up to an almighty 'squeeze' so presciently anticipated by Ray Davies's 'Sunny Afternoon', three male diarists sought to summarise them:

> Today we heard of Harold Wilson's stringent economic measures to save the pound. More purchase tax and other economic limitations. I do not profess to know the intricacies of the problem but there is no doubt that the country's financial condition is in a parlous state. *(James Allen)*
>
> I heard a bit of what Wilson was saying, during the time he was saying it, from 3.45 onwards. We heard of price freeze and wage freeze, of cuts in government spending, of increase in surtax, hire-purchase lump sums raised to 40% for cars and a reduction in the time for paying off the whole . . . *(Kenneth Preston)*
>
> Big increases in taxes on liquor, tobacco & petrol, & tightening up on H.P. are the main moves. They will doubtless have some effect, but nothing fundamental. The pound is reported to be perking up, but I don't think the financial world will be happy until there's a lot of unemployment, & quite frankly I would prefer the pound to continue its slow decline. *(Keith McBride)*

To which they might have added, most worryingly for those Kensington mothers, a limit of £50 on travel allowances outside the sterling area. Not, of course, that all the diarists this Wednesday the 20th were focused on Wilson's statement. 'Very heavy rain and strong winds,' noted Dee, 'a bit rough on my hay which was ready for cocking'; while across on the Lancashire coast, it was for Betty Allen, doctor's wife and anxious parent, 'another lovely day', weather-wise anyway: 'I rang Mr Hudson up about John – he was very kind & hopes he will be transferred to the A class next time – I do hope he will. Still in quite a state about him & smoked like mad all day! Did quite a lot of gardening. John much happier tonight. David on call & out till midnight.'

The politics continued during the evening: *Coronation Street* interrupted by a newsflash saying that Brown was resigning; continued attempts by sympathetic MPs and indeed by the PM to get him to change his mind; Wilson ('looking tired and drawn') on television justifying the measures ('This is our chance to show what we are made of. We are under attack . . .'); a newly emboldened PM then changing tack and telling Brown that he was not unduly bothered if he went; an offended Brown in turn deciding to step back from the brink; and, just before midnight, standing on the steps of No. 10 and declaring to waiting pressmen that 'it is my duty to stay in the Government to work for the success of our policies and to make Britain strong again'. All of which somewhat overshadowed England's final group match at Wembley: a 2–0 win over France (Marks confessing he was 'becoming a little bit concerned about the bet I've had', but still fairly confident); both goals scored by Liverpool's Roger Hunt; a bad shin injury for Greaves, though (like Pelé the night before) having to play on in the absence of substitutes; and an outraged France actually reduced to ten men, after their perhaps most skilful player, Jacques Simon, had been forced to leave the field following a tackle by England's combative, gap-toothed, very Lancastrian working-class midfielder Nobby Stiles that was, as the *Daily Mirror*'s Ken Jones accurately noted, 'far too late to be excused as bad timing'. Why, he was asked afterwards, had he done it? Because, explained Nobby, the Frenchman had called him – and one has to imagine the accent – 'Norbert'.[28]

20

Not Rocking the Boat

'We've been through it all before,' a Ford worker in Dagenham told a journalist later in the week, as he sat in his shiny new Cortina. 'Cut back, go forward. That's the story of life round here. But we still eat, sleep, laugh and bring up the kids.' An undeniable realism – yet, just the same, there *was* something different about the 20 July measures. 'The massive package thumped down before parliament on Wednesday', reckoned *The Economist*, 'means that Mr Wilson's Government is now following a right-wing policy of deflation more resolutely, more ruefully, more reactionarily – although unfortunately more messily – than any of its predecessors since the war'; similarly emphatic was *New Society*'s verdict (in an editorial called 'Axemanship') that 'the decision of the government to deal with our present economic troubles by means chiefly of a strong internal deflation represents a defeat for whatever kind of new economic policymaking the Labour Party and its advisers may have had in mind when they came to power'; while the *Guardian*'s financial editor, William Davis, reflected that 'although Mr Wilson still has four years to go before the next general election, traditional Labour supporters will not easily forget what he has made a Socialist Government do'.[1] How, wondered many Labour loyalists at the time as well as historians subsequently, had it come to this? How had a government elected and then re-elected on the seemingly plausible promise of economic growth and expansion in order to reverse relative economic decline, been reduced to such straits? Could it have been otherwise? Had serious mistakes been made?[2] But on one thing almost everyone was agreed: for Harold Wilson and his Labour government, never glad confident morning again.

An 'aching tooth' was what Wilson – privately and understandably – called the whole vexed issue of sterling. Should he have extracted the wretched thing by, at some point between October 1964 and July 1966, accepting as an inexorable and inevitable reality the case for devaluation?[3]

It would indeed soon become the conventional wisdom that he should have done just that, at a stroke making British goods more competitive in foreign markets and thereby going a long way to solve the balance-of-payments problem that so exercised sterling's holders. 'There is little doubt,' declared the economist Wilfred Beckerman in his 1972 overview of the Wilson government's economic record, 'that the decision to give absolute priority to the maintenance of the exchange rate [$2.80 to the £] was the one great mistake of economic policy'; while according to Keith Middlemas, writing in 1990 in his magisterial history of the post-war settlement, the decision not to go for an early devaluation trapped the government in 'an ineluctable form of conditionality', by which 'modernisation of industry and the rest of the economy had to be carried through at the existing parity of sterling, while repaying heavy external borrowings and *before* the expansion which ought to have provided, for TUC and CBI members, the necessary trade-off for their co-operation'. Barbara Castle would not have dissented, declaring in 1988 that 'this decision put the government in a straitjacket'; Michael Foot in 1997 looked back wistfully on the failure to grasp 'the remedy'; while Wilson's biographer, Ben Pimlott, reckoned in 2000 that 'if devaluation might have taken place in 1964, and could have taken place in a measured way in the months that followed, it certainly should have been carried out in 1966'.

However, not all economic historians over the years have agreed that the economic consequences of non-devaluation were necessarily so negative. Take Sidney Pollard, noting that although 'the clinging to a particular dollar exchange rate was irrational', even so devaluation, whenever it came, 'was merely a means of registering the fact that Britain's productivity had fallen far behind that of others while money incomes had risen at about the same rate', with nothing fundamental having been done 'to arrest the process of relative decline which had made it necessary in the first place'. So, too, Jim Tomlinson (pointing to how the mid-1960s data 'show no clear, strong trend in the deterioration of British trade competitiveness that would require devaluation'), Glen O'Hara (arguing that 'devaluation would have necessitated just as much deflation as did fighting for the parity', that 'indeed, it might have required more, given the blow to confidence engendered by immediate devaluation'), and Scott Newton (emphasising how, because of the increasing availability of central bank and IMF credit, the defence of the pound did not involve 'any sacrifice of the post-war nation state's commitment to the preservation of full employment').

Yet, ultimately, the issue was not about economics. Aching tooth it may have been, but Wilson between 1964 and 1966 did not hesitate to identify the defence of sterling as a very personal as well as national crusade, typified by an address he gave in April 1965 in New York to American bankers and industrialists. After restating his government's 'unalterable determination to maintain the value of the pound', he went on to assure them that he was speaking 'with absolute frankness as befits a representative of Britain talking to an audience of friends, not least because as a Yorkshireman who believes in speaking his mind I sometimes get a little tired of the cant and mumbo-jumbo with which issues of this kind are cloaked'. Put another way, Wilson turned a technical economic decision, full of competing arguments, into a high-stakes political gamble – or, as Crossman reflected later that year, 'if you commit yourself to the view that devaluation is the end of everything and then fail to defend the pound, then it really is the end and you go down in catastrophe'. A last word goes to David Marquand. 'The more Wilson staked his authority on not devaluing, and maintaining the exchange rate of the pound, the bigger would be the cost to him in authority and reputation if in the end there was a devaluation,' he recalled three decades later. 'It was like he was a general throwing new armies into the battle. Each new army he threw in made it harder for him to retreat and so by '66 he had already committed an awful lot of himself, of his own political capital, to not devaluing.'[4]

Such was the whole issue's totemic importance that Wilson and those around him went to extraordinary lengths to discourage free and dispassionate debate. In the immediate wake of the October 1964 post-election decision by Wilson, Callaghan and Brown not to devalue, Crosland dared to offer a sceptical voice to Brown, who brusquely told him that 'the subject was never, *never* to be raised again'; about the same time, when Callaghan's economic adviser Nicky Kaldor made similar noises, the chancellor riposted that 'if you want to work for me, you must not argue against things that have already been decided'; and the following month, Wilson decreed to Whitehall that he never wished to see or read the word 'devaluation' again. Obviously, that did not stop advisers and senior civil servants talking among themselves about 'the unmentionable', as it was henceforth coyly referred to – indeed, the former and future economic journalist Samuel Brittan, at this stage based at the Department of Economic Affairs as a temporary civil servant, privately noted in June 1965 that 'everyone seems to be talking of the unmentionable'. Even so, given this taboo-like atmosphere, it is hard to disagree with the assertion of the historian David Blaazer that 'the most powerful and authoritative voices in the devaluationist cause were, quite literally, silenced until the actual moment [November 1967] of devaluation, leaving the field open for the development of a public discourse in which devaluation was represented as an object of dread'. That external trepidation, to be fair, was not entirely novel. 'To the general public,' Marquand had observed in 1963 (writing about the Attlee government's 1949 devaluation), 'money is an arcane mystery to be approached with reverence and dread; and the price of a nation's currency is a measure of its standing in the world.' And he added that whereas 'to the economist the news that the price of the pound sterling has fallen in terms of the dollar means only that prices have risen in the sterling area faster than they have done in the dollar area, to the man in the street it means that Great Britain and the sterling area have suffered a humiliation as terrible as it is inexplicable'. The pound, in short, as a powerful – if barely understood – national virility symbol; and Castle's biographer, Anne Perkins, tellingly notes how, in relation to the pound's fortunes in the foreign exchange market, Callaghan apparently would 'anxiously stop colleagues to update them on its health, as if it was a favourite aunt'.[5]

Certainly, neither the Bank of England nor the City more generally encouraged open discussion about any option that seemingly threatened sterling's standing as an international reserve currency. When a paper from Kaldor, arguing for floating the pound, landed on Cromer's desk in July 1965 (in the middle of a sterling crisis), the governor scribbled on it in red biro a series of palpably angry comments, including that he felt 'ashamed to read such a paper on HM Treasury stationery'. But given Cromer's personally acrimonious relationship with Wilson, probably just as influential a voice in Wilson's ear was the increasingly prominent – and manifestly intellectual – merchant banker Siegmund Warburg, knighted in 1966 and whose unwavering views on the matter were summarised in November 1964 in a *Times* letter (co-authored with fellow merchant banker Jack Hambro) in which he described devaluation as 'a measure which means abusing the confidence of those who have placed their trust in sterling; which would be demoralising to the whole nation; which would represent a permanent and substantial movement of the terms of trade against us; and finally which would give, at best, only a very temporary fillip to our competitive position'. Also trusted by Wilson was Leslie O'Brien, Cromer's replacement just in time for the fateful July 1966 sterling crisis. 'A totally professional, cool and competent central banker,' recalled the PM, 'his calm and reasoned advice made a deep impression on my colleagues and myself.' O'Brien was quite as implacably opposed to devaluation as Cromer had been; but the way he got across his message, expressing a degree of human sympathy for the government's plight, arguably made all the difference at a point where the policy outcome might very plausibly have gone the other way.

What about the role of the fourth estate? Brittan in December 1965 jotted down an illuminating reflection:

> Wilson protected from frank discussion of devaluation by:
> a. positive correlation between advocates of devaluation and sympathy for Labour Government.
> b. playing game and 'not rocking the boat' (FT etc).

FT was of course the *Financial Times*, by the mid-1960s increasingly required reading not just in the City, but in Westminster, Whitehall, universities and the business world at large. Its long-standing editor was Gordon Newton: cautious by instinct; deeply patriotic; highly averse to any charge of having, in a sensitive situation, undermined the national interest; and, like Warburg, knighted by Wilson in 1966. Accordingly, he ensured during this charged period that in his pink pages there was virtually a complete absence of any sense of a debate about whether Wilson & Co. were justified in sticking to their apparently adamantine non-devaluation line. Still, it was 'FT etc', and Newton was far from alone. The crucial context, surprisingly little written about over the years, was the so-called 'self-denying ordinance', by which the British press agreed not to discuss the possibility of devaluation, for fear, so the reasoning ran, that such a mention would be self-fulfilling and cause a perhaps decisive run on the pound in the world's foreign exchange markets. *The Economist*, *The Times*, the *Telegraph* – in none of these titles was space given for a proper airing of the issue; and when on 10 July 1966 the *Observer* did make its plea to the government to devalue, it correctly noted that 'even to mention this ugly word is to court the ugly charges of being irresponsible and unpatriotic'. Instead, the press as a whole continued to beat the patriotic drum. '*The £ could be strong if the British people had the ears to hear, the eyes to see, and the will to recover their native sense and energy*,' proclaimed *The Times*, in very deliberate italics, during the March 1966 election. '*They have done it time and again in wars; why can they not do it just once in peace?*' While in the July 1966 crisis itself, typical was the *Daily Telegraph* on the 14th: 'Let us hope that in the moment of their despair our rulers will not spontaneously reach for the biggest gimmick of all – devaluation', before ending: 'Devaluation is no soft option. France's one really successful devaluation, in 1958, owed its success to President de Gaulle's toughness in enforcing the most severe financial discipline. There are no de Gaulles visible on the British political scene.'

Inevitably, at a time when many economists were increasingly pro-devaluation, all this involved for many journalists a degree of intellectual dishonesty – or at the least, a reluctant participation in what was in effect a conspiracy of silence. Was a future chancellor part of that conspiracy? Nigel Lawson became editor of the *Spectator* at the start of 1966; in March, in his weekly notebook in the magazine, he condemned the difficulty of discussing devaluation 'in a calm and rational manner' as 'the last taboo in a permissive age'; and in April he was reported by Alec Cairncross as giving 'a disquisition' at the Political Economy Club 'on the necessity of devaluation'. Yet it was not until 29 July – *after* the sterling crisis, *after* Wilson had ensured there would be no jettisoning of the $2.80 parity – that he came out publicly in his magazine in favour of devaluation. Or put another way, and not just in relation to the *Spectator*, that rather unexpected government minister (in retrospect anyway), Lord Longford, surely called it right when, at the end of the crisis, he told the eminent government economist Sir Donald MacDougall that he 'thought the press had behaved rather well over devaluation and had refrained from playing up rumours about George's [i.e. Brown's] intention to resign and his conviction that we ought to devalue'.[6]

In the end, though, it all came down to one man. After all, by summer 1965 not only were all the government's special economic advisers in favour of devaluation, but they were joined by several of the bigger-picture members of the Cabinet, including Brown; while a year later, even Callaghan famously wobbled, before pulling back. Harold Wilson's subsequent reputation may have become – not always fairly – that of a trimmer and a fixer, a man of flexible principles, but on this issue he stood absolutely firm. Why? The reasons are not difficult to identify, and they include a fourfold anxiety about how devaluation might have led to an almost immediate cut in real wages, to instability at large in the international monetary order, to a downgrading of Britain's general position on the world stage and to Labour being labelled (less than two decades after 1949) as the party of devaluation. But there were at least three other reasons. The first was the American factor, with Lyndon Johnson having made it clear to him in 1964 that American financial support for sterling was predicated on a no-devaluation policy, and Wilson giving a pledge to that effect. 'Having given your personal assurance, particularly to the president of the United States, then it becomes very hard to say, "Oh, I was only joking",' reflected Robert Sheldon, a Labour backbencher keenly interested in financial and economic matters, many years later. The second was Wilson's underlying conviction that the 'real' economy somehow transcended finance – and that Labour's economic approach, a mixture of planning, modernisation and restructuring, would sort out Britain's long-running balance-of-payments sore far more effectively and permanently than any jiggery-pokery to do with the exchange rate. Finally, and befitting someone with his roots in northern nonconformity, there was the quasi-moral dimension. 'There are many people overseas, including governments, marketing boards, central banks and others, who had left their money in the form of sterling balances on the assumption that the value of sterling would be maintained,' he explained in August 1965 to an interviewer about the October 1964 decision. 'To have let them down would have been not only a betrayal of trust, it would have shaken their faith about holding any further money in the form of sterling.' And, in the same interview, he made it unequivocally clear that that decision remained, in his word, 'permanent'.

The situation had its obvious piquancy. It was almost as if, and not just in the 1960s, the relationship between financial orthodoxy (as embodied by the Bank of England) and Labour had a sado-masochistic quality to it. 'Collectively, Labour governments (and the present one is no exception) are willing to sacrifice anything – life, liberty, the pursuit of happiness – to the maintenance of sterling, its position, its parity and its prestige,' the political commentator Alan Watkins wrote soon after the July 1966 crisis, the turning point that failed to turn. 'No burdens are too great to bear, no price too high to pay,' he went on. 'Stand up, stand up, for sterling!'[7] The historical jury remains out on the economic consequences; and perhaps it does too on the political. For if Wilson through his obstinacy was indeed setting himself up for a high price to pay if devaluation was eventually forced on him, his shade might have smiled wryly at the political price paid in 2022 when a hubristic PM and her willing chancellor dared to defy the high priests.

At the heart of the Labour government's creation in October 1964 of the Department of Economic Affairs (DEA) was – over and above the thorny matter of finding a central role for George Brown – the concept of economic planning, seen as the key to attaining a long-term growth rate well in excess of the ambitions of the fiscally preoccupied and institutionally conservative Treasury. Exactly what sort of planning? Essentially the model was French-style 'indicative' planning, defined by Andrew Shonfield in his seminal *Modern Capitalism* (1965) as 'a system which relies on pointing out desirable ends rather than giving orders to achieve them'. Even so, in an illuminating passage, the strongly pro-planning Shonfield, convinced that red-in-tooth-and-claw capitalism had by now been permanently tamed, was at pains to emphasise that in practice, if not necessarily in public presentation, the French approach went some way beyond the purely voluntary:

> It must not be forgotten that 'planning' initially during the postwar period, and in some countries throughout the 1950s, was a dirty word; it was associated with extreme forms of *dirigisme* [especially Soviet-style planning]. Naturally, the pioneers of the method in the West were eager to insist that what they were offering was nothing of the sort. Instead, they produced the image of something like a university seminar in continuous session or an orchestra successfully playing a score which they [i.e. the planners and the planned] had composed together, without a conductor in sight. The typical form in which this was expressed during the 1950s was to say that the Plan was 'indicative' and never 'imperative'. But these simplified labels tended to blur an important issue of method: granted that the Plan was not imposed by direct compulsion, it was still open to the government to engage its greatly enlarged resources in an act of persuasion. If the government used all its considerable power, either to persuade the recalcitrant or to reward the obedient, the pressure behind the Plan could become well-nigh irresistible. The intellectual exercise would then have a different and lesser role.

In Britain itself, the Conservative government had started the 1960s planning journey, with the National Economic and Development Council (Neddy) being in existence from 1962; but lacking powers, it barely developed from being a fairly ineffectual talking shop. Wilson and Brown intended something altogether different – a dedicated planning ministry. Three decades later, at a witness seminar, survivors of the era would look back on the DEA's short life. 'I think it was a complete misconception from start to finish,' declared Alec Cairncross (never himself in the DEA):

> It was intended to accelerate growth, but it simply did not understand how growth could be accelerated . . . It was based on a French model which was completely misunderstood. Nobody ever went

> over to France to ask what the French did. If you went over, you found that the plan was prepared in the French Treasury, not in some separate thing called a commissariat, and you found that the French would not claim to have accelerated growth, they simply had what they regarded as a high and satisfactory rate of growth, on which they planned for the coming year. So the idea that the French somehow had a lesson to teach us was absolute nonsense. Nor were they the fastest-growing country on the Continent: Germany and Italy were growing much faster.

'If you take "stop-go", which was the great war cry,' added Cairncross, 'stop-go was no worse in Britain than it was on the Continent.' A dissenting voice came from Sir Ronald McIntosh, who had been a senior civil servant at the DEA. 'When one looks back on these periods of history, it is very important to get the mood at the start and the perceptions that people had,' he quite reasonably pointed out. 'It doesn't really matter whether people were right or wrong in thinking that the French experiment was one worth following, that was what they did believe at the time.'[8]

'Brown v. Callaghan' was the title in early 1965 of Michael Posner's piece, as the *New Statesman*'s economics correspondent contrasted the DEA with its 'expansionist' instincts and the Treasury with its 'contractionist'. 'By all means let us have discussion and argument,' he concluded, 'but in the end we must have clear decisions clearly explained without mystification.' Alas, the so-called 'concordat' that the two sides had agreed to, not long after Labour coming to power, was seemingly designed for the reverse. 'The functions of the two departments were to reflect "the unity in diversity of economic policy",' recalled ruefully one of the DEA's junior ministers, Bill Rodgers:

> Both departments would be 'centres of coordination', and each would consult the other before proposing any substantial departure from agreed policies. The DEA would be 'primarily responsible' ('primarily' was underlined in the typescript) for long-term aspects of economic policy and the Treasury 'primarily responsible' (also underlined) for short-term. But, to make the position doubly clear – or doubly opaque – neither distinction was 'absolute'.

> Primary concern or responsibility did not mean either 'only' or 'exclusive' . . .

Or in fine, in the words of the eminent economist Sir Eric Roll, one of the many outsiders (or 'irregulars') recruited to the DEA, it was all 'a pretty hopeless mish-mash', unable to resolve 'a great deal of almost medieval disputation' between the two departments. Yet as to which of the two was going to come out on top in the overall battle, it was probably never really a contest. 'Once the heady first days had gone and the novelty had worn off,' remembered Brown himself, 'the Treasury began to reassert itself, and with its absolutely superb mastery of the government machine gradually either filched things back or – more to the point – made it rather difficult for us to effect the grand design we had in mind.' And crucially, he might have added, the Treasury held from the outset – and continued to hold – almost all the highest cards when it came to the day-to-day running of the economy: external financial relations; managing the balance of payments; operating monetary policy; controlling public expenditure. Not that this stopped a series of turf wars and an accumulation of misplaced energy. 'The DEA's attention', reckoned Cairncross at the time, 'seems to me to wander irresistibly towards the short end of the spectrum and to desert a wide range of major problems of longer-term strategy that would repay study.' And whereas, he went on, 'in the Treasury the economists are inclined to be frustrated because they cannot give sufficient time to long-range problems, the economists in the DEA seem to be frustrated if they cannot gravitate to short-term issues'.[9]

For a flavour of life in the new department, together with the reflections of a highly intelligent outsider on Whitehall more generally, our best source is the Samuel Brittan diary, especially the early months:

> Gloomy toilet with no soap or towels. I donated a piece of soap to the toilet, which afterwards vanished. Apparently suggestion of a modern type ticking roller towel has never got anywhere in Whitehall! One has to keep a horrible towel and soap in a drawer. A laundry then comes round with a fresh piece of soap and a towel every week (or is it every fortnight?), if one is at one's desk at the time. *(2 November 1964)*

Have got own 'secretary' – an elderly audio-typist who is trying to cope! *(5 November 1964)*

Officials attend so many meetings with other officials at top and medium level that most of time taken up. Very little time to think. The sheer job of getting something out and agreed (or clearly disagreed) exerts a great pressure for orthodoxy and following precedent. Any solution must involve more rugged edges, less co-ordination and more breaking up tasks into individual jobs. Different departmental policies should be allowed to emerge. Only high level questions at point of crucial decision should have to involve agreed unified Government action. Too high a price is paid for the myth of Government unity. *(24 November 1964)*

Where does power lie? At top seems to lie with 'experts'; at assistant secretary level in departments. But people at that level have to work in restricted policy framework which they are in no position to question. Policy is dictated by external events and general climate of opinion, which causes them; or are they 'statistically' determined? or even randomly? Tolstoy's theory of powerlessness. *(4 January 1965)*

Fantastic wastes of time: spent long time last week on draft of how export measures might be presented. Now PM insists on swallowing them in a lot of other measures, including defence, which will get all the publicity. *(12 January 1965)*

Endless committee meetings and talk; then everything is done in an excessive hurry. *(7 February 1965)*

Fantastic team loyalties bind people together in common attitudes towards particular groups. These are shared by people who have only recently met each other, e.g. industrial group is contemptuous of Committees unless an industrial adviser happens to be on it. Then it is the real stuff. Take it for granted that if one of their members reports on something, e.g. British Productivity Council, then report will be all right. (In contrast to any previous reports!) Similar loyalties within planning group. Will only take seriously reports coming from their number. *(10 February 1965)*

Civil Servants very good at drafting so as not to offend anyone. Very necessary because of possible shower from all sides if anything offensive in drafts. Keeping in touch with what everyone is doing, and writing so as to take in everything without offending anyone is

> a full time job, but can be a quiet life. No wonder lack of dynamism. *(1 March 1965)*
>
> ER [Eric Roll] admits that in present set-up DEA can only come in when it can show that its interests are affected. Very little DEA stuff so far to impinge on [Callaghan's] Budget. Interests now are in matters difficult to prove. Effects of measures on confidence or regions – very intangible. *(23 March 1965)*

The sequence ends on April Fool's Day. 'Treasury still has privileged position,' reflected the author of the recent book *The Treasury under the Tories, 1951–1964*, almost as if he had now viscerally realised something for the first time. 'Fantastic that whole of overseas finance, fiscal and monetary policy completely outside Cabinet, interdepartmental Committees, or Cabinet Committees. A private mystique, an empire of its own. Like foreign policy before first world war.'

Might the DEA have had a chance if it had had a different political chief? 'Immense drive and energy, but unsettling habits and an underlying insecurity' would be Rodgers's fair-minded characterisation of George Brown; while Brittan in January 1965 had, despite everything, an essentially positive take: 'GB's unpredictable and intolerable behaviour is the only way to stir things up in this country. GB works at extra rational level. Perhaps one has got to be a bit of a bastard to get anything done.' Arguably it was Crossman who, over time, got it more right than anybody. Although at the start of 1965 he was praising Brown for his 'outstanding' leadership of the DEA, by June he felt forced to concede that Brown-style leadership ('gifted, brilliant, ebullient, gay, erratic') was sadly 'not the kind of leadership necessary to face the Treasury on equal terms'; while as for the DEA's whole *raison d'être*, he had to admit the following month that its top man 'just isn't a planner by nature'.[10] And of course, as Crossman well knew, the demon drink played its part, too.

'This is a plan to provide the basis for greater economic growth,' affirmed the opening sentence of the National Plan itself, published in September 1965 and rather grudgingly endorsed by both sides of industry. On the whole, historians have given it low marks, typified by the Middlemas verdict:

> Never a synoptic plan for modernisation of industry: it had no jurisdiction over science and technology, nor the vast fiefdom of Defence. It had little to do with Trade or the significance of transnational corporations as harbingers of new techniques and managerial skills . . . The National Plan was prepared at great speed and may, *au fond*, have been intended more as a declaration of intent (to reassure industry about continuity and priorities) than as a precise agenda for change . . . The only real innovation – a purely declaratory one – turned out to be the schedule of programmes of action, which itself depended on a hypothetical balance of payments surplus . . .
>
> Quite apart from its dependence on a surplus, the Plan had no remedy for the DEA's lack of macro-economic priority, other than waiting patiently for long-term adjustment to occur, through the slow growth of exports and reduction in import penetration of home markets. It had no mechanism by which to adjust targets and programmes to events, and its targets remained absurdly at variance with actual rates of investment or productivity levels. On complex issues dating from the 1930s – such as the choice between making existing plant more efficient, and renewing plant for long-term competitiveness – it said virtually nothing; for action, it assumed a rationality and a simple perception of the national interest, which was never likely to fit with known patterns of behaviour.

A notably close examination comes from Glen O'Hara, emphasising that – because of ministerial pressure, and ignoring well-justified scepticism from the Treasury and the Board of Trade – the Plan 'progressed on the basis of deciding the four per cent growth rate *first* (to reach an overall figure of 25 per cent growth by 1970) and *only then* deciding on measures to fit around the target'. Accordingly, when companies, trade associations, development councils and suchlike were 'asked for their projections for employment, use of raw materials, investment, training and a balance of imports and exports, the crucial mistake was to imagine that this was actually *what would happen*, rather than a statistical exercise: most industries took the 25 per cent target at face value, as an increase in demand for their industry, as none could even begin to calculate how growth *overall* would affect them'. The result, inevitably, was a series of deeply flawed, unreliable forecasts. Nor did it help, notes O'Hara, that 'the balance of payments assumptions behind the Plan were particularly suspect', with the planners not knowing (through no fault of their own) 'the answers to critical questions, such as when the import surcharge [introduced soon after Labour had come to power] would be removed, or the relative priorities the Cabinet gave to the balance of payments and growth'. So, too, while simultaneously downplaying the Plan's novelty, Jim Tomlinson:

> Reflecting a political imperative to be seen to aim at breaking out of Tory stop-go, and aiming to generate the resources upon which Labour could deliver its improvements, it was already out of date by the time of publication, having been undermined by successive deflationary measures designed to defend the balance of payments . . . In many respects the use of the word 'planning' mis-states what was involved in Labour's approach as embodied in the National Plan. It involved no significant new deviations from the scale of state activity that existed under the Conservatives. Some new ideas that might enhance the government's role were discussed (for example, greater use of government purchasing to shape industry), but by and large the Plan was never even intended to involve anything beyond a more co-ordinated and effective deployment of public resources combined with a similarly co-ordinated use of existing or marginally reshaped sticks and carrots in the private sector.

'It ran into problems,' he concludes, 'not because it tried to tell the private sector what to do in an economically or politically unsustainable fashion, but essentially because it simultaneously fudged the macro-economic arithmetic and exaggerated how far such fudging could be offset by micro-economic improvement over the relatively short run.'[11]

In that story of how the Plan played out in real time, Tomlinson's phrase 'already out of date' is particularly suggestive. In early August, some six weeks before the Plan was due to be published, the key contribution in Cabinet discussion came from Crosland, as (in Crossman's words) 'he asked how we could talk about a plan based on a 4-per-cent average increase of production each year when we now knew perfectly well that for the next eighteen months at least production wasn't going to rise by anything like that – in fact when the Government was actually cutting back production by its deflationary measures', i.e. the previous month in response to the latest sterling crisis. 'Crosland is the only member of the Cabinet,' added Crossman in his account, 'who comes right out with these honest-to-God economic judgements.' Ben Pimlott, in his biography of Wilson, is justly critical of Crosland's colleagues, including Wilson himself, arguing that in backing the Plan they were guilty of an act of collective self-delusion – in fact, of 'behaving as if they were able omnipotently to defy the laws of gravity'.

In any case, after all the generally (if far from universally) positive reception that the Plan received on publication, helped by Brown being in his most compelling bravura mode, it was not all that long before the shine wore off. 'Don't knock the plan!' was the suggestive title of the *Listener*'s printed version of a Third Programme talk given in December 1965 by the economist Peter Oppenheimer, who largely sought to defend it from criticism, while fully acknowledging not only that it had 'serious shortcomings' (including how 'some of the key statistics have been derived in a manner which makes one feel very uncomfortable'), but also that 'the practical difficulties of making such a Plan work are enormous' ('the stepping-up and co-ordination of investment, the improvement of labour mobility and other features of the Plan cannot be realized simply by publishing documents and making speeches'). The following March saw the National Plan playing only a relatively marginal role in the general election, such was its apparent lack of impact so far; while soon afterwards, looking ahead to post-election economic prospects, the *New Statesman*'s Posner referred almost dismissively to 'the Plan' as 'that much neglected but presumably important document'. The fateful July measures were, as it turned out, just three months away; and when they arrived, almost all observers realised at once that Brown's bold growth predictions of the previous September, together indeed with much of the Plan itself, were now for the birds.[12]

In effect – because of the chronic balance of payments problem, because of sterling's travails, because of the obstinate refusal to devalue – Labour's 1960s-style planning moment never really happened. Even so, its perceived failure still had, and would continue to have for many years in retrospect, an emblematic quality. Emblematic, too, were two other aspects of the Wilson government in economic action: on the one hand, Mintech; on the other, the AGR decision.

Mintech was the common name for the Ministry of Technology, the new ministry created in October 1964 that was intended to fulfil Wilson's celebrated 'white heat' promise of almost exactly a year earlier.[13] Headed by Frank Cousins, its minister in the Lords was the newly elevated 'corridors of power' novelist C. P. Snow, but who lasted only a year and would be remembered by Tam Dalyell as 'that pompous, vain, lazy man'. While as for Cousins himself, described by his largely admiring biographer Geoffrey Goodman as 'not a good administrator', it was hardly a natural fit, not helped by a paucity of support from Wilson in the inevitably difficult early months; and by May 1965 he was telling Crossman that 'he had been thinking of resigning for some time owing to his dissatisfaction with his job'. Mintech – situated high in Millbank Tower, and with its task defined at the outset as being to 'guide and stimulate a major national effort to bring advanced technology and new processes into British industry' – had two main areas of responsibility, of roughly equal status until 1966: explicitly technological or scientific, including control of the National Research Development Corporation, most of the Department of Scientific and Industrial Research, and the Atomic Energy Authority; and 'industrial', including from the outset a 'sponsorship' role in relation to four industries (computers, electronics, telecommunications and machine tools) all identified as suitably high-tech. Of the four, it particularly concentrated, in these first two years anyway, on computers (including arranging a short-term rescue of International Computers and Tabulators (ICT) as well as setting up in Manchester a National Computing Centre) and machine tools (including a package announced in June 1965 involving government guarantees to enable firms to experiment with highly expensive advanced prototypes). But one close and instinctively sympathetic observer, Frank Kearton of Courtaulds (and from early 1966 first chairman of the Industrial Reorganisation Corporation (IRC)), believed that a golden chance was being missed to reshape the whole relationship between the state and industry. 'I urged Frank Cousins to be much tougher,' he told Goodman in 1973. 'He ought to have been much bolder both with the machine tool industry and the computer industry. I told him so at the time. As a matter of fact Frank thought I was a bit wild.'

Others seem to have broadly shared that perspective. 'Mr Cousins goes slow' was the title in April 1965 of a long piece in the *Sunday Times* by Anthony Howard, judging Mintech's record to date as 'sadly disappointing' and accusing Cousins of having apparently been 'content to make a care and protection order for the present structure of British technology'; six months later, in the *Observer*, John Davy not only cited a recent negative report on Mintech ('slow, top heavy') by the Estimates Committee, but declared that it would need considerably more 'imagination, mobility and enterprise' to be shown than was currently being displayed if 'a fruitful relationship between science, industry and Government' was to be achieved; and in May 1966, the *Sunday Times*'s Bryan Silcock remained unpersuaded even after interviewing the minister, admittedly someone by politicians' standards attractively averse to self-promotion. 'Mr Cousins does not give the impression of being frustrated and itching to put revolutionary schemes into effect,' reflected Silcock. 'He talks continually of persuasion and setting an example. This approach has produced a lot of useful measures which will no doubt continue. But are they enough? From Mr Wilson's [1963 'white heat'] Scarborough speech onwards we were led to expect major surgery rather than a bottle of pills.'[14] Yet at this point, of course, Cousins was almost on borrowed time, about to resign over Brown's compulsory incomes policy. A new, energetic, more obviously suitable minister (Tony Benn) would replace him in July 1966; and Mintech, having already been the inspiration behind the recently established big-is-best IRC, was about to become exponentially more directly involved in matters industrial.

In retrospect, Mintech can plausibly be seen as part of what has been called 'techno-nationalism' – that attempt (pre-dating Wilson's white heat but exemplified by it) to take on American technological might by utilising home-grown scientific achievements. 'If we were not to enjoy the prestige of empire,' recalled Edmund Dell in the 1970s about this distinctive moment, 'we would seek prestige through advanced technology, by becoming leaders in aerospace and nuclear energy.' Indeed, it was nuclear energy which arguably saw the absolute high tide of British techno-nationalism. 'I am quite sure that we have hit the jackpot with this,' Fred Lee, Minister of Power, boasted to the Commons in May 1965. 'As one looks at the AGR tender, and the longer the life one attributes to the reactor, the more favourably it comes out for the AGR.' AGR stood for advanced gas-cooled reactor; and, on the advice of both the Central Electricity Generating Board (CEGB) and the Atomic Energy Authority (AEA), he announced that, for Dungeness B which would spearhead the new generation of nuclear power stations, he had selected the reactor tendered by a British consortium (Atomic Power Construction) – chosen by the government ahead of its two American-designed rivals, namely Westinghouse's pressurised water reactor (PWR) and General Electric's boiling water reactor (BWR).

In reality, though, it had not been a dispassionate decision made on a level playing field. One historian, David Edgerton, explicitly calls it 'a rigged contest'; another, Tom Kelsey in his more detailed account, not only quotes Cairncross's shrewd suspicion soon after the announcement that the AGR's apparently lower construction costs were at least partially artificial, but emphasises the 'deep admiration of the AEA among many Labour ministers', very reluctant accordingly not to follow its techno-nationalist steer. 'The mystery of how that AGR decision was reached has remained one of the industry's most closely-kept secrets,' noted in 1989 the *FT*'s veteran science correspondent, David Fishlock. 'Those involved have always denied that they were strong-armed to promote a British design. However, Lord Marshall, the present CEGB chairman and a long-standing opponent of the AGR programme, sent later for the records and found that no discussion had been recorded.'

It certainly proved a disastrous decision. 'By the early 1970s, when Dungeness B was scheduled to come into service,' recalled Fishlock, 'all five AGR stations were on order – and all five were in deep trouble, with no relief in sight. In the words of one engineer, it was "watch-making on a tonnage scale." The problem was that an intricate mechanical system had to behave faultlessly at dull-red heat in a gas compressed to the density and turbulence of a tidal wave!' By contrast, Westinghouse's spurned PWR was already by this time becoming, outside Britain and Canada, 'almost a world standard and the prototype for some of the most successful nuclear programmes'. All of which meant that, far from the AGR fulfilling its international purpose to (in Kelsey's words) 'usher in British dominance of the atomic future', including through large-scale exports of the reactor, it would instead largely be a case of 'saving face and scaling back'.[15] So, a jackpot indeed, but sadly not on this side of the herring pond.

Whether it was planning or the role of Mintech, let alone decisions about nuclear reactors, it is unlikely that much of this was being talked about at the proverbial Dog and Duck. Four days after the launching of the National Plan, a survey by Mark Abrams found that barely a third had heard or read about it, while only 7 per cent rated its chances of succeeding as 'very good'. Popular versions of the Plan were disseminated – *Working for prosperity*, aimed at trade union officials in particular, and *Upswing*, a factory-wall newspaper in tabloid style – but there is no evidence that they made any great impact; and for all George Brown's valiant efforts to sell to the unions the concept of 'planned wage growth', involving a significant component of the 'social wage' in the form of increased government expenditure on welfare and suchlike, it was all too clear by the summer of 1966 that an incomes policy based on a voluntary approach had run out of road. 'Now at last the British people are slowly becoming aware of the realities,' Siegmund Warburg wrote to an old German friend soon after Wilson had announced the thoroughly deflating as well as deflationary July measures. Looking ahead, he went on to declare that 'the real question for Britain is whether in the next ten to twenty years the strong and vital elements of the country will prove to be superior to the weak and morbid ones'. And, added this remarkable merchant banker with an outsider's unsentimental perspective, 'needless to say that the hotbed of the weak and morbid elements is mainly in the City of London . . .'[16]

Economic planning and the City had never been natural partners; the justifiably feared if barely understood power of the latter had carried the day; and Labour was now left without a plausible central focus for a generation or more.

21

It Is Now

'The dusty old recipe of deflation' (*Daily Express*), 'drab old-style unemployment' (*Daily Mail*), 'The measures must be swallowed painful though they are' (*Guardian*), 'First aid only' (*Sun*) – the tone of the daily press on Thursday, 21 July, the morning after Wilson had announced his save-the-pound measures, was largely negative-cum-regretful, with the major exception being the *Daily Mirror*'s declaration that 'The nation is behind the Prime Minister now that he is demonstrating that Labour CAN govern with guts!' Among the commentariat, perhaps the most striking piece was John Grigg's in the *Guardian*. Almost a decade after (as Lord Altrincham) he had become a national hate figure for laying into the Queen and her circle because of their lack of the common touch, he now argued that Labour's 'best chance of governing successfully lies in removing Mr Wilson from the leadership':

> His political gifts are beyond question. As a short-term fixer he is a nonpareil. Adroitness in debate and resourcefulness in party manoeuvre have given him a local ascendancy which few modern Prime Ministers have equalled. Yet he is almost entirely deficient in those larger qualities which would enable him to put that ascendancy to constructive use.
>
> His reputation has been boosted by the silly notion that a Prime Minister in our day should be an expert, and preferably an economic expert. Actually, the job of a national leader is to exercise judgement and imagination, and to take firm and farsighted decisions. Mr Wilson may be a trained economist, but he seems to have very poor

> judgement, no imagination, and an extreme reluctance to take any decisions which are not forced upon him by events.

'Above all,' insisted Grigg, 'he lacks the power to evoke from the British people their latent patriotism and idealism. So long as he is Prime Minister, the British miracle will obstinately refuse to occur.'[1]

Elsewhere in the papers this Thursday, *The Times* praised Paul Scott's *The Jewel in the Crown* ('the whole is told with a Conradian obliquity that suggests depth and subtlety and removes the novel from the simplicities of anti-imperial protest'), while a full-page advertisement in the *Daily Express* launched what would be Shell's incredibly successful 'Make Money' promotion, involving one half of a mock banknote on the purchase of petrol at a Shell station and the hope of acquiring the matching half in order to claim a cash prize; outside Parliament, an ultra-enthusiastic crowd of some 2,000, singing the National Anthem and waving Welsh flags, acclaimed Plaid Cymru's Gwynfor Evans as he took his seat; and Dennis Dee 'turned the hay tonight'. Next day was release date for 'The Beano Album' (John Mayall's *Blues Breakers*, with his lead guitarist, Eric Clapton, pictured on the cover moodily reading the comic); later on, Dee 'turned the hay, hope it stays fine while the morning'; for Betty Allen, off the Lancashire coast, 'busy, busy day getting ready to go away – wonder sometimes whether it's worth it!'; for her namesake James near Colchester, a thinly attended choir practice prompting him to reflect that 'it seems to be getting more difficult to get these young people along'; and in the Commons, the day's main event undoubtedly the second reading of David Steel's Medical Termination of Pregnancy Bill. After noting that recent opinion polls had indicated some three-quarters of the public being in favour of legalising abortion, he argued with impressive clarity that 'those who wish to oppose the Bill have to consider the effect of their opposition':

> If they were opposing the Bill because they could devise some other means by which abortions would stop tomorrow and by which there would be no unwanted pregnancies and none of the tide of human misery which is developed by our uncertain state of the law, then they would have a strong case. But, as the Home Office statistics show, over the last few years an average of some 25 to 30 women

> have died as a result of complications following illegal abortions. Many more have been cluttering up hospital beds with the treatment required following these operations. Many lives have been lost through suicide following conditions in which it was impossible to obtain an abortion, or in which abortion was in some way involved.

Among the vocal dissenters, Edgbaston's Tory MP, Jill Knight, declared that if society was going to be in the business of ridding itself of inconvenient encumbrances like unwanted babies, then why not 'put down' elderly parents, too? And Walsall's Labour MP, William Wells, similarly provoked shocked 'Ohs' as he graphically imagined a future daughter of Steel's becoming a nurse and telling him about how she had been in an operating theatre terminating pregnancies and then burning the embryos. It was a free vote – albeit the home secretary, Roy Jenkins, making it clear where he stood, describing the existing law as harsh and archaic – and in the event a triumph for Steel: 223 votes (including Margaret Thatcher's) in favour of his bill and only 29 (including Enoch Powell's) against.[2] Now would come the tricky business of the bill making its way through the parliamentary system, but it had been the clearest of signals.

Saturday was quarter-finals day in the World Cup, a tournament of the people's game in which coverage by commercial TV had been falling seriously short. 'A complete disaster, a shambles, on the basis that (1) we hadn't enough experience in production and commentary, and (2) the great moguls of the day decided to run *Coronation Street* at 8 o'clock, which was when the football was starting,' recalled John Bromley, ITV's head of sport. 'They thought the viewers would watch *Coronation Street* then stay on for the football, but clearly everyone went to the BBC to watch the whole football match.' That left Kenneth Wolstenholme, BBC's main man, as almost *de facto* the voice of football, as indeed he had already been for well over a decade. 'It wasn't particularly brilliant, it wasn't particularly vivid, it wasn't even especially professional,' remembered Simon Barnes about his commentary style after Wolstenholme's death. Rather, it was 'boyish, keen, and, as befits a pioneer, primitive, a bit of a blunt instrument'. Even so, BBC research after the World Cup found that most viewers had been satisfied, as indeed they had been with all the BBC commentators, with David Coleman the most favourably mentioned. Who were the viewers? Conventional wisdom has it that July 1966 was when football, traditionally seen as an almost exclusively working-class pastime, suddenly became fashionable; but research by Fabio Chisari reveals that 'middle-class viewers were considerably less inclined to view the pictures, and to listen to the commentaries, than were those from the working class'. What was happening, though, was many women watching football on TV for the first time, especially as the tournament went on. 'Some housewives, one understands, are complaining that the BBC is devoting too much time to the televising of the matches,' reported the *Listener* shortly before it began; but as Mrs Jean Spencer wrote to England's manager, Alf Ramsey, after it was all over: 'Although my husband, my father & son know a fair amount about the game, I'm afraid I know nothing, but I really must say again how I enjoyed the hours spent watching your team on the T.V.'

Ramsey himself had from the 23rd what turned out to be his definitive team, with Geoff Hurst now replacing the injured Jimmy Greaves. Unsurprisingly, the eleven immortals came from an overwhelmingly working-class background, with the major exception being Liverpool's awkward but tireless striker Roger Hunt, whose family ran a haulage business. A very different family background for the goalkeeper, Leicester City's Gordon Banks, born in Abbeydale, Sheffield, in 1937, youngest of four brothers and growing up in Tinsley:

> His father worked in a steel foundry, while his mother worked part-time cooking and cleaning in the large home of a steel magnate [noted his *Times* obituary in 2019]. The family had their only bath on a Friday night in a tin tub by the fire. As the youngest, Gordon was last in, by which point the water was almost black.
>
> Much of the grime came from the thirteen chimneys billowing smoke from the steelworks at the end of the road. 'When the wind was blowing in the wrong direction we couldn't see to the bottom of the street,' he said. 'My mother would rush out and take the clothes from the washing line to prevent the soot from sticking to them.'
>
> He would recall holidays in the seaside town of Bridlington, when the Banks family would cram into a Standard Eight car with bald tyres that regularly punctured . . .

Six decades on, it is hard not to be struck by the unfashionable clubs some of the team came from: not only Leicester City, but also Fulham, Huddersfield Town and Blackpool; with no one from Spurs or Arsenal or Chelsea, but of course the trio (Bobby Moore, Geoff Hurst, Martin Peters) from West Ham United, an altogether more homely, less glamorous London club. And Ramsey? Born in 1920 in thoroughly working-class Dagenham, close to thoroughly working-class Barking where his captain Moore came from, his father would be variously described as a smallholder, a dustman, a rag-and-bone man, and the catch-all 'general labourer'; and his route to the England manager's job was steering humble, unpretentious Ipswich Town to becoming unexpected League champions in 1961–2. Deeply cautious, emotionally remote, unsentimental, putting the highest of premiums on discipline and hard work, patriotic to the point of xenophobia, often prickly about his social position – one way and another, he was hardly a 'Sixties' man. 'In the evening I usually have a long read, for I have found that serious reading has helped me develop a command of words so essential when you suddenly find yourself called upon to make a speech,' Ramsey had written in 1952 while still a player (the calmest, most conscientious of full-backs) at Spurs. 'People, remember, are inclined to forget that speechmaking may not be your strong point. With this in mind, I always try hard to put up some sort of show when asked to say a few words.' Or as his biographer Leo McKinstry justly remarks, 'even the keenest advocate of the Victorian philosophy of self-help could not have put it better'.[3]

This latter-day Samuel Smiles was in his familiar tracksuit as, on a very hot Saturday, England took on Argentina. Elsewhere in the quarter-finals, there would be wins for Russia and West Germany, while in a remarkable encounter at Goodison Park, the Eusebio-inspired Portugal would come back from three down against North Korea to win 5–3. Almost all English eyes, though, were on events at Wembley; and the match report comes from a by now ultra-preoccupied Laurence Marks ('I haven't told a soul about my bet and have to pretend I want England to win the world cup, but I can't afford to take 52/- out of my meagre wage packet and give it away'):

> Argentina defends fiercely and my dad says he thinks they will break out and score a goal and then shut their defence down and

> so we won't get near their goal. But it doesn't look like that in the first half because the ball seems to always be in the Argentina half. But Argentina is really tough and their tackling flies everywhere and at any height. The referee from West Germany takes lot of names of Argentina players who commit terrible fouls. Kenneth Wolstenholme says, 'He'll have a library before the game's finished.'
>
> Argentina have loads of fans inside Wembley Stadium this afternoon and they are really cheering their team on, although they just don't look like scoring. And while we are watching play on the pitch, something is happening on the other side of the pitch. After warning him about three times, I think the referee has sent off the Argentina captain, Rattin, but he won't leave the pitch. The match is held up for a long time and my dad says, 'He should be banned from football for arguing with the referee.' After about ten minutes delay, Rattin eventually walks around the pitch to the tunnel, waving to fans on his way. He is still arguing with the referee, the England fans and even the England players. Argentina is down to ten men and now we have a real chance of winning this match.
>
> The only goal of the match comes just around 12 minutes left to play. It starts when Ray Wilson slides a pass to Martin Peters, who is sort of playing on the left wing, and he crosses the ball into Argentina's penalty box and his teammate Geoff Hurst seems not to be marked and from about five yards out he heads the ball into the far corner of the net. He holds his arms in the air and Alan Ball jumps all over him. Could this be the winning goal? Yes, it is, and at the end George Cohen goes to exchange shirts with an Argentina forward and Alf Ramsey comes dashing onto the turf and prevents an exchange taking place. He later calls the Argentine team 'animals', which is silly.

England's chief had indeed used the derogatory word. 'We have still to produce our best,' he told Wolstenholme in a post-match interview, 'and this best is not possible until we meet the right type of opposition and that is a team that comes out to play football and not act as animals.' Under pressure from the FA, a grudging apology eventually followed, while for Marks, he could only pray that Eusebio would save his bacon, even as he tried to enjoy a night in the West End. 'Everyone seems to be waving flags and cheering for England. If this is what it's like around Piccadilly Circus when we win a quarter final, what might it be like next Saturday night if we win the world cup? I can't imagine. My dad says to me it will be like V.E. Night, but I wasn't around for that, so it means little to me.'

Other diarists this Saturday, for example the unrelated Allens, allowed themselves non-footballing concerns. 'Set off soon after dinner for the caravan & got there well before tea,' recorded Betty after arriving in the Lake District, somewhere near Kendal. 'Found the van had been left rather dirty, so had to start cleaning up a bit! Not very pleased.' While for James, oblivious to a competing attraction: 'This afternoon we had the children's Sunday School sports on the Recreation ground . . . Afterwards there was tea at the Village Hall . . . I was disappointed that no members of the Church Council appeared except Cicely Poland . . . Neither of the Churchwardens appeared and I think they ought to do so.' That evening, Veronica Lee and her boyfriend were at Stratford, where David Warner 'made Hamlet so much more plausible than ever before'; the TV cameras were at the Albert Hall for the ritual First Night of the Proms – touted as Sir Malcolm Sargent's 500th Promenade Concert (though in fact merely his 473rd) and earning a handsome RI of 76, with viewers especially appreciating the maestro's 'agreeable moments of greeting'; and *The Likely Lads* bowed out, seemingly for good, with the final episode of their third series. Called 'Goodbye To All That', it featured Bob joining the Army in order to see the world; an initially appalled Terry deciding to keep him company; but right at the end, only Terry going, after Bob had failed his medical on account of flat feet.[4]

'The Labour Party has not unnaturally been rocked by the abandonment of all it stood for,' ran next day the *Sunday Telegraph*'s not unduly partisan take on the aftermath of the government's measures four days earlier. 'The National Plan, already moribund, is now defunct.' Still, light relief that afternoon with BBC1's latest offering of *Tich and Quackers*, those lovable glove puppets (one a small boy somewhere in the north of England, the other his pet duck) masterminded by ventriloquist Ray Alan. Yet for one viewer it summed up 'the prevailing confusion about moral values':

> Tich [wrote Mary Whitehouse not long afterwards] was about to sit for an examination and bribed Quackers (who generally does

> what Tich suggests) to steal the answers the night before. He then felt confident that he would pass and Ray Alan promised him five shillings if he did. At the examination he artfully pretended that he found the questions difficult – and later realized that the answers did not fit the questions he was being asked at all. They turned out to be the answers to a competition that Ray and Quackers had entered. So Ray discovered that Tich had tried to cheat. Just then the prize money for Quackers winning the competition came in. Tich was quickly forgiven, and off they all went to spend the prize on an evening out. No suggestion that Tich deserved any punishment, or that he should be sorry that he had done wrong. Nor was the question of Quackers taking the bribe and stealing the answers ever brought up . . .

Other, less morally challenging, entertainments followed in the evening. For Florence Turtle, listening on the Home Service to *Grand Hotel* (featuring this week Reginald Leopold with the Palm Court Orchestra), then a game of Patience 'for an hour or so'; for BBC1 viewers, *The Ken Dodd Show*, generating only modified enthusiasm (RI of 55), with one viewer referring to his 'pretty footling' patter; for those watching ITV and expecting Tony Hancock to present *The Blackpool Show*, the regular host absent (in a nursing home with 'nervous exhaustion') and instead the Irish comedian Dave Allen doing the honours; and for Philip Larkin, his regular Sunday letter to Monica Jones. 'You know, I fancy my bed *does* cave in the middle,' he informed her. 'I wonder if I ought to buy a new one? I've a good mind to. Espinasse [Paul 'Espinasse, zoology professor at Hull] advises Vi-Spring or Vi-Sprung – know it?'[5]

On Monday the 25th, work began on a twenty-two-storey block of flats in Canning Town, to be built employing the Larsen-Nielsen method (large pre-cast concrete panels bolted together) and to be called Ronan Point; Wilson had a couple of difficult meetings, first with the TUC economic committee (even its more right-wing members deeply unhappy about the proposed pay freeze), then with his parliamentary party (extracting from Wilson the promise that unemployment would not rise above 2 per cent); West Germany that evening beat Russia 2–1 at Goodison Park to secure a place in the final. Next morning, a letter from the Scottish peer Lord Lovat, sent as befitting a war hero from the Guards Club, appeared in *The Times*, where he pointed out that

England on Saturday had committed thirty-three fouls to Argentina's nineteen, before declaring that 'England, in spite of the fanfares of the Press in every paper except your own, have got through to the last four by a lucky disqualification [presumably a reference to Rattin being sent off] and the crippling of two Frenchmen in an earlier round'; and Marks at work ran into his potential nemesis, Phil Chiltern:

> He says to me, before I have a chance to speak, 'You must be quite worried, Laurence. England will win tonight and go on to win the world cup final and I will go on to win £2/12 shillings from you.' I remained firm. 'I don't think England will beat Portugal tonight.' 'I bet they do,' says Phil. He then invites me into his office because he has a demo of a track from the Beatles next LP and wants to play it to me. He doesn't say how he got it but it's called 'She Said, She Said' and it's weird and very un-Beatles-like. I listened to the words and it includes the line 'You don't know what it's like to be dead', and I think, who does? It doesn't sound like the usual Beatles records. It's a bit of a dirge.

That evening, while Wilson hatched an agreement with the TUC leaders that they would 'acquiesce' in the incomes policy in return for the PM undertaking (in his subsequent words) 'to give consideration to the proposal that the lowest-paid workers and men involved in genuine productivity agreements should escape the full rigours of the freeze', the two other semi-finalists duly met at Wembley:

> A good match and I was sorry one side had to lose. *(Judy Haines)*
>
> Poor Eusebio . . . No nice little North Koreans bobbing all round him, but someone called Stiles who seemed to stand between him and that beckoning goal all the time like an immovable monument. *(Vere Hodgson)*
>
> T.V. pack up – middle of England match. *(Avril Sandall)*
>
> The Portuguese as sporting as the Argentinians were unsporting. England won 1 nil I think but was ironing & bathing all the time. *(Florence Turtle)*

England did indeed win, but 2–1, with both goals scored by Bobby Charlton; and inevitably, not a great evening for the rash young gambler. 'England take the lead and my head goes into my hands. "What you so upset about?" asks my dad. I change the subject.' While at the end: 'My only hope of not losing my bet now rests with West Germany and who wants the Germans to win anything?'[6]

This was also the week of a legal judgment attracting widespread attention. The case involved four Ealing parents – who claimed to represent 10,000 others – attempting to stop their local education authority from introducing a comprehensive school system. 'If the intention to introduce comprehensive schools was carried out the whole face of the educational pattern in the Ealing area would be changed,' argued their QC on Monday. 'The local authority might say that all they would be doing was to do away with selective entry by allowing boys and girls who would not have been able to get into a school to do so without a qualifying examination, but the consequence of that would be that a child would enter a grammar school without any test of its ability to meet the necessary standards, and the school would be thrown open to all, so that the whole character and purpose of the school would be changed in a vital and fundamental manner . . .' Two days later, however, Mr Justice Goff rejected their contention that, under the 1944 Education Act, they had a right to have their children educated in accordance with their wishes; rather, their right to be consulted was restricted to the question of the curriculum, which excluded more structural matters. 'We deprecate the fact that education has become political,' one of the parents, Louis Rubens, declared immediately afterwards. 'It is ridiculous that children's education should depend on what party is in power.' But in truth, whatever the judgment, the comprehensive juggernaut was by now rolling irresistibly – and, in the event of an adverse judgment, the law could always be changed if a Labour education secretary was sufficiently committed, as Crosland was, to ending selection as much as he could.

Another name for 'comprehensive' school was 'neighbourhood' school, with talk inevitably starting by now to increase about whether Britain was poised to follow the North American example of parents changing residence in order to maximise their children's educational chances. Indeed, a conservative American commentator, James Koerner, drew the parallel in a *Daily Telegraph* article this very week. After noting how 'the quality of a given school is often dictated by housing patterns', he went on:

> And housing patterns are becoming more, not less, homogeneous with middle-class parents fleeing the cities to the desirable suburbs and lower-class families concentrating more than ever in undesirable areas . . . The social effect of such schools is then to reinforce rather than combat class consciousness.

No stauncher defender of the comprehensive principle, in any type of neighbourhood, than the prominent sociologist Peter Townsend. 'They really do try to live by their beliefs and principles,' reflected Phyllis Willmott on Tuesday about recently bumping into him and his wife Ruth at a party. 'They have foregone the privilege of manipulating the educational system to get something better (as the middle classes can and do) for their own children. That is, they "believe" in comprehensive *and* send their children to one.'[7]

'Desperate medicine not a tonic' was the *FT*'s view on Thursday the 28th of the wage freeze, after the TUC general council the day before had voted 20–12 to accept it; the *Telegraph* reported that 'the machine which the BBC has been using to show television pictures within seconds in slow motion during World Cup matches' was 'an invention of the Corporation's design department' and would be used again for the final on Saturday; pouring rain in the Lake District had Betty Allen and her family heading home early, but another diarist, Kenneth Preston in Keighley, was able to make a wedding anniversary trip with his wife to Harewood House, prompting some mulling about how 'taxes and death duties' were bound to finish off it and similar places of 'such cultural ease'. 'I suppose such palaces', he continued, 'are only possible because some folk were in desperate penury but I cannot myself feel convinced that there will be any equality when all the Harewoods have become comprehensive schools or old folks' homes.' The latest weeklies included Nigel Lawson in the *Spectator* unequivocally backing devaluation, on the grounds that the price of defending the pound had become too high, and mixed reviews for *Revolver* (*NME* rather doubtful about its 'new sounds and new ideas'; *Melody Maker* acclaiming 'a brilliant album which underlines once and for all that The Beatles have definitely broken the bounds of what we used to call pop'; Ray Davies in *Disc Weekly* reckoning it inferior to *Rubber Soul* and declaring, 'I just don't think the fans like the newer electronic stuff – the Beatles are supposed to be like the boy next door only better'); while in Chingford this Friday morning, it was good news in the post for Judy Haines: 'Nabisco-Frears sorry about my experience with stale Ritz Crackers. Sent me vouchers for two free packets and one of Premium Crackers, and refunded postage. Very nice of them. Sent them p.c. acknowledging courtesy.' At noon the government published its White Paper on the prices and incomes standstill, confirming that six months of a complete freeze would be followed by six further months of 'severe restraint', though with Brown at pains to emphasise, as he introduced the document, that this did not involve 'dictatorial' powers; the rain continued ('too wet for the hay again,' recorded Dee); two road accidents this day were Sir Stanley Matthews in his car (resulting in immediate surgery at North Staffordshire Infirmary) and Bob Dylan, back in the States, on his motorbike; the first Laker Airways flight, a Britannia with 100 passengers, took off from Gatwick to Paris; and that evening, the world's first supergroup had its surprise debut gig at Manchester's the Twisted Wheel. Cream, comprising Eric Clapton, Jack Bruce and Ginger Baker, had only recently come together, and their commercially minded manager, Robert Stigwood, had been expected to launch them two days later at the National Jazz & Blues Festival in Windsor. Still, given how Elton John would remember 'those kids' in the Twisted Wheel in the mid-sixties as 'so clued-up, so switched-on, so much hipper than anyone else in the country', somehow it was more appropriate – not least coming as it did on the eve of an historic morrow, impossible to top.[8]

Saturday, 30 July 1966. To be remembered by Anthony Heap (no interest in football) as 'a cool, unsettled day of showers and "bright periods".' A morning of predictions. England to 'just about win on their "home" ground' (Geoffrey Green, *The Times*); England 'to beat Germany by two goals' (Peter Lorenzo, *Sun*); 'England will win because they are men of courage and adventure' (Desmond Hackett, *Daily Express*). Ramsey announces his team at eleven o'clock: unchanged, with no place for the recovered Greaves. BBC TV coverage, introduced by David Coleman at Wembley, starts at twelve: a series of mini-features over the next two-plus hours (The Wembley

Scene, How They Got There, People At The Match, Meet The Teams, Inside Wembley). Wilson, after visits to Washington and Ottawa, returns to London Airport at 1.10 and heads to Wembley, privately predicting a 2–1 win for England. ITV coverage starts at 1.10. The crowd (96,924, producing gate receipts of £204,805, new world record for any football match) gathers at the Empire Stadium. Among them, fifteen-year-old Blake Morrison, his father unhappy about the 2s. 6d. 'daylight robbery' being charged for the souvenir programme; eleven-year-old Patrick Wintour, disconcerted to have just been told by his father Charles (editor of the *Evening Standard*) that he does not like England's opponents, as he reels off the names of family members killed in the two world wars; Hunter Davies, in the posh seats with a £5 ticket; Arthur Hopcraft, unfavourably struck by how too many of those around him are not real football followers, but seemingly instead rugby men in blazers asking in their Home Counties accents about who is in the England team; and Ken Baily, aka 'World Cup Willie', in top hat, red tailcoat and Union Jack waistcoat. In Dorset, the annual Loders Fete (held as usual at Loders Court, at the kind invitation of the Honourable Mrs Alexander Hood) has a lowish turnout, with small boys clutching transistors. At Wembley, the band of the Royal Marines, complete with pith helmets, plays a tune for each of the sixteen competing nations, including 'Oriental Patrol' for North Korea. Nearby, at 2.48, a sharp burst of rain at Hampstead Cricket Club sees the players gratefully racing for the pavilion and the TV there. Across Britain, some 30.5 million others are also now settled in front of the box, all but 4 million of them preparing to watch the match on BBC rather than ITV (Hugh Johns the spurned commentator). One diarist, the TV-less Frederick Ward in Bristol, is invited next door; another, Laurence Marks, is at his Auntie Miri's (second-floor council flat in Green Lanes, north London) with two male cousins and his dad; in Birmingham, David Lodge and Malcolm Bradbury, neither of them possessing a TV, are watching in the flat of the absent Stuart Hall; in Scarborough, the holidaymaking Clark family sneak into a backstreet British Legion club (12-inch TV set positioned high above a bingo caller), where they make the major tactical mistake of winning on the one-armed bandit and, as the price of being allowed to stay, are only permitted to keep a small portion of the silver sixpences that have noisily poured out; in Wiltshire, as they take a break from filming *Dr Dolittle*, three stars (Rex Harrison, Samantha Eggar, Chee-Chee the chimpanzee) sit watching a set placed on a table in the middle of a field; in Riddings, Derbyshire, the Wheeldon family is ready, with curtains drawn, to munch their way through a box of forty-eight packets of Golden Wonder salt-and-vinegar crisps; and thirteen-year-old Graham Gooch, staying with his family at a holiday camp on the Isle of Wight, is one of some fifty campers assembled anxiously in the dining hall around the site's only TV, which refuses to work until one of them picks up the primitive aerial ('a sort of coathanger') and eventually finds the perfect spot – three yards directly *behind* the screen, where he is implored to stay standing and, heroically, agrees. No TV joy, though, for Michael Chaplin (putting up tents in the pouring rain at a Scout camp in Swaledale) or for Keith Allen (caught by a policeman stealing a tennis ball from Woolworths and now in solitary confinement in his room); while the Charltons' father, Bob, works his shift cutting coal at Linton Colliery and the Scottish footballer Denis Law opts to play golf. At last the teams come out: West Germany in white, England in red. 'Why if we are the home team do we change from our usual white shirts?' Laurence Marks asks his father. 'Because we are gentlemen,' he replies. 'The Germans wouldn't have done that for us. You could never trust the Germans to do anything sportsmanlike.' The two teams are presented to the Queen. She takes her place in the royal box. The national anthems are played. And a minute or two later, Kenneth Wolstenholme gives the green light: *The rain has stopped . . . the excitement is intense . . . the ground in many places is soft . . . and the 1966 World Cup Final is under way.*[9]

Also happening this afternoon, inviting posterity's pity but raising no eyebrows on the day, are not only the Loders Fete, but also the Royal Tournament at Earl's Court, the Kensington Kitten and Neuter Cat Club Show at the Royal Horticultural Society's Old Hall in Vincent Square, agricultural shows at Blackburn and Durham, a sea-angling festival at Gourock, the Wiltshire International Scout jamboree at Marlborough, the Country Landowners' Association game fair at Chatsworth House, the 2.30–5.30 segment of the National Jazz & Blues Festival at Royal Windsor Racecourse, the matinee performance at Drury Lane of *Hello, Dolly!* (Dora Bryan starring), and, starting at the Royal Court just as West Germany kick off, Max Wall in *Ubu Roi*. At Wembley itself, *ten minutes gone, no score*; but soon after

(Wolstenholme again), *Wilson penalised, taking Seeler's ankles ... Haller to Seeler ... Schnellinger now to Held, number 10 ... Ooh ... to Haller ... a goal ... West Germany have scored ... 12 minutes gone ... Helmut Haller has put West Germany in the lead ...* In a flat in Green Lanes, my dad is 'really put out', whereas 'I have to do all I can to control myself by not jumping out of my seat in joy'. Still, Wolstenholme consoles the watching millions, *if English hearts now have slumped, let me tell them that this is the fourth World Cup Final I have seen, and in the previous three the team that scored first lost.* And some five minutes later, even as German supporters in the unsegregated stadium are making all the noise, *Moore moving up to the attack ... And brought down by Overath ... Moore with the free kick ... England ... equaliser ... Last Saturday Geoff Hurst got that vital goal which knocked out Argentina. Now he's got a vital goal which has put England back into this game ... 18 minutes gone ... It's one goal each ... Now it's bubbling ...* While in Green Lanes, 'our lounge goes mad', but 'I have mixed feelings'. Midway through the half, the sun comes drizzlingly out. At half-time, score still 1–1, the marching massed bands play 'Colonel Bogey', instantly evoking the comforting wartime thought, 'Hitler Has Only Got One Ball'. *Torrential rain as England start the second half ... And may I just remind you that if the scores are level after 90 minutes, there is half an hour's extra time. And if they're still level, a replay here Tuesday night.* 'Oh my, what a referee!' sing the crowd as Mr Dienst makes some fussy decisions. The sun starts to peep out. *Certainly becoming a test of stamina now ...* The Isle of Wight holiday camper continues selflessly to hold the aerial, but in his Staffordshire hospital bed, the watching, post-op Stanley Matthews falls asleep. Then at 4.28, with less than a quarter of an hour to go, *Corner kick ... Remember, the day before the competition began, Billy Wright saying that the last 20 minutes will be in England's favour on this pitch. The crowd seem to sense it ... Ball with the corner ... Hurst ... And a chance ... a goal ... Peters ... the goal which could well win the World Cup for England ...* 'Oh, dear me' in Green Lanes. *All smiles in the Royal Box Ten minutes left ... Can England now hold on to this 2-1 lead ... The Germans tired, leg-weary ... Eight minutes to go. ... Seven minutes left ... 2-1 for England ... The tension now becoming unbearable ... The England team superbly fit ... Rule Britannia now being sung by the crowd . . . Fantastic how many people have brought along the St George's Cross instead of the Union Jack to wave . . . Four minutes left . . . The clouds have parted, the sun now is streaming down on Wembley . . .* In Highgate, Phyllis Willmott is woken from her afternoon nap by 'great yells and "Oh's"' from her husband and two sons in the sitting room, comes downstairs intending to go out to a shop, but finds herself 'trapped' by the unfolding drama. A northern fan sitting next to Peter Cook opens a bottle of champagne and pronounces, 'It's all over.' *Here comes Hurst . . . He's got Hunt with him, he's got Ball with him . . .* [groans from the crowd as Hurst shanks it wide] . . . *Just three minutes left, it doesn't really matter, it just gains a bit of time, even though the shot is wide . . .* In the sitting room at 4 Baker Avenue, Benson, Oxfordshire, my father (an Army officer, a man of few words) stands up, shakes his fist at the screen, and shouts, 'Of course it fucking matters!' And of course it does, it does:

> *Thirteen years ago the Hungarians came and showed that England were no longer masters of football. And in those thirteen years England has fashioned a team which is on the threshold of being the world champions . . . And it's a free-kick to West Germany . . . One minute to go, just 60 seconds . . . Every Englishman coming back, every German going forward . . . Now will the Germans snatch a dramatic equaliser and bring us to extra time? . . . It's Emmerich coming in, and it's . . . Oh yes, it must go . . . They have done. Weber has scored in the last seconds . . . 30 seconds from the end, and Weber has equalised. What a dramatic end . . . We are now in injury time, there goes the whistle for the end of 90 minutes . . .*

In Green Lanes, a diarist's 'huge sigh of relief'; in Norwich, a five-year-old David Taylor sits silently on the parquet floor and weeps; in Romford, a twelve-year-old Tony Parsons, with his father out at work, says 'Fuck' in front of his mother; in Rotherhithe, the father of nine-year-old Danny Baker goes puce, grabs the set off its stand, swears that it is all Wolstenholme's fault, and is so angry that the boy flees the house; while in the stadium, as loud boos ring out and English fans chant 'We won the war!' at the Germans, Peter Cook turns to his neighbour and says, 'If you open your fucking mouth in extra time I'll kill you.'[10]

Only a briefish pause as the shattered England players regroup and Ramsey tells them to do it all over again. *Off we go. Fifteen minutes each way.* For Gill Haynes and her mother, the tension so unbearable that they leave the room and sit on the stairs – their hands over their ears, but Gill's father with strict instructions to tell them if England score. *Never has a World Cup Final produced such a finish ... And the sun really shining now ... Bobby Charlton now with stockings rolled down ... Two goals each ... Just 20 minutes of the game left ...* Gooch's new hero still doing his stuff and about to miss seeing the most controversial moment. *Here's Ball running himself out ...* [indecipherable as Ball crosses, Hurst shoots, the ball comes down off the bar, the English players celebrate a goal, the Swiss referee runs over to consult the linesman, and in Green Lanes there is unanimity that it's not a goal] ... *Yes, yes, no, no, the linesman says no, the linesman says no ... It's a goal! It's a goal ... And the Germans don't like it ... The linesman who can only speak Russian and Turkish ... So, England are in the lead again, 3–2 ... And I thought for a moment the linesman had said no, he seemed to be shaking his head ...* The disgruntled Germans kick off, the game goes on, Chris Barber tops the afternoon bill at Windsor. *And the whistle goes for the end of the first period of extra time.* A quick turn-round, and *away we go.* Unable to bear to watch, notwithstanding Wolstenholme's admirably phlegmatic, non-hysterical commentary, I retreat upstairs to my bedroom and play a side of a Nancy Sinatra album, reckoning it will see both me and England through. Danny Baker eventually finds somewhere (round at Tommy Hodges's) where he has managed to knock loud enough to be heard and let in to watch. *Eight minutes left ... England supporters doing all they can to urge their men on ... Six minutes left ... Four minutes now left to play and the crowd biting fingernails down to the knuckles ... Certainly the whole of England can be proud of England's footballers today ... One minute twenty seconds left to play ... One minute to go ... The referee looks at his watch ... Any second now, it will all be over. Thirty seconds by our watch and the Germans are going down and they can hardly get up ... It's all over, I think ... No, it's ...* As I come downstairs, *And here comes Hurst, he's got some people on the pitch, they think it's all over ... It is now ...* An instantly iconic photo has everyone on the England bench standing up – all except one stony-faced man, the most important man. In an Isleworth living room, film critic David Thomson roars; baby son Matthew cries in alarm; his mother comes in and tells his father not to scare him so. Herr Dienst brings the match to an end. England have won 4–2.

Other fathers, in the immediate aftermath, are able to seize the moment. David Taylor's father, John, celebrates defeating Germany for the third time in a row – in the conflicts that really matter – by presenting his son with the almost unimaginable sum of a one pound note; John Bungey's father, less emotional, remarks, 'Well, they won't be able to call us the sick man of Europe any more.' Among diarists, Marks reflects bitterly enough ('I have lost a big bet . . . I shall remember the heartache of this afternoon'); Keith McBride is semi-detached ('a pretty good game on the whole'); eighteen-year-old Roger Darlington is exuberant ('What a final! What a final!); Phyllis Willmott is secretly pleased about the result ('would have seemed yet another indication of our "fall" to have lost to the Germans'); and Pamela Hansford Johnson is relieved it is all over ('felt I would scream if the noise didn't stop'). The cameras focus on the far side of the pitch, where England's reserves, dressed in smart civvies, have come across the touchline to greet and congratulate the England players. *One man has not come on the pitch. Alf Ramsey, the man who schemed all this, is still as calm and as cool as ever.* Soon it is time for the winners to head up the nearby stairs to the Royal Box. *Bobby Moore comes up to receive the Jules Rimet Trophy for England . . . Her Majesty the Queen . . . It's only 12 inches high, solid gold, and it means England are the world champions . . .* Then the National Anthem, with close-ups of Elizabeth and Philip – and, as it ends, a huge roar in the stadium. And then, back on the pitch, Moore on his teammates' shoulders holds aloft the trophy. *What a day this is – a day none of us privileged to be here will ever forget.* To the sound of the band playing and the crowd singing 'When the Reds Go Marching In', and with German spectators raising their flags alongside the Union Jacks, the team does its lap of honour. *I have never seen Nobby Stiles like this before . . . What a great moment for English football . . .* The crowd file out. A future football historian, Tony Mason, comments to the person next to him, 'Well, we did it . . . but only just.' A Frenchman, perhaps mulling over England's third goal, overhears and, misunderstanding, says to Mason, 'Yes, you won, but it was not just.' BBC's TV coverage has finished, and it is time – at 5.40, barely a quarter of an hour after the last kick – for the next programme. The panel this week on *Juke Box Jury* comprises Dave Cash, Joy Marshall, Jackie Stewart and Susan Hampshire. One of the records is Nancy Sinatra's 'Friday's Child'. It gets the thumbs-down.[11]

Not everyone is quite clued into the enormity of what has happened. Newly appointed deputy news editor at the *Observer* is 28-year-old Donald Trelford, appalled to discover there are no plans to cover the footballing triumph on next day's front page. 'If you think it's that important,' he is told, 'you'd better write it,' and he duly does so. Regular Saturday evening life does, of course, go on. Many cinemas are showing *Those Magnificent Men in Their Flying Machines*; and there is greyhound racing at Brighton, Catford, Clapton, Crayford, Hackney, Oxford, Poole, Ramsgate, Reading, Rochester, Romford, Slough, Southend, Walthamstow and White City, though the meeting at New Cross is abandoned after the second race because of a power cut. At Windsor the line-up is topped by the Who and the Yardbirds. On a busy evening, the police find time to arrest Charlie Richardson and his gang, some four months after the violent death of George Cornell at the Blind Beggar in Whitechapel. Away from it all is the poet Mary Casey, living in Mappowder, Dorset. 'A glorious evening with the wind west again, gold and blue gulfs in the storm-dark heaven. Best of all the prospects from the high ridges between here and Maiden Newton, a most exciting drive whirling down into those narrow bottoms, racing over the hills in a gale as though in air . . .' Different aesthetics in London's West End, where Laurence Marks and three mates head for their favourite club, the Scene. 'Every car that drives down Shaftesbury Avenue, Piccadilly, Haymarket, Lower Regent Street are blasting on the car horns. It's non-stop. It's deafening. Union Jacks seem to be waving everywhere. People are dancing in the streets. People are crying. Grown men. Girls are removing their clothes and climbing up Eros. Is this what my dad meant by V.E. Night?' And when they try to get into a pub for a celebration drink, 'we can't get near the door to any pub, let alone get inside. Everyone has gone mad. I ask one chap what the England footballers are doing tonight and he tells me that they are in the Royal Garden Hotel, Kensington.' So indeed they are – London's first post-war hotel, built by Richard Seifert, brand-new, and now hosting FIFA's official banquet. A huge crowd swarms round the team's coach as it arrives; chanting is continuous of 'Ramsey, Ramsey' and 'England, England'; politicians inside include Wilson and Brown, the latter as the evening goes on leading his table in singing the West Ham anthem 'I'm Forever Blowing Bubbles'; players' wives are banished to a side room; and on the glass-and-concrete balcony, the team display to the crowd below not only the trophy, but Pickles the dog, held aloft by Moore and Bobby Charlton. Across the country, millions wait for the BBC's edited highlights of the match, to be shown at 10.20. The cream of the New Left, including E. P. Thompson and Ralph Miliband, are gathered at Mervyn Jones's house off Blackheath Common; and once it starts, they get so irritated by Clancy Sigal's exuberance over a German defeat, his lamentable lack of 'comradely internationalism', that eventually Thompson and the American have it out in fisticuffs in the back garden. Due to be playing by this time at an outdoor event at Pinhoe, Devon, are the Kinks. But having delayed leaving London until after the afternoon's drama is over, they fail to arrive until 11.45, two hours late. The show has to end at midnight, so they play for just ten minutes, to a visibly angry crowd of some 6,000, booing them loudly.[12] An unhappy end to a largely happy day. And for this future chronicler, a fifteenth birthday to cherish.

Abbreviations

Abrams	Mark Abrams Papers (Churchill Archives Centre, Churchill College, Cambridge)
Amis	Zachary Leader (ed.), *The Letters of Kingsley Amis* (2000)
AJ	*Architects' Journal*
AR	*Architectural Review*
BBC WAC	BBC Written Archives Centre (Caversham)
Benn	Ruth Winstone (ed.), *Tony Benn, Out of the Wilderness: Diaries 1963–67* (1987)
Bonham Carter	Mark Pottle (ed.), *Daring to Hope: The Diaries and Letters of Violet Bonham Carter, 1946–1969* (2000)
Brandreth	Gyles Brandreth, *Something Sensational to Read in the Train* (2009)
Castle	Barbara Castle, *The Castle Diaries: 1964–1976* (1990)
Crossman	Richard Crossman, *The Diaries of a Cabinet Minister*, vol. 1 (1975)
Darlington	Diary of Roger Darlington (private collection of Roger Darlington)
Dee	Diary of Dennis Dee (East Riding of Yorkshire Archives, Beverley)
D Ex	*Daily Express*
DM (1)	*Daily Mail*
DM (2)	*Daily Mirror*
DS	*Daily Sketch*
DT	*Daily Telegraph*
E	*The Economist*
ES	*Evening Standard*

Fowles (1)	Charles Drazin (ed.), John Fowles, *The Journals*, vol. 1 (2003)
Fowles (2)	Charles Drazin (ed.), John Fowles, *The Journals*, vol. 2 (2006)
FT	*Financial Times*
G	*Guardian*
GDP	Great Diary Project (Bishopsgate Institute, London)
Hague	Frances and Gladys Hague Papers (Keighley Library)
Haines	Dairy of Alice (Judy) Haines (Mass-Observation Archive, University of Sussex, The Keep, Brighton)
Heap	Diary of Anthony Heap (The London Archives)
Hill	Diary of Jennie Hill (Hampshire Record Office, Winchester)
Hodgson	Diary of Vere Hodgson (Kensington Central Library)
Ind	*Independent*
Ironside	Diary of Virginia Ironside (private collection of Virginia Ironside)
Kynaston	David Kynaston, *The City of London*, vol. 4 (2001)
L	*Listener*
Langford	Diary of Gladys Langford (Islington Archives)
Larkin	Anthony Thwaite (ed.), Philip Larkin, *Letters to Monica* (2010)
Larkin	Unpublished letters of Philip Larkin to Monica Jones (Bodleian Library, Oxford)
Last	Diary of Nella Last (Mass-Observation diarist 5353, Mass-Observation Archive, University of Sussex, The Keep, Brighton)
Lee	Diary of Veronica Lee (later Porter) (private collection of Veronica Porter)
LRB	*London Review of Books*
Marks	Diary of Laurence Marks (private collection of Laurence Marks)
MM	*Melody Maker*
MRC	Modern Records Centre (University of Warwick)
NME	*New Musical Express*
New Soc	*New Society*
NS	*New Statesman*
NVLAA	National Viewers' and Listeners' Association Archive (Special Collections, Albert Sloman Library, University of Essex)
Ob	*Observer*
P	*Punch*
Partridge	Frances Partridge, *Other People* (1993)

Preston	Diary of Kenneth Preston (Bradford Archives, Bradford Central Library)
RT	*Radio Times*
St John	Diary of Henry St John (Ealing Local History Centre)
Scott	Diary of Patricia Scott (Mass-Observation Archive, University of Sussex, The Keep, Brighton)
Spec	*Spectator*
ST	*Sunday Times*
S Tel	*Sunday Telegraph*
T	*The Times*
TLS	*Times Literary Supplement*
Turtle	Diary of Florence Turtle (Wandsworth Heritage Service)
Williams	Russell Davies (ed.), *The Kenneth Williams Diaries* (1993)
Willmott	Diary of Phyllis Willmott (Churchill Archives Centre, Churchill College, Cambridge)

All books are published in London unless otherwise stated.

Notes

CHAPTER 1 BACK IN HIS CAGE

1. Keith McBride, GDP/379/1964–5, 7 Feb 1965; Betty Allen, GDP/450/1963–7, 7 Feb 1965; Grace Taylor, GDP/318/1965, 7 Feb 1965; *Sun*, 8 Feb 1965.
2. *Sun*, 9 Feb 1965; London Chamber of Commerce (London Metropolitan Archives), Ms 16, 479, 9 Feb 1965; https://coronationstreet.fandom.com/wiki/Episode_434; BBC WAC, R9/7/7–VR/65/71, 9 Feb 1965; Keith McBride, GDP/379/1964–5,10 Feb 1965; *Sun*, 11 Feb 1965; *Williams*, p. 252; *T*, 12 Feb 1965; *Crossman*, p. 155; Darlington, 11 Feb 1965; *Salford City Reporter*, 12 Feb 1965; *Liverpool Echo*, 12 Feb 1965; Julia Cook (née McLaughlin), GDP/373/1965, 12 Feb 1965.
3. This account of Malcolm X's visit to Smethwick is largely based on: *Birmingham Evening Mail*, 12 Feb 1965, *Smethwick Telephone*, 19 Feb 1965. See also: Peter Goldman, *The Life and Death of Malcolm X* (1974), p. 255; *Ind*, 3 Mar 1993 (Chris Arnot); Joe Street, 'Malcolm X, Smethwick, and the Influence of the African American Freedom Struggle in British Race Relations in the 1960s', in *Journal of Black Studies*, Jul 2008, pp. 939–40; Saladin Ambar, *Malcolm X at Oxford Union* (Oxford, 2014), pp. 159–62; David Jesudason, 'Avtar Singh Jouhl', *G*, 7 Dec 2022.
4. Frederick Ward, GDP/145/1965, 13 Feb 1965; Doug Hinman, *The Kinks* (San Francisco, 2004), p. 48; *DT*, 16 Feb 1965; *Castle*, p. 8; *Williams*, p. 253; Simon Farquhar, 'Frank Finlay', *Ind*, 2 Feb 2016; *DM (1)*, 17 Feb 1965; *ES*, 17 Feb 1965; Daphne Meryon, GDP/44/1965, 17 Feb 1965; *TLS*, 22 May 2020 (Geoffrey Wheatcroft); *Spec*, 19 Feb 1965; BBC WAC, R9/7/73–VR/65/95, 20 Feb 1965; *Ob*, 21 Feb 1965; *T*, 22 Feb 1965.
5. BBC WAC, R9/7/73–VR/65/99, 22 Feb 1965, R9/74/2, Apr 1965 (No. 199), 23 Feb 1965, R9/7/73–VR/65/102, 24 Feb 1965; *P*, 24 Feb 1965; *G*, 24 Feb 2025 ('Sixty years ago this week'); *New Soc*, 25 Feb 1965.
6. Stephen Dixon, 'Charlie Drake', *G*, 28 Dec 2006; David Frost, *An Autobiography* (1993), pp. 145–50; Kevin Cann, *Any Day Now* (2010), p. 49; *Peterborough Standard*, 5 Mar 1965; Neville Braybrooke (ed.), *The Letters of J. R. Ackerley* (1975), p. 260; Larkin, Ms. Eng. c. 7430, 27 Feb 1965, fos 1–2; Hinman, p. 49; *Williams*, p. 254; *Ob*, 28 Feb 1965; *Williams*, p. 254.
7. *DT*, 2 Mar 1965; Crossroads Appreciation Society, 'The Crossroads Years' (online), Mar 1965, episode 86; *Williams*, p. 254; *DT*, 3 Mar 1965; *G*, 3 Mar 1965; Paul Foot, *Immigration and Race in British Politics* (Harmondsworth, 1965), pp. 151–2; British Cartoon Archive, 'Arthur Stuart Michael Cummings'; *DT*, 4–5 Mar 1965; Veronica Horwell, 'Molly Parkin', *G*, 6 Jan 2026; *DM (1)*, 4 Mar 1965; *DT*, 6 Mar 1965; *Bournemouth Times*, 5 Mar 1965; *D Ex*, 5 Mar 1965; Foot, p. 152; *(Sheffield) Star*, 6 Mar 1965; *DT*, 6 Mar 1965; *NME*, 12 Mar 1965.
8. *ST*, 7 Mar 1965; *NS*, 12 Mar 1965; *DM (1)*, 11 Mar 1965; Ironside, 14 Mar 1971; *DM (1)*, 11 Mar 1965; Keith McBride, GDP/379/1964–5, 7 Mar 1965; *DT*, 8 Mar 1965; *BBC On This Day*, 7 Mar 1965, 'Goldie the eagle evades capture again'; 'Barry Took', *T*, 1 Apr 2002; *G*, 9 Mar 1965; James Stourton, *Kenneth Clark* (2016), p. 312;

Hertfordshire Express, 12 Mar 1965; *DT*, 10–11 Mar 1965; Keith McBride, GDP/379/1964–5, 10 Mar 1965.

9. *Benn*, pp. 229–32; *Williams*, p. 254; Alec Cairncross, *The Wilson Years* (1997), p. 43; Grace Taylor, GDP/318/1965, 10 Mar 1965; Frederick Ward, GDP/145/1965, 10 Mar 1965.

CHAPTER 2 WHY DIDN'T THEY SEND US *HAMLET* INSTEAD?

1. *Ripon Gazette*, 11 Mar 1965; *D Ex*, 11 Mar 1965; *G*, 12 Mar 1965 (Jean Stead); *Ind*, 1 Jan 1996; Tam Dalyell, 'Richard Buchanan', *Ind*, 24 Jan 2003; *The Roundhegian*, Jul 1965, p. 5; *DT*, 12 Mar 1965; James Allen, GDP/172/1965–66, 11 Mar 1965; *Ob*, 21 Mar 1965 (Nigel Gosling), 14 Mar 1965; *ST*, 14 Mar 1965; *Spec*, 19 Mar 1965.
2. *MM*, 13 Mar 1965, 20 Mar 1965; *G*, 15 Mar 1965 (Eric Todd); BBC WAC, R9/7/74–VR/65/136, 13 Mar 1965; James Allen, GDP/172/1965–66, 14 Mar 1965, 17 Mar 1965; 'Dee Wells', *T*, 9 Jul 2003; https://coronationstreet.fandom.com/widi/Episode_445; *DT*, 23 Jul 1965.
3. Paul Harrison, *The Black Flash* (Skipton, 2012), pp. 199–200; 'Kathy Kirby', *T*, 21 May 2011; *Williams*, p. 255; *Ind*, 1 Apr 2005 (Adam White); James Booth (ed.), Philip Larkin, *Letters Home, 1936–1977* (2018), pp. 398–9; *G*, 24 Mar 1965 (Francis Boyd); *T*, 28 Apr 2015 (Christopher Maguire); *Fowles (1)*, p. 627; Peter Bartram, *David Steel* (1981), p. 54; Adam Sisman, *Hugh Trevor-Roper* (2010), p. 359; *DM (1)*, 25 Mar 1965; 'Kevin Burke', *T*, 25 Aug 2023; *G*, 26 Mar 1965; BBC WAC, R9/7/74–VR/65/162, 25 Mar 1965.
4. Christopher Bray, *Michael Caine* (2005), p. 78; *Ob*, 21 Mar 1965; *P*, 31 Mar 1965; Bray, p. 76; *Ob*, 28 Mar 1965; *S Tel*, 28 Mar 1965; *Wikipedia*, 'List of best-selling albums of the 1960s in the United Kingdom'. See also: Travis Elborough, *Through the Looking Glasses* (2021), chap. 10.
5. *Illustrated London News*, 3 Apr 1965; *G*, 3 Apr 1965; *G*, 27 Mar 1965; *T*, 13 Sep 2017; *DT*, 27 Mar 1965; *S Tel*, 28 Mar 1965; Phil Davison, 'Tommy Smith', *Ind*, 18 Mar 2013; Nigel Fountain, 'Peter Boizot', *G*, 7 Dec 2018, *New European*, 2 May 2024 (Josh Barrie); *Ob*, 27 Jul 2025 (Jude Rogers); *DT*, 29–30 Mar 1965,
6. Hague, 30 Mar 1965; Alan Strachan, 'David Halliwell', *Ind*, 5 Apr 2006; Michael Coveney, *The World According to Mike Leigh* (1996), p. 67; *G*, 2 Apr 1965, *LRB*, 22 Sep 2022 (Florence Sutcliffe-Braithwaite); James Allen, GDP/172/1965–66, 1 Apr 1965; Mark Lewisohn, *The Complete Beatles Chronicle* (1996 edn), p. 190; *P*, 14 Apr 1965.
7. *Crossman*, pp. 243–4, 221, 227, 204; Alec Cairncross, *The Wilson Years* (1997), p. 47; *Kynaston*, pp. 311–12; *FT*, 7 Apr 1965; *Crossman*, p. 234; Cairncross, p. 66.
8. Aubrey Jones, *Industrial Order* (1950), pp. 26, 13; *T*, 18 Mar 1965; *G*, 25 Mar 1965; *T*, 20 Mar 1965; *Ob*, 21 Mar 1965 (Michael Frayn, 'The wage of reason dawns'); *G*, 9 Apr 1965, 1 May 1965; Geoffrey Goodman, *The Awkward Warrior* (1979), p. 451; *Benn*, p. 274.
9. *Crossman*, pp. 210–11; Mervyn Jones, *Michael Foot* (1994), p. 289; Ben Pimlott, *Harold Wilson* (1992), p. 359; Robert J. Wybrow, *Britain Speaks Out, 1937–87* (Basingstoke, 1989), p. 75; *Castle*, p. 14; *NS*, 9 Apr 1965; Paul Foot, *The Politics of Harold Wilson* (Harmondsworth, 1968), p. 214; Francis Wheen, *Tom Driberg* (1990), p. 354; *DT*, 5 Apr 1965; *Private Eye*, 30 Apr 1965; Jones, *Foot*, p. 293; *S Tel*, 13 Jun 1965, *G*, 12 Jun 1965; *G*, 17 Jun 1965; *Ob*, 20 Jun 1965.

10. *Castle*, p. 20; *Crossman*, p. 250; *Benn*, p. 273; Pimlott, pp. 385–6; Wybrow, pp. 75–6; Raymond Williams, *Politics and Letters* (1979), p. 372; Pimlott, p. 394.
11. BBC WAC, R9/10/12–VR/65/337, 3 Apr 1965; Marks, 6 Apr 1965; Terence Dooley (ed.), *So I Have Thought of You: The Letters of Penelope Fitzgerald* (2008), p. 35; *G*, 8 Apr 1965; Betty Allen, GDP/450/1963–1967, 8 Apr 1965; Darlington, 10 Apr 1965; *T*, 12 Apr 1965; Paul Stephenson and Lilleith Morrison, *Memoirs of a Black Englishman* (Bristol, 2011), p. 66; *NME*, 16 Apr 1965; BBC WAC, R9/7/74–VR/65/193, 11 Apr 1965; *DT*, 13 Apr 1965; *NME*, 5 Mar 1965; St John, 12 Apr 1965.
12. Andrew Weir, 'Jimmy O'Connor', *G*, 3 Oct 2001; Paul Ferris, *Sir Huge* (1990), p. 193; BBC WAC, R9/7/74–VR/65/199, 14 Apr 1965; ITC archives at BFI, Audience Research Boxes, 1965 box, 'A Report on a Study of Television Play Viewing, April 1965'.
13. Haines, SxMOA99/34/8/18, 16 Apr 1965; *Ob*, 18 Apr 1965; Duncan Hamilton, *Immortal* (2013), pp. 95–6; *ST*, 18 Apr 1965; Michael Bilington, *How Tickled I Am* (1977), p. 32; Antony Hayward, 'Ted Rogers', *Ind*, 4 May 2001; *P*, 28 Apr 1965; Haines, SxMOA99/34/8/18, 19 Apr 1965; *DT*, 4 Oct 2003.
14. John Pearson, *The Profession of Violence* (1984 edn), pp. 201–3; *ST*, 11 Apr 1965; Andrew Barrow, *Gossip* (1980 edn), p. 244; 'Cal McCrystal', *T*, 11 Aug 2021; Haines, SxMOA99/34/8/18, 21 Apr 1965; James Allen, GDP/172/1965–66, 21 Apr 1965; *Manchester Evening Herald* (Connecticut), 22 Apr 1965; *G*, 24 Apr 1965; 'John Hollins', *DT*, 16 Jun 2023; *Ob*, 27 Dec 2015 (Robin McKie); Robert Colls, 'When we lived in communities', in Robert Colls and Richard Rodger (eds), *Cities of Ideas* (Aldershot, 2004), pp. 283–4; *G*, 27 Apr 1965; Paul Sutton (ed.), Lindsay Anderson, *The Diaries* (2005), p. 109; Claudia Elliott, 'A Brand New Beat', *BBC online*, 2 May 2015; *NS*, 7 May 1965; *T*, 1 May 1965; *G*, 1 May 1965.
15. Joe Boyd, *White Bicycles* (2006), pp. 64, 82; Julia Cook (née McLaughlin), GDP/373/1965, 5 May 1965; Robert Shelton, *No Direction Home* (1986), p. 293; *(Newcastle) Evening Chronicle*, 4 Jul 2006; *ST*, 9 May 1965 (Nicholson); Haines, SxMOA99/34/8/18, 9 May 1965; *DM (1)*, 10 May 1965; Colin Harper, *Dazzling Stranger* (2000), p. 151; *New Soc*, 20 May 1965.
16. Haines, SxMOA99/34/8/18, 12 May 1965; *Country Life*, 13 May 1965; *Benn*, p. 258; Haines, SxMOA99/34/8/18, 15 May 1965; BBC WAC, R9/7/75–VR/65/261, 15 May 1965; Jack Powell, *Gone But Not Forgotten* (Merthyr Tydfil, nd), p. 51; *S Ex*, 16 May 1965; Matthew Engel, *The Reign: Part 1* (2022), p. 287.
17. Julia Cook (née McLaughlin), GDP/373/1965, 18 May 1965; Tom Vallance, 'Ken Russell', *Ind*, 29 Nov 2011; James Allen, GDP/172/1965–66, 18 May 1965; *DM (1)*, 19 May 1965; BBC WAC, R9/74/3, Jul 1965 (No 305); Doug Hinman, *The Kinks* (San Francisco, 2004), p. 55; BBC WAC, R9/74/2, Jul 1965 (No. 202); *Crossman*, p. 224; Louis Jebb, 'John Smith', *Ind*, 1 Mar 2007; *DM (1)*, 24 May 1965; Willmott, WLMT 1/31, 24 May 1965.
18. Michael De-La-Noy, *Mervyn Stockwood* (1996), p. 160; *DT*, 25 May 1965; *T*, 25 May 1965; *DM (1)*, 25 May 1965; Graham Payn and Sheridan Morley (eds), *The Noël Coward Diaries* (1982), p. 600; *DM (1)*, 25 May 1965; *DT*, 27 May 1965; Rachel Reeves, *Alice in Westminster* (2017), p. 131; *G*, 28 May 1965.
19. Dennis Dean, 'The Race Relations Policy of the First Wilson Government', in *Twentieth Century British History*, 2000 (11/3), p. 279; *DT*, 8 Apr 1965, 26 May 1965, 25 Jun 1965; Sheila Patterson, *Immigration and Race Relations in Britain, 1960–1967* (1969), p. 38; *Crossman*, pp. 149–50; Paul Foot, *Immigration and Race in British*

Politics (Harmondsworth, 1965), pp. 192–3; Vernon Bogdanor, *Making the Weather* (2024), p. 73; *Benn*, p. 261; Patterson, pp. 38–9; *Crossman*, p. 270.

20. *North Wales Chronicle*, 28 May 1965; *G*, 28 May 1965; *DT*, 28 May 1965; Barry Miles, *Ginsberg* (1990), p. 371; *ES*, 29 May 1965; Lee, 30 May 1965; Leicestershire Record Office, Misc 488/1, scrapbook of Mowsley and Laughton WI (1965); *Birmingham Evening Mail*, 1 Jun 1965; BBC WAC, R9/7/75–VR/65/296, 2 Jun 1965.
21. *L*, 3 Jun 1965; Michael Coveney, 'Ann Jellicoe', *G*, 4 Sep 2017; *S Tel*, 6 Jun 1965; Les Gurl Papers, Mss 57/1, p. 10, 3 Jun 1965 (Oxfordshire History Centre); *G*, 4 Jun 1965; Heap, Acc 2243/39/1, 3 Jun 1965; Peter Hall, *Making an Exhibition of Myself* (1993), pp. 190–1; Miles, *Ginsberg*, p. 371.
22. *North Wales Chronicle*, 4 Jun 1965; Lewisohn, *Beatles*, p. 190; BBC WAC, R9/40/10, 4 Jun 1965; *NS*, 11 Jun 1965; BBC WAC, R9/7/75–VR/65/302, 5 Jun 1965; 'The Rev Angus Smith', *T*, 6 Sep 2019; *G*, 8 Jun 1965; Lee, 8 Jun 1965; John Clay, *R. D. Laing* (1996), p. 122; Morton Schatzman, 'Mary Barnes', *Ind*, 11 Jul 2001.
23. *G*, 11 Jun 1965; David Eastwood, 'History, Politics and Reputation', in *History*, Oct 2000, p. 646; *G*, 12 Jun 1965 (Norman Shrapnel); Christopher Logue, *Prince Charming* (1999), p. 321; *Ob*, 8 May 1966; Miles, *Ginsberg*, p. 372; Marks, 15 Jun 1965; *Noël Coward Diaries*, p. 602; Barrow, *Gossip*, p. 245; *Benn*, p. 273; *NS*, 25 Jun 1965; *DT*, 16 Jun 1965, 19 Jun 1965; Haines, SxMOA99/34/8/18, 17 Jun 1965; see also: Dominic Sandbrook, *The Great British Dream Factory* (2015), pp. 57–60.
24. Peter Mandelson, *The Third Man* (2010), p. 41; BBC WAC, R9/7/75–VR/65/318, 12 Jun 1965; *Evening News*, 15 Jun 1965; BBC WAC, R9/7/75–VR/65/324, 16 Jun 1965; Heap, Acc 2243/39/1, 17 Jun 1965; *Crossman*, p. 254; Lewisohn, *Beatles*, p. 196.
25. Betty Allen, GDP/450/1963–1967, 19 June 1965; BBC WAC, R9/7/75–VR/65/328, 19 Jun 1965, R9/7/75–VR/65/331, 21 Jun 1965; *DT*, 22 Jun 1965 ('Hotspur'); *Ob*, 8 Feb 2009; Ferris, *Sir Huge*, pp. 195–6; BBC WAC, R9/7/75–VR/65/334, 24 Jun 1965; Humphrey Carpenter, *That Was Satire That Was* (2000), p. 312; *DT*, 30 Jun 1965; Haines, SxMOA99/34/8/18, 29 Jun 1965.
26. *DT*, 1 Jul 1965; Lee, 30 Jun 1965; *TLS*, 1 Jul 1965; Anthony Hayward, 'Ed Stewart', *G*, 11 Jan 2016; Spencer Leigh, 'Simon Dee', *Ind*, 2 Sep 2009; *G*, 4 Jan 2003 (Claire Cozens); BBC WAC, R9/7/76–VR/65/363, 7 Jul 1965; Dick Hobbs, 'Ronnie Biggs', *Ind*, 19 Dec 2013; Marks, 8 Jul 1965; *Scarborough Evening News*, 8–9 Jul 1965; *Castle*, p. 25; BBC WAC, R9/7/76–VR/65/378, 13 Jul 1965; *T*, 14 Jul 1965.

CHAPTER 3 ONE HUGE HANDICAP EVENT

1. Anthony Sampson, *Anatomy of Britain Today* (1965), p. 191; *NS*, 16 Apr 1965; Caroline Benn and Brian Simon, *Half Way There* (Harmondsworth, 1972 edn), p. 54; *New Soc*, 5 Nov 1964 (Tyrrell Burgess); *T*, 29 Dec 1964; *NS*, 8 Jan 1965 (Francis Williams); *S Tel*, 3 Jan 1965; *T*, 18 Jan 1965.
2. *Crossman*, pp. 132–3; Dick Stroud, *The Secondary Mod* (2021), p. 317; Roy Jenkins, *A Life at the Centre* (1991), pp. 169–71; *G*, 22 Jan 1965; Kevin Jefferys, *Anthony Crosland* (1997), pp. 103–4; Susan Crosland, *Tony Crosland* (1982), p. 148; Alan Kerckhoff et al., *Going Comprehensive in England and Wales* (1996), pp. 27–8.
3. Brian Simon, *Education and Social Order, 1940–1990* (1991), pp. 278–9; *Liverpool Daily Post*, 24 Feb 1965; Jad Adams, *Tony Benn* (1992), p. 242; Charles Moore, *Margaret Thatcher*, Volume One (2013), pp. 204–5; *G*, 1 Apr 1965, 25 Apr 1965;

Ob, 25 Apr 1965; Kerckhoff et al., p. 113; *Half Way*, p. 76; D. N. Holly, 'Profiting from a Comprehensive School', in *British Journal of Sociology*, Jun 1965, pp. 156–7; Kerckhoff et al., pp. 95–6; Beverley Shaw, *Comprehensive Schooling* (Oxford, 1983), pp. 67–8.

4. *T*, 14 Jul 1965; Shaw, p. 58; *G*, 14 Jul 1965; *DT*, 14 Jul 1965; Peter Hitchens, *A Revolution Betrayed* (2022), p. 44.
5. William Hampton, *Democracy and Community* (1970), pp. 238–40; Mark Abrams, 'Social Class and Politics', in *20th Century*, spring 1965, pp. 46–8; *G*, 18 Jun 1965; Paul Barker, 'The Ups and Downs of the Meritocracy', in Geoff Dench et al. (eds), *Young at Eighty* (Manchester, 1995), p. 160; Peter Housden, *The Passing of a County Grammar School* (Edinburgh, 2015), p. 74; *Where?*, spring 1965, pp. 16–17.
6. *G*, 15 Jul 1965; David Ayerst, *Understanding Schools* (Harmondsworth, 1967), pp. 120–3; *New Soc*, 11 Feb 1965; Ayerst, p. 121; *Ob*, 16 May 1965; Dennis Dean, 'Circular 10/65 Revisited', in *Paedagogica Historica*, 1998 (1), p. 89; *T*, 14 Jul 1965; *Half Way*, p. 73.
7. *Spec*, 18 Dec 1964, 29 Jan 1965; Maurice Kogan, *The Politics of Education* (Harmondsworth, 1971), p. 155; Dean, 'Circular', p. 78; Nicholas Hillman, 'The Public Schools Commission', in *Contemporary British History*, Dec 2010, p. 514; A. H. Halsey, *No Discouragement* (1996), p. 131; *Crossman*, pp. 278–9; Jenkins, *Life*, p. 170; Wendy Pollard, *Pamela Hansford Johnson* (2014), pp. 360–1; Dennis Marsden, 'Lord Snow's Middle-class Dilemma', in *20th Century*, spring 1965, p. 6.
8. Sampson, *Anatomy*, p. 221; BBC 4, *TV on Trial: 1960s*, 28 Mar 2005; Rodney Lowe, *The Welfare State in Britain since 1945* (Basingstoke, 1999 edn), p. 229; D. C. Watt, 'Expansion at the London School of Economics', in C. B. Cox and A. E. Dyson (eds), *Fight for Education* (1968), p. 32; Sampson, *Anatomy*, p. 218; *Ob*, 11 Apr 1965, 18 Apr 1965.
9. Simon Dixon, 'The University of Leeds and the British Higher Education System, 1963–2004', in *Northern History*, Sep 2006, p. 304; Glen O'Hara, 'British economic and social planning 1959–1970' (University of London PhD, 2002), p. 201; Dixon, p. 305; O'Hara, p. 201; Alan Roff and Tom Carty, 'Eric Robinson', *G*, 10 Mar 2011.
10. Brian Jackson and Dennis Marsden, *Education and the Working Class* (1962), p. 224; Patricia Hollis, *Jenny Lee* (Oxford, 1997), p. 297; Asa Briggs, *Michael Young* (Basingstoke, 2001), p. 199; *G*, 3 Apr 1965; *DT*, 3 Apr 1965; *T*, 3 Apr 1965; *G*, 3 Apr 1965; Williams, *Politics*, p. 371. For a full account of the creation of the Open University, see: Hollis, chaps 10–11.
11. Adam Kirsch (ed.), *Life in Culture: Selected Letters of Lionel Trilling* (New York, 2018), p. 319; *NS*, 5 Mar 1965; Alan Little and John Westergaard, 'The Trend of the Class Differentials in Educational Opportunity in England and Wales', in *British Journal of Sociology*, Dec 1964, p. 312; Joan Abbott, 'Students' Social Class in Three Northern Universities', in *British Journal of Sociology*, Sep 1965, pp. 206–20; *G*, 29 Aug 1966; Francis Green and David Kynaston, *Engines of Privilege* (2019), pp. 85–6; George Smith, 'Schools', in A. H. Halsey (ed.), *Twentieth-Century British Social Trends* (Basingstoke, 2000), pp. 216–17; *Ob*, 13 Mar 2016. For detailed discussions on education and social mobility, see: Peter Mandler, *The Crisis of the Meritocracy* (Oxford, 2020), pp. 189–95; Selina Todd, *Snakes and Ladders* (2021), pp. 194–212.
12. *ST*, 6 Jan 1980 (Roy Hattersley); *TLS*, 21 Apr 2023 (Emily Baughan, reviewing Eve Worth's *The Welfare State Generation*); *FT*, 3 Nov 1990 (Simon Holberton); Sampson, *Anatomy*, p. 564; *T*, 3 Sep 1964; *Kynaston*, chaps 7–9; Sean Nixon, *Hard*

Sell (Manchester, 2013), p. 27; *G*, 20 May 2021 (Amelia Gentleman); Alan Macfarlane, *Oxford Postgraduate, 1963–1966* (nd), p. 218.

13. *Prospect*, Oct 2013 (Philip Collins), citing John H. Goldthorpe's paper, 'Understanding – and Misunderstanding – Social Mobility in Britain' (Oxford, 2012); Anthony Heath and Clive Payne, 'Twentieth Century Trend in Social Mobility in Britain' (Centre for Research into Elections and Social Trends, Jun 1999).
14. Martin Johnes, *Wales in 1939* (Manchester, 2012), p. 135; *G*, 6 Jan 2003 (Hugh Richards); *Fowles (1)*, pp. 592, 620; *Fowles (2)*, p. 25.
15. *G*, 6 May 2017; Bill Williamson, *The Temper of the Times* (Oxford, 1990), p. 207; 'Mavis Cheek', *T*, 4 Jul 2023; *G*, 7 Dec 2024 (Simon Hattenstone); 'Sir Harold Evans', *T*, 25 Sep 2020; *Ind*, 26 Jun 1996 (Judith Judd); *Ind*, 3 Dec 1998; Tony Judt, *Thinking the Twentieth Century* (2012), pp. 113–14; Wikipedia, 'Mervyn King, Baron King of Lothbury'; *G*, 29 Oct 2020, 6 May 2017; Martin Westlake, *Kinnock* (2001), pp. 41–2; *G*, 6 May 2017; Duncan Campbell, 'Howard Marks', *G*, 12 Apr 2016; Julia Langdon, 'Mo Mowlem', *G*, 20 Aug 2005; John Forrester, 'Roy Porter', *Ind*, 6 Mar 2002; *NS*, 11 Oct 2014 (Sophie McBain); *Ind*, 30 Aug 1994 (Andrea Lambert); Malcolm Read, *Educating the Educators* (2003); *G*, 6 May 2017; *Ob*, 28 Nov 2021 (Rachel Cooke); Polly Toynbee, *An Uneasy Inheritance* (2023), pp. 52–4.
16. *New European*, 2 Nov 2023; Mary Ingham, *Now We Are Thirty* (1981), pp. 51–2, 75–82, 96–7, 82–5, 116–17; Roy Greenslade, *Goodbye to the Working Class* (1976), pp. 65–8, 1, 48, 80–2, 162; Peter Willmott, *Adolescent Boys of East London* (Harmondsworth, 1969 Pelican edn), pp. 86–7, 101–3, 114, 120; BBC WAC, *Woman's Hour*, 10 Feb 1964.
17. *Big Issue*, 17 Feb 2025; Hanif Kureishi, *My Ear at His Heart* (2004), pp. 47–8; Marks, 12 May 1965, 16 Jun 1965, 2 Aug 1965, 4 Aug 1965, 6–7 Aug 1965, 27 Aug 1965, 7 Oct 1965, 8 Dec 1965.

CHAPTER 4 BROADSTAIRS BOY MAKES GOOD

1. Frederick Ward, GDP/145/1965, 14 Jul 1965; *Hansard*, 15 Jul 1965, col. 911; *TLS*, 15 Jul 1965; David Oswell, *Television, Childhood and the Home* (Oxford, 2002), p. 146; *Benn*, p. 293; Frederick Ward, GDP/145/1965, 15 Jul 1965; *DT*, 16 Jul 1965; *G*, 17 Jul 1965; Alec Cairncross, *The Wilson Years* (1997), p. 68; Scott, SxMOA99/97/1/14, 17 Jul 1965; Darlington, 17 Jul 1965; *ST*, 18 Jul 1965.
2. Frederick Ward, GDP/145/1965, 19 Jul 1965; Diana Griffith, GDP/7/1965–9, 19 Jul 1965; *G*, 20 Jul 1965; *T*, 10 May 1999 (Helen Rumbelow); Jonathan Coe, *Like A Fiery Elephant* (2004), p. 196; *Benn*, p. 294; *G*, 22 Jul 1965; *P*, 28 Jul 1965; BBC WAC, R9/7/76–VR/65/396, 21 Jul 1965; Heap, Acc 2243/39/1, 21 Jul 1965; *G*, 23 Jul 1965 ('London letter'); *DT*, 23 Jul 1965; Cairncross, p. 71; Mark Garnett and Ian Aitken, *Splendid! Splendid!* (2002), p. 68; Preston, 6D87/6, 22 Jul 1965, fo. 1434; James Allen, GDP/172/1965–66, 22 Jul 1965; Sheila Rowbotham, *Promise of a Dream* (2019), p. 100.
3. *DT*, 22 Jul 1965; BBC WAC, R9/7/76–VR/65/397, 22 Jul 1965; Marks, 22 Jul 1965; Simon Heffer, *Like the Roman* (1998), p. 382; *The Cecil King Diary, 1965–1970* (1972), p. 25; *ES*, 24 Jul 1965 (John Clarke); *Crossman*, p. 286; *ES*, 23 Jul 1965.
4. Scott, SxMOA99/97/1/14, 24 Jul 1965; Kennetta Hammond Perry, *London Is The Place For Me* (2015), p. 211; *T*, 26 Jul 1965; Keith McBride, GDP/379/1964–1965, 25

Jul 1965; Larkin, Ms. Eng. c. 7430, 25 Jul 1965, fo. 125; John Campell, *Edward Heath* (1993), p. 182; *Benn*, p. 299; Sir Gerald Nabarro, *NAB 1* (Oxford, 1969), p. 58; Last, 26 Jul 1965.

5. *Crossman*, p. 290; *T*, 28 Jul 1965; *Castle*, p. 27; *Crossman*, p. 291; *Benn*, p. 301; *NS*, 30 Jul 1965; *P*, 4 Aug 1965 (Francis Williams); Lewis Baston, *Reggie* (Stroud, 2004), pp. 260–3.

6. Heap, Acc 2243/39/1, 27 Jul 1965; Keith McBride, GDP/379/1964–1965, 27 Jul 1965; *Benn*, p. 301; *Crossman*, pp. 292–3; D. R. Thorpe, *Supermac* (2010), p. 597; *P*, 4 Aug 1965 (Francis Williams); Lord Hill of Luton, *Both Sides of the Hill* (1964), pp. 241–2; Heffer, p. 385; Campbell, p. 181; Charles Moore, *Margaret Thatcher*: Volume One (2013), p. 178; Baston, pp. 254–5; Edward du Cann, *Two Lives* (Upton upon Severn, 1995), pp. 113–14.

7. *G*, 28 Jul 1965; *ST*, 18 Jul 1965; Heffer, pp. 380–2; *New Soc*, 22 Jul 1965; *P*, 4 Aug 1965; *Ob*, 21 Mar 1965 (Colin McGlashan).

8. Sheila Patterson, *Immigration and Race Relations in Britain, 1960–1967* (1969), p. 43; *Crossman*, p. 299; Robert J. Wybrow, *Britain Speaks Out, 1937–87* (Basingstoke, 1989), p. 76; Keith McBride, GDP/379/1964–1965, 2 Aug 1965.

9. Janet Street-Porter, *Baggage* (2004), pp. 222–3; BBC WAC, R9/7/76–VR/65/412, 30 Jul 1965; Brian Henry (ed.), *British Television Advertising: The First 30 Years* (1986), p. 107; https://www.strawbsweb.co.uk/progs/camb65.asp; *Ob*, 1 Aug 1965; Campbell, pp. 191–2; *G*, 24 Aug 2019 ('The late August bank holiday comes too late'); *DM (1)*, 3 Aug 1965; Scott, SxMOA99/97/1/14, 2–3 Aug 1965; *Crossman*, pp. 300–1.

10. *New Soc*, 12 Aug 1965; *Cecil King Diary*, p. 27; *Crossman*, p. 305–6; *Kynaston*, pp. 313–14; *DM (1)*, 11 Aug 1965.

11. 'Rick Parfitt', *T*, 26 Dec 2016; Ivan Hewett, 'Sir Harrison Birtwistle', *G*, 19 Apr 2022; *Wikipedia*, 'Allan Smethurst'; Donovan Leitch, *The Hurdy Gurdy Man* (2005), p. 106; *G*, 28 Oct 2016 (Alex Godfrey); Cliff Goodwin, *When the Wind Changed* (1999), pp. 400–1; David Lister, *In the Best Possible Taste* (1996), p. 38; Danny Baker, *Going to Sea in a Sieve* (2012), p. 49; John Cooper Clarke, *I Wanna Be Yours* (2020), pp. 172–3; Kwaku, 'Notting Hill Carnival: The Genesis Story' (online).

12. Hazel Holt and Hilary Pym (eds), Barbara Pym, *A Very Private Eye* (1984), p. 330; Hilary du Pré and Piers du Pré, *A Genius in the Family* (1997), p. 171; *Ob*, 22 Aug 1965 (Penelope Gilliatt); *DM (1)*, 20 Aug 1965; *Spec*, 27 Aug 1965 (David Benedictus); *DT*, 20 Aug 1965 (W. A. Darlington); Stephen Fay, *Power Play* (1995), p. 179; *DM (1)*, 14 Aug 1965; *NME*, 20 Aug 1965.

13. *Wikipedia*, 'Keith Peacock'; Antony Thwaite (ed.), *Selected Letters of Philip Larkin* (1992), p. 376; *G*, 25 Aug 1965; Scott, SxMOA99/97/1/14, 25 Aug 1965; Frederick Ward, GDP/145/1965, 26 Aug 1965; *Salford City Reporter*, 27 Aug 1965; *ES*, 28 Aug 1965; Julia Cook (née McLaughlin), GDP/373/1965, 28 Aug 1965; BBC WAC, R9/7/76–VR/65/463, 28 Aug 1965; Heap, Acc 2243/39/1, 30 Aug 1965; *DM (1)*, 1 Sep 1965.

14. *Castle*, p. 32; Robert Taylor, 'The trade union "problem" in the Age of Consensus, 1960–1979', in Ben Pimlott and Chris Cook (eds), *Trade Unions in British Politics* (Harlow, 1991 edn), pp. 183–4; *G*, 9 Sep 1965.

15. *LRB*, 6 Sep 2007 (David Cannadine); *DM (1)*, 7 Sep 1965; Paul Sutton (ed.), Lindsay Anderson, *The Diaries* (2004), p. 134; Scott, SxMOA99/97/1/14, 7 Sep 1965; NVLAA, Box 39; *NS*, 10 Sep 1965; Darlington, 10 Sep 1965; James Allen, GDP/172/1965–66, 12 Sep 1965; Julia Cook (née McLaughlin), GDP/373/1965, 13 Sep 1965; Heap, Acc

2243/39/1, 13 Sep 1965; *Sun*, 15 Sep 1965; *Crossman*, p. 327; Kevin Cann, *Any Day Now* (2010), p. 64; *Vogue*, 15 Sep 1965.

16. *G*, 17 Sep 1965; *Benn*, p. 321; *Spec*, 17 Sep 1965; BC WAC, *Any Questions?*, 10 Sep 1965; Andrew Rosthorn, 'The Proof: Paul Simon, Homeward Bound and Widnes Station' (online, sent by the author in Jan 2024).

CHAPTER 5 IS THAT ALL?

1. 'Rowley Atterbury', *T*, 9 Apr 2011; *G*, 17 Dec 1965; *S Tel*, 12 Sep 1965; Margaret Drabble, *The Millstone* (1965), pp. 19, 27; Simon Raven, 'Class and the Contemporary Novel' in Richard Mabey (ed.), *Class* (1967), p. 119; Michael Frayn, 'Festival', in Michael Sissons and Philip French (eds), *Age of Austerity* (Oxford, 1986 edn), pp. 307–8. See also about *The Millstone*: D. J. Taylor, *After the War* (1993), pp. 163–6; *G*, 19 Mar 2011 (Margaret Drabble).
2. Peter Catterall (ed.), *The Macmillan Diaries*: Volume II (2011), p. 552; *T*, 16 Sep 1965; William J. Mann, *Edge of Midnight* (2004), p. 247; *S Tel*, 19 Sep 1965; *TLS*, 5 Aug 2022 (Graham Daseler, reviewing Melvyn Stokes et al., *Cinema Memories*).
3. Anthony Blond, 'Lord Goodman', *Ind*, 15 May 1995; Brian Brivati, *Lord Goodman* (1999), chaps 7–9; Fiona MacCarthy, 'Robert Harling', *G*, 2 Jul 2008; Artemis Cooper, *Elizabeth David* (1999), pp. 237–50; Juliet Gardiner, *Joining the Dots* (2017), pp. 107–10; 'Iris Murdoch', *T*, 9 Feb 1999; David Jays, 'Jocelyn Rickards', *G*, 14 Jul 2005; Liz Thomson, 'Tom Maschler', *G*, 17 Oct 2020; Phil Baines, 'Germano Facetti', *Ind*, 15 Apr 2006; John Sutherland, 'Karl Miller', *G*, 27 Sep 2014; 'Sir Jonathan Miller', *T*, 28 Nov 2019; Philip Purser, 'Robert Robinson', *G*, 15 Aug 2011; Eric Homberger, 'George Steiner', *G*, 8 Feb 2020; Michael Billington, *The Life and Work of Harold Pinter* (1996), p. 162; James Stourton, *Kenneth Clark* (2016), p. 316.
4. BFI, *screenonline*, 'Late Night Line-Up'; Allen Eyles, 'Ivo Jarosy', *Ind*, 7 May 1996; Robertson/Russell/Snowdon, *Private View* (Edinburgh, 1965), pp. 295, 3; Viv Albertine, *To Throw Away Unopened* (2018), pp. 222–3; P. H. Mann, 'Surveying a Theatre Audience', *British Journal of Sociology*, Mar 1967, pp. 75–90.
5. Kevin Cann, *Any Day Now* (2010), p. 64; *MM*, 18 Sep 1965; *NME*, 17 Sep 1965; Julia Cook (née McLaughlin), GDP/373/1965, 18 Sep 1965; *T*, 18 Sep 1965; Frank Lewis (Glamorgan Record Office), D51/1/220, 19 Sep 1965; Frederick Ward, GDP/145/1965, 18 Sep 1965; Scott, SxMOA99/97/1/14, 19 Sep 1965; Cann, p. 64; *S Tel*, 26 Sep 1965; *Illustrated London News*, 2 Oct 1965; Lewis, 22 Sep 1965; *L*, 23 Sep 1965; Tom Jaine, 'Derek Cooper', *G*, 21 Apr 2014; Michael McManus, *Jo Grimond* (Edinburgh, 2001), p. 237.
6. Tony Shaw, 'The BBC, the State and Cold War Culture', in *English Historical Review*, Dec 2006, p. 1, 366; Diana Griffith, GDP/7/1965–9, 24 Sep 1965; Brian Simon, *A Life in Education* (1998), p. 103; *Benn*, p. 324; BBC WAC, *Any Questions?*, 24 Sep 1965; *T*, 25 Sep 1965.
7. Grace Taylor, GDP/318/1965, 25 Sep 1965; Diana Griffith, GDP/7/1965–9, 25 Sep 1965; diary of Celia Kent, 26–7 Sep 1965; Haines, SxMOA99/34/8/18, 28 Sep 1965; BBC WAC, R9/7/77–VR/65/532, 28 Sep 1965, R9/7/77–VR/65/534, 28 Sep 1965; *DT*, 29 Sep 1965; Anne Francis, *Julian Wintle* (1986), p. 85; *ST*, 26 Sep 1965; Anthony Hayward, 'Laurie Johnson', *G*, 24 Feb 2024; Francis, p. 85; *Ob*, 3 Oct 1965; *ST*, 3 Oct

1965; Anthony Hayward, 'David Graham', *G*, 23 Sep 2024; Simon Farquhar, 'Sylvia Anderson', *Ind*, 17 Mar 2016; 'Sylvia Anderson', *DT*, 17 Mar 2016.

8. Wendy Pollard, *Pamela Hansford Johnson* (2014), pp. 364–5; *Crossman*, p. 337; 'Peter Townend', *T*, 18 Jul 2001; *Benn*, p. 329; *Crossman*, p. 339; *Ob*, 27 Nov 2016 (Rachel Reeves); *Crossman*, p. 333; *Spec*, 1 Oct 1965; *E*, 2 Oct 1965.

9. *AR*, Oct 1965, p. 311; *Fowles (1)*, p. 642; *Sun*, 2 Oct 1965; *G*, 13 Mar 2018 (Alexis Petridis); Frederick Ward, GDP/145/1965, 2 Oct 1965; *DM (1)*, 4 Oct 1965; Celia Kent, 3–4 Oct 1965; David Hendy, *Life on Air* (Oxford, 2007), p. 48; BBC WAC, R9/7/77–VR/65/546, 4 Oct 1965; *DT*, 5 Oct 1965 (Norman Hare); Anthony Hayward, 'Maggie Fitzgibbon', *G*, 9 Jul 2020; 'Wendy Richard', *Ind*, 27 Feb 2009; BBC WAC, R9/7/77 – VR/65/550, 5 Oct 1965; *Wikipedia*, 'The War Game'; Jimmy Hill, *My Autobiography* (1998), p. 130; 'David Smith', *DT*, 2 Jul 2012; Carol Ann Lee, *One of Your Own* (Edinburgh, 2010), chaps 15–16.

10. John Prescott, *Prezza* (2008), p. 81; Anderson, *Diaries* (2004), p. 138; Betty Allen, GDP/450/1963–67, 7 Oct 1965; John Caughie, 'Progressive Television and Documentary Drama', in Tony Bennett et al. (eds), *Popular Television and Film* (1981), p. 331; *DT*, 8 Oct 1965; *T*, 21 Oct 1994 (Peter Waymark); *Ind*, 14 Aug 2001 (Jay Merrick); *ES*, 21 Feb 2024 (Jonathan Prynn); *DT*, 12 Oct 1965, 11 Oct 1965 (Donald Saunders); *Sun*, 11 Oct 1965, 13 Oct 1965; *P*, 13 Oct 1965; *G*, 15 Oct 1965; *NME*, 15 Oct 1965; *DM (1)*, 15 Oct 1965; Scott, SxMOA99/97/1/14, 12–15 Oct 1965.

11. *NS*, 15 Oct 1965; *Crossman*, p. 352; *DM (1)*, 11 Oct 1965; *New Soc*, 14 Oct 1965.

12. James Allen, GDP/172/1965–66, 8 Oct 1965; Sir Gerald Nabarro, *NAB 1* (Oxford, 1969), p. 243; *S Tel*, 17 Oct 1965; James Allen, GDP/172/1965–66, 23 Oct 1965; *DT*, 27 Oct 1965; *Crossman*, p. 361; Ben Pimlott, *Harold Wilson* (1992), p. 371; *S Tel*, 31 Oct 1965.

13. *T*, 21 Sep 2021 (Henry Winter); *Crossman*, p. 351; Robert Brown, *Basingstoke* (Chichester, 1994), unpaginated; BBC WAC, R9/7/77–VR/65/583, 17 Oct 1965; Keith McBride, GDP/379/1964–65, 17 Oct 1965; *Crossman*, p. 352; *RT*, 14 Oct 1965; *Sun*, 19 Oct 1965; *RT*, 14 Oct 1965; St John, 68/50, 19 Oct 1965; *RT*, 14 Oct 1965; *Ob*, 24 Oct 1965 (Nigel Gosling); *G*, 6 Nov 1965 (Norbert Lynton); *Sun*, 21 Oct 1965; *RT*, 14 Oct 1965; Martin Johnes, *Wales Since 1939* (Manchester, 2012), p. 233; *T*, 23 Oct 1965; *G*, 23 Oct 1965; *G*, 30 Oct 1965; *G*, 30 Dec 2008 (George Monbiot); Richard King, *Brittle with Relics* (2022), p. 39.

14. *Spec*, 22 Oct 1965; *RT*, 14 Oct 1965; Keith McBride, GDP/379/1964–65, 22 Oct 1965; Jonathan Coe, *Like a Fiery Elephant* (2004), pp. 201–2; Kenneth Roy, *The Invisible Spirit* (Prestwick, 2013), pp. 333–4; Scott, SxMOA99/97/1/14, 23 Oct 1965; *T*, 27 Oct 1965; *G*, 26 Oct 1965; *Sun*, 26 Oct 1965; Avril Sandall, GDP/343/1965, 25 Oct 1965; *G*, 26 Oct 1965; *DM (1)*, 26 Oct 1965; Hague, 27 Oct 1965; *Sun*, 27 Oct 1965; Robert Dougall, *In and Out of the Box* (1973), pp. 257–9; *G*, 11 Nov 2009 (Hunter Davies).

15. Haines, SxMOA99/34/8/18, 26 Oct 1965; *Edinburgh Live*, 13 Nov 2022 (David McLean); *Sun*, 27 Oct 1965; *NME*, 29 Oct 1965; Frederick Ward, GDP/145/1965, 29 Oct 1965; *Partridge*, p. 181; Lee, 29 Oct 1965; Martin Westlake, *Kinnock* (2001), p. 42; Neville Braybrooke (ed.), *The Letters of J. R. Ackerley* (1975), p. 276; *Sun*, 30 Oct 1965; *Ob*, 31 Oct 1965; *DM (1)*, 1 Nov 1965.

16. *DT*, 4 Nov 2014; *G* 2 Nov 1965 (Michael Parkin); 'Corriepedia' (online), Episode 510; *Benn*, p. 343; Hodgson, 3 Nov 1965; *DM (1)*, 4 Nov 1965; Michael Billington, *State of the Nation* (2007), p. 183; *DM (1)*, 4 Nov 1965 (Peter Lewis); Heap, Acc 2243/39/1, 3 Nov 1965; *T*, 4 Nov 1965; *DT*, 4 Nov 1965; *D Ex*, 4 Nov 1965; *New Soc*, 25 Nov 1965 (Irving Wardle); *G*, 9 Sep 2006.

17. *ST*, 7 Nov 1965; Anthony Hayward, *Which Side Are You On?* (2004), p. 53; Clair Wills, 'Quickening or How to Plot an Abortion', in *LRB*, 16 Mar 2023; BBC WAC, R9/7/78–VR/65/619, 3 Nov 1965; Nigel Smurthwaite, 'Carol White', *Ind*, 5 Oct 1991; *NS*, 12 Nov 1965; *ST*, 7 Nov 1965; *DM (2)*, 4 Nov 1965; *Sun*, 4 Nov 1965; Hayward, p. 58; *Sun*, 5 Nov 1965; Hayward, p. 58; *Ob*, 7 Nov 1965.
18. *Country Life*, 4 Nov 1965; *G*, 4 Nov 1954; *Sun*, 6 Nov 1965; Geoffrey Wansell, *An Evil Love* (1996), p. 47; Daniel Percival, 'John Percival', *Ind*, 9 Feb 2005; Avril Sandall, GDP/343/1965, 4 Nov 1965; *G*, 5 Nov 1965; *DM (1)*, 5 Nov 1965; *T*, 6 Nov 1965: Adam Sharr and Stephen Thornton, *Demolishing Whitehall* (Farnham, 2013), p. 229; Johnes, *Wales*, p. 99; Leonard Miall (ed.), *Richard Dimbleby, Broadcaster* (1966), pp. 165–6; Last, 5 Nov 1965.
19. *Williams*, p. 266; *G*, 5 Nov 2005 (Sean Magee), 8 Nov 1965; *T*, 29 Sep 2023 (Keith Elliott); Marks, 6 Nov 1965; *Ob*, 7 Nov 1965; *ST*, 7 Nov 1965; *DT*, 8 Nov 1965; Roy Galton and Alan Simpson, *Steptoe and Son* (2002), p. 112; *DM (1)*, 10 Nov 1965; *T*, 10 Nov 1965; Nicholas Hilman, 'The Public Schools Commission', in *Contemporary British History*, Dec 2010, p. 514; Gerald T. Rimmington, *The Comprehensive Issue in Leicester 1945–1974 and other essays* (Peterborough, 1984), p. 18; Haines, SxMOA99/34/8/18, 9 Nov 1965.
20. *DM (1)*, 10 Nov 1965; *G*, 10 Nov 1965; *T*, 10 Nov 1965; *Sun*, 10 Nov 1965; Heap, Acc 2243/39/1, 10 Nov 1965; *D Ex*, 11 Nov 1965; Grace Taylor, GDP/318/1965, 10 Nov 1965; Frederick Ward, GDP/145/1965, 11 Nov 1965.
21. Lee, 11 Nov 1965; *Sun*, 12 Nov 1965; Austin Mitchell and David Wienir, *Last Time* (1997), pp. 180–1; *The Cecil King Diary, 1965–1970* (1972), pp. 42–3; Patrick Cosgrave, 'Lord Amery of Lustleigh', *Ind*, 5 Sep 1996; *DT*, 16 Nov 1965; *DM (1)*, 15 Nov 1965, 18 Nov 1965; Hodgson, 10 Nov 1965; *Pontefract and Castleford Express*, 18 Nov 1965.
22. *Ob*, 14 Nov 1965; Haines, SxMOA99/34/8/18, 13 Nov 1965; Kathleen Tynan, *The Life of Kenneth Tynan* (1987), p. 236; *NS*, 19 Nov 1965 (D. A. N. Jones); *Spec*, 19 Nov 1965 (Stuart Hood); Joe Moran, *Armchair Nation* (2013), p. 7; Marks, 13 Nov 1965; *Ob*, 14 Nov 1965; *Sun*, 16 Nov 1965; *G*, 13 Oct 2012 (Allan Jones); *T*, 15 Nov 1965; *New Soc*, 25 Nov 1965 (Irving Wardle); Tynan, *Tynan*, p. 237; *Sun*, 16 Nov 1965; Ned Sherrin, *A Small Thing – Like an Earthquake* (1983), p. 113; *D Ex*, 16 Nov 1965; *G*, 1 Feb 2019 (Mark Brown); *T*, 20 Apr 2022 (David Smith); *G*, 18 Nov 1965; Frederick Ward, GDP/145/1965, 18 Nov 1965.
23. *G*, 15 Nov 1965; *Benn*, p. 350; *G*, 17 Nov 1965; Dennis Dean, 'Circular 10/65 Revisited', in *Paedagogica Historica*, 1998 (1), p. 89; Kevin Jefferys, *Anthony Crosland* (1999), p. 107.
24. Daphne Meryon, GDP/44/1965, 19 Nov 1965; BBC WAC, *Any Questions?*, 19 Nov 1965; *Sun*, 20 Nov 1965; Larkin, Ms. Eng. c. 7431, 20 Nov 1965, fos 91–2; Grace Taylor, GDP/318/1965, 20 Nov 1965; Daphne Meryon, GDP/44/1965, 20 Nov 1965; Heap, Acc 2243/39/1, 21 Nov 1965; Daphne Meryon, GDP/44/1965, 21 Nov 1965.
25. *Crossman*, pp. 345, 363–4, 376–7, 382–3; *E*, 27 Nov 1965; *DT*, 25 Nov 1965; *T*, 25 Nov 1965; *E*, 27 Nov 1965; *G*, 25 Nov 1965.
26. *Sun*, 26 Nov 1965; *Castle*, p. 34; *G*, 26 Nov 1965; *Ob*, 28 Nov 1965; *DT*, 27 Nov 1965; Scott, SxMOA99/97/1/14, 27 Nov 1965; Guy Atkins, 'Alvin Atkins', *G*, 22 Jul 2019; BBC WAC, *Any Questions?*, 26 Nov 1965; *NS*, 26 Nov 1965.
27. *DT*, 30 Nov 1965; Mary Whitehouse, *A Most Dangerous Woman?* (Tring, 1982), p. 70; *Bonham Carter*, p. 305; John Clay, *R. D. Laing* (1996), pp. 117–18; Brian Simon,

Education and the Social Order, 1940–1990 (1991), p. 251; David Crook, 'Edward Boyle', in *History of Education*, Mar 1993, p. 54; *T*, 2 Dec 1965; *TLS*, 2 Dec 1965 (Douglas Hewitt); *Sun*, 3 Dec 1965 (David Nathan); *G*, 3 Dec 1965 (Peter Jenkin); *MM*, 4 Dec 1965; *NME*, 10 Dec 1965 (Alan Smith).

28. Tony Jasper, *The Top Twenty Book* (1994 edn), pp. 112–14; *G*, 4 Dec 1965; *Sun*, 4 Dec 1965; *Ob*, 5 Dec 1965; Preston, 6D87/6, 5 Dec 1965, fo. 1463; Haines, SxMOA99/34/8/18, 5 Dec 1965; Mark Lewisohn, *The Complete Beatles Chronicle* (1996), p. 209; *S Tel*, 5 Dec 1965; Olive Cook, *The Stansted Affair* (1967), pp. 31–3; Lee, *One of Your Own*, p. 261; *G*, 8 Dec 1965; Lewisohn, *Beatles*, p. 209; Lee, *One of Your Own*, pp. 75–6.
29. *Wikipedia*, 'Race Relations Act, 1965'; *Sun*, 9 Dec 1965; W. Stephen Gilbert, *Fight and Kick and Bite* (1995), p. 131; Humphrey Carpenter, *Dennis Potter* (1998), pp. 169, 172; *Sun*, 9 Dec 1965; BBC WAC, R9/7/78–VR/65/689, 8 Dec 1965; *TLS*, 9 Dec 1965; James Allen, GDP/172/1965–66, 9 Dec 1965; Betty Allen, GDP/540/1963–67, 9 Dec 1965.
30. *NS*, 10 Dec 1965; *G*, 28 Jul 2025 (Dalya Alberge); Scott, SxMOA99/97/1/14, 10 Dec 1965; Rogan Taylor and Andrew Ward, *Kicking and Screaming* (1995), p. 258; Frederick Ward, GDP/145/1965, 11 Dec 1965; *Ob*, 12 Dec 1965; *Benn*, p. 358; Lewisohn, *Beatles*, p. 209; *G*, 13 Dec 1965; Carpenter, *Potter*, p. 173; *Benn* p. 359; *Wikipedia*, 'List of *Jackanory* episodes'; Anthony Hayward, 'Barbara Murray', *G*, 6 Jun 2014; Lee, *One of Your Own*, p. 262; Jeremy Gavron, *A Woman on the Edge of Time* (2015), pp. 1–3; *Sun*, 15 Dec 1965.
31. *G*, 15 Dec 1965; *Sun*, 15 Dec 1965; *DM (1)*, 16 Dec 1965; Lee, *One of Your Own*, pp. 262–3; Diana Griffith, GDP/7/1965–69, 15 Dec 1965; Keith McBride, GDP/379/1965–68, 15 Dec 1965; Heap, Acc 2243/39/1, 15 Dec 1965; *DM (1)*, 16 Dec 1965; *Sun*, 16 Dec 1965; Dennis Potter, *The Nigel Barton Plays* (Harmondsworth, 1967), p. 121; Carpenter, *Potter*, p. 172; *P*, 22 Dec 1965; BBC WAC, R9/7/78–VR/65/702, 15 Dec 1965.
32. Diana Griffith, GDP/7/1965–69, 16 Dec 1965; Anthony Hayward, 'Anthony Simmons'), *G*, 11 Mar 2016; *Ob*, 19 Dec 1965; Lee, *One of Your Own*, p. 263; BBC WAC, *Any Questions?*, 17 Dec 1965; *NS*, 31 Dec 1965.
33. *Ob*, 19 Dec 1965; *DT*, 20 Dec 1965; *DM (1)*, 21 Dec 1965; *G*, 21 Dec 1965; *Wikipedia*, 'List of Jackanory Episodes'; Miall, *Dimbleby*, p. 166; *Sun*, 21 Dec 1965; *T*, 21 Dec 1965; *DT*, 21 Dec 1965 (W. A. Darlington); *G*, 21 Dec 1965 (Benedict Nightingale); *DM (2)*, 21 Dec 1965 (Arthur Thirkell); *Sun*, 21 Dec 1965; *DM (1)*, 21 Dec 1965 (Bernard Levin); *DM (2)*, 21 Dec 1965 (Thirkell); Heap, Acc 2243/39/1, 20 Dec 1965; Tom Vallance, 'Lionel Bart', *Ind*, 5 Apr 1999; Peter Rankin, *Joan Littlewood* (2014), p. 168; *G*, 22 Dec 1965; Frederick Ward, GDP/145/1965, 21 Dec 1965; *Sun*, 22 Dec 1965; Stuart Laing, 'Banging in Some Reality', in John Corner (ed.), *Popular Television in Britain* (1991), pp. 142–3.
34. John Campbell, *Edward Heath* (1993), p. 205; John Campbell, *Roy Jenkins* (2014), pp. 255–6; *Sun*, 23 Dec 1965; *G*, 27 May 2003 (Anne Perkins); *DM (1)*, 23 Dec 1965; *T*, 23 Dec 1965; Francis Green and David Kynaston, *Engines of Privilege* (2019), p. 43; *T*, 23 Dec 1965; Simon, *Education and the Social Order*, pp. 322, 340; *Sun*, 23 Dec 1965.
35. Richard Burton, *A Strong Song Tows Us* (Oxford, 2013), p. 396; *DT*, 23 Dec 1965; Hayward, *Which Side?*, p. 48; Mark Lewisohn, *Radio Times Guide to TV Comedy* (2003 edn), pp. 383–4; *DM (1)*, 23 Dec 1965; Marks, 22 Dec 1965; James Allen, GDP/172/1965–66, 22 Dec 1965; Marks, 22 Dec 1965; *Sun*, 23 Dec 1965.

CHAPTER 6 BAKED BEANS FOR US

1. *Sun*, 23 Dec 1965; Michael Sullivan, *The Politics of Social Policy* (Hemel Hempstead, 1993), p. 122; *G*, 23 Dec 1965; Pat Thane, *Divided Kingdom* (Cambridge, 2018), p. 268; *G*, 24 Dec 1965; Pat Thane and Ruth Davidson, *The Child Poverty Action Group* (2016), pp. 6–9; Frank Field, 'Harriett Wilson', *G*, 26 Jul 2002; *G*, 24 Dec 1965; Thane and Davidson, p. 10; *RT*, 16 Dec 1965; Thane and Davidson, p. 10.
2. *NS*, 31 Dec 1965; *Crossman*, pp. 204, 276–7; Stephen Thornton, 'A Case of Confusion and Incoherence', in *Contemporary British History*, Sep 2006, p. 449; *Crossman*, pp. 410–11.
3. David Vincent, *Poor Citizens* (Harlow, 1991), pp. 162–3; *G*, 18 Jan 1966, 22 Mar 1965, 18 Sep 1965; Nicholas Timmins, *The Five Giants* (2001 edn), p. 257.
4. *G*, 22 May 1969 (Ann Shearer); *TLS*, 24 Jul 1969 (Sheila Jackson); Dennis Marsden, *Mothers Alone* (Harmondsworth, 1973 Pelican edn), pp. 38–73.
5. Last, 1 Jan 1966; Keith McBride, GDP/379/1965–68, 2 Jan 1966; Leonard Miall (ed.), *Richard Dimbleby* (1966), pp. 170–2; Hodgson, 13 Jan 1966.
6. Brandreth, pp. 96–7; *Castle*, p. 49; Anne Perkins, *Red Queen* (2003), p. 214; Larkin, Ms. Eng. c. 7432, 23 Jan 1966, fo. 39, 25 Jan 1966, fos 43–4; Tariq Ali, *Street Fighting Years* (2005), p. 136; *Benn*, p. 380; Paul Foot, *The Politics of Harold Wilson* (Harmondsworth, 1968), p. 165. On the by-election, see also: *LRB*, 4 Dec 2025 (Tom White).
7. Michael Newman, *Ralph Miliband and the Politics of the New Left* (2002), pp. 110–12; Ali, pp. 136–7; *G*, 1 Feb 2006; Perry Anderson, 'Socialism and Pseudo-Empiricism', in *New Left Review*, Jan–Feb 1966.
8. *G*, 26 Jan 1966; Geoffrey Owen, *The Rise and Fall of Great Companies* (Oxford, 2010), p. 87; *Ob*, 30 Jan 1966; *G*, 26 Jan 1966; *FT*, 26 Jan 1966; *T*, 26 Jan 1966; *DT*, 26 Jan 1966; *G*, 26 Jan 1966, 28 Jan 1966; *Ob*, 30 Jan 1966; *ST*, 30 Jan 1966.
9. Andrew Taylor, *The NUM and British Politics*: Volume 1 (Aldershot, 2003), p. 216; Clive Jenkins Papers (MRC), 79/6/CJ/3/24a; Keith McBride, GDP/379/1965–68, 9–10 Feb 1966; Heap, Acc 2243/040, 11 Feb 1966; Turtle, D103/1/31, 12 Feb 1966; Geoffrey Goodman, 'Lord Greene of Harrow Weald', *G*, 28 Jul 2004; *Castle*, pp. 55–6; Linda McDougall, *Marcia Williams* (2023), p. 103.
10. *Wikipedia*, 'Adlestrop railway station'; *BBC News*, 'Leicester Forest East service station marks 50th birthday', 14 Feb 2016; *T*, 26 Jan 1966; Barbara Weinberger, *The Best Police in the World* (Aldershot, 1995), pp. 72–4; Berry Ritchie, 'Sir Freddie Laker', *Ind*, 11 Feb 2006; 'Sir Freddie Laker', *T*, 11 Feb 2006; *DT*, 9 Feb 1966.
11. *NS*, 7 Jan 1966, 14 Jan 1966; *G*, 18 Feb 1966; John Vaizey, *Education for Tomorrow* (Harmondsworth, 1966 edn), p. 47; *G*, 18 Feb 1966; Brian Simon, *Education and the Social Order, 1940–1990* (1991), p. 322; *G*, 22 Feb 1966; *Hansard*, 23 Feb 1966, cols 229, 246, 275, 320, 323.
12. *G*, 8 Jan 1966; Nirmala Rao, 'Labour and Education', in *Contemporary British History*, summer 2002, p. 111; David Crook, 'Edward Boyle', in *History of Education*, 1993, p. 54; *New Soc*, 27 Jan 1966; Caroline Benn and Brian Simon, *Half Way There* (Harmondsworth, 1972 edn), p. 76; Leeds City Council, *Agendas & Verbatim Reports, 1966*, 5 Jan 1966.
13. *ST*, 13 Feb 1966; *Partridge*, p. 199; *G*, 12–13 Feb 1966; *DT*, 12 Feb 1966; *Castle*, p. 54; 'Colm Brogan', *DT*, 29 Jan 1977, 'Mr Colm Brogan', *T*, 29 Jan 1977; *DT*, 18 Feb 1966.

14. *S Tel*, 30 Jan 1966 (Michael Pearson); *G*, 9 Jan 1966; *DT*, 4 Feb 1966; *G*, 10 Feb 1966; Keith Hindell, *A Guilded Vagabond* (Brighton, 2012), p. 181.
15. *Ob*, 13 Feb 1966, 20 Feb 1966, 27 Feb 1966; *ST*, 23 Jan 1966; *T*, 4 Feb 1966; *Ob*, 6 Feb 1966; *T*, 8 Feb 1966, 16 Feb 1966; *Encounter*, Apr 1966, pp. 51–2. On the Nairn/Esher episode, see also: Otto Saumarez Smith, *Boom Cities* (Oxford, 2019), p. 139.
16. Heap, Acc 2243/040/3 Feb 1966; *T*, 26 Feb 2014 (Dominic Maxwell); *ST*, 6 Feb 1966; *Ob*, 6 Feb 1966 (Penelope Gilliatt); Michael Billington and Mike Leigh, 'David Halliwell', *G*, 22 Mar 2006.
17. 'Bob Bura', *T*, 15 May 2018; *Wikipedia*, 'Watch With Mother'; BBC WAC, R9/7/79–VR/66/10, 5 Jan 1966, VR/66/120, 23 Feb 1966; Susan Sydney-Smith, *Beyond Dixon of Dock Green* (2002), pp. 181–91; BBC WAC, R9/7/79 – VR/66/11, 5 Jan 1966; *NS*, 25 Feb 1966 (John Holmstrom); Harry Thompson, *Peter Cook* (1997), p. 197; Anthony Hayward, 'Leslie Duxbury', *Ind*, 21 Oct 2005; Last, 26 Jan 1966.
18. Kevin Cann, *Any Day Now* (2010), p. 71; 'Spencer Davis', *T*, 21 Oct 2020; Andrew Barrow, *Gossip* (1978), p. 250; *NME*, 11 Feb 1966; Johnny Rogan, *Ray Davies* (2015), pp. 256–7; *NME*, 25 Feb 1966 (Derek Johnson); *MM*, 26 Feb 1966; *G*, 5 Apr 2014.
19. *RT*, 27 Jan 1966; *G*, 30 May 2017; *ST*, 20 Feb 1966; Heap, Acc 2243/040, 16 Feb 1966; Twiggy Lawson, *Twiggy* (1997), pp. 47–8; *G*, 3 Sep 2001 (Emma Brockes); *NS*, 26 Apr 2013 (Philip Maughan); *G*, 24 Feb 1966.
20. Langford, S/GHL/1, 12 Jan 1966; Haines, SxMOA99/34/8/19, 13 Jan 1966; St John, 68/50, 18 Jan 1966; Haines, SxMOA99/34/8/19, 19 Jan 1966; Keith McBride, GDP/379/1965–68, 19 Jan 1966; Diana Griffith, GDP/7/1965–69, 27 Jan 1966; *Williams*, p. 273; Heap, Acc 2243/040, 14 Feb 1966; Scott, SxMOA99/97/1/15, 19 Feb 1966; Betty Allen, GDP/450/1963–67, 19 Feb 1966; Frederick Ward, GDP/145/1966, 19 Feb 1966; Betty Allen, GDP/450/1963–67, 20 Feb 1966; Last, 24 Feb 1966; Turtle, D103/1/31, 27 Feb 1966; Frederick Ward, GDP/145/1966, 1 Mar 1966.

CHAPTER 7 A CHANCE TO CONTINUE

1. James Allen, GDP/172(4)/1966, 1 Mar 1966; Barbara Hulanicki, *From A to Biba* (1983), p. 88; Turtle, D103/1/31, 1 Mar 1966; Kenneth O. Morgan, *Callaghan* (Oxford, 1997), pp. 234–5; Haines, SxMOA99/34/8/19, 1 Mar 1966; Diana Griffith, GDP/7/1965–69, 2 Mar 1966; Cliff Goodwin, *When the Wind Changed* (1999), p. 414; *ES*, 4 Mar 1966; Robin Jones, *Beeching: 50 Years of the Axeman* (2011), pp. 64–5; 'Kenneth McKellar', *T*, 17 Apr 2010; Dave Laing, 'Kenneth McKellar', *G*, 13 Apr 2010; *G*, 8 Mar 1966; Harold Wilson, *The Labour Government, 1964–1970* (1971), pp. 216–17; Dick Hobbs, 'Charlie Richardson', *Ind*, 21 Sep 2012; Alan Thornett, *From Militancy to Marxism* (1987), pp. 64–5; Mervyn Jones, *Michael Foot* (1994), p. 295; Thornett, pp. 64–5; *G*, 10 Mar 1966.
2. Winston G. Ramsey, *The East End Then and Now* (Old Harlow, 1997), pp. 504–5; *Kynaston*, pp. 317–18; *T*, 10 Mar 1966; *DM (2)*, 10 Mar 1966; *DM (1)*, 10 Mar 1966; *The Cecil King Diary: 1965–1970* (1972), pp. 60–1; *Crossman*, p. 477; Heap, Acc 2243/040, 10 Mar 1966; John Cleese, *So, Anyway . . .* (2014), pp. 267–70; Marks, 10 Mar 1966; David Frost, *An Autobiography* (1993), pp. 173–7; Derek Schofield, 'Julie Felix'), *G*, 25 Mar 2020; *T*, 11 Mar 1966; *Ob*, 13 Mar 1966; Frost, pp. 181, 186–7.
3. *Sun*, 12 Mar 1966; Thornett, pp. 67–8; *Ob*, 13 Mar 1966; Edward du Cann, *Two Lives* (Upton upon Severn, 1995), p. 127; *G*, 11 Mar 1966; *Benn*, p. 397.

4. Betty Allen, GDP/450/1963–67, 12 Mar 1966; *DT*, 12 Mar 1966 (D.A.W.M.); *T*, 'Christopher Nupen', 11 May 2023; Barry Took with Mat Coward, *The Best of Round the Horne* (2000), p. 58; Kevin Cann, *Any Day Now* (2010), p. 78; *Crossman*, p. 478; *G*, 14 Mar 1966; BBC WAC, R9/7/80–VR/66/154, 14 Mar 1966; *FT*, 15 Mar 1966; *Sun*, 16 Mar 1966; *DM (1)*, 26 Mar 1966; Keith McBride, GDP/379/1965–68, 16 Mar 1966; *G*, 17 Mar 1966, *Sun*, 17 Mar 1966; *New Soc*, 31 Mar 1966 (Colin Seymour-Ure); Heap, Acc 2243/040, 17 Mar 1966; *G*, 17 Mar 2010 (Frank Keating); *L*, 7 Apr 1966; Charles Moore, *Margaret Thatcher*, Volume One (2013), p. 186; BBC WAC, *Any Questions?*, 18 Mar 1966; Frederick Ward, GDP/145/1966, 18 Mar 1966; *From Roots to Boots* (online), 'The First Gig'; *Crossman*, p. 482; *When Saturday Comes*, Jul/Aug 2018, p. 34 (Paul Brown); Marks, 20 Mar 1966; Scott, SxMOA99/97/1/15, 21 Mar 1966; *G*, 23 Mar 1966; *Wikipedia*, 'Jack Hargreaves'; *Sun*, 23 Mar 1966; *T*, 23 Mar 1966; *Sun*, 24 Mar 1966; *T*, 25 Mar 1966.
5. John Hill, *Sex, Class and Realism* (1986), p. 165; *Ob*, 27 Mar 1966; *Sun*, 22 Mar 1966; Virginia Nicholson, *How Was It For You?* (2019), p. 244.
6. D. E. Butler and Anthony King, *The British General Election of 1966* (1966), pp. 204–7; Michael Randle, 'Pat Arrowsmith', *G*, 3 Oct 2023; Kenneth Roy, *The Invisible Spirit* (Prestwick, 2013), p. 351; *G*, 17 May 2017 (Martin Kettle); 'Christopher Frere-Smith', *T*, 9 Nov 2000; Judy Hillman and Peter Clarke, *Geoffrey Howe* (1988), p. 74; 'Baroness Knight of Collingtree', *T*, 13 Apr 2022; 'Baroness Lestor of Eccles', *T*, 30 Mar 1998; Colin Brown, *Fighting Talk* (1997), p. 97; 'Derek "Red Robbo" Robinson', *DT*, 1 Nov 2017; Ben Savill, 'Dudley Savill', *G*, 2 Feb 2023; 'Ben Whitaker', *DT*, 13 Oct 2014; Lawrence Daly Papers (MRC), 302/3/4, 5 Apr 1966 (Dalyell); Rosa Prince, *Comrade Corbyn* (2016), p. 30.
7. *NS*, 25 Mar 1966; Paul Foot, *The Rise of Enoch Powell* (Harmondsworth, 1969), p. 92; *Ob*, 20 Mar 1966 (Colin McGlashan); Butler and King, p. 252 (James Byrne); Foot, *Powell*, p. 94; *Ob*, 20 Mar 1966 (McGlashan); Butler and King, p. 105; *Sun*, 21 Mar 1966.
8. *T*, 25 Mar 1966; John Campbell, *Margaret Thatcher*, Volume One (2000), p. 167; Simon Courtauld, *To Convey Intelligence* (1999), p. 120; Geoffrey Goodman, *The Awkward Warrior* (1979), pp. 484–5; 'Reg Tweedie', *DT*, 2 Aug 1999; *DT*, 28 Mar 1966; D. R. Thorpe (ed.), Kenneth Rose, *Who's In, Who's Out* (2018), p. 323; Frederick Ward, GDP/145/1966, 26 Mar 1966; *T*, 29 Mar 1966; *When Saturday Comes*, Jul/Aug 2018, p. 34 (Paul Brown); Heap, Acc 2243/040, 28 Mar 1966; *T*, 29 Mar 1966; BBC WAC, R9/7/80–VR/66/175, 29 Mar 1966; *FT*, 30 Mar 1966; Haines, SxMOA99/34/8/19, 30 Mar 1966; Keith McBride, GDP/379/1965–68, 30 Mar 1966.
9. *Williams*, p. 275; Daphne Meryon, GDP/44/1966, 31 Mar 1966; Lee, 31 Mar 1966; Frederick Ward, GDP/145/1966, 31 Mar 1966; diary of Elsie Johnston (records of Yorkshire Archaeological and Historical Society, Brotherton Library, Leeds), YAS MS1722, 31 Mar 1966; Marks, 31 Mar 1966; Turtle, 31 Mar 1966; Lee, 31 Mar 1966; Preston, 31 Mar 1966; Marks, 1 Apr 1966; Frederick Ward, GDP/145/1966, 1 Apr 1966; Betty Allen, GDP/450/1963–67, 1 Apr 1966; Hague, 1 Apr 1966; James Allen, GDP/172(4)/1966, 1 Apr 1966; Turtle, 1 Apr 1966; Denis Judd (ed.), *The Private Diaries of Alison Uttley* (Barnsley, 2009), p. 279; Larkin, Ms. Eng. c. 7432, 1 Apr 1966, fo. 117.
10. Roy, *Invisible Spirit*, p. 352; *Jane Rossington's The Crossroads Years* (1988), pp. 19–20; *G*, 23 May 2015 (Chris Birch); Michael White, 'Andrew Faulds', *G*, 1 Jun 2000; 'Peter Griffiths', *DT*, 28 Nov 2013; Foot, *Powell*, p. 95; Nicholson, *How Was It For You?*,

p. 249; Butler and King, p. 210; *Benn*, p. 399; Janie Hampton (ed.), *Joyce & Ginnie* (1997), p. 330.

11. Hodgson, 6 Apr 1966; Robert J. Wybrow, *Britain Speaks Out, 1937–87* (Basingstoke, 1989), pp. 77–8; BBC WAC, *Any Questions?*, 1 Apr 1966; *Spec*, 8 Apr 1966; records of Cazenove & Co, 'Betting Book', 1 Apr 1966.

CHAPTER 8 CHAINS AT CRADLEY, SPRINGS AT WEST BROMWICH, LEATHERS AT WALSALL

1. Christine Greenhalgh and Andrew Kilmister, 'The British Economy, the State and the Motor Industry', in Teresa Hayter and David Harvey (eds), *The Factory and the City* (1993), p. 27; Duncan Gallie, 'The Labour Force', in A. H. Halsey and Josephine Webb (eds), *Twentieth-Century British Social Trends* (Basingstoke, 2000), p. 283; Sidney Pollard, *The Development of the British Economy* (1983 edn), p. 304; Michael Roper, *Masculinity and the British Organization Man Since 1945* (Oxford, 1994), p. 47; Leslie Hannah, *The Rise of the Corporate Economy* (1983 edn), p. 144; Pollard, *Development*, p. 304.
2. *S Tel*, 28 Nov 1965; unpublished memoir by David Warren; *T*, 27 Apr 1967; Warren.
3. David Edgerton, *The Rise and Fall of the British Nation* (2018), p. 312; *FT*, 30 Jul 1966; Michael Dintenfass, *The Decline of Industrial Britain, 1870–1980* (1992), pp. 5, 8.
4. Mark Keighley, *Wool City* (Ilkley, 2007), chaps 25–6; John Singleton, 'The Decline of the British Cotton Industry since 1940', in Mary B. Rose (ed.), *The Lancashire Cotton Industry* (Preston, 1996), pp. 297, 310; Peter Pagnamenta and Richard Overy, *All Our Working Lives* (1984), p. 44; Vic Keegan, 'Lord Kearton', *G*, 9 Jul 1992; Robert Heller, 'Joe Hyman', *G*, 12 Jul 1999; *ST*, 24 Apr 1966; Singleton, 'Decline', p. 296. More generally, see also: John Singleton, *Lancashire on the Scrapheap* (Oxford, 1991), chaps 6–10; Geoffrey Owen, *The Rise and Fall of Great Companies* (Oxford, 2010), chap. 3.
5. Geoffrey Owen, *From Empire to Europe* (1999), p. 133; Pollard, *Development*, p. 293; Owen, *Empire*, pp. 236, 230; Pollard, *Development*, p. 289; *Ob*, 13 Nov 1966; *ST*, 4 Sep 1966 ('24 kinds of aircraft'); Keith Hayward, *The British Aircraft Industry* (Manchester, 1989), p. 201; Graham Turner, *Business in Britain* (Harmondsworth, 1971 edn), pp. 375–6; Owen, *Empire*, pp. 192–4; *E*, 9 Oct 1965.
6. Jad Adams, *Tony Benn* (1992), p. 273; Edward Lorenz and Frank Wilkinson, 'The Shipbuilding Industry, 1880–1965', in Bernard Elbaum and William Lazonick (eds), *The Decline of the British Economy* (Oxford, 1986), p. 116; *G*, 25 Mar 1966; *Ob*, 27 Mar 1966. More generally about Geddes and the larger shipbuilding story around this time, see: Anthony Burton, *The Rise & Fall of British Shipbuilding* (1984), pp. 221–35; Lewis Johnman and Hugh Murphy, *British Shipbuilding and the State since 1918* (Ithaca, New York, 2002), chap. 6.
7. Neil K. Buxton, *The Economic Development of the British Coal Industry* (1978), pp. 237–8; Michael P. Jackson, *The Price of Coal* (1974), pp. 102–8; Buxton, p. 244; Jackson, p. 105; *G*, 26 Nov 1965.
8. Clair Wills, *Lovers and Strangers* (2017), p. xx; *E*, 6 Nov 1965; Jim Phillips et al., 'Deindustrialization, the Linwood Car Plant and Scotland's Political Divergence from England in the 1960s and 1970s', in *Twentieth Century British History*, 2019 (30/3), p. 402; Jim Phillips et al., *Deindustrialisation and the Moral Economy in Scotland Since 1955* (Edinburgh, 2021), pp. 86–8; Jim Phillips, 'The Meanings of Coal Community

in Britain since 1947', in *Contemporary British History*, 2018 (32/1), pp. 39–59; *G*, 29 Dec 2018 (Jack Seale); *G*, 23 Mar 2019, 15 Aug 2015, 26 Oct 2013; Oscar Marzaroli, *Shades of Scotland, 1956–1988* (Edinburgh, 1989), pp. 97–109, *Shades of Grey: Glasgow, 1956–1987* (Edinburgh, 1987), pp. 51–63; Archie Hind, *The Dear Green Place & Fur Sadie* (Edinburgh, 2008 Polygon edn), pp. 62–3; *ST*, 20 Jan 1963.

9. Graham Turner, *The North Country* (1967), p. 310; John W. House, *The North East* (Newton Abbot, 1969), pp. 77, 175; *T*, 21 Jan 2023 (Robert Crampton); Ron French and Ken Smith, *Lost Shipyards of the Tyne* (Newcastle, 2004), pp. 90–2; Graham Day, *Community and Everyday Life* (Abingdon, 2006), p. 83; Geoffrey Moorhouse, *Britain in the Sixties: The Other England* (Harmondsworth, 1964), p. 166; Huw Beynon and Ray Hudson, *The Shadow of the Mine* (2021), p. 62; Moorhouse, *Other England*, pp. 168–9; Beynon and Hudson, pp. 187–8; John Tomaney et al., *Social Infrastructure and Left Behind Places* (2024), pp. 75–6; *NS*, 29 Nov 2013. On deindustrialisation in the north-east, and its consequences, see also: *LRB*, 4 Dec 2025 (James Meek).

10. *E*, 4 Mar 1967; Moorhouse, *Other England*, pp. 155–6; *NS*, 6 Nov 2015; *Big Issue*, 27 Dec 2019; Jack Ramsay, *Made in Huddersfield* (Huddersfield, 1989), pp. 29, 66–7, 98–9.

11. Otto Saumarez Smith, *Boom Cities* (Oxford, 2019), pp. 76–7; Moorhouse, *Other England*, pp. 121, 123; Turner, *North Country*, p. 29; Derek Beattie, *Blackburn* (Halifax, 1992), p. 166; Saumarez Smith, p. 75; Andrew Taylor, *20th Century Blackburn* (Barnsley, 2000), p. 94; John Cooper Clarke, *I Wanna Be Yours* (2020), p. 117.

12. *T*, 3 Dec 1964; *E*, 2 Apr 1966; Ian Lowe, 'Leonard Brammer', *Ind*, 1 Jul 1994; *DT*, 8 Sep 1967.

13. *E*, 2 Apr 1966; *TLS*, 14 Oct 2022 (Adrian Smith); Moorhouse, *Other England*, p. 91; *ST*, 12 Jul 2015; Brian Griffin, *The Black Country* (Stockport, 2013), pp. 13, 19, 83.

14. Hywel Francis and David Smith, *The Fed* (1980), pp. 452–7; *NS*, 10 Jan 2020 (Jude Rogers); email from Stephen Moss, 24 Jan 2014.

15. Jerry White, *London in the Twentieth Century* (2001), p. 206; *Ind*, 27 Mar 1999 (Ian Jack); White, *London*, p. 206; *Ind*, 25 Apr 2000; White, *London*, pp. 198, 202–3; Piotr Stolarski, *Ealing in the 1960s* (2013), pp. 164–7; John Marriott, *Beyond the Tower* (Newhaven, 2011), p. 344; *ST*, 30 Oct 1966 (Keith Richardson); *G*, 16 Nov 1966 (David Fairhall); *DT*, 7 Aug 1967 (John Petty); Richard Roberts and David Kynaston, *City State* (2001), chaps 4, 6, 9.

16. *New Soc*, 9 Feb 1967; *E*, 15 Jan 1966; Anthony Sampson, *Anatomy of Britain Today* (1965), p. 511; *FT*, 7 Jan 1965 (Patrick Coldstream).

17. *FT*, 16 Nov 1998 (Chris Tighe); Richard King, *Brittle with Relics* (2022), pp. 91–2; Richard Hart, *The Vauxhall Story* (Leighton Buzzard, 2002 edn), pp. 70–81; David Kynaston, *Cazenove & Co* (1991), p. 240; *Spec*, 7 Jul 2012; *Yorkshire Imperial*, summer 1966, pp. 14–37.

18. E. P. Thompson, 'The Moral Economy of the English Crowd in the Eighteenth Century', in *Past and Present*, Feb 1971 (50/1), p. 79; Phillips et al., *Deindustrialisation and the Moral Economy*, pp. 43, 6; Ewan Gibbs, *Coal Country* (2021), pp. 55, 69.

19. Phillips et al., *Deindustrialisation and the Moral Economy*, pp. 1–2, 106–8, 123–8; *Ob*, 2 Jan 1966 (David Howarth); Phillips et al., *Deindustrialisation and the Moral Economy*, p. 128; Burton, *Shipbuilding*, p. 231.

20. David Tuckett, 'Work, Life-Chances, and Life-Styles', in David Tuckett (ed.), *An Introduction to Medical Sociology* (1976), p. 115; Gallie, 'Labour Force', p. 288; Selina

Todd, *The People* (2014), pp. 276–7; Cooper Clarke, *Wanna*, pp. 179–80; Turner, *North Country*, p. 29; H. A. Turner et al., *Labour Relations in the Motor Industry* (1967), p. 168; 'Morris Motors in the 1960s', in *History Workshop*, autumn 1983, p. 109.

21. Peter Smith, 'Consett, Co. Durham – some notes' (sent to me, 2014); Tuckett, 'Work', pp. 110–11; Gallie, 'Labour Force', p. 303; Dominic Sandbrook, *The Great British Dream Factory* (2015), pp. 5–9; *Wikipedia*, 'Tony Iommi'.
22. Tuckett, 'Work', pp. 110–11; *Economic History Review*, 2008 (61/2), pp. 514–15 (Joseph Melling review of Arthur McIvor and Ronald Johnston, *Miners' Lung* (Aldershot, 2007)); *ST*, 31 Oct 1965; Ronald Johnston and Arthur McIvor, '"Dust to Dust"', in *Oral History*, autumn 2001, pp. 51–5; 'Doctor Morris Greenberg', *T*, 11 Sep 2021; *G*, 8 Jul 2019 (Frances Perraudin); *Docklands & East London Advertiser*, 28 Jun 2018 (Mike Brooke); Danny Baker, *Going to Sea in a Sieve* (2012), pp. 66–7. See also: *Ind*, 25 Nov 1997 (Barbara Birchall); 'Molly Newhouse', *DT*, 13 Mar 2000; Geoffrey Tweedale, *Magic Mineral to Killer Dust* (Oxford, 2000), pp. 123–8; oral testimony in Johnston and McIvor, '"Dust to Dust"'. See also: Tom White, *Bad Dust* (2025); *Prospect*, Mar 2025 (Charlotte Bailey).
23. *New Soc*, 25 Jul 1963 (J. Walker); Singleton, *Scrapheap*, pp, 178–9; Turner, *Labour Relations*, p. 176; James Foreman-Peck et al., *The British Motor Industry* (Manchester, 1995), p. 170; *New Soc*, 2 Jan 1964.
24. Gallie, 'Labour Force', p. 288; Adrian Smith, 'An Oval Ball and a Broken City', in *International Journal of the History of Sport*, Dec 1994, p. 511; Pagnamenta and Overy, *Working Lives*, p. 191; Turner, *North Country*, pp. 30–1; W. W. Daniel, 'A Comparative Consideration of Two Industrial Work Groups', in *Sociological Review*, Mar 1966, pp. 42–4.
25. Jane Lewis, *Women in Britain Since 1945* (Oxford, 1992), p. 65; Gallie, 'Labour Force', p. 297; Chris Wrigley, 'Women in the Labour Market and in the Unions', in John McIlroy et al. (eds), *British Trade Unions and Industrial Politics*: Volume Two (Aldershot, 1999), pp. 45–63; Simon Phillips, 'The Changing Social & Economic Role of Women within the Valley Community of Merthyr Tydfil during the Twentieth Century' (Keele University, 1992), unpaginated; *New Soc*, 2 Jan 1964 (Stephen Aris); Richard Vinen, 'Second City' (2022), p. 268; Cooper Clarke, *Wanna*, p. 164; *G*, 17 Sep 1966.
26. *G*, 30 Sep 2024 (Jane Croft); 'Old King Coal', *T*, 30 Sep 2024.

CHAPTER 9 KAZAM!

1. *New Soc*, 11 Feb 1965; Jim Yelling, 'The incidence of slum clearance in England and Wales, 1955–85', in *Urban History*, Aug 2000, pp. 236–7; *YouTube*, 'Unit 4 + 2 – Concrete and Clay'. In general for this and the next two chapters, see also: Simon Gunn et al. (eds), *The Modern British City: 1945–2000* (2025), a major collection of essays published too late to be taken into account here.
2. John R. Gold, *The Practice of Modernism* (Abingdon, 2007), pp. 138–9; *FT*, 14 Mar 2004 (Colin Amery); *Sun*, 9 Feb 1967; Architects' Lives (National Life Stories, British Library), C467/05, p. 24; Tony Aldous, *Goodbye Britain?* (1975), p. 92; *Kynaston*, pp. 132–6; Miles Glendinning and Stefan Muthesius, *Tower Block* (1994), p. 267; Bridget Cherry et al., *London 5 East* (2005), pp. 92, 656; Elain Harwood, *Space Hope and Brutalism* (2015), p. 87; Patrick Dunleavy, *The Politics of Mass Housing in Britain,*

1945–1975 (Oxford, 1981), pp. 237–8; John Grindrod, *Concretopia* (Brecon, 2013), p. 203; Joseph Bullman et al., *The Secret History of Our Streets* (2012), pp. 123–34; Andrew Duncan and Liz Bartlett (eds), *Taking on the Motorway* (1992), pp. 13–14; *TLS*, 26 Feb 2021; Will Noble, *Croydonopolis* (2024), pp. 132 (Audrey Powell), 136; *ST*, 10 Jul 1966 (Robert Troop); Ian Nairn, *Nairn's London* (Harmondsworth, 1966), p. 203.

3. *NS*, 26 Feb 1965; *New Soc*, 3 Nov 1966; Gordon E. Cherry, *Birmingham* (Chichester, 1994), p. 202; Elain Harwood, 'John Madin', *G*, 28 Jan 2012; *G*, 21 Sep 2015 (Maev Kennedy); Stefan Muthesius and Miles Glendinning, *Towers for the Welfare State* (Edinburgh, 2017), p. 186; Richard Vinen, *Second City* (2022), p. 243; Cherry, *Birmingham*, pp. 177, 179; William Dargue, 'A History of Birmingham Places & Placenames from A to Y' (online); Cherry, *Birmingham*, p. 169; Norman Bartlam, *Ladywood Lives* (Stroud, 2004), pp. 17, 26–7.
4. David Nash and David Reeder, *Leicester in the Twentieth Century* (Stroud, 1993), p. 149; Ben Beazley, *Postwar Leicester* (Stroud, 2006), pp. 62–4; Elain Harwood, 'White Light/White Heat', in *Twentieth Century Architecture*, 2002, p. 66; Muthesius and Glendinning, *Towers*, p. 192; Harwood, 'White Light', pp. 66–7; Nottinghamshire Archives, *Turning Back the Pages in Maid Marian Way* (Nottingham, 2011), p. 2.
5. *Darts*, 26 Nov 1964; *Housing Review*, Jan–Feb 1974, pp. 15–16; Glendinning and Muthesius, *Tower Block*, p. 262; *Star*, 27 Mar 2023 (Robert Cumber); *Darts*, 26 Nov 1964.
6. *Crossman*, p. 127; Simon Gunn, 'The Rise and Fall of British Urban Modernism', in *Journal of British Studies*, Oct 2010, p. 851; Jim Appleby, *Bygone Bradford* (Derby, 1995), p. 108; Gunn, 'Rise and Fall', p. 857; Appleby, pp. 146, 151, 157; Gavin Stamp, *Britain's Lost Cities* (2007), p. 24; Alistair Kefford, *The Life and Death of the Shopping City* (Cambridge, 2024), p. 194; *E*, 4 Mar 1967; *DT*, 3 Jan 2004 (Saul Brookfield); Preston, 6D87/6, 23 Jul 1966, fo. 1506.
7. *G*, 28 Oct 2024; John J. Parkinson-Bailey, *Manchester* (Manchester, 2000), p. 184; Graham Turner, *The North Country* (1967), p. 68; Paul Morley, *The North* (2013), p. 18; *Crossman*, pp. 124–5; Stamp, *Lost*, p. 139; Parkinson-Bailey, pp. 193–4. In general re Hulme, see: Peter Shapely et al., 'Civic Culture and Housing Policy in Manchester, 1945–79', in *Twentieth Century British History*, 2004 (15/4), pp. 424–7.
8. Kefford, *Life and Death*, pp. 188–91; *Wikipedia*, 'St John's Shopping Centre', 'St John's Market'; Tam Dalyell, 'Lord Sefton of Garston', *Ind*, 12 Sep 2001; *P*, 8 Sep 1965 (Patrick Skene Catling); Muthesius and Glendinning, *Towers*, p. 201; *G*, 22 Apr 1966; *T*, 13 Oct 1977 (Peter Godfrey); Dan Warner, 'High-Rise Sites: Reflections on the Piggeries' (Open Eye Gallery, online).
9. Noel Hanson, 'Getting About', in Anna Flowers and Vanessa Histon (eds), *Water under the Bridges* (Newcastle, 1999), pp. 54–5; Graham Sault, 'Re-Graingerising Brasilia', in *Northern Review*, 2002–3, pp. 54, 56; Harwood, *Space*, p. 546; *G*, 1 Dec 2003; Thomas Faulkner, 'Architecture in Newcastle', in Robert Colls and Bill Lancaster (eds), *Newcastle upon Tyne* (Chichester, 2001), p. 240; Ray Marshall, *Newcastle West End* (Stroud, 2004), p. 48; Jon Gower Davies, *The Evangelistic Bureaucrat* (1972), pp. 149–57.
10. *E*, 6 Nov 1965; Glendinning and Muthesius, *Tower Block*, p. 224; W. W. Knox, *Industrial Nation* (Edinburgh, 1999), p. 263; Miles Horsey, *Tenements and Towers* (Edinburgh, 1990), p. 45; Muthesius and Glendinning, *Towers*, p. 238; *Wikipedia*, 'Sighthill, Glasgow'; John Boughton, *A History of Council Housing in 100 Estates*

(2023), p. 178; Glendinning and Muthesius, *Tower Block*, p. 233; Knox, p. 263; *AJ*, 9 Nov 1966, 22 Jun 1966; *LRB*, 4 Nov 2021.

11. Muthesius and Glendinning, *Towers*, p. 246; Adam Fergusson, *The Sack of Bath* (2010, Persephone edn), pp. 24, 26; Andrew Taylor, *20th Century Blackburn* (Barnsley, 2000), p. 98; Derek Beattie, *Blackburn* (Halifax, 1992), p. 171; Otto Saumarez Smith, *Boom Cities* (Oxford, 2019), pp. 115–18; *Liverpool Echo*, 25 Jun 1965; John Winstone, *Bristol As It Was, 1963–1975* (Bristol, 1990), pp. 19–20; Bristol Civic Society, *The Fight for Bristol* (Bristol, 1980), pp. 29, 31; Muthesius and Glendinning, *Towers*, p. 178; Sarah Mass, 'Commercial Heritage as Democratic Action', in *Twentieth Century British History*, Sep 2018, p. 467; Adrian Smith, *The City of Coventry* (2006), p. 109; Stamp, *Lost*, p. 58; Glendinning and Muthesius, *Tower Block*, p. 238; *NS*, 9 Dec 1966 (Nicholas Taylor); Stamp, *Lost*, pp. 67–8; Ray Rooney et al. (eds), *Home Is Where The Heart Is* (Castleford, 1989), p. 33; Geoffrey Moorhouse, *Britain in the Sixties: The Other England* (Harmondsworth, 1964), pp. 57–8; *Ob*, 5 Mar 1967; Muthesius and Glendinning, *Towers*, p. 219; Moorhouse, *Other England*, pp. 173–4; *Liverpool Echo*, 27 Aug 1965; Glendinning and Muthesius, *Tower Block*, p. 237; Oldham Local Studies, *Oldham Remembered* (Oldham, 2002), pp. 33, 39; Morley, *North*, pp. 16–17; David Hunt, *A History of Preston* (Preston, 1992), p. 260; *Crossman*, p. 340; Muthesius and Glendinning, *Towers*, p. 209; *G*, 16 Oct 2017 (Josh Halliday); Trevor Rowley, *The English Landscape in the Twentieth Century* (2006), p. 148; Roy Bullock, *Salford, 1940–1965* (Salford, 1996), pp. 62–3; Boughton, *Council Housing*, pp. 176–7; Morley, *North*, p. 351; Howard Salt, 'Etruria' (online), chap. 7; *Crossman*, p. 341; *AR*, Nov 1966, pp. 349–50; *G*, 28 Nov 1964.

CHAPTER 10 HEART-WEARY WITH IT ALL

1. *Liverpool Echo*, 1 Oct 1965; *Manchester Evening News*, 25 Nov 1966.
2. R. Wilkinson, 'A Statistical Analysis of Attitudes to Moving', in *Urban Studies*, May 1965, p. 1; *Official Architecture and Planning*, May 1965, pp. 645–7 (Joan Ash); John Rex and Robert Moore, *Race, Community, and Conflict* (1967), pp. 73–4, 109; *New Soc*, 11 Mar 1965 (Robert McKie); R. K. Wilkinson and E. M. Sigsworth, 'Attitudes to the Housing Environment', in *Urban Studies*, Jun 1972, p. 197; Norman Dennis, *People and Planning* (1970), p. 333; Jon Gower Davies, *The Evangelistic Bureaucrat* (1972), p. 45; Robert McKie, *Housing and the Whitehall Bulldozer* (1971), p. 48; John English et al., *Slum Clearance* (1976), pp. 156, 158. See also: J. A. Yelling, 'Residents' Reactions to Post-War Slum Clearance in England', in *Planning History*, 1999 (21/3), pp. 5–12 – though one might qualify his conclusion that 'councils did have general support for clearance policies among the residents affected'.
3. Bob Hudson, 'Norman Dennis', *G*, 29 Nov 2010; Dennis, *People and Planning*, pp. 187–293; *Official Architecture and Planning*, May 1965, pp. 645–7; Wilkinson and Sigsworth, 'Attitudes', p. 202; *New Soc*, 24 Nov 1966 (Robin H. Best); Patrick Dunleavy, *The Politics of Mass Housing in Britain, 1945–1975* (Oxford, 1981), p. 94; *Ind*, 1 Jun 2013; Dunleavy, p. 94.
4. Dennis, *People and Planning*, pp. 261–2, 265, 302, 346, 185, 348–52; Ruth I. Johns, *St Ann's Nottingham* (Warwick, 2002), p. 226; Ray Gosling, *Personal Copy* (Nottingham, 2010 edn), pp. 188–90.
5. Jim Yelling, 'The incidence of slum clearance in England and Wales, 1955–85', in *Urban History*, Aug 2000, pp. 234, 241; Andrew Gibb, *Glasgow* (Beckenham, 1983),

p. 170; N. R. Fyfe, 'Contested visions of a modern city', in *Environment and Planning A*, 1996 (28/3), p. 397; Dennis, *People and Planning*, pp. 350–1.

6. Dennis, *People and Planning*, p. 293; Katie McAdam, 'Rubbish, Rubble and Rodents' (University of Huddersfield thesis, 2019), p. 50; *Manchester Evening News*, 25 Nov 1966; *Bolton Evening News*, 12 Jan 1966, 5 Feb 1966 (O. J.); Colin Hyde, *Walnut Street Past, Present and Future* (Leicester, *c.* 1996), p. 72; N. S. Power, *The Forgotten People* (Evesham, 1965), pp. 43, 45; Michael Collins, *The Likes of Us* (2004), pp. 164, 179; Scott, SxMOA99/97/1/15, Jan–Jul 1966. Katie McAdam's thesis is a fascinating piece of work, though more about the late 1960s than the mid-1960s.
7. James Tucker, *Honourable Estates* (1966), pp. 77–8; R. K. Wilkinson and Valerie Talbot, 'An Investigation of the Attitudes of Families Rehoused from Slum and Twilight Areas in Batley, Leeds and York', in *Social and Economic Administration*, Oct 1971, pp. 236–62; *AJ*, 7 Apr 1965; *Liverpool Echo*, 1 Oct 1965; Tucker, *Estates*, p. 77; *G*, 10 Oct 1966; *Wythenshawe Express*, 22 Sep 1966; *DT*, 8 May 1967; Norman Bartlam, *Ladywood* (Stroud, 1999), p. 142; Power, *Forgotten*, pp. 47, 55; *ST*, 3 Apr 1966; Graham Turner, *The North Country* (1967), p. 33.
8. *New Soc*, 11 Nov 1965 (John Barr); *Official Architecture and Planning*, Jan 1966, p. 71; Glen O'Hara, *From Dreams to Disillusionment* (Basingstoke, 2007), pp. 159–60; Martin Johnes, *Wales Since 1939* (Manchester, 2012), pp. 128–9; *G*, 10 Oct 1966, 13 Aug 1968.
9. BBC online website, 20 Nov 2011 (Glencairn, Motherwell); *G*, 13 Mar 2010 (Ian Jack); finding of Séan Damer, historian of Glasgow.
10. *T*, 29 Apr 1974; Otto Saumarez Smith, *Boom Cities* (Oxford, 2019), p. 85; *Liverpool Echo*, 11 Nov 1965; *G*, 11 Aug 1964; Selina Todd, 'Phoenix Rising', in *Journal of British Studies*, Jul 2015, pp. 698–700; *Lancashire Evening Telegraph*, 7 Nov 1964, 9 Nov 1964, 31 Dec 1964.
11. Alistair Kefford, *The Life and Death of the Shopping City* (Cambridge, 2022), p. 255; Oliver Marriott, *The Property Boom* (1967), p. 230; *G*, 4 Apr 1966; Kefford, pp. 257–8; Gordon Bentley, GDP/344/1957–66, May 1965, Nov 1965, Jun 1965.

CHAPTER 11 QUITE MAGNIFICENT SCHEMES

1. Andrew Denham & Mark Garnett, *Keith Joseph* (Chesham, 2001), p. 116; Otto Saumarez Smith, *Boom Cities* (2019), p. 39; John Boughton, *Municipal Dreams* (2018), p. 127; J. Dickson Mabon, 'Rebuilding Scotland: The Role of Government', in Miles Glendinning (ed.), *Rebuilding Scotland* (East Linton, 1997), p. 58.
2. *T*, 20 Jun 2017; Miles Glendinning and Stefan Muthesius, *Tower Block* (1994), p. 279; *Crossman*, pp. 340, 281–19; *NS*, 16 Dec 2002.
3. *Birmingham Evening Mail*, 27 May 1965; *E*, 6 Nov 1965; *Manchester Evening News*, 5 Jan 1966; *G*, 17 Feb 1965 ('London letter'); *Camden New Journal*, 9 Oct 2009 (obituary of Brack); Holly Smith, *Up in the Air* (2025), p. 89; *AJ*, 1 Dec 1965. In general on the high-rise phenomenon and lived experience, Smith's survey is an invaluable contribution.
4. *Lancashire Evening Telegraph*, 11–12 Nov 1964; Peter Shapely et al., 'Civic Culture and Housing Policy in Manchester, 1945–79', in *Twentieth Century British History*, 2004 (15/4), p. 424; *Liverpool Echo*, 25 Jun 1965; Local Studies Library, Sheffield, MP 1117 M (includes the June 1966 brochure); Will Noble, *Croydonopolis* (2024), chap. 11; *FT*, 6 Apr 2024 (Jo Ellison); *Liverpool Echo*, 25 Jun 1965. In general on local

boosterism and a post-industrial future, see: Shapely et al., 'Civic pride'; Saumarez Smith, *Boom Cities*, pp. 75–82.

5. *Crossman*, pp. 541–2; Glendinning and Muthesius, *Tower Block*, p. 192; Alistair Kefford, *The Life and Death of the Shopping City* (Cambridge, 2022), chap. 4; Barnabas Calder, *Raw Concrete* (2016), p. 224; Peter Jones, 'Re-thinking corruption in post-1950 urban Britain', in *Urban History*, 2012 (39/3), pp. 523, 515; Martin Tomkinson and Michael Gillard, *Nothing to Declare* (1980), chaps 2–3; *Wikipedia*, 'Winstanley and York Road Estate'; Boughton, *Municipal Dreams*, pp. 133, 136.
6. Tomkinson and Gillard, chap. 5; *AJ*, 28 Apr 1965; University of Newcastle upon Tyne, *Speeches Delivered by the Public Orator when Presenting Candidates for Honorary Degrees at a Congregation in King's Hall on Wednesday, 23rd March 1966* (Newcastle, 1966), unpaginated; Wilfred Burns, *Newcastle* (1967), pp. 3, 96; *G*, 28 Oct 2024; J. F. Griffiths, 'Mr Newcastle: The Career of T. Dan Smith' (University of Northumbria, PhD thesis, 2019); *G*, 2 Nov 2024; Burns, *Newcastle*, pp. 32–3; David Byrne, 'T. Dan Smith', in *North East Labour History*, 1994 (Bulletin No 28), p. 24; John Pendlebury, 'Alas Smith and Burns?', in *Planning Perspectives*, 2001 (16), p. 115. See also: Raymond Fitzwalter and David Taylor, *Web of Corruption* (1981).
7. Saumarez Smith, *Boom Cities*, p. 6; *G*, 2 Nov 2024; *AJ*, 1 Sep 1965; Gavin Stamp, *Britain's Lost Cities* (2007), pp. 112–13; Percy Johnson-Marshall, *Rebuilding Cities* (Edinburgh, 1966), chap. 8.
8. *Ob*, 7 Mar 2004; Alan Lipman, 'The architectural belief system and social behaviour', in *British Journal of Sociology*, Jun 1969, pp. 190–204; Elain Harwood, *Space Hope and Brutalism* (2015), p. 383.
9. Joe Moran, *Queuing for Beginners* (2007), p. 132; Simon Gunn, 'The Rise and Fall of British Urban Modernism', in *Journal of British Studies*, Oct 2010, pp. 854–9; Clara H. Greed, *Women and Planning* (1994), chaps 8–9; *L*, 18 Mar 1965; Willmott, WLMT 1/31, 27 May 1965; Norman Dennis, *People and Planning*, pp. 339, 352; David Byrne, 'The Reconstruction of Newcastle', in Robert Colls and Bill Lancaster (eds), *Newcastle upon Tyne* (Chichester, 2001), pp. 348–9; *TLS*, 19 Feb 2021. In general on planners and sociologists, see: *Ob*, 13 Jun 1965 (Colin McGlashan); Anne Buttimer, 'Sociology and Planning', in *Town Planning Review*, Apr 1971, pp. 145–80.
10. Patrick Dunleavy, *The Politics of Mass Housing in Britain, 1945–1975* (Oxford, 1981), p. 361; Peter Shapely, *The Politics of Housing* (Manchester, 2007), pp. 164–5; *DT*, 23 Mar 1965; John Winstone, *Bristol As It Was, 1963–1975* (Bristol, 1990), p. 19; *NS*, 26 Jun 1965; *New Soc*, 4 Nov 1965. In general on Banham, see: Nigel Whiteley, 'Banham and "Otherness"', in *Architectural History*, 1990, pp. 188–221.
11. *Master Builders 10: Architecture or Revolution*, BBC1, 19 Jun 1966; Elain Harwood, 'David Bernstein', *G*, 17 Feb 2018; *Ob*, 21 Jun 2015 (Rowan Moore); *AJ*, 15 Dec 1965; *AR*, Jul 1965, p. 41; *Country Life*, 25 Nov 1965; *Birmingham Post*, 28 May 1964; *Liverpool Echo*, 6 May 1966; Glen O'Hara, *From Dreams to Disillusionment* (Basingstoke, 2007), pp. 158–9; *Ob*, 5 Dec 1965; *New Soc*, 9 Sep 1965; Candida Lycett Green (ed.), John Betjeman, *Letters*: Volume Two (1995), p. 319.
12. Peter Hall, *Cities of Tomorrow* (Oxford, 2002 edn), p. 245; *T*, 22–3 Jul 1966.
13. *G*, 15 Jun 1966; Simon Jenkins, *A Short History of London* (2019), p. 269; Ben Campkin, *Remaking London* (2013), pp. 80–4; Thom Gorst, *The Buildings Around Us* (1995), p. 134. Also on Aylesbury, see: John R. Gold, *The Practice of Modernism* (Abingdon, 2007), pp. 190–1; Boughton, *Municipal Dreams*, pp. 129–30; Michael Romyn, *London's Aylesbury Estate* (Basingstoke, 2020).

14. *TLS*, 3 Jan 2025; *G*, 3 Jan 2025; John Campbell, *Edward Heath* (1993), p. 162; *Sheffield Forward*, Aug 1965.
15. *FT*, 13 Feb 2010 (Matthew Engel); Jeff Young, *Ghost Town* (Bridport, 2020), p. 85; N. R. Fyfe, 'Contested visions of a modern city', in *Environment and Planning A*, 1996 (28/3), pp. 398–9; Edwin Morgan, *Poems of Thirty Years* (Manchester, 1982), pp. 162–3; *AJ*, 21 Jul 1965.

CHAPTER 12 I CAN'T PUT MY FINGER ON IT

1. *Lancashire Evening Post*, 25 May 1965; *New Soc*, 17 Jun 1965; *Lancashire Evening Post*, 25 May 1965; *New Soc*, 17 Jun 1965; *Lancashire Evening Post*, 8 Jun 1965, 15 Jun 1965.
2. Sheila Patterson, *Immigration and Race Relations in Britain, 1960–1967* (1969), Appendix VIII (Marsh), pp. 423–30; *New Soc*, 14 Dec 1967; *G*, 21 Dec 1965; *New Soc*, 5 Jan 1966, 27 Jan 1966.
3. Brian Cohen, 'The Demographic as Statistical Background', in Simon Abbott (ed.), *The Prevention of Racial Discrimination in Britain* (1971), p. 66; Mike Phillips & Trevor Phillips, *Windrush* (1998), p. 198; Cohen, p. 66; Richard Vinen, *Second City* (2022), p. 337; *(Wolverhampton) Express & Star*, 3 May 1966.
4. *T*, 27 Jan 1965; Clair Wills, *Lovers and Strangers* (2017), p. 121; John R. Lambert, *Crime, Police, and Race Relations* (1970), pp. 186–7; *New Soc*, 3 Nov 1966 (Paul Barker); *NS*, 17 Feb 1967; John Rex and Robert Moore, *Race, Community, and Conflict* (1967), pp. 79–83.
5. *G*, 23 Jul 1965 (Dennis Barker); Panikos Panayi (ed.), *The Impact of Immigration* (Manchester, 1999), pp. 140–1; *NS*, 13 Aug 1965; *Birmingham Evening Mail*, 31 Mar 1965, 1 Apr 1965.
6. *Birmingham Evening Mail*, 14 Aug 1965; *(Wolverhampton) Express & Star*, 12 Aug 1965, 14 Aug 1965, 16 Aug 1965.
7. Shirin Hirsch, *In the Shadow of Enoch Powell* (Manchester, 2018), chap. 2; *DT*, 4 May 1965; Simon Heffer, *Like the Roman* (1998), pp. 378–9; Elizabeth Burney, *Housing on Trial* (1967), pp. 212–13.
8. *Crossman*, p. 195; *Birmingham Evening Mail*, 6 May 1965, 27 May 1965; *G*, 26 Oct 1965; Kamal Ahmed, *The Life and Times of a Very British Man* (2018), p. 91; *NS*, 1 Jan 1965.
9. *T*, 27 Jan 1965; *Flamingo*, Feb 1965, p. 59; *DT*, 24 Feb 1965, *S Tel*, 7 Mar 1965, *DT*, 16 Mar 1965; *Ind*, 4 Mar 2003 (Jason Burt); Piotr Stolarski, *Ealing in the 1960s* (2013), p. 248; *T*, 12 Aug 1965; *NS*, 20 Aug 1965, 10 Sep 1965; Martin Johnes, *Wales Since 1939* (Manchester, 2012), pp. 140–1; *Sun*, 1 Nov 1965; *DM (1)*, 3 Nov 1965; John Platts-Mills, *Muck, Silk and Socialism* (Wedmore, Somerset, 2002), p. 391; Bill Hagerty, 'Dennis Hackett', *G*, 22 Sep 2016; *Sunday Mercury*, 13 Feb 1966 (Anthony Hancox); Anthony Thwaite (ed.), *Larkin*, p. 356; *(Wolverhampton) Express & Star*, 25 May 1966; *New Soc*, 23 Jun 1966; *Brixton Advertiser*, 2 Sep 1966.
10. Graham Clark, *Coronation Baby Council House Kid 70s Soulboy* (Slough, 2021), p. 161; Alan Thornett, *From Militancy to Marxism* (1987), p. 127; Norwell Roberts, *I Am Norwell Roberts* (2022), pp. 61–2; Panayi, *Impact*, pp. 143–4; Robin Bunce and Samara Linton, *Diane Abbott* (2020), p. 16; Anton Rippon, *A Derby Boy* (Stroud, 2007), pp. 128; Tony Bullimore, *Saved* (1997), pp. 74–7, 100–2.

11. *Loughborough Monitor*, 13 Aug 1965, 20 Aug 1965; Graham Turner, *The North Country* (1967), pp. 216–17, 220–6.
12. *New Soc*, 10 Dec 1964 (Fenner Brockway), 24 Feb 1966 (Derrick Sington); *Flamingo*, Feb 1965, pp. 6–11.
13. Clifford S. Hill, *How Colour Prejudiced Is Britain?* (1967 Panther edn), pp. 42–3, 79, 116; Anthony H. Richmond, *Migration and Race Relations in an English City* (1973), pp. 81, 177, 185, 199, 216–19; Daniel Lawrence, *Black Migrants: White Natives* (Cambridge, 1974), pp. 81, 85, 114, 210–13; Hugh Wilson et al., *Change or Decay: Final Report of the Liverpool Inner Area Study* (1977), pp. 91–2; Dennis Brooks, *Race and Labour in London Transport* (1975), pp. 334–5, 71–98, 105–6, 111–12.
14. Mark Abrams, 'The Incidence of Race Prejudice in Britain', in E. J. B. Rose, *Colour and Citizenship* (1969), p. 551; *Ob*, 23 Apr 1967 (Colin McGlashan); Abrams, pp. 552–65; Lawrence, *Black Migrants*, pp. 48–52; Abrams, pp. 566–7, 570, 585, 588; W. W. Daniel, *Racial Discrimination in England: Based on the PEP Report* (Harmondsworth, 1968), pp. 199–205, 155–9, 182–94, 171–2, 175–6, 76, 118, 74–5, 133–7, 87–9, 108.
15. Donley T. Studlar, 'British Public Opinion, Colour Issues, and Enoch Powell', in *British Journal of Political Science*, Jul 1974, p. 374.

CHAPTER 13 IT HURTS YOU DEEP INSIDE

1. Valerie Jackson, 'The Evidence from the Two Censuses', in E. J. B. Rose, *Colour and Citizenship* (1969), pp. 99, 83; Ceri Peach et al., 'Immigration and Ethnicity', in A. H. Halsey (ed.), *Twentieth-Century British Social Trends* (Basingstoke, 2000), p. 156.
2. Richard Vinen, *Second City* (2022), pp. 321, 345–6; Clair Wills, *Lovers and Strangers* (2017), p. 363; Colin Grant, *Homecoming* (2019), p. 124; Wills, p. 309; *Flamingo*, Sep 1964, pp. 6–7, Dec 1964, pp. 2–3, Jan 1965, pp. 11–12; *L*, 23 Sep 1965; Samuel Selvon, *The Housing Lark* (1965), p. 24; Barbara Maria Nnameka, *Granddaughter of the Windrush* (Brighton, 2013), p. 48; *G*, 1 Aug 2020; Donald Hinds, *Journey to an Illusion* (1966), p. 135 ; David Matthews, *Voices of the Windrush Generation* (2018), pp. 99, 104–5; Helen McCarthy, *Double Lives* (2018), p. 289; Wills, *Lovers*, p. 354.
3. John Rex and Robert Moore, *Race, Community, and Conflict* (1967), pp. 102–4; Daniel Lawrence, *Black Migrants: White Natives* (Cambridge, 1974), pp. 19–20, 36–7.
4. Lawrence, pp. 25, 35; Rex and Moore, pp. 121–4.
5. Rex and Moore, pp. 162–3, 157, 163–6.
6. Sheila Patterson, *Immigration and Race Relations in Britain, 1960–1967* (1969), pp. 112–13; Rose, *Colour and Citizenship*, pp. 443, 449; Stephen Ward et al., 'Cowley in the Oxford Economy', in Teresa Hayter and David Harvey (eds), *The Factory and the City* (1993), p. 84.
7. Shakil Salam et al. (eds), *Humlog* (Oldham, 1997), pp. 14, 22, 24, 42, 54; Graham Turner, *The North Country* (1967), pp. 227–8; Geoff Dench et al., *The New East End* (2006), pp. 25, 42; Sarfraz Mansoor, *Greetings from Bury Park* (2007), pp. 8–11.
8. Patterson, *Immigration and Race Relations*, pp. 8, 12–13, 143–4, 148; Arthur Wesley Helweg, *Sikhs in England* (New Delhi, 1979), pp. 58–79; *T*, 19 Jan 1965; *Loughborough Monitor*, 27 Aug 1965.
9. W. W. Daniel, *Racial Discrimination in England: Based on the PEP Report* (Harmondsworth, 1968), pp. 41–2; Lawrence, pp. 39–43; Darshan S. Tatla, 'A Passage to England', in *Oral History*, autumn 2002, pp. 61–72.

10. *New Soc*, 10 Dec 1964; *T*, 9 Aug 1965; John Davis, *Waterloo Sunrise* (Oxford, 2022), pp. 309–10; Patterson, p. 421; Davis, p. 310.
11. Michael Banton, 'White and Coloured in Britain', in Melvin M. Tumin (ed.), *Comparative Perspectives on Race Relations* (Boston, USA, 1969), pp. 63–5, 73, 78; Kenneth Little, 'Some Aspects of Color, Class, and Culture in Britain', in *Dædalus*, spring 1967, pp. 517–18, 524.
12. *New Soc*, 19 Nov 1964 (John Barr), *Sunday Mercury*, 13 Feb 1966 (Anthony Hancox); Kieran Connell, *Multicultural Britain* (2024), pp. 138–9; Wills, *Lovers*, pp. 229–30; *G*, 4 Apr 2014.
13. David Beetham, *Immigrant School Leavers and the Youth Employment Service in Birmingham* (1967), pp. 2–3; *New Soc*, 4 Apr 1968; Malorie Blackman, *Just Sayin'* (2022), pp. 14–16.

CHAPTER 14 ABSOLUTELY NOTHING OLD HAT

1. Christopher Hitchens, *Hitch-22* (2010), p. 82.
2. *FT*, 7 Mar 2006 (John Kay); *Oldie*, Apr 2015 (Keith Giles); *FT*, 27 Jan 2001 (Kevin Done); *Sun*, 30 May 1966 (Elizabeth Prosser); Dick Godfrey, 'Swinging Newcastle', in Anna Flowers and Vanessa Histon (eds), *Water under the Bridges* (Newcastle, 1999), p. 130; Joanna Bourke, *Working-Class Cultures in Britain, 1890–1960* (1994), p. 48; Alison Ravetz, *The Place of Home* (1995), pp. 128, 190–3; *S Tel*, 26 Apr 2015 (Elizabeth Anderson); Clive D. Field, *Secularization in the Long 1960s* (2017), pp. 164, 51, 110; *G*, 24 Mar 2012 (MacCarthy); *TLS*, 8 May 2020 ('J. C.'); Bourke, p. 31; Ruth Adam, *A Woman's Place* (1975), p. 270; Alva Myrdal & Viola Klein, *Women's Two Roles* (1968 edn), p. 54; *Ob*, 17 Jul 2005 (Savage); *NS*, 9 Apr 1965 (Bishop of Woolwich), 18 Jun 1965 (Madeleine Simms), 11 Jun 1965 (West), 3 Jun 1966 (Jones), 11 Jun 1965 (Ridley), 4 Feb 1966 (C. H. Rolph); *Brentwood Review*, 20 May 1966 (Maureen Odell); Callum G. Brown, *The Death of Christian Britain* (2001), p. 191; *New Soc*, 28 Oct 1965 (O. R. McGregor), 2 Feb 1967 (A. Kaldegg); James H. Mills, *Cannabis Nation* (Oxford, 2013), p. 124; *Ind*, 19 May 2001 (Matthew Sweet); Eric Dunning et al., 'Spectator violence at football matches', in *British Journal of Sociology*, Jun 1986, p. 239; *Pontefract and Castleford Express*, 9 Dec 1965; John Pearson and Graham Turner, *The Persuasion Industry* (1965), p. 29; *Oldie*, May 2000 (Alan Thomas); Philip Corrigan, 'Film Entertainment as Ideology and Pleasure', in James Curran and Vincent Porter (eds), *British Cinema History* (1983), p. 30; *FT*, 17 Nov 1964; Peter Haydon, *Beer and Britannia* (Stroud, 2001), p. 293; Brian Bennison, 'Drink in Newcastle', in Robert Colls and Bill Lancaster (eds), *Newcastle upon Tyne* (Chichester, 2001), p. 188; *G*, 24 Apr 2004 (Jack); Simon Winder, *The Man Who Saved Britain* (2006), pp. 228–9; *Ind*, 20 Jul 2000 (Moggach); 'George Curtis', *T*, 20 Aug 2021; *ES*, 26 Jun 2024 (Dylan Jones, quoting Smith); *G*, 4 Sep 2020 (John Hodgkinson); *T*, 22 Feb 1966; *TLS*, 3 Feb 1966; Leslie Brown, *Three Worlds* (1981), pp. 190–1; *News of the World*, 1 May 1966 (Johnson); *Manchester Sketch*, Aug 1966; *Daily Sketch*, 11 Jan 1966; Michael White, *Tolkien* (2001), p. 224; Helena Barrett and John Phillips, *Suburban Style* (1987), p. 206; *T*, 17 Jan 1975 (Caroline Moorehead); Barrett and Phillips, p. 204; Anthony Sampson, *Anatomy of Britain Today* (1965), pp. 619–20; Harold Perkin, *The Rise of Professional Society* (2002 edn), p. 434; Paul Ferris, *Sex and the British* (1993), p. 188; Virginia Nicholson, *How Was It For You?* (2019), p. 193; *Kynaston*, pp. 147–8; David

Lodge, *Quite a Good Time to Be Born* (2015), p. 422 (Hoggart); Martin Johnes, *Wales Since 1939* (Manchester, 2012), p. 100; Alan Travis, *Bound and Gagged* (2000), pp. 218–21; Roger Hood and Andrew Roddam, 'Crime, Sentencing and Punishment', in A. H. Halsey (ed.), *Twentieth-Century British Social Trends* (Basingstoke, 2000 edn), p. 680; Laurie Dennett, *A Sense of Security* (Cambridge, 1998), pp. 310, 330; Ferris, p. 185; Peter Parker (ed.), *Some Men in London*, vol. 2 (2024), pp. 303–10, quoting from Hunter Davies (ed.), *The New London Spy* (1966); John Davis, *Waterloo Sunrise* (Oxford, 2022), pp. 109–10; Joe Moran, *Queuing for Beginners* (2007), pp. 50–1; Mary Ingham, *Now We Are Thirty* (1981), p. 100; Christina Hardyment, *Slice of Life* (1995), p. 88 (Deighton); Nell Dunn, *Talking to Women* (2018 edn), p. 38; Anne Sebba, *Laura Ashley* (1990), p. 64; Hugh McLeod, *The Religious Crisis of the 1960s* (Oxford, 2007), p. 105; Ian Mole, *Michelle My Umbrella* (2018), p. 59; Mary Abbott, *Family Affairs* (2003), p. 118; Alexandra Pringle, 'Chelsea Girl', in Sara Maitland (ed.), *Very Heaven* (1988), p. 38; Leila Berg, *Risinghill* (Harmondsworth, 1968), p. 219; Nicholson, *How Was It For You*, p. 222.

3. *Independent on Sunday*, 5 Jul 1992 (Maureen Freely); Sebba, *Ashley*, p. 63; Isobel Emmett, 'Blaenau Boys in the Mid-1960s', in Glyn Williams (ed.), *Social and Cultural Change in Contemporary Wales* (1978), p. 96; A. H. Halsey, 'Further and Higher Education', in Halsey, *Trends*, pp. 225–7; McLeod, *Religious Crisis*, p. 102; Myrdal & Klein, *Two Roles*, p. xi; Jeffrey Weeks, *Sex, Politics and Society* (Harlow, 1989 edn), p. 250; *Fowles (1)*, p. 611.
4. See, for example, Callum G. Brown, *Religion and Society in Twentieth Century Britain* (2007), and review in *TLS*, 14 Dec 2007 (Bernice Martin).
5. Eleanor M. Wright, 'The Representation of Women and Girls in Post War Secondary School English Course Books', in *History of Education Society Bulletin*, spring 1983, pp. 26–7; Abigail Walls, 'Delinquency, Masculinity and Citizenship in England 1950–1970', in *Past and Present*, May 2005, pp. 159–60, 179; *Ob*, 3 Jun 2018; Fiona MacCarthy, 'Mary Stott', *G*, 18 Sep 2002; Willmott, WLMT 1/25, 7 Nov 1962; 'Susanne Puddefoot', *T*, 11 Dec 2010; *T*, 11 Apr 1967; *G*, 20 Mar 1967.
6. *T*, 2 Mar 2016 (Janice Turner); *G*, 5 Mar 2016; *T*, 2 Mar 2016; Brown, *Death*, pp. 176–7; Cynthia L. White, *Women's Magazines, 1693–1968* (1970), p. 223; *Independent on Sunday*, 16 Feb 1992; Stuart Hall, 'Class and the Mass Media', in Richard Mabey (ed.), *Class* (1967), p. 109; H. G. Cocks, 'Saucy stories', in *Social History*, Nov 2004, p. 482; Marcus Collins, 'The Pornography of Permissiveness', in *History Workshop*, spring 1999, pp. 111–12. On *Jackie*, see also: Alison Light, *Red, Red Robin* (2026), pp. 204–5.
7. Johnes, *Wales*, p. 107; Meic Stephens, 'John Rowlands', *Ind*, 18 May 2015; Christopher Hilliard, *A Matter of Obscenity* (Princeton, 2021), pp. 125–9; *New Soc*, 26 Jan 1967; 'The original Generation X', in *BBC News Magazine* (online), 1 Mar 2014 (Alan Dein); Ingham, *Thirty*, pp. 87–8.
8. Hilliard, pp. 111–13; *NS*, 25 Jun 1965 (Pritchett); Bruce Carson, 'Comedy, sexuality and "Swinging London" films', in *Journal of Popular British Cinema*, 1998, pp. 48–9; Selina Todd, *Tastes of Honey* (2019), pp. 162–3; *ES*, 4 Sep 2023 (Joe Bromley interview with John Pearse); 'Alan Blaikley', *DT*, 7 Jul 2022; *Ob*, 19 Jun 2005 (Smith); Richard Williams, 'Penny Valentine', *G*, 13 Jan 2003; Brown, *Death*, pp. 178–9; Mat Snow, *Mojo*, Nov 2002, p. 117 (reviewing *Forty Licks*); Peter Doggett, *Growing Up* (2021), p. 178.
9. *G*, 6 Nov 2007 (Chris Arnot); Andy Medhurst, *A National Joke* (Abingdon, 2007), pp. 98–9; *G*, 16 Mar 2013 (Mark Brown), 8 Jun 2017 (Savage); Claire Langhamer, *The*

English in Love (Oxford, 2013), pp. 201, 192; McLeod, *Religious Crisis*, p. 241; *NS*, 11 Nov 2022.

10. Cate Haste, *Rules of Desire* (1992), p. 195; Hall, 'Class', p. 111; Charles Stuart (ed.), *The Reith Diaries* (1975), p. 519; Jeremy Lewis, *Shades of Greene* (2010), p. 444; *T*, 24 May 1966 (Gillian Stathen). Also on Fox, see: *T*, 28 Nov 2001 (letter), 21 Jul 2015 (obituary).
11. Abbott, *Family Affairs*, p. 121; McLeod, *Religious Crisis*, p. 224; Jane Lewis and Patrick Wallis, 'Fault, Breakdown, and the Church of England's Involvement in the 1969 Divorce Reforms', in *Twentieth Century British History*, 2000 (11/3), pp. 308–32; Callum G. Brown, *The Battle for Christian Britain* (Cambridge, 2019), chaps 1–4, 6–7; Sam Brewitt-Taylor, *Christian Radicalism in the Church of England and the Invention of the British Sixties, 1957–1977* (Oxford, 2018), pp. 25–6.
12. Barbara Wootton, *In A World I Never Made* (1967), pp. 163–4; Meredith Veldman, *Fantasy, the Bomb, and the Greening of Britain* (Cambridge, 1994), pp. 218–20; *New Soc*, 9 Mar 1967. In general on progressive-minded pressure groups, see: Helene Curtis and Mimi Sanderson, *The Unsung Sixties* (2004).
13. *Ind*, 1 Jul 1997 (Rupert Cornwall), *NS*, 11 Jun 1965; *Partridge*, pp. 199–200; David Hendy, *The BBC* (2022), pp. 422–3; *G*, 17 Nov 2012 (Saskia Baron), Penny Warren, 'Michael Baron', 29 Jan 2026; 'Canon G. B. Bentley', *T*, 20 Sep 1996; *Ob*, 26 Nov 2023 (Rob Walker, citing Sue Tate); Janet Watts, 'Margaret Bramall', *G*, 17 Aug 2007; *G*, 3 Jan 1991 (Rebecca Abrams); Steve Bryson, 'Gwen Bryson', *G*, 1 Jul 2021; Alessandro Gallenzi, 'John Calder', *G*, 22 Aug 2018; Paul Oestreicher, 'Sydney Carter', *G*, 17 Mar 2004; Ferris, *Sex*, pp. 194–5, Callum G. Brown, 'Sex, Religion, and the Single Woman *c.* 1950–75', in *Twentieth Century British History*, 2011 (22/2), p. 202 (Chesser); Brown, *Battle*, p. 239, Doggett, *Growing Up*, pp. 300–1 (Cole); *LRB*, 22 Feb 2024 (Florence Sutcliffe-Braithwaite, on Comfort); *Spec*, 11 Mar 2006, *New Soc*, 11 Mar 1965 (Cooper); Bruce Wilkinson, 'Dave Cunliffe', *G*, 14 Jul 2021, 22 Feb 1964 (Jim Burns); *Unsung Sixties*, p. 435 (Elisabeth Hoodless); Malcolm Potts, 'Peter Diggory', *G*, 4 Jan 2010; *Ob*, 14 Sep 2025 (Bernardine Evaristo), *G*, 25 May 2024 (Alex Needham); 'A. E. Dyson', *T*, 13 Aug 2002; Veronica Horwell, 'Rose Evansky', *G*, 27 Jan 2017; 'Barry Fantoni', *T*, 23 May 2025; Richard Davenport-Hines, *The Pursuit of Oblivion* (2001), pp. 307–10; Haste, *Rules*, p. 213, Lewis and Wallis, 'Fault', p. 323; Jonathan Glancey, 'Patrick Garnett', *G*, 8 Jun 2006; *Ob*, 24 Jun 2007 (Geraldine Bedell); Jonathon Green, *All Dressed Up* (1998), pp. 131–2, 151–7, 168–70; *G*, 12 Mar 2026; Tom Deveson, 'David Holbrook', *G*, 2 Sep 2011; Joe Boyd, *White Bicycles* (2006), pp. 133–4; Peter Scott-Presland, 'Allan Horsfall', *Ind*, 11 Sep 2012; Richard Weight, *Mod!* (2013), p. 208; Patrick Marnham, *The Private Eye Story* (1982), pp. 112, 97, 90; Brewitt-Taylor, pp. 92, 41, 229; Rachel Reeves, *Alice in Westminster* (2017), pp. 136–7; Suzie Hayman, 'Sheila Kitzinger', *G*, 13 Apr 2015; Elizabeth Butler-Schloss, 'Lane (née Coulborn), Dame Elizabeth Kathleen', in *Oxford Dictionary of National Biography*, vol. 32 (Oxford, 2004), p. 420; 'Danny La Rue', *T*, 2 Jun 2009; Peter Stanford, *Lord Longford* (1994), pp. 327–9; Elizabeth Wilson, *Only Halfway to Paradise* (1980), p. 196; David Marquand, *Britain Since 1918* (2008), p. 220; Valerie Grove, *A Voyage Around John Mortimer* (2007), pp. 198–9; *NME*, 5 Aug 1966 (Keith Altham); Kenneth Leech, 'Valerie Pitt', *Ind*, 14 Jan 1999; Alistair Service, 'Nancy Raphael', *G*, 12 Mar 2003; Audrey Leathard, *The Fight for Family Planning* (1980), pp. 139, 144; Elisabeth Rivers-Bulkeley, *T*, 12 Feb 2007; Veronica Horwell, 'Tommy Roberts', *G*, 22 Dec 2012; Dennis Barker, 'Egon Ronay', *G*, 14 Jun 2010, 'Jonathan Routh', *G*, 9 Jun 2008; Linda Watson, 'William

Scholl', *Ind*, 1 Apr 2002; Brown, *Battle*, pp. 220, 216; Brewitt-Taylor, pp. 83–8; Jeremy Reed, *The King of Carnaby Street* (2010), pp. 122, 26, *G*, 8 Jun 2017 (Jon Savage), *TLS*, 1 Apr 2011 (Davenport-Hines); Michael De-La-Noy, *Mervyn Stockwood* (1996), p. 160; 'Anthony Storr', *T*, 20 Mar 2001; Simon Tisdall, 'Merry Tisdall', *G*, 23 Mar 2017; David Clark, 'Guidance, counselling, therapy', *Sociological Review*, Nov 1991, pp. 765–78; *NS*, 1 Nov 2024; Jill Gardiner, 'Gina Ware', *Ind*, 3 Aug 2001, 'Gina Ware', *T*, 22 Aug 2001; Ann Oakley, *A Critical Woman* (2011), p. 286.

14. David Simonelli, '"Meet the new boss/same as the old boss"' (University of Tulane PhD thesis, 2001), pp. 167, 172; *ES*, 29 May 1965; *MM*, 3 Jul 1965 (Nick Jones); Reed, *King*, pp. 129–30; *G*, 8 Jun 2017; *NME*, 23 Jul 1965.
15. *DM (1)*, 24 Oct 1966, 11 Jun 1966; Scottish Life Archive, W. Ms 1991/17/2, 'Mary Quant Cosmetics Ltd', undated; *DM (1)*, 14 Jun 1966; 'Dame Mary Quant', *T*, 14 Apr 2023; *G*, 14 Apr 2023 (Jess Cartner-Morley); *ES*, 6 Apr 1967; *DM (1)*, 11 Jun 1966; *G*, 28 Oct 2021; *Ob*, 17 Mar 2019 (Kate Kellaway). See also: Veronica Horwell, 'Dame Mary Quant', *G*, 14 Apr 2023.
16. *G*, 3 Dec 2005; *Independent on Sunday*, 4 Aug 1996.

CHAPTER 15 WHITE SHIRT! BLACK SHOES AND SOCKS!

1. David Lodge, *Quite a Good Time to Be Born* (2015), pp. 389–90; Paul Morley, *The North* (2013), pp. 178–9; Jeanette Winterson, *Why Be Happy When You Could Be Normal?* (2011), pp. 55, 87, 90–1, 94; Brian Griffin, *The Black Kingdom* (Stockport, 2013), pp. 15, 25; Martin Newell, *This Little Ziggy* (2001), pp. 29–30; *TLS*, 17 Nov 2006; Michael Collins, *The Likes of Us* (2004), pp. 163, 170, 173.
2. *Ind*, 11 Nov 2002 (Deborah Ross); *G*, 7 Sep 2024 (Esther Addley); Stuart Laing, *Representations of Working-Class Life, 1957–1964* (Basingstoke, 1986), p. 28; James Obelkevich, 'Consumption', in James Obelkevich and Peter Catterall (eds), *Understanding Post-war British Society* (1994), p. 145; John and Elizabeth Newson, *Four Years Old in an Urban Community* (1968), p. 33; Geoff Dyer, *Homework* (2025), pp. 15–17; *DM (1)*, 10 Sep 1965 (Lionel Clay).
3. *New Soc*, 4 Feb 1965 (John Barr); *Ob*, 29 Mar 1964; Graham Turner, *The North Country* (1967), p. 35; Anne Secord, 'David Elliston Allen', in *Archives of Natural History*, 10 Jun 2024 (51/1); D. Elliston Allen, *British Tastes* (1968), pp. 57, 72, 80, 96, 116–17, 129, 137, 162–3, 173, 201, 219. In general on food, see also: Nigel Slater, *Toast* (2003); *G*, 9 Apr 2003 (John Haney); Ian Mole, *Tiddle-ee-aye-go!* (2017), chap. 14.
4. *T*, 6 Jun 1966, 2 Jun 1966, 31 May 1966; Stephen McGann, *Flesh and Blood* (2017), p. 174; Avram Taylor, *Working Class Credit and Community Since 1918* (2002), pp. 161–3; *LRB*, 6 Nov 2025 (Rosemary Hill); Simon Gunn, 'People and the car', in *Social History*, 2013 (38/2), p. 224; John Urry, 'Holiday-Making in Britain since 1945', in *Contemporary Record*, summer 1991, p. 58; Gunn, 'People', p. 229; Richard Vinen, *Second City* (2022), pp. 255, 257; Margaret Hanson et al., *The Inner Circle* (Stroud, 2002), p. 7.
5. Duncan Hamilton, *Immortal* (2013), p. 98; *G*, 12 Aug 1993 (Henry Porter); Polly Pattullo, 'David Hessayon', *G*, 26 Feb 2025; John Littlewood, *The Stock Market* (1998), p. 271; *G*, 10 Sep 2010 (Andrew Roberts), 1 Apr 2006 (Blake Morrison); Peter Bird, *The First Food Empire* (Chichester, 2000), pp. 348–54; *Ind*, 21 Mar 1994 (Peter Dunn); *G*, 16 Apr 2016 (Ian Jack); *ES*, 7 Jan 2016 (Sophia Sleigh and Jonathan Prynn);

T, 11 Jan 2021; John Davis, *Waterloo Sunrise* (2022), p. 5; Turner, *North Country*, p. 35; Viv Albertine, *To Throw Away Unopened* (2018), p. 235; *(Wolverhampton) Express & Star*, 20 May 1966; Morrissey, *Autobiography* (2013), p. 28.

6. Otto Newman, 'The sociology of the betting shop', in *British Journal of Sociology*, Mar 1968, pp. 22–3, 31; Mole, *Tiddle*, chap. 29; Matthew Taylor, *The Association Game* (Harlow, 2008), p. 266; Arthur Hopcraft, *The Football Man* (1968), p. 189; *ES*, 25 Apr 2001.
7. Laurence Saywood, 'Identifying the Vicwardian Continuum in British Popular Music' (Goldsmith's, University of London PhD, 2024), p. 71; *Ind*, 8 Jul 2006; Turner, *North Country*, p. 251; Clancy Sigal, *The London Lover* (2018), p. 203; *NS*, 22 Jul 1966; Saywood, 'Vicwardian', pp. 60–73; Dave Russell, 'Glimpsing *La Dolce Vita'*, in *Journal of Social History*, 2013 (47/2), p. 299; Max Wall, *The Fool on the Hill* (1975), pp. 213–16; Jonathan Margolis, 'Bernard Manning', *Ind*, 19 Jun 2007; *NS*, 11 Jun 1965; Russell, 'Glimpsing', pp. 307–12. On WMCs, see also: Pete Brown, *Clubland* (Manchester, 2022).
8. Russell, p. 311; Ian Wallace, 'Max Jaffa', *Ind*, 1 Aug 1991; *New Soc*, 22 Dec 1966 (Benedict Nightingale); Saywood, 'Vicwardian', pp. 130–5.
9. 'Val Doonican', *T*, 3 Jul 2015, Dennis Barker, 'Val Doonican', *G*, 3 Jul 2015; Saywood, 'Vicwardian', pp. 135–40; Dave Harker, 'Still crazy after all these years', in Bart Moore-Gilbert and John Seed (eds), *Cultural Revolution?* (1992), pp. 239–40; *NS*, 24 Feb 1967; Harker, p. 241.
10. Martin Johnes, *Wales Since 1939* (Manchester, 2012), p. 115; Ian Mole, *Michelle My Umbrella* (2018), pp. 99–100; 'Peter Rogers', *T*, 16 Apr 2009; Andy Medhurst, *A National Joke* (Abingdon, 2007), p. 133; Marion Jordan, 'Carry On . . . Follow that Stereotype', in James Curran and Vincent Porter (eds), *British Cinema History* (1983), pp. 318–22; *Oldie*, Aug 2018, pp. 14–15.
11. Jeremy Ridgman, 'Inside the liberal heartland', in *Cultural Revolution?*, p. 140; Patrick Campbell, *My Life and Easy Times* (1967), p. 208; *P*, 25 Mar 1964 (Bernard Hollowood); Tom Jaine, 'Zena Skinner', *G*, 17 Apr 2018; *G*, 26 Jul 2014 (Ian Jack); Stephen Dixon, 'Eric Sykes', *G*, 5 Jul 2012; *Wikipedia*, 'Crossroads'; BBC WAC, R9/7/79–VR/66/60, 26 Jan 1966; *P*, 29 Apr 1964; Saywood, 'Vicwardian', pp. 144–52.
12. *G*, 15 Jan 2004; *NS*, 1 Sep 1965; *G*, 11 Jan 2003 (Ian Jack); Colin Seymour-Ure, *The British Press and Broadcasting Since 1945* (Oxford, 1991), Table 3.2; 'Barry Appleby', *T*, 21 Mar 1996; *NS*, 24 Dec 1965.
13. Julian Demetriadi, 'The golden years', in Gareth Shaw and Allan Williams (eds), *The Rise and Fall of British Coastal Resorts* (1997), p. 57; Tim Lott, *The Scent of Dried Roses* (1996), pp. 120–2; Roger K. Bingham, *Lost Resort?* (Milnthorpe, 1990), chap. 6; Wilfrid F. Simms, *The Littlehampton Miniature Railway, 1948–1998* (Rustington, 1998), p. 10; 'Fred Darrington', *T*, 23 Aug 2002; *G*, 13 May 2024 (Mark Brown); John Benson, *The Rise of Consumer Society in Britain, 1880–1980* (Harlow, 1994), p. 89; Turner, *North Country*, pp. 130, 134–5; John K. Walton, *Blackpool* (Edinburgh, 1998), p. 141; *Ind*, 28 Jul 2001 (Matthew Sweet).

CHAPTER 16 WHIPPED AT THE CART'S TAIL

1. Michael Christie (ed.), Derek Jarman, *At Your Own Risk* (Woodstock, New York, 1993), p. 42; Paul Bailey (ed.), *The Stately Homo* (2000), pp. 88–9; Bryan Magee, *One*

in Twenty (1966), pp. 65, 60, 66–7; BBC WAC, R9/7/74–VR/65/130, 10 Mar 1965; *Lancashire Evening Post*, 8 Jun 1965; Langford, S/GHL/1, 7 Oct 1966; *TLS*, 21 Dec 2012 (Richard Davenport-Hines); *NS*, 4 Feb 1966 (C. H. Rolph); *DM (1)*, 28 Oct 1965; *L*, 28 Jan 1965; *Independent on Sunday*, 4 Aug 1996. Generally on the homosexual experience by the mid-sixties, see also: Peter Parker (ed.), *Some Men in London*, vol. 2 (2024); Hugo Greenhalgh, *The Diaries of Mr Lucas* (2024).

2. Magee, *One*, pp. 61–2; Olive Stevenson, *Reflections on a Life in Social Work* (Buckingham, 2013), p. 48; Peter Doggett, *Growing Up* (2021), pp. 148–9; John Lahr (ed.), *The Orton Diaries* (1998 Methuen edn), p. 127.
3. Janet Street-Porter, *Baggage* (2004), pp. 220–1; *LRB*, 8 May 2025; *NS*, 28 Jul 2017 (David Kynaston). For an excellent biography of Ramsey, see: Leo McKinstry, *Sir Alf* (2006).
4. Jeffrey Weeks, *Sex, Politics and Society* (Harlow, 1989 edn), pp. 255–6; *P*, 28 Jul 1965 (Patrick Skene Catling); Liz Stanley, *Sex Surveyed, 1949–1994* (1995), p. 45; Christie Davies, *Permissive Britain* (1975), pp. 62–70; Geoffrey Gorer, *Sex & Marriage in England Today* (1971), pp. 4, 30, ix; Elizabeth Roberts, *Women and Families* (Oxford, 1995), p. 65; Graham Turner, *The North Country* (1967), p. 224.
5. Weeks, *Sex*, p. 331; Martin P. M. Richards and B. Jane Elliott, 'Sex and Marriage in the 1960s and 1970s', in David Clark (ed.), *Marriage, Domestic Life and Social Change* (1991), p. 43; Colin Gibson, 'The association between divorce and social class in England and Wales', in *British Journal of Sociology*, Mar 1974, p. 79; *New Soc*, 28 Oct 1965 (O. R. McGregor); Kenneth More, *More or Less* (1978), chaps 12–13; Robin Douglas-Home, *Hot for Certainties* (1964), p. 3.
6. Roberts, *Women*, p. 78; *NS*, 17 Jun 1966 (Cynthia Walton); draft autobiography of Veronica Porter (née Lee), pp. 113–14; *NS*, 17 Jun 1966 (Walton); Virginia Nicholson, *How Was It For You?* (2019), pp. 245–6; *NS*, 30 Sep 2016 (Kay Smith).
7. Porter, p. 114; Cate Haste, *Rules of Desire* (1992), p. 205; Gorer, *Sex & Marriage*, p. 139; Doggett, *Growing Up*, p. 312; Roberts, *Women*, p. 80; *New Soc*, 10 Nov 1966 (C. B. Goodhart); Nicholson, *How Was It For You?*, pp. 119–201; *New Soc*, 10 Nov 1966 (Goodhart); Street-Porter, *Baggage*, pp. 221–2; *LRB*, 16 Mar 2023.
8. Ken Livingstone, *You Can't Say That* (2011), p. 36; *G*, 11 Apr 2009; Pat Thane and Tanya Evans, *Sinners? Scroungers? Saints?* (Oxford, 2012), p. 121; Dennis Marsden, *Mothers Alone* (Harmondsworth, 1973 Pelican edn), p. 111; Gillian Clark, 'The Role of Mother and Baby Homes in the Adoption of Children Born Outside Marriage in Twentieth-Century England and Wales', in *Family & Community History*, May 2008, pp. 54–5; *ES*, 17 Oct 2002 (Cohen); Rachel Langham, 'Veronica Smith', *G*, 2 Oct 2024; Callum G. Brown, *Becoming Atheist* (2017), p. 93; Marsden, *Mothers*, p. 239; Thane and Evans, *Sinners?*, p. 133; Langford, S/GHL/1, 7 Oct 1966. For other heartbreaking stories of forced adoption, see: *Ob*, 27 Oct 2013 (Yvonne Roberts), *G*, 27 May 2021 (Harriet Sherwood), 28 May 2021 (Gaby Hinsliff).
9. 'Fay Kramrisch', *T*, 11 Nov 2023; *G*, 8 Mar 2021; April Carter, *The Politics of Women's Rights* (Harlow, 1988), p. 40; Gorer, *Sex*, pp. viii, 92; Selina Todd, *The People* (2014), p. 280.
10. Porter, p. 141; Penelope Mortimer, *About Time Too* (1993), p. 74; Jeanette Winterson, *Why Be Happy When You Could Be Normal?* (2011), p. 46; Roberts, *Women*, p. 106; Tim Lott, *The Scent of Dried Roses* (1996), pp. 125–7.

11. Martin Johnes, *Wales Since 1939* (Manchester, 2012), p. 116; Pete Brown, *Clubland* (Manchester, 2022), pp. 239–40; Laurence Saywood, 'Identifying the Vicwardian Continuum in British Popular Music' (Goldsmiths, University of London PhD, 2024), p. 78; Michael Wolfers, 'The North', in Richard Mabey (ed.), *Class* (1967), pp. 149–50; Turner, *North Country*, p. 361; *G*, 8 Feb 2020; David Horspool, *More Than a Game* (2023), p. 233; Andrew Ward & John Williams, *Football Nation* (2009), pp. 120–7; John Williams, *Football in Wind and Rain* (Chichester, 2024), p. 234. For an overall history of women's football in Britain, see: Suzanne Wrack, *A Woman's Game* (2022).
12. Ysenda Maxtone Graham, *Jobs for the Girls* (2023), pp. 13, 22, 27–8, 36, 34, 50; Ruth Adam, *A Woman's Place, 1910–1975* (Persephone edn, 2000), p. 274; Nicholson, *How Was It For You?*, p. 256; Carol Dyhouse, 'Education', in Ina Zweiniger-Bargielowska (ed.), *Women in Twentieth-Century Britain* (Harlow, 2001), pp. 127, 124; Mary Abbott, *Family Affairs* (2003), p. 136; Dyhouse, 'Education', p. 127; Nicholson, *How Was It For You?*, p. 257; Mary Ingham, *Now We Are Thirty* (1981), pp. 103–10.
13. 'Dame Ann Leslie', *T*, 28 Jun 2023; Steve Humphries and John Taylor, *The Making of Modern London, 1945–1985* (1986), p. 74; *Kynaston*, pp. 148–9; *G*, 24 Jan 2004 (Zoe Williams); Maxtone Graham, *Jobs*, pp. 154–5, 248, 241–2, 251.
14. Hugh Beynon and Ray Hudson, *The Shadow of the Mine* (2021), p. 193; Michael Chaplin, *Newcastle United Stole My Heart* (2021), p. 17; Jeremy Gavron, *A Woman on the Edge of Time* (2015), pp. 229–30; Roberts, *Women*, pp. 129–31; Maxtone Graham, *Jobs*, p. 265; Paul Jennings, *The Living Village* (1968), p. 188.
15. Helen McCarthy, *Double Lives* (2020), pp. 234, 247, 243–4, 250, 258–9. See also: Penelope Labovitch and Rosemary Simon, *Late Start* (1966), including a supportive preface from Marjorie Proops; Pat Williams, *Working Wonders* (1969); Dolly Smith Wilson, 'A New Look at the Affluent Worker: The Good Working Mother in Post-War Britain', in *Twentieth Century British History*, 2006 (17/2), pp. 206–29; Jane Lewis, 'The Failure to Expand Childcare Provision and to Develop a Comprehensive Childcare Policy in Britain during the 1960s and 1970s', in *Twentieth Century British History*, 2013 (24/2), pp. 249–74.
16. Sarah Aiston, 'A Good Job for a Girl?', in *Twentieth Century British History*, 2004 (15/4), pp. 366–7; Carter, *Politics*, pp. 30, 33; Nicholson, *How Was It For You?*, p. 248; McCarthy, *Double Lives*, p. 276; *Kynaston*, pp. 159–60; David Kynaston, *Till Time's Last Sand* (2017), pp. 545–6; David Lascelles, *Other People's Money* (2005), p. 101; Nicholson, *How Was It For You?*, p. 249; Anne Perkins, *Red Queen* (2003), p. 209.
17. Cynthia L. White, *Women's Magazines, 1693–1968* (1970), pp. 222, 228; 'Barbara Boxall', *T*, 6 Apr 2017; White, p. 229. On *Woman's Own*, see also: Myriam Wilks-Heeg, 'How slimming became an obsession with women in post-war Britain', 'The Conversation' (online), 3 Jul 2017.
18. 'Trevor Hill', *T*, 7 Nov 2023; Maggie Brown, 'Nan Winton', *G*, 31 May 2019; *NS*, 31 Jan 1964; Joan Bakewell, *The Centre of the Bed* (2003), p. 176; *T*, 11 Sep 2021 (Roger Lewis); Sheila Rowbotham, *Promise of a Dream* (Verso edn, 2019), p. 131; Maggie Andrews, 'Butterflies and Caustic Asides', in Stephen Wagg (ed.), *Because I Tell a Joke or Two* (1998), p. 52; Maxtone Graham, *Jobs*, p. 18; *Big Issue*, 22 Feb 2016; Nicholson, *How Was It For You?*, pp. 192, 243; *Wikipedia*, 'Action Man' ; Alex Comfort, *The Anxiety Makers* (1967), p. 177; Doggett, *Growing Up*, p. 98; Anne Robinson, *Memoirs of an Unfit Mother* (2002 pbk edn), p. 59.

CHAPTER 17 NOT A GUITAR IN SIGHT

1. Michael Williams, *Born Rebel* (2022), pp. 158–9; *G*, 26 May 2007; *DT*, 24–5 Aug 1964; Jane Torday and Roger Mortimer, *Dearest Jane . . .* (2014), pp. 72–4; *Wikipedia*, 'Roger Mortimer (racing)'.
2. Elizabeth Roberts, *Women and Families* (Oxford, 1995), pp. 51–3; Ronald Fletcher, *The Family and Marriage in Britain* (Harmondsworth, 1973 edn), pp. 118–21; Lawrence Black, *Redefining British Politics* (Basingstoke, 2010), p. 77; James H. Mills, *Cannabis Nation* (Oxford, 2013), p. 121; David Kynaston, *A Northern Wind* (2023), pp. 414–15; Thomas Loughran et al., 'A Coming of Age', in *Contemporary British History*, Feb 2021, pp. 294–5; *DT*, 20 Jul 1967.
3. Viv Albertine, *To Throw Away Unopened* (2018), p. 107; Leila Berg, *Risinghill* (Harmondsworth, 1968), p. 271; Kenneth Roy, *The Invisible Spirit* (Prestwick, 2013), p. 321; *T*, 31 Mar 2021; Mary Abbott, *Family Affairs* (2003), p. 130; *NS*, 16 May 2025; *Ob*, 14 Sep 2014; Paul Morley, *The North* (2013), p. 168; Ian Mole, *Michelle My Umbrella* (2018), pp. 7, 22–8.
4. David Fowler, *Youth Culture in Modern Britain, c. 1920–c. 1970* (Basingstoke, 2008), p. 167; *Big Issue*, 3 Feb 2014; *G*, 26 Nov 2005; Anton Rippon, *A Derby Boy* (Stroud, 2007), p. 132; *T*, 13 Aug 2024; *TLS*, 2 May 2025 (Fay Bound Alberti); *Ob*, 30 Mar 2025; *G*, 29 Mar 2025.
5. *G*, 18 Nov 2017, 22 Feb 2014; David Frost and Antony Jay, *To England With Love* (1967), pp. 15, 115; Harold Perkin, *The Rise of Professional Society* (2002 edn), pp. 455–6; Mike Savage, 'Sociology, Class and Male Manual Work Cultures', in John McIlroy et al. (eds), *British Trade Unions and Industrial Politics*: Volume Two (Aldershot, 1999), chap. 1.
6. Rippon, *Derby Boy*, p. 125; *G*, 18 Feb 2006, 1 Dec 2012; *Crossman*, p. 344; *Prospect*, Jul 2007, p. 47; *NS*, 22 Jul 1966.
7. Martin Francis, 'The Labour Party', in Becky Conekin et al. (eds), *Moments of Modernity* (1999), pp. 169–70; *P*, 4 Aug 1965 (Patrick Skene Catling); Frank Mort, 'Social and Symbolic Fathers and Sons in Postwar Britain', in *Journal of British Studies*, Jul 1999, p. 367; Geoff Dyer, *Homework* (2025), p. 92; John Cleese, *So, Anyway . . .* (2014), pp. 251–3.
8. *G*, 11 Jul 2025; The Wives' Fellowship, *The Spirit of Wives* (2016), p. 53; Christie Davies, *The Strange Death of Moral Britain* (2004), pp. 300, 400; Roy Wallis, 'Moral Indignation and the Media', in *Sociology*, May 1976, pp. 291, 294; BBC WAC, T/5/782/3, 7 Oct 1966.
9. Clive D. Field, *Secularization in the Long 1960s* (2017), pp. 97, 91; *New Soc*, 27 May 1965 (Ronald Goldman); *Ind*, 5 Apr 2014; *Mail on Sunday*, 17 Jan 1999 (Stewart Steven).
10. *Banffshire Herald*, 14 May 1966; *Haltwhistle Echo*, 13 May 1966; *Clitheroe Advertiser*, 13 May 1966; *Fraserburgh Herald*, 13 May 1966; *Gourock Times*, 13 May 1966; *Brechin Advertiser*, 19 May 1966; *Dunoon Observer and Argyllshire Standard*, 21 May 1966; *Dalkeith Advertiser*, 19 May 1966; *Littlehampton Gazette*, 20 May 1966; *Pontypridd Observer*, 20 May 1966; *Kidderminster Times*, 20 May 1966; *North Bucks Times*, 25 May 1966; *Dewsbury Reporter*, 21 May 1966; *Cambrian News*, 27 May 1966; *Marlborough Times*, 27 May 1966; *Brecon & Radnor Express*, 26 May 1966; *Llanelli Star*, 28 May 1966; *Felixstowe Times*, 27 May 1966; *Reading Mercury*, 28 May 1966; *Andover Advertiser*, 27 May 1966; *Ilkley Gazette*, 27 May 1966; *County*

Times, 4 Jun 1966; *Peterborough Standard*, 27 May 1966; *Leith Gazette*, 27 May 1966; *Glossop Chronicle*, 20 May 1966, 3 Jun 1966; *Holyhead & Anglesey Mail*, 27 May 1966.

CHAPTER 18 TURN IT DOWN!

1. Haines, SxMOA99/34/8/19, 1 Apr 1966; *D Ex*, 2 Apr 1966; *News of the World*, 3 Apr 1966; Frederick Ward, GPD/145/1966, 4 Apr 1966; 'William Davis', *DT*, 5 Feb 2019; *T*, 7 Apr 1966; BBC WAC, R9/7/80–VR/66/189, 6 Apr 1966; Marks, 6 Apr 1966; Mark Lewisohn, *The Complete Beatles Chronicle* (1996), pp. 216–17; *Crossman*, p. 498.
2. *TLS*, 7 Apr 1966; Adam Sisman, *A. J. P. Taylor* (1994), p. 338; David Frost, *An Autobiography* (1993), pp. 182–3; *Radio Times*, 31 Mar 1966.
3. *NME*, 8 Apr 1966; BBC WAC, R9/7/80–VR/66/192, 8 Apr 1966; *News of the World*, 10 Apr 1966; Hugo Vickers (ed.), *Beaton in the Sixties* (2003), p. 111; Heap, Acc 2243/040/10 Apr 1966; *Sun*, 11 Apr 1966; *G*, 7 Apr 2006 (Will Hodgkinson); *ST*, 4 Apr 1976; Christopher Hitchens, *Hitch-22* (2010), p. 81; Doug Hinman, *The Kinks* (San Francisco, 2004), p. 80; Johnny Rogan, *Ray Davies* (2015), pp. 266–7.
4. BBC WAC, R9/7/80–VR/66/202, 12 Apr 1966; *Ob*, 3 Apr 1966; Turtle, 15 Apr 1966; *Sun*, 15 Apr 1966; Haines, SxMOA99/34/8/19, 14 Apr 1966; *NS*, 22 Apr 1966 (James Cameron); Heap, Acc 2243/040, 15 Apr 1966; Paul Foot, *The Rise of Enoch Powell* (Harmondsworth, 1969), p. 97; *Sun*, 16 Apr 1966; *News of the World*, 17 Apr 1966; *Sun*, 18 Apr 1966; *News of the World*, 17 Apr 1966; *Sun*, 18 Apr 1966.
5. *ST*, 17 Apr 1966; *P*, 20 Apr 1966; *Sun*, 13 Apr 1966; *NS*, 15 Apr 1966; Heap, Acc 2243/040, 13 Apr 1966; *G*, 15 Apr 1966; Janie Hampton (ed.), *Joyce & Ginnie* (1997), p. 331; Richard Huggett, *Binkie Beaumont* (1989), p. 491; *DT*, 12 Apr 1966; John Lahr, *Prick Up Your Ears* (2002 pbk edn), p. 212; *G*, 12 Apr 1966.
6. Heap, Acc 2243/040, 18 Apr 1966; *Wikipedia*, 'West Coast Main Line'; Keith McBride, GDP/379/1965–68, 19 Apr 1966; *Sun*, 20 Apr 1966; *Spec*, 22 Apr 1966 (Ludovic Kennedy); *P*, 20 Apr 1966; Carol Ann Lee, *One of Your Own* (Edinburgh, 2010), p. 269; Jack Common Papers (University of Newcastle Library, Special Collections), box 77, 20 Apr 1966.
7. *T*, 21 Apr 1966; Eric Dunning et al., *The Roots of Football Hooliganism* (1988), p. 151; *T*, 22 Apr 1966; *Castle*, p. 61; *NS*, 22 Apr 1966; Paul Foot, *The Politics of Harold Wilson* (Harmondsworth, 1968), p. 172; *Hansard*, 22 Apr 1966, col. 315; Scott, SxMOA99/97/1/15, 23 Apr 1966; BBC WAC, R9/7/80–VR/66/222, 23 Apr 1966; *Williams*, p. 278; *P*, 4 May 1966 (Francis Williams).
8. *Wikipedia*, '*Morning Star* (British Newspaper)'; *Kynaston*, pp. 318–19; Betty Allen, GDP/450/1963–67, 25 Apr 1966; BBC WAC, R9/7/80–VR/66/228, 25 Apr 1966; Geoffrey Wheatcroft, *Churchill's Shadow* (2021), pp. 423–4; *T*, 26 Apr 1966; *NS*, 29 Apr 1966 (Jacobson); Frederick Ward, GDP/145/1966, 26 Apr 1966; *DT*, 27 Apr 1966.
9. *Benn*, p. 405; Tam Dalyell, 'Tom Iremonger', *Ind*, 26 May 1998; https://coronationstreet.fandom.com/wiki/Episode_561; *Larkin*, p. 358; Willmott, WLMT 1/32, 28 Apr 1966; *Country Life*, 28 Apr 1966; *G*, 30 Apr 1966; Edward Leeson, *Dusty Springfield* (2001), pp. 75–7; *Sun*, 30 Apr 1966; Kevin Cann, *Any Day Now* (2010), pp. 81–2.
10. *Charwell*, 4 May 1966; Harold Wilson, *The Labour Government, 1964–1970* (1971), pp. 226–7; *Benn*, p. 406; Lee, 1 May 1966; *Uncut*, Feb 2006, pp. 44–8 (Steve

Sutherland); Mojo, *Days that Shook the World* (2002), p. 46 (Johnny Black); *T*, 2 May 1966; Kenneth O. Morgan, *Callaghan* (Oxford, 1997), p. 239; *Crossman*, p. 510; *Castle*, p. 62; https://coronationstreet.fandom.com/wiki/Episode_562; *T*, 3 May 1966; *DT*, 4 May 1966; Turtle, D103/1/31, 3 May 1966; *Kynaston*, p. 319.

11. *Sun*, 5 May 1966; Turtle, D103/1/31, 4 May 1966; https://coronationstreet.fandom.com/wiki/Episode_563; *Ind*, 21 Dec 1996 (Glenn Moore); *Ob*, 1 May 1966; John Campbell, *Margaret Thatcher*, Volume One (2000), p. 171; Turtle, D103/1/31, 5 May 1966; Hodgson, 5 May 1966; *G*, 7 May 1966 (Geoffrey Whiteley); Haines, SxMOA99/34/8/19, 6 May 1966; Marks, 6 May 1966; Turtle, D103/1/31, 8 May 1966; *Ob*, 8 May 1966; *Sunday Express*, 8 May 1966; Terence Morris, 'Myra Hindley', *Ind*, 16 Nov 2002; *DM (2)*, 16 May 2017; *Big Issue*, 22 May 2017.
12. 'John Fowles', *T*, 8 Nov 2005; *Ob*, 1 May 1966; *Fowles (2)*, p. 14; *ST*, 1 May 1966; *S Tel*, 1 May 1966; *T*, 5 May 1966; *DT*, 5 May 1966; *L*, 5 May 1966; *TLS*, 5 May 1966; *New Soc*, 5 May 1966; *G*, 6 May 1966; *Spec*, 6 May 1966; *NS*, 6 May 1966; *Fowles (2)*, p. 14; Peter Guttridge, 'John Fowles', *Ind*, 8 Nov 2005.
13. *Ob*, 8 May 1966; *News of the World*, 8 May 1966; *Benn*, p. 409; *G*, 11 May 1966; Clinton Heylin, *Bob Dylan: A Life in Stolen Moments* (1996), p. 100; Foot, *Politics of Harold Wilson*, p. 172; *G*, 13 Sep 2006 (Peter Lewis); Jenny Uglow (ed.), Angela Carter, *Shaking a Leg* (1997), p. 324; *Castle*, p. 65; Heap, Acc 2243/040, 12 May 1966; Heylin, p. 100; *Sun*, 13 May 1966; *NS*, 13 May 1966; Philip Ziegler, *Wilson* (1993), p. 251; Turtle, D103/1/31, 13 May 1966; Keith McBride, GDP/379/1965–68, 13 May 1966; *Sun*, 14 May 1966; 'Jimmy Gabriel', *T*, 22 Jul 2021; Heylin, p. 100; *News of the World*, 15 May 1966; *T*, 16 May 1966, 14 May 1966; https://www.facebook.com/photo/?fbid=10158217358195875@set=a.236419465874.
14. Edwin Way Teale, *Springtime in Britain* (1971), pp. 4, 19, 23, 42, 51, 62, 93, 126, 174, 196, 200, 225–8, 257, 276, 287, 291, 348, 388, 29–30; *S Tel*, 11 Apr 1971; *G*, 17 Mar 1966; *Ob*, 20 Mar 1966, 27 Mar 1966, 3 Apr; *G*, 11 Apr 1966, 3 May 1966, 31 May 1966, 14 Mar 1966; Anthony Hayward, 'Betty Paul', *Ind*, 13 Apr 2011; *DT*, 22 Jun 1966; *G*, 8 Aug 1966; Hayward, 'Betty Paul'; *G*, 9 Apr 1966.

CHAPTER 19 MOANING MINNIES

1. *T*, 16 May 1966; *Castle*, p. 65; Keith Jeffery and Peter Hennessy, *States of Emergency* (1983), p. 230; Clinton Heylin, *Bob Dylan: A Life in Stolen Moments* (1996), p. 101; James Allen, GDP/172/1966 (5), 17 May 1966; Caryl Phillips, *Foreigners* (2007), pp. 154–5; *Kidderminster Times*, 20 May 1966; Keith McBride, GDP/379/1965–68, 17 May 1966; Mark Lewisohn, *Radio Times Guide to TV Comedy* (2003 edn), p. 33; 'Derek Nimmo', *T*, 25 Feb 1999; *DT*, 18 May 1966 (Sean Day-Lewis); *Ind*, 26 Feb 1994 (E. J. Taylor); *Bob Dylan Live 1966: The Bootleg Series*, Vol. 4 (1998 CD). See also: C. P. Lee, *Like the Night: Bob Dylan and the road to the Manchester Free Trade Hall* (1998); Andy Kershaw, 'Ghosts of Electricity', Radio 3, 25 Sep 2005; Martin Scorsese's 2005 documentary film, *No Return Home*, for the crucial footage.
2. *(Portsmouth) Evening News*, 19 May 1966; *Castle*, p. 66; *Benn*, p. 413; *DT*, 28 May 1966 (Terence Mullaly); Heylin, p. 102; Robert Harris, *Good and Faithful Servant* (1990), p. 43; *DT*, 4 May 1966; James Booth, *Philip Larkin* (2014), p. 302; *T*, 7 Feb 2009; Heylin, p. 102; Keith McBride, GDP/379/1965–68, 20 May 1966; Larkin,

Ms. Eng. c. 7433, 22 May 1966, fo. 40; Tony Gould, *Inside Outsider* (1993), pp. 191–4; *DT*, 24 May 1966, 4 May 1966; *S Tel*, 22 May 1966; *Wikipedia*, '*The Incredible String Band* (album)'; *G*, 24 May 1966; Harold Wilson, *The Labour Government, 1964–1970* (1971), p. 231; Langford, S/GHL/1, 24 May 1966; Haines, SxMOA99/34/8/19, 24 May 1966; *Clitheroe Advertiser*, 27 May 1966; 'Reg Varney', *T*, 17 Nov 2008; *DT*, 26 May 1966; John McVicar, *McVicar by Himself* (1974), pp. 187–8; https://coronationstreet.fandom.com/wiki/Episode_569; BBC WAC, R9/7/81–VR/66/284, 25 May 1966; John R. Cook, '"Between Grierson and Barnum"', in *Journal of British Cinema and Television*, 2004 (1/2), p. 225.

3. *G*, 27 May 1966; Terry Pattinson, 'Jim Slater', *Ind*, 31 May 1993; *New Soc*, 26 May 1966; *Ob*, 8 May 1966 (Hawarth); *G*, 27 May 1966; *Crossman*, p. 524; Mervyn Jones, *Michael Foot* (1994), p. 297; *Crossman*, pp. 529–30; Robert J. Wybrow, *Britain Speaks Out, 1937–87* (Basingstoke, 1989), p. 78; Turtle, D103/1/31, 18 May 1966; Kier Thorpe, 'The "Juggernaut" Method', in *Twentieth Century British History*, 2001 (12/4), pp. 476–7; Paul Foot, 'The Seamen's Struggle', in Robin Blackburn and Alexander Cockburn (eds), *The Incompatibles* (Harmondsworth, 1967), p. 195.
4. Heylin, p. 103; *MM*, 4 Jun 1966; Tony Jasper (ed.), *The Top Twenty Book* (1994 edn), p. 119; Peter Doggett, *Growing Up* (2021), p. 231; *G*, 30 May 1966; Jonathan Croal (ed.), A. S. Neill, *All the Best, Neill* (1983), p. 19; James Allen, GDP/172(4)/1966, 29 May 1966; Frederick Ward, GDP/145/1966, 30 May 1966; *Manchester Sketch*, Jun 1966 (Max Murphy); *Sun*, 1 Jun 1966; *DM (1)*, 1 Jun 1966; Haines, SxMOA99/34/8/19, 1 Jun 1966; *DT*, 2 Jun 1966; *G*, 2 Jun 1966; *T*, 2 Jun 1966; *Sun*, 2 Jun 1966 (Noel Whitcomb).
5. *Sun*, 2 Jun 1966; Angus Fraser, 'Bill Frindall', *Ind*, 3 Feb 2009; *Benn*, p. 421; *NS*, 10 Jun 1966 ('Taurus'); Keith McBride, GDP/379/1965–68, 3 Jun 1966; Grace Taylor, GDP/318/1966, 4 Jun 1966; *Ob*, 5 Jun 1966; Larkin, Ms. Eng. c. 7433, 4 Jun 1966, fo. 54; *ST*, 12 Jun 1966; Hague, 5 Jun 1966; *T*, 6 Jun 1966; Willmott, WLMT 1/32, 6 Jun 1966; Betty Allen, GDP/450/1963–67, 6 Jun 1966; John Heilpern, *John Osborne* (2006), pp. 325–6; *DM (1)*, 7 Jun 1966; *T*, 7 Jun 1966; *DT*, 7 Jun 1966; *DM (1)*, 7 Jun 1966; *S Tel*, 12 Jun 1966; *ST*, 12 Jun 1966; *Sun*, 7 Jun 1966.
6. *Manchester Evening News*, 7 Jun 1966; *G*, 9 Jun 1966; *DM (1)*, 10 Jun 1966; Johnny Rogan, *Ray Davies* (2015), pp. 268–74; Julie Walters, *That's Another Story* (2008), p. 43; *T*, 10 Jun 1966; *Sun*, 10 Jun 1966; *DT*, 11 Jun 1966; 'Norman "Nobby" Pilcher', *T*, 26 Jul 2023; Heilpern, *Osborne*, p. 326; *D Ex*, 10 Jun 1966; BBC WAC, *Any Questions?*, 10 Jun 1966.
7. *G*, 14 Jun 1966; *Sun*, 14 Jun 1966; Heap, Acc 2243/040, 13 Jun 1966; Paul Boyle (ed.), *Cassandra at his finest and funniest* (1967), pp. 62–5; *Sun*, 14 Jun 1966; *Castle*, p. 69; *Crossman*, p. 538; Foot, 'Seamen's Struggle', p. 203; Thorpe, '"Juggernaut"', pp. 464–5; *Benn*, pp. 427–8; Heap, Acc 2243/040, 14 Jun 1966.
8. Foot, 'Seamen's Struggle', p. 203; *G*, 11 Dec 2002; John Prescott, *Prezza* (2008), p. 91; Colin Brown, *Fighting Talk* (1997), pp. 102–3; *G*, 11 Dec 2002; *DT*, 17 Jun 1966; Wybrow, p. 78.
9. *Kynaston*, p. 320; Betty Allen, GDP/450/1963–67, 15 Jun 1966; Heap, Acc 2243/040, 15 Jun 1966; Michael Coveney, 'Terence Frisby'; *G*, 25 Apr 2020; *DT*, 16 Jun 1966; Richard Boston, *Osbert* (1989), p. 171; *TLS*, 16 Jun 1966; Larkin, Ms. Eng. c. 7433, 27 Jun 1966, fo. 75; Peter Oborne, *Basil D'Oliveira* (2004), p. 105.
10. Mark Lewisohn, *The Complete Beatles Chronicle* (1996), p. 225; *DM (1)*, 17 Jun 1966; *G*, 27 May 1966; *DT*, 17 Jun 1966; *G*, 17 Jun 1966.

11. Ben Pimlott, *Harold Wilson* (1992), p. 406; *Wisden Cricketers' Almanac, 1967* (1967), p. 298; Lee, 17 Jun 1966; *MM*, 18 Jun 1966; *DM (1)*, 20 Jun 1966 (John Walker); Charles Marowitz, *Burnt Bridges* (1990), pp. 154–5; *TLS*, 6 Jan 2006; *DM (1)*, 20 Jun 1966; *Ob*, 19 Jun 1966 (Peter Marsh); *London Magazine*, Aug 1966, pp. 80–1; John Fisher, *Tony Hancock* (2008), p. 423; Roger Wilmut, *Tony Hancock 'Artiste'* (1986 edn), pp. 152, 252; Alec Cairncross, *The Wilson Years* (1997), p. 142.
12. *TLS*, 6 Jan 2006; Pimlott, *Wilson*, pp. 406–7; *Crossman*, p. 544; 'Lord Prescott', *T*, 22 Nov 2024; *Castle*, p. 70; *Benn*, p. 437; *Castle*, p. 70; *Crossman*, p. 544; *Wikipedia*, 'Reg Calvert'; Larkin, Ms. Eng. c. 7433, 21 Jun 1966, fos 68–9; *Benn*, pp. 436–7; *T*, 22 Jun 1966; Paul Sutton (ed.), Lindsay Anderson, *The Diaries* (2004), p. 161; *Crossman*, p. 547; *T*, 24 Jun 1966; 'Kathy Kirby', *T*, 21 May 2011; BBC WAC, R9/7/81–VR/66/338, 23 Jun 1966; Jones, *Foot*, p. 298; *T*, 25 Jun 1966.
13. Foot, 'Seamen's Struggle', pp. 196–7; *DM (1)*, 25 Jun 1966; Heap, Acc 2243/040, 25 Jun 1966; *T*, 30 Dec 2022 (Michael Grant); *G*, 27 Jun 1966; Thorpe, "'Juggernaut"', p. 477; Joanna Moorhead, *New Generations* (Chesterton, 1996), p. 43; *Crossman*, p. 550; *T*, 28 Jun 1966; *Sun*, 28 Jun 1966; *T*, 28 Jun 1966.
14. *Castle*, p. 71; *T*, 29 Jun 1966; *Benn*, p. 439; Scott, SxMOA99/97/1/15, 28 Jun 1966; Kathleen Tynan (ed.), Kenneth Tynan, *Letters* (Random House edn, New York, 1998), pp. 347–52; Frederick Ward, GDP/145/1966, 28 Jun 1966; *DT*, 1 Jul 2016 (James Titcomb); Marks, 29 Jun 1966; *P*, 29 Jun 1966 (Furlong); *T*, 30 Jun 1966; *Benn*, p. 440; *Castle*, p. 72; Heap, Acc 2243/040, 29 Jun 1966.
15. *DM (1)*, 30 Jun 1966; Adam Sharr and Stephen Thornton, *Demolishing Whitehall* (2013), p. 232; Rogan, *Davies*, p. 282; 'Lord O'Brien of Lothbury', *T*, 25 Nov 1995; *LRB*, 4 Jul 2024 (Rosemary Hill); *G*, 2 Jul 1966; Denis Judd (ed.), *The Private Diaries of Alison Uttley* (Barnsley, 2009), p. 280; Donald Coggan, *Cuthbert Bardsley* (1989), p. 176; Dee, DDX 829/3, 2 Jul 1966.
16. Geoffrey Goodman, *The Awkward Warrior* (1979), pp. 495–9; *Benn*, p. 443; Jones, *Foot*, p. 298; Wilson, *Labour Government*, p. 245; Haines, SxMOA99/34/8/19, 3 Jul 1966; Graham Payn and Sheridan Morley (eds), *The Noël Coward Diaries* (1982), p. 633; Dee, 3 Jul 1966; *Crossman*, p. 557; Douglas Jay, *Change and Fortune* (1980), p. 344; *T*, 5 Jul 1966; Lewis Baston, *Reggie* (Stroud, 2004), p. 272; *RT*, 30 Jun 1966; Diana Griffith, GDP/7/1965–69, 5 Jul 1966; Geoffrey K. Fry, 'Parliament and "Morality"', in *Contemporary British History*, spring 1998, p. 142; *G*, 6 Jul 1966; Dee, 5 Jul 1966.
17. *NS*, 1 Jul 1966; *G*, 1–2 Jul 1966, 5 Jul 1966; *T*, 6 Jul 1966; Goodman, *Awkward Warrior*, pp. 500–1; *Benn*, pp. 445–6.
18. Bank of England Archives, G3/264, 6 Jul 1966 (J.V.O.); *G*, 7 Jul 1966; *TLS*, 7 Jul 1966; Pimlott, *Wilson*, p. 414; https://www.lightstraw.uk/ate/main/ris/16.html ('The Post Office "Dial-a-Disc" Service'); Doug Hinman, *The Kinks* (San Francisco, 2004), p. 86; Martin Johnes, *Wales Since 1939* (Manchester, 2012), pp. 99–100; Harris, *Good and Faithful Servant*, p. 45; *Kynaston*, p. 320; *G*, 11 Jul 1966; Haines, SxMOA99/34/8/19, 9 Jul 1966; *Ob*, 10 Jul 1966; Fisher, *Hancock*, p. 423; Lavinia Greacen (ed.), *J. G. Farrell in his Own Words* (Cork, 2009), p. 93; *Crossman*, p. 566; Wilmut, *Hancock*, pp. 156, 252; Samuel Brittan, *Steering the Economy* (Harmondsworth, 1971 edn), p. 332; Pimlott, *Wilson*, pp. 415–16; *Crossman*, pp. 566–7; *RT*, 7 Jul 1966.
19. *Four Four Two*, 11 Jul 2018 (Steve Morgan); Marks, 15 Apr 1966; Rosa Prince, *Comrade Corbyn* (2016), pp. 31–2; BBC WAC, R9/7/82–VR/66/372, 10 Jul 1966; *P*, 6 Jul 1966; *NS*, 8 Jul 1966; *RT*, 7 Jul 1966; Uttley, p. 280; Marks, 11 Jul 1966; John Cleese, *So, Anyway . . .* (2014), p. 286.

20. *ST*, 10 Jul 1966; Richard Batley et al., *Going Comprehensive* (1970), p. 98; *DT*, 4 Aug 1966; Scott, SxMOA99/97/1/15, 7 May 1966.
21. *G*, 12 May 1966; *T*, 24 Jun 1966; *New Soc*, 12 May 1966; *NS*, 24 Jun 1966 (Alan R. Wolfe); *New Soc*, 19 May 1966 (J. M. Ross and P. Case).
22. *Ob*, 12 Jun 1966; Kit Hardwick, *Brian Jackson* (Cambridge, 2003), p. 22; Brian Jackson and Dennis Marsden, *Education and the Working Class* (Harmondsworth, 1966 Pelican edn), pp. 249–50.
23. *Crossman*, pp. 567–8; Roy Jenkins, *A Life at the Centre* (1991), p. 191; Brittan, *Steering*, p. 332; Preston, 6D87/6, 12 Jul 1966, fo. 1503; Betty Allen, GDP/450/1963–67, 12 Jul 1966; Avril Sandall, GDP/343/1966, 12 Jul 1966; *DT*, 13 Jul 1966 (R. H. Williams); *G*, 13 Jul 1966.
24. Dee, DDX 829/3, 13 Jul 1966; Jay, *Change*, pp. 344–5; Kenneth O. Morgan, *Callaghan* (Oxford, 1997), p. 241; Pimlott, *Wilson*, pp. 417–19; *Castle*, p. 74; Cairncross, *Wilson*, p. 151; Goodman, *Awkward Warrior*, p. 509; *NS*, 23 Sep 1966 (Brian Parkyn); Michael Crick, *Michael Heseltine* (1997), p. 130; *G*, 15 Jul 1966; *NS*, 2 Oct 2020 (E. Pritchard); John Davies, 'Wales in the Nineteen-sixties', in *Llafur*, 1987 (4/4), p. 87; Brittan, *Steering*, p. 332; John Littlewood, *The Stock Market* (1998), p. 151; *Kynaston*, pp. 321–2; Pimlott, *Wilson*, p. 420.
25. Preston, 6D87/6, 15 Jul 1966, fo. 1504; *G*, 16 Jul 1966; *DT*, 16 Jul 1966; Harold Mayes (ed.), The Football Association, *World Cup Report 1966* (1967), pp. 109–11, 139–42; Peter Doggett, *Growing Up* (2021), p. 299; *Benn*, p. 454; *Kynaston*, p. 322; Preston, 6D87/6, 16 Jul 1966; Dee, DDX 829/3, 16 Jul 1966; Langford, S/GHL/1, 16 Jul 1966; Larkin, Ms. Eng. c. 7433, 16 Jul 1966, fo. 88; *DT*, 18 Jul 1966; 'Fred Jordan', *T*, 13 Aug 2002; Marks, 16 Jul 1966; Gavin McOwan, 'Sir Bobby Charlton', *G*, 23 Oct 2023; *Ob*, 17 Jul 1966.
26. Fisher, *Hancock*, p. 424; Dee, DDX 829/3, 18 Jul 1966; *Crossman*, p. 574; Morgan, *Callaghan*, p. 245; *Castle*, pp. 75–6; *Crossman*, p. 574.
27. Jenkins, *Centre*, pp. 194–5; *Castle*, p. 76; Pimlott, *Wilson*, pp. 423–4; Hodgson, 18–19 Jul 1966; *G*, 20 Jul 1966; Arthur Hopcraft, *The Football Man* (1968), p. 220; *G*, 20 Jul 1966 (Eric Todd), 30 Dec 2022 (Williams).
28. *P*, 20 Jul 1966; *FT*, 20 Jul 1966; *Crossman*, p. 578; Pimlott, *Wilson*, p. 425; *Crossman*, p. 578; *NS*, 22 Jul 1966; James Allen, GDP/172(4)/1966, 20 Jul 1966; Preston, 6D87/6, 20 Jul 1966; Keith McBride, GDP/379/1965–68, 20 Jul 1966; Dee, DDX 829/3, 20 Jul 1966; Betty Allen, GDP/450/1963–67, 20 Jul 1966; Pimlott, *Wilson*, p. 426; *DT*, 21 Jul 1966; Pimlott, *Wilson*, pp. 426–7; *G*, 21 Jul 1966; Marks, 20 Jul 1966; *DM (2)*, 21 Jul 1966; personal memory.

CHAPTER 20 NOT ROCKING THE BOAT

1. *Ob*, 24 Jul 1966; *E*, 23 Jul 1966; *New Soc*, 28 Jul 1966; *G*, 21 Jul 1966.
2. For two particularly helpful overall analyses of the Labour government and the economy between October 1964 and July 1966, see: Jim Tomlinson, *The Labour Governments, 1964–70*: Volume 3: *Economic Policy* (Manchester, 2004); Glen O'Hara, *From Dreams to Disillusionment* (Basingstoke, 2007), especially chaps 3–5, 8.
3. *NS*, 28 Feb 2000 (Ben Pimlott). Valuable accounts of the non-devaluation decision include: Jock Bruce-Gardyne and Nigel Lawson, *The Power Game* (1976), chap. 5; Rob Stones, 'Government-finance relations in Britain, 1964–7', in *Economy and*

Society, Feb 1990, pp. 36–42; Austin Mitchell and David Wienar, *Last Time* (1997), chap. 6; David Blaazer, '"Devalued and Dejected Britons"', in *History Workshop Journal*, spring 1999, pp. 123–4; Tim Bale, 'Dynamics of a Non-Decision', in *Twentieth Century British History*, 1999 (10/2), pp. 192–217.

4. *Power Game*, p. 118; Keith Middlemas, *Power, Competition and the State*: Volume 2 (Basingstoke, 1990), p. 119; *Castle*, p. ix; *Last Time*, p. 195; *NS*, 28 Feb 2000; Sidney Pollard, *The Wasting of the British Economy* (Beckenham, 1984 edn), p. 45; Tomlinson, *Labour Governments*, p. 223; Glen O'Hara, '"Dynamic, Exciting, Thrilling Change"', in *Contemporary British History*, Sep 2006, p. 386; Scott Newton, 'The Sterling Devaluation of 1967, the International Economy and Post-War Social Democracy', in *English Historical Review*, Aug 2010, p. 944; Samuel Brittan, *Steering the Economy* (Harmondsworth, 1971 edn), p. 307; *Crossman*, p. 305; *Last Time*, p. 199.
5. Peter Paterson, *Tired and Emotional* (1993), p. 183; Blaazer, pp. 123–4; Roger Middleton (ed.), *Inside the Department of Economic Affairs* (Oxford, 2012), p. 99; Blaazer, pp. 124, 131–2; Anne Perkins, *Red Queen* (2003), p. 242.
6. *Kynaston*, pp. 312–13; Niall Ferguson, *High Financier* (2010), pp. 279–81; Harold Wilson, *The Labour Government, 1964–1970* (1971), p. 251; *Kynaston*, p. 322; *Inside*, p. 141; David Kynaston, *The Financial Times: A Centenary History* (1988), pp. 328–9; *Ob*, 10 Jul 1966; Blaazer, p. 130; *DT*, 14 Jul 1966; *Spec*, 18 Mar 1966; Alec Cairncross, *The Wilson Year* (1997), p. 130; *Spec*, 29 Jul 1966; Cairncross, *Wilson*, p. 153.
7. O'Hara, *Dreams*, p. 43; Edmund Dell, *A Strange Eventful History* (1999), pp. 347–9; *Last Time*, p. 207; *Power Game*, pp. 124–5; Ben Pimlott, *Harold Wilson* (1992), pp. 412–13; *G*, 6 Aug 1965; *Encounter*, Sep 1966, p. 61.
8. Andrew Schonfield, *Modern Capitalism* (1965), pp. 84, 145–6; Stewart Wood, 'Why "Indicative Planning" Failed', in *Twentieth Century British History*, 2000 (11/4), pp. 431–2; Christopher Clifford and Alistair McMillan (eds), 'The Department of Economic Affairs', in *Contemporary British History*, summer 1997, p. 126.
9. *NS*, 19 Feb 1965; Bill Rodgers, *Fourth Among Equals* (2000), p. 88; Eric Roll, *Crowded Hours* (1985), p. 152; George Brown, *In My Way* (1971), p. 92; Peter Hennessy, *Whitehall* (1989), p. 187, quoting Sir Douglas Wass; O'Hara, 'Dynamic', p. 396.
10. *Inside*, pp. 51, 53, 60–1, 71, 73, 78, 81, 84–5, 89, 91; Rodgers, *Fourth*, p. 81; *Inside*, p. 71; *Crossman*, pp. 116, 238, 277.
11. Rodgers, *Fourth*, p. 91; Middlemas, *Power*, pp. 123–4; O'Hara, *Dreams*, pp. 55–8; Tomlinson, *Labour Governments*, p. 88.
12. *Crossman*, p. 300; Pimlott, *Wilson*, p. 363; *L*, 30 Dec 1965; Pimlott, *Wilson*, p. 363; *NS*, 8 Apr 1966; typically, *Ob*, 24 Jul 1966 (Rudolf Klein).
13. See in general on Mintech: David Edgerton, *Warfare State* (Cambridge, 2006), chap. 6.
14. Richard Coopey (ed.), 'Ministry of Technology 1964–70', in *Contemporary Record*, summer 1991, p. 130; Geoffrey Goodman, *The Awkward Warrior* (1979), pp. 413, 407; *Crossman*, p. 213; Richard Bailey, *Managing the British Economy* (1968), p. 58; Tomlinson, *Labour Governments*, p. 103; Richard Coopey, 'The White Heat of Scientific Revolution', in *Contemporary Record*, summer 1991, pp. 119–23; Goodman, *Awkward Warrior*, pp. 438, 443, 445; *ST*, 4 Apr 1965; *Ob*, 3 Oct 1965; *ST*, 29 May 1966.
15. Tom Kelsey, 'The Retreat from "High Technology" in Post-War Britain', in *English Historical Review*, Oct/Dec 2023, p. 1,368; *G*, 26 May 1965; David Edgerton, *The Rise and Fall of the British Nation* (2018), p. 293; Kelsey, 'Retreat', pp. 1,375–6; *FT*,

2 Dec 1989; Kelsey, 'Retreat', pp. 1,369, 1,379. See also for an accessible and well-informed account of the AGR fiasco: Tony Hall, *Nuclear Politics* (1986), pp. 83–102.

16. Jim Tomlinson, 'Managing the economy, managing the people', in *Economic History Review*, Aug 2005, pp. 571–2, 577; Ferguson, *High Financier*, p. 275.

CHAPTER 21 IT IS NOW

1. *NS*, 29 Jul 1966 ('Magnus Turnstile'); *G*, 21 Jul 1966.
2. *T*, 21 Jul 1966; *Oldie*, summer 2014 (Alan Thomas); Martin Johnes, *Wales Since 1939* (Manchester, 2012), pp. 223–4; Dee, DDX 829/3, 21 Jul 1966; 'John Mayall', *T*, 25 Jul 2024; Dee, DDX 829/3, 22 Jul 1966; Betty Allen, GDP/450/1963–67, 22 Jul 1966; James Allen, GDP/172(4)/1966, 22 Jul 1966; Rachel Reeves, *Alice in Westminster* (2017), pp. 140–1; *G*, 23 Jul 1966; Reeves, *Alice*, pp. 141–2; *G*, 23 Jul 1966; Geoffrey K. Fry, 'Parliament and "Morality"', in *Contemporary British History*, spring 1998, p. 143.
3. Rogan Taylor and Andrew Ward, *Kicking and Screaming* (1995), p. 318; *T*, 27 Mar 2002; BBC WAC, R9/10/13–VR/66/407, Aug 1966; Fabio Chisari, 'When Football Went Global', in *Historical Social Research*, 2006 (1), pp. 51–3; Brian Glanville, 'Roger Hunt', *G*, 29 Sep 2021; 'Gordon Banks', *T*, 13 Feb 2019; Leo McKinstry, *Sir Alf* (2006), pp. 5, 23.
4. Marks, 23 Jul 1966; McKinstry, *Sir Alf*, pp. 311–12; Marks, 23 Jul 1966; Betty Allen, GDP/450/1963–67, 23 Jul 1966; James Allen, GDP/172(4)/1966, 23 Jul 1966; Lee, 23 Jul 1966; *LRB*, 6 Sep 2007 (David Cannadine); BBC WAC, R9/7/82–VR/66/393, 23 Jul 1966; Mark Lewisohn, *Radio Times Guide to TV Comedy* (2003 edn), p. 470.
5. *S Tel*, 24 Jul 1966; Mary Whitehouse, *Cleaning up TV* (1967), p. 164; Turtle, D103/1/31, 24 Jul 1966; BBC WAC, R9/7/82–VR/66/397, 24 Jul 1966; John Fisher, *Tony Hancock* (2008), p. 425; Larkin, Ms. Eng. c. 7433, 24 Jul 1966, fo. 99.
6. Lindsey Hanley, *Estates* (2007), pp. 106–7; Harold Wilson, *The Labour Government, 1964–1970* (1971), p. 261; *Crossman*, p. 585; *T*, 26 Jul 1966; Marks, 26 Jul 1966; Wilson, *Labour Government*, p. 262; Haines, SxMOA99/34/8/19, 26 Jul 1966; Hodgson, 1 Aug 1966; Avril Sandall, GDP/343/1966, 26 Jul 1966; Turtle, D103/1/31, 26 Jul 1966; Marks, 26 Jul 1966.
7. *T*, 26 Jul 1966; *DT*, 28 Jul 1966; Richard Batley et al., *Going Comprehensive* (1970), p. 14; Nirmala Rao, 'Labour and Education', in *Contemporary British History*, summer 2002, p. 112; Willmott, WLMT 1/33, 26 Jul 1966.
8. *FT*, 28 Jul 1966; Robert Taylor, 'The trade union "problem" in the Age of Consensus, 1960–1979', in Ben Pimlott and Chris Cook (eds), *Trade Unions in British Politics* (Harlow, 2nd edn, 1991), p. 184; *DT*, 28 Jul 1966; Betty Allen, GDP/450/ 1963–67, 28 Jul 1966; Preston, 6D87/6, 28 Jul 1966; *Spec*, 29 Jul 1966; *NME*, 29 Jul 1966; *MM*, 30 Jul 1966; *Disc*, 30 Jul 1966; Haines, SxMOA99/34/8/19, 29 Jul 1966; *T*, 30 Jul 1966; Dee, DDX 829/3, 29 Jul 1966; *T*, 30 Jul 1966; Clinton Heylin, *Dylan: A Life in Stolen Moments* (1996), p. 105; *DM (1)*, 30 Jul 1966; Paul Sexton, 'First Spoonful', www.udiscovermusic.com, 29 Jul 2023; Elton John, *Me* (2019), p. 38.
9. Heap, Acc 2243/040, 30 Jul 1966; *T*, 30 Jul 1966; *Sun*, 30 Jul 1966; *D Ex*, 30 Jul 1966; Marks, 30 Jul 1966; Wilson, *Labour Government*, p. 266; *S Tel*, 31 Jul 1966; Harold Mayes (ed.), The Football Association, *World Cup Report 1966* (1967), p. 273; *G*, 30 Jul 2016 (Morrison), 10 Jul 2021 (Wintour); *NS*, 22 Apr 2016 (Davies); Arthur

Hopcraft, *The Football Man* (1968), pp. 221–2; Leigh Hatts, 'Ken Baily', *Ind*, 13 Dec 1993; Reverend Oliver Leonard Willmott, *The Parish Notes of Loders, Dottery & Askerswell*: Volume II (Shrewsbury, 1996), Jul/Aug 1966 (unpaginated); *DM (2)*, 1 Aug 1966 (Peter Wilson); *Ob*, 31 Jul 1966 (Hugh McIlvanney); *S Tel*, 31 Jul 1966; Chisari, 'Global', p. 51; Frederick Ward, GDP/145/1966, 30 Jul 1966; Marks, 30 Jul 1966; David Lodge, *Quite a Good Time to be Born* (2015), pp. 402–3; Normal Shiel, *Voices of 1966* (Stroud, 2000), pp. 107–8; *Sun*, 1 Aug 1966; *G*, 3 Aug 2016 (Bill Taylor); *Spec*, 18 Nov 2006 (Frank Keating); Michael Chaplin, *Newcastle United Stole My Heart* (2021), p. 38; *G*, 9 Mar 2013 (Allen); *NS*, 6 Nov 2020 (Robert Colls); Denis Law, *The King* (2003), pp. 206–7; Marks, 30 Jul 1966. The full match, including Wolstenholme's commentary, is available on YouTube.

10. *T*, 30 Jul 1966; Marks, 30 Jul 1966; Jonathan Coe, *Like a Fiery Elephant* (2004), p. 210; *G*, 30 Jul 2016 (Blake Morrison); *T*, 1 Aug 1966 (Geoffrey Green); *Spec*, 18 Nov 2006; *D Ex*, 1 Aug 1966; Marks, 30 Jul 1966; Willmott, WLMT 1/33, 30 Jul 1966; Harry Thompson, *Peter Cook* (1997), p. 231; Marks, 30 Jul 1966; *NS*, 14 Aug 2020 (D. J. Taylor); *Ind*, 27 Apr 1998 (Parsons, interviewed by Deborah Ross); *T*, 17 Feb 2001 (Baker); John Hughson, *England and the 1966 World Cup* (Manchester, 2016), pp. 163–4; Thompson, *Cook*, p. 231.
11. Shiel, *Voices*, p. 112; *Spec*, 18 Nov 2006; Marks, 30 Jul 1966; https://www.ukrockfestivals.com/windsor-festival-66.html; *T*, 17 Feb 2001 (Baker); Duncan Hamilton, *Answered Prayers* (2023), p. 258; David Thomson, *4–2* (1996), p. 201; *NS*, 14 Aug 2020; *T*, 30 Jul 2016; Marks, 30 Jul 1966; Keith McBride, GDP/379/1965–68, 30 Jul 1966; Darlington, 30 Jul 1966; Willmott, WLMT 1/33, 30 Jul 1966; Wendy Pollard, *Pamela Hansford Johnson* (2014), p. 376; Thomson, p. 205; *News of the World*, 31 Jul 1966 (Frank Butler); Dilwyn Porter and Christoph Wagner, 'Over the Line?', in Anthony Waine and Kristian Naglo (eds), *On and Off the Field* (Wiesbaden, 2014), p. 68; *RT*, 28 Jul 1966.
12. Stephen Bates, 'Donald Trelford', *G*, 28 Jan 2023; *ES*, 30 Jul 1966; *News of the World*, 31 Jul 1966; https://www.ukrockfestivals.com/windsor-festival-66.html; *S Tel*, 31 Jul 1966; Judith M. Lang and Louise de Bruin (eds), *A Net In Water: A Selection from the Journals of Mary Casey* (Kilmersdon, 1994), p. 68; Marks, 30 Jul 1966; National Life Story Collection (National Sound Archive, British Library), Architects' Lives, Richard Seifert, C467/05, p. 42; *News of the World*, 31 Jul 1966; Wilson, *Labour Government*, p. 266; Matthew Engel, *The Reign: Part 1* (2022), p. 268; *S Tel*, 31 Jul 1966; Clancy Sigal, *The London Lover* (2018), pp. 199–200; Doug Hinman, *The Kinks* (San Francisco, 2004), pp. 87–8.

Acknowledgements

The following kindly gave permission to reproduce copyright material: Roger Darlington; Pamela Hendicott (Judy Haines); Sue Lowndes (Vere Hodgson); Veronica Porter; Laurence Marks; Diana Griffith; Celia Kent; Virginia Ironside; Josh Benn (The Estate of Tony Benn); Islington Archives (Gladys Langford); Ruth Walton (Betty Allen); BBC Written Archives Centre (BBC copyright content reproduced courtesy of the British Broadcasting Corporation; all rights reserved); Michael and Lewis Willmott (Phyllis and Peter Willmott); Fred Ward (Frederick Ward); Julia Cook; Daphne Roach (James Allen); Virginia Crossman (Richard Crossman); Kevin Saint (Gordon Bentley); Yorkshire Archaeological and Historical Society (Elsie Johnston); Bessie White (Keith McBride); Ian Mole; Judy Hebert, Nonie Insall, Clare Joyce and Richard Meryon (Daphne Meryon); Brian Sandall (Avril Sandall); Neil and Lorna Franklin (Grace Taylor); Michael Williams; Geoff Dyer; Emanuel Lipton (Michael Lipton); Faber & Faber (*To Throw Away Unopened* © Viv Albertine); *The Castle Diaries 1964-1976* by Barbara Castle (Macmillan); reproduced by permission of David Higham Associates; *So, Anyway* by John Cleese (Penguin Random House); *The Likes of Us* by Michael Collins (Granta Books); the estate of John Fowles (© John Fowles 2003); *Hitch 22* by Christopher Hitchens (Atlantic Books); Faber & Faber (*Letters Home, Selected Letters* and *Letters to Monica* © Philip Larkin); from *Quite A Good Time to be Born* by David Lodge published by Harvill Secker. Copyright © David Lodge, 2015. Reprinted by permission of The Random House Group Limited; from *The Scent of Dried Roses* by Tim Lott published by Penguin. Copyright © Tim Lott, 1996.

Reprinted by permission of Penguin Books Limited; Nella Last and Pat Scott, reproduced with permission of Curtis Brown, London on behalf of the Trustees of the Mass Observation Archive © The Trustees of the Mass Observation Archive; Edwin Morgan; *Centenary Selected Poems* (Carcanet); *The North* by Paul Morley (Bloomsbury Publishing); *The Orton Diaries* by Joe Orton (Methuen); *Baggage* by Janet Street Porter (Headline); extract from *Why Be Happy When You Could Be Normal?* by Jeanette Winterson reprinted by permission of Peters Fraser & Dunlop on behalf of Jeanette Winterson; 'The Dear Green Place' by Archie Hind, reproduced with permission of the Licensor through PLSclear; from *My Ear at His Heart* by Hanif Kureishi published by Faber & Faber. Copyright © Hanif Kureishi, 2004. Reprinted by permission of Faber & Faber; 'My Passage to England' by Madho Ram Bahini, published in the Autumn 2022 issue of *Oral History*.

As ever, I am grateful to archivists and various others for help along the way. These include (with apologies for any inadvertent omissions): Emma Anthony; Sophie Bridges; Kate Clarke; Stefan Dickers; Alison Light; Duncan Marlor; Louise North; Polly North; Jonathan Oates; Dil Porter; Andrew Riley; Andrew Rosthorn; Laurence Saywood; Jessica Scantlebury; Peter Shapely; Adrian Smith; Peter Smith; Joy Webb; Jack Winkler.

I owe a particular debt to friends who looked at all or part of the draft, in varying proportions, and gave me a mixture of suggestions and encouragement: Steve Bates; Chris and Nicola Beauman; Lewis Biggs; Mike Brearley; Ian Greaves; Nick Hornby; Sara Marsh; Jack Ozanne; Veronica Porter; Harry Ricketts; Laurence Saywood; Holly Smith; David Warren; and Richard Williams.

Many thanks also to Amanda Howard (Superscript Editorial Services) for transcribing my audio tapes; to Richard Collins for his copy edit; to Vicki Robinson for compiling the index; to Catherine Best and Patric Dickinson for reading the proofs; to my agent Georgia Garrett and her assistant Ivy Pottinger-Glass; and at Bloomsbury, to my editor Jasmine Horsey and her colleagues Francisco Vilhena, Gurdip Ahluwalia and Ros Ellis.

My greatest debt remains to my wife Lucy. And, this time round, a special nod to our grandchildren Wolfie, Larkspur and Eli.

Finally, a very belated 'thank you' to the readers of these *Tales*: whether sticking with them or just dipping in and out. I'm truly grateful for all the positive feedback. 'How many more to go?' I am sometimes asked. Well, my intention from here is, broadly speaking, to lengthen my stride – not least because it would be nice to get to that Francis of Assisi moment one day in early May.

New Malden
May 2026

Image credits

John, Paul, George and Ringo play a little ditty on live TV: Trinity Mirror/Mirrorpix; clothing factory in Tredegar, Blaenau Gwent: Western Mail Archive/Mirrorpix/Getty Images; the Gorbals, Glasgow: Joseph McKenzie Archive/Bridgeman Images; slum clearance, Hulme: Graham/Manchester Evening News Archive/Mirrorpix via Getty Images; Abinger Hammer: Evening Standard/Hulton Archive/Getty Images; Gleadless Valley, Sheffield: Historic England Archive/Heritage Images via Getty Images; Coventry precinct: copyright Guardian News & Media Ltd 2026; fares, please: Central Press/Hulton Archive/Getty Images; Julie Christie travelling in the London Underground: David Hurn/Magnum Photos; Jim Clark returns to home village of Chirnside: Rolls Press/Popperfoto via Getty Images; Malcolm X in Smethwick: Daily Express/Archive Photos/Getty Images; ice cream van on terraced street, Manchester: Estate of Shirley Baker/Mary Evans Picture Library; a woman hangs up her laundry on a street in Halifax: John Bulmer/Popperfoto via Getty Images.

Allen Ginsberg by the Albert Memorial: M. Stroud/Daily Express/Hulton Archive/Getty Images; family meal: Central Press/Getty Images; matron's daily conference: The Times/News Licensing; the last remaining shop in Hulme: Estate of Shirley Baker/Mary Evans Picture Library; T Dan Smith studies a giant wall map of the northern region in his office: © AmberSide Collection; the Red Road flats, 1966: © Oscar Marzaroli Collection, courtesy Street Level Photoworks; anti-Vietnam War demonstration on Regent Street, London: Clive Limpkin/Express/Hulton Archive/Getty

Images; Carnaby Street life: Fox Photos/Getty Images; the Hull docks: Roger Mayne Archive/Mary Evans Picture Library; Marine Gardens, Skegness: The J Salmon Image Archive/Mary Evans Picture Library; holidays in Brighton: Science & Society Picture Library/Getty Images; Harold Wilson takes the train: Stan Meagher/Express/Getty Images; street decorations near Goodison Park: Ray Green/Paul Popper/Popperfoto via Getty Images; England's third goal in the World Cup final: Robert Stiggins/Express/Getty Images.

Index

A Note on the Author

David Kynaston was born in Aldershot in 1951. His many books include *King Labour* (1976, a study of the Victorian working class), *The City of London* (1994–2001, a widely acclaimed four-volume history), *Arlott, Swanton and the Soul of English Cricket* (2018, co-written with Stephen Fay) and *Richie Benaud's Blue Suede Shoes* (2024, co-written with Harry Ricketts). Since 2001 his main focus has been on 'Tales of a New Jerusalem', a multi-volume history of post-war Britain. He continues to support Aldershot Town, subject of his diary *Shots in the Dark* (2020).

A Note on the Type

The text of this book is set in Linotype Stempel Garamond, a version of Garamond adapted and first used by the Stempel foundry in 1924. It is one of several versions of Garamond based on the designs of Claude Garamond. It is thought that Garamond based his font on Bembo, cut in 1495 by Francesco Griffo in collaboration with the Italian printer Aldus Manutius. Garamond types were first used in books printed in Paris around 1532. Many of the present-day versions of this type are based on the *Typi Academiae* of Jean Jannon cut in Sedan in 1615.

Claude Garamond was born in Paris in 1480. He learned how to cut type from his father and by the age of fifteen he was able to fashion steel punches the size of a pica with great precision. At the age of sixty he was commissioned by King Francis I to design a Greek alphabet, and for this he was given the honourable title of royal type founder. He died in 1561.